THE
PRACTICE OF
SOCIAL WORK

THE

PRACTICE OF

SOCIAL WORK

FOURTH EDITION

Charles Zastrow
University of Wisconsin — Whitewater

Wadsworth Publishing Company
Belmont, California
A Division of Wadsworth, Inc.

Social Work Editor: Peggy Adams
Editorial Assistant: Tammy Goldfeld
Production Editor: Stacey C. Sawyer, Sawyer & Williams
Print Buyer: Randy Hurst
Designer: Mary Ellen Podgorski
Copy Editor: Patterson Lamb
Photo Researcher: Judy Mason
Cover Designer: Adriane Bosworth
Cover Photographer: H. Mark Weidman
Compositor: TypeLink, Inc., San Diego

*This book is printed on acid-free paper that meets
Environmental Protection Agency standards for recycled
paper.*

2 3 4 5 6 7 8 9 10 — 96 95 94 93 92

Library of Congress Cataloging in Publication Data

Zastrow, Charles.
    The practice of social work / Charles Zastrow. — 4th ed.
        p.   cm.
    Includes bibliographical references and index.
    ISBN 0-534-17004-8
    1. Social service.   2. Social service — Psychological aspects.
3. Counseling.   I. Title.
HV40.Z273 1991
361.3'2 — dc20   91-28066
                                                  CIP

To Kris and Vicki

Preface   xiv

PART I   Introduction   1

CHAPTER 1   Overview of Social Work Practice   2

Purpose of This Chapter   2
History of Social Work   3
Definition of Social Work   6
Relationship between Social Work and Social
   Welfare   6
What Is the Profession of Social Work?   8
Generalist Social Work Practice   9
   The Change Process   9
   A Variety of Roles   14
Medical Model versus Ecological Model of Human
   Behavior   15
   Medical Model   17
   Ecological Model   17
Goals of Social Work Practice   19
   *Goal 1: Enhance the Problem-Solving, Coping, and
      Developmental Capacities of People*   19
   *Goal 2: Link People with Systems That Provide Them
      with Resources, Services, and Opportunities*   19
   *Goal 3: Promote the Effectiveness and Humane
      Operation of Systems That Provide People with
      Resources and Services*   20
   Goal 4: Develop and Improve Social Policy   20
A Problem-Solving Approach   20
Micro, Mezzo, and Macro Practice   20
   Social Casework   20
   Case Management   21
   Group Work   21
   Group Therapy   24
   Family Therapy   24
   Community Organization   24
   Administration   24
Knowledge, Skills, and Values Needed for Social Work
   Practice   25
   Knowledge   25
   Core Practice Skills   27
   Values   29
Key Objectives of This Text   29

Which Intervention Strategies Should Social Workers
 Learn? 30
Summary 31
Exercise 32

CHAPTER 2 Social Work Values 33

Value Dilemmas 33
Knowledge and Values 36
Value Dilemmas of Clients versus Workers 37
Client's Right to Self-Determination 40
Confidentiality 42
 Privileged Communication 45
 Explaining Confidentiality to Clients 46
Other Values 47
 The Institutional Orientation 47
 Advocacy and Social Action 48
 Focus on Family 48
 Accountability 49
Summary 50
Exercises 51

PART II Social Work Practice 55

CHAPTER 3 Assessment 56

A Focus on Strengths 58
Sources of Information 58
 Verbal Report from Client 58
 Forms That Client Completes 59
 Collateral Sources 59
 Psychological Tests 59
 Nonverbal Behavior of Client 60
 *Interactions with Significant Others and
  Home Visits 60*
 Worker's Intuition from Direct Interactions 60
Knowledge Used in Making an Assessment 61
Environmental Systems Emphasis 62
Assessing Problems 64

A Systems Perspective 70
 Overview of Systems Theory 70
 Pincus-Minahan Model 71
Summary 82
Exercises 82

CHAPTER 4 Social Work with Individuals:
    Interviewing 85

Three Types of Social Work Interviews 85
 Informational or Social History Interviews 85
 Diagnostic Interviews 86
 Therapeutic Interviews 86
The Place of the Interview 90
Opening the First Interview 92
 When Interviewee-Initiated 92
 When Interviewer-Initiated 92
Closing an Interview 93
Questioning 94
Note Taking 96
Tape Recording and Videotaping 97
Videotaping for Training Purposes 97
Summary 99
Exercise 99

CHAPTER 5 Social Work with Individuals:
    Counseling 101

Counseling from the Helper's Perspective 101
Counseling from the Helpee's Perspective 102
 Stage I — Problem Awareness 102
 Stage II — Relationship to Counselor 103
 Stage III — Motivation 104
 Stage IV — Conceptualizing the Problem 106
 Stage V — Exploration of Resolution Strategies 110
 Stage VI — Selection of a Strategy 110
 Stage VII — Implementation of the Strategy 111
 Stage VIII — Evaluation 116
Reactions of Clients to Having a Personal
 Problem 117
 Kübler-Ross's Five Stages 118
Summary 122
Exercises 122

CHAPTER 6   Social Work with Groups: Types of Groups and Guidelines for Leading Them   127

Types of Intervention Groups   128
  Recreation Groups   128
  Recreation-Skill Groups   129
  Educational Groups   129
  Problem-Solving and Decision-Making Groups   132
  Self-Help Groups   138
  Socialization Groups   142
  Therapeutic Groups   142
  Encounter Groups   143
How to Start, Lead, and Terminate Groups   149
  Homework   149
  Session Planning   151
  Relaxing before a Meeting   152
  Cues upon Entering the Meeting Room   152
  Seating Arrangements   153
  Introductions   153
  Role Clarification   154
  Agenda   154
  Additional Guidelines for Leading a Group   154
  Terminating a Group   155
Summary   158
Exercises   159

CHAPTER 7   Social Work with Groups: Concepts and Skills   161

Membership and Reference Groups   161
Stages in Group Development   163
Task and Maintenance Roles   165
Leadership Theory   165
  The Trait Approach   166
  The Style Approach   166
  The Distributed Functions Approach   168
Social Power Bases in Groups   169
Personal Goals and Group Goals   171
Conformity   172
  Idiosyncratic Credits   173
Competitive and Cooperative Groups   174
Controversy and Creativity   175

The Win-Lose Approach versus the Problem-Solving Approach   175
Handling Disruptive Behavior   177
Group Size   178
Starting, Leading, and Ending Therapy Groups   178
  Building Rapport   179
  Exploring Problems in Depth   180
  Exploring Alternative Solutions   181
  Ending a Session   182
  Ending a Group   183
Summary   185
Exercises   186

CHAPTER 8   Social Work with Families   189

Diversity of Family Forms   189
Societal Functions of Families   192
Problems in Families   192
The Nature of Social Work with Families   193
Family Therapy in Systems Perspective   195
Three Approaches to Family Therapy   199
  Virginia Satir   199
  Salvador Minuchin   201
  Jay Haley   203
Problem-Solving Stages   204
  Beginning the Counseling Process   206
  Continuing the Counseling Process   210
  Restructuring the Family System   214
  Maintenance of Gains and Termination of Counseling   218
Summary   218
Exercise   219

CHAPTER 9   Social Work Community Practice   223

Personal Problems and Community Problems   225
Generalist Skills and Macropractice   225
Knowledge of the Community   226
Knowledge of Organizations   227
Knowledge of Funding Sources and Funding Cycles   230

Skills for Macropractice — Group Decision-
  Making Skills   231
  Brainstorming   231
  Nominal Group Technique   233
  Needs Assessment   233
Public Relations Skills/Communicating with
  the Public   235
Relationships with Media Representatives   236
Skills for Media Utilization   237
Fund-Raising   237
Methods of Fund-Raising   238
Political Activity and Lobbying   239
Community Practice — A Problem-Solving
  Process   239
  Preplanning: The Questions to Ask   240
  Planning: Plans to Make   241
  Impact: Steps to Take   243
Values and Macropractice   244
Models of Community Practice   246
Summary   250
Exercises   251

CHAPTER 10   Evaluating Social Work
              Practice   253

What Is Evaluation?   253
The Single-System Evaluation Approach   255
  Specify the Goal   255
  Select a Suitable Measure(s)   255
  Measurement Methods   255
General Issues in Measurement   258
  Record Baseline Data   259
  Implement Intervention and Continue
    Monitoring   260
  Assess Change   261
  Infer Effectiveness   266
  Threats to Validity   266
Single-System Designs   267
  The Basic AB Design   267
  Withdrawal Designs   267
Evaluating Programs   268
Computer Applications in Social Work Practice
  270
  Office Management   272
  Client Information Systems   273

Decision Support   273
Clinical Assessment   273
Direct Intervention   273
Electronic Networking   273
Education and Training   274
Research and Information Retrieval   274
Issues in Computer Applications   274
Summary   274
Exercises   275

CHAPTER 11   Social Work Practice with Diverse
              Groups   279

Problems and Barriers   280
  Native American Clients   281
  African-American Clients   281
  Latino Clients   283
  Gays and Lesbians   283
  Rural Settings   284
  Feminist Social Work   284
  Other Examples   285
Knowledge of Self   286
Knowledge of Differences   286
Application of Knowledge — Techniques of
  Intervention   289
  African-American Client — White Worker   290
  Latino Client — Non-Latino Worker   291
  Native American Client — Non-Native American
    Worker   294
  Female Client — Male Worker   296
  Gay and Lesbian Clients   299
  Rural Settings   300
  Other Differences Affecting Practice   301
Some General Observations   302
Summary   303
Exercises   303

CHAPTER 12   Surviving and Enjoying
              Social Work   308

Common Concerns of Students   308
  Will I be able to make it in field placement?   308
  Will I conduct a satisfactory interview with my
    first client?   309

I'm really depressed, because my supervisor is able to handle an interview much better than I — will I ever be able to do that well? 310

How should I separate the role of counselor from that of friend? 311

How can I avoid becoming too emotionally involved with clients' problems? 312

Do I really want to have a career in social work? 314

Burnout 314
  Definitions and Symptoms of Burnout 315
  Burnout Is One of the Reactions to High Stress 315
  Structural Causes of Stress That May Lead to Burnout 318
  Approaches to Manage Stress and Prevent Burnout 319
  Goal Setting and Time Management 320
  Positive Thinking 320
  Changing the Thoughts That Produce Burnout 320
  Relaxation Techniques 321
  Exercise 321
  Outside Activities 321
  Pleasurable Goodies 321
  Social Support Systems 322
  Variety at Work 323
  Humor 323
  Changing or Adapting to Distressing Events 323
Surviving in a Bureaucracy 323
Enjoying Social Work and Your Life 327
  Becoming a Positive Thinker 328
  Developing an Identity 329
  Using Rational Challenges to Develop a Success Identity 331
Summary 337
Exercises 338

PART III   Contemporary Theories of Counseling   341

CHAPTER 13   Psychoanalysis   342

Sigmund Freud 343
The Mind 343
  Emphasis on the Unconscious 343
  The Id, Superego, and Ego 344

Psychosexual Development (Personality Development) 346
  1. Oral Stage 346
  2. Anal Stage 347
  3. Phallic Stage 347
  4. Latency Stage 347
  5. Genital Stage 348
Psycopathological Development (Development of Emotional and Behavioral Problems) 348
Psychoanalysis (Theory of Therapy) 348
  Hypnosis 349
  Free Association 349
  Dream Analysis 350
  Transference 352
Evaluation 353
Summary 354
Exercises 355

CHAPTER 14   Client-Centered Therapy   357

Carl Rogers: Central Concepts 358
Theory of Personality Development and of Psychopathology 359
Theory of Therapy 360
  1. Clarification, or Reflection of Feeling 361
  2. Restatement of Content 361
  3. Simple Acceptance 361
Evaluation 363
Summary 365
Exercise 366

CHAPTER 15   Gestalt Therapy   367

Fritz Perls: Gestalt Psychology 368
Theory of Personality and of Psychopathology 369
Theory of Therapy 371
Evaluation 375
Summary 376
Exercise 377

CHAPTER 16   Transactional Analysis   379

Eric Berne: Theory of Personality Development 380
  Personality Structure 380
  Psychosocial Drives 382

Types of Transactions   383
Common Games   385
Life Scripts   386
Theory of Psychopathology   389
Theory of Therapy   392
Game Analysis   393
Script Analysis   394
Evaluation   395
Summary   397
Exercises   397

CHAPTER 17   Reality Therapy   400

William Glasser: Theories of Personality
   Development and Psychopathology   401
Control Theory   401
Identity Theory   402
Theory of Therapy   404
1. Encourage Responsible Behavior   404
2. Recognize Mental Illness Labels as
   Destructive   404
3. Foster Involved Relationships   405
4. Focus on Present and Future   405
5. Focus on Behavior Rather Than on Feelings   406
6. Encourage Value Judgments   406
7. Encourage Planning   406
8. Reject Excuses   406
9. Eliminate Punishment   407
10. Do Not Offer Sympathy   407
11. Rarely Ask Why   407
12. Praise Responsible Behavior   407
13. Question Traditional Case Histories   407
14. Foster Success Experiences   410
Evaluation   410
Summary   410
Exercise   412

CHAPTER 18   Rational Therapy   413

Albert Ellis: Theory of Personality Development and
   Psychopathology   414
Self-Talk Determines Our Feelings and Actions   414
Personality Development and Self-Concept
   Formations   415
Additional Aspects of Self-Talk   417
Understanding Deviant Behavior   418

Theory of Therapy   419
Rational Self-Analysis   420
Therapy Is an Educational Process   421
An Eclectic Approach   421
Common Irrational Beliefs   426
Evaluation   428
Summary   430
Exercises   430

CHAPTER 19   Behavior Therapy   433

Founders   433
Types of Learning Processes   434
Operant Conditioning   434
Respondent Conditioning   434
Modeling   435
Theory of Psychotherapy   435
Assertiveness Training   437
Overview of Assertiveness Training   437
Steps in Assertiveness Training   438
Helping Others Become More Assertive   440
Token Economies   442
Contingency Contracting   443
Systematic Desensitization   444
In Vivo Desensitization   445
Implosive Therapy   446
Covert Sensitization   447
Aversive Techniques   448
Cognitive Behavior-Modification Techniques   449
Thought Stopping and Covert Assertion   449
Diversion Techniques   450
Reframing   450
Evaluation   452
Summary   453
Exercises   454

CHAPTER 20   Sex Counseling and Therapy   458

Knowledge   459
Assumptions   459
Words   460
Levels of Intervention   460
AIDS   466
AIDS and the Sexual Revolution   466
Transmission of AIDS   468

Symptoms of AIDS 468
Testing for AIDS 468
Who Are the Persons with AIDS? 469
Sexual Problems 470
Treatment of Sexual Dysfunction 471
Sexual Dysfunctions Defined 472
Sex Therapy 472
  The Intake 473
  The History 475
  The Roundtable 475
  The Physiology Session 477
  Subsequent Treatment Sessions 479
Summary 479
Exercises 480

**CHAPTER 21   Neuro-Linguistic
                        Programming** 483

NLP Defined 484
Representational Systems 484
Representational System Predicates 485
Eye-Accessing Cues 490
The Four-Tuple 490
Causing Change by Communicating in
  Metaphor 491
Reframing 492
Therapeutic Change Often Occurs without the Cause
  of the Problem Being Known 493
Evaluation 494
Summary 495
Exercises 495

**CHAPTER 22   Prominent Specific Treatment
                        Techniques** 497

Milieu Therapy 497
Psychodrama 498
Play Therapy 500
Parental Education: Parent Effectiveness
  Training 502
  Parents Are Persons, Not Gods 502
  Who Owns the Problem? 502
  Active Listening 503
  I-Messages 504

No-Lose Problem Solving 505
Resolving Collisions of Values 506
Crisis Intervention 507
Task-Centered Practice 511
Mediation 512
Muscle Relaxation Approaches 514
Deep Breathing and Imagery Relaxation
  Approaches 519
Meditation 520
Hypnosis and Self-Hypnosis 522
Biofeedback 526
Summary 529
Exercises 530

**CHAPTER 23   Analysis of Therapy
                        Approaches** 534

Comparison of Counseling Theories 534
Insight versus Resolution Approaches 536
Is Counseling Effective? 538
What Really Causes Psychotherapy Change? 543
  *What Causes Disturbing Emotions and Ineffective
      Actions? 544*
  *Could Restructuring Thinking Be the Key
      Psychotherapeutic Agent? 544*
  Nontraditional Psychotherapy Techniques 546
Does Mental Illness Exist? 548
  What Is Schizophrenia? 548
  The Controversy over the Mental Illness Approach 549
A Perspective from Rational Therapy 550
  A Bizarre Murder 551
Labeling as a Cause of Chronic "Mental Illness" 552
Summary 554
Exercises 555

APPENDIX A   The NASW Code of Ethics 558

**APPENDIX B   Suggested Counselor's Responses
                        to Client's Statements** 565

Bibliography 567

Index 585

PREFACE

This text provides the theoretical and practical knowledge needed for entry levels of practice in social work. Material is presented covering generalist practice, social work values, confidentiality, principles of interviewing, contemporary theories of counseling, sexual therapy, social work with individuals, social work with groups, social work with families, social work community practice, assessment, evaluation, general systems theory, cross-cultural social work, working within a bureaucratic system, burnout, and the frustrations and satisfactions of being a social worker. A number of case examples are included to illustrate the theory that is presented.

The Practice of Social Work, Fourth Edition, is designed for use in practice courses in social work at both the undergraduate and graduate levels. Social work practitioners will also find the text valuable as it describes a variety of approaches to social work practice, including sexual treatment techniques, hypnosis, biofeedback, relaxation approaches, mediation, neurolinguistic programming, milieu therapy, task-centered practice, systematic desensitization, family counseling concepts, Gestalt therapy, transactional analysis, reality therapy, rational therapy, and behavior therapy. In presenting these diverse types of therapies, the author uses an eclectic approach. After each therapy approach is described, a critical review of the theory is presented to help the reader assess its merits and shortcomings.

This book is unique in that it combines the key components in existing practice texts, both traditional and contemporary, into one text. As much as possible, jargon-free language is used so that the reader can more readily grasp the theory. Exercises for students are presented at the end of each chapter to illustrate key concepts and to help students learn how to apply the theoretical material to social work practice.

PLAN OF THE BOOK

Part I is an introductory section with two chapters. The first chapter conceptualizes social work practice. It describes what social workers do, explains how social work is distinct from other professions, and summarizes the knowledge, values, and skills needed for beginning-level social work practice. This chapter also describes the goals of social work practice, gives a brief history of social work, indicates that social work is a multiskilled profession, and summarizes professional activities performed by social workers, including casework, case management, group work, group therapy, family counseling, and community organization. Various role models of social work practice are defined, including that of an enabler, broker, advocate, and activist. Generalist practice in social work is also defined and described.

The second chapter summarizes social work values. Values described include self-determination, individualization, confidentiality, belief in the institutional approach for the delivery of services, focus on family, advocacy for those being discriminated against, and accountability.

Part II has several chapters that describe social work practice. Social work with individuals, social work with groups, social work with families, and social work community practice are covered in depth. Techniques for interviewing and counseling clients are given considerable attention. Eight stages of a problem-solving approach to counseling clients are presented. Guidelines are also provided on how to begin and end interviews, on how to phrase interview questions, and on how to take notes while interviewing. Chapters are also included on assessment on evaluating social work practice. Material is summarized on computer applications in social work practice, and on systems analysis.

This part also covers material on a variety of other crucial aspects of social work practice: changing the delivery system to serve clients better, cross-cultural social work (for example, white workers and Native American clients), surviving and enjoying social work, concerns of students considering a career in social work, burnout, and surviving in a bureaucracy. This part concludes with a discussion of the importance for social workers (as well as other people) of developing a positive identity, and provides guidelines on how to develop a positive sense of self.

Part III presents and critiques the prominent theories of counseling that are widely used in the helping professions: psychoanalysis, client-centered therapy, Gestalt therapy, transactional analysis, reality therapy, rational therapy, behavior therapy, sex therapy ap-

proaches, task-centered practice, and neuro-linguistic programming. A number of specific treatment techniques are also described, including assertiveness training, token economies, systematic desensitization, implosive therapy, covert sensitization, aversive techniques, milieu therapy, psychodrama, crisis intervention, parent effectiveness training, mediation, muscle relaxation approaches, deep breathing relaxation, imagery relaxation, meditation, hypnosis, and biofeedback.

It is not necessary for the instructor to cover all of the theories of intervention presented in this text. Rather it is suggested that the instructor (with the consultation of the other faculty in the program) make decisions as to which intervention theories are most important for students to learn in order to best serve clients in the geographic area in which the campus is located.

This part also has a concluding chapter that analyzes and compares prominent theories of counseling. The question "What really causes psychotherapy change" is raised, and an explanation is advanced as to why all of the above-mentioned therapy approaches may lead to positive changes. The part ends with a review of the mental illness (medical model) approach to personal problems and discusses the effects of labeling.

ACKNOWLEDGMENTS

I wish to express my deep appreciation to the following people who made this book possible. Special thanks to the contributing authors and to the following colleagues who provided comments on the manuscript for this edition: John Bertsche, University of Montana; Norman Cobb, University of Texas/Arlington; Dana Cole, Central Washington University; Kevin Marett, University of Nevada/Las Vegas; and Mary Pegram, Bowling Green State University.

A sincere thank you to Vicki Vogel, Ralph Navarre, Diane Sonsthagen, and Kristine Zastrow who assisted in conceptualizing various chapters and helped in a number of ways with the writing of this text.

Charles Zastrow

CONTRIBUTING AUTHORS

WALLACE J. GINGERICH, MSW, Ph.D.
Professor, Mandel School of Applied Social Sciences
Case Western Reserve University
Cleveland, Ohio

GRAFTON H. HULL, JR., MSW, Ed.D.
Chairperson and Professor, Social Work Department
University of Wisconsin — Eau Claire
Eau Claire, Wisconsin

KAREN K. KIRST-ASHMAN, MSW, Ph.D.
Professor, University of Wisconsin — Whitewater
Whitewater, Wisconsin

DONALD NOLAN, MSSW, BCD
Clinical Social Worker
South Central Psychiatric Center
Janesville, Wisconsin

LLOYD G. SINCLAIR, MSSW, ACSW
Certified Sex Educator, Sex Therapist, and Sex Therapist Supervisor
Midwest Center for Sex Therapy
Madison, Wisconsin

CAROLYN WELLS, MSW, Ph.D.
Associate Professor, Social Work Program
Marquette University
Milwaukee, Wisconsin

JAMES P. WINSHIP, MSW, DPA
Assistant Professor
University of Wisconsin — Whitewater
Whitewater, Wisconsin

I

INTRODUCTION

The Practice of Social Work, Fourth Edition, is intended for use in social work practice courses. The focus of this book is on the theoretical and practical knowledge that students need to do the tasks of a beginning-level social worker. This book is designed to be read by students preparing for, or already in, field placement.

1

OVERVIEW OF SOCIAL WORK PRACTICE

PURPOSE OF THIS CHAPTER

What do social workers do? How is social work different from psychology, psychiatry, guidance and counseling, and other helping professions? What is the relationship between social work and social welfare? What knowledge, skills, and values do social workers need to be effective? Since there are hundreds of intervention techniques available, which ones should social workers learn? This chapter will seek to address these questions. There have been a number of other efforts to address these same issues. (See Baer and Federico, 1978; Bartless, 1970; *Classification Processes for Social Service Positions: Part I–IV*, 1981; "Conceptual Frameworks II," 1981; "Curriculum Policy for the Master's Degree & Baccalaureate Degree Programs in Social Work Education," 1982; Germain and Gitterman, 1980; Lowenberg and Dolgoff, 1971; Pincus and Minahan, 1973; "Special Issue on Conceptual Frameworks," 1977; *Standards for the Classification of Social Work Practice*, 1982; *Standards for the Regulation of Social Work Practice*, 1976; *Standards for Social Service Manpower*, 1973.) This chapter is largely an effort to integrate these prior conceptualizations. The purpose of this chapter is to describe social work as a profession and thereby assist social workers and other interested persons in understanding and articulating what social work is and what is unique about the social work profession. We will begin by taking a brief look at the history of social work.

HISTORY OF SOCIAL WORK

Social work as a profession is of relatively recent origin. To attempt to meet the needs of people living in urban areas, the first social welfare agencies were developed in the early 1800s. These agencies, or services, were private and were developed primarily at the initiation of clergymen and religious groups. Up until the early 1900s these services were provided exclusively by clergymen and affluent "do-gooders" who had no formal training and little understanding of human behavior or of how to help people. The focus of these private services was on meeting such basic physical needs as food and shelter and on attempting to cure emotional and personal difficulties with religious admonitions.

An illustration of an early social welfare organization was the Society for the Prevention of Pauperism, founded by John Griscom in 1820 (Bemner, 1962, p. 13). This society aimed to investigate the habits and circumstances of the poor, to suggest plans by which the poor could help themselves, and to encourage the poor to save and economize. One of the remedies used was house-to-house visitation of the poor (a very elementary type of social work).

By the latter half of the 1800s there were a fairly large number of private relief agencies that had been established in large cities to help the unemployed, the poor, the ill, the physically and mentally impaired, and orphans. Programs of these agencies were uncoordinated and sometimes overlapping. Therefore an English invention — the Charity Organization Society (COS) — caught the interest of a number of American cities (Cohen, 1958). Starting in Buffalo, New York, in 1877, COS was rapidly adopted in many cities. In charity organization societies private agencies joined together to (1) provide direct services to individuals and families — in this respect they were forerunners of social casework and of family counseling approaches, and (2) plan and coordinate the efforts of private agencies to meet the pressing social problems of cities — in this respect they were precursors of community organization and social planning approaches. Charity organizations conducted a detailed investigation of each applicant for services and financial help, maintained a central system of registration of clients to avoid duplication, and used volunteer *friendly visitors* extensively to work with those in difficulty. The friendly visitors were primarily "doers of good works" as they generally gave sympathy rather than money and encouraged the poor to save and to seek employment. Poverty was viewed as a personal shortcoming. Most of the friendly visitors were women.

Concurrent with the COS movement was the establishment of settlement houses in the late 1800s. Toynbee Hall was the first settlement house, established in 1884 in London; many others were soon formed in larger U.S. cities. Many of the early settlement house workers were daughters of ministers. The workers were from the middle and upper classes who would live in a poor neighborhood so they could experience the harsh realities of poverty. Simultaneously, they sought to develop ways in cooperation with neighborhood residents to improve living conditions. In contrast to friendly visitors they lived in impoverished neighborhoods and used the missionary approach of teaching residents how to live moral lives and improve their circumstances. They sought to improve housing, health, and living conditions; find jobs; teach English, hygiene, and occupational skills; and sought to change environmental surroundings through cooperative efforts. Settlement houses used change techniques that are now called social group work, social action, and community organization.

On the one hand settlement houses placed their emphasis on "environmental reform," while at the same time "they continued to struggle to teach the poor the prevailing middle-class values of work, thrift, and abstinence as the keys to success" (Becker, 1968, p. 85). In addition to dealing with local problems by local action, settlement houses played important roles in drafting legislation, and in organizing to influence social policy and legislation. The most noted leader in the settlement house movement was Jane Addams of Hull House in Chicago, who summarized what a settlement house was as follows:

The Settlement, then, is an experimental effort to aid in the solution of the social and industrial problems which are engendered by the modern conditions of life in a great city. (Addams, 1959, pp. 125–26)

Settlement house leaders believed that by changing neighborhoods, they would improve communities; and through altering communities, they would develop a better society.

It appears that the first paid social workers were executive secretaries of charity organization societies in the late 1800s (Dolgoff and Feldstein, 1980, pp. 233–34). In the late 1800s charity organization societies received some contracts from the cities in which they were located to administer relief funds. In administering these programs, COS hired people as executive secretaries to organize and train the friendly visitors and to establish accounting procedures to show accountability for the funds received. To improve the services of friendly visitors, executive secretaries needed to establish standards and training courses. In 1898 a training course was first offered by the New York Charity Organization Society. By 1904 a one-year program was offered by the New York School of Philanthropy. Soon after this time, colleges and universities began offering training programs in social work. Initially, social work education focused on environmental reform approaches to meet social problems. (Environmental reform approaches focus on changing the system to better meet the needs of people. The enactment of the Social Security Act in 1935 to meet the needs of the poor and the unemployed is an example of an environmental reform approach.)

Richard Cabot introduced medical social work into Massachusetts General Hospital in 1905 (Dolgoff and Feldstein, 1980, pp. 233–34). Gradually social workers were employed in schools, courts, child guidance clinics, and other settings.

In 1917 Mary Richmond published *Social Diagnosis*, a text that presented for the first time a theory and methodology for social work. The book focused on how the worker should intervene with individuals. The process is still used today and involves study (collecting information), diagnosis (stating what is wrong), prognosis, and treatment planning (stating what

should be done to help clients improve). This book was important as it formulated a common body of knowledge for casework.

In the 1920s Freud's theories of personality development and therapy became popular. The concepts and explanations of psychiatrists appeared particularly appropriate for social workers, who also worked in one-to-one relationships with clients. The psychiatric approach emphasized intrapsychic processes and focused on enabling clients to adapt and adjust to their social situations. Therefore, social workers switched their emphasis from reform to therapy for the next three decades. In the 1960s, however, there was a renewed interest in sociological approaches, or reform, by social workers. Several reasons account for this change. Questions arose about the relevance and appropriateness of talking approaches with low-income clients who tend to be nonverbal and who have urgent social and economic pressures. Furthermore, the effectiveness of many psychotherapeutic approaches has been questioned (Eysenck, 1961). Other reasons for the renewed interest include the increase in status of sociology and the mood of the 1960s, which raised questions about the relevancy of social institutions in meeting the needs of the population. Social work at the present time embraces both the reform and the therapy approaches.[1]

Not until the end of World War I did social work begin to be recognized as a distinct profession. The depression of the 1930s and the enactment of the Social Security Act in 1935 brought about an extensive expansion of public social services and job opportunities for social workers. Since 1900 there has been a growing awareness by social agency boards and the public that professionally trained social workers are needed to provide social services competently. In 1955 the National Association of Social Workers was formed to represent the social work profession in this country. The purpose of this association is to improve social

---

[1]Note: The author believes there is little difference between the terms *psychotherapy* and *counseling* (for emotional and behavioral problems), and therefore these terms will be used interchangeably in this text.

Relief agencies prior to the twentieth century focused on meeting the basic needs of the poor, the unemployed, and the ill. Two engravings from Harper's Weekly — *"For the Poor" and "Visiting the Sick" — present an admiring view of the roles played by the church and the upper class in ministering to the needy.*

conditions in society and promote high quality and effectiveness in social work practice.

In recent years there has been considerable activity in developing a system of registration or licensing of social workers. Such a system helps in assuring the public that qualified personnel are providing social work services, and it also advances the recognition of social work as a profession. Most states have now passed legislation to license or regulate the practice of social work.

Social work is a relatively young profession, but it constitutes one of the most important professions in our society in terms of the number of people affected, the human misery treated, and the amount of money spent.

DEFINITION OF SOCIAL WORK

Social work has been defined by the National Association of Social Workers (NASW) as follows (*Standards for Social Service Manpower*, 1973, pp. 3–4):

Social work is the professional activity of helping individuals, groups, or communities to enhance or restore their capacity for social functioning and to create societal conditions favorable to their goals.

Social work practice consists of the professional application of social work values, principles, and techniques to one or more of the following ends: helping people obtain tangible services; providing counseling and psychotherapy for individuals, families, and groups; helping communities or groups provide or improve social and health services and participating in relevant legislative processes.

The practice of social work requires knowledge of human development and behavior; of social, economic, and cultural institutions; and of the interaction of all these factors.

The term *social worker* is generally applied to graduates (either with bachelor's or master's degrees) of schools of social work who are employed in the field of social welfare. A social worker is a *change agent*, a helper who is specifically employed for the purpose of creating planned change (Pincus and Minahan, 1973, p. 54). As a change agent a social worker is expected to be skilled at working with individuals, groups, and families, and in bringing about community changes.

RELATIONSHIP BETWEEN SOCIAL WORK AND SOCIAL WELFARE

The goal of social welfare is to fulfill the social, financial, health, and recreational requirements of all individuals in a society. Social welfare seeks to enhance the social functioning of all age groups, both rich and poor. When other institutions in our society (such as the market economy and the family) fail at times to meet the basic needs of individuals or groups of people, then social services are needed and demanded.

Along with many other concepts, social welfare has not been precisely defined. The National Association of Social Workers states (*Encyclopedia of Social Work*, 1971, p. 1446):

Social welfare generally denotes the full range of organized activities of voluntary and governmental agencies that seek to prevent, alleviate, or contribute to the solution of recognized social problems, or to improve the well-being of individuals, groups or communities. Such activities use a wide variety of professional personnel, such as physicians, nurses, lawyers, educators, engineers, ministers, and social workers.

Examples of social welfare programs and services are foster care, adoption, day care, Head Start, probation and parole, public assistance programs (such as Aid to Families with Dependent Children), public health nursing, sex therapy, suicide counseling, recreational services (Boy Scouts and YWCA programs), services to minority groups and veterans, school social services, medical and legal services to the poor, family planning services, Meals on Wheels, nursing home

FIGURE 1.1

Examples of Professional Groups within the Field of Social Welfare

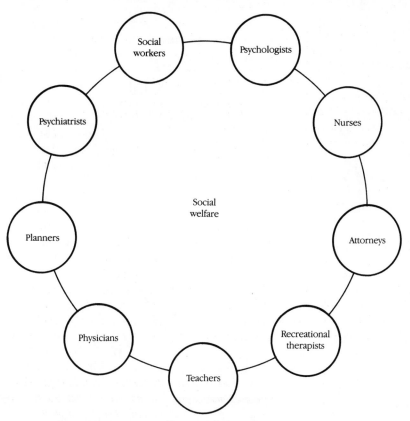

Professional people staffing social welfare services include attorneys providing legal services to the poor; urban planners in social planning agencies; physicians in public health agencies; teachers in residential treatment facilities for the emotionally disturbed; psychologists, nurses, and recreational therapists in mental hospitals; and psychiatrists in mental health clinics.

services, shelters for battered spouses, services to persons with acquired immune deficiency syndrome (AIDS), protective services for victims of child abuse and neglect, assertiveness training, encounter groups and sensitivity training, public housing projects, family counseling, Alcoholics Anonymous, runaway services, services to people with developmental disabilities, and sheltered workshops.

Almost all social workers are employed in the field of social welfare. There are, however, many other professional and occupational groups working in the field of social welfare, as illustrated in Figure 1.1.

Social services seek to improve the quality of life for all age groups. Above, a Meals on Wheels volunteer makes a home delivery with a week's worth of frozen dinners.

WHAT IS THE PROFESSION OF SOCIAL WORK?

The National Association of Social Workers defines the social work profession as follows:

The social work profession exists to provide humane and effective social services to individuals, families, groups, communities, and society so that social functioning may be enhanced and the quality of life improved. . . .

The profession of social work, by both traditional and practical definition, is the profession that provides the formal knowledge base, theoretical con-

cepts, specific functional skills, and essential social values which are used to implement society's mandate to provide safe, effective, and constructive social services.[2]

Social work is thus distinct from other professions (such as psychology and psychiatry) as it is the profession that has the responsibility and mandate to provide social services.

A social worker needs training and expertise in a wide range of areas to be able to effectively handle problems faced by individuals, groups, and the larger community. While most professions are increasingly becoming more specialized (for example, most medical doctors now specialize in one or two areas), social work continues to emphasize a generic (broad-based) approach. The practice of social work is analogous to the old general practice of medicine. A general practitioner in medicine (or family practice) has training to handle a wide range of common medical problems faced by people, while a social worker has training to handle a wide range of common social and personal problems faced by people. The case example on page 10 highlights some of the skills needed by social workers.

GENERALIST SOCIAL WORK PRACTICE

There used to be an erroneous belief that a social worker was either a caseworker, a group worker, or a community organizer. Practicing social workers know that such a belief is faulty because every social worker is involved as a change agent in working with individuals, groups, and community groups. The amount of time spent at these levels varies from worker to worker, but every worker will, at times, be assigned and expected to work at these three levels and therefore needs training in all of them.

---

[2]Published 1982, National Association of Social Workers, Inc. Reprinted with permission, from *Standards for the Classification of Social Work Practice*, Policy Statement 4, p. 5. Copyright National Association of Social Workers, Inc.

The Council on Social Work Education (the national accrediting entity for baccalaureate and master's programs in social work) requires all bachelor's level and master's level programs to train their students in generalist social work practice. (MSW programs, in addition, usually require their students to select and study in an area of specialization. MSW programs generally offer several specializations, such as family therapy, administration, corrections, and clinical social work.)

A generalist social worker is trained to assess and treat people (who have a variety of social and personal problems) with a large number of assessment and intervention techniques. Anderson (1981) has identified three characteristics of a generalist social worker: (*a*) The generalist is often the first professional to see clients as they enter the social welfare system; (*b*) the worker must therefore be competent to assess their needs and to identify their stress points and problems; and (*c*) the worker must draw on a variety of skills and methods in serving clients.

D. Brieland, L. B. Costin, and C. R. Atherton (1985, pp. 120–21) define and describe generalist practice as follows:

The generalist social worker, the equivalent of the general practitioner in medicine, is characterized by a wide repertoire of skills to deal with basic conditions, backed up by specialists to whom referrals are made. This role is a fitting one for the entry-level social worker.

The generalist model involves identifying and analyzing the interventive behaviors appropriate to social work. The worker must perform a wide range of tasks related to the provision and management of direct service, the development of social policy, and the facilitation of social change. The generalist should be well grounded in systems theory that emphasizes interaction and independence. The major system that will be used is the local network of services. . . .

The public welfare worker in a small county may be a classic example of the generalist. He or she knows the resources of the county, is acquainted with the key people, and may have considerable influence to accomplish service goals, including obtaining jobs, different housing, or emergency food and clothing.

The activities of the urban generalist are more complex, and more effort must be expended to use the array of resources.

The crux of generalist practice involves a view of the situation in terms of the person-in-environment conceptualization (described in an upcoming section in this chapter) and the capacity and willingness to intervene at several different levels, if necessary, while assuming any number of roles. The case example on page 13 illustrates the approach of responding at several different levels in a variety of roles.

This text should facilitate readers' learning a generalist practice approach in social work by describing a variety of assessment and intervention strategies. Through learning these strategies, readers can then select those approaches that hold the most promise in facilitating positive changes in clients (who may be individuals, groups, families, or communities).

The Change Process

A social worker uses a *change process* in working with clients. (Clients include individuals, groups, families, organizations, and communities.) The change process can be conceptualized as involving five phases:

Phase I: Intake

Phase II: Data Collection and Assessment

Phase III: Planning and Contracting

Phase IV: Intervention and Monitoring

Phase V: Evaluation and Termination

Each of these phases will be briefly described.

PHASE I: INTAKE   This phase involves the social worker gathering initial information from the client about his or her problems and reasons for seeking help. Intake also involves an assessment of the degree of match, or fit, between the client's needs and the agency's eligibility requirements and resources. The service may be terminated for a lack of fit. The client may be referred elsewhere for service, perhaps because of the presumed superiority of some other agency's resources. Or, the fit may be deemed appropriate, and the social worker and the client then move on to Phase II. During

Rape

D r. Richard Carr referred Kay Barber to Lakeside Counseling Center (a mental health center). Kay is 17 years old and a senior at West High School. The previous evening she had been raped by four males in a parking lot near West High. The rape had occurred after Kay had left a school dance, about 1:00 A.M. The intake worker assigned the case to Karen Bowman, a social worker who in the recent past had counseled most of the agency's sexual assault cases. Ms. Bowman immediately met with Kay.

Kay was in tears, was badly bruised, and was still shaking from terror. She was angry, confused, and deeply hurt emotionally. In the next 50 minutes she briefly described the details of the assault and some of her feelings. She was getting into her dad's car, alone, when she was grabbed by two youths and pulled into some bushes. Behind the bushes were two other youths, one of whom she recognized as being the son of a college professor in the community. Following the assault, the youths warned her there would be serious trouble if she informed anyone. Hurt (emotionally and physically) and terrified, she returned home. Her mother was awake when she returned and immediately recognized that something had happened. Kay informed her parents. Kay's mother was horrified and angry, but attempted to comfort Kay. Kay indicated that her father was even more upset, and even today was talking about shooting the rapists if he could find out who they were (Kay had not as yet informed him that she knew one of the attackers for fear of what her father might do).

Kay indicated that upon hearing of the assault her parents took her to the police station. There she was questioned by two male police officers. Kay indicated that she revealed only sketchy details of the rape to the police officers as she was in tears, still terrified, and was on the defensive because she felt many of the officers' questions suggested she contributed to the rape. She also felt the officers may not have even believed she was assaulted.

Earlier this morning her parents took her to the family doctor, Richard Carr, who provided medical attention and then referred the case to the counseling center.

Kay was especially confused about a number of issues. Should she seek to press charges against the youths, particularly the one she knew? If she pressed charges, would she have to appear in court? What might this do to her reputation if she went to court? If she didn't press charges, might not these youths rape others, or perhaps even herself in the future? In either case how would she face the other students in school who she felt would hear, one way or the other, about the attack? Why did the police officers doubt her story about being raped, and why did the officers imply she may have contributed to the assault? What were her chances of getting pregnant? If she were pregnant, what would she do then? (Ms. Bowman indicated that the medical services she received might well have prevented her from now being pregnant—and this could be checked with Dr. Carr.) Should she inform her father that she knew one of the assailants? If she did, what might be the consequences? How could she ever learn to deal with the terror she experienced? She also indicated that she felt she would never go out in the evening, alone or with anyone else, in the future, unless she went with a member of her family. And, she wondered why this had to happen to her.

Ms. Bowman listened attentively, and conveyed warmth, empathy, support, and a sincere sense of caring. After Kay had ventilated her concerns, Ms. Bowman expressed her understanding that Kay had been deeply hurt and was now feeling overwhelmed by this situation. Ms. Bowman gradually informed Kay that something could be done about all of her present concerns. The way to proceed would be to take her concerns, one by one, and work on resolving them. Ms. Bowman asked Kay to indicate her most urgent concerns. Kay thought awhile and said they were whether to inform her parents that she knew one of the attackers, whether to press charges, and how to react to schoolmates who might make cruel remarks related to the rape.

Kay was then asked to elaborate her concerns in each of these three areas. Her concerns about telling her parents centered around what her father might do. Her concerns about pressing charges focused on wanting to know the procedures involved and what might be the consequences to her of a long drawn-out court trial. In regard to cruel remarks from others, Ms. Bowman suggested to Kay that they role-play how she might respond to such remarks. Ms. Bowman first played Kay's role to model a few assertive strategies to respond to cruel remarks. The roles were then reversed, with Ms. Bowman role-playing someone giving a crude remark, and Kay practicing responding to them.

After this initial hour and 40-minute meeting, Kay became a little more relaxed. Kay mentioned that she was really worried about what her father might do. Ms. Bowman suggested her parents (who were in the waiting room) might be brought in to discuss their concerns. Kay agreed. A rather lengthy meeting was then held with the Barbers. They began by ventilating a great deal of anger, wanting to find out who did this. Mr. Barber indicated he was going to shoot whoever did this. Ms. Bowman mentioned Kay was partially upset, now, by what her father might do if he found out, and asked Mr. Barber if he was aware of this. Following a lengthy discussion of the negative consequences of taking the law into one's own hands, tears came to Mr. Barber and he acknowledged he would not carry out his threats, and that he was only saying this because he felt so helpless. After Mr. Barber gave full assurance that he would not do anything illegal, he was informed that Kay thought she knew one of the attackers. The pros and cons of pressing charges were then discussed. The procedures involved were described. Another meeting was arranged for the next day with the Barbers to talk further about this, partially because they wanted additional time to think about what to do. Time was also set aside for tomorrow for Kay and Ms. Bowman to meet to talk further about her concerns.

As indicated earlier, this case was only one of several sexual assault cases that Ms. Bowman was handling. These cases led her to conclude that the area she was living in (320,000 population) needed a well-publicized rape crisis center. She began by gathering data on the incidence of sexual assault in the community—from the police department (many cases go unreported) and from other social service agencies in the community. She then convinced the director of the counseling center to form a committee of representatives from other interested social service agencies in the community and from certain women's organizations in the community. After formation of the committee (of which Ms. Bowman

Continued

CASE EXAMPLE   *Continued*

was a member) a questionnaire to obtain further information on the incidence of sexual assault was constructed. It was distributed by members of the committee at a large shopping
center in town to women as they shopped in the mall (respondents in this way remained
entirely anonymous). The results suggested less than one rape in ten was being reported to
the police, which further documented the need for a rape crisis center that would be well
publicized so that victims would know where help was available. Another proposed service
of the center would be to provide speakers to schools and other organizations on how to
avoid becoming a victim and on what to do if an assault occurred. The center would also
work with the police department and with the court system to "humanize" the reporting
and processing of sexual assault cases. The committee then wrote a grant proposal. After
eleven months of searching for funding, the proposal was funded for a three-year test period by the city and the United Way. Because of her capacities in this area, Karen Bowman
was appointed assistant director of this rape crisis center.

*   *   *   *   *

*This case illustration documents a wide range of knowledge and skills displayed by Ms.
Bowman: interviewing skills, ability to counsel effectively individuals and families during a
crisis, ability to work effectively with other agencies, research and grant-writing skills, public
speaking capacities, program development and fundraising skills, and knowledge of how
to handle ethical/legal issues that arise.*

*Perhaps the most basic skill that a social worker needs is to be able to counsel clients ef-
fectively. If one is not able to do this, one should probably not be in social work, certainly
not in direct service. Another key skill is to be able to interact effectively with other groups
and professionals in the area. Social workers need to learn a wide range of skills and intervention techniques that will enable them to intervene effectively with (a) the common
personal and emotional problems of clients, and (b) the common social problems faced by
groups and the larger community.*

Intake (and during the other phases) it is important
that the worker seeks to establish and continue a working relationship. A working relationship is facilitated by
the worker's encouragement and by the reflection of empathy, warmth, and genuineness. (See Chapter 5 for an
elaboration of skills and techniques to establish rapport.)

PHASE II: DATA COLLECTION AND ASSESSMENT   This phase
focuses on the collection and analysis of data to allow
the social worker to understand the client's situation.

Assessment is the process of analyzing the data in order
to make sense of it. The processes of collecting data
and arriving at valid assessments are described in
Chapter 3.

PHASE III: PLANNING AND CONTRACTING   This phase involves the assessment of the situation. It involves the
specification of goals; the generation and consideration of various action strategies to reach these goals;
the selection of one or more action strategies; and the

CASE EXAMPLE

Generalist Practice Involves Options Planning

Jack Dawson is a social worker at a high school in a midwestern state. Four teenagers are expelled (consistent with school board policy) for being caught drinking alcoholic beverages at the school during school hours. Mr. Dawson assesses the situation and identifies the following potential courses of action. He can serve as an advocate for the youths by urging the school board and the administration to reinstate the youths. Mr. Dawson is aware that the expulsions are upsetting not only to the youths and their parents but also to the police department and the business community (because expelled youths tend to spend the day on the streets of the city). He can seek to involve the four teenagers in one-to-one counseling about their expulsion and their drinking patterns. He can involve these youths (along with others having drinking problems) in group counseling at the school. He can function as a broker to have the youths receive individual or group counseling from a counseling center outside the school system. He can ascertain the willingness of the parents of these teenagers to become involved in family therapy and serve as a broker to link the interested families with a counseling center that offers family therapy. He can raise the issue (to parents, to the business community, to the police department, to the school administration, and to the school board) of whether expulsion from school for drinking alcoholic beverages is a desirable policy. (Perhaps a better policy is to give the youths the choice of either participating in counseling or receiving supervision from the juvenile probation department. Expulsion is a drastic measure that may adversely affect the futures of these youths.) He can serve as an organizer and a catalyst to encourage interested parents and school staff to use the incident as a rationale for incorporating educational material on alcohol and other drugs into the curriculum. (The selected course of action will depend on a variety of factors, including a cost-benefit analysis of each course.)

---

development of an informal or formal contract with the client that is designed to reach the specified goals. The Planning and Contracting phase is a bridge between the Assessment phase and the Intervention phase. Planning and contracting are described in Chapters 5, 6, 7, 8, and 9.

PHASE IV: INTERVENTION AND MONITORING   This is the point at which the intervention or action strategies are applied and monitored. Monitoring involves keeping

track of the interventions being employed and continuously evaluating the extent to which these interventions are achieving the goals of the change process. Intervention and monitoring are described in Chapters 5, 8, 9, and 10.

PHASE V: TERMINATION AND EVALUATION   In this phase, the worker ends contact with the client for this change process and also ends the process of assessing the extent to which the interventions or action strategies have achieved the specified goals. If a close working relationship has formed between the worker and the client, termination is often a painful process — especially for the client and sometimes also for the worker. In the change process, sensitive issues are often addressed, considerable effort is frequently made to make constructive changes, dependency may develop, and as a result the client is apt to experience a sense of loss when termination occurs. The client may also feel angry and rejected.

The final evaluation involves more than the assessment of what occurred during monitoring, because it places a value on the usefulness of the change process. The final evaluation is also extremely significant to the agency, because it provides information about whether, for this situation, the agency's services have been beneficial. Each agency needs composite evaluations of all their services to all clients in order to provide documentation to funding sources of the extent to which the agency's services are worthy of continued funding. Termination and evaluation are described in Chapters 5, 6, 7, 8, 9, and 10.

A Variety of Roles

In working with individuals, groups, families, and communities, a social worker is expected to be knowledgeable and skillful in filling a variety of roles. The particular role that is selected should (ideally) be determined by what will be most effective, given the circumstances.

ENABLER   In this role a worker *helps* individuals or groups to articulate their needs, to clarify and identify their problems, to explore resolution strategies, to select and apply a strategy, and to develop their capacities to deal with their own problems more effectively. This role model is perhaps the most frequently used approach in counseling individuals, groups, and families. The model is also used in community organization — primarily when the objective is to help people organize to help themselves.

BROKER   A broker links individuals and groups who need help (and do not know where help is available) with community services. For example, a wife who is frequently physically abused by her husband might be referred to a shelter home for battered women. Nowadays even moderate-sized communities have 200 or 300 social service agencies/organizations providing community services. Even human services professionals are often only partially aware of the total service network in their community.

Some agencies (such as neighborhood centers, mental health clinics, public welfare departments, agencies serving the elderly, and agencies providing family planning services) may employ *community outreach workers* whose function is to inform residents about available services, identify individuals and families with problems, and link such families with available services.

ADVOCATE   The role of an advocate has been borrowed from the law profession. It is an active directive role in which the social worker is an advocate for a client or for a citizen's group. When a client or a citizen's group is in need of help and existing institutions are uninterested (and sometimes openly negative and hostile) in providing services, then the advocate's role may be appropriate. In such a role, the advocate provides leadership for collecting information, for arguing the correctness of the client's need and request, and for challenging the institution's decision not to provide services. The object is not to ridicule or censure a particular institution but to modify or change one or more of its service policies. In this role the advocate is a partisan who is exclusively serving the interests of a client or of a citizen's group.

ACTIVIST   An activist seeks basic institutional change; often the objective involves a shift in power and resources to a disadvantaged group. An activist is concerned about social injustice, inequity, and deprivation. Tactics involve conflict, confrontation, and negotiation. Social action is concerned with changing the social environment in order to better meet the recognized needs of individuals. The methods used are assertive and action-oriented (for example, organizing welfare recipients to work toward improvements in services and increases in money payments). Activities of social action include fact-finding, analysis of community needs, research, the dissemination and interpretation of information, organizing activities with people, and other efforts to mobilize public understanding and support in behalf of some existing or proposed social program. Social action activity can be geared toward a problem that is local, statewide, or national in scope.

In addition to these roles, it is important for social workers to be skilled at public speaking and public education. Potential clients and service providers are often unaware of present services or gaps in services. Social workers occasionally talk to a variety of groups (e.g., high school classes, public service organizations such as Kiwanis, police officers, staff at other agencies) to inform them of available services, or to advocate the need to develop new services for clients having unmet needs. In recent years a variety of new services have been identified as being needed (for example, runaway centers, services for battered spouses, rape crisis centers, services for persons with AIDS, and group homes for youth). Social workers who have public speaking skills are not only better able to interpret services to groups of potential clients, but probably also earn a few thousand dollars more each year.

MEDICAL MODEL VERSUS ECOLOGICAL MODEL OF HUMAN BEHAVIOR

Medical Model

From the 1920s to the 1960s most social workers used a medical model approach to assessing and changing human behavior. This approach was initiated primarily by Sigmund Freud. It views clients as *patients*. The task of the provider of services is first to diagnose the causes of a patient's problems and then to provide treatment. The patient's problems are viewed as being inside the patient.

In regard to emotional and behavioral problems of people, the medical model conceptualizes such problems as *mental illnesses*. People with emotional or behavioral problems are then given medical labels, such as schizophrenic, psychotic, or insane. Adherents of the medical approach believe the disturbed person's mind is affected by some generally unknown, internal condition. That unknown, internal condition is thought to result from a variety of possible causative factors: genetic endowment, metabolic disorders, infectious diseases, internal conflicts, unconscious uses of defense mechanisms, and traumatic early experiences that cause emotional fixations and prevent future psychological growth.

The medical model has a lengthy classification of mental disorders that are defined by the American Psychiatric Association. The major mental disorders are listed in Table 1-1 on the following page.

In DSM-III-R (American Psychiatric Association, 1987) numerous mental disorders are defined. Examples of a few of these disorders are the following:

SCHIZOPHRENIA   A large group of disorders, usually of psychotic proportion, manifested by characteristic disturbances of language and communication, thought, perception, affect, and behavior that last longer than six months.

PARANOIA   A rare condition characterized by the gradual development of an intricate, complex, and elaborate system of thinking based on (and often proceeding logically from) misinterpretation of an actual event. A person with paranoia often considers himself endowed with unique and superior ability or has systematized delusions of persecution.

HYPOCHONDRIASIS   A chronic maladaptive style of relating to the environment through preoccupation with shifting somatic concerns and symptoms, a fear or conviction that one has a serious physical illness, seeking of medical treatment, inability to accept reassurance, and either hostile or dependent relationships with caregivers and family.

BIPOLAR DISORDER   A major affective disorder in which there are episodes of both mania and depression; formerly called manic-depressive psychosis. Bipolar disorder may be subdivided into manic, depressed, or mixed types on the basis of currently presenting symptoms.

TABLE 1.1

Major Mental Disorders According to the American Psychiatric Association

DISORDERS USUALLY FIRST EVIDENT IN INFANCY, CHILDHOOD, OR ADOLESCENCE

Include, but are not limited to, mental retardation, attention deficit disorders (including hyperactivity), eating disorders (including anorexia), pervasive developmental disorders (e.g., infantile autism), and others.

ORGANIC MENTAL DISORDERS

Can be induced by substances (alcohol, drugs) or can be organic brain syndromes (delirium, dementia, etc.).

SUBSTANCE USE DISORDERS

Abuse of alcohol, barbiturates, amphetamines, and so on.

SCHIZOPHRENIC DISORDERS

All forms of schizophrenia.

DELUSIONAL (PARANOID) DISORDERS

All forms of paranoia and persistent irrational delusions. Often there is a fear of persecution.

MOOD DISORDERS

Emotional disorders such as depression or exaggerated mood swings, including manic behavior.

ANXIETY DISORDERS

Phobias, panic, extreme anxiety, and stress from traumatic experiences, (for example, battle shock).

SOMATOFORM DISORDERS

Psychological problems that manifest themselves as symptoms of physical disease (for example, hypochondria).

DISSOCIATIVE DISORDERS

Problems in which part of the personality is dissociated from the rest (for example, multiple personalities and amnesia).

SEXUAL DISORDERS

Sexually related problems such as transsexualism, exhibitionism, and inhibited sexual desire.

SLEEP DISORDERS

Insomnia and other problems with sleep.

DISORDERS OF IMPULSE CONTROL

The inability to control certain undesirable impulses (for example, kleptomania, pyromania, and pathological gambling).

ADJUSTMENT DISORDERS

Difficulty in adjusting to the stress created by such common events as unemployment or divorce.

PERSONALITY DISORDERS

Inflexible and maladaptive patterns of sufficient severity to cause either significant impairment in adaptive functioning or subjective distress.

Source: American Psychiatric Association, *DSM-III-R (The Diagnostic and Statistical Manual of Mental Disorders, Third Edition, Revised)* (Washington, D.C.: American Psychiatric Association, 1987).

PHOBIA An obsessive, persistent, unrealistic, intense fear of an object or situation. A few common phobias are the following:

Acrophobia: Fear of heights

Algophobia: Fear of pain

Claustrophobia: Fear of closed spaces

Erythrophobia: Fear of blushing

PERSONALITY DISORDERS Deeply ingrained, inflexible, maladaptive patterns of relating, perceiving, and thinking of sufficient severity to cause either impairment in functioning or distress. Listed below are some personality disorders and their characteristics:

Antisocial: A lack of socialization along with behavior patterns that bring a person repeatedly into conflict with society; incapacity for significant loyalty to others or to social values; callousness; irresponsibility; impulsiveness; and inability to feel guilt or learn from experience or punishment.

Borderline: Instability in a variety of areas, including interpersonal relationships, behavior, mood, and self-image.

Compulsive: Restricted ability to express warm and tender emotions; preoccupation with rules, order, organization, efficiency, and detail; excessive devotion to work and productivity to the exclusion of pleasure; indecisiveness.

Narcissistic: Grandiose sense of self-importance or uniqueness; preoccupation with fantasies of limitless success; need for constant attention and admiration; and disturbances in interpersonal relationships such as lack of empathy, exploitativeness, and relationships that vacillate between the extremes of overidealization and devaluation.

Passive-aggressive: Aggressive behavior manifested in passive ways such as obstructionism, pouting, procrastination, intentional inefficiency, and obstinacy.

Schizoid: Manifested by shyness, oversensitivity, social withdrawal, frequent daydreaming, avoidance of close or competitive relationships, and eccentricity. Persons with this disorder often react to disturbing experiences with apparent detachment and are unable to express hostility and ordinary aggressive feelings.

The medical model approach arose in reaction to the historical notion that the emotionally disturbed were possessed by demons, were mad, and were to be blamed for their disturbances. These people were "treated" by being beaten, locked up, or killed. The medical model led to viewing the disturbed as one in need of help, stimulated research into the nature of emotional problems, and promoted the development of therapeutic approaches.

The major evidence for the validity of the medical model approach comes from studies suggesting that some mental disorders, such as schizophrenia, may be influenced by genetics (heredity). The bulk of the evidence for the importance of heredity comes from studies of twins. For instance, Hofer and Polin (1970) found a concordance rate (if one has it, both have it) for schizophrenia of 15.5 percent for identical twins and 4.4 percent for fraternal twins in a sample of over 15,000 twins. Critics of such studies argue that the findings may be flawed, claiming that the physical similarity of identical twins leads their family and friends to treat them alike. However, there is some research (Kety, 1976) suggesting a higher concordance rate for schizophrenia among identical twins even when they have been raised apart.

Ecological Model

In the 1960s social work began questioning the usefulness of the medical model. Environmental factors were shown to be at least as important in causing a client's problems as internal factors. Research also was demonstrating that psychoanalysis was probably ineffective in treating clients' problems (Stuart, 1970).

In the 1960s social work shifted at least some of its emphasis to a *reform approach*. A reform approach seeks to change systems to benefit clients. The enactment of the antipoverty programs (such as Head Start) in the 1960s is an example of an effort to change systems to benefit clients.

In the past several years social work has increasingly focused on using an *ecological approach*. This approach integrates both treatment and reform by conceptualizing and emphasizing the dysfunctional transactions between people and their physical and social

FIGURE 1.2

Person-in-Environment Conceptualization

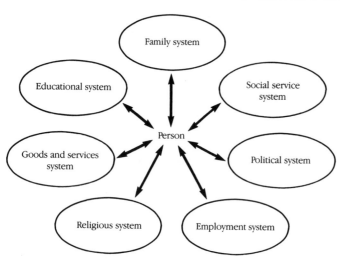

People in our society continually interact with many systems, some of which are listed in this figure.

environments. Human beings are viewed as developing and adapting through transactions with all elements of their environments. An ecological model gives attention to both internal and external factors. It does not view people as passive reactors to their environments, but rather as being involved in dynamic and reciprocal interactions with them.

It tries to improve the coping patterns of people and their environments so that a better match can be attained between an individual's needs and the characteristics of his/her environment. One of the emphases of an ecological model is on the person-in-environment. The person-in-environment conceptualization is depicted in Figure 1.2.

Figure 1.2 suggests that people interact with many systems. With this conceptualization, social work can focus on three separate areas. First, it can focus on the person and seek to develop his problem-solving, coping, and developmental capacities. Second, it can focus on the relationship between a person and the systems he or she interacts with and link the person with needed resources, services, and opportunities. Third, it can focus on the systems and seek to reform them to meet the needs of the individual more effectively.

The ecological model views individuals, families, and small groups as having transitional problems and needs as they move from one life stage to another. Individuals face many transitional changes as they grow older. Examples of some of the transitions are learning to walk, entering first grade, adjusting to puberty, graduating from school, finding a job, getting married, having children, having children leave home, and retiring.

Families also have a life cycle. The following are only a few of the events that require adjustment: engagement, marriage, birth of children, parenting, children going to school, children leaving home, and loss of a parent (perhaps through death or divorce).

Small groups also have transitional phases of development. Members of small groups spend time getting acquainted, gradually learn to trust each other, begin to self-disclose more, learn to work together on tasks, develop approaches to handle interpersonal conflict, and face adjustments to the group eventually terminating or some members leaving.

A central concern of an ecological model is to articulate the transitional problems and needs of individuals, families, and small groups. Once these problems and needs are identified, intervention approaches are then selected and applied to help individuals, families, and small groups resolve the transitional problems and meet their needs.

An ecological model can also focus on the maladaptive interpersonal problems and needs in families and groups. It can seek to articulate the maladaptive communication processes and dysfunctional relationship patterns of families and small groups. These difficulties cover an array of areas, including interpersonal conflicts, power struggles, double binds, distortions in communicating, scapegoating, and discrimination. The consequences of such difficulties are usually maladaptive for some members. An ecological model seeks to identify such interpersonal obstacles and then apply appropriate intervention strategies. For example, parents may set the price for honesty too high for their children. In such families children gradually learn to hide certain behaviors and thoughts, and even learn to lie. If the parents discover such dishonesty, an uproar usually occurs. An appropriate intervention in such a family is to open up communication patterns and help the parents to understand that if they really want honesty from their children, they need to learn to be more accepting of their children's thoughts and actions.

Two centuries ago people interacted primarily within the family system. Families were nearly self-sufficient. In those days, the *person-in-family* was a way of conceptualizing the main system which individuals interacted with. Our society has become much more complex. Today, a person's life and quality of life are interwoven and interdependent upon many systems, as shown in Figure 1.2.

GOALS OF SOCIAL WORK PRACTICE

Social work practice has been conceptualized as having four major goals (*Standards for the Classification of Social Work Practice*, 1982, p. 17):

Goal 1: Enhance the Problem-Solving, Coping, and Developmental Capacities of People

Using the person-in-environment concept, the focus of social work practice at this level is on the "person." With this focus a social worker serves primarily as an *enabler*. In the role of an enabler, the worker may take on activities of a counselor, teacher, care giver (i.e, providing supportive services to those who cannot fully solve their problems and meet their own needs), and behavior changer (i.e., changing specific parts of a client's behavior).

Goal 2: Link People with Systems That Provide Them with Resources, Services, and Opportunities

Using the person-in-environment concept, the focus of social work practice at this level is on the relationships between persons and the systems they interact with. With this focus a social worker serves primarily as a *broker*.

Goal 3: Promote the Effectiveness and Humane Operation of Systems That Provide People with Resources and Services

Using the person-in-environment concept, the focus of social work practice at this level is on the systems people interact with. One role a worker may fill at this level is that of an advocate. Additional roles at this level are the following:

Program developer: In this role the worker seeks to promote or design programs or technologies to meet social needs.

Supervisor: The worker seeks in this role to increase the effectiveness and efficiency of the delivery of services through supervising other staff.

Coordinator: The worker seeks in this role to improve a delivery system through increasing communications and coordination between human service resources.

Consultant: The worker seeks in this role to provide guidance to agencies and organizations through suggesting ways to increase the effectiveness and efficiency of services.

Goal 4: Develop and Improve Social Policy

Similar to goal three, the focus of social work practice at this level is on the systems people interact with. The distinction between goal three and goal four is that the focus of goal three is on the available resources for serving people, while the focus of goal four is on the statutes and broader social policies that underlie such resources. Major roles of social workers at this level are *planner* and *policy developer*. In these roles, workers develop and seek adoption of new statutes or policies and propose elimination of ineffective or inappropriate statutes and policies. In these planning and policy

development processes, social workers may take on an advocate role and, in some instances, an activist role.

A PROBLEM-SOLVING APPROACH

In working with individuals, families, groups, and communities, social workers use a problem-solving approach. Steps in the problem-solving process can be stated in a variety of ways. Below is a simple statement of this process:

1. Identify as precisely as possible the problem or problems.
2. Generate possible alternative solutions.
3. Evaluate the alternative solutions.
4. Select a solution or solutions to be used, and set goals.
5. Implement the solution(s).
6. Follow up to evaluate how the solution(s) worked.

MICRO, MEZZO, AND MACRO PRACTICE

Social workers practice at three levels: (*a*) micro—working on a one-to-one basis with an individual, (*b*) mezzo—working with families and other small groups, and (*c*) macro—working with communities or seeking changes in statutes and social policies.

The specific activities performed by workers can be described as follows:

Social Casework

Aimed at helping individuals on a one-to-one basis to meet personal and social problems, casework may be geared to helping the client adjust to his/her environment, or to changing certain social and economic pressures that are handicapping an individual. Social casework services are provided by nearly every social welfare agency that provides direct services to people. Social casework encompasses a wide variety of activities, such as counseling runaway youths; helping unemployed people secure training or employment; counseling someone who is suicidal; placing a homeless child in an adoptive or foster home; providing protective services to abused children and their families; finding nursing homes for stroke victims who no longer need to be confined in a hospital; counseling individuals with sexual dysfunctions; helping alcoholics to acknowledge they have a drinking problem; counseling those with a terminal illness; being a probation and parole officer; providing services to single parents; and working in medical and mental hospitals as a member of a rehabilitation team.

Case Management

Recently a number of social service agencies have labeled their social workers *case managers*. The tasks performed by case managers are similar to those of caseworkers. The job descriptions of case managers vary from service area to service area. For example, case managers in a juvenile probation setting are highly involved in supervising clients, providing some counseling, monitoring clients to make certain they are following the rules of probation, linking clients and their families with needed services, preparing court reports, and testifying in court. On the other hand, case managers at a sheltered workshop are apt to be involved in providing job training to clients, counseling clients, arranging transportation, disciplining clients for unacceptable behavior, acting as an advocate for clients, and acting as liaison with the people who supervise clients during their nonwork hours (which may be at a group home, foster home, residential treatment facility, or their parent's home). Hepworth and Larsen (1986, p. 563) describe the role of a case manager as follows:

Case managers link clients to needed resources that exist in complex service delivery networks and orches-

Depression and emotional problems

trate the delivery of services in a timely fashion. Case managers function as brokers, facilitators, linkers, mediators, and advocates. A case manager must have extensive knowledge of community resources, rights of clients, and policies and procedures of various agencies and must be skillful in mediation and advocacy.

Group Work

The intellectual, emotional, and social development of individuals may be furthered through group activities. In contrast to casework or group therapy, it is not primarily therapeutic, except in a broad sense. Different groups have different objectives, such as socialization, information exchange, curbing delinquency, recreation, changing socially unacceptable values, and helping to achieve better relations between cultural and racial groups. For example, a group worker at a neighborhood center may through group activities seek to curb delinquency patterns and change socially unacceptable values; or a worker at an adoption agency may

Drinking and drug problems

Crime

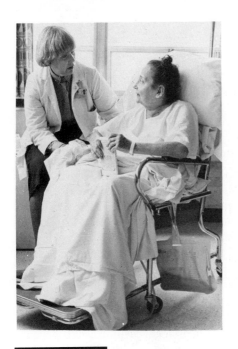

Old age and physical limitations

Poverty and substandard housing

Children learn by repetition.

You don't have to hit to hurt.

San Francisco
Child Abuse Council
(415) 668-0494

Child abuse

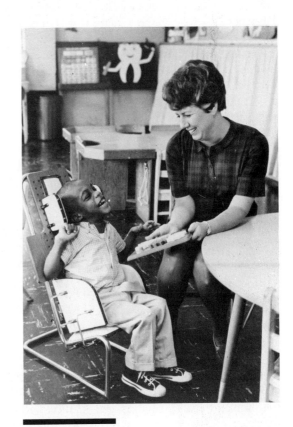

Parentless children

23

meet with a group of applicants to explain adoption procedures and to help applicants prepare for becoming adoptive parents. Activities and focuses of groups vary: arts and crafts; dancing; games; dramatics; music; photography; sports; nature study; woodwork; first aid; home management; information exchange; and discussion of such topics as politics, sex, marriage, religion, and selection of a career.

Group Therapy

Although aimed at facilitating the social and emotional adjustment of individuals through the group process, participants in group therapy usually have adjustment difficulties. Group therapy has within the past two decades become used much more extensively. It has several advantages over one-to-one counseling, such as the operation of the *helper therapy* principle, which maintains it is therapeutic for the helper (who can be any member of a group) to feel he or she has been helpful to others. In contrast to one-to-one counseling, group pressure is often more effective in changing maladaptive behavior of individuals, and group therapy is a time saver as it enables the therapist to treat several people at the same time. A few examples in which group therapy might be used are for individuals who are severely depressed, have drinking problems, are victims of a rape, are psychologically addicted to drugs, have a relative who is terminally ill, are single and pregnant, are recently divorced, or have an eating disorder.

Family Therapy

A type of group therapy aimed at helping families with interactional, behavioral, and emotional problems, family therapy can be used with parent-child interaction problems, marital conflicts, and conflicts with grandparents. A wide variety of problems are dealt with in family therapy or family counseling, such as disagreements between parents and youths on choice of friends, drinking and other drug use, domestic tasks, curfew hours, communication problems, sexual values

and behavior, study habits and grades received, and choice of dates.

Community Organization

The aim of community organization is stimulating and assisting the local community to evaluate, plan, and coordinate efforts to provide for the community's health, welfare, and recreation needs. It perhaps is not possible to define precisely the activities of a community organizer, but such activities are apt to include encouraging and fostering citizen participation, coordinating efforts between agencies or between groups, public relations and public education, research, planning, and being a resource person. A community organizer acts as a catalyst in stimulating and encouraging community action. Agency settings where such specialists are apt to be employed include community welfare councils, social planning agencies, health planning councils, and community action agencies. The term *community organization* is now being replaced in some settings by such labels as *planning, social planning, program development, policy development,* and *macro practice.*

Administration

Administration is the activity that involves directing the overall program of a social service agency. Administrative functions include setting agency and program objectives, analyzing social conditions in the community, making decisions relating to what services will be provided, employing and supervising staff members, setting up an organizational structure, administering financial affairs, and securing funds for the agency's operations. In a small agency these functions may be carried out by one person, while in a larger agency several people may be involved in administrative affairs.

Other areas of professional activity in social work include research, consulting, supervision, and teaching (primarily at the college level). Social casework, case management, group work, group therapy, family therapy, and community organization constitute the primary professional areas that beginning-level social workers are apt to get involved in. All of these activities require that social workers have counseling skills. (Counseling involves helping individuals or groups resolve social and personal problems through the process of developing a relationship, exploring the problem(s) in depth, and exploring alternative solutions—this process is described in Chapter 5.) Caseworkers, group workers, group therapists, and family therapists obviously need a high level of counseling skills in working with individuals and groups. Community organizers need relationship skills, need to be perceptive, and need skills in assessing problems and developing resolution strategies—skills that parallel or are analogous to counseling skills. Therefore, a major emphasis of this text will be on counseling.

Counseling skills, however, are not the only skills needed by social workers. For example, some additional skills needed by caseworkers are being able to do social histories and being able to link clients with other human services. In some agencies such skills as public speaking, preparing and presenting reports to courts and to other agencies, teaching parents better parenting techniques, and so forth are also called for.

KNOWLEDGE, SKILLS, AND VALUES NEEDED FOR SOCIAL WORK PRACTICE

Knowledge

The knowledge needed for effective social work practice has been identified by NASW as follows:

Knowledge *of casework and group work theory and techniques.*

Knowledge *of community resources and services.*

Knowledge *of basic federal and state social service programs and their purposes.*

Knowledge *of community organization theory and the development of health and welfare services.*

Knowledge *of basic socioeconomic and political theory.*

Knowledge *of racial, ethnic, and other cultural groups in society—their values and lifestyles and the resultant issues in contemporary life.*

Knowledge *of sources of professional and scientific research appropriate to practice.*

Knowledge *of the concepts and technques of social planning.*

Knowledge *of the theories and concepts of supervision and the professional supervision of social worker practice.*

Knowledge *of theories and concepts of personnel management.*

Knowledge *of common social and psychological statistical and other research methods and techniques.*

Knowledge *of the theories and concepts of social welfare administration.*

Knowledge *of social and environmental factors affecting clients to be served.*

Knowledge *of the theories and methods of psychosocial assessment and intervention and of differential diagnosis.*

Knowledge *of the theory and behavior of organizational and social systems and of methods for encouraging change.*

Knowledge *of community organization theory and techniques.*

Knowledge *of the theories of human growth and development and of family and social interaction.*

Knowledge *of small-group theory and behavioral dynamics.*

Knowledge *of the theories of group interaction and therapeutic intervention.*

Knowledge *of crisis intervention theories and techniques.*

Knowledge *of advocacy theory and techniques.*

Knowledge *of the ethical standards and practices of professional social work.*

Knowledge *of teaching and instructional theories and techniques.*

Knowledge *of social welfare trends and policies.*

Knowledge *of local, state, and federal laws and regulations affecting social and health services.*[3]

(In regard to the knowledge base of social work, this text summarizes a number of intervention approaches at the micro, mezzo, and macro levels of practice.)

The Council on Social Work Education has categorized the knowledge needed by social workers in four broad content areas. Every accredited social work educational program is expected to provide the following content, which is excerpted from the 1988 curriculum policy statement ("Curriculum Policy for the Master's Degree & Baccalaureate Degree Programs in Social Work Education," 1988, pp. 126–27.)

Human Behavior and the Social Environment

In keeping with social work's person-in-environment focus, students need knowledge of individuals as they develop over the life span and have membership in families, groups, organizations, and communities; students need knowledge of the relationships among human biological, social, psychological, and cultural systems as they affect and are affected by human behavior.

Social Welfare Policy and Services

The major aims of study in this area are to prepare professionals to function as informed and competent practitioners in providing services and as knowledgeable and committed participants in efforts to achieve change in social policies and programs. Students are expected to develop skills in the use and application of scientific knowledge to the analysis and development of social welfare policy and services. They should know the structure of service programs and the history of the organized profession and other social welfare institutions. Social work students should also gain an understanding of the political process

and the means to further the achievement of social work goals and purposes.

Social Work Practice

Social work practice embraces multiple methods and models, including generalist practice and a variety of concentrations defined according to the size of the client populations and other means of classification. Social work practice occurs with individuals, families, small groups, organizations, and communities. This variety and range represent the current state of the art in social work practice.

The curriculum content relating to practice must include the knowledge base, that is, theory, research, and practice wisdom. It must also include the practice skills: exploration and data-gathering, differential assessment and differential planning, intervention, and evaluation relevant to social work practice. The plan for teaching practice should explicitly demonstrate how content on practice relates to the knowledge base and skills that are included in the curriculum content of research.

The practice skills taught for use in any practice context and with any size system must reflect an integration of professional purposes, knowledge, and values.

Research

Informed criticism and a spirit of inquiry are the basis of scientific thinking and of systematic approaches to the acquisition of knowledge and the application of it to practice. Every part of the professional foundation curriculum should therefore help to bring students to an understanding and appreciation of the necessity of a scientific, analytic approach to knowledge building and practice. The ethical use of scientific inquiry should be emphasized throughout.

The content of research should impart scientific methods of building knowledge for practice and of evaluating service delivery in all areas of practice. It should include quantitative and qualitative research methodologies; designs for the systematic evaluation of the student's own practice; and the critical appreciation and use of research and of program evaluation. The plan for teaching research should be explicit

---

[3]Published in 1982, National Association of Social Workers, Inc. Reprinted with permission, from *Standards for the Classification of Social Work Practice*, Policy Statement 4, p. 17. Copyright National Association of Social Workers, Inc.

in showing how content on research relates to the knowledge base and practice skills that are included in the curriculum content of social work practice.

The professional foundation content in research should thus provide skills that will take students beyond the role of consumers of research and prepare them to evaluate their own practice systematically.[4]

This text provides material primarily in the social work practice content area.

Core Practice Skills

One of the most serious issues facing social work education is to articulate clearly the skills needed for social work practice and to spell out the relationship between specific skills and service outcome. At the present time there is a lack of agreement as to the core skills needed by social workers. Unlike many professionals, a social worker does not bring many tangible resources to a helping situation. (A physician, for example, has a wide range of equipment to help diagnose problems and a wide range of tangible treatment techniques, such as medication.) During the early 1980s there were sharp cutbacks in social welfare programs and in social work positions. While there are many reasons for these cutbacks, one is that the social work profession has not been very successful in articulating to the general public the unique and essential skills possessed by social workers. If social work is to continue to grow and develop as a profession, the core practice skills need to be conceptualized more clearly.

There have been a number of efforts to articulate the essential skills for entry-level social work practice positions. A few of these conceptualizations will be presented to indicate contemporary thinking about core practice skills. It should be noted that there are a number of similarities between these conceptualizations, but as yet there is *not* full agreement on these core skills.

Federico (1973, pp. 146–47) has indirectly described social work skills by outlining roles and activities:

1. Outreach worker—*reaching out into the community to identify need and follow up referrals to service contexts.*
2. Broker—*knowing services available and making sure those in need reach the appropriate services.*
3. Advocate—*helping specific clients obtain services when they might otherwise be rejected, and helping to expand services to cover more needy persons.*
4. Evaluation—*evaluating needs and resources, generating alternatives for meeting needs, and making decisions between alternatives.*
5. Teacher—*teaching facts and skills.*
6. Mobilizer—*helping to develop new services.*
7. Behavior changer—*changing specific parts of a client's behavior.*
8. Consultant—*working with other professionals to help them be more effective in providing services.*
9. Community planner—*helping community groups plan effectively for the community's social welfare needs.*
10. Care giver—*providing supportive services to those who cannot fully solve their problems and meet their own needs.*
11. Data manager—*collecting and analyzing data for decision-making purposes.*
12. Administrator—*performing the activities necessary to plan and implement a program of services.*

Baer (1979, p. 106) has identified the following ten competencies as being essential for successfully performing the responsibilities of entry-level positions:

1. *Identify and assess situations in which the relationship between people and social institutions needs to be initiated, enhanced, restored, protected, or terminated.*
2. *Develop and implement a plan for improving the well-being of people, based on problem assessment*

---

[4]This excerpt was first published by the Council on Social Work Education, and is reprinted here with its permission. Reprinted from "Curriculum Policy for the Master's Degree & Baccalaureate Degree Programs in Social Work Education," in *Handbook of Accreditation Standards and Procedures* (Alexandria, Va.: Council on Social Work Education, 1988), pp. 126–27.

and the exploration of obtainable goals and available options.

3. *Enhance the problem-solving, coping, and developmental capacities of people.*

4. *Link people with systems that provide them with resources, services, and opportunities.*

5. *Intervene effectively on behalf of populations most vulnerable and discriminated against.*

6. *Promote the effective and humane operation of the systems that provide people with services, resources, and opportunities.*

7. *Actively participate with others in creating new, modified, or improved service, resource, or opportunity systems that are more equitable, just, and responsive to consumers of services; work with others to eliminate unjust systems.*

8. *Evaluate the extent to which the objectives of the intervention plan were achieved.*

9. *Continually evaluate one's professional growth and development through assessment of practice behaviors and skills.*

10. *Contribute to the improvement of service delivery by adding to the knowledge base of the profession as appropriate and supporting and upholding the standards and ethics of the profession.*

These ten competencies were originally developed by Baer and Federico (1978). They have generated considerable discussion among social work educators, and a fair number of social work programs have designed their practice courses to develop these competencies in students.

NASW has identified the following skills as being essential for social work practice:

Skill *in listening to others with understanding and purpose.*

Skill *in eliciting information and in assembling relevant facts to prepare a social history, assessment, and report.*

Skill *in creating and maintaining professional helping relationships and in using oneself in relationships.*

Skill *in observing and interpreting verbal and nonverbal behavior and in using a knowledge of personality theory and diagnostic methods.*

Skill *in engaging clients in efforts to resolve their own problems and in gaining trust.*

Skill *in discussing sensitive emotional subjects in a nonthreatening supportive manner.*

Skill *in creating innovative solutions to clients' needs.*

Skill *in determining the need to end therapeutic relationships and how to do so.*

Skill *in interpreting the findings of research studies and professional literature.*

Skill *in mediating and negotiating between conflicting parties.*

Skill *in providing interorganizational liaison services.*

Skill *in interpreting or communicating social needs to funding sources, the public, or legislators.*[5]

Closely related to conceptualizing essential skills, NASW has identified the following abilities as being needed for social work practice:

Ability *to speak and write clearly.*

Ability *to teach others.*

Ability *to respond supportively in emotion-laden or crisis situations.*

Ability *to serve as a role model in a professional relationship.*

Ability *to interpret complex psychosocial phenomena.*

Ability *to organize a workload to meet designated responsibilities.*

Ability *to identify and obtain resources needed to assist others.*

Ability *to assess one's performance and feelings, and to use help or consultation.*

Ability *to participate in and lead group activities.*

[5]Published 1982, National Association of Social Workers, Inc. Reprinted with permission, from *Standards for the Classification of Social Work Practice*, Policy Statement 4, pp. 17–18. Copyright National Association of Social Workers, Inc.

Ability *to function under stress.*

Ability *to deal with conflict situations or contentious personalities.*

Ability *to relate social and psychological theory to practice situations.*

Ability *to identify the information necessary to solve a problem.*

Ability *to conduct research studies of agency services or one's practice.*[6]

The acquisition of social work skills depends partly on innate abilities of people and partly on learning experiences. Social work educational programs facilitate learning of such skills by theoretical material (e.g., material on how to interview), by practicing such skills (e.g., videotaping students in simulated counseling situations), and by extensively supervising students in practicum courses.

Values

Should the primary objective of imprisonment be rehabilitation or punishment? Should a father committing incest be prosecuted with the likelihood of such publicity in the community leading to family breakup, or should an effort first be made, through counseling, to stop the incest and keep the family intact? Should a wife who is occasionally abused by her husband be encouraged to remain with him? Should an abortion be suggested as one alternative for resolving the problems of someone who is single and pregnant? Should youths who are claimed to be uncontrollable by their parents be placed in correctional schools? If a client of a social worker threatens serious harm to some third person, what should the worker do? All of these questions involve making decisions based not on knowledge but on values. Much of social work practice is dependent upon making decisions based on values.

NASW has identified the following broad-based values as being needed for social work practice:

Commitment *to the primary importance of the individual in society.*

Respect *for the confidentiality of relationships with clients.*

Commitment *to social change to meet socially recognized needs.*

Willingness *to keep personal feelings and needs separate from professional relationships.*

Willingness *to transmit knowledge and skills to others.*

Respect *and appreciation for individual and group differences.*

Commitment *to developing clients' ability to help themselves.*

Willingness *to persist in efforts on behalf of clients despite frustration.*

Commitment *to social justice and the economic, physical, and mental well-being of all in society.*

Commitment *to a high standard of personal and professional conduct.*[7]

Because values play a key role in social work practice, it is essential that social work educational programs (*a*) help students clarify their values, and (*b*) foster the development of values in students that are consistent with professional social work practice. Social work values will be expanded upon in Chapter 2.

KEY OBJECTIVES OF THIS TEXT

In regard to the knowledge, skills, and values needed for social work practice, this text uses an *integrative* approach that presents the prominent approaches to social work practice. In summary form, the key objectives of this text are to present material designed to accomplish the following:

---

[6]Published 1982, National Association of Social Workers, Inc. Reprinted with permission, from *Standards for the Classification of Social Work Practice*, Policy Statement 4, p. 18. Copyright National Association of Social Workers, Inc.

[7]Published 1982, National Association of Social Workers, Inc. Reprinted with permission, from *Standards for the Classification of Social Work Practice*, Policy Statement 4, p. 18. Copyright National Association of Social Workers, Inc.

Prepare students for generalist social work practice by informing them of the contemporary assessment and intervention strategies.

Develop the interviewing and counseling skills and capacities of students so that they can intervene effectively with individuals, families, and groups.

Develop students' skills and capacities in community development and community organization efforts.

Help students to develop a philosophical value orientation that is consistent with social work practice.

Develop students' capacities to function effectively as brokers, enablers, advocates, and activists.

Develop in students an awareness, understanding, and appreciation of how to intervene effectively with people of diverse racial, ethnic, and cultural backgrounds.

Develop students' capacities to evaluate and modify human service programs and systems in order to make human services more equitable, humane, and responsive to consumers.

Develop philosophical conceptual skills so graduates will be able to evaluate critically and further develop their intervention techniques throughout life.

Help students to develop a positive sense of self and an awareness and appreciation of the importance of continuing to evaluate their professional skills and their professional growth.

FIGURE 1.3

Partial List of Intervention Therapies at Micro and Mezzo Levels

Treatment Approach

Task-centered therapy	Assertiveness training
Psychoanalysis	Token economies
Client-centered therapy	Contingency contracting
Transactional analysis	Systematic desensitization
Gestalt therapy	In vivo desensitization
Rational-emotive therapy	Implosive therapy
Reality therapy	Covert sensitization
Crisis intervention	Aversive techniques
Behavior modification	Thought-stopping
Provocative therapy	Sex therapy
Radical therapy	Milieu therapy
Adlerian therapy	Play therapy
Analytical therapy	Parent effectiveness
Existential therapy	training
Encounter therapies	Muscle relaxation
Ego psychology approaches	Deep breathing relaxation
Cognitive approaches	Imagery relaxation
General systems approaches	Meditation
Role theory approaches	Hypnosis
Time management	Self-hypnosis
Biofeedback	Encounter groups
Marathon groups	Sensitivity groups
Alcoholics Anonymous	Parents Anonymous
Weight Watchers	Neuro-linguistic
Psychodrama	programming

WHICH INTERVENTION STRATEGIES SHOULD SOCIAL WORKERS LEARN?

There are literally hundreds of intervention approaches that have been developed at the micro, mezzo, and macro levels of practice. A partial list of available tech-

niques which can be used at the micro and mezzo levels of practice appears in Figure 1.3.

It is impossible for any social worker to have an effective working knowledge of all these treatment approaches. What social workers should do, however, is to continue throughout their careers to learn additional approaches and to learn to apply more effectively those approaches with which they are already acquainted. Social work agencies encourage this continual learning through offering in-service training and workshops, sending workers to conferences, and encouraging workers to take additional college courses in the helping professions.

Workers should continue to learn a wide variety of intervention approaches so that they can select from their "bag of tricks" the intervention approach that (given each client's unique set of problems and circumstances) is apt to be most effective. It should be noted that the selection of an intervention approach is also based on a worker's personality. Workers soon become aware that their own personalities partially determine which therapy approaches they are more comfortable and effective in applying.

Because there are so many intervention techniques (as suggested in Figure 1.3) readers are apt to be bewildered about which treatment approaches they should attempt to learn. It is therefore crucial that the faculty of social work educational programs give direction to social work students by (*a*) as a group making carefully thought-out decisions regarding the intervention theories that are most useful for students in their geographic area to learn; (*b*) giving an overview of many of these theories so that students have familiarity with a wide number of theories; and (*c*) conveying material on the merits and shortcomings of each of the theories which are covered. Future chapters in this text summarize most of the therapies listed in Figure 1.3. *It is suggested that the instructor of this course, along with the other social work faculty members, make decisions as to which therapies to cover in this class.*

After the student graduates and obtains employment, the work setting will also be a factor in focusing the worker's attention on which treatment approaches to acquire a working knowledge of. If a worker is assigned to working with shy or aggressive people, assertiveness training may be recommended. Alcoholics Anonymous may be recommended for people with drinking problems, rational therapy for people who are depressed, systematic desensitization for people who have phobias, and so on.

An effective social worker generally has a working knowledge of a variety of treatment approaches. In working with clients, the worker should focus on selecting the most effective treatment approaches to help clients solve their problem(s) rather than trying to redefine the clients' problems so as to be able to use the worker's favorite treatment approach.

SUMMARY

Social work is the professional activity of helping individuals, families, groups, or communities to enhance or restore their capacity for social functioning and to create societal conditions favorable to their goals. The term *social worker* is generally applied to graduates (either with bachelor's or master's degrees) of schools of social work who are employed in the field of social welfare. A social worker is a change agent who is skilled at working with individuals, groups, and families, and in bringing about community changes. Almost all social workers are employed in the field of social welfare.

The profession of social work is distinct from other helping professions as it has the responsibility and mandate to provide social services. Social work is also distinct as it uses the person-in-environment concept with the following four goals: (1) enhance the problem-solving, coping, and developmental capacities of people; (2) link people with systems that provide them with resources, services, and opportunities; (3) promote the effectiveness and humane operation of systems that provide people with resources and services; and (4) develop and improve social policy.

A social worker needs training and expertise in a wide range of areas to be able to effectively handle problems faced by individuals, groups, and the larger community. While most professions are becoming increasingly more specialized, social work continues to emphasize a generalist (broad-based) approach.

Social work uses a problem-solving approach. Social workers practice at three levels: micro, mezzo, and macro. Specific activities performed by workers include social casework, case management, group work, group therapy, family counseling and family therapy, community organization, planning, program development, policy development, research, consulting, supervision, and administration. The knowledge, skills, and values needed for social work practice were summarized.

There are literally hundreds of intervention approaches that have been developed for social work practice. It is impossible for any social worker to have an effective working knowledge of all these theories.

Educational programs have an obligation to provide social work students with an overview of the commonly used theories and to convey information on the merits and shortcomings of these approaches. Social workers have an obligation to continue to learn throughout their careers a variety of intervention approaches. In working with clients, a worker should focus on selecting the most effective intervention approaches to help clients solve their problems rather than trying to redefine the clients' problems in order to use the worker's favorite intervention approach.

EXERCISE

Breaking the Ice

GOAL: Starting a new class can be both exciting and anxiety producing for students and for the instructor. This exercise is designed to facilitate getting acquainted and to reduce anxiety.

Step 1: Explain the purpose of the exercise. Ask students to brainstorm about what they would like to know about other members of the class. Examples might include marital status, hometown, work or volunteer experience in social work, and most unforgettable experience. These characteristics should be written on the blackboard.

Step 2: Have each student then give answers to the items listed on the blackboard.

Step 3: Ask the students what they would like to know about the instructor. The instructor should attempt to answer these questions.

Step 4: (This is an additional, optional step.) Divide the class into subgroups of two. Ask each member to share an experience that has had a profound effect on his or her life. Listeners should be encouraged to ask questions to seek clarification. After each person in the subgroups has spoken, reform the class and have the students report on what they learned about their partners.

2

SOCIAL WORK VALUES

VALUE DILEMMAS

Let's assume that you are a social worker and are assigned the following case. What would you do to help this family?

Mrs. Kehl is two months pregnant. She works part-time in a shoe factory and is paid at the minimum wage. Her husband is a janitor in a business office and earns only slightly more. They already have seven children and are living in substandard, poverty conditions. They do not wish to have additional children and the pregnancy has resulted partially from a failure of the birth control method they were using. The family is Catholic and attends church regularly. On one hand they want to have an abortion as they feel their family is already being hurt because of a lack of money. On the other hand they believe having an abortion may be immoral as it may mean taking the life of an unborn child.

This case raises a number of questions about values. As a social worker, how would you help this family weigh their moral views against abortion with their values about wanting to limit their family size in order to improve living conditions?

This case is not unique. Most situations that clients face involve, at least partially, value dilemmas. A few more examples follow:

Mr. Ritter is eighty-two years old and has terminal cancer. He has lived a full life but now is in severe pain. He is rather depressed and is seriously considering taking his own life. Should he be allowed to?

Mr. and Mrs. Sinclair have a two-year-old profoundly retarded child who needs extensive medical care. They have three older children. The family's emotional and physical resources are being severely drained, and family relationships are becoming increasingly tense. Yet the family feels the retarded child will develop at a faster pace in their home than in an institution. What should they do?

Mr. and Mrs. Fedders have been married for six years and have two children. Their love for each other has been practically nonexistent for the past three years. Mr. Fedders recently discovered his wife has been having an affair. They both hold religious beliefs against divorce, but they are seriously considering

Abortion: A value dilemma

terminating their marriage. How should a counselor help them?

Mr. Franzene is on probation for two years for theft. For the past year and one-half he has stayed out of trouble. He inadvertently reveals to his probation officer that he took two pens from a discount store. Should his probation officer make a report on this?

LaVonne Hall recently left a mental hospital and was helped by her aftercare worker to obtain a filing job. Ms. Hall calls her worker while intoxicated and angry and informs the worker that she has been fired. She says that she is going to shoot her former employer, then hangs up. What should the worker do?

Mr. Townsend's neighbors occasionally hear cries of anguish from Mr. Townsend's two children. The

neighbors make a report to the public welfare department as they suspect abuse. A protective service worker investigates, and Mr. Townsend and the children report the cries are the result of spankings. How does the worker decide when harsh spanking should be considered abuse?

Mr. and Mrs. Stonek's only child was taken away two years ago and placed in a foster home because of neglect. The husband drank excessively, and the mother was very depressed. Over the past two years the Stoneks occasionally have made efforts to improve their lives but have always "slid back." For the past two months Mr. Stonek has been involved in Alcoholics Anonymous (AA) and only occasionally has gotten drunk. Mrs. Stonek presently seems less depressed and

feels having her son back would help make her life more meaningful. The Stoneks ask to have their child returned. Should the child be returned? How would you as worker arrive at a decision?

Mrs. Barta seeks counseling at a comprehensive mental health center. She states her husband is having intercourse with their eleven-year-old daughter. The counselor arranges a joint meeting with the Bartas. Mr. Barta first denies the accusation, but then admits it after being confronted with what his wife has seen and heard. How should the worker attempt to help this family?

Mrs. Johnson is a caseworker at a public welfare agency in a rural county. She observes and collects evidence that the director makes a range of decisions that deny migrant workers in the area (most of whom are Mexican-Americans) public assistance benefits for which they are eligible. Mrs. Johnson believes if she confronts the director with this evidence, she will be fired, or at least denied merit increases and promotions at work. What should she do?

Mrs. Gordon seeks counseling from a sex therapist. She indicates she is fairly content with her marriage and has an enjoyable sex life with her husband.

Yet, she feels substantial guilt about her desire and following through on her desire to masturbate. How can the therapist help her?

A community worker in an inner city is working with residents to organize a rent strike against a landlord who neglects making essential repairs. The building also does not have adequate heat and has rats and roaches. The organizer wonders whether she should fully inform the residents of the risks involved in a rent strike (such as being evicted). She fears that if she fully informs the tenants of the risks, they probably will decide not to strike, which will mean essential improvements in living conditions will not be made. What should she do?

The examples highlight the fact that much of social work practice involves value dilemmas. Social work is both an art and a science. Because social work is partly an art, a worker frequently must make decisions based on values rather than on knowledge. It also means the change techniques used by workers are often based on theory and value assumptions, rather than on proven therapy techniques.

One of the value assumptions of social work that is frequently useful in helping clients resolve value dilemmas is the principle of self-determination. This principle asserts that clients have the right to hold and express their own opinions and to act upon them, as long as in so doing they do not infringe upon the rights of others. When clients face a value dilemma, a worker can often proceed effectively by helping the clients first to define their problems precisely and then to examine fully the merits and shortcomings of each of the various alternatives to resolving the problem. After this is done, clients are then given the responsibility to decide which course of action they desire to pursue. This problem-solving format might be useful for many of the case situations listed above. For example, the Kehls who are considering having an abortion might make a list of all their reasons for and against having an abortion, and then make a decision. This same approach might also be useful in helping the Sinclairs to make a decision about whether to place their profoundly retarded child in an instittion and in helping the Fedders to decide whether to terminate their marriage.

Although this self-determination principle may be useful in some cases, *there are no absolutes in social work practice.* Guidelines are simply guidelines. What works in one situation may not resolve problems in others. Suppose, for example, that Mr. Ritter makes a list of the reasons for and against taking his life and decides that there is no rational reason for him to endure further pain. Such a decision on his part may raise a value dilemma for the social worker regarding whether he should attempt to stop Mr. Ritter from taking his life. Or, suppose the Bartas decide they do not want further counseling on the incestuous relationship between Mr. Barta and his daughter because they both conclude that delving further into it will break up their marriage and their family. What should the worker do then?

Much of social work practice is dependent upon the worker's professional judgment. Directors of social welfare agencies frequently tell me that their best workers are those who have common sense and are able to "trust their guts" (that is, trust their feelings, intuition, and perceptions). This chapter will spell out value assumptions and principles of social work practice. *These guidelines (and all other guidelines presented in this text) are not to be applied as absolutes, but simply as concepts that may be useful in working with people.* An effective worker has an understanding of these guidelines and is then able to make a professional judgment of whether a guideline is, or is not, useful when working with particular people.

KNOWLEDGE AND VALUES

It is important for workers to be able to distinguish between values and knowledge and to be aware of the role each plays in social work practice.

Pincus and Minahan (1973, p. 38) concisely define the difference between values and knowledge as follows:

Values are beliefs, preferences, or assumptions about what is desirable or good for man [humans]. An example is the belief that society has an obligation to help each individual realize his fullest potential. They are not assertions about how the world is and what we know about it, but how it should be. As such, value statements cannot be subjected to scientific investigation; they must be accepted on faith. Thus we can speak of a value as being right or wrong only in relation to the particular belief system or ethical code being used as a standard.

What we will refer to as knowledge statements, on the other hand, are observations about the world and man [humans] which have been verified or are capable of verification. An example is that black people have a shorter life expectancy than white people in the United States. When we speak of a knowledge statement as being right or wrong, we are referring to the extent to which the assertion has been confirmed through objective empirical investigation.

The distinction between values and knowledge can be illustrated in some of the above cases. First, let us take the abortion question. Suppose a person questions the abortion procedure because she feels it may be immoral. The person believes it means killing an unborn baby. Implicit in this value statement is the belief that life begins at or shortly after conception. Deciding whether life does in fact begin at conception is a belief that is not verifiable.

On the other hand, if a person has qualms about an abortion because she fears the risks of the medical procedure or fears there is a high probability of feeling remorseful after the abortion, then informational questions are raised. Knowledge, or empirical evidence, can in these situations be presented showing that the health risks of having an abortion are less than those of carrying the child to full term, and evidence can be presented showing that only a small percentage of women who have an abortion have severe remorse (Hyde, 1990).

Mrs. Gordon's guilt over masturbating may also be used as an illustration. If she feels guilty because she believes masturbating is immoral and sinful, she then obviously has a value system that asserts it is wrong to masturbate. For her to resolve this value dilemma would either involve having her change her belief system, or stop masturbating. On the other hand, if she feels guilty because she fears she is hurting herself physiologically or hindering her sex life with her hus-

band, she could be shown that both of these beliefs are erroneous by pointing out that most married men and women masturbate, masturbation is highly recommended by sex therapists, and masturbation usually fosters rather than hinders a sexual relationship (Masters and Johnson, 1966).

As these case illustrations suggest, it is much easier to change a belief of a client that conflicts with current knowledge. Changing a belief of a client that is based on a value is much more difficult, as the "rightness" or "wrongness" of the belief cannot be determined with empirical evidence.

VALUE DILEMMAS OF CLIENTS VERSUS WORKERS

Also, it is important (as will be discussed later in this text) for social workers to distinguish just who has the value dilemma. An important guideline in social work practice is not to become overly emotionally involved in a client's case. (If you find yourself frequently taking your clients' problems home with you so that your dwelling on their problems interferes with your life, then you are overly involved.) If a client faces a value dilemma about whether to obtain a divorce, or have an abortion, or place a member of the family in an institution, it is important for you to be aware that it is the *client's* dilemma, and not yours. By being aware that it is not your dilemma, you will best be able to remain objective and thereby by most helpful to a client.

On the other hand, if you feel strongly that a client is doing something immoral (for example, if you believe abortions are unethical), then *you* face a value dilemma. In such situations it will be very difficult for you to remain objective.

When you face a value dilemma about what a client is doing, or planning to do, the following guidelines are sometimes helpful.

The first step in coping with such a value question is to recognize its existence. Such self-awareness is often difficult to obtain. Ethical questions are often ambiguous and make us feel uncomfortable. Therefore we like to avoid them.

Every human being is unique in a variety of ways — value system, personality, goals in life, financial resources, emotional and physical strengths, personal concerns, past experiences, peer pressures, emotional reactions, self-identity, family relationships, and deviant behavioral patterns. In working with a client a social worker needs to perceive and respect the uniqueness of the client's situation.

Individualization is relatively easy for a social worker to achieve when the worker is assisting clients who have values, goals, behavioral patterns, and personal characteristics similar to the worker's. Individualization is harder to achieve when a worker is assigned clients who have values or behavioral patterns that the worker views as disgusting. For example, a worker holding traditional middle-class values may have difficulty in viewing a client with respect when that client has raped a young girl, or is involved in an incestuous relationship, or has killed a member of his family, or has severely abused a child. A general guideline in such situations is that the worker should seek to accept and respect the client but not accept the deviant behavior that needs to be changed. If a worker is unable to convey acceptance of the client, a helping relationship will not be established. If such a relationship is not established, then the worker will have practically no opportunity to help the client change deviant behaviors. A second guideline is that if a worker views a client as being disgusting and is unable to establish a working relationship, then the worker should transfer the case to another worker. There should be no disgrace or embarrassment in having to transfer a case for such reasons; it is irrational for a worker to expect to like every client, or for every client to like the worker (Ellis and Harper, 1977b).

Social workers occasionally encounter "raw" situations. For a while I worked in a mental hospital for the criminally insane and had a variety of clients who had committed a wide range of asocial and bizarre acts including incest, rape, decapitation of a girlfriend, sodomy, sexual exhibitionism, and removing corpses from graves. I've worked in a variety of other settings and encountered other raw situations. Achieving an attitude of respect for people who commit bizarre actions

is difficult at times to achieve, but rehabilitation will not occur unless it is achieved.

Social psychologists have firmly established the theoretical principle that people's images of themselves develop largely out of their interactions and communications with others. A long time ago Charles Cooley (1902) called this process the *looking glass self-concept*. The looking glass says that people develop their self-concept in terms of how other people relate to them. Specifically, if people receive respect from others and are praised for their positive qualities, they will feel good about themselves, gradually develop a positive sense of worth, be happier, and will seek in responsible and socially acceptable ways to continue to maintain the respect of others.

On the other hand, if a person commits a deviant act, and *then* is shunned by others, viewed as different, and treated with disrespect, that person will develop a *failure identity*. According to Glasser (1972), people with failure identities either withdraw from society, become emotionally disturbed, or express their discontent in delinquent and deviant actions.

For example, if a neighborhood identifies a youth as being a troublemaker (a delinquent) the neighbors are apt to relate to the youth as if he were not to be trusted, may erroneously accuse him of delinquent acts, and will label his semidelinquent and aggressive behavior as being delinquent. In the absence of objective ways to gauge whether he is, in fact, a delinquent, the youth will rely on the subjective evaluations of others. Thus, gradually, as the youth is related to as being a delinquent, he is apt to perceive himself in that way and will begin to enact the delinquent role.

Compton and Galaway (1975, pp. 106–7) expand on the importance of social workers' attending carefully to their communications with clients:

Social workers and other professionals intervening in the lives of people are well advised to be constantly sensitive to the messages they are extending to others about their worth. Do we, in the little things we do, communicate to the other person that he is a unique individual to be highly prized? What, for example, is the message communicated when we safeguard time and provide a client with a specific time to be seen as opposed to a catch-me-on-a-catch-as-catch-can basis for visits? Do appointments in advance communicate to the client a higher sense of respect than unannounced visits or hurriedly arranged telephone appointments? And, speaking of telephoning, how about the all too frequently overlooked return call? What message does the client get from the worker in terms of the client's worth when the worker does not have the courtesy or good sense to return telephone calls promptly? How about the ability to listen to clients, to secure from them their own account of their situation, and to avoid prejudgments? And does not privacy, both in terms of how the social worker conducts the interviews and how he treats the material gained from interviews, communicate something to clients about the esteem in which they are held? A worker attempting to operationalize the premise of individual uniqueness and dignity may find it useful to repeatedly inquire of himself, "What does this action on my part communicate to the client about my perception of his personhood?"

The principle of individualization also plays a key role in social work treatment. Various problems, needs, goals, and values of clients involve different patterns of relationships with clients and different methods of helping. For example, consider the needs of a teenage male who is placed in a group home for being beyond parental control. At times he may need an understanding but firm counselor who sets and enforces strict limits. At times he may need encouragement and guidance in how to perform better at school. If conflicts develop between the youth and other boys at the group home, the counselor may need to play a mediating role. If the youth is shy, counseling on how to be more assertive may be needed. If his parents are fairly ineffective in their parenting role, the counselor may seek to have the parents enroll in a Parent Effectiveness Training program (Gordon, 1970). If the youth is being treated unfairly at school or by the juvenile court, the counselor may play an advocate role for the youth and attempt to change the system. If the youth has behavior problems, the reasons need to be explored and an intervention program developed.

A thorny problem facing social workers involves striking an effective balance between classification and individualization. There is a need in all human service

areas to generalize beyond individuals and to organize data on the basis of common characteristics. Classification is essential in order to make sense out of a mass of data and is an essential part of developing theories. The danger of classifying people into a particular category is that such a classification may lead social workers to respond to people as objects rather than as individuals. Compton and Galaway (1975, p. 107) comment about the labeling process:

The pitfalls of this process are being documented in a growing body of literature from sociologists studying deviance from a labeling perspective. Not only does labeling or classification lead to a distortion of individual differences, but, as labeling theorists and their supporting research are noting, a person labeled deviant, those doing the labeling, and the surrounding audience frequently respond to the deviant on the basis of the label rather than on the basis of individual characteristics. This creates conditions for the development of a self-fulfilling prophecy in which the person becomes what he has been labeled.

In the same vein, Hans Toch (1970, p. 15) notes:

Playing the classification game in the abstract, as is done in universities, is a joyful, exhilarating experience, harmless and inconsequential. Classifying people in life is a grim business which channelizes destinies and determines fate. A man becomes a category, he is processed as a category, plays his assigned role, lives up to the implications. Labeled irrational, he acts crazy; catalogued dangerous, he becomes dangerous or he stays behind bars.

This labeling process, most simply stated, occurs due to Cooley's *looking glass self* (described earlier) in which people define who and what they are in terms of how others relate to them. Those labeled mentally ill, or delinquent, or an ex-con, or a welfare mother are then apt to define themselves in terms of these labels, and unfortunately begin playing these roles.

Social workers have to continue to be alert to the dangers of labeling and should interact with each client (or judge, attorney, professor, and so forth) as being a person rather than a label.

One final comment will be made about individualization. Because of individualization, this author dislikes the term *caseworker. Webster's Ninth New Collegiate Dictionary* (1981) defines a case as "a set of circumstances or conditions"; " situation requiring investigation or action (as by the police)"; "the object of investigation or consideration." With such definitions, the term *caseworker* connotes someone who performs primarily an investigative function. The term thereby does not convey the importance of the uniqueness of each person, nor does it convey the importance of building a working relationship with clients. This author believes a term such as *counselor* or *social worker* conveys a more realistic image of the skills, functions, and approach of professionals identified as caseworkers.

CLIENT'S RIGHT TO SELF-DETERMINATION

As indicated earlier, social workers believe that clients have the right to express their own opinions and to act upon them, as long as by so doing clients do not infringe upon the rights of others. This principle is in sharp contrast to the layperson's views that a social worker seeks to "remold" clients into a pattern chosen by the worker. Instead, the efforts of social workers are geared to enhancing the capability of clients to help themselves. Client self-determination derives logically from the belief in the inherent dignity of each person. If people have dignity, then it follows that they should be permitted to determine their own lifestyles as far as possible.

Social workers believe that making all decisions and doing everything for a client is self-defeating as it leads to increased dependency rather than greater self-reliance and self-sufficiency. In order for people to grow, to mature, to become responsible, they need to make their own decisions and to take responsibility for the consequences. Mistakes and emotional pain will at times occur. But that is part of life. We learn by our mistakes and by trial and error. The respect for the clients' ability to make their own decisions is associated with the principle that social work is a cooperative endeavor between clients and workers (client participation). Social work is done *with* a client, and not *to* a

client. Plans imposed on people without their active involvement have a way of not turning out well.

There are four points that should be made in operationalizing the principle of client self-determination.

First, self-determination implies that clients should be made aware that there are alternatives for resolving the personal or social problems they face. Self-determination involves having clients make decisions — that is, making a choice selected from several courses of action. If there is only one course of action, there is no choice and therefore clients would not have the right of self-determination. As will be expanded upon in later chapters the role of a social worker in helping clients involves (*a*) building a helping relationship; (*b*) exploring problems in depth with clients; and (*c*) exploring alternative solutions with the client, then choosing a course of action. This third step is the implementation of the principle of self-determination.

Second, self-determination means that the client, not the worker, is the chief problem solver. Workers need to recognize that it is the client who *owns* the problem and therefore has the chief responsibility to resolve the problem. This is an area in which social work differs markedly from most other professions. Most other professionals, such as physicians and attorneys, advise clients as to what they believe clients ought to do. Doctors, lawyers, and dentists are viewed as being experts in advising clients. Clients' decision making after receiving the expert's advice in such situations is generally limited to the choice of whether or not to accept the professional's advice.

In sharp contrast, social workers should not seek to establish an expert-inferior relationship, but a relationship between equals. The expertise of the social worker does *not* lie in knowing or recommending what is best for the client. Rather, the expertise lies in assisting clients to define their problems, develop and examine the alternatives for resolving the problems, maximize clients' capacities and opportunities to make decisions for themselves, and help clients to implement the decisions they make. In conjunction with this principle Matthew Dumont (1968, p. 60) notes:

The most destructive thing in psychotherapy is a "rescue fantasy" in the therapist — a feeling that the therapist is the divinely sent agent to pull a tormented soul from the pit of suffering and adversity and put him back on the road to happiness and glory. A major reason this fantasy is so destructive is that it carries the conviction that the patient will be saved only through and by the therapist. When such a conviction is communicated to the patient, verbally or otherwise, he has no choice other than to rebel and leave or become more helpless, dependent, and sick.

Third, self-determination does not prohibit or restrict social workers from offering an opinion or making a suggestion. In fact, social workers have an obligation to share their viewpoints with clients. Compton and Galaway (1975, p. 111) note:

Workers have the obligations of sharing with clients their own thinking, perhaps their own experiences, not as a way of directing the clients' lives but rather as an additional source of information and input for the clients to consider in their own decision making. It is imperative, however, that the social worker's input be recognized as information to be considered and not an edict to be followed.

The key to implementing this principle is for the social worker to phrase the alternative as a suggestion rather than as advice. For example, if a client is worried about how her elderly mother, who is living alone, will be able to have her physical, emotional, and social needs met, the social worker should not advise: "The best thing for you to do is to place her in a nursing home." Instead the worker should offer a suggestion for the client to consider — "Have you thought about placing your mother in a nursing home?"

Fourth, client self-determination is possible and should be encouraged even in areas in which the social worker has the additional function to protect society. Three areas in social work for which the worker has this additional function are in protective services, in prisons, and in probation and parole. Compton and Galaway (1975, p. 112) note:

*A probation agency, for example, may enforce the legal requirement that the probationer must report to the probation officer; this is not a matter for client self-determination. But the sensitive probation officer can allow for considerable client self-determination in the frequency of reporting, the length of the inter-*views, *the time of reporting, and the content to be discussed during the interviews.*

Actually probationers, in one sense, also can be informed that they even have a choice in reporting to the probation officer. In working with involuntary clients who are angry with the legal authority held by the social worker, it is often helpful for the worker to inform the clients that they do have a choice regarding whether they are willing to meet the minimum legal requirements. The consequences of not cooperating (such as being sent to prison, or having their children taken away in the case of abusive parents) are also made clear to them. This approach appears to be useful as it reduces the clients' inclination to view the social worker as a parent or a cop. Instead of playing the game of how much they can get away with, this approach puts the responsibility for their future squarely on the clients. They in fact are faced with the decision of reporting or suffering the consequences of not reporting; of deciding whether to stop abusing their children or of suffering the consequences of making no effort to refrain from abusing their children. In this connection Gerald O'Connor (1972, pp. 485–86) notes:

The recognition of man's [a person's] right to free choice guarantees that he may choose to run his life as he sees fit. This choice may run counter to society's welfare and even his own, yet essentially it is his choice and his prerogative. Society may censure, but it cannot take from him his right; nor should society strip him of his dignity by a censure. The criminal then has a right to say "crime is my choice and I am willing to pay the price. If you send me to prison, I am paying my debt to society and refuse to submit to your attempts to reform me." The principle of self-determination makes it incumbent upon society to honor such a plea.

In working with involuntary clients whose actions have adversely affected other people in the past (for example, abusive parents) it is the worker's obligation to outline clearly the minimum legal requirements (for example, no further incidents of abuse), and to specify clearly the consequences that will result if these clients decide not to meet these requirements. Clients, even in such situations, have a choice in deciding whether they will meet the requirements. If they are not met by a client, then the worker must follow through on implementing the consequences in order to maintain credibility with the client. Often the consequences have therapeutic shock value as clients learn they can no longer manipulate the system and that they are responsible for the consequences they suffer.

CONFIDENTIALITY

Confidentiality is the implicit or explicit agreement between a professional and a client to maintain the private nature of information about the client. An *absolute* implementation of this principle means that disclosures made to the professional will not be shared with anyone else, except when authorized by the client in writing or required by law. Because of the principle of confidentiality, professionals can be sued if they disclose information that the client is able to document has a damaging effect upon said client.

One of the reasons confidentiality is important is that clients will not be apt to share their hidden secrets, personal concerns, and asocial thoughts and actions with a professional if they believe that information will be revealed to others. A basic principle of counseling is that clients must feel comfortable in fully revealing themselves to the professional without fear that their secret revelations will be used against them.

Confidentiality is absolute when information revealed to a professional is *never* passed on to anyone or anything in any form. Such information would never be shared with other agency staff, fed into a computer, or written in a case record. A student or beginning practitioner tends to think in absolutes and may even naively promise clients *absolute confidentiality*.

Absolute confidentiality is seldom achieved. Social workers today generally function as part of a larger agency. In such an agency much of the communication is written into case records and shared orally with other staff in the system as part of the service-delivery process. Social workers share details with supervisors, and many work in teams with whose members they are

expected to share information. Therefore, instead of absolute confidentiality, it is more precise to indicate that a system of *relative confidentiality* is being used in social work practice (Wilson, 1978, p. 3).

Confidentiality is a legal matter, and at the present time there is a fair amount of uncertainty as to what is an unlawful violation and what is not. There have been few test cases in court to determine what is, and what is not, an unlawful violation of confidentiality. Let me provide a brief summary of how agencies are now handling issues related to confidentiality.

Practically all agencies allow (and in fact encourage) their workers to discuss a client's circumstances with other professionals who are employed at the same agency. At many agencies (such as a mental hospital) the input of many professionals at the agency (psychiatrist, psychologist, social workers, nurses, physical therapist, and so forth) is used in assessing a client and developing a treatment plan.

Many agencies feel it is inappropriate to share or discuss a client's case with a secretary. (Yet, the secretary does the typing and usually knows as much about each client as the professional staff does.)

Most agencies believe it is inappropriate to discuss a client's case with professionals at another agency unless the client first signs a release of information form (Figure 2.1). (Yet, informally, professionals employed by different agencies do at times share information about a client without the client's authorization.)

At the present time nearly all agencies share case information with social work interns. (Whether it is legally permissible to share information with student interns has not been determined.)

It is certainly permissible to discuss a case for educational purposes with others if no identifying information about the specific person is given. Yet, this is another gray area, as the person talking about the case will not be able to determine precisely when identifying information is being given. Take the following example:

Some years ago I was employed at a maximum security hospital for the criminally insane and had on my caseload a young male who had decapitated his seventeen-year-old girlfriend. Such a criminal offense is indeed shocking and rare. People in the client's local

FIGURE 2.1

Release of Information Form (Sample Copy of a Suggested Format)*

Lakeside Counseling Center
Consent for Release of Confidential Information

_____ at Lakeside Counseling Center requests permission from _____
　　　　　(Name of social worker)

_____ to release confidential information about _____. This information will be released to:
　　(Name of client)　　　　　　　　　　　　　　　　　　　　　(Name of client)

Name: _____　　Address: _____

Position: _____　　_____

Agency: _____

Material to be released: _____

_____

_____

Reason for this disclosure: _____

_____

_____

_____ must abide by the following limitations in their
　　(name of person and the agency receiving the information)
use of the information received: _____

_____

My signature verifies that I know what information is being disclosed and have had the opportunity to correct the data to make certain it is accurate. I am aware that this consent can be revoked (in writing) at any time. I am also aware of the consequences that might occur as a result of signing this form or of my refusal to do so.

　　My signature means that I have read this form and/or have had it read and explained to me in language I can understand. I have checked this form, and upon signing it will receive a copy.

　　This consent form expires on _____ unless revoked by me in writing prior to that date.
　　　　　　　　　　　　　　　　　(Date)

_____　　_____　　_____
　　(Client's signature or "X")　　　　　　　(Date signed)　　　　　　　　　　(Witness)

_____　　_____　　_____
　(Client's guardian—if applicable)　　　　　(Date signed)　　　　　　　　　　(Witness)

_____　　_____
　　(Lakeside Counseling Center representative)　　　　　　　　(Date signed)

*One of the sources from which this release of information form was adapted by Suanna J. Wilson, *Confidentiality in Social Work: Issues and Principles* (New York: Free Press, 1978).

area will never forget the offense. If I were to discuss this case in a class at a university (which I occasionally do), I would never be fully assured that no one would be able to identify the offender. There is always the chance that one of the students may have lived in the client's home community and recognize the offender.

A question that is sometimes raised in relation to confidentiality is whether clients have a right to see the agency's records on them. The 1974 Federal Privacy Act legislated that any agency receiving federal funds must allow clients to see their records. Furthermore, if a client requests a copy of the record, the agency must provide one. (It is probably a good idea not to put anything into a client's record that you do not want a client to see.) A number of voluntary agencies also now have policies to allow clients access to their records.

Another problematic area is the thorny question of when a professional should violate confidence and inform others. Again, there are many gray areas surrounding this question (Wilson, 1978).

Most state statutes permit or require the professional to inform the appropriate people when a client admits to a past or intended *serious* criminal act. Yet, the question of how serious a crime must be before there is an obligation to report it has not be resolved. On the extreme end of the severity continuum it has been established that a professional *must* inform the appropriate people.

A precedent-setting case occurred in the case of *Tarasoff v. Regents of the University of California, 1974* (*University of Pittsburgh Law Review*, 1975). In this case a university student informed his psychiatrist that he was going to shoot his girlfriend. The psychiatrist informed the campus police of this threat but did not inform the intended victim or her parents. Campus security picked up and questioned the student and soon released him, concluding that he "appeared rational." Shortly afterward he murdered his girlfriend. Her parents sued the psychiatrist, and the Supreme Court ruled (*University of Pittsburgh Law Review*, 1975, p. 159):

When a doctor or a psychiatrist, in the exercise of his professional skills and knowledge, determines, or shall determine that a warning is essential to avert

danger arising from a medical or psychological condition of his patient, he incurs a legal obligation to give that warning.

The court also concluded (*University of Pittsburgh Law Review*, 1975, p. 161):

The public policy favoring protection of the confidential character of patient-psychotherapist communication must yield in instances in which disclosure is essential to avert danger to others. The protective privilege ends where the public peril begins.

Thus, the court set a precedent holding that a professional is liable for failure to warn the intended victim. This precedent has continued to be upheld in recent court decisions involving a helping professional's obligation to inform the intended victim (Schwartz, 1989, pp. 225–26).

In regard to the question of how serious a crime must be before it is reported, Wilson (1978, pp. 116–17) notes:

How serious must a crime be in order for the professional to take protective measures? Obviously, crimes involving someone's life are sufficiently serious. But what about destruction of personal property, theft, and the hundreds of misdemeanors that are so minor that they are rather easily overlooked? Unfortunately, there seems to be no clear-cut definition of what constitutes a serious crime, and it appears that this will have to be determined by the courts in individual case rulings.

Without guidelines, professionals at the present time must use their own best judgment of when a client's actions or communications warrant protective measures and what those measures should be. Student interns or beginning practitioners are advised to ask their supervisors when questions in this area arise.

Several years ago I was the faculty supervisor for a student in a field placement at a public assistance agency. The student intern had an unmarried AFDC mother (Aid to Families of Dependent Children Program) on his caseload. A trusting, working relationship between the intern and the mother was developed. The mother then informed the student she was dating a person who was sometimes abusive to her when he was drunk. The mother further indicated there was a warrant for the boyfriend's arrest in another state for an armed robbery charge. The student intern contacted me inquiring whether it was his obligation to inform the police, thereby violating confidentiality. My response was that he should discuss this with his agency supervisor to find out the agency's policy in regard to this question.

Wilson (1978, p. 121) further concludes:

In summary, a professional whose client confesses an intended or past crime can find himself in a very delicate position, both legally and ethically. There are enough conflicting beliefs on how this should be handled, so that clear guidelines are lacking. Social workers who receive a communication about a serious criminal act by a client would be wise to consult an attorney for a detailed research of appropriate state statutes and a review of recent court rulings that might help determine the desired course of action.

There are number of other areas in which a professional is permitted, expected, or required to violate confidentiality.[1] These areas include the following:

When a client formally (usually in writing) authorizes the professional to release information.

When a professional is called to testify in a criminal case (state statutes vary regarding guidelines on what information may be kept confidential in such criminal proceedings, and therefore practitioners must research their own particular state statutes in this area).

When a client files a lawsuit against a professional (e.g., for malpractice).

When a client threatens suicide and a professional may be forced to violate confidentiality to save the client's life. While the treating professional is encouraged to violate confidentiality in such circum-

stances, there is not necessarily a legal requirement to do so.

When a client threatens to harm his therapist.

When a professional becomes aware that a minor has committed a crime, when a minor is used by adults as an accessory in a crime, or when a minor is a victim of criminal actions. In such situations most states require that counselors inform the legal authorities. Again, the question arises of how serious the crime must be before it is reported.

When there is evidence of child abuse or neglect. Most states require professionals to report the evidence to the designated child-protection agency.

When a client's emotional or physical condition makes his employment a clear danger to himself or others (for example, when a counselor discovers a client who is an airplane pilot has a serious drinking problem).

In all these areas professional judgment must be used in deciding when the circumstances justify violating confidentiality (for example, making a judgment as to when child abuse or neglect may be occurring).

Privileged Communication

Privileged communication is closely related to confidentiality, but is narrower in scope. Privileged communication refers only to the legal right that protects clients, under certain circumstances, from having their communication with a professional revealed in court without their permission. Bernstein (1975, p. 521) has defined privileged communication as follows:

In states where certain professional groups are granted privileged communication, the client or his attorney has the privilege of preventing the professional from answering questions about their communication when called as a witness in court.

It should be noted that privileged communication protects the client, and the right to exercise this privilege belongs to the client, not to the professional. Many state statutes contain exceptions to privileged communication whereby the professional must testify in court.

---

[1]An extended discussion of these areas is contained in Suanna J. Wilson, *Confidentiality in Social Work: Issues and Principles* (New York: Free Press, 1978).

A listing of these exceptions is contained in Wilson (1978). Examples of such exceptions are the following:

- The client waives privilege.
- The client sues his counselor.
- The client commits or threatens a criminal act.
- The client's condition makes his employment hazardous to others.

Social workers in the past few decades have been fighting for enactment of state legislation that recognizes social worker–client privileged communication in order to avoid forced disclosures in court of confidential information. In states in which social workers are not granted privileged communication, they can be subpoenaed by any party to a court action and thereby forced to testify in court, fully and under oath, to all that transpired between the client and the social worker. If they fail to testify, they can be found in contempt of court by the judge and either fined, sent to jail, or both. Such court appearances can be detrimental to the client-worker relationship, and to future work with the client.

Social workers in recent years have been successful in most states in securing passage of legislation that licenses social workers. A section of such legislation usually contains a provision that recognizes social worker–client privileged communication. In various states a number of other professionals have been licensed and have secured recognition of privileged communication with clients. These professionals include attorneys, accountants, physicians, the clergy, guidance counselors, marriage counselors, nurses, psychiatrists, and psychologists.

Explaining Confidentiality to Clients

Given all the above material on confidentiality, how should a worker respond to questions about confidentiality that clients have? It should be noted that clients often wonder when they seek services how the information they reveal will be used. Clients need to be assured the information they divulge will be kept confidential; otherwise they are unlikely to share their secret concerns. Compare the following two explanations involving a question asked by a husband who is seeking marriage counseling for himself and his wife:

First response:

HUSBAND: Will what we say here be told to others?

WORKER: Our agency operates on a system of relative confidentiality. This means I may discuss certain aspects of your case with other staff members at this agency, but I will not discuss your case with anyone else outside the agency. There is one exception to this: if I am subpoenaed by a court (which might happen if you decide to get a divorce and the divorce is contested), then I would have to reveal what we talked about. I guess there might be one additional exception. Should the need arise for me to talk with professionals at other agencies (for example, your doctor) then I would first ask you to sign a release-of-information form allowing me to discuss your case.

Second response:

HUSBAND: Will what we say here be told to others?

WORKER: No, what you say here will be kept within this agency. I know when clients first come to an agency they often wonder how the information they reveal will be used. I assure you that what we talk about will be kept confidential.

The second response is probably the most desirable at agencies when the chances of court subpoenas are unlikely. The first response, while more thorough, is apt to suggest to clients that there is a moderate chance that information they reveal will be used against them at some future time, which will inhibit them from sharing their "secret" concerns.

However, if a worker is providing services in an area with a moderate or high chance of court action, then clients should be informed about the limits of confidentiality. For example, a probation and parole officer should inform clients (early in the supervision period) about the probation officer's obligations to the court if a client reveals he has violated the conditions of probation (for example, by committing another offense) as illustrated in the following excerpt from an interview:

PROBATION OFFICER: [to probationee] I'm here to help you in any way that I can. If you have personal concerns and want to talk to someone, I'd be happy to talk with you. If you choose to talk with someone else, that's certainly OK with me. The important thing is that when you have personal concerns, you get them worked out. We all have personal concerns at times. If you choose to talk to me, it will be kept confidential. The only information that will not be kept confidential is a violation by you of the conditions of probation, which we have discussed and which you have a copy of. If you violate the conditions of probation, and I find out, either by your telling me, or in some other way, I am required to make a report to the court of the violation. Do you have questions about this?

PROBATIONEE: No.

PROBATION OFFICER: All right, if you have some concerns, now, or in the future, I'll be happy to talk with you.

PROBATIONEE: There is one concern I have. My girlfriend's parents as yet don't know I've been arrested and placed on probation. He's a minister, and his wife is a school teacher. I don't know what they will say when they find out I'm in trouble. How do you think I should handle this? [The interview continues— and a trusting, helping relationship is beginning to develop.]

OTHER VALUES[2]

Additional values and principles of social work practice will briefly be summarized.

The Institutional Orientation

Currently there are two conflicting views of the role of social welfare in our society (Wilensky and Lebeaux, 1965). One of these roles has been termed *residual*, a gap-filling or first-aid role. This view holds that social welfare services should be provided only when an individual's needs are not properly met through other societal institutions, primarily the family and the market economy. With the residual view, it is thought that social services and financial aid should not be provided until all measures or efforts have failed, after the exhaustion of the individual's or the family's resources. In addition, this view asserts that funds and services should be provided on a short-term basis (primarily during emergencies), and are to be withdrawn when the individual or the family again becomes capable of being self-sufficient.

The residual view has been characterized as being "charity for unfortunates" (Wilensky and Lebeaux, 1965, p. 14). Funds and services are seen not as a right (something to which one is entitled) but as a gift, with the receiver having certain obligations (for example, in order to receive financial aid the recipient may be required to perform certain low-grade work assignments). Associated with the residual view is the belief that the causes of recipients' difficulties are rooted in their own malfunctioning (that is, recipients are

---

[2]The reader is also urged to study the Code of Ethics of the National Association of Social Workers, which is presented in the Appendix and summarizes important practice ethics for social workers. The National Association of Social Workers is the largest professional association representing the social work profession in the United States.

brought to their predicament through their own fault, because of some personal inadequacy, or ill-advised activity, or sin).

Under the residual view there is usually a stigma attached to receiving services or funds. The prevalence of the residual stigma can be shown by your asking yourself, "Have I ever in the past felt a reluctance to seek counseling for a personal or emotional situation that I faced because I was wary of what others might think of me?" For almost everyone the answer is yes, and the reluctance to seek help is due to the residual stigma.

The opposing point of view, which has been called the *institutional view*, holds that social welfare programs are to be "accepted as a proper, legitimate function of modern industrial society in helping individuals achieve self-fulfillment" (Wilensky and Lebeaux, 1965, p. 14). Under this view there is no stigma attached to receiving funds or services; recipients are viewed as being entitled to such help. Associated with this view is the belief that individuals' difficulties result from causes largely beyond their control (e.g., the reason a person is unemployed may well be a lack of employment opportunities).

The residual approach characterized social welfare programs from our early history to the depression of the 1930s. Since the Great Depression, both approaches have been applied to social welfare programs with some programs being largely residual in nature while others are more institutional in design and implementation. Social workers believe in the institutional approach, and strive to develop and provide programs with this orientation.

Advocacy and Social Action

Social workers have recognized an obligation to be an advocate for those who are oppressed or dispossessed. Social work believes that society has a responsibility to all of its members to provide security, acceptance, and satisfaction of basic cultural, social, and biological needs. It is thought that only when individuals' basic needs are met is it possible for them to develop their maximum potentials. Since social work believes in the value of the individual, it has a special responsibility to protect and secure civil rights based upon democratic principles. Social workers have a moral responsibility to work toward eradicating discrimination for any reason. Civil rights of clients need to be protected in order to preserve human dignity and self-respect.

Focus on Family

Often the focus of social work services is on the family. A family is seen as an interacting independent system. The problems faced by any person are usually influenced by the dynamics with a family, as illustrated in the following example.

A school teacher became concerned when one of her pupils was consistently failing, and she referred the child for psychological testing. Testing revealed a normal IQ, but failure was found to be due to a low self-concept (the girl was reluctant to do her academic work because she saw herself as being incapable of doing it). A school social worker met with the family and observed that the low self-concept was primarily a result of the parents' ridiculing and criticizing the child, and from seldom giving emotional support, encouragement, or compliments.

Since a family is an interacting system, change in one member affects others. For example, with some abusive families it has been noted that the abused child is at times a scapegoat on which the parents vent their anger and hostility. If the abused child is removed from a home, another child within the family is at times selected to be the scapegoat (Leavitt, 1974).

Another reason for the focus on the family rather than on the individual is that the other family members are often needed in the treatment process. For example, other family members can put pressure on an alcoholic in order to have him acknowledge that a problem exists. The family members may also need counseling to help them cope with the person when he is drinking, and these family members may play important roles in providing emotional support for the alcoholic's efforts to stop drinking.

On October 11, 1987, over 500,000 people gathered for the National March on Washington for Lesbian and Gay Rights. Maintaining dignity and self-respect through the protection of individual civil rights is a basic belief of social work.

Accountability

Increasingly, federal and state governmental units and private funding sources are requiring that the effectiveness of service programs be measured. Gradually, programs found to be ineffective are being phased out. While some social workers view accountability with trepidation and claim the paperwork involved interferes with serving clients, members of the social work profession have an obligation to funding sources to provide the highest quality services. Two hundred years ago bloodletting was thought to be an effective treatment technique. Only a few decades ago lobotomies were erroneously thought to be effective. At the present time the value of electroshock therapy, psycho-

analysis, and other therapy techniques is being questioned. Program outcome studies have also demonstrated that orphanages are not the best places to serve homeless children, long-term hospitalization is not the best way to help those who are emotionally disturbed, probation generally has higher rehabilitative value than long-term confinement in prison, the Job Corps program of the 1960s was too expensive for the outcomes achieved, mentally retarded children can be better served in their home communities through local programs than by confinement in an institution, and so on.

Social workers need to become skilled at evaluating the extent to which they are being effective in providing services. At the agency and program levels a wide variety of evaluation techniques are now available to assess effectiveness of current services and to identify unmet needs and service gaps. One of the most useful approaches is management by objectives (MBO). This technique involves specifying the objectives of a program, stating in measurable terms how and when these objectives are to be met, and then periodically measuring the extent to which the objectives are being met.

Management by objectives is perhaps also the most useful approach that social workers can use to assess their effectiveness. Many agencies are now requiring each of their workers, *with the involvement of their clients*, to (*a*) identify and specify what will be the goals for each client—generally this is done together with clients during the initial interviews; (*b*) write down in detail what the client and the worker will do in order to accomplish the goals—deadlines for accomplishing these tasks are also set; and (*c*) assess, when treatment is terminated (and perhaps periodically during the treatment process), the extent to which the goals have been achieved.

If goals are generally not being achieved the worker needs to examine the underlying reasons. Perhaps unrealistic goals are being set. Perhaps the program or the treatment techniques are ineffective. Perhaps certain components of the treatment program are having an adverse effect. Perhaps the reasons account for the low success rate. Depending on the reason that the goals are not being achieved, appropriate changes need to be made.

On the other hand, if the goals are generally being met, workers can use this information to document to funding sources and to supervisors that high-quality services are being provided.

SUMMARY

Several values underlying social work practice and their implications for practice were presented. It was concluded that social work is both an art and a science. Because social work is partly an art, a worker fre-

quently must make decisions based on values rather than on knowledge. It should also be noted that change techniques used by workers are often based on theory and value assumptions rather than on proven therapy techniques.

Values were distinguished from knowledge. Values are beliefs, preferences, or assumptions about what is desirable or good for people. Knowledge statements are observations about the world and people that have been verified or are capable of verification. It is much easier to change a belief of a client that conflicts with current knowledge than it is to change a belief that is based on values. Guidelines were presented for how a worker should handle a value conflict between the worker and the client.

An important value of social work is respect for the dignity and uniqueness of the individual. The importance of individualizing each client was discussed, and guidelines were presented on how to relate to clients whose behavior is viewed as disgusting by the worker. Involved in individualization is the ability to accept clients but not the deviant behavior to be changed, careful attendance to clients' communications, and the discreet use of labeling.

Self-determination is the clients' right to express their own opinions and to act upon them, as long as clients do not infringe upon the rights of others. Clients should be made aware that there are alternatives for resolving the personal and social problems they face. Self-determination means that the client, not the worker, is the chief problem solver, although the worker has an obligation to offer suggestions of resolution approaches that the client may not be aware of.

Confidentiality is the implicit or explicit agreement between a professional and a client to maintain the private nature of information about the client. In professional practice a system of *relative confidentiality* currently exists, rather than a system of *absolute confidentiality*. A number of unresolved questions surrounding confidentiality were raised, and some guidelines on how beginning practitioners should handle such questions were presented. At times, circumstances arise in which a professional is permitted, expected, or required to violate confidentiality, and a number of these circumstances were listed — for example, when a client admits to a past or intended serious criminal act.

Other values of social work practice were summarized: belief in the institutional approach for the delivery of social services rather than the residual approach, advocacy and social action for those being discrimi-nated against, focus on family instead of the individual in treatment, and accountability.

In presenting guidelines for social work practice the reader was advised that such guidelines are not to be applied as absolutes, but simply as concepts that *may* be useful in working with people.

EXERCISES

1. Confidentiality

GOAL: This exercise is designed to help students learn guidelines about when to uphold, and when to violate, confidentiality.

Step 1: State the purpose of the exercise. Divide the class into subgroups of about five students. Ask each subgroup to arrive at answers to questions raised in the following vignettes.

1. You're a social worker at a public school and have been working with a family that has multiple problems. Two of the children are in special education programs for the emotionally disturbed. The mother has occasionally been hospitalized for emotional problems. The father has been investigated for child abuse by protective services in the past. Mother and father are having marital problems and are presently separated. The father comes to your office and demands to see a copy of the school's records on his children and his family. As a social worker, would you show him a copy of these records?

2. You're a social worker at a mental health center and are working with a client who appears emotionally upset. He states he has heard that his girlfriend is seeing someone else. While saying this, he becomes enraged and says he intends to shoot her. He asks you not to tell anyone that he has said this. As you seek to discuss his threat he continues to become more upset and walks out, stating, "I'll make sure she doesn't cheat on me." Should you violate confidentiality and inform someone? If you believe you should inform someone, who would you inform?

3. You're a social worker at a drug abuse treatment center and you're working with a twenty-three-year-old female. You establish a good working relationship with her. She says something has been bothering her for a long time, but she states she won't discuss it unless you agree not to tell anyone. You assure her that what she reveals will be kept confidential. She then reveals that in the past she had an incestuous relationship with her stepfather that started when she was fourteen and lasted for nearly three years. She believes her unresolved feeling about this experience is one of the reasons she sometimes drinks too much. In a staffing that is held on this client would you reveal what she has said to the other staff at this agency?

Step 2: (Answers to these questions are found in the chapter and involve (*a*) the 1974 Federal Privacy Act, (*b*) the 1974 *Tarasoff v. Regents of the University of California* decision, and (*c*) guidelines about sharing information with other staff.) Ask the subgroups what they arrived at, and then provide the answers that are given in the text.

Step 3: Explain that in social work practice a system of relative rather than absolute confidentiality is used. Present the guidelines (outlined in this chapter) as to when to uphold and when to violate confidentiality.

2. Clarifying Values

GOAL: This exercise is designed to help students clarify their values in regard to a number of prominent issues in social work.

Step 1: State the purpose of this exercise. Explain that social workers need to be aware of their personal values and aware of professional values so that they know when they should take a nonjudgmental position in working with clients, and when they should seek to sell to clients (or enforce to clients) a particular set of values. Have the class form subgroups of three. Instruct each subgroup to arrive at answers, and reasons for their answers, to each of the following 10 questions. (Distribute the following questions on a handout, or have the students read the questions from this text.)

1. Assume that you are a protective service worker and that you have evidence that a father is committing incest with his ten-year-old daughter. Would you seek to end the incest by (*a*) seeking to provide counseling services to all members of the family in order to keep the family intact, or (*b*) bringing legal charges against the father, or (*c*) seeking to do both at the same time?
2. Do you support a constitutional amendment to make abortions illegal?
3. Assume you are a parent. Would you send your child to a school in which one or more of his classmates has AIDS?
4. Do you support affirmative action programs which assert that certain minority groups and women should be given preference in hiring over white males?
5. Do you believe the severely and profoundly retarded who will never be able to function at a level at which they can sit up should be kept alive indefinitely at taxpayer's expense?
6. Do you believe our country should support an extensive program to develop the capacity to clone human beings?
7. Do you believe in capital punishment for certain crimes?
8. Do you think a teacher who is a homosexual should be allowed to teach in elementary and secondary schools?
9. If there were a war, do you think women in the military service should fight in combat?
10. Do you support mercy killing when the victim is terminally ill and in intense pain?

Step 2: After the subgroups have arrived at answers, take each question (one at a time) and have the subgroups present and discuss their answers. (Indicate that the purpose of this exercise is to help students clarify their values and definitely is not to sell any particular value system.)

Step 3: Have the students discuss their feelings about how they felt when others in class expressed views with which they strongly disagreed.

3. *New Frontier to Rings of Fire*

GOAL: This exercise is designed to help students clarify their values about humanity.

Step 1: State the purpose of the exercise. Have the class form subgroups of about five. Read the following vignette to the subgroups.

The United States has recently completed building a remarkable spaceship, named *New Frontier,* that is capable of carrying seven people to planets in other galaxies. *New Frontier* uses nuclear power and is guided by a new computer system that does not require a pilot to fly the spaceship.

Our government has recently discovered a new planet in a faraway galaxy that is very similar to our Earth's atmosphere and appears capable of supporting life. This planet has been named Rings of Fire as it has a red hue and several rings around it similar to those of Saturn.

Your subgroup has been chosen by the president of the United States to select the seven people who will take the first flight. *New Frontier* is presently located on a remote Samoan island.

Suddenly a nuclear war breaks out in the Middle East, and the superpowers quickly enter the conflict. The bombs and the radioactive fallout will destroy civilization as we know it. The chief scientist frantically calls your group. She indicates there are fifteen minutes available to select the seven people to go on *New Frontier* to Rings of Fire. A country we are fighting in this war has sent a nuclear missile to this Samoan island to destroy *New Frontier*. There are thirteen people close enough to board *New Frontier*. The chief scientist wants your subgroup to select the seven people so that these thirteen people do not begin fighting among themselves. If your subgroup does not select seven people in fifteen minutes, there is a danger the human race will cease to exist. The seven people selected may well be the only hope for continuing the human race. Your subgroup has only the following information about the thirteen people.

1. Chief scientist, fifty-seven years old, has a husband and three children who are in Beaumont, Texas.
2. Male Korean medical student, twenty-four years old.
3. White male rabbi, twenty-eight years old.
4. Female Samoan prostitute who has herpes, thirty-five years old.
5. White male professional baseball player, twenty-six years old and gay.
6. Protestant male child, eight years old.
7. Ten-year-old white female who is moderately retarded from not having enough oxygen at birth.
8. Twenty-seven-year-old white Catholic male who is unemployed and has cerebral palsy.
9. Thirty-four-year-old white male truck driver who has a history of not getting along with people and of getting into numerous fights.
10. Twenty-two-year-old Samoan farmer who has had a vasectomy.
11. Twenty-seven-year-old female Japanese stockbroker.
12. Thirty-five-year-old white female who is depressed and has a long history of being hospitalized for emotional problems.
13. Twenty-six-year-old white female who is a millionaire via inheritance and detests working.

Step 2: Distribute copies of this list to the subgroups. Give the subgroups fifteen minutes to complete the task and inform them when they have the following time remaining (in minutes): ten, five, three, and one. Call time at the end of fifteen minutes.

Step 3: Have each subgroup state its choices and the reasons for its selections. Seek to ask questions to reveal the values underlying the selections. End the exercise by asking the students their thoughts about the merits and shortcomings of this exercise.

II

SOCIAL

WORK

PRACTICE

3

ASSESSMENT

Assessment is a critical process in social work practice. The selection of goals and treatment interventions depends largely on the assessment. An inaccurate or incomplete assessment will probably lead to inappropriate goals being set and inappropriate interventions being used. When an inaccurate or incomplete assessment is made, positive changes in the targeted client are unlikely to occur.

Hepworth and Larsen (1986, p. 165) define assessment as follows:

Assessment is the process of gathering, analyzing, and synthesizing salient data into a formulation that encompasses the following vital dimensions: (1) the nature of clients' problems, including special attention to the roles that clients and significant others play in the difficulties; (2) the functioning (strengths, limitations, personality assets, and deficiencies) of clients and significant others; (3) motivation of clients to work on the problems; (4) relevant environmental factors that contribute to the problems; and (5) resources that are available or are needed to ameliorate the clients' difficulties.

Assessment has sometimes been referred to as *psychosocial diagnosis* (Hollis, 1972). But the term *diagnosis* focuses on what is wrong with the client, family, or group that is being diagnosed—such as having a disease, dysfunction, or mental problem. Because diagnosis has a negative connotation, the term *assessment* is preferred by this author and many other social work educators. Assessment includes not only what is wrong with the client[1] but also the resources, strengths, motivations, functional components, and other positive factors that can be utilized in resolving difficulties, in enhancing functioning, and in promoting growth. In fact, assessment in its broadest sense is the base for the development of a treatment plan.

The nature of the assessment task varies significantly with the type of setting in which the social worker

---

[1]The term *client* in this chapter will often be used in a generic sense to refer to an individual, family, group, or community that a practitioner is working with.

practices, although the process that one uses in different settings is similar. A social worker in a nursing home who is assessing an applicant for potential placement will look at variables that are radically different from those examined by a social worker in a protective service setting who is assessing an allegation of child abuse.

In some settings (as in many protective services programs) the social worker makes an independent assessment. With independent assessments, the social worker may consult with colleagues or professionals in other disciplines on complicated cases. In other settings (for example, mental health clinics, schools, and medical hospitals), the social worker is apt to be a member of a clinical team that makes an assessment. Other team members may include a psychologist, psychiatrist, nurse, and perhaps professionals from other disciplines. With clinical teams, each team member has a circumscribed role in the assessment process, which is based on his special professional expertise. A psychologist, for example, would focus primarily on psychological functioning and would probably administer a variety of psychological tests (including personality and intelligence tests). A social worker usually compiles a social history that assesses family background, marital dynamics, environmental factors, and employment and educational background. In settings in which the social worker is the primary assessor, the assessment is generally completed in one, two, or three sessions. With a clinical team approach, the case is usually more complicated, and assessment by the various professionals may take several weeks.

Assessment is sometimes a product and sometimes an ongoing process. As a product, an assessment is a formulation at a point in time regarding the nature of a client's difficulties and resources. An illustration is the completion of a mental status assessment at a psychiatric hospital. Such an assessment is first focused on determining whether the client is sane or psychotic. If the client is assessed as psychotic, a psychiatric label is assigned and a recommended treatment approach is then stated. Even when an assessment is a product, the assessment will usually have to be updated and revised months or sometimes years later. An assessment is, in essence, a working hypothesis of a client's difficulties

and resources that is based on the current data. As time passes, the client will change and so will environmental factors that impact him. Based on such changes, assessments have to be updated and revised periodically.

Assessment can also be viewed as an ongoing process from the initial interview to the termination of the case. The length of time a client receives services may be weeks, months, or even years. During this time the professionals working with a case are continually receiving and analyzing new information that gradually emerges. In the early stages of contact with a client the focus is primarily on gathering information to assess the client's problems and resources. Once these are tentatively specified, the problem-solving phase has a greater emphasis—as resolution strategies are suggested, analyzed, and then one or more strategies are selected and implemented. But even in the problem-solving phase, new information related to the client's difficulties and resources is apt to emerge, necessitating a revision of the assessment. In fact, as contact between a professional and a client continues, the client may disclose additional problems that need to be assessed and then resolved. It is common in initial contact for a client to withhold vital information from fear of condemnation by the professional. For example, a parent who is abusing a child is apt initially to deny that the abuse is occurring. As time passes, if the parent comes to trust the worker, the parent may disclose that she at times loses control and then hits the child. As new information is provided, the initial assessment needs to be revised.

Hepworth and Larsen (1986, p. 166) note that assessment continues to occur even during the termination phase:

The process of assessment continues even during the terminal phase of service. During the final interviews, the practitioner carefully evaluates the client's readiness to terminate, assess the presence of residual difficulties that may cause future difficulties, and identifies possible emotional reactions to termination. The practitioner also considers possible strategies to assist the client to maintain improved functioning or to achieve additional progress after formal social work service is concluded.

A FOCUS
ON STRENGTHS

For most of the past several decades, social work and the other helping professions have had a primary focus on diagnosing the pathology, shortcomings, and dysfunctions of clients. One reason may be because Freudian psychology was the primary theory that was used in analyzing human behavior. (Freud's theories of personality development and psychopathology are summarized in Chapter 13.) Freudian psychology is based on a medical model and thereby has concepts that are geared to identify illness or pathology in clients. It has very few concepts to identify strengths. As described in Chapter 1, social work is now shifting to use an ecological model in assessing human behavior. An ecological model focuses on identifying both strengths and weaknesses.

It is essential that social workers include clients' strengths in the assessment process. In working with clients, social workers focus on the strengths and resources of clients to help them resolve their difficulties. In order to utilize clients' strengths effectively, social workers must first identify those strengths.

Unfortunately, Maluccio found that many social workers focus too much on the perceived weaknesses of clients and underestimate or are blind to their strengths. Malucci (1979, p. 401) concludes:

There is a need to shift the focus in social work education and practice from problems or pathology to strengths, resources, and potentialities in human beings and their environments.

There is a danger that a primary focus on weaknesses will impair a worker's capacity to identify the growth potential of clients. Social workers strongly hold the value that clients have the right (and should be encouraged) to develop their potentialities fully. Focusing on pathology often undermines this value commitment.

Another reason for attending to clients' strengths is that many clients need help in enhancing their self-esteem. Many have feelings of worthlessness, feelings of inadequacy, a sense of being a failure, and a lack of self-confidence and self-respect. Glasser (1972) has

noted that low self-esteem often leads to emotional difficulties, withdrawal, or criminal activity. In order to assist clients in viewing themselves more positively, it is crucial that social workers first view their clients as having considerable strengths and competencies. Berwick (1980, p. 270) underscores this point in working with neglectful parents of children who fail to thrive:

Self-esteem is already at a low ebb in many of the parents of these children, and the success of the hospital in nourishing a child when the mother has failed only serves to accentuate the pain of failure. . . . Even in the few cases that require foster care, the health care team's task is to seek strengths and to develop a sense of competence in both the parents and the child that will permit a synchronous nurturant relationship to emerge.

SOURCES
OF INFORMATION

Data used in making an assessment are derived from a variety of sources. The following are the primary sources.

Verbal Report from Client

The verbal report from a client is often the primary source and in some cases is the only source. (For example, social workers in private practice sometimes obtain information only from the client.) A variety of information may be obtained from the client: description of the problems, feelings about the problems, views of his personal resources to combat the problems, motivations to make efforts to resolve the problems, the history of the problems, views of the causes, a description of what has already been done in attempting to resolve the problems, and so on.

Although clients are often fairly accurate in describing their difficulties and resources, a worker should be aware that verbal reports from clients are sometimes distorted by embarrassments, biases, distorted perceptions, and strong emotional feelings. For example, a married woman whose husband has left her for someone else may have such strong emotional reactions that she may not be objective about the role she played in the breakup of her marriage. In some settings clients deliberately try to conceal, or even distort, information. Abusive parents, for example, may deny they have abused their children. Alcoholics, because of the nature of the addictive process, are apt to deny they have a drinking problem. Correctional clients may try to conceal some of their illegal activities.

Clients' verbal reports should be respected as valid until additional information indicates otherwise. In some settings, as in protective services, it is often necessary to verify a client's denial that a problem exists by checking with other sources — such as neighbors, relatives, and school personnel.

Forms That Client Completes

Many agencies, prior to or after the first interview, ask clients to complete certain forms that request such information as name, address, telephone number, employer, years of school completed, marital status, description of problem, names of family members, and so on. Such information often is most efficiently collected by having the client fill out a form.

There are also several self-report forms that can be used in the assessment process. Some clients, particularly adolescents, may be more relaxed and potentially more truthful if they can answer questions on a form, while being assured that only helping professionals at the agency will see the answers. Examples of self-report forms for children and adolescents are the Piers-Harris Children Self-Concept Scale (Piers and Harris, 1969), and the Personal Problems Checklist for Adolescents (Schinka, 1985). Both of these instruments repeat questions in different ways so that the examiner can get a sense of reliability — that is, the extent to which the respondent answers the same question in the same way. These instruments also have validity indexes. There are also self-report instruments for adults, such as the Forty-Eight Item Counseling Evaluation Test: Revised (McMahon, 1971).

If a worker chooses to utilize a self-report instrument (such as one of the above) the worker needs to become knowledgeable about the instrument and guidelines for its use. Research on the instrument's reliability and validity should be carefully studied in order to evaluate its value. Also, the worker needs to use "common sense" in making interpretations of the results. Like so many other parts of the assessment process, a test result is a starting point and not an end product.

Collateral Sources

Information is sometimes collected from a variety of collateral sources: friends, relatives, neighbors, physicians, other social agencies, teachers, and others who may be able to provide relevant information. In some cases clients have received social services from a number of other agencies. Summary information about such clients is often obtained from these agencies.

Some workers make the mistake of overlooking collateral sources; as a result, potentially valuable information is not collected. Less frequently, some workers spend too much time gathering collateral information. In social work practice a practitioner needs to exercise prudence in deciding what information is needed. In many circumstances it is essential to get the client's verbal consent and have the client sign release-of-information forms before collateral sources are contacted. (See Chapter 2 for a description of confidentiality and release-of-information forms.)

Psychological Tests

There are a variety of personality and intelligence tests. Most psychological tests are designed to be administered by psychologists. An exception to this rule is the limited number of tests that have been developed by Hudson (1982) for clinical social workers. This package of tests gathers information on self-esteem, contentment, marital satisfaction, sexual satisfaction, parent's attitudes towards child, child's attitudes toward mother, child's attitudes toward father, attitudes toward family as a whole, and peer relations.

Caution should be used with psychological tests, as most tests are not designed to be administered or interpreted by social workers. Such administration and interpretation is the responsibility of psychologists. In addition, most personality tests have low validity and reliability and therefore should be used with extreme caution, if at all.

Nonverbal Behavior of Client

Nonverbal behavior of clients provides a valuable source of information. As practitioners become more experienced, they give greater attention to and become more competent in identifying and interpreting nonverbal cues. Such cues are invaluable in identifying what clients are actually thinking and feeling. There are a wide variety of nonverbal cues: gestures, posture, breathing patterns, tension in facial and neck muscles, facial color, eye movements, choice of clothes, physical appearance, eye contact, and tone of voice. Such cues give information about stress levels, kinds of feelings being experienced, and whether the client is telling the truth. For example, a client who folds his arms over his chest and frowns every time a worker brings up a particular topic is conveying valuable information about his feelings related to that topic.

Interactions with Significant Others and Home Visits

Observation of a client interacting with people who are important in her life reveals a lot of information. These significant others include family members, other close relatives, peers, friends, and neighbors. The way a client presents herself in an office may be dramatically different from the way she interacts at home. In an office setting a client may seek to portray an image that is atypical for her. A home visit will provide information not only about how a client interacts with significant others but also on environmental factors that are impacting the client. For example, a home visit investigating a charge that a single mother is neglecting her children will reveal information about home cleanliness, available food and diet, presence of animals (including pets and rats), presence of cockroaches and insects, available clothing, possible drug abuse by the parent, home interactions between mother and children, interactions between the mother and neighbors, type of neighborhood, and financial circumstances.

It is important for practitioners to remember that an office setting is an unnatural arena for family interaction. In an unnatural setting, families are less apt to interact as they do at home. As with any source of information, there are chances of errors in observing interactions. For example, the way a family interacts while being observed may be atypical for how they interact when they know they are not being observed.

Additionally, clients will often feel some discomfort if the worker is better educated and has a higher societal status than the client. A home visit may help such clients to feel more accepted and less anxious, as most people are more relaxed in their own home.

Worker's Intuition from Direct Interactions

A worker's reactions to the way a client interacts with him provides clues to how others react to this client. This is because clients often manifest similar interactional patterns in their general social relationships. The way clients interact with a worker therefore provides clues to probable difficulties or successes in interactions with others. Some of the many ways in which a worker may experience clients are nonassertive, passive, submissive, aggressive, withdrawn, passive-aggressive, personable, caring, manipulative, highly motivated, insecure, and dependent. Such intuition may provide valuable information about problematic behavior facing a client. For example, I recently counseled a twenty-two-year-old college coed who complained that her roommates used her as a "doormat" by frequently borrowing her car, failing to pay for gas, wearing her clothes without asking, and eating the food she bought without asking. In the interview she came across as nonassertive (with her verbal and nonverbal communication) and as making extraordinary efforts to please me. These specific behaviors were pointed out to her, and I inquired whether she thought she had indirectly communicated these kinds of behaviors that she would not object to her roommates' "using her things." She thought about it for awhile and acknowledged that that assessment was probably accurate. She was then instructed in how to express her concerns assertively to her roommates. With role-playing, she gradually acquired the confidence to confront her roommates about these concerns.

It should be noted that there are cautions and limitations to using one's intuition to assess a client's interactions with others. A client may interact atypically with a social worker because he may want to convey an atypical image. Just as some people change their patterns when interacting with a police officer, so do some clients seek to convey an atypical image when interacting with a worker.

Also the personality of a worker may lead clients to interact atypically. For example, if a worker comes across as being aggressive and highly confrontive, two reactions of clients are common: one is to become passive and submissive, and the other is to respond by also being aggressive. Therefore, in order to use one's intuition effectively in assessing client's behaviors, it is important for the worker to have substantial awareness of self and an awareness of how he tends to affect others during interactions. It is also important for the worker to convey a nonjudgmental attitude to clients. For lasting change to occur, most clients need to feel competent. In order to feel competent, most clients need to value and believe in themselves.

KNOWLEDGE USED IN MAKING AN ASSESSMENT

An *extensive* knowledge of human behavior and the social environmet is needed in order to have a high degree of accuracy in assessing the problems of a client system. Hepworth and Larsen (1986, p. 172) note:

To assess the problems of a client system (individual, couple, or family) . . . requires extensive knowledge

about that system as well as careful consideration of the multifarious systems (e.g., economic, legal, educational, medical, religious, social, interpersonal) that impinge upon the client system. Moreover, to assess the functioning of an individual entails evaluating various aspects of that person's functioning. For example, one must consider dynamic interactions among the biophysical, cognitive, emotional, cultural, behavioral, and motivational subsystems and the relationships of those interactions to problematic situations.

As identified by Hepworth and Larsen, conducting an assessment may require a broad array of knowledge about

- Multifarious systems
- Biophysical factors
- Cognitive factors
- Emotional factors
- Cultural factors
- Behavioral factors
- Motivational factors
- Family systems
- Environmental factors

At first glance learning about all these factors seems overwhelming, but such knowledge is obtained in college from a variety of social work courses. A key course in most social work programs that includes these factors is a course in human behavior and the social environment. Practice and policy courses also cover some of these areas. Other disciplines providing background information are sociology, psychology, anthropology, biology, political science, women's studies, ethnic studies, history, communication, philosophy, religious studies, and economics.

In addition, the overall purpose of an assessment adds considerable focus to what knowledge is needed. For example, a social worker doing an assessment of an elderly applicant for a placement at a nursing home would first of all need to know the criteria used by the nursing home for accepting applicants. Such criteria may include variables involving financial resources, medical conditions, physical strengths and impairments, emotional and behavioral patterns, special needs, level of cognitive functioning, and degree of willingness to enter a nursing home. Based on the nursing home's criteria, the social worker would then seek to obtain information from the client, from family members, from physicians, and from other relevant sources to determine the extent to which the client meets the criteria of the nursing home.

The purpose of an assessment *always* gives focus to the kinds of factors that are examined. For example, for a fourth-grade child who is performing considerably below his grade level in school work, the following variables are apt to be examined: Does he have a learning disability? What is his I.Q. as measured by intelligence tests? Is he having some emotional difficulties? Does he have a low self-esteem which may be contributing to his low level of performance? Does he have a visual or hearing impairment, or other medical problems? Are there factors in his home and family life that may be influencing his school performance? What specific educational subjects and tasks is he doing fairly well at, and which is he having the most trouble with? How does he interact with peers and with his teachers? Has he experienced significant traumas in the past that may still be affecting him? Is he involved in using and perhaps abusing drugs? Is he motivated to do his best in school? How does he feel about his school performance?[2]

The theory or theories used by a practitioner have a major influence on what is examined when conducting an assessment. For example, Freudian psychology focuses on pathology, or unconscious processes, on fixations during a child's development, on sexuality, and on traumatic experiences during childhood. In contrast, rational therapy asserts that thinking patterns determine emotions and actions, and therefore the focus is on identifying the self-talk of clients that leads to unwanted emotions and dysfunctional behaviors. (Chapter 18 summarizes rational therapy.) What a worker looks for in conducting an analysis also has a large effect on determining the outcome. For example, practially everyone has traumatic early childhood experiences—so it is not surprising that when an adherent of Freudian psychology does an assessment that he is apt to identify some traumatic early childhood experiences that are then hypothesized as being causes of the current problems of clients. Similarly, all individuals talk to themselves in negative ways at times, so it is not surprising that a rational therapist will find evidence to support his "theory" in any assessment he does. Another example follows. Adherents of Freudian psychology are much more apt to assess a person as psychotic (because they believe mental illness exists) than are adherents of reality therapy, who believe that mental illness is a myth. (Freudian psychology is summarized in Chapter 13, and reality therapy is described in Chapter 17.)

Most theories of human behavior have not been proven. Many practitioners make the mistake of assuming their favorite theory or theories are factual. When an assessment is based on a theory of human behavior, the practitioner should be aware that the results of the assessment rest upon the accuracy of the theory, which has not yet been proven. Practitioners need to be aware that their assessment of someone is not "gospel," but only a hypothesis that is based on unproven theories.

---

[2]There is additional material elsewhere in this text that may be valuable in conducting an assessment: Chapter 4, how to write a social history; Chapters 4 and 5, interviewing and counseling (helpful when gathering information from clients and from collateral resources); Chapter 6 and 7, group dynamics; Chapter 8, family functioning and family systems (useful in assessing families); Chapter 9, how to assess community needs and how to conduct a community needs assessment; Chapter 11, ethnic groups, racial groups, and gender roles; Chapters 13–18, contemporary theories of personality development and psychopathology; Chapter 19, summary of learning theory approaches to conceptualizing behavioral dysfunctions; Chapter 20, assessing sexual dysfunctions; Chapter 21, a communication model that has useful concepts in assessing human behavior.

ENVIRONMENTAL SYSTEMS EMPHASIS

As described in Chapter 1, social work is increasingly using an ecological perspective in assessing human behavior. The ecological perspective involves considering the adaptive fit of human beings and their environments. The ecology of people in their "life space," which includes all the components of the social and physical environments that impact them. In doing an assessment of a client, an ecological perspective asserts the importance of assessing the person in the environment. Such an assessment therefore includes a focus not only on the person but also on the environmental systems that impact him.

When one is assessing the environment of a client, attention should be limited to those elements of the environment that are affecting (positively or negatively) the problem situation. In some cases the elements may be obvious (e.g., substandard housing and serious financial problems). In other cases the elements may be subtle (e.g., having aloof parents who give little encouragement).

Although the assessment of environmental factors should be limited to those that impact the client's problematic situations, there are a number of basic environmental needs that are universal. A partial list of these follows:

1. Adequate housing
2. Safety from hazards and safety from air, noise, and water pollution
3. Opportunities for a quality education
4. Adequate social support systems (e.g., family and relatives, neighbors, friends, and organized groups)
5. Access to quality health care
6. Access to recreational facilities
7. Adequate police and fire protection
8. Adequate financial resources to purchase essential items for an acceptable standard of living
9. Sufficient food and opportunities for a nutritional diet
10. Adequate clothing
11. Emotional support from significant others
12. Support from significant others to be drug free

Some students majoring in social work have the misconception that what a social worker does is sit in an office and counsel clients. True — counseling is one of the functions that social workers perform. But a worker has many more responsibilities — such as working with groups, working with families, and as-

sessing community needs and working with a variety of groups to meet unmet needs. For most social workers in-office counseling constitutes only a small fraction of the total services provided. A major part of working with individuals, families, groups, and communities is assessing environmental systems and then seeking to make changes in those systems that are negatively impacting clients. In seeking to change environmental systems, a worker may use a variety of skills — such as brokering, advocacy, program development, mediation, research, enabling, and case management. The following are some examples:

- A protective service worker may remove a child from a family by whom she is being sexually abused and place her in a foster home.

- A worker may arrange for visiting nurses and Meals on Wheels (home-delivered hot meals for homebound persons) to serve an elderly couple so that they can continue to live independently.

- A worker may arrange for homemaker services to be provided to a single mother with three young children; such services may involve shopping, cleaning, budgeting, preparing balanced meals, doing the laundry, and teaching these same skills to the mother.

- A worker may get involved with a women's group to work toward developing a shelter for battered women and their children in the community.

- A worker may help a community to develop local chapters of needed self-help groups — such as Alcoholics Anonymous, Narcotics Anonymous, and Parents Anonymous.

- For a family in which the husband has a terminal illness, a worker may make a referral to a hospice program.

- A practitioner may work with parents of children with special needs to establish closer collaboration with schoolteachers in order to enhance the children's functioning in school.

- A worker may join with other health professionals in seeking to raise the state's licensing standards for residential treatment centers, nursing homes, or day-care centers.

Social workers are increasingly looking at "life space" or how people are affected by their social and physical environments.

ASSESSING PROBLEMS

As indicated earlier, assessments are always focused on evaluating the needs and problems of clients. In assessing needs and problems it is helpful to use the concept *problem system*. Hepworth and Larsen (1986, p. 174) have defined a problem system as follows:

The configuration of the client(s), other people, and elements of the environment that interact to produce the problematic situation are designated as the problem system. The problem system revolves around the

client's concerns and is limited to those persons and factors directly involved in the client's ecological context.

The following fifteen questions are useful guides for assessing problem systems:

1. What specifically are the problems?   Many problems have several dimensions. It is crucial in an assessment to articulate the subproblems and dimensions of the problem as specifically and accurately as possible. For example, a twenty-seven-year-old wife with two children whose husband is killed in a traffic accident caused by a drunk driver may have a variety of needs and problems. She will probably undergo several emotional reactions to the death including denial of the tragedy, depression, anger at the drunk driver, possible guilt over unresolved conflicts she had with her husband, anger that the husband has left her with two children to raise alone, and nightmares. Since grieving intensively is highly stressful, she may come down with one or more stress-related illnesses (such as skin rashes, ulcers, or hypertension). She may seek to escape her problems by using drugs. She is apt to have financial difficulties caused by loss of income from her husband. She will have a need for companionship. She will need emotional support from others. Her children may have a variety of emotional reactions to the death, which they will need help in handling. She may need help in learning to take on the child care responsibilities that were previously performed by her husband. She may face a sharp reduction in her standard of living with the loss of her husband's income. She may be forced to seek a job (if she is not working) or be forced to seek a higher paying job. She may be forced to apply for AFDC benefits and have to cope with the embarrassment she may feel about being on welfare. She may need legal help in receiving any death benefits she is entitled to. At some point in the future she may have to make a decision about whether she should begin dating again. In order for the social worker to do an accurate assessment, it is essential that the problems and subproblems be precisely identified, prioritized, and specified. Those subproblems that are not identified in an assessment will not be combatted in the problem-solving phase.

2. How does the client view the problems? The meanings that clients assign to negative events in their lives are often as important, or more important, than the negative events. For example, a woman may end a relationship with a man she has been engaged to for over a year. The man's view of the breakup will largely determine the problems he faces. Let's assume he tells himself the following: "Life is not worth living. My life is ruined forever. I might just as well end it right now." Such a person will be very depressed and perhaps suicidal. These are the problems he then needs help with.

On the other hand, let's assume he tells himself the following: "I'll miss her somewhat, but it's probably best we end it now. The last three or four months we apparently grew in different directions. I'm somewhat relieved she broke up with me, as I was thinking about ending the relationship myself. It's easier with both of us wanting out of the relationship. I'll soon find someone else to date." In this case the man will probably be somewhat sad but also relieved that the relationship is over. With such views he may have little need for social services.

3. Who is involved in the problem system? The problem system includes all the people who are involved in producing the problematic situation. In the example above where a husband was killed in a traffic accident, the problem system would definitely include the surviving wife and her two children. The problem system may also include others who are highly involved with this family, such as in-laws, other relatives, neighbors, friends, or employers. Such people may need help for the grief they are experiencing, and some may also be part of the intervention process by becoming a social support system for the wife and her children. Another problem system that may or may not be identified is the drunk driver and his close family members. The drunk driver and his family may need help for the guilt and remorse they are experiencing, and the driver is probably also in need of help for his drinking problem.

4. How are the participants involved? In this aspect of the assessment process, the focus is on identifying the roles that each person plays in the problem system. Some systems become very complex. For example, a multiproblem family may require considerable analysis to determine the roles that are played by each member. In a multiproblem family there are several problems that need to be identified. For each problem, each family member may be playing one or more roles. Detailed information is needed about how each person affects and is affected by others and about consequences of events that tend to perpetuate problematic behavior.

5. What are the causes of the problems? Frequently identifying the causes or determinants of problems will suggest ways to intervene. If a husband abuses his wife when he is angry, then instructing him in learning alternative ways to vent his anger (such as jogging or expressing his feelings in an assertive rather than an aggressive manner) may be constructive. If he abuses his wife when under stress, then instructing him in stress management techniques (such as relaxation techniques) may be useful. If he abuses his wife only when intoxicated, he is apt to have a drinking problem and may benefit from an alcohol treatment program.

In making an assessment it is useful to remember that all human behavior is purposeful. A powerful way of analyzing human behavior is in terms of

Antecedents → Thought Processes →
Behavior → Consequences

The following is an example:

ANTECEDENT:	John Shaw comes home from work intoxicated.
THOUGHT PROCESSES OF MRS. SHAW:	"John is spending all of our money on booze. This is awful. My evening is ruined as I'll now have to listen to his foolish talk. I am angry at him, and he needs to feel as bad as I do."
BEHAVIOR OF MRS. SHAW:	Yelling and screaming at her husband for coming home intoxicated.
CONSEQUENCES:	Mr. Shaw becomes defensive. He thinks the verbal abuse from his wife is unwarranted, so he decides to "put her in her place" by becoming verbally and physically abusive to her.

In this situation the wife may not be able to stop her husband from drinking or from coming home intoxicated. But she has the power to stop the physical and verbal abuse that she has been suffering when her husband comes home intoxicated. She can, for example, go shopping or make arrangements to stay with someone else whenever her husband comes home intoxicated. She can also decide to separate from her husband. Analyzing behavior in terms of the above model often enables practitioners to suggest new response patterns to clients that will break dysfunctional cycles and reduce the damage generated by the problematic behaviors.

What each participant says and does during the problematic event needs to be determined, as the response of each participant is a stimulus to the other participants. Analyzing problematic behavior in terms of the above model frequently identifies the stimuli that lead to problematic behaviors. Once the stimuli are identified, interventions can be made to change the stimuli in order to break the dysfunctional cycles.

6. Where does the problematic behavior occur? Problematic behavior tends to occur in certain locations and not in others. A child may throw temper tantrums at home, but not at school or when visiting relatives. Perhaps the child has learned that having a tantrum at home will manipulate his parents into giving him what he wants; perhaps he has also learned that throwing a tantrum elsewhere will result in his being ridiculed instead of getting what he wants. Identifying where problematic behavior does *not* occur is as important as identifying where it does occur—as both may provide clues to identifying factors that trigger the problematic behavior and factors that prevent the problematic behavior from occurring. For example, a married couple may get into heated arguments when visiting the wife's parents but not when visiting the husband's parents. Perhaps there are factors that lead to increased tension when the couple visits the wife's parents—such as the husband's feeling he is being "put down" and not accepted by the wife's parents. An excellent way for determining why arguments occur at the wife's parents is to ask each spouse what the arguments were about, and to ask each to describe why they believe the arguments occurred.

7. When does the problematic behavior occur? Closely related to *where* the problematic behavior occurs is the question of *when* it occurs. The process of identifying when problematic behavior occurs and when it does not occur frequently reveals valuable clues to factors that trigger the behavior. If someone frequently becomes depressed at a certain time of year, it may be the result of grieving about a serious loss that occurred at that time some years ago—such as the death of a loved one or a divorce. It may also suggest seasonal affective disorder (SAD). Identifying when serious arguments occur for a married couple may suggest factors that trigger the conflict—such as one or both drinking at a party, one having contact with someone she or he dated in the past, one spouse participating in activities that the other is excluded from, and a misbehaving child (the parents may disagree about discipline). A child may feign a headache or throw a temper tantrum whenever he has to go someplace he does not want to go, or when he is told to do something (such as studying his spelling words) that he views as unpleasant. A male in a romantic relationship may start talking about taking his life whenever his woman friend suggests that they stop dating. A person with a drinking problem may drink to excess whenever he has intense unwanted emotions—such as anger, frustration, depression, and feeling insecure. Once the antecedents that trigger the problematic behavior are identified, the intervention phase can then focus on making the kinds of changes that will reduce the frequency of the problematic behavior.

8. What is the frequency, intensity, and duration of the problematic behavior? Someone who becomes intoxicated once or twice a year may not have a drinking problem, while someone who becomes intoxicated once or twice a week probably does. Someone who becomes depressed for a day or two every three months probably does not have a serious problem with depression, but someone who is depressed daily certainly does.

Closely related to the frequency of the problematic behavior is its intensity. Someone who is mildly depressed is much more functional than someone who is so severely depressed that he sleeps fifteen hours a day, cries frequently during his waking hours, and cannot think rationally. For many other problematic behaviors there are varying degrees of intensity—such as extent of intoxication, extent of violent behavior when angry, intensity of family arguments, and extent of overeating.

The duration of problematic behavior also is an important assessment variable. For example, when someone is intoxicated, how long does she continue to drink to maintain the intoxication? Or, if he is angry or depressed or under high stress, what is the typical duration of problematic behavior? A marital disagreement that lasts three weeks is obviously much more serious than one that lasts twenty minutes.

An assessment of the frequency, intensity, and duration of the problematic behavior helps to specify its severity and also helps to clarify the impact of the problematic behavior on the client and members of his family.

9. What is the history of the problematic behavior? An assessment of the history of a problem often identifies the events that originally acted as antecedents in triggering the dysfunctional behavior. For example, if an eighth-grade child develops a school phobia, an assessment of the history of the problem would first seek to identify when the phobia began to occur. Once identified, the assessment would focus on seeking to identify what was happening in the child's life at this time that was making him fearful about going to school. Perhaps he was not getting the grades he hoped he would. Perhaps his classmates were making life miserable for him. Perhaps his parents were having severe marital conflict and he may erroneously have believed that by staying home he could help ease the marital conflict. Perhaps it is part of a larger anxiety-related problem that has been developing for years. Identifying such antecedents may help in designing an intervention plan to reduce the frequency and severity of the problematic behavior.

It should be noted that identifying the antecedents that initially caused the dysfunctional behavior may not fully provide answers to the question of what are the current factors that are maintaining the problematic behavior. For example, a child may have developed a school phobia because two of his classmates were "bullying" him around. It is possible that those two classmates may have moved to another city. Other factors may now be causing the child to want to stay home—such as being able to watch television, being able to play all day long, and not having any schoolwork to do.

For voluntary clients it is also often revealing to seek out the *precipitating events* that led them to seek help. Often, their problems have existed for months and even years. Identifying the precipitating events often yields valuable information. For example, a person who has been bulimic for two and one-half years sought help after she noticed there was blood in her vomit—which suggested she might have internal bleeding; she was referred to a physician who found that her esophagus was severely damaged. A married couple who had been arguing periodically for three years sought counseling after they had their first serious physical fight; both were fearful their feuding had entered a new phase that could potentially be life-threatening to both. The precipitating events can usually be identified by the practitioner's asking (and probing) clients to identify the reasons for seeking help at this time.

Involuntary clients usually have a crisis, or a series of crises, that results in their being seen by a practitioner. A practitioner needs to identify as many data about these crises as possible (often from collateral sources) in order to determine why an involuntary client is being referred and what his problems are. Such information is also useful in confronting the involuntary client with the problem. (Involuntary clients frequently deny they have a problem.)

10. What does the client want? A key social work value is to start where the client is. Too often assessment of problematic situations is made from the practitioner's perspective rather than the client's. An adult services worker for a public welfare department was assigned the following case. A seventy-eight-year-old man was living alone in a house on a farm where he had been born and raised. The house was a shambles; it was filthy and had no running water or toilet facilities. Dishes were washed (when they were washed) in rainwater. A small wood-burning stove in the kitchen was used to heat the house. The elderly man was mentally alert but suffered from a variety of minor medical problems: he was overweight and had gout and hypertension. The man drank to excess and also rolled and smoked his own cigarettes—which was a potential fire hazard, especially when he was intoxicated. The worker for the case decided it was best for the man to be placed in a nursing home where adequate care could

be given. To the worker's surprise, the man refused and bluntly stated, "You know I was born and raised here, and I'm going to die here. If you would get a court order to place me in a nursing home, which I don't believe you will be able to get, I'll give up the will to live, and die quickly there." The worker was shocked. She discussed the case with her supervisor, and her supervisor pointed out that she may have been viewing the situation from what she wanted rather than what the client wanted. The worker agreed.

This case example points out that what a worker views as being a problematic situation may not be viewed as a problem by a client. If a client chooses to live in a substandard living situation, that is *his* choice—and he was a right to do so, *as long as he is not hurting anyone else in the process*. If, for example, young children were living with this elderly man, then child neglect might have been occurring. In that case, changes in living conditions might need to be made, or the children might need to be removed from the home.

In any assessment it is crucial to obtain accurately the client's view of the problem and what the client wants. If the client's desires are realistic and obtainable, satisfying them should generally be a major goal of the helping process. If what the client wants is not realistic, the reasons that his desires cannot be fulfilled need to be tactfully explained to the client.

11. How has the client attempted to handle the problem? The ways in which clients have attempted to cope with their problems provide valuable information during an assessment. Clients may have tried some ways of resolving their problems that did not work. Those strategies can be eliminated from consideration in the problem-solving phase.

Perhaps clients have tried some strategies that were partially successful. Perhaps with increased effort or some modifications in these strategies they will work. For example, a client suffering from a high level of stress had learned in the past to relax by using imagery relaxation. However, she did not think of using the technique when she was highly anxious or frustrated. The client was instructed to set aside fifteen minutes every morning before going to work and fifteen minutes in the evening, to practice the technique. (See

Chapter 22 for a description of imagery relaxation.) Structuring imagery relaxation into daily activities proved to be a useful way of helping her to combat the stress.

Examining the strategies that clients have used to try to resolve their problems may also reveal valuable information about their coping and problem-solving skills. If clients have marked deficits in problem solving perhaps it may be helpful to instruct them in the "no-lose" problem-solving approach (see Chapter 22 for a description of this approach).

Some clients may respond to interpersonal difficulties by being passive or nonassertive. Others may respond to interpersonal conflict by being aggressive. If either is the case, it may be desirable to instruct clients in handling interpersonal conflict by being assertive (see Chapter 19 for a description of assertiveness training).

Some clients have good problem-solving and interpersonal skills in some situations but not in others. For example, a schoolteacher was able to handle disruptive students in her classroom but was ineffective in dealing with her own children. A closer examination revealed that she was divorced and was fearful that if she disciplined her children they would want to live with her ex-husband. Through counseling she came to realize that her children would respect her more if their behavioral limits were more clearly specified and enforced by her. Once this was accomplished, she was able to use the same child management skills she used in the classroom with her own children.

12. What skills does the client need to combat the problem? An assessment of a problematic situation should also identify the skills that clients need to resolve their difficulties. If a parent is having difficulties with a child, specific skills that may be needed by the parent are listening, negotiating, setting limits, following through on consequences, and nurturing. If a couple is having marital conflicts, they may need problem-solving, communication, listening, and conflict management skills. (Sometimes helping such a couple learn the above skills may be more productive in the long run than helping them to resolve their present conflicts.) If a client frequently loses considerable

sums of money while gambling, he may need to learn how to say no assertively when his friends ask him to play poker or go to the racetrack. If a client is depressed, he may need to learn what he can do to counter the depression (see Chapter 18 for some strategies).

13. What external resources are needed to combat the problem? An assessment should identify not only the skills that clients need to combat their problems but also the external resources that are needed. A single mother on AFDC may need day-care services, transportation, and job training to help her become employable. Someone addicted to gambling may need a self-help group, such as Gamblers Anonymous, to give him the emotional support and guidance he needs to combat his addiction. A bulimic may need medical attention to assess and treat physical damage from binging and purging, one-to-one counseling to stop the binge-purge cycle, support from a self-help eating disorders group, and instruction in what is a nutritious and well-balanced diet. Once an assessment is made, a social worker often acts as a broker or case manager in connecting clients with needed services and resources. Frequently some or all of the needed services are not provided by the practitioner's agency and therefore arrangements need to be made for the services to be provided by other agencies, organizations, self-help groups, and natural support systems (such as neighbors, family members, fellow workers, church groups, and social groups).

14. What are the client's resources, skills, and strengths? As mentioned earlier in this chapter, a quality assessment also identifies the resources, strengths, and skills that clients already possess to combat their problems. The importance of identifying such strengths has already been described. Sometimes problems are resolved by enabling clients to apply to their problematic behavior the resources and skills they already possess. Clients who have frequent stress-related illnesses may, through counseling, learn that greater application of the following will help them to relax and reduce their high stress levels: positive thinking, problem solving rather than "awfulizing" about their problems, greater use of social support systems, and being more assertive with significant others in expressing their feelings and concerns. A couple who has marital problems may find their relationship improving when they seek to treat each other with the same kind of respect that they give to strangers and acquaintances; many spouses use tact in communicating with acquaintances but not in communicating with each other. A person who is grieving about the death of a loved one may find that discussing her grief with friends and relatives not only helps to ventilate her grief but also helps in developing a social support system for putting her life back together.

15. What are the recommended courses of action? The recommended courses of action have also been called the *treatment plan* and the *intervention plan.* Once a client's difficulties and strengths have been assessed, the next step is to set goals and arrive at a course of action to accomplish the goals. Some authorities conceptualize goal setting and specifying recommended courses of action to be a process that follows an assessment. However, in social work practice most assessments contain a recommended course of action; therefore, this process is discussed briefly here.

The goals should be jointed agreed to by both the client and the worker and should be realistic and obtainable. The goals should be geared to resolving the identified problems and should be stated in such a way that they are operational and measurable. An *operational goal* is one that can be directly translated into a course of action so that the goal can be accomplished. For example, for a nonassertive client, an operational goal might be to learn to be assertive with significant others; assertiveness training can be used as the course of action to accomplish this goal. A *measurable goal* is one that can be measured in its contribution to achieving the goal. One way to measure whether a client is making progress in becoming more assertive with significant others is for the client to record for two weeks the number of times he is assertive and nonassertive in interactions with significant others. The client is then given training in being assertive. After the training he again records for another two weeks the number of times he is assertive and nonassertive in interactions with significant others. If the proportion of being assertive after treatment is higher than before treatment,

measurable progress toward accomplishing the goal has occurred.

The stated courses of action should be realistic and obtainable. They also should usually be agreed to by the client; if the client disagrees with these courses of action he is unlikely to carry them out. (With some involuntary clients there are exceptions to the guideline that clients should agree with the recommended courses of action. For example, a parolee may not agree with the parole officer's assessment that the parolee's violation of the rules of parole warrants a recommendation to the court for a return to prison.)

The stated courses of action should usually be selected through the following process. After a goal has been set, the client and worker should generate a list of feasible courses of action to accomplish the goal. The strengths and shortcomings of each alternative should be considered. Then, the client and worker should usually select the course of action.

In some settings the worker or the clinical team selects the recommended courses of action, with minimal input from the client. For example, when an assessment is done for an elderly person's admission application for a nursing home, the recommendation will usually be based on the extent to which the elderly person's characteristics meets the nursing home's criteria for admission.

A SYSTEMS PERSPECTIVE[3]

Overview of Systems Theory

A systems perspective emphasizes looking beyond the presenting problems of a client in order to assess

---

[3]The material on a systems perspective was especially written for this text by Donald Nolan, M.S.S.W., BCD (Board Certified Diplomate in Clinical Social Work). Mr. Nolan is a clinical social worker in private practice.

the complexities and interrelationships of problems. Through a systems analysis of a case, the most effective intervention targets and strategies can usually be identified.

A systems perspective is based on systems theory. Key concepts of general systems theory are *wholeness*, *relationship*, and *homeostasis*.

The concept of wholeness means that the objects or elements within a system produce an entity that is greater than the additive sums of the separate parts. Systems theory is antireductionistic as it asserts no system can be adequately understood or totally explained once it has been broken down into its component parts. (For example, the central nervous system is able to carry out thought processes that would not occur if only the parts were observed.)

The concept of relationship asserts that the patterning and structuring among the elements in a system are as important as the elements themselves. For example, Masters and Johnson (1970) have found that sexual dysfunctions occur primarily because of the nature of the relationship between husband and wife rather than because of the psychological makeup of the partners in a marriage system.

Systems theory opposes simple cause-and-effect explanations. For example, whether a child will be abused in a family is determined by a variety of variables and patterning of these variables, such as parents' capacity to control their anger, relationships between child and parents, relationships between parents, degree of psychological stress, characteristics of child, and opportunities for socially acceptable ways for parents to ventilate anger. All these variables need to be assessed if one is to arrive at a plan of action that has a good chance of success. A systems approach is not a "Band-aid" approach.

The concept of homeostasis suggests that most living systems seek a balance to maintain and preserve the system. Jackson (1965), for example, has noted that families tend to establish a behavioral balance or stability and to resist any change from that predetermined level of stability. Emergence of the state of imbalance (generally either within or outside the marriage) ultimately acts to restore the homeostatic balance of the family. If one child is abused in a family, that abuse

often serves a function in the family as indicated by the fact that if that child is removed, a second child is often selected to be abused. Or, if one family member improves through seeking counseling, that improvement will generally upset the balance within the family and other family members will have to make changes (such changes may be adaptive or maladaptive) to adjust to the new behavior of the improved family member.

Pincus-Minahan Model

To understand how to use systems theory and systems analysis, one can work from many systems models. The most publicized systems model in social work literature is the Pincus-Minahan (1973) approach.

In 1973 Allen Pincus and Anne Minahan wrote *Social Work Practice: Model and Method*, which to many has become the primary way of applying systems analysis to social work practice. Their basic premise is that there is a *common core* of skills and concepts that are essential to the practice of social work (Pincus and Minahan, 1973, p. xi). Assessment skills are part of the common core of skills that are needed by social work practitioners.

Pincus and Minahan theorize that there are four basic systems in social work practice: a change agent system, a client system, a target system, and an action system. The *change agent* system is composed of professionals who are employed specifically for the purpose of creating planned change. Also part of the change agent system are the employing organizations of the change agents (Pincus and Minahan, 1973, p. 54). The term *employing organization* is important as Pincus and Minahan view only *paid* individuals as change agents. A change agent, then, is a professional who is employed specifically for the purpose of creating planned change.

The *client system* is composed of the people who sanction or *ask* for the change agent's services, who are the expected beneficiaries of the service, *and* who have a working agreement or contract with the change agent (Pincus and Minahan, 1973, p. 56). *Client* is used

FIGURE 3.1.

Basic Conceptualizations of Client System, Change Agent System, Target System, and Action System in the Pincus-Minahan Model

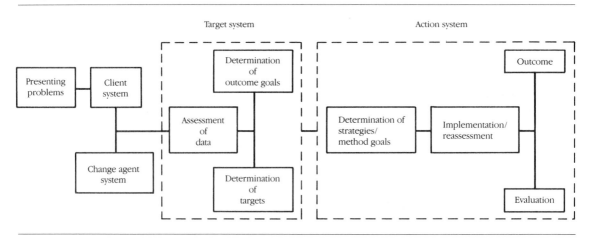

here in a more limited sense than is often used by social workers, precluding the possibility of "doing things" for people or organizations without their knowledge or agreement.

The *target system* is composed of the people, agencies, and/or organizational practices whom one wishes to change in some *measurable* way in order to reach the goals of the change agent(s) (Pincus and Minahan, 1973, p. 59). Through analyzing the changes of the target system one can measure effectiveness and provide a mechanism for accountability.

The last defined system is the *action system*. This term is used to describe those with whom the social worker works to accomplish the tasks and achieve the goals of the change effort (Pincus and Minahan, 1973, p. 61). One may need to involve a number of different

action systems in different aspects of a planned change effort to accomplish all the different goals of the change agent(s). The concepts of strategies and outcome goals are also used to further differentiate how action systems and target systems are developed and utilized. Figure 3.1 displays the basic conceptualizations in the Pincus-Minahan model.

Although assessment of data is formally displayed in this model as occurring within the target system, it is important to note that assessment also occurs within the client system and the change agent system. As specified earlier in this chapter, specifying the problem and its causes is a step in assessment. The assessment process also involves an analysis of the client's perception of the problem and an assessment of who and how others are involved in the client system. In developing

FIGURE 3.2

Examples of the Association and Overlap between Various Systems in the Pincus-Minahan Model

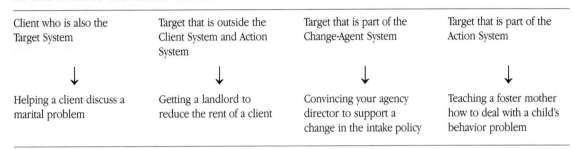

Client who is also the Target System	Target that is outside the Client System and Action System	Target that is part of the Change-Agent System	Target that is part of the Action System
↓	↓	↓	↓
Helping a client discuss a marital problem	Getting a landlord to reduce the rent of a client	Convincing your agency director to support a change in the intake policy	Teaching a foster mother how to deal with a child's behavior problem

a target system, the practitioner must consider the history of problematic behavior as well as where and when it occurs. Assessing the frequency and intensity of problematic behavior and past attempts to solve the problem are also important in the development of goals within a target system. This systems approach also helps a practitioner in developing targets for change; it presents a framework for analyzing client needs and wants and the external resources that may have to be developed or modified. Changes that a client needs to make in order to improve also become targets for change through a comprehensive assessment. The information thus acquired is then put into an action plan through which recommended courses of action are developed. Ongoing assessment continues to occur in the implementation and evaluation phases.

It should be noted that the four systems presented in Figure 3.1 are not mutually exclusive but can and do overlap in many cases. Such overlap is illustrated in Figure 3.2.

The Pincus-Minahan model is illustrated by the case example on the next page.

Another example (page 79) demonstrates how systems analysis can be applied in a clinical setting. Psychiatric social work has long been seen as different or distinct from other types of social work practice: its roots are more clinical and psychoanalytic than those of generalist social work practice. Also some authorities view a clinical approach as being more limited in scope (e.g., social action and macropractice approaches are seldom used) than a generalistic practice approach. In regard to assessment, it is important to note that the assessment process is similar in all settings, although comprehensiveness and specifics may be different. In this example the major focus of a systems analysis approach is on analyzing the presenting problem of the client. This analysis is done by a social worker who has had extensive training in systems analysis and considerable experience in using the approach. The case example demonstrates that after a practitioner gains experience in using the approach she can do much of the analysis "in her head," rather than writing out the components in diagrams, as was done with the previous example.

CASE EXAMPLE

In a School Setting

Richard Thomas is a social worker in a school setting. He gets a referral from a teacher, Mr. Phillips, that one of his students, John Hecht, a third-grade boy, is not behaving well in class (not complying with teacher directions, not listening, and not completing assignments). The teacher asks that Mr. Thomas do some counseling with the student to improve his attitude—simple enough referral, and one in which the problem could be seen as one of motivation and/or attitude. A number of counseling sessions could be beneficial and, given time limitations, is often the way social workers would intervene in this case. The implicit assumption is that there is an identified problem (the student), and to solve this problem the student must change. However, by not analyzing the problem more fully, one may miss a number of other problems in this situation.

In using systems analysis as an approach to assess a problem, Mr. Thomas would first list the presenting problems and then decide who his client is in this situation. Using the prior definition of what determines a client, only the teacher and in some sense the employing organization of Mr. Thomas can be defined as clients at this point. John and/or his parents may be potential clients in the future (see Figure 3.3 on page 76).

The next part of analyzing this case is to establish clear targets. Going back to Figure 3.1, this part of the analysis involves more thorough investigation and assessment of the data and then the development of long-range or outcome goals as one determines targets. Figure 3.4 (page 77) shows the beginning step in this assessment stage.

Within the assessment of data phase, outcome goals need to be developed. Then targets must be established to accomplish these outcome goals. This continuing process of assessment is diagrammed in Figure 3.5. (page 77).

At this point goals and targets have been identified and it is now necessary to develop an action system. The first part of this process, as seen in Figure 3.1, is the determination of strategies. (Determination of strategies is a later part of the assessment process.) These strategies must be linked to the targets and must be individualized to meet the needs of the target population. Systems analysis firmly requires that the intervention strategies that are applied should not be based on the worker's favorite techniques but on most effectively meeting the needs of the clients. For example, a worker may desire to use small group intervention skills at which she is particularly adept, but these skills would be applied only when systems analysis suggests such an approach is the best way to change a target and ultimately to accomplish a goal. Figure 3.6 (page 78) shows the development of strategies as the first step in developing an action system.

Now that consistent outcome goals, targets and strategies have been developed, the next step of applying systems analysis is to plan the *implementation stage* of the action system (see Figure 3.1). Often the social worker must use personal judgment as to what is practical and feasible at the time. Additionally, the worker can prioritize needs according to the most immediate and pressing needs of the client(s). Of course, the worker must also be prepared to reassess the strategies as intervention progresses, through observing the extent to which the desired *outcomes* are occurring. There may also be changes in client and change agent systems along the way as continuing assessment occurs. In this case the change agent system now includes not only the school social worker but also the school principal, the referring teacher as he alters his teaching style, the school guidance counselor, and social workers from the County Social Services Department in the areas of financial assistance, child management training, and protective services. In addition, some potential clients (such as John and his mother) may also become actual clients during the implementation phase of the action system.

It should be noted that in forming action systems that involve other agencies and other professionals, a key social work goal is to keep the process moving along. Often the referring social worker should serve as an advocate of the client and of the outcome goals of the systems analysis. It will often be necessary to restate these goals to others and to find ways to encourage other change agents to continue to provide services when "roadblocks" are encountered. In fact, monitoring or continuing to assess the progress should be expected as a systems analysis approach implies that there will be a group of people working *together* and thus there will be a need for coordination and direction.

It is also imperative to *evaluate* and stabilize the change effort after a prescribed amount of time. This evaluation (another part of overall assessment) should seek to measure the extent to which the *initial outcome goals* of the target system are being accomplished.

Not all cases are as complicated as this one or involve as many targets and action systems. This case did in fact exist, and assessment and strategy were developed as described. However, many, and perhaps most, social work cases are complicated. As such, systems analysis can help the worker understand the complexities of the case and the overall complexities of assessment. Systems analysis can be applied by virtually all social workers.

FIGURE 3.3

First Steps of the Systems Analysis Approach in the Case of John Hecht

---

Presenting problems

John Hecht, a third-grade
student, is

a. not complying with teacher's directions.

b. not listening.

c. not completing assignments.

Client system

Actual:

The teacher (Mr. Phillips) has asked for help, expects to benefit, and has a contract through the school system for the social worker to provide help. The school system that employs Mr. Thomas is also a client.

Potential:

John and/or his family may want to ask for help in the future. They may also be expected beneficiaries of help in the future. As yet, they have not contracted for help.

Change agent system

a. School social worker, Mr. Thomas.

b. The school system that employs Mr. Thomas.

Note: Additional change agents may be included later when the systems analysis approach is further developed and more thorough assessment is completed.

FIGURE 3.4

■■■■■■■■■■■■■■■■■■

Assessment of Data in the Case of John Hecht

The social worker, Mr. Thomas, seeks to develop a target system. He begins by collecting the following data:

A. The student's behavior in class is more complicated than originally reported. The student is often belittled by the teacher and frequently ignored when he asks for help. Additional observations of John in his class show that many other students also demonstrate inappropriate behavior. The teacher, Mr. Phillips, appears to have difficulty with classroom control. Also, conversations with Mr. Phillips reveal that he has a pattern of negative comments toward low-income students.

B. The student's attendance is a matter of concern. Over the past two years John has averaged approximately twenty-five percent nonattendance. As was previously mentioned, he also is not completing much of his school work, is not following directions, and is being disruptive. Further assessment also shows that John is not relating very well to his peers.

C. Upon talking with John's mother, who is a single parent, Mr. Thomas finds a pattern of school absences by the other two children in the family, and generally finds a home situation reflecting economic problems, family disorganization, and questionable knowledge of parenting skills. In discussions with other teachers that John has had, and other school faculty who "know of" the family, the social worker finds concerns about parental supervision at home, including the suspicion that John's mother, Mrs. Hecht, has problems with alcohol abuse and is often not home.

FIGURE 3.5.

■■■■■■■■■■■■■■■■■■

Determination of Outcome Goals and of Targets in the Case of John Hecht

Determination of Outcome Goals	Determination of Targets
(These goals represent the goals that were set in John Hecht's case, and relate to the three sets of problems identified in the beginning assessment of data stage in Figure 3.4).	(These targets identify the focuses of the change effort.)

A. Improve the teacher's classroom control and attitude toward students.	A. Target: Mr. Phillips, the teacher
	  1. Attitudes toward low-income students.
	  2. Shortcomings in classroom control.

B. Improve John's behavior, attendance, and peer relationships in school.	B. Target: John Hecht
	  1. Inappropriate attitudes and behaviors in school.
	  2. Inadequate peer relationships.
	  3. Frequent absences from school.

C. Bring more stability to John's home situation.	C. Target: The Hecht family
	  1. Financial difficulties.
	  2. Mrs. Hecht's lack of management skills and inadequate supervision of children.
	  3. The possibility of alcohol abuse by Mrs. Hecht.

FIGURE 3.6

Determination of Strategies in the John Hecht Case

A. Target: Mr. Phillips, a third-grade teacher.

1. The social worker will discuss concerns about Mr. Phillips's attitudes toward low-income students with the school principal and ask that the principal help by providing educational supervision in this area; that is, by arranging an in-service training session for teachers on (a) the societal conditions that contribute to the financial and family change problems that are occurring in the area, (b) the destructive effects on low-income students of negative attitudes by teachers, and (c) the benefits for low-income students of a nonjudgmental attitude by teachers. The social worker will also ask that the principal help Mr. Phillips to individualize more of his assignments for students so that he can better recognize individual differences in students, and can give students academic work that is at their individual grade level.

2. The social worker will discuss the issues of classroom management with Mr. Phillips and provide material on behavioral strategies of positive and negative reinforcement. The social worker will also explore with Mr. Phillips the benefits of developing some type of student charting system so that John (and potentially other students) can work toward goals on a daily basis. Finally, the social worker will consult with the teacher periodically about problematic behavior in his classroom, problem solve these situations, and provide suggestions on more effective techniques for controlling disruptive student behavior.

B. Target: John Hecht.

1. The social worker will provide supportive counseling to John regarding issues of developing more constructive ways of confronting others, developing goals as a learner, and developing responsibility for his actions. The need for supportive counseling is evident in order to develop rapport with John, to help John develop more effective problem-solving skills, and to demonstrate a positive adult role model.

2. The social worker will talk to the school guidance counselor about the possiblity of John's joining one of the small groups the counselor is currently leading, or joining one in the future. This could help John to improve his relationships with other students. Additionally, the social worker will discuss with the counselor the need for developing a classroom guidance program, perhaps for the entire school, directed toward improving human relations.

3. The social worker will refer the problem of frequent absences to the protective services unit of the County Social Services Department, as a case of unexcused absences or truancy. This referral will bring to the change effort the resources of another agency to help with the overall family difficulties. This referral also provides the County Social Services Department with an access point to the family.

C. Target: The Hecht family.

1. The social worker will inform Protective Services of the family's economic difficulties and will ask that Protective Services investigate whether the family is receiving all the financial assistance they are eligible for, and whether financial counseling is needed to better budget the family's resources.

2. The social worker, after assessing the seriousness of the home management difficulties, will refer this matter to the County Social Services Department. Realistically, this difficulty will involve the same protective service worker (at least as a case manager) who received the referral for truancy and financial assistance. The protective service worker may well ask other workers to provide certain services to this family, such as involving the mother in a Parent Effectiveness Training class (see Chapter 22). In this family it is important that timing the involvement of several workers not overwhelm the family. The school social worker, together with Mrs. Hecht and the social workers from the County Social Services Department, will develop a treatment plan to help Mrs. Hecht improve her knowledge of child development and parenting/behavioral practices. This plan may involve individual counseling, involvement in a parenting group, or demonstrating behavioral practices through modeling.

3. The social worker will investigate the alleged alcohol abuse further and then decide whether to refer Mrs. Hecht for alcohol and other drug abuse assessment, which is provided by the County Social Services Department. Since Mrs. Hecht also appears somewhat depressed and lacking in energy, an adult psychiatric referral may also be considered in the future. Additionally, since alcohol problems are also not unidimensional, it will be suggested that the County Social Services Department assist Mrs. Hecht in finding employment or in receiving job training. Also, it is likely that Mrs. Hecht will need some support (either through group or individual counseling) to help meet the demands of being a single parent.

CASE EXAMPLE

In a Clinical Setting

Jane Angell comes to a private mental health facility with vague concerns of unhappiness. She is referred by a friend. The psychiatric social worker explains that a thorough assessment needs to occur before a treatment plan can be developed. Ms. Angell is the client system at this point. Terra Montana (a social worker), and the clinic where she practices, compose the initial change agent system. Because there are complaints that suggest a possibility of depression, Ms. Montana needs to identify and examine Ms. Angell's symptoms as part of the assessment. Some types of depression are now viewed as having contributing factors that are considered "medical" in nature. Depression is an affective disorder with a number of distinguishing symptoms. Some current research suggests that depression is partly caused by chemical imbalances within the brain and central nervous system (Coryell, Endicott, and Andreasen, 1988; Rasmussen and Tsuang, 1986). Imbalances in chemicals, called neurotransmitters, that transmit messages from one nerve cell to another are theorized to cause problems with dysphoria (marked and persistent unhappiness, often without specific cause) as well as difficulties with concentration and often worry and guilt.[4] Environmental stressors also play a role and are often seen as "triggers" that may eventually lead to neurotransmitter imbalance in susceptible individuals. Ms. Montana, in assessing mental health issues in the client, needs to find out the following:

1. What is the client's current perception of her problems? What is the history of the depression including history of past treatment, successful or not?

2. Are there disturbances of sleep, including nightmares or night terrors, sudden awakening, early morning awakenings, insomnia or excessive sleep? What is the overall quality and history of sleep behaviors?

3. Are there disturbances of appetite, including loss or lack of appetite, periods of bingeing or purging of food and/or specific *avoidance* of certain foods?

4. Is there history of headaches? If so, specifically when and how often do these headaches occur? Do the headaches cause accompanying nausea, fatigue, or difficulty going outside because of light sensitivity? Do they cluster together? Is there history of sinus trouble and if so has this been medically assessed?

5. Is there history of stomachaches or other gastrointestinal difficulties, such as chronic constipation or diarrhea? Did these difficulties also occur in childhood?

6. Is there history of other somatic or physical complaints, such as backaches, joint or knee pains, a general feeling of malaise or not feeling well? Has the individual sought

Continued

There are several excellent resources for a comprehensive discussion of depression: Nancy Andreasen, *The Broken Brain* (New York: Harper & Row, 1985), and Paul Wender and D. Klein, *Mind, Mood and Medicine* (New York: Meridian Publishers, 1968). Additionally, specific diagnostic criteria for depression are found in *The Diagnostic and Statistical Manual of Mental Disorders*, (3rd ed., rev.) (*DSM-III-R*), (Washington, D.C.: American Psychiatric Association, 1987).

CASE EXAMPLE   *Continued*

medical care? If so, is there history of "doctor hopping," perhaps because physicians cannot find medically diagnosable conditions?

7. Is there history of anxiety and/or worry? How dysfunctional is this? Are there specific phobias that interfere in the person's lifestyle? Is there history of panic behaviors—a sudden feeling of intense anxiety and uneasiness that is often accompanied by rapid heart beat, difficulties in breathing, intense perspiring, and at times fear?

8. How does the client perceive what are normally pleasant times, such as birthdays, and holidays? Is there any seasonal nature to the depression?[5]

9. Are there difficulties in sexual functioning and/or desire? If there are, how does the client interpret these? Is there past history of rape or incest?

10. What is the client's prevalent mood? Is there history of fearfulness and crying, ruminating, worry, feelings of worthlessness, and/or thoughts of death or suicide? Has her mood generally been stable and predictable or are there substantial variations sometimes associated with excess energy or manic feelings?

11. Does the client have difficulty concentrating and remembering things?

12. How is the client functioning at home, at her job, and within her social context? Is she chronically tired? Does she feel "slowed down"? What are her family or friends telling her about her actions or moods? If married, what is the status of the marital relationship? If there are children in the family, how is the client relating to them?

13. Is there history of obsessive unwanted thoughts or compulsive actions, such as pacing or hand wringing?

14. Is there current alcohol or drug abuse, including abuse of prescription medications (such as Valium or other minor tranqualizers)? Is the client in denial of these problems? Is there any past history of treatment?

15. What is the client's history as a child and teenager and how does she view her parent(s)? Does she view her parent(s) as contributing or helping with past or current problems? Are there dysfunctional ways of thinking that were developed in childhood (e.g., the client viewing herself as a "bad child" as a result of being an adult child of an alcoholic)?

16. How did the client function in school, including history of past learning problems or disabilities, social interactions, patterns of dealing with school stresses and pressures, and possible past feelings of failure?

---

[5]There is a condition called seasonal affective disorder (SAD) that seems to coincide with winter seasons and corresponding low amounts of daylight.

17. What is the client's personal medical history including relevant illnesses, exposure to toxins, medications used, allergies and accidents? Has specialized medical care or previous psychiatric consultation occurred? How does the client view medical practitioners? If female and previously pregnant, were there problems associated with postpartum depression or possible termination of pregnancies?

18. What is the client's genetic history? Since certain types of depression are often seen as biologically or genetically influenced, a very careful and thorough history is essential.

Although this type of assessment is time-consuming, it is necessary in psychiatrically oriented social work practice. In developing change agent, client, target, and action systems for this case, information related to the above areas is utilized in combination with information about environmental stressors and client strengths to develop a treatment plan. In the above example, Ms. Angell, the client, is assessed as having many of the physical and emotional symptoms of depression. Since she has not seen her personal physician in some time, she needs a comprehensive physical. She will then need a psychiatric consultation to confirm a diagnosis of depression and to determine whether any medications may help in an overall treatment plan. Because depression is seen, at least in part, as being an imbalance of neurotransmitters, medications may be necessary to restore the balance. Ms. Angell, who is married and has two young children, also is assessed to have difficulties in these family relationships. Family therapy will become part of the action system, with targets of her husband and children. Mr. Angell does not understand his wife's difficulties with depression. He is often angry with her and blames her for being depressed. He needs to understand better why she is depressed and to be aware of what he and the children can do to help alleviate the depression. The children have behavioral problems at home, and therefore he and his wife need to develop (together with the therapist) an agreed-upon discipline plan. The couple also needs to increase their capacities to listen and to communicate with each other. Ms. Angell also has past feelings of worthlessness, derived in part from feeling that her parents viewed her as a failure. She needs individual therapy to counter and change her negative views of herself (see Chapter 20), and to improve her capacities to be assertive with her husband and her parents (see Chapter 21). Stresses at her job also appear to trigger problems with depression. Ms. Angell may need to reconsider her job demands (or her vocation itself); she may even need career counseling. Thus, a presenting problem of generalized unhappiness becomes a system of interrelating difficulties and numerous targets. As targets and action strategies are developed, client and change systems are also more fully developed. The overall change effort with this case involves the development of a treatment plan that evolves from a systems analysis of Ms. Angell's problems and life circumstances.

SUMMARY

Assessment is a critical process in social work practice. The selection of goals and treatment interventions largely depends upon the assessment. An assessment should include not only what is wrong with a client but also the resources, skills, and strengths of the client that can be utilized in resolving difficulties and in promoting growth. Too often in the past assessments have focused only on shortcomings and pathology of clients.

The nature of the assessment process varies significantly with the type of setting in which the social worker practices. In some settings the social worker makes an independent assessment, and in other settings the social worker is a member of a clinical team that makes an assessment. An assessment is, in essence, a working hypothesis of a client's difficulties and resources that is based on current data. As time passes, assessments have to be revised and updated as changes occur in the client and in his environment.

Data used in making an assessment are derived from various sources: verbal report from the client, forms that the client completes, collateral sources, psychological tests, nonverbal behavior of client, home visits, observation of client interacting with significant others, and the worker's gut feelings from interacting with the client.

A worker needs an extensive knowledge of human behavior and the social environment in order to do a quality assessment. An assessment may require knowledge about multifarious systems, biophysical factors, behavioral factors, motivational factors, family systems, and environmental factors. Such knowledge is obtained from a variety of courses that social work majors typically take in college. The purpose of an assessment always serves to give focus to the kinds of factors that are examined.

The theory or theories of human behavior that a practitioner uses in making an assessment will have a major influence on what is examined during the assessment. What a worker examines in conducting an assessment has a large effect on the outcome. Since most theories of human behavior have not been proven, practitioners need to be aware that their assessment of someone is only a hypothesis that is based on unproven theories.

Social work is increasingly using an ecological perspective in assessing human behavior. An ecological perspective asserts that it is important to assess the person-in-environment. The chapter presents fifteen questions that serve as guides for what to examine in conducting an assessment.

Systems theory is a way of conceptualizing problems and forming action/treatment plans. Through a systems analysis of a situation, the social worker can attempt to understand the relative importance of the many influences in the client's life. As a way of expanding upon a presenting problem, the social worker can conceptualize issues in terms of client, change agent, target, and action systems in order to determine goals and strategies in a planned change effort. A systems perspective highlights the importance of looking beyond the presenting problems of a client in order to assess the complexities of his or her life. A dynamic balance exists between individuals and their environments. Assessment, using a systems analysis approach, seeks to understand this balance so that compensating changes can improve the life of the client within an environment of systems that are included in the change effort.

EXERCISES

1. Writing an Assessment

GOAL: This exercise is designed to give students experience in writing an assessment.

Step 1: Explain the purpose of the exercise. Summarize the fifteen questions in the chapter as guides for information to focus on in writing an assessment. (As an alternative, the students may read these questions in the text.)

Step 2: Ask a student to volunteer to come up with a *contrived* problem prior to the next class period. At the next class period the instructor should interview the volunteer about the contrived problem. The other students in the class should then independently write up an assessment that covers the following topics:

a. Specific problems.
b. Client's views of problems.
c. People involved in the problem system.
d. Roles of participants in problem system.
e. Causes of problems.
f. Where problematic behavior occurs.
g. When problematic behavior occurs.
h. Frequency, intensity, and duration of problematic behavior.
i. History of the problematic behavior.
j. Goals of client regarding this problematic behavior.
k. Strategies client has used to handle the problem.
l. Skills needed by client to resolve the problem.
m. External resources needed to combat the problem.
n. Client's resources, skills, and strengths.
o. Recommended courses of action.

During the interview the instructor should ask questions that will provide the data to be written up for all the topics except the last. The instructor should then inform the students that they need to cover all of the above topics, with a significant percent (perhaps 40 percent) of their grade for this assignment being based on the quality of their response to "Recommended courses of action."

Step 3: Have the students write up the assessment and turn in at a later class period. Grade the papers. Before returning the papers, read one or two responses (without identifying the names of the writers) to the section "Recommended courses of action" in order to give the students one or two examples of a high-quality recommendation.

Step 4: End the exercise by having the students discuss the merits and shortcomings of this assignment.

2. Identifying Client and Change Agent Systems*

GOAL: The purpose of this exercise is to give students practice in determining client and change agent systems.

Step 1: Explain the goal of this exercise and then review the definitions of client and change agent systems.

---

*Exercises 2 and 3 were specially written for this text by Donald Nolan, M.S.S.W., BCD (Board Certified Diplomate in Clinical Social Work). Mr. Nolan is a clinical social worker in private practice.

Step 2: In each of the following situations have *students* individually write down who is part of the client system and change agent system. Students can identify actual and potential categories in each of these systems.

1. A mother and her son come to a social services agency seeking food and shelter.
2. A social worker employed by a public mental health center asks a psychiatrist for a consultation regarding whether a young woman the social worker has seen is clinically depressed.
3. A social worker in a hospital setting is asked by a nurse to talk with a single mother who has just given birth to her first child. The young woman's parents may also have some concerns and are presently visiting her.
4. A high school student is taken by his parents to a social worker in private practice because the parents are concerned with instances of violence and destructive behavior on their son's part.

Step 3: Discuss each one of these situations with the class, asking students to share their answers. Use a blackboard if possible to write down the answers given by students.

Step 4: Discuss how each of these situations may change over time, thereby changing the elements in the client and change agent systems. Use situation (4) to show this process by adding more data and a time sequence to the case.

3. Forming Target and Action Systems

GOAL: The purpose of this exercise is to give students practice in developing target systems and action systems.

Step 1: Review Figure 3.1 with the students, writing it on a blackboard if possible.

Step 2: Using the following situation, devise outcome goals, targets, and strategies. Remember that there should be some logical consistency between each outcome goal, the targets for that goal to be achieved, and the strategies to be used for achieving that goal (see Figures 3.5 and 3.6).

You are a social worker employed by a family services agency. Through your involvement with the juvenile court with a number of delinquency cases, a judge refers to you a group of teenagers who are required to attend weekly court-ordered counseling sessions. In your data gathering or assessment process, you find out that these teenagers all come from the same large public housing complex in a low-income section of the city. This part of the city is considered a problem area by the police department because of high rates of crime and high unemployment among adults. A number of social service and volunteer organizations are involved with this part of the community, but there seems to be no coordination among them. There is a neighborhood organization, but few people attend its meetings. The school is concerned about a high truancy rate and a high dropout rate among children living in this area. You have heard that the managers of the public housing complex in the area have generally discouraged the formation of tenant organizations, and there are serious problems in the maintenance of the apartments. As a result, there is a high rate of mobility in and out of the complex.

Step 3: Now go back and have the class identify the client systems and change agent systems in this situation.

Social work practice with individuals is aimed at helping individuals on a one-to-one basis to meet personal and social problems. Perhaps the two most essential skills needed by social workers in working with individuals are interviewing and counseling. This chapter presents material on how to interview; the next chapter focuses on how to counsel. This chapter covers types of social work interviews, how to begin and close interviews, how to phrase questions, note taking, and use of audiotapes and videotapes while interviewing. Workers spend a great deal of their time interviewing, and much of what they are responsible for depends on interviewing.

4

SOCIAL WORK WITH INDIVIDUALS: INTERVIEWING

THREE TYPES OF SOCIAL WORK INTERVIEWS

The purposes of most social work interviews can be classified as being informational (to obtain data for a social study or for writing a social history), diagnostic (to arrive at an appraisal), or therapeutic (to help clients change). Often, there is overlap among these three types. For example, a protective service worker in the initial interview with a couple suspected of child abuse often will obtain background information about the family members and seek to arrive at an appraisal of whether child abuse has occurred. If abuse is occurring, the worker may also begin helping the families to make changes to end further abuse. These three types of interviews, in spite of overlap, differ in the way they are structured and conducted.

Informational or Social History Interviews

Informational interviews are designed to obtain background or life history material related to the personal or social problem faced by a client. The purpose is not to learn all there is to know about a client's background but to seek information that will enable the worker (or agency) to better understand the client so that decisions can be made regarding the kinds of services that should be provided. Information that is sought includes both objective facts and subjective feelings and attitudes. People interviewed or contacted in addition to the client may include parents, friends, other relatives, employers, and other agencies having contact with the client (such as social service agencies, police departments, and schools). The specific information desired in a social history varies somewhat from agency to agency. An adoption agency, for example, would be more interested in information about child-rearing philosophies of potential adoptive parents as compared to a sheltered workshop, which would be more interested in specific work capacities of potential clients. As the social history example in Figure 4.1 shows, a social history usually has fact sheet information (e.g., name, age, occupation, and so on) and then information about the presenting question or problem, early childhood experiences and development, family background, school performance, dating and marital history, employment history, contact with other agencies, and general impressions. The desired objectives and format of social histories vary greatly from agency to agency.

A few examples of informational interviews will be mentioned. A social worker at a mental hospital may seek background information to better understand the problems and social functioning of an inpatient. A probation officer may be asked to do a social investigation to guide the court in dealing with someone charged with a felony. A worker for a community welfare council may be asked to interview people in a multiproblem neighborhood to identify what the residents view as being their most urgent unmet needs. A worker at a nursing home may do a social history on a new resident to obtain information on current social and personal problems and on special interests of the resident, so that the resident can be better understood.

Diagnostic Interviews

Appraisal or decision-making interviews are generally more focused in purpose than informational inter-

views. Diagnostic interviews differ from informational interviews in that the questions asked in diagnostic interviews are focused more on making *specific* decisions involving human services. Examples include the following. A protective service worker investigates a child abuse complaint to make a judgment about whether abuse is occurring. A public assistance worker interviews an unmarried woman who is pregnant to determine eligibility for a grant. A vocational rehabilitation counselor interviews a mentally handicapped client to determine eligibility for a range of services including financial assistance, vocational training, and sheltered workshop participation. A social worker at a residential facility for the developmentally disabled interviews the parents of a profoundly retarded child to obtain decision-making information that will be used by the admissions committee of the center to determine whether the child should be admitted to the center. A director of a group home for adolescent boys interviews a youth on juvenile probation who is having severe conflict with his parents to determine whether the youth might benefit from the group home, or perhaps needs to be placed in a correctional school.

Therapeutic Interviews

The purpose of therapeutic interviews is to help clients make changes, or to change the social environment to help clients function better, or both. Examples of the first type include the following. A parent who is shy may be counseled on how to be more assertive. A client who is depressed, or lonely, or suicidal may be counseled on how to handle such problems better. A client on probation may be counseled on how to apply for and find a job. A couple who is having marital problems may be counseled on how to communicate and handle their problems better. A newly married couple distressed by the husband's premature ejaculation may be counseled on how to resolve such a dysfunction (Belliveau and Richter, 1970). A couple that has problems in disciplining their children might be given instructional sessions in Parent Effectiveness Training techniques (Gordon, 1970).

FIGURE 4.1

Example of a Social History*

Wiscon State Hospital
Social History

Donald Cooper

Birth date: June 30, 1963

Home Address: 2030 Lincoln Drive
Milwaukee, Wisconsin

Occupation: Accountant
Race: White
Religion: Unaffiliated
Marital status: Divorced, and currently engaged
Height: 5'10"
Weight: 180

Phone: 414 726-4567

Presenting Problems: Mr. Cooper was committed to this hospital by Judge Cherwenka of Washington County for a sixty-day observation period. Mr. Cooper was arrested on August 1 on the charge of sexually molesting a minor earlier in the day. The reported victim was an eight-year-old girl whom Mr. Cooper reportedly enticed into his car at the girl's school, and then fondled her genitals after driving to a secluded area.

Mr. Cooper has been arrested on three previous occasions for fondling young girls; each time the charges were dropped after Mr. Cooper consented to receiving psychiatric care. Besides minor traffic violations, he has no other arrest record.

Family Background and Early History: Mr. Cooper's father, Dave Cooper, has been a dairy farmer near Stevens Point all his life. His income has been marginal through the years. Dave Cooper gave the impression of being a meek, submissive person who reportedly has a drinking problem. Dave Cooper indicated he has no idea why his son would become involved in his current difficulties.

David Cooper's wife died when Donald was eight years old, after being ill with cancer for a relatively short time. Dave Cooper mentioned this was a substantial blow to the children and to himself. He added that he has not as yet fully adjusted to his wife's death.

Donald has one sibling, Mary, who is one year older. She is currently married to a serviceman and they are now stationed in Germany.

Dave Cooper reported his son's developmental milestones were normal, except he sometimes was enuretic until age five. Dave Cooper reported Donald had a very close relationship with his mother, but seemed to adjust satisfactorily to his mother's death. Dave Cooper continued to provide and care for the two children after his wife died.

School Performance: Mr. Cooper received slightly above average grades in elementary and high school and received a two-year associate degree in accounting from Portage County Vocational School. Mr. Cooper reported he neither disliked nor liked school, and that he was somewhat of a loner during his school years.

General Health: Mr. Cooper reports his health has been good. He had a hernia operation at age twenty with no lingering complications.

Marital History: Mr. Cooper was married at age nineteen to Nancy Riehle whom he met in high school. It was a forced marriage and ended after one year because of "incompatibility." His ex-wife was interviewed and had no explanation for his involvement in his current difficulties. She is currently receiving $140 per month in child support, and is currently a typist and caring for their ten-year-old daughter. The daughter has not been informed of her father's current confinement; she seldom has contact with her father. The ex-wife appeared to be very dominating and overly critical of Donald whom she views as "morally immature."

Continued

---

*Names and other identifying information have been changed in this social history.

FIGURE 4.1

━━━━━━━━━━

(Continued)

Mr. Cooper is currently engaged to Mary Gautier, and the marriage was planned for December 2 of this year. Miss Gautier indicated she is now reconsidering the upcoming marriage. She is a charming, attractive, petite person who is currently employed at Jones High School as a secretary. She mentioned she was shocked upon being informed of her fiancé's arrest, and had not previously known about his prior arrests. She mentioned she still loves Donald, but feels that unless his reported involvement with young girls is discontinued, it would be better for them to break their engagement. She mentioned she has had sexual relations with Mr. Cooper about twice a week for the past six months which she described as "satisfying" for her, and she also thought for her fiancé.

Employment History: Mr. Cooper has been employed as an accountant at Paul Realty Company for the past five years. His supervisor, John Namman, reported his work is reliable, that he associates well with other employees, but is sometimes "moody." Mr. Cooper reported he likes his current job and hopes he can return after his confinement.

Prior to this position, Mr. Cooper worked as an accountant for two other firms where his work was also reported as acceptable. While in high school and in vocational school, he helped his father on the farm.

Prior Contact with Social Agencies: Since Mr. Cooper's first arrest for fondling young girls six years ago, he has been seeing Dr. Timmer at Midwest Psychiatric Center occasionally.

Dr. Timmer reported Mr. Cooper's difficulty is due to the following past history. (Mr. Cooper also related these events in an interview.)

Mr. Cooper mentioned his family life was fairly normal until his mother died when he was eight years old. His father then began drinking. When sober, his father was considerate, quiet, and an adequate family provider. However, when intoxicated, he was verbally, and sometimes physically, abusive to the children. The children became terrified when they knew their father was drinking. Therefore, when they heard him coming home, they learned to hide by crawling under a blanket. While under the blanket, in fear, they began fondling each other, which seemed to make them feel better. Now, Mr. Cooper mentioned when he feels "moody" or depressed, he seeks young girls to fondle, hoping to feel better again.

In treating Mr. Cooper, Dr. Timmer has been using a modified psychoanalytic approach, but he admits the therapy has as yet apparently not curbed Mr. Cooper's involvement with young girls.

General Impressions: In the interviews, Mr. Cooper appeared to be very concerned about his fondling behaviors with young girls and displayed motivation to curb the deviant behavior. He appears to have traditional middle-class values. He is fairly attractive, and has a pleasant personality.

Mr. Cooper, however, has had repeated incidents of involvement with young girls, even while under psychiatric care. The latest incident occurred at a time when Mr. Cooper is engaged; and as he reported, when he is having satisfying relations with his fiancée. His deviant behavior is apparently deeply entrenched. Sexual activities such as Mr. Cooper's are difficult to change. Perhaps covert sensitization, a form of behavior therapy, might be attempted.[†] Or, rational therapy might be used to teach him other ways of handling his emotions of depression and moodiness, instead of through seeking to fondle young girls.[‡] Also an arrangement might be made with the local mental health center to have Mr. Cooper call and receive immediate counseling (perhaps staying overnight at the center) whenever he has a strong urge to fondle young girls.

[†]See Chapter 19.
[‡]See Chapter 18.

Taking a social history

Other therapeutic interviews might be geared to changing the social environment to facilitate a client's social functioning. The spouse of a client with a drinking problem might be counseled on how to help the spouse stop drinking and develop a meaningful life separate from alcohol. Alfred Kadushin (1972, p. 19) gives other examples:

Interviews may have a therapeutic purpose but the person for whom the therapeutic change is sought may not be present. These include interviews with persons important in the client's life, where the social worker acts as a broker or advocate in the client's behalf. The social worker engaged in brokerage or advocacy may interview people in strategic positions in an attempt to influence them on behalf of the client. The purpose of the interview is to change the balance
of forces in the social environment in the client's favor. The school social worker may interview a teacher in order to influence her to show more accepting understanding of a client. The social worker at the neighborhood service center may interview a worker at the housing authority or at the local department of public welfare in order to obtain for his client full entitlement to housing rights or to assistance. Or a social worker may accompany an inarticulate client to an employment interview in an effort to influence the decision in the client's favor. In each instance the scheduled interview has a definite, and in these cases, therapeutic purpose on behalf of the client.[1]

---

[1]Alfred Kadushin, *The Social Work Interview.* Copyright © 1972, Columbia University Press, New York. Reprinted by permission.

*A therapeutic interview: A twenty-three-year-old man with a developmental disability is being coun-
seled by a social worker.*

Therapeutic interviews are the most common in social work, and therefore this text will focus mainly on this type.

THE PLACE OF THE INTERVIEW

Social work interviews can take place anywhere—in the office, the client's home, on street corners, in restaurants and taverns, and in institutions. Office inter-
views permit control of the physical setting, usually make the interviewer comfortable, and can usually be arranged to assure privacy. Office interviews also reduce worker's travel time between interviews.

Home visits have an advantage in helping the inter-
viewer to better understand the living conditions of the interviewee. Family interactions can also be observed. Some clients find it difficult or impossible to travel to an office (e.g. clients with severe disabilities), and therefore home visits are common in social work. Other clients find an office to be "foreign" to them and,

A home visit

therefore, are more comfortable in their home or in other settings.

The home visit also offers more opportunities for the worker to enter the life of the interviewee as a participant—opening a stuck door, moving furniture, holding a crying baby. However, there is also the chance that the interviewer may have to respond to conflict between family members if it occurs, and some clients may feel that a home visit may suggest that the worker is spying on them. Another disadvantage of home visits is that distractions are more apt to occur—for example, telephone calls, TV programs that other family members want to watch, friends dropping by to visit.

In practice I have found that while the physical setting may have an initial effect on the start of an interview, these effects can almost always be handled by a skillful interviewer. For example, on a home visit where there are a number of other people present, the worker can suggest to the client that they go to a restaurant where they can have a soda and talk in private. The skills of the interviewer are almost always more important in determining the productivity of an interview than the place of the interview.

OPENING THE FIRST INTERVIEW

When Interviewee-Initiated

If someone has asked to see a counselor and has come, it is best to let that person state just what he is concerned about. The counselor should, of course, greet the client with something like "Hi, I'm Jane Bernes and I'm a counselor at this agency." After the client has been seated, the client often begins indicating his concerns. If the client does not begin to relate his concerns, the worker should say something brief and neutral (so as not to sidetrack the client) to help the client get started, such as: "You came in here to see me about something today," or "Please feel free to tell me what's on your mind."

Openings that are *not* as desirable are the following: (*a*) "I'm glad you came in this afternoon," because the client may know that you are being superficial and may not in fact be glad to hear what the client has to say; (*b*) "In what way can I help you?" because the worker should not erroneously convey that the worker is the chief problem solver — the client owns the problem and is the primary problem solver; (*c*) "You have a problem?" as the word *problem* in a counseling situation may suggest to the client that the worker is viewing the client as a psychiatric case.

Benjamin (1974, p. 13) recommends the following about small talk at the beginning of an interview:

Sometimes at the outset there is room or need for small talk on the interviewer's part, something to help the interviewee get started. But we should attempt this only when we truly feel that it will be helpful. Brief statements such as the following may break the ice: "With traffic the way it is around here, you must have found it hard to get a parking place" or "It's nice to have a sunny day after all that rain, isn't it?"[2]

Kadushin (1972, pp. 130–31) gives the following suggestions on how to start an interview:

It is helpful if the interviewer can greet the interviewee by name. She invites her in, goes through the familiar social amenities — taking her coat, offering her a chair, and demonstrating her concern that she is reasonably comfortable. The interviewer gives the interviewee a chance to get settled — to compose herself, to absorb first impressions, to get her bearings, to catch her breath. She needs a little time to get used to the room and the interviewer. . . .

It is helpful, particularly at the beginning and the end of the contact, to make general conversation rather than engage in an interview. . . . The preliminary chit-chat may be about the weather, parking problems, cooking, baseball, or the high cost of living.

This socializing is not a waste of time. It eases the client's transition from the familiar mode of conversational interaction into a new and unfamiliar role which demands responses for which he has little experience. The conversation has the additional and very important advantage of permitting the interviewee to become acquainted with and size up the interviewer as a person.[3]

When Interviewer-Initiated

Whether talking to a client, or to relatives of clients, or to professionals at other agencies, the worker should indicate her role or position at the agency and then state the purpose of the interview. Thus a school counselor may say to a student who is receiving failing grades, "Hi, John. I'm Mr. Roberts, a counselor at this school. I asked that you see me today because I was looking at your grade report. It looks like you are having difficulty in some of your courses. Perhaps we can talk about the reasons why." A protective service worker might say, "Hi, I'm Mary Seely, a protective

---

[2]Alfred Benjamin, *The Helping Interview*, 2d ed. Copyright © 1974, by Houghton Mifflin Company, used by permission.

[3]Alfred Kadushin, *The Social Work Interview*. Copyright © 1972, Columbia University Press, New York. Reprinted by permission.

service worker with Rock County Social Services. Information which raises questions about the care your child is receiving has come to our attention. I realize there are always two sides to any such report, and therefore I would like to talk with you about this."

CLOSING AN INTERVIEW

Closing is not always easy. Ideally, both the interviewer and interviewee should accept the fact that the interview is ending, and subjects being discussed should not be left hanging in the middle. Saying something like, "Well, you really have serious problems, but I've got to catch my ride. When can we talk further?" is too abrupt and unprofessional. Such abrupt endings are apt to be perceived by the interviewee as being discourteous and uncaring.

There are some useful guidelines on how to terminate an interview. Kadushin (1972, p. 207) recommends:

Preparation for termination begins with the very beginning of the interview. The interviewee should be informed explicitly at the beginning that a definite period of time has been allotted for the interview, that she is free to use some, or all, of this time but that going beyond the time limit is clearly discouraged. Unless an unusual situation develops, it is understood that the interview will terminate at the end of the allotted time.[4]

When the allotted time is nearly up, the interviewer may inform the interviewee by saying something like: "Well, our time is just about up. Is there anything you'd like to add before we look at where we arrived, and where we now go from here?" It is often helpful to summarize what was discussed at the end of the interview. If the interview focused only on exploring prob-

lems that the client has, another interview should be set up for fuller exploration and to begin looking at alternatives.

I have found it is very helpful to give clients "homework" assignments between interviews. A couple who is having trouble communicating with each other might, for example, be encouraged to set aside a certain amount of time each evening to discuss their personal thoughts with each other. At the next interview this "homework" assignment is then reviewed.

Reid and Shyne (1969) have found that if an agency establishes a set, limited time period for contact with the client (including both the number of interviews and the length of each interview) both the worker and client make more productive use of the time as they mobilize their efforts to accomplish the tasks within the designated time.

Ideally, the interviewee should be emotionally at ease when the interview ends, and therefore the interviewer should not introduce emotionally charged content at the end, but should seek a reduction in intensity of emotion.

If an interviewee displays a reluctance to end the interview it is sometimes helpful to confront this directly by saying, "It appears to me that you wished we had more time." The reasons for the interviewee's reluctance can then be discussed, and perhaps another appointment can be made.

Just as it is sometimes advisable to begin an interview with small talk, a short social conversation at the end may be useful as it provides a transition out of the interview. There are many styles of closing. The style used will depend on the interviewer, the interviewee, and what was said during the interview.

At times an interview can be closed with a restatement of the way both the interviewer and interviewee agreed to proceed: for example, "I'm glad you have decided to have the pregnancy test. If it's positive, give me a call so we can arrange another time to further discuss the options that we briefly talked about."

At times a more explicit summation may be made by the interviewer of what was discussed, what decisions were arrived at, what questions remain to be resolved, and what actions will be taken. A somewhat different approach is to ask the interviewee to state what

---

[4]Ibid.

was discussed, what was learned from the interview, and/or plans for the future.

Sometimes in closing an interview, concerns that were alluded to but not fully discussed might be mentioned as topics that will be discussed at the next interview. I have found some clients will first reveal their most serious concerns at the end of the interview, perhaps because they are ambivalent about whether they are ready to fully explore these concerns with the interviewer. In such instances the interviewer has to make a professional judgment of whether to extend the interview beyond the allotted time or to set up another appointment to discuss these concerns.

Benjamin (1974, p. 32) observes:

Closing is especially important because what occurs during this last stage is likely to determine the interviewee's impression of the interview as a whole. We must make certain that we have given him full opportunity to express himself, or, alternatively, we must set a mutually convenient time for this purpose. We should leave enough time for closing so that we are not rushed, since this might create the impression that we are evicting the interviewee.[5]

QUESTIONING

Questions are asked for a variety of purposes—to obtain information, to help a client tell his story, to help build a relationship, to help a client look at alternative solutions, and to help a client select an alternative.

The tone in which the question is asked is often as important as the question itself. For a client who is depressed, an appropriate tone should indicate caring and understanding. For someone who is angry, the tone should imply recognition of the anger and a willingness to examine the anger. For someone anxious, the tone should convey reassurance.

In exploring both problems of clients and alternative solutions, usually a series of questions having an increasingly specific focus is advisable. Kadushin (1972, p. 149) expands on this point.

The successive questions should act as a funnel, moving from general to more specific aspects of the content being discussed. As discussion of one area is completed at the more specific end of the funnel, the new content area introduced for discussion should start with another general, open-ended question. The movement is from "Could you tell me what it is like for you to live on an AFDC budget?" to "What did you do about food for the children the last time you ran out of money before the next check was due?"[6]

A common question that I find useful is, "How do you feel about that?" for a variety of situations; for example, when a client is pregnant, or is involved in a romance that is failing. Another common question that I ask when a client has a problem that involves someone else is to ask that client, "Could you describe what kind of a person (*name*) is?" Such a question usually facilitates getting a rapid impression of the client's thoughts and feelings about the other person.

Probing questions are often used by skilled interviewers to help clients elaborate on the specific details of their concerns and to help clients look in greater detail at the merits, shortcomings, and consequences of possible resolution strategies. For example, probing questions with a client who feels her husband drinks too much include the following: "How much does he drink?" "How often does he drink?" "How does he act when intoxicated?" What specifically does she find offensive about his drinking (for example, possible loss of job, embarrassment over his behavior, possible abuse to her or to their children, decline in sexual satisfaction, fear of a driving accident). These concerns also need to be explored in depth with her, using such probing questions as the following: "Given his drinking, how do you now feel about him?" "Does he recognize he may have a drinking problem?" "Do you think he would be willing to come in to talk about these concerns?" Probes should not be used in a cross-examination fashion but in a manner that gradually permits the

---

[5]Benjamin, *The Helping Interview*.

[6]Kadushin, *The Social Work Interview*.

FIGURE 4.2

Phrasing Questions

Errors in Phrasing Question	More Desirable Neutral Formulation
The loaded question: (This question assumes an action is occurring that is not known.)	
"When did you last hit your wife?"	"Have you ever hit your wife?"
"What are you going to do when John breaks up with you?"	"Do you think John is considering breaking up with you?"
The suggestive, or leading, question: (The interviewer suggests a "desired" answer.)	
"Don't you think it's high time you stop drinking and shape up?"	"Do you think you have a drinking problem?"
"You're really making good progress—aren't you?"	"What progress do you think you're making?"
Yes-no question: (Such questions do not encourage elaboration.)	
"Do you ever do anything together with your husband?"	"What kinds of things do you and your husband do together?"
"You really don't like Mary—do you?"	"How do you feel toward Mary?"
Either-or question: (The interviewee might prefer both or neither or a third.)	
"Would you like to talk about your marriage or your job this morning?"	"What would you like to talk about this morning?"
"Have you and Tim decided to get married or have an abortion?"	"What alternatives have you and Tim talked about?"
Bombarding: (Asking two or more questions at the same time.)	
"How are you feeling today, and did you and your husband get a chance to further discuss what we talked about last week?"	(Such questions should be asked separately.)
"What were your parents' reactions when you told them you were pregnant? Did they suggest getting an abortion? How do you know feel about having an abortion?"	
"Since graduating from high school have you found a job, a place to live, and are you still dating the same person?"	
Garbled question: (Such questions usually occur when the interviewer is unclear about what he wants to ask.)	
"You've been considering, uh, what was it, oh ya, something about what we talked about last time—now how do you feel about that?"	(The interviewer needs to be clear what he wants to ask before speaking. Silence is better than asking garbled questions.)
"Have you thought about—no, that wouldn't work, another possible thing you could do is—I don't know. What were we talking about?"	

interviewer and the interviewee to see the situations more clearly.

There are a variety of errors that should generally be avoided in phrasing questions. A number of these are shown in Figure 4.2 (page 95). The questions in the figure that are classified as "errors" should not be used unless a worker has a *specific, constructive* purpose for phrasing the question in that fashion.

NOTE TAKING

Note taking is an integral part of counseling. Workers need notes to refresh their memory of past interviews, to record the contracts made with clients, to record information for social histories, to share important facts with professional colleagues, and to note what has been done or left undone.

Benjamin (1974, p. 58) observes:

In our culture, when note taking is discriminately handled, it is not resented. On the contrary, its absence may be looked upon as negligence or lack of respect. Usually no explanation of our recording practice is required. However, should an explanation be requisite because of the needs of either or both partners in the interview, it can be easily provided.[7]

Note taking should be subordinate to interviewing. Don't let note taking interfere with the flow of the interview; for example, avoid saying or conveying, "I wish you would talk slower as I can't write that fast." Don't turn note taking into cross-examination; for example, "Let's see if I got it right, you state you sometimes think about getting a divorce because you find marriage confining." Convey that you are relaxed and comfortable with note taking; don't be secretive about taking notes as this may cause the client to become suspicious or anxious.

Note taking presents a possible distraction to interview interaction. When a worker breaks eye contact

and then makes notes, there is a danger that the focus on the interview may shift from what is *being* said to what *has been* said. Ideally, workers should acquire the capacity to take notes unobtrusively without seeming to shift their attention from the client to what is being written.

At times it is important for a worker to record certain kinds of information in order to demonstrate an interest in the client; such expected information that generally needs to be recorded includes certain addresses, names, telephone numbers, contract goals, and tasks.

Kadushin (1972, p. 206) advises,

The effect of note taking needs to be assessed periodically during the interview. If at any point the interviewee appears to be upset or made hesitant by note taking, this should be raised for explicit discussion. If, despite the interviewee's stated assent, note taking appears to be a disruptive tactic, one might best forget it.[8]

Note taking generally decreases in quantity as a worker gains experience. In recording, don't emphasize the importance of note taking by, for example, sitting with a pen and paper between you and the client, or by recording most of what clients say. Most experienced interviewers find that in therapeutic interviews they often do not need to make notes during the interview. Frequently, writing down a few key phrases and points after an interview will enable the worker in the future to recall the important points that were discussed.

Benjamin (1974, p. 60) stressed the importance of honesty with clients in taking notes:

I am certain of one thing: we must be honest. If the notes taken are to be used for the purpose of research, we should state this at the outset. In the event that the information gathered cannot be kept confidential, we should frankly indicate this, too. Above all, we should not promise confidentiality if we are not certain that we can provide it.[9]

---

[7]Benjamin, *The Helping Interview*.

[8]Kadushin, *The Social Work Interview*.
[9]Benjamin, *The Helping Interview*.

TAPE RECORDING AND VIDEOTAPING

Audiotape and videotape recordings of interviews are increasingly being used. Both have the advantage over note taking because they provide a full recording of what was said. However, one can hardly refer to tapes as readily as to written notes. Tapes, of course, may be transcribed, but this usually is quite expensive.

Tape recordings and note taking are generally used for different purposes. They are used as a mirror to reflect either to the interviewer or to the interviewee exactly what was said and how things were said. As such they have a *self-confrontation* or *sensitivity* value as they reflect how a person interacts with others. Playing back tapes to clients can help show areas where clients have interactional problems (for example, in being shy). For interviewers, tapes can be used for training purposes to help develop counseling and interviewing skills.

An initial concern of interviewers in deciding whether to use tape recordings is how the interviewee will react to being taped. I have used both audiotaping and videotaping extensively for the past several years and have found that clients soon forget the interview is being taped. A number of other authorities agree. Benjamin (1974, p. 62), for example, says:

I am firmly convinced that after the first few minutes he will not react to it at all for he will no longer notice it. It is my belief that, as a manner of ethics, the fact that the interview is being taped should not be concealed. If I tell him that it is my custom to record interviews to learn from them afterwards and that the tape will be kept confidential, he will usually not object. He will not be uneasy unless he feels that I am. If I can say that he, too, may listen to the tapes to learn, so much the better. If after all this the interviewee still objects, it is probably best to respect his feelings. Some people are simply afraid or suspicious. In areas or cultures in which the tape recorder is seldom used or seen, for the interviewer to insist might prove harmful indeed. When one finds he is working with suspicious people, the wise thing to do is to get at the suspicious-

ness and leave the tape recorder alone for the time being.[10]

Some counselors now routinely videotape interviews so that the client can more fully grasp what was said and also gain valuable feedback on how she "comes across" to others.

Videotaping allows both the interviewer and the interviewee to study stimultaneously their verbal and nonverbal communication.

VIDEOTAPING FOR TRAINING PURPOSES

Most educational programs in social work and counseling now use videotaping of simulated counseling situations to help students develop and assess their interviewing and counseling skills. Our program (similar to a growing number of other programs) also uses videotaping as one approach to screen out from social work those students who do not have the aptitude to be social workers.

It is our belief that an essential capacity social workers must possess is the ability to counsel and relate to people. We believe this capacity is necessary in order to be an effective caseworker or group worker. Also, since a community organizer works primarily with groups, we believe the capacity to relate to people effectively is a necessary component for performing competently in macro practice.

In the first practice course of our program each student has to demonstrate a level of counseling and interviewing skills that will give field placement agencies substantial assurance that the students will be able to counsel clients. Students are required to demonstrate their interviewing and counseling capacities via videotaped role-playing. Each student in the class is videotaped in the role of a counselor while counseling

---

[10]Ibid.

someone else in the class who has a contrived problem. This videotape is later reviewed jointly by the student and instructor. Students are graded on a pass/fail basis on this videotaped role-play. They are permitted to videotape a role-playing situation as many times as they want. If they fail to make an acceptable tape, they are not allowed to pass the course and are encouraged to transfer to another major. This course, therefore, serves as a first step in "counseling out" students from the program. The emphasis of the course, however, is not on culling students from the program, but on helping them to develop their interviewing and counseling techniques. If the student feels the review of the tape by the instructor of the course is unfair, an appeal process is available in which the student can take the tape to other social work faculty members for their review.

We have received some grants to study the effectiveness of using videotapes as a training tool and have found (Zastrow and Navarre, 1979) the following. Students were, at the beginning of the course, quite apprehensive (and some students extremely apprehensive) about participating in the videotape role-playing. This apprehensiveness was partially reduced by didactic material and discussions in class on "how to counsel," and by role-playing counseling situations in class (generally two students counseling two other students who have a contrived problem). Following the videotaped role-playing, students expressed considerable increased confidence in their capacities to counsel and a substantial reduction in their apprehensiveness about being videotaped in the future.

The following responses by students of how videotaping was helpful are typical (Zastrow and Navarre, 1979, pp. 201–2):

"It helped make me comfortable in a counseling situation. I was able to test out different ways in helping a client and when reviewing the tape I saw what things I did well, and what I need to work on to become a better counselor."

"I became aware of my own voice, posture, and gestures and the importance they play in counseling."

"I was able to see an actual picture of myself, not what I thought I looked like, and was able to see where I made my mistakes and could have done something different."

"I feel that the best way to learn something is to actually do it, instead of just talking about it. I also thought it was useful to watch the tape and look for your mistakes. This is the best way to correct them."

"I became aware of exactly how I came across to the client and I noticed that I was suggesting things to him—which I didn't even realize before reviewing the tape."

"Made me more aware of my self-presence (mannerisms). Gave me the opportunity early in my academic career to have a slight taste of what counseling is about and what I might be in store for!"

"I was not confident in my counseling skills at first. But after seeing the videotape I saw that I could do it. Videotaping is a good confidence builder."

The advantage of using videotaped role-playing to assess and develop counseling skills appear to be the following:

1. Students report it is a valuable tool in learning how to counsel.

2. Problems that students have in counseling and relating to people can be identified, shown to the student; then efforts can be made to make improvements.

3. Students whose capacities lie elsewhere can be identified early in their college career and counseled into some other major.

4. Videotaping links theory with practice and thereby makes the course more meaningful and relevant.

5. Students report videotaping provides considerable feedback on themselves and on how they relate to others.

6. Students report videotaping builds their confidence for counseling "real" clients, and gives them an opportunity to test out their skills and interpersonal behaviors in a relatively safe setting.

7. This laboratory approach helps students make the transition from having intellectual ideas of what should be done to trying out their ideas.

8. The approach provides assurance to field placement agencies that student interns will have an acceptable level of counseling capacities.

We also found that almost all students are able (perhaps after three or four attempts) to develop their interviewing and counseling skills to an acceptable level. It is interesting that the few students who have been identified with this approach not to have the aptitude for social work have, for the most part, voluntarily decided to switch to another major. They generally conclude after viewing their videotapes that they do not have the capabilities to be a social worker.

SUMMARY

The purposes of most social work interviews can be classified as informational (to obtain data for a social study or for writing a social history), diagnostic (to arrive at an appraisal), or therapeutic (to help clients change). Often, there is overlap between these three types. Therapeutic interviews are the most common in social work. The purpose of therapeutic interviews is either to help clients make changes, or to change the social environment to help clients function better, or both.

Social work interviews can take place anywhere. Most commonly they are either in the interviewer's office or the client's home. Although the place of an interview does have an effect on an interview, the skills of the interviewer are almost always more important in determining the productivity of an interview.

Material on how to begin and how to end interviews was presented. In interviewee-initiated interviews the beginning focus should be on helping clients to become comfortable and to help the clients get started in relating their concerns. In interviewer-initi-ated interviews the beginning focus, after the introductions, is for the interviewer to state the purpose concisely, and then to begin the dialogue. There are a variety of ways to close interviews—the style used depends on the interviewer, the interviewee, and what was said during the interview. Ideally, both the interviewer and the interviewee should accept the fact that the interview is ending, and topics being discussed should not be left hanging. Most interviews end with either the interviewer or the interviewee giving a summary of what was said, or a summary of what course of action is now planned.

Questions in interviews are used for a variety of purposes—to gather information, to help a client tell her story, to help a client look at alternative solutions, and to help a client select an alternative. The tone in which a question is asked is often as important as the question itself. Probing questions are common in social work practice. There are several types of questions that should usually be avoided: loaded questions, suggestive questions, yes-no questions, either-or questions, clustered questions (bombarding), and garbled questions.

Note taking is an integral part of counseling, and should be done in an unobtrusive way so that it does not interfere with the flow of the interview.

Audiotape and videotape recordings are increasingly being used. They provide a full recording of what was said and are generally used for different purposes than note taking. For clients, reviewing tapes helps them to grasp more fully what was said and gives them valuable feedback on how they "come across" to others. For counselors, reviewing tapes is particularly valuable in helping them to assess and further develop their interviewing skills.

EXERCISE

Writing a Social History

GOAL: The purpose of this exercise is to give students practice in writing a social history.

Step 1: At a prior class session inform the class there will be an exercise in a future session that is designed to instruct them on how to write a social history. Instruct them to read the material contained in this chapter on how to write a social history. Inform the students they can either use the format and subheadings contained in the case example of a social history in this chapter or use an adaption of it. Ask for a volunteer to develop a contrived story of (*a*) some unusual incident that has led him or her to become a client of an agency, and (*b*) background information covering the following material:

Birth date
Religion
Occupation
Marital status
Height
Weight
Address
Home phone
Why referred
    By whom
Early developmental history
    Toilet trained (what age)
    Walk (what age)
    Talk (what age)
    Relationship to parents, brothers, sisters
Education
    Kindergarten
    Grade school   Places, grades, relationships to other students,
    Junior high   and attitudes about these schools
    High school
Employment history
    Where worked
    How long
Health
Family life
    Dating
    Courtship
Prior contact with other social agencies

    Inform the class that at a future session you will interview the "client" and that each student will have to write a social history based on this interview. (The volunteer may be excused from having to write the social history.) Inform the students that a significant part of their grade for this project will depend on their *realistic* recommendations on how to intervene effectively to help this "client." Indicate that if some students want to bring tape recorders to record the interview for their write-ups, that is acceptable.

Step 2: Interview the "client" at a future class session covering the information contained in Step 1. In this interview explore problems, but end the interview before the client chooses specific courses of action to resolve the situation, as a major focus of this exercise is to give students practice in arriving at recommendations for how to intervene. (Set a deadline when students are to hand in their social histories.) After grading them, read one or two to the class (without naming the writers) that were particularly well done.

5

SOCIAL WORK WITH INDIVIDUALS: COUNSELING

Counseling someone with personal problems is neither magical nor mystical. Although training and experience in counseling is beneficial, everyone has the potential of helping others by listening and talking through their difficulties. Counseling with an effective outcome can be done by a friend, neighbor, relative, the local barber, hairdresser, banker, and bartender, as well as by social workers, psychiatrists, psychologists, guidance counselors, and the clergy. This is not to say that everyone will be effective at counseling. Professional people, because of their training and experience, have a higher probability of being effective, but competence and rapport, rather than degrees or certificates, are the keys to desirable outcomes. The focus of this chapter is on how professional counseling should be done. Since all of us at one time or another counsel others, the closer the counseling (including friend-to-friend counseling) approaches professional counseling, the higher the probability of a successful outcome.

COUNSELING FROM THE HELPER'S PERSPECTIVE

Most simply stated there are three phases to counseling: (1) building a relationship, (2) exploring problems in depth, and (3) exploring alternative solutions with the client then selecting a course of action. (These phases are components of the problem-solving approach, described in Chapter 1.) Successful counseling

This chapter is adapted from three other chapters written by this author: (a) Charles Zastrow, "How to Counsel," in *The Personal Problem Solver*, edited by Charles Zastrow and Dae H. Chang, © 1977, pp. 267–74. Adapted by permission of Prentice-Hall, Inc., Englewood Cliffs, New Jersey; (b) Charles Zastrow, "Self-Talk in Counseling," in *Talk to Yourself: Using the Power of Self-Talk* © 1979, pp. 266–79. Adapted by permission of Prentice-Hall, Inc., Englewood Cliffs, New Jersey; (c) Charles Zastrow, "The Counseling Process," in *Introduction to Social Welfare Institutions*, 2nd ed. (Homewood, Ill.: Dorsey Press, 1982), pp. 484–86.

gradually proceeds from one phase to the next, with some overlap of these stages. For example, in many cases while exploring problems the relationship between the counselor and the counselee continues to develop, and while they are exploring alternative solutions the problems are generally being examined in greater depth. At the end of a series of counseling interviews there is often the fourth phase of termination and evaluation. (Guidelines on the counselor's role in each of these phases are presented in the next section.)

Many times before the initial interview a counselor is unaware of the concerns (or problems) that new clients have. The question arises as to what the counselor's objective should be in the first interview. In such initial interviews the counselor should seek to build a helping relationship, and to begin exploring the client's problems. The third phase — examining alternative solutions — may or may not be arrived at in the initial interview. Every interview has a goal or objective, and the counselor should use this goal to give focus to the interview.

On many occasions the first problem that clients present may not be the one that they are most concerned about. Clients sometimes initially present problems that they believe are more socially acceptable in order to test how objective, understanding, and helpful the counselor will be. I once had a client who mentioned six "presenting" problems prior to sharing with me the one she was most concerned about — which was the guilt she experienced over masturbating.

COUNSELING FROM THE HELPEE'S PERSPECTIVE

The counseling process can also be conceptualized from the client's point of view. In order for counseling to be successful, clients must arrive at a progressive series of "self-talk" statements (that is, clients must arrive at having certain thoughts and beliefs). These self-talk stages are the following:

Stage I   Problem awareness: "I have a problem."

Stage II   Relationship to counselor: "I think this counselor has what it takes to help me."

Stage III   Motivation: "I want to improve my situation and am willing to put forth the effort to do so."

Stage IV   Conceptualizing the problem: "My problem is not overwhelming but has specific components that can be changed."

Stage V   Exploration of resolution strategies: "I see there are several courses of action that I might try in order to do something about my situation."

Stage VI   Selection of strategy: "I think this approach might help and I am willing to try it."

Stage VII   Implementation: "This approach is helping me."

Stage VIII   Evaluation: "Although this approach takes a lot of my time and effort, it's worth it."

The advantage of this conceptualization of the counseling process is that it presents a framework for assessing and improving the effectiveness of counseling. When counseling is not producing positive changes in clients, this framework helps in identifying the reasons for a lack of progress. Once such reasons are identified, needed changes can then be made in the counseling process.

Stage I — Problem Awareness

At this initial stage counselees must say to themselves, "I have a problem — I need to do something about my situation." If people with problems refuse to acknowledge they have a problem they will, of course, not be motivated to make the efforts needed to change. In some areas of counseling, (for example, working with problem drinkers) it is sometimes difficult to have people acknowledge that they have a problem. Involuntary clients are particularly apt to deny a problem exists. Involuntary clients are clients who are forced to seek counseling. There are a variety of settings in which social workers encounter involuntary clients: protective services; corrections; certain public school settings; group homes; mental health facilities; nursing homes; and hospitals.

For people who deny a problem exists, constructive changes are not apt to occur unless the counselor finds a way to convince them that there is a problem. When a person denies the problem, counseling needs to focus on this denial by exploring why the counselee believes a problem does not exist and by gathering evidence to document the existence of the problem to the counselee. The client then needs to be confronted (in a tactful manner) with this evidence by the counselor. If after such a confrontation the client still denies a problem exists, the counselor should be aware that the client *owns* the problem, and there is little more that the counselor can do constructively at this time, except perhaps to indicate she will be available in the future if the client wants to talk.

At times a person who acknowledges a problem exists may prefer to try to resolve it alone without receiving help from others. A person with a problem is the "owner" of the problem, and therefore has a right to decide how he wants to handle it. If the person decides to work on it alone, the counselor should respect this decision, but also indicate that he or she will be available in the future by saying something like, "If you do decide later that you'd like to talk further about it, my door will always be open."

Stage II — Relationship to Counselor

This stage overlaps the first stage and all other stages in the counseling process. In order for counseling to be effective, the counselee must arrive at the point where his self-talk is, "I think this counselor has what it takes to help me." If the counselee instead has the self-talk, "This counselor can't help me. I don't need a head shrinker. I just don't trust this counselor," counseling will fail unless a more positive relationship is estab-

One-to-one counseling

lished. Throughout the counseling process, and especially in the initial meetings, the counselor must be aware and give attention to the kind of relationship that is developing between the counselor and the counselee.

Eriksen (1979, p. 54) emphasizes the importance of a helping relationship being formed with clients:

The relationship that develops between worker and client is the very cornerstone of helping. Through the helping relationship, the client and worker come together to unblock communication that is preventing problem solving. . . .

Through the vehicle of the helping relationship, the client can communicate to the worker what she thinks, knows and feels about her problem. This kind of in-depth communication, when reinforced by effective responses by her worker, will strengthen the helping relationship itself and will soon open the door to problem solving.

The following are some guidelines on how to build a constructive relationship:

a. The counselor should seek to establish a non-threatening, comfortable atmosphere where the counselee feels safe to communicate fully his or her troubles while feeling accepted as a person.

b. In initial contacts with the counselee, the counselor needs to "sell" herself, not arrogantly, but as a knowledgeable, understanding person who may be able to help and who wants to try.

c. Be calm, do not laugh or express shock when the counselee begins to open up about his problems. Emotional outbursts, even if subtle, will lead the counselee to believe that you are not going to understand his difficulties, and he will usually stop discussing them. Remaining calm is not always easy. I remember one interview with a client who had brutally murdered his estranged partner by decapitating her. It took forty-five minutes for the client to explain his reasons for killing her and for recounting how he had planned and carried out this murder. Many details were shocking, but I had to continue to tell myself to take a professional approach, to remain calm, and to continue to maintain a nonthreatening atmosphere so that he would feel free to relate what occurred.

d. Generally be nonjudgmental, not moralistic. Show respect for the counselee's values and do not try to sell your own. The values that work for you may not be best for someone else in a different situation. For example, if the counselee is premaritally pregnant, do not attempt to force your values toward adoption or abortion, but let the counselee decide on the course of action after a full examination of the problem and an exploration of alternative solutions.

e. View the counselee as an equal. "Rookie" counselors sometimes made the mistake of thinking that because someone is sharing their intimate secrets, the counselor must be very important, and they end up arranging a superior-inferior relationship. If the counselee feels that he or she is being treated as an inferior, he or she will be less motivated to reveal and discuss personal difficulties.

f. Use a shared vocabulary. This does not mean that the counselor should use the same slang words and the same accent as the counselee. If the counselee sees the counselor as being artificial in use of slang or accent, it may seriously offend him. The counselor should use words that the counselee understands and that are not offensive.

g. The tone of the counselor's voice should convey the message that the counselor empathetically understands and cares about the counselee's feelings.

h. Keep confidential what the counselee has said. People unfortunately have nearly irresistible urges to share "juicy secrets" with someone else. If the counselee discovers that confidentiality has been violated, a working relationship may be quickly destroyed.

i. If you are counseling a relative or a friend, there is a danger that, because you are emotionally involved, you may get upset or enter into an argument with the other person. If that happens it is almost always best to drop the subject immediately, as tactfully as possible. Perhaps after tempers cool the subject can be brought up again, or perhaps it may be best to refer the counselee to someone else. When counseling a friend or relative, you should be aware that when you find yourself becoming upset, further discussion will not be productive. Many professional counselors refuse to counsel friends or relatives because they are aware that they are emotionally involved. Emotional involvement interferes with the calm, detached perspective that is needed to help clients objectively explore problems and alternative solutions.

Stage III — Motivation

Counselees must come to say to themselves, "I want to improve my situation and am willing to put forth the effort in order to do so." Unless a counselee becomes motivated to change, constructive changes are not apt to occur. In counseling, the key variable in determining whether a client will improve his circumstances is the client's motivation to want to improve and put forth the necessary effort (Losoncy, 1977).

A counselor can best seek to motivate discouraged or apathetic people by being an encouraging person. According to Losoncy (1977) an encouraging person has the following characteristics:

Has complete acceptance for the discouraged person, and conveys "I accept you exactly as you are, with no conditions attached." (The counselor should not, however, convey acceptance of the deviant behavior that needs to be changed.)

Has a nonblaming attitude so that the discouraged person no longer feels a need to lie, pretend, or wear a mask.

Conveys empathy that the counselor is aware and can to some extent feel what the discouraged person is feeling. Empathy occurs, as described by Kadushin (1972, p. 52) when a counselor

feels *with the client rather than for him. Feeling* for *the client would be a sympathetic rather than an empathic response. Somebody once said that if you have a capacity for empathy you feel squat when you see a squat vase and feel tall when you look at a tall vase. Empathy is entering imaginatively into the inner life of someone else. It is not enough simply to be empathically understanding; one needs to communicate to the client that one accurately perceives and feels his situation.*

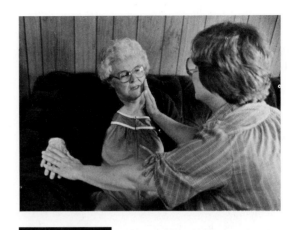

Communicating . . . through touching

Conveys to the discouraged person that the counselor is genuinely interested in his progress, and conveys that the counselee is an important, worthwhile person.

Conveys to the discouraged person that the counselor has confidence in the capacity of the discouraged person to improve.

Conveys sincere enthusiasm about the discouraged person's interests, ideas, and risk-taking actions. In order for discouraged persons to believe in themselves, they generally need an encouraging person who conveys they are important, worthwhile persons.

Has the capacity to be a nonjudgmental listener so that the discouraged person's real thoughts and feelings can be expressed freely, without fear of censure.

When the counselor meets with the discouraged person (particularly during the beginning of the relationship) the counselor should notice (reward) every small instance of progress — for example, if the person is wearing something new, say "That's new, isn't it? It really looks good on you."

Motivating a discouraged person takes a long, long time. Discouraged people generally have a long his-

tory of failures. To reverse this trend requires that the counselor have the time to spend listening and understanding this person as fully as possible.

The counselor should have a sincere belief in the discouraged person's ability to find a purpose in life.

The counselor should allow the person to take risks without judging him.

The counselor should reinforce *efforts* made by the discouraged person. The important thing is that one tries, not necessarily succeeds. By making efforts to improve, there is hope.

The counselor should help the discouraged person to see the falsehood and negative consequences of self-defeating statements (such as "I'm a failure"). Every person has skills and deficiencies, and every person should be encouraged to improve both his strengths and weaknesses.

The counselor should recognize that all that can be done is to give one's best efforts in trying to motivate a discouraged person. Success in motivating such a client is not guaranteed. To give up hope of motivating her means the counselor will no longer be effective in working with this discouraged person.

The counselor should be skilled at looking for uniquenesses and strengths in an individual. These uniquenesses are communicated to the discouraged person so that he begins to realize he is special and worthwhile. This process leads to a sense of improved self-worth and strengthens the courage to take risks and change.

The counselor should be aware of the negative consequences of overdependency in a relationship. When the discouraged person is on the way to taking risks and making constructive changes, the counselor should start to help her to develop self-encouragement, in which the counselee is encouraged to make and trust her own decisions, and encouraged to take more risks.

(Note: these guidelines on motivating clients are also useful in building a relationship with clients.)

Stage IV — Conceptualizing the Problem

In order for counseling to be effective a client needs to recognize, "My problem is not overwhelming, but has specific components that can be changed." Many clients tend to view their situation initially as being so complex that they become highly anxious or emotional, and thereby are unable to see that their problem has a number of components that they can change in a step-by-step fashion. Several years ago I counseled a teenager who had missed her menstrual period for the past three months and was so overwhelmingly afraid of being pregnant that she was unable to figure out on her own that the first step was to have a pregnancy test. (When she finally took the test the results showed she was not pregnant.) In order to help clients conceptualize their problems, the counselor needs to explore the problems together in depth with the client. The following are some guidelines on how to explore problems in depth:

a. Many "rookie" counselors make the mistake of suggesting solutions as soon as a problem is identified, without exploring the problem area in depth. For example, an advocate of abortions may advise this solution as soon as a single female reveals that she is pregnant, without taking the time to discover whether this person is strongly opposed to abortions, really wants a baby, or intends to marry soon.

b. In exploring problems in depth, the counselor and counselee need to examine such areas as the severity of the problem, how long the problem has existed, what the causes are, how the counselee feels about the problem, and what physical and mental capacities and strengths the counselee has to cope with the problem, prior to exploring alternative solutions. For example, if a single female is pregnant, the counselor and counselee need to explore the following questions: How does the person feel about being pregnant? Has she seen a doctor? About how long has she been pregnant? Do her parents know? What are their feelings and concerns if they know? Has she informed her sexual partner? What are his feelings and concerns if he knows? What does she feel is the most urgent situation to deal with first? Answers to such questions will determine the future direction of counseling. The most pressing, immediate problem might be to inform her parents (who may react critically) or it might be to secure medical services.

c. When a problem area is identified, there are usually a number of subproblems that can be identified. Explore all these; for example, how to tell the father, obtaining medical care, obtaining funds for medical expenses, deciding where to live, deciding whether to leave school or stop working during the pregnancy, deciding whether to terminate the pregnancy, making plans for what to do after the child is delivered or the pregnancy terminated.

d. In a multiproblem situation, the best way to decide which problem to handle first is to ask the counselee which problem he or she perceives as most pressing. If the problem can be solved, start with exploring that subproblem in depth and developing together a strategy for the solution. Success in solving a subproblem will increase the counselee's confidence in the counselor, and thereby further solidify the relationship.

e. Convey empathy, not sympathy. Empathy is the capacity to show that you are aware of and can to some extent feel what the counselee is saying. Sympathy is also a sharing of feelings, but it has the connotation of offering pity. The difference is subtle, but empathy is problem-solving-oriented and sympathy is usually problem-prolonging. Giving sympathy usually causes the counselee to dwell on his or her emotions without taking action to improve the situation. For example, if one gives sympathy to a depressed person, that person will keep telling you his sad story over and over, each time having an emotional outpouring supported by your sympathy, without taking any action to improve the situation. Telling the story over and over only reopens old wounds and prolongs the depression.

Benjamin (1974, p. 47) further describes how to be empathic:

The empathic interviewer tries as much as he possibly can to feel his way into the internal frame of reference of the interviewee and to see the world through the latter's eyes as if that world were his own world. The words "as if" are crucial for although the interviewer is empathic, he never loses sight of the fact that he remains his own self. Knowing all the time that he is distinct from the interviewee, he tries to feel his way about in the internal world of thought and feeling of the other in order to come as close to him as possible, to understand with him as much as possible.[1]

The difference between sympathy and empathy can be shown in responses to the following statement by a client whose male friend has recently ended their three-year relationship, "How could he do this to me, after all I've done for him? He's hurt me so much."

Sympathic response by the interviewer: "Yes, he sure is a schnook. With what he did to you, I don't see how you can even face the world. You're probably going to be miserable for a long, long time."

Empathic response by the interviewer: "I know ending this relationship has deeply hurt you. You also appear confused as to why he said he wants to end the relationship. Have you discussed this with him?"

Keith-Lucas (1972, pp. 80–81) gives a cogent example separating sympathy, pity, and empathy:

Consider three reactions to someone who has told us that he strongly dislikes his wife. The sympathetic person would say, "Oh, I know exactly how you feel. I can't bear mine, either." The two of them would comfort each other but nothing would come of it. The pitying person would commiserate but add that he himself was most happily married. Why didn't the other come to dinner sometime and see what married life could be like? This, in most cases, would only increase the frustration of the unhappy husband and help him to put his problem further outside himself, on to his wife or his lack of good fortune. The empathetic person might say something like, "That must be terribly difficult for you. What do you think might possibly help?" and only the empathetic person, of the three, would have said anything that would lead to some change in the situation.

f. "Trust your guts." The most important tool that counselors have is themselves (their feelings and perceptions). Counselors should continually strive to place themselves in the client's situation (with the client's values and pressures). To use the earlier example, if the client is seventeen years old, single and pregnant, and has parents who are very critical of the situation and who want her to have an abortion, a competent counselor will continually strive to feel what she is feeling and to perceive the world from her perspective, with her goals, difficulties, pressures, and values. It probably never happens that a counselor is 100 percent accurate in placing herself in the counselee's situation, but 70 to 80 percent is usually sufficient to gain an awareness of the counselee's pressures, problems, and perspectives. This information is very useful in assisting the counselor in determining what additional areas need to be explored, what she should say, and what might be possible solutions. Stated in a somewhat different way, a counselor should ask herself, "What is this person trying to tell me and how can I make it clear that I understand not only intellectually but empathically?"

g. When you believe that the client has touched upon an important area of concern, further communication can be encouraged in the following ways:

---

[1]Alfred Benjamin, *The Helping Interview*, 2d ed. Copyright © 1974, by Houghton Mifflin Company, used by permission.

1. Nonverbally showing interest.

2. Pauses. "Rookie" counselors usually become anxious when there is a pause, and they hasten to say something, anything, to have conversation continue. This is usually a mistake, especially when it leads to a change in an important topic. A pause will also make the counselee anxious, give him time to think about the important area of concern, and then usually motivate him to continue conversation in that area.

3. Neutral probes. "Could you tell me more about it?" "How do you feel about that?" "I'm not sure I understand what you have in mind."

4. Summarizing what the client is saying. "During this past hour you made a number of critical comments about your spouse; it sounds like some things about your marriage are making you unhappy."

5. Reflecting feelings. "You seem angry" or "You appear to be depressed about that."

b. Approach socially unacceptable topics tactfully. Tact is an essential quality of a competent counselor. Try not to ask a question in such a way that the answer will put the respondent in an embarrassing position. Suppose, for instance, that you are an adult who has a good relationship with a teenager and you have reason to suspect that this person has "hangups" about masturbation. How would you tactfully bring up the subject to discuss? One possible approach is, "When I was your age, I had a number of hangups about masturbating. That was unfortunate. Most teenagers masturbate, but many have strong feelings of guilt or shame about it. Although masturbation has been stigmatized, it is in reality a natural outlet for sexual feelings and is not harmful. In fact, most sex therapists recommend masturbation as it is a way to release sexual tensions. I'm wondering if you may have some questions or concerns about masturbation that perhaps it would be helpful for us to discuss?" Informing the youth that you also had hangups about this subject personalizes it and tells the teenager that you have experienced some of the concerns he is currently facing. Communication and relationship building are fostered.

A question occasionally arises as to when a counselor should self-disclose by sharing experiences from her past. There is a danger that when such experiences are shared the client may come to view the counselor as being in need of counseling. (The client is particularly apt to reach this conclusion if the counselor reveals, by nonverbal and verbal communication, that she still has unresolved issues surrounding these experiences.) Also when working in certain settings (for example, drug treatment centers) a statement by a counselor that she continues to engage in behaviors that the client needs to change (such as getting drunk or smoking pot) may be used as an excuse for the client to maintain problematic behaviors. A good rule to follow in deciding whether to self-disclose is for the counselor to first ask herself, "If I share these personal experiences are they apt to have a constructive effect?" If not, don't share the experience.

i. When pointing out a limitation that a counselee has, mention and compliment him on any assets. When a limitation is being mentioned, the counselee will literally feel that something is being laid bare or taken away. Therefore, compliment him in another area to give something back.

j. Watch for nonverbal cues. A competent counselor will generally use such cues to identify when a sensitive subject is being touched upon, as the client will generally become anxious and show anxiety by a changing tone of voice, fidgeting, tightening of facial or neck muscles, yawning, stiff posture, or a flushed face. Some counselors even claim they can tell when a client becomes anxious by observing when the eye pupils are dilating.

k. Be honest. An untruth always runs the risk of being discovered. If that happens, the counselee's confidence in the counselor will be seriously damaged, and perhaps the relationship will be seriously jeopardized. If a client asks an important question that the counselor cannot answer, it is usually best for the counselor to say, "Unfortunately I do not know the answer to that important question, but let me check into it and I'll let you know by ——— (a specified time)." Being honest goes beyond not telling lies. The counselor should always tactfully inform the client of the shortcomings that the client has that are in vital need of attention. For example, if someone is being fired from jobs because

Exploring alternatives with a client and a nurse

---

of poor grooming habits, this fact needs to be brought to that person's attention. Or, if a trainee's relationship skills and intervention capacities are not suited for the helping profession, that trainee needs to be "counseled out" in the interest of clients and in the trainee's own best interests.

l. Listen attentively to what the counselee is saying. Trying to view his words, not from your perspective but from the counselee's. Unfortunately, many people are caught up in their own interests and concerns, and they do not tune out those thoughts while the counselee is speaking. This guideline seems very simple, but it is indeed difficult for many to follow. Kadushin (1972, p. 188) expands on why listening attentively is difficult:

The nature of spoken communication presents a special hazard, seducing the interviewer into an easy nonlistening. The hazard lies in the great discrepancy between the number of words that are normally spoken in one minute and the number of words that can be absorbed in that time. Thought is much more rapid than speech. The average rate of spoken speech is about 125 words per minute. We can read and understand an average of about 300-500 words per minute. There is, then, a considerable amount of dead time in spoken communication, during which the listener's mind can easily become distracted. The listener starts talking to herself to take up the slack in time. Listening to the internal monologue may go on side by side with listening to the external dialogue. More often, however, it goes on at the expense of listening to the external dialogue. The interviewer becomes lost in some private reverie—planning, musing, dreaming.[2]

Kadushin (1972, p. 190) gives the following suggestions on how to listen effectively:

Rather than becoming preoccupied as a consequence of the availability of the spare time between the slow spoken words, the good interviewer exploits this time in the service of more effective listening. The listener keeps focused on the interviewee but uses the time made available to the mind by slowness of speech to move rapidly back and forth along the path of the interview, testing, connecting, questioning: How does what I am hearing now relate to what I heard before? How does it modify that I heard before? How does it conflict with it, support it, make it more understandable? What can I anticipate hearing next? What do I miss hearing that needs asking about? What is he trying to tell me? What other meanings can the message have? What are his motives in telling me this?[3]

Stage V — Exploration of Resolution Strategies

After (or sometimes while) a subproblem is explored in depth, the next step is for the counselor and the counselee to consider alternative solutions. In exploring alternative solutions it is almost always best for the counselor to begin by asking something like "Have you thought about ways to resolve this?" The merits, shortcomings, and consequences of the alternatives thought of by the counselee should then be tactfully and thoroughly examined. If the counselee has not thought of certain viable alternatives, the counselor should mention these, and the merits and shortcomings of these alternatives should also be examined.

Each client is unique, and so are his problems. What works for one client may not be in the best interest of another. An abortion, for example, may be compatible with one client's values and circumstances, but may well be undesirable for another unmarried pregnant woman who has a different set of values and goals. If counseling is going to be effective the client needs to say to himself, "I see there are several courses of action that I might try in order to do something about my situation." Unless a client comes to realize there are some resolution strategies, counseling is apt to fail.

Stage VI — Selection of a Strategy

After the counselor and client discuss the probable effects and consequences of possible resolution strategies, it is essential that the client conclude, "I think this approach might help me and I am willing to try it." If a client is indecisive or refuses to make an honest commitment to trying a course of action, constructive change will not occur. For example, if a client says to himself, "I know I have a drinking problem, but am unwilling to take any action to cut down on my drinking," counseling probably will not be successful.

The counselee usually has the right to self-determination, that is, to choose the course of action among

---

[2]Alfred Kadushin, *The Social Work Interview.* Copyright © 1972 Columbia University Press, New York. Reprinted by permission.
[3]Ibid.

possible alternatives. The counselor's role is to help the counselee clarify and understand the likely consequences of each available alternative but generally not to give advice or choose the alternative for the counselee. If the counselor were to select the alternative, there are two possible outcomes: (1) the alternative may prove to be undesirable for the counselee, in which case, the counselee will probably blame the counselor for the advice and the future relationship will be seriously hampered, and (2) the alternative may prove to be desirable for the counselee. This immediate outcome is advantageous, but the danger is that the counselee will then become overly dependent on the counselor, seeking the counselor's advice for nearly every decision in the future and generally being reluctant to make decisions on his own. In actual practice, most courses of action have desirable and undesirable consequences. For example, if an unmarried mother is advised to keep her child, she may receive considerable gratification from being with and raising the child, but at the same time she may blame the counselor for such possible negative consequences as long-term financial hardships and an isolated social life.

The guideline of not giving advice does *not* mean that a counselor should not suggest alternatives that a client has not considered. On the contrary, it is the counselor's responsibility to suggest and explore all viable alternatives with a client. A good rule to follow is that when a counselor believes a client should take a certain course of action, this should be phrased as a suggestion, "Have you thought about . . .?" rather than as giving advice, "I think you should . . ."

The counselee's right to self-determination should be taken away only if the selected course of action has a high probability of seriously hurting others or the counselee. For example, if it is highly probable that a parent will continue to abuse a child, or if the counselee attempts to take his or her own life, intervention by the counselor is suggested. For most situations, however, the counselee should have the right to select his or her alternative, even when the counselor believes that another alternative is a better course of action. Frequently, the counselee is in a better position to know what is best for him or her, and if the alternative is not the best, the counselee will probably learn from the mistake.

Stage VII — Implementation of the Strategy

Counseling will be successful only if the client follows through on her commitment to try a resolution approach and then concludes, "This approach is beginning to help me." If the client follows through on the commitment, but instead concludes, "I don't believe this approach is helping me," counseling again is failing. If this occurs, the reasons for no gain need to be examined, and perhaps another resolution strategy needs to be tried. The following are some guidelines on how to implement a resolution approach:

a. The counselor should attempt to form explicit, realistic "contracts" with counselees. When the counselee does select an alternative, the counselee should clearly understand what the goals will be, what tasks need to be carried out, how to do the tasks, and who will carry out each of them. Frequently, it is desirable to write the "contract" for future reference, with a time limit set for the accomplishment of each task. For example, if an unmarried mother decides to keep her child and now needs to make long-range financial plans, this goal should be understood and specific courses of action decided upon — seeking public assistance, seeking support from the alleged father, securing an apartment within her budget, and so on. Furthermore, who will do what task within a set time limit should be specified.

When a contract is negotiated (and perhaps renegotiated in future interviews) it helps bring a focus to the interview. Client and counselor are less likely to get sidetracked by extraneous issues, and the interview's productivity can be sustained.

If client and counselor differ in their expectations of desired goals, or in their expectations of who will do what tasks, the process of negotiating a contract will force the client and counselor to discuss and hopefully resolve their differences.

b. Counseling is done *with* the counselee, not *to* or *for* the counselee. The counselee should have the responsibility of doing many of the tasks necessary to improve the situation. A good rule to follow is that the counselee should take responsibility for those tasks

Counseling Principles

Our social work program (similar to social work programs at other universities) places students in social service agencies for an internship. As social work interns, students observe, and soon begin to do, the kind of work that social workers do. A frequent "reality shock" reported by students is that many clients are apathetic and discouraged and simply are not motivated to improve. The result often is that clients do not "follow through" on commitments made during counseling sessions to make certain efforts to improve their circumstances.

Several years ago, at a county social services agency (county welfare department), I was supervising a student who became quite surprised and frustrated when clients failed to follow through on commitments. The student was working with a small caseload of AFDC mothers (Aid to Families of Dependent Children Program). The student commented, "The case examples discussed in textbooks are always successes, and I as yet have seen no improvement in my cases." I reassured the student that she was not at fault and that lack of improvements is more often the rule than the exception. I added that textbooks are very selective in that they usually present success cases to illustrate theory, rather than presenting typical cases. Yet, I cautioned that if she became discouraged and gave up being an "encouraging person" then there would be *no* hope of her being effective in helping her clients to improve. Upon further discussion she developed an approach in which she used the principles presented earlier. By the end of her internship, not all of the AFDC mothers she was working with showed substantial improvement. Yet, by the end of the semester she had formed a respected working relationship with all her clients, and some were making significant efforts to improve their circumstances. At the end of the semester the student wrote the following summary about her contacts with one of her clients:

I was assigned the case of Mrs. H. She was thirty-three years of age and had three children, ages fifteen, eleven, and seven. She had been receiving AFDC assistance for the past six years, ever since her husband deserted her. During the past four years the agency had made several efforts to get her a job, without success. The records showed Mrs. H did not want a full-time job as she felt she was too busy taking care of her children. She applied for several part-time jobs but was not hired. Mrs. H felt she was not skilled, and the reality of the situation was that a low-paying job would result in a reduction of her AFDC check, with the end result being that financially a part-time job would hardly be beneficial.

I was assigned Mrs. H's case when she requested a social worker's help with a problem she was having with her fifteen-year-old son. Mrs. H had found some "pot" in her son's clothes drawer and didn't know how to handle the situation. I met with Mrs. H. Her home had a general unclean appearance. Mrs. H's physical appearance gave the impression she had been through a war. Her clothes were wrinkled and had what appeared to be food stains on several places. Her hair was greasy, she was quite obese, and she had few teeth left in her mouth. Dark circles were under her eyes, suggesting a great deal of fatigue and stress.

We met for about an hour and a half, and Mrs. H related much of her life history. She had never held a full-time job, having a "forced marriage" shortly after she graduated from high school. Her husband had been a road construction worker and had a drinking problem. She had not heard from him in six years. She felt if he did come back, she would not even want to see him. She had heard he had moved to a distant state with another woman when he left.

My aim in the first interview was to build a working relationship, obtain Mrs. H's trust, and help her explore what she saw as her problems. Her immediate problem appeared to be what to do about her discovery of "pot." We discussed to some extent the legalities of smoking marijuana and the effects and consequences of the drug. I also said I could bring over some brief reading material on the drug the next day, and she responded by saying she would very much appreciate receiving such material.

We then role-played how she might bring up the subject of smoking marijuana with her son. First I played her role in order to model a possible approach, and she played her son. Then we reversed roles to give her practice in trying out an approach. Before discussing the subject with her son, she mentioned she wanted to look at the reading material I had promised her. I dropped off this material the next day. We also set another meeting for the following week.

At our next appointment Mrs. H indicated she had discussed smoking marijuana with her son. Her son responded first with some surprise and some displeasure that Mrs. H had gone through his clothes drawer. The son, Jerry, indicated he had tried smoking marijuana only twice and was not that interested in smoking in the future. Mrs. H added that a somewhat greater concern with Jerry appears to be his interest in occasionally drinking beer with some of his friends, and that she and Jerry have some moderate disagreements in this area which they are working on.

I asked if she felt she needed help from our agency for this issue. She responded, "No, not at this time." I then asked if she needed any other additional help from our agency. She thanked me for the help I had given and said she was not aware of other areas where she needed help. I could have left, but I thought since I had a good relationship established with her, and had been of some prior help, that this might be an opportunity to have her take a look at her future.

I began by asking her what she would like to see herself doing ten years from now. She responded by saying, "I haven't given that much thought. I probably will be doing what I'm doing now." I asked if she was satisfied with her current life. She rather firmly said no, and went on at length about how difficult it is to live on an inadequate AFDC budget and to raise three children by herself. She was also critical of her husband, who placed her in this situation by deserting her.

I conveyed an understanding of her concerns and mentioned that it was certainly true that past events had led to her current circumstances. But I added that what she wanted for the present and the future was largely up to her. She asked what I meant.

I said, "Take your financial situation for example. You have a choice between staying home or seeking a job. Now, I know at the present time that working would not improve your finances very much. But if you don't begin learning an employable skill now, and

Continued

CASE EXAMPLE   *Continued*

gradually working your way up in a job, what's going to happen in ten years? In ten or eleven years your youngest child will no longer be eligible for AFDC payments. Then what will you do? There are also other areas that we could work on; for example, dental care. But the choice is totally up to you. If you want to work on some of these areas, I'm very interested in working with you. If you aren't interested at the present time, there's little I can do to change your mind."

Mrs. H responded by indicating she was aware that her teeth needed attention, but added she didn't have the money to pay a dentist. I indicated the expenses were covered under her medical card (Medicaid Program). She expressed surprise, and indicated she would make an appointment with a dentist. She thanked me for the information, and I noted her face showed a spark of interest.

I then asked if she had thought about obtaining a job. She mentioned that would be nice, but then started citing a number of reasons why she thought that it would not be possible. Many of these appeared to me to be "self-defeating self-talk" that she was giving herself. The following is a summary of her negative self-talk, along with a more positive view for each reason that I suggested to her:

Mrs. H's reasons for not seeking a job	A more positive, alternative view for each reason
1. "I've tried finding a job several times in the past and was not able to obtain one."	1. "Having tried in the past and failed, does not mean you can't obtain a job at this time. We could provide you with work training in an area that you were interested in, and also help you obtain a job after the training."
2. "Even if I worked, it would not significantly add to my total income, as my AFDC grant would be reduced."	2. "There is some truth in this. However, a job would add some money to your total income. Also, you need to start thinking about your future, because when your children become adults, you will no longer be eligible for AFDC. Having a job now will help you prepare for the future. Also, there are other benefits in working, such as the opportunity to get to know other people."
3. "I'm really not skilled at any job. It frankly is very embarrassing to be turned down when I apply."	3. "Nothing ventured, nothing gained. As far as not having a skill, we can enroll you in a work-training program. We can also help you in finding a job. You are not alone in being turned down for a job. I have a friend who applied to sixty-seven teaching positions before being hired. This person was becoming quite discouraged but kept on trying. She finally found one and really likes it. The key is to keep on trying and hoping."

Mrs. H's reasons for not seeking a job	A more positive, alternative view for each reason
4. "I won't be able to work and also take care of my home and family."	4. "A working mother does have a lot to do and limited time to get it all done. However, many mothers are able to do both." (At this point I asked if she would be interested in discussing this area with a friend of mine, Mrs. S. Mrs. S is also on AFDC, has four children, but now works full-time as a secretary. Mrs. S is an "encouraging" person. She got her job by first having work training, then volunteering at an agency to do clerical work. By volunteering she developed her typing skills, and after a year the agency hired her. Mrs. H indicated she would be interested in talking with Mrs. S.)
5. "Frankly, my personal appearance is such that I don't think that anyone would hire me."	5. "You're selling yourself short. Our agency can help you with dental care and in getting some new clothes. When you meet with Mrs. S you will see she probably will not win a beauty contest, but has an inner beauty (personality) that helped her get a job. I think with a more positive attitude, people would note an inner beauty on your part."
6. "I wouldn't, if I worked, be able to watch some of my favorite game shows and soap operas during the day. My present daily routine would be greatly altered."	6. "This is true. But you would be able to meet more people if you worked, and perhaps grow more as a person. Also, would not your children be prouder of you if you worked? Are you really satisfied and contented with your present circumstances and current daily routine?"
7. "I don't own a car, and therefore don't have a way to get to a job even if I did get one."	7. "We can help you here by paying the cost of transportation and by helping you to arrange for transportation. For example, we have volunteer drivers who would be able to provide transportation when you go for job interviews."

At this point I asked her to think over what we had talked about, and indicated that I would ask Mrs. S to contact her.

A week later I stopped by to see Mrs. H. She mentioned she had had an "inspirational" talk with Mrs. S. At that point she asked to be enrolled in our work-training program. I

Continued

CASE EXAMPLE   *Continued*

praised her decision. Within three months she had obtained a receptionist job for a new car dealer. Equally important, she appeared to have a renewed interest in living and had improved her personal appearance with increased grooming attention, some new clothes, and a set of dentures. For me as a student social work intern, this turned out to be a deeply rewarding, gratifying person to work with.

This case example is adapted from a case illustration that appeared in Charles Zastrow, *Talk to Yourself: Using the Power of Self-Talk*, © 1979, pp. 75–79. Adapted by permission of Prentice-Hall, Inc. Englewood Cliffs, New Jersey.

that he has the capacity to carry out, while the counselor should attempt to do only those that are beyond the capacities of the counselee. Doing things *for* counselees, similar to giving advice, runs the risk of creating a dependency relationship. Furthermore, successful accomplishment of tasks by counselees leads to personal growth and prepares them better for taking on future responsibilities.

c. For a number of tasks the counselee lacks confidence or experience in carrying out, it is helpful to "role-play" the tasks. For example, if a pregnant single woman wants help in knowing how to tell her male friend about the pregnancy, role-playing the situation will assist the woman in selecting words and developing a strategy for informing him. The counselor can first play the woman's role and model an approach, with the woman playing the male role. Then the roles should be reversed so that the woman gains practice in telling her male friend.

Stage VIII — Evaluation

If constructive change is apt to be long lasting or permanent, the client must conclude, "Although this approach takes a lot of my time and effort, it's worth it." On the other hand, if he concludes, "This approach has helped a little, but it's really not worth what I'm sacrific-

ing for it," then counseling will either be ineffective, or an alternative course of action needs to be developed and implemented.

When counselees meet commitments, reward them verbally or in other ways. Rewarding them increases their self-esteem and self-respect, and also further motivates them to continue working on improving their circumstances.

One of the biggest reality shocks of new trainees entering the helping professions is that many clients, even after making commitments to improve their situations, do not carry out the steps outlined.

If a counselee fails to meet the terms of the "contract" that has been developed, generally do not punish. Punishment usually increases hostility without producing positive lasting changes. Also, do not accept excuses when commitments are not met. Excuses let people off the hook; they provide temporary relief, but they eventually lead to more failure and to a failure identity. Simply ask, "Do you still wish to try to fulfill your commitment?" If the counselee answers affirmatively, another time deadline acceptable to the counselee should be set.

Whether the counselee reaches all the goals that have been set, careful attention should be given to terminating the relationship. If the counselee still has unresolved problems that the counselor is unable to help with, a referral should be made to an appropriate agency or professional person. Care should be taken in terminating the contact so that the client does not erroneously conclude that the counselor is rejecting him. Also, the counselee should be asked whether she has additional concerns that she would like help with. If there are no concerns, the counselee should be informed the counselor's "door will be open" if help is needed in the future.

At the final interview, or a few weeks after termination, it is usually beneficial to ask the client (verbally or with a brief questionnaire) the following questions:

a. Did the counseling help you? If yes, how? If no, why did it not help?

b. What did the counselor do well?

c. What were the shortcomings of the counseling that was received?

d. What suggestions do you have for improving counseling services at this agency?

e. Do you have some concerns for which you desire additional counseling?

Such information is very useful in improving the counseling process and in determining whether additional help is needed by the counselee.

The above guidelines on counseling should not be followed dogmatically as they will probably work only 70 to 80 percent of the time. The most important tool that a counselor has is herself (feelings, perceptions, relationship capacities, and interviewing skills).

One final important guideline—the counselor should refer the counselee to someone else, or at least seek another professional counselor to discuss the case with, for any of the following situations: (*a*) if the counselor feels unable to empathize with the counselee; (*b*) if the counselor feels that the counselee is choosing unethical alternatives (such as seeking an abortion) that conflict with the counselor's basic value system; (*c*) if the counselor feels that the problem is of such a nature that she will not be able to help; (*d*) if a working relationship is not established. A competent and secure counselor knows that it is possible to work with and help some people but not all, and that it is in the counselee's and the counselor's best interests to refer those she cannot help to someone else who may be able to provide the counseling needed.

REACTIONS OF CLIENTS TO HAVING A PERSONAL PROBLEM

In counseling clients there is another crucial area that counselors need to be aware of and learn to handle effectively: the emotional reactions of clients to having a personal problem. The following example involving Lee Askew underscores the importance of this area. Mr. Askew has been an alcoholic for many years, yet his reaction to his drinking problem is *denial*. Why? When Mr. Askew was first seen in counseling nearly three years ago he had experienced a variety of problems related to his drinking. The following is a summary of the intake history on Mr. Askew:

Lee Askew is forty-three years old and has been drinking heavily since he was sixteen years of age. For the past several years he has drunk an average of a quart of vodka each day. His second marriage is in trouble because his wife claims their money is being spent on alcohol rather than on paying their bills. Also, his wife, Callie, has informed him she can no longer tolerate his drunken behavior—nearly every evening he is in a druken stupor and rambles on repeating himself until he finally falls asleep, often by passing out. Mr. Askew's first wife divorced him because of his drinking. When he is sober he is friendly, and enjoyable to be with. But as the day moves along, he increasingly becomes intoxicated and his behavior becomes intolerable. Five years ago he had a serious automobile accident while intoxicated and was nearly killed. Three and one-half years ago he was arrested for drunken driving. In the past ten years he has held a variety of sales jobs and been fired from three of these jobs for being intoxicated. Last night Mr. Askew physically abused his wife for the first time. This morning Mrs. Askew informed Lee that he must either seek help for his drinking or she will leave. Mr. Askew apologized for hitting his wife, claiming he had had a bad day at work. Lee, however, refuses to acknowledge he has a drinking problem.

Mr. Askew's denial of having a drinking problem is not unique. Clients display a variety of emotional reactions when confronted with evidence they have a personal problem. The effectiveness of counseling frequently depends on the counselor's understanding such emotional reactions in order to assist clients in recognizing they do have a personal problem and are in need of certain services.

In spite of the importance of understanding the emotional reactions of clients to having a personal problem, there is a paucity of literature in this area.[4] An important contribution, however, has been made by Elizabeth Kübler-Ross. In *On Death and Dying*, Kübler-Ross (1969) presents five stages of dying that terminally ill people typically proceed through. These stages are not absolute as not everyone goes through each one. But helping professionals who counsel the terminally ill have found this paradigm, when used in a flexible, insight-producing way, to be valuable in explaining why a patient may be behaving the way he is. The five stages are also typical of any individual's reaction when confronted with a serious personal problem of any kind.

The following section has three objectives.

a. Summarize Kübler-Ross's five stages of dying for the terminally ill. These five stages are in actuality five distinct emotional reactions that people display upon being informed they have a terminal illness.

b. Suggest that these five stages are emotional reactions that are not unique to the terminally ill, but are emotional reactions that all clients typically display when confronted with evidence that they have a personal problem.

c. Show how a counselor's awareness of why clients are reacting as they are can be used to develop intervention approaches that will lead clients to acknowledge that they do have a personal problem and are in need of services.

---

[4]For several articles in this area, see Simos, 1977; Smith, 1978; and Wiseman, 1975.

Kübler-Ross's Five Stages

Hans O. Mauksch (1975, p. 10) provides a concise summary of Kübler-Ross's five stages that terminally ill people typically proceed through:

1. Denial—"No, not me." This is a typical reaction when a patient learns that he or she is terminally ill. Denial, says Dr. Ross, is important and necessary. It helps cushion the impact of the patient's awareness that death is inevitable.

2. Rage and anger—"Why me?" The patient resents the fact that others will remain healthy and alive while he or she must die. God is a special target for anger, since He is regarded as imposing, arbitrarily, the death sentence.

3. Bargaining—"Yes, me, but . . ." Patients accept the fact of death but strike bargains for more time. Mostly they bargain with God—"even among people who never talked with God before." They promise to be good or to do something in exchange for another week or month or year of life. Notes Dr. Ross: "Why they promise is totally irrelevant, because they don't keep their promises anyway."

4. Depression—"Yes, me." First, the person mourns past losses, things not done, wrongs committed. But then he or she enters a state of "preparatory grief," getting ready for the arrival of death. The patient grows quiet, doesn't want visitors. "Why a dying patient doesn't want to see you anymore," says Dr. Ross, "This is a sign he has finished his unfinished business with you, and it is a blessing. He can now let go peacefully."

5. Acceptance—"My time is very close now and it's all right." Dr. Ross describes this final stage as "not a happy stage, but neither is it unhappy. It's devoid of feelings but it's not resignation, it's really a victory."

In presenting these five stages, Kübler-Ross (1969) warns it is a mistake to expect that all terminally ill patients will methodically pass through all five stages. Some never reach the fifth stage of acceptance. Others may display reactions from two stages at the same time, for example, anger and denial. Still others may waver from one stage to another—reaching the depressed stage, and then returning to an earlier stage of denial or anger.

EMOTIONAL REACTIONS TO OTHER PROBLEMS   It is asserted here that Kübler-Ross's five stages are common emotional reactions that clients have when they are confronted with evidence that they have a personal problem. Denial, rage and anger, bargaining, depression, and acceptance are in the author's experiences common reactions in the following situations: a husband is informed his wife is having an affair; a single teenager is informed she is pregnant; an employee is fired for incompetence; a woman is informed she has a malignant tumor in her breast; a woman informs her fiancé she is ending their engagement; a college coed is raped; a young couple is informed their youngest child is mentally retarded; an elderly male discovers he is losing his sexual potency; a student intern is informed he does not have the capacities to become a competent counselor; a teacher is informed her contract will not be renewed for the next year. This list could perhaps be infinitely expanded, as it appears that clients are likely to have the above emotional reactions to practically any personal problem.

To illustrate the above, Lee Askew's case will be presented for each stage.

STAGE 1 — DENIAL ("NO, NOT ME")   For clients to admit they have a problem is difficult as they may often (erroneously) perceive themselves as weak, sinful, or irresponsible. Also, recognizing a problem exists means a client has to acknowledge that change is inevitable. When such change is inevitable clients often mourn the loss of that which must be changed. For example, for alcoholics to admit they have a drinking problem generally means they will be expected to give up their drinking. This is especially difficult as their social activities and their lifestyles are centered around drinking. Unless clients have already developed an openness or reaching out pattern with others it will be very difficult for them to share a new problem openly. Denial is often important and necessary as it helps cushion the impact of the client's awareness that change is inevitable.

For people who are denying a problem exists, constructive changes are not apt to occur unless the counselor finds a way to convince them that there is a problem. When a client denies a problem exists, counseling needs to focus on the denial by exploring why the person believes there is no problem and by gathering evidence to document the existence of the problem to the client. The client then needs to be confronted in a tactful manner with this evidence by the counselor.

Mr. Askew has been denying for over twenty years that he has a drinking problem. He believes that he needs alcohol to get through each day. He feels such a strong need for alcohol that he has allowed his drinking to end his first marriage, and he will not face reality that his drinking is also ruining his second marriage. Because he believes alcohol is such a necessity for him, he will not acknowledge that he nearly lost his life while driving when intoxicated, nor will he acknowledge that he has lost several jobs because of his drinking.

Mrs. Askew gave her husband an ultimatum — either he sees a counselor or she is leaving now. Mr. Askew reluctantly chose to see a counselor. In counseling Mr. Askew denied he had a drinking problem. He had excuses for everything that happened to him. His automobile accident resulted from slippery roads. He was fired because his employers did not like his suggestions for how to increase sales. He ended his first marriage because his wife was a "nag." He denied that he had more than a couple of drinks each day.

STAGE 2 — RAGE AND ANGER ("WHY ME?")   The client resents the fact that he has to make changes while others do not. Also, the client may be resentful that old friends, relatives, or society at large are doing the things that the clients must change. Anyone may be the target for the anger. Sometimes the anger is used to avoid discussing the issue at hand. At other times the anger may be directed at the counselor for confronting him with the reality of the "real problem."

The underlying reasons generating the client's anger need to be remembered during this stage. There are some therapeutic techniques that are often helpful during this stage. Allowing clients to ventilate their anger serves to reduce the intensity of the anger; once the intensity is reduced, they are better able to examine their difficulties realistically. Conveying empathy and emotional support helps create an atmosphere in

which they feel more comfortable examining their difficulties. Often during this stage clients feel overwhelmed by their problems, which is a factor in their
intensely felt "Why me?" If clients feel overwhelmed,
they need to see that their problems are not overwhelming but can be broken down into subproblems
that are resolvable in a gradual step-by-step fashion.
During this stage it is also helpful for counselors to
realize that when clients are angrily attacking them, the
reason for the anger is probably being generated by
the client's saying "Why me?" and should not be personalized by counselors. Reacting personally or angrily
to the client's anger will only prolong the client's hostile behavior.

Lee Askew at times displayed anger while in counseling with Paul Decker. As indicated earlier, Mr. Askew
at first denied he had a drinking problem. He had excuses for all the problems that were being caused by
drinking. Mr. Decker knew counseling would not be
productive unless this denial was broken through. Mr.
Decker suggested that at the next session a joint meeting be held with the Askews to get both their perceptions of their marital problems. Mr. Askew reacted angrily to this, castigating his wife for making up stories
about him, particularly his drinking. The counselor allowed Mr. Askew to ventilate his anger, and then asked,
"Are you fearful of what your wife might say?" Mr.
Askew stated no, and agreed to a joint meeting.

Several meetings were jointly held with the Askews.
Mr. Askew frequently continued to deny he had a
drinking problem. These denials were countered by
the counselor's asking Mrs. Askew questions that
served to confront Mr. Askew with his drinking problem. Such questions included how much he drinks
each day, how he acts while drunk, how Mrs. Askew
feels about seeing her husband intoxicated, whether
his drinking has gotten him into trouble at work and
with the police. At times Mr. Askew reacted angrily to
such confrontations. (It appeared he was using anger
to try to manipulate the counselor and his wife into
refraining from forcing him to acknowledge that he
has a drinking problem.) Mr. Decker let Mr. Askew
"spit fire" and ventilate his anger. On a few occasions
after Mr. Askew calmed down Mr. Decker would ask,
"Why are you reacting angrily to what is being said?" or
"It appears we are touching a sensitive chord with you."

Such questions were designed to help Mr. Askew gain
an awareness of why he was reacting angrily.

At other times, Mr. Askew would go into a tirade
about the fact that many of his friends drank and had a
good time. He angrily wondered why his wife was putting pressure on him to stop drinking. He was clearly
illustrating "Why me?" After being allowed to ventilate
his anger, it was pointed out to him that unlike social
drinkers, his drinking was a serious problem for him
because alcohol was controlling him; he was not in
control of his drinking. Specific incidents of difficulties
created when he was intoxicated were also tactfully
mentioned.

On one occasion Mr. Askew, with his wife present,
began castigating Mr. Decker for meddling in his family
affairs. The counselor calmly listened, and then replied, "Are you feeling angry at me because I'm forcing
you to see that you face a choice between giving up
drinking or losing your wife?" Mr. Askew at first reacted
angrily to this but later acknowledged the statement
was true. Again, anger was a reaction of Mr. Askew to
being forced to face his drinking problem.

STAGE 3—BARGAINING ("YES, ME, BUT . . .")   During
this stage clients are beginning to accept the problem,
but will bargain for such things as "just one more time."
They promise to be good or to do something in exchange for another week or month before they use the
alternatives presented to them to change. During this
stage a counselor should confront clients with the reality of the circumstances and their bargaining efforts.

During the bargaining stage clients will usually try
to change a few circumstances in their lives and they
generally believe that if these circumstances change
they can continue in their old ways. They are telling
themselves that "if such and such changes I can still
continue to . . ." Bargaining is a common reaction.
People who are urged to lose weight bargain for
"strawberry shortcake"; smokers who are urged to quit
bargain to smoke when tense; some spouses seek to
preserve a marriage that is in trouble via a pregnancy.

Mr. Askew, in counseling, tried several bargaining
efforts. At first he asked if he continued in counseling
whether he could continue to drink socially. Both the
counselor and Mrs. Askew doubted that Mr. Askew
could quit after a few drinks and expressed their mis-

givings. Social drinking was tried for a week, and Mr. Askew became intoxicated on three occasions. At the next session Mrs. Askew again stated her ultimatum, "Stop drinking, or I'm leaving." Efforts were then made to supplement this counseling by getting Mr. Askew involved in Alcoholics Anonymous (AA) meetings. Initial results in AA were good. Then a wedding came up and Mr. Askew bargained with his wife (outside of counseling) that he would continue in AA if he could socially drink at special occasions such as the wedding. His wife struck the bargain on the condition that he quit after a few drinks. Mr. Askew became intoxicated at the wedding, and his actions (including wetting his pants) were immensely embarrassing to Mrs. Askew. At the next counseling session, Mrs. Askew again stated her ultimatum, "Stop drinking completely, or else I'm leaving." After a few other similar bargaining efforts, Mr. Askew was confronted by Mr. Decker with the statement that it appeared he was not committed to giving up drinking but was striking bargains to continue his drinking. Mr. Askew at first reacted angrily (back to the anger stage) but gradually acknowledged he was bargaining.

STAGE 4 — DEPRESSION ("YES, ME") Clients at the depression stage usually become very quiet. They have, by now, stopped denying their problem. Their anger has subsided and they no longer try to bargain. They have gained insight into their particular problem and realize they must make changes in their lives. Alternatives, however, are as yet not perceived as being viable solutions for them. They are blaming themselves in a "self-downing" manner for their problems and frequently mourn the loss of what they will have to change in their lives. During this stage counselors need to convey empathy and help clients see that their problems are not overwhelming. At this stage clients need to be given hope; frequently this can be accomplished by developing resolution strategies with them.

Mr. Askew and his wife had been coming to weekly counseling for three and one-half months. During this time Mr. Askew made some efforts to give up drinking. At times he would go for a week or two without drinking, but always returned to the bottle. In counseling sessions he often vacillated between making excuses for his drinking (denial) and displaying anger, or bar-

gaining when confronted with the need to stop drinking. Generally at the counseling session following a drinking episode he would usually be depressed, acknowledging he was ruining his life by drinking. He would deprecate himself and beg his wife to give him one more chance. When she did, a week or two later he would find an excuse to start drinking again.

After three and one-half months, Mr. Askew came into counseling one day a little hung over, and very depressed. He indicated he had gotten drunk the day before, and he and his wife had gotten into an argument. He wasn't certain, but he thought he may have slapped her face a few times; she had packed a bag last night and indicated she was going to file for divorce. Mr. Askew stated life was not worth living without his wife. He fully acknowledged he had a drinking problem and had to abstain completely. The counselor and Mr. Askew discussed various alternatives. Mr. Askew stated with emotion that he would never take another drink, and that he would demonstrate this to his wife. He further decided to wait for two weeks before contacting her so that she could sort out her feelings and thoughts. Mr. Askew left the interview depressed, realizing that his drinking may now have ruined his marriage forever.

STAGE 5 — ACCEPTANCE ("I HAVE A PROBLEM, BUT IT'S ALL RIGHT" "I CAN") Clients now will make a concentrated effort at this stage to work out alternatives. Not only those suggested earlier in treatment but also some of their own. They have the attitude now of "I can do it." There is hope. A plan for rehabilitation can be presented if one was lacking or dismissed in the earlier stages. Fear is still present but very much reduced with the prospect of hope.

After two weeks Mr. Askew called his wife. They talked, and she agreed to attend the next counseling session. At this session, Mrs. Askew indicated she was ambivalent about ending her marriage, but she had totally had it with her husband's drunken behavior. They agreed to live apart for the next four months. If Lee participated in AA meetings and did not drink at all, they then would live together again, on the condition that he would never drink again.

That was over two years ago. Lee Askew has not had a drink, and he is active in AA helping other problem drinkers. He is also active in a speaker's bureau in which he talks to high school students and to businesses and organizations about the dangers of alcohol and about treatment programs. After three months of being separated, his wife returned, and both report their marriage and their careers are going well.

SUMMARY

From the counselor's perspective counseling can be divided into three phases: (1) building a relationship, (2) exploring problems in depth, and (3) exploring alternative solutions, with the client then selecting a course of action. Successful counseling gradually proceeds from one phase to the next, with some overlap of these stages. At the end of a series of counseling interviews there is often the fourth phase of "termination and evaluation."

The counseling process can also be conceptualized from the client's perspective. In order for counseling to be successful, clients must give themselves a progressive series of "self-talk" (that is, clients must arrive at having certain thoughts and beliefs). These self-talk stages are listed below:

Stage I   Problem awareness: "I have a problem."

Stage II   Relationship to counselor: "I think this counselor has what it takes to help me."

Stage III   Motivation: "I want to improve my situation and am willing to put forth the effort to do so."

Stage IV   Conceptualizing the problem: "My problem is not overwhelming but has specific components that can be changed."

Stage V   Exploration of resolution strategies: "I see there are several courses of action that I might try in order to do something about my situation."

Stage VI   Selection of strategy: "I think this approach might help and I am willing to try it."

Stage VII   Implementation: "This approach is helping me."

Stage VIII   Evaluation: "Although this approach takes a lot of my time and effort, it's worth it."

The advantage of this conceptualization of the counseling process is that it presents a framework for improving the effectiveness of counseling. This framework indicates when counseling is not helpful, the reasons for no progress can be identified by examining the self-talk of clients about the counseling they are receiving. Once these reasons are identified, needed changes can be made in the counseling process.

In counseling clients there is another crucial area that counselors need to be aware of and learn to effectively handle: the emotional reactions of clients to having a personal problem. Material is presented demonstrating that Kübler-Ross's (1969) five stages are emotional reactions that are not unique to the terminally ill but are typical reactions that any client is apt to display when confronted with evidence of having a personal problem. These five stages are denial, rage and anger, bargaining, depression, and acceptance. Only when clients reach the fifth stage of acceptance are they ready to work effectively on alternatives for resolving their problems. With a better understanding of these emotional reactions, counselors will be more effective in selecting appropriate intervention strategies.

EXERCISES

1. Understanding Clients' Reactions to Having a Personal Problem

GOAL: This exercise is designed to help students understand client's reactions to having a personal problem.

Step 1: Explain the purpose of the exercise. Indicate that when a person acknowledges he has a personal problem, almost always that person experiences a loss of some kind. The loss may involve giving up something one has had (such as an alcoholic giving up drinking). Or, the loss may involve recognition that a desired goal is not obtainable (for example, parents who have a retarded child may feel the loss of not having a child of normal intelligence). When a loss is experienced, the person almost always has the emotional reactions described by Kübler-Ross. Describe the following reactions to students: denial, anger and rage, bargaining, depression, and acceptance.

Step 2: Ask students to volunteer to describe a loss they have had, and have them comment on whether they experienced the five reactions described by Kübler-Ross.

Step 3: Explain that clients are frequently not ready emotionally to work on resolving a personal problem or a loss until they reach the fifth stage of acceptance. Ask the students who describe a loss if in fact they had to reach the stage of accepting their loss before they were able to make a concentrated effort to work on alternatives for resolving the problems.

2. *Learning How to Counsel through Role-Playing*

GOAL: The purpose of this exercise is to help students develop their counseling skills
        through role-playing counseling situations.

Step 1: Describe the goal of the exercise. Indicate that the counseling process from the counselor's view can be divided into five phases: (1) starting the interview; (2) building a relationship; (3) exploring problems in depth; (4) exploring alternative solutions with the client(s), then choosing one or more of the alternatives; and (5) ending the interview. (Material on these five phases is summarized in Chapters 4 and 5 of this text.) Briefly summarize guidelines on how a counselor should handle each of these phases.

Step 2: Ask two students to volunteer to role-play being clients. Allow the "clients" to come up with their own contrived problems. Indicate the following as examples of possible problems:

a.   Two college students are roommates. One believes the other has a drinking problem while the other refuses to acknowledge a problem exists.

b.   Two siblings are concerned about their mother living alone. Her health is failing, and her husband has recently died. The siblings also believe they are unable to care for their mother as each is married and has a family, and the mother is not easy to live with.

c.   A husband and wife both want children but the husband is infertile. The wife wants to become pregnant through artificial insemination (with the donor being someone rather than her husband). The husband objects to his wife getting pregnant through artificial insemination.

Step 3: The instructor should then counsel the two students who have contrived problems in order to demonstrate the five phases of counseling. After the counseling is completed, the class should discuss the strengths and shortcomings of the counseling that was given.

Step 4: Four more students should be asked to volunteer—two as clients having contrived problems and two as counselors for the two "clients." (It is useful to have two people, at this early stage, volunteer to be counselors in order to offset the potential problem of one counselor becoming "stuck" by not knowing what to say.) Role-play the interview.

Step 5: As an additional step, you may require each student in the class to role-play as counselor and also as client (for some other student who role-plays being a counselor). Ideally each student should be videotaped in the role of the counselor, and this videotape should then be played back so students can access the interview. (As described in Chapter 4, the videotaping may be used not only to help students develop their counseling skills but also as a screening device to counsel out students from the social work major if they are unable, after several tries, to make an acceptable videotape.)

Step 6: If the instructor decides to show each videotape to the class, a brief class discussion should be held after each tape is shown. This discussion should review the strengths and shortcomings of the counseling and also look at what else might be done. If each tape is shown to the class, it is helpful for each student to fill out the following Interviewer Skills Rating Sheet, which is then given to the "counselor" for feedback purposes. (One advantage of showing each tape to the class is that students learn aspects of what should and should not be done in counseling from viewing tapes.)

Note: Role-playing contrived counseling situations (and also videotaping of such situations) can be structured in a variety of ways. This exercise presents some ideas, but the instructor of course has the autonomy to structure the role-playing in ways that she believes will be most beneficial.

INTERVIEWER SKILLS RATING SHEET			
Student _____ Date _____			
Skills	**Need Improvement**	**Satisfactory**	**Excellent**
1. Opening remarks			
2. Explanation of counselor role			
3. Voice quality and volume			
4. Body posture			
5. Eye contact			
6. Behavioral congruence/facial expression (therapist's words match his/her outward appearance)			
7. Frequency of open-ended questions (not yes-no or multiple-choice questions)			
8. Amount of therapist's verbal activity			
9. Verbal following behavior (sequencing questions with client's answers preparing client for shift in subject matter)			
10. Clarity of questions			
11. Ability to confront client with inconsistencies			
12. Use of humor			
13. Warmth/ability to put client at ease			
14. Use of silence			

Interviewer Skills Rating Sheet (*continued*)			
Skills	**Need Improvement**	**Satisfactory**	**Excellent**
15. Ability to help client define problems			
16. Ability to have client specify goals			
17. Paraphrasing			
18. Reflection of client's feelings			
19. Summarization of client information			
20. Ability to answer client's questions — provide useful information			
21. Extent to which interviewer presented him/herself as a professional			
22. Extent to which necessary data about the problem was obtained			
23. Ending the interview/length of interview			
24. Completeness of interview			
25. Extent to which a helpful relationship was developed			
26. Extent to which alternative solutions to the problem were begun to be explored			

Positive Comments about Strengths Demonstrated during the Interview

Areas Needing Attention

3. Responding Effectively to Critical Statements from Clients

GOAL: This exercise is designed to help students learn how to respond more effectively to highly emotional and complex statements from clients.

Step 1: The instructor should explain the purpose of the exercise. The instructor should then read the first client statement and ask the class for their suggestions on the most effective way for a counselor to respond. There are a variety of effective responses. (One way of responding to each of these statements is presented in Appendix B.) A class discussion of the merits and shortcomings of some of the suggested responses by students is apt to be a productive learning experience.

Step 2: After the class responds to and discusses the first statement, the instructor should read the second statement and again seek responses and discussion from the students. This process continues with the remaining statements.

Client Statements

1. *Male client* (fifth interview). "There's something that's been bothering me for the past few weeks (pause). I'm beginning to feel that you're not really interested in me as a person. I have the feeling that the only reason you're meeting with me is because you're getting paid to see me."

2. *Engaged female*, age twenty: "I'm engaged to marry Kent. My uncle thinks he's terrific, but my parents are telling me I'm making the biggest mistake of my life to marry him. They dislike him and also think I'm too young to marry. I'm so confused about what I should do. Kent is putting a lot of pressure on me to elope."

3. *Juvenile probationee*, age sixteen, who is recognized as being a con artist — in required weekly visit with probation agent: "Your office is really cool. You've really got it made. I admire your taste in furnishing this office. You deserve what you've got in life. I admire you. Those are cool photographs on the wall — Did you take them?"

4. *Male client*, age twenty-seven (fourth interview): "I'm feeling real tense today. I've got a lot on my mind (pause). I don't think we've made much progress in the last three meetings, although I am gradually coming to trust you (pause). I haven't been fully honest with you. You know the marital problems I've been having? Well, the main reason our marriage hasn't gone well, and Karen doesn't even know this, is because for the past few years I've been involved with someone else — who happens to be a male. Karen no longer turns me on because I guess I'm more attracted to males."

5. *Black client* from an inner city who has a white therapist: "You honkies don't know what life is really like for us who live in a ghetto. You say you want to help me, but I don't buy that jive. How can you possibly help me when you have no idea what it is like to be black and living in a ghetto?"

6. *Teenage male delinquent* caught with marijuana in his possession at a correctional institution: "Please don't report this. You know I've been doing really well here at school and have a clean record. If you report this, my stay will be extended. I was only holding the drugs for a friend here. I'm not using any of it myself. Give me a break — everyone needs one in life."

6

SOCIAL WORK WITH GROUPS: TYPES OF GROUPS AND GUIDELINES FOR LEADING THEM

The practice of social work in groups is not a new phenomenon. The ideological roots of social group work can be traced most directly to the settlement houses, informal self-help recreational organizations (YMCA, YWCA), Jewish centers, and scouting, all of which developed during the first three decades of this century. It was during this period that many social workers found group-based methods of intervention effective and efficient for confronting a variety of personal and social problems. The last sixty years have witnessed a progressive interest in, and expansion of, group services in our society. The involvement of the social work profession in groups has broadened accordingly. Today it is not uncommon to find social workers as both group leaders and participants in a myriad of settings, helping to solve or ameliorate human or social problems, and planning for and creating change. There are many reasons behind the attractiveness of groups for members and for practitioners. Hartford (1971, p. 26) defines a group as

at least two people—but usually more, gathered with common purposes or like interests in a cognitive, affective, and social interchange in single or repeated encounters sufficient for the participants to form impressions of one another, creating a set of norms for their functioning together, developing goals for their collective activity, evolving a sense of cohesion so that they think of themselves and are thought of by others as an entity distinct from all other collectivities.

From this description we can see that the members of a group relate to one another within a context of sensing they form a distinct entity, that they share a common goal or purpose, and that they have confidence that together they can accomplish as much or more than would be possible were they to work separately. This commonality is characteristic of a wide variety of groups dealing with a multitude of societal

Material in this chapter is adapted from Charles Zastrow, "Social Work Practice with Groups," in *Introduction to Social Welfare Institutions*, 2nd ed. (Homewood, Ill.: Dorsey Press, 1982), pp. 507–29.

Community organizations such as the YWCA may offer space and equipment for group recreation.

problems. The beginning social worker is likely to be surprised at the diversity of groups in existence and excited by the challenge of practicing social work in groups. The period from 1960 to the present has witnessed an explosion in the number of groups and group-based techniques utilized by the social work profession. We have described below a significant sample of the types of groups in which social workers may become involved. This listing is not intended to be exhaustive; only the creativity of the helping professional and the client group served will provide such limits.

TYPES OF INTERVENTION GROUPS

Recreation Groups

The objective of recreation groups is to provide activities for enjoyment and exercise. Often such activities are spontaneous and the groups are practically

Learning how to swim: A recreation skill group

leaderless. The group service agency (such as YMCA, YWCA, or neighborhood center) may offer little more than physical space and the use of some equipment. Spontaneous playground activities, informal athletic games, and an open game room are examples. Some group agencies providing such physical space claim that recreation and interaction with others helps to build character and helps prevent delinquency among youth by providing an alternative to the street.

Recreation-Skill Groups

The objective of a recreation-skill group is to improve a set of skills while at the same time providing enjoyment. In contrast to recreational groups, this group has an adviser, coach, or instructor; also there is more of a task orientation. Examples of activities include golf,

basketball, needlework, arts and crafts, and swimming. Competitive team sports and leagues may emerge. Frequently such groups are led by professionals with recreational training rather than social work training. Social service agencies providing such services include YMCA, YWCA, Boy Scouts, Girl Scouts, neighborhood centers, and school recreation departments.

Educational Groups

The focus of educational groups is to help members acquire knowledge and learn more complex skills. The leader generally is a professional person with considerable training and expertise in the subject area. Examples of topics include child-rearing practices, assertiveness training, techniques for becoming a more effective parent, preparing to be an adoptive parent,

CASE EXAMPLE
_____

Assertiveness Training — An Educational Group

Assertiveness training can be provided to almost any new or already existing educational group. There are several advantages of group over individual assertiveness training. A group provides a "laboratory" for testing or experimenting with new assertive behaviors. A group has a broader base for social modeling as each person sees several others trying out a variety of assertive approaches. A wider variety of feedback is also offered by a group. Furthermore, a group is generally understanding and supportive. Finally, group pressure and expectations motivate members to conscientiously develop and practice new assertive responses.

A typical format for an assertiveness training group is as follows: The size of such groups generally ranges from five to twenty members. The first session is devoted to a lecture presentation on the differences between assertive, nonassertive, and aggressive behavior. The specific steps in assertive training are then summarized. (These steps are presented in Chapter 19 of this text.) Several examples of typical situations are also given to illustrate that assertive responses are generally more effective than aggressive or nonassertive responses.

In the following sessions specific situations involving assertive responses are then examined. At first it may be desirable to begin with situations that are not brought forth by members of the group (group members may at first be reluctant to reveal personal situations they face). Alberti and Emmons (1975, pp. 183–84) suggest the following situations be practiced:

1. Starting a conversation with a small group of strangers who are already engaged in conversation at a party.

2. Saying "no" assertively when a roommate or friend asks to borrow something that you do not want to lend to others.

3. Returning faulty or defective items to a store.

4. Asking someone next to you to extinguish a cigarette.

5. Asking someone to turn down a stereo that is too loud, or not talk so loudly in the library, theater, and so forth.

6. Asking for a date/refusing a date on the telephone and face-to-face.

7. Expressing positive feelings; "soft assertions."

8. Responding assertively to a date or spouse who is giving you "put down" comments.

9. Assertively refusing to take an alcoholic beverage from a friend when you prefer not to drink.

For each situation the following steps are used: (*a*) each member is asked to fantasize his/her response, (*b*) one member is selected to role-play an assertive response, (*c*) the group briefly discusses the strategy after it is role-played, (*d*) if a more effective response is desired, a new assertive response is role-played by a member, and (*e*) the group then discusses the strategy.

Following this exercise, group members are then encouraged to bring to the group real-life situations that are troubling them. These are often complicated and involve close, intimate relationships. Such situations may not have pat, simple resolutions. The following steps are recommended for group leaders in helping members become more assertive.

1. Help each group member to identify the situations/interactions in which it would be to his benefit to be more assertive. Usually group members will bring up these situations themselves. Some members, however, may be reluctant to reveal problem interactions, or they may be unaware they could handle certain situations better by being more assertive. Considerable tact and skill by the leader is necessary in initiating problem areas of the latter type. (One approach that usually works is to have the members anonymously write the situations they want role-played on a note card.)

2. When a problem interaction is identified each member of the group is asked to fantasize a response silently. For complicated situations with no simple solutions considerable discussion may arise about possible ways of resolving the matter.

3. A member (often someone other than the person with the problem situation) is asked to role-play an assertive response. The member with the problem may be asked to play the role of the person with whom he is having difficulty. The situation is then role-played.

4. The group briefly discusses the merits of the assertive strategy that was modeled in step three.

If it is effective and the person with the problem is comfortable with it, that person is then asked to role-play the approach. If the group believes there may be a more effective approach, steps three and four are repeated. If the person with the problem is uncomfortable about using a strategy that is effective, the reasons for the discomfort are then explored. For example, for very shy people, certain attitudes, such as "don't make waves" or the "meek shall inherit the earth" may need to be dealt with.

5. The person with the problem is asked to rehearse an assertive strategy silently, thinking what he will say and what are apt to be the consequences.

6. The person with the problem then is asked to role-play an assertive strategy.

7. Feedback is given by the group about the merits of the strategy. Generally the person is praised for the effective aspects and coached on how to improve other aspects. This

Continued

CASE EXAMPLE   *Continued*

approach is practiced via role-playing until it is perfected and the person has developed sufficient comfort and self-confidence for the "real event." For feedback purposes, if possible, the approach is recorded on audiotape or videotape.

8. The person tries out the new response pattern in an actual situation.

9. The person describes at the next group meeting how the real-life test went. The person is complimented on the degree of success attained, and assistance is given on aspects that could be improved.

and training volunteers to perform a specialized task for a social service agency. Educational group leaders often function in a more didactic manner and frequently are social workers. These groups may resemble a class, with considerable group interaction and discussion being encouraged. The example shows how assertiveness training can be taught in an educational group.

Problem-Solving and Decision-Making Groups

Both providers and consumers of social services may become involved in groups concerned with problem solving and decision making.

Providers of services use group meetings for such objectives as developing a treatment plan for a client or a group of clients, deciding how to best allocate scarce resources, deciding how to improve the delivery of services to clients, arriving at policy decisions for the agency, deciding how to improve coordination efforts with other agencies, and so on.

Potential consumers of services may form a group to study an unmet need in the community and to advocate the development of new programs to meet the need. Data on the need may be gathered, and the group

may be used as a vehicle either to develop a program or to influence existing agencies to provide services. Social workers may function as stimulators and organizers of such group efforts as well as participants (see Chapter 9 on community organization).

In problem-solving and decision-making groups each participant normally has some interest or stake in the process and may gain or lose, depending on the outcome. Usually, there is a formal leader of some sort, although other leaders sometimes emerge during the process. There are three issues of importance to problem-solving and decision-making groups: group versus individual decision making, groupthink, and decision by consensus versus decision by majority vote.

GROUP VERSUS INDIVIDUAL DECISION MAKING   Is group decision making superior to individual decision making? There is evidence that group decision making is usually superior to individual decision making (Johnson and Johnson, 1975, p. 60). This conclusion applies even when the individual decision is made by an expert.

There appear to be several reasons that group decision making is generally superior (Watson and Johnson, 1972). First, through group interaction the knowledge, abilities, and resources of each member are pooled. An individual acting alone often is lacking some of the information, skills, or resources needed to arrive at the highest quality decision. Second, working in the presence of others motivates a person to put forth more effort, to be more careful, and to increase the quality of the work. Third, having more people working on a problem increases the probability that someone in the group will suggest the highest quality solution. Fourth, through group interaction the members can build on each other's ideas and develop a high-quality decision that is based on this building block approach. Fifth, through group discussion there is a greater chance of identifying the positive and negative consequences of each alternative. Therefore, the negative consequences of an inferior decision are more apt to be identified. Sixth, it is easier to identify other people's mistakes than it is to identify your own. Through group interaction we are more apt to identify the problem areas in the favorite alternatives of others, and others are more apt to identify the problem areas in our favorite alternative.

In general the effectiveness of group decision making is enhanced when there is high involvement by all group members in making decisions. High involvement increases the willingness of members to share their information and abilities in making a decision, increases their allegiance to the group, increases their commitment to implementing the decision, and increases their commitment to working for the group in the future. Most groups can become more effective than they are now by seeking to increase the involvement of all group members in making decisions.

There are only a few situations in which decisions might best be made by one or a few individuals: (*a*) when a decision has to be made so quickly it is not possible to have a meeting, (*b*) when the decision is relatively unimportant and the person making the decision follows precedents previously set by the group, and (*c*) when the decision is relatively unimportant, does not require committed action by most members of a group, and there is no reason to believe the group will object to the decision.

But there are some problems with group decision making that take place in real life. At times a subgroup will seek to "railroad" a decision that will benefit them but be counterproductive for the whole group or for certain people outside the group. (Hitler, for example,

A session on AIDS for service employees: An educational group

used many tactics to sway groups he worked with to begin World War II and to exterminate six million Jews.) Tactics of "railroading" include pressuring a group to make a quick decision without giving the members time to analyze all the consequences, withholding information that is adverse to the desired decision, buying votes with promises, and suggesting there may be negative consequences for members who do not vote for the desired decision.

Another problem in group decision making is that friendships and paybacks for past favors sometimes lead members to vote for "the person" rather than for a decision based on thorough analysis of the consequences of the alternatives. Republicans and Democrats in Congress, for example, largely vote for the position taken by their party on issues.

CASE EXAMPLE

Nominal Group Approach — A Problem Identification Technique for Problem-Solving Groups

The nominal group approach was developed by Delbecq and Van de Ven (1971) for use as a problem identification technique in social program development efforts. The approach involves meeting with potential users of a service. A nominal group is defined as "a group in which individuals work in the presence of others but do not verbally interact" (Van de Ven and Delbecq, 1971, p. 205). This need-identification approach emphasizes the importance of understanding clearly the view of the population that one is trying to serve, and asserts that potential consumers of new services should articulate their needs, problems, and goals. The main orientation is to respond to consumers' needs rather than independently developing programs for them. To accomplish this objective, the nominal group approach is designed to receive input from all group members rather than just the more vocal or aggressive ones, as often happens in conventional group discussions. This technique has been successfully used in such applications as determining the housing difficulties of college students, reasons that have led delinquent youth into difficulty with police (Zastrow, 1973), and specific course topics wanted by students enrolling in social work courses (Zastrow and Navarre, 1977).

Research indicates that the nominal group approach is superior to brainstorming and to other types of interacting groups in generating information relevant to a problem situation. Both quantity and quality of suggestions are enhanced with this technique (Van de Ven and Delbecq, 1971). Several features appear to be involved in leading to this superiority. The approach has a game mystique that stimulates the interest of participants. Creative tension is stimulated by the presence of others, which fosters individual commitment to the task. Evaluation of items is avoided, which substantially reduces the pressure against expressing minority opinions or unconventional ideas. Conflicting, incompatible ideas are tolerated. Furthermore, the approach appears to be "a time-saving process since it can be activated and concluded with greater rapidity than interacting group processes" (Van de Ven and Delbecq, 1971, p. 210).

Sometimes groups reach incorrect or ineffective decisions because of a phenomenon known as *groupthink.*

GROUPTHINK   Irving Janis (1971) has identified groupthink as an unusual condition that can prevent effective problem solving. Janis studied groups who advised presidents of the United States and found that powerful social pressures were often exerted whenever a dissident began to voice objections to what otherwise appeared to be a group consensus. Groupthink is a problem-solving process in which proposals are accepted

The mechanics of conducting a nominal group are as follows:

1. Gather together a group of participants, any size, ranging up to about 100, and explain the nature of the study. Emphasize the importance of their ideas related to this topic. Care should be taken to obtain a representative cross-section of the populations of interest.

2. Randomly divide the participants into small groups ranging in size from five to eight. Each group is seated around a separate table or in desks arranged in a circle.

3. Distribute a sheet of paper that contains the question to which the participants are asked to respond. For example, the wording for determining desired course content might be

    What specific subject topics do you want covered in this course?
PLEASE—NO TALKING

4. For fifteen to twenty minutes, the participants privately list items they feel are in response to the question being asked; no talking is permitted during this period.

5. A round-robin listing technique is then used in which each individual in turn is given the opportunity to disclose one item at a time to the group. This listing is done separately for each group with one of the members acting as a recorder. Ideas may be recorded on flip-chart paper or on a blackboard. This round-robin listing continues until all members indicate they have no further ideas to share. Until this point is reached there is no discussion or evaluation of ideas presented.

6. Following the listing of all ideas, the flip-chart sheets are posted on the wall with masking tape. There is a brief, informal discussion of the items, which is focused on clarifying what the ideas mean. There are two different approaches to reviewing the items: (*a*) all items are made known to all participants, (*b*) each group briefly reviews only the items recorded for their group. Both approaches appear to work. For smaller-sized groups, the first is usually used while with larger groups, in which the total number of listed items becomes very large, the latter is generally used.

7. Once the participants are familiar with the items listed, each is asked to write privately on index cards the five items he feels are the most important.

8. These selections are then tabulated and posted. The highest ranked problems or topics represent those considered most important by the group members.

---

without a critical, careful review of the pros and cons of the alternatives, and in which considerable social pressure is brought to bear against expressing opposing points of view. Groupthink occurs partially because the norms of the group hold that it is more important to bolster group morale than to evaluate all alternatives

critically. Another group norm that increases groupthink is that members should remain loyal to the group by sticking with the policies to which the group has already committed itself, although those policies are not having the intended effects, or are even having disturbing unintended consequences.

Janis (1971) has listed a number of factors that promote groupthink:

a. Members have an illusion of being invulnerable, which leads them to become overly optimistic about their selected courses of action, leads them to take extraordinary risks, and causes them to fail to respond to clear warnings of danger.

b. Members have an unquestioning belief in the moral rightness of their group, which leads them to ignore the ethical consequences of their decisions.

c. The group applies social pressures of disapproval toward any member who momentarily questions the basic policies of the group or who raises questions about a policy alternative favored by the majority.

d. The group constructs rationalizations to discount warnings and other forms of negative feedback that would, if taken seriously, lead the members to rethink basic assumptions about policies that are not working out well.

e. Group members hold stereotyped views of the leaders of opposing groups. These leaders are viewed as either being so evil that it would be a mistake to try genuinely to negotiate differences, or they are viewed as so stupid or so weak that they will not be able to prevent the group from attaining its objectives.

f. Members sometimes assume "mind guard" roles in which they attempt to protect their leader and the group from negative information that might lead them to question the morality and effectiveness of past decisions.

g. Members keep quiet about their misgivings and even minimize to themselves the importance of these misgivings. Through self-censorship members avoid deviating from what appears to be group consensus.

h. The members believe practically everyone in the group fully agrees on the policies and programs of the group.

There are a number of poor decision-making practices that result from groupthink. The group limits its discussion to only those courses of action that are consistent with past decisions and policies; as a result, more divergent strategies (some of which are viable) are not considered. The group fails to reexamine a selected course of action, even when they discover the risks, drawbacks, and unintended consequences that they had not previously considered. The group makes little effort to get cost-benefit information on possible strategies from experts who might be able to supply more accurate information. Members seek primarily to obtain facts and listen to opinions that support their preferred policy and tend to ignore facts and opinions that do not. The group fails to work out contingency plans to cope with foreseeable setbacks, and it spends little time considering how the chosen strategy might be sabotaged by political opponents or hampered by bureaucratic red tape.

CONSENSUS VERSUS MAJORITY VOTING   Decision making by consensus is usually the most effective approach for getting all members to support and work for the decision. Consensus means that everyone is willing to go along with the decision, at least temporarily. This approach is also the most time consuming because the concerns of each member need to be dealt with. For many decisions, consensus is difficult to achieve as members are apt to have diverse opinions about what should be done.

To use consensus effectively, the group members need to have a certain mind-set and the group has to have a trusting, cooperative atmosphere. For consensus to be arrived at, members need to feel free to present their views as clearly and logically as possible but to avoid blindly arguing their own individual views. They need to listen and respect the views of other members. Members should *avoid* going along with the group if they believe the majority opinion is a mistake. It is a mistake to yield to the majority if the only reason is to avoid conflict and to appear united. Members, however, might yield to the majority opinion if that position appears to have merit and is a position they believe has a fair chance of having positive outcomes.

To make consensus work effectively, differences of opinion are sought out and respectfully dealt with. It is recognized that disagreements and divergent views are advantageous as they increase the chances that all crucial aspects will be reviewed, that members will build on the views of others, and that viable decisions will be made.

With consensus, the participation of all members is encouraged. The emphasis is on finding the best solution that everyone can agree on and support. If a group becomes stalemated between two possible alternatives, a vote is not taken to allow one subgroup to win while the other loses. Instead, a third alternative is sought to incorporate the major desires of both subgroups.

There are a number of benefits to consensus. Since consensus resolves controversies and conflicts, it increases the ability of the group to make future high-quality decisions.

If group members feel they have participated in the decision and support it, they are more apt to contribute their resources to implement the decision. Consensus is useful in making important, serious, and complex decisions in which the success of the decision depends upon the commitment of all members.

There are some disadvantages to consensus. It takes a great deal of time and psychological energy. There is a danger that the pressure for group consensus may lead to groupthink. In this situation members go along with what they believe is the majority opinion, even when they have evidence or information (which they fail to share for fear of making waves) that the probable decision will be unproductive or even destructive. In addition, consensus will not work in many groups for a variety of reasons. A high level of trust may not exist in the group, thereby not allowing candor, honesty, and directness. Some members may seek to dominate or manipulate the group rather than listen and support each other as individuals. The slow process required to arrive at consensus by members is experienced at times by some members as being painful, aggravating, and time wasting.

Most groups make decisions by simple majority vote. With this approach, issues are discussed until they are clarified and a simple majority of the members have arrived at an alternative. A vote is then taken.

There are several advantages to this type of decision making. Decisions are arrived at much faster than with the consensus approach. Most decisions in a group are not so important that full support of all members is necessary to achieve the objectives of the decision. Also, majority vote does not require, to as great an extent, the characteristics that are essential for consensus (such as trust, open communication, and willingness to give up one's favorite position).

There are also shortcomings of the simple majority approach. Minority opinions are not always safeguarded. Racial groups, women, certain ethnic groups, homosexuals, and people with disabilities are minority groups that in the past have suffered from adverse decisions made by simple majority voting. Majority voting frequently splits a group into winners and losers, with the losers often becoming angry, frustrated, and apathetic. Sometimes the group of losers is nearly as large in size as the winners (such as having 49 percent of the vote), but they wind up feeling their concerns are receiving no attention. A large-sized minority that feels it has been outvoted may not lend its resources to implementing the decision and may even work to subvert or overturn it. If the final vote alienates a minority, the future effectiveness of the group is diminished. There is a danger that the majority rule approach may be interpreted by the minority as being an unfair means of control and manipulation by the majority. Therefore, in order to maintain effective group functioning, groups that use majority voting should seek to create a climate in which members feel they have had their day in court, and where members feel an obligation to go along with the group decision.

A compromise between consensus and simple majority is a high percentage majority vote (such as two-thirds or three-fourths). This approach requires more time to arrive at a decision than a simple majority since more votes are needed. But it takes less time than consensus as not everyone has to be convinced or persuaded. A strong minority (such as 45 percent) can block a decision they dislike, but a small majority cannot force its views on a strong minority. However, a small minority may still feel it is being controlled and manipulated by a high percentage majority vote. A high percentage majority vote will generally draw stronger support from group members than the simple majority approach, but it will not generate as much support as the consensus approach.

Self-Help Groups

Self-help groups are becoming increasingly popular and are often successful in helping individuals with certain social or personal problems. Katz and Bender (1976, p. 9) provide a comprehensive definition of self-help groups:

Self-help groups are voluntary, small group structures for mutual aid and the accomplishment of a special purpose. They are usually formed by peers who have come together for mutual assistance in satisfying a common need, overcoming a common handicap or life-disrupting problem, and bringing about desired social, and/or personal change. The initiators and members of such groups perceive that their needs are not, or cannot be, met by or through existing social institutions. Self-help groups emphasize face-to-face social interactions and the assumption of personal responsibility by members. They often provide material assistance as well as emotional support; they are frequently cause-oriented, and promulgate an ideology or values through which members may attain an enhanced sense of personal identity.

Katz and Bender (1976) have also formulated the following classification of self-help groups:

1. Groups that focus on self-fulfillment or personal growth. Examples of such groups include Alcoholics Anonymous, Recovery Inc. (for former mental patients), Gamblers Anonymous, and Weight Watchers.

2. Groups that focus on social advocacy. Examples of such groups include Welfare Rights Organizations, MADD (Mothers Against Drunken Drivers), and the Committee for the Rights of the Disabled. Katz and Bender (1976, p. 38) note that the advocacy "can be both on behalf of broad issues, such as legislation, the creation of new services, change in the policies of existing institutions and so on, or it can be on behalf of individuals, families, or other small groups."

3. Groups whose focus is to create alternative patterns for living. Examples of such groups include Gay Liberation and certain religious cults such as the Moonies.

4. *Outcast haven* or *rock bottom* groups. Katz and Bender (1976, p. 38) define this type as follows:

   These groups provide a refuge for the desperate, who are attempting to secure personal protection from the pressures of life and society, or to save themselves from mental or physical decline. This type of group usually involves a total commitment, a living-in arrangement or sheltered environment, with close supervision by peers or persons who have successfully grappled with similar problems of their own.

   Examples of this type include Synanon, at least in its early years, and many other ex-drug addict organizations.

5. Groups of mixed types that have characteristics of two or more categories. One such group is Parents Without Partners, which promotes personal growth, advocacy, and social events for its members. Examples of other self-help groups and their primary focus are shown in Table 6.1.

Many self-help groups stress (*a*) a confession by members to the group that they have a problem, (*b*) a testimony by members to the group recounting their past experiences with the problem and their plans for handling the problem in the future, and (*c*) support, that is, when a member feels an intense urge of a recurrence (such as to drink or to abuse a child) a member of the group is called, and that member comes over to stay with the person until the urge subsides.

There appear to be several other reasons why such self-help groups are successful. The members have an internal understanding of the problems, which helps them to help others. Having experienced the misery and consequences of the problem, they are highly motivated and dedicated to finding ways to help themselves and their fellow sufferers. The participants also benefit from the *helper therapy principle*: the helper gains psychological rewards by helping others (Riessman, 1965). Helping others makes a person feel good and worthwhile; it also enables the helper to put his own problems into perspective as he sees that others have problems that may be as serious, or even more serious, than his own.

TABLE 6.1

Examples of Self-Help Groups

Organization	Service Focus
Abused Women's Aid in Crisis	For battered wives and other abused women
Adoptee's Liberty Movement Association	For adoptees searching for their natural parents
Alcoholics Anonymous	For adult alcoholics
American Diabetes Association	Clubs for diabetics, their families, and friends
Brain Tumor Support Group	For persons with brain tumors or their loved ones
Burns Recovered	For burn victims
Caesarian Birth Association	For those expecting a caesarian birth
Candlelighters	For parents of young children with cancer
Checks Anonymous	For persons in debt
Concerned United Birthparents	For parents who have surrendered children for adoption
Depressives Anonymous	For depressed persons
Divorce Anonymous	For divorced persons
Emotions Anonymous	For persons with emotional problems
Emphysema Anonymous	For those with emphysema
Fly without Fear	For people who are afraid of flying
Fortune Society	For ex-offenders and their families
Gam-Anon	For families of gamblers
Gray Panthers	An intergenerational group
Make Today Count	For persons with cancer and their families
Mensa	For persons with high IQs
Naim Conference	For widowed persons
The National Conference of Stutterers	For adult stutterers
National Organization for Women	For women's rights
Overeaters Anonymous	For overweight persons
Parents Anonymous	For parents of abused children
Phobia Self-Help Groups	For persons with phobias
Prison Families Anonymous	For family members of prisoners
Resolve	A support group for infertile people
Stroke Clubs	For those who have had strokes and their families
Survivors of Suicide Victims	For the relatives and friends of suicide victims
We Care	Support group for divorced and separated persons

Note: Alan Gartner and Frank Riessman in *Help: A Working Guide to Self-Help Groups* (New York: Franklin-Watts, 1980) describe more than two hundred self-help groups.

CASE EXAMPLE

Parents Anonymous — A Self-Help Group

Parents Anonymous (PA) is a national self-help organization for parents who have abused or neglected their children. PA was originally established in 1970 by Jolly K in California, who was desperate to find help to meet her needs. For four years prior to this time she struggled with an uncontrollable urge to severely punish her daughter. One afternoon she attempted to strangle her daughter. Desperate, she sought help from the local child-guidance clinic. She was placed in therapy. When asked by her therapist what she could do about this situation, she developed an idea; as she explained (Zauner, 1974, p. 247), "if alcoholics could stop drinking by getting together, and gamblers could stop gambling, maybe the same principle would work for abusers, too." With her therapist's encouragement she formed "Mothers Anonymous" in 1970, and started a few local chapters in California. Nearly every major city in the United States and Canada now has a chapter, and the name has been changed to Parents Anonymous (since fathers who abuse their children are also eligible to join).

PA uses some of the basic therapeutic concepts of Alcoholics Anonymous. PA is a crisis intervention program that offers two main forms of help: (1) a weekly group meeting in which members share experiences and feelings and learn better control of their emotions, and (2) personal and telephone contact among members during periods of crisis, particularly when a member feels a nearly uncontrollable desire to take their anger or frustration out on a child.

Parents may be referred to PA by a social agency (including protective services), or may be self-referrals of parents who are aware they need help.

Cassie Starkweather and S. Michael Turner (1975, p. 151) describe why some parents who abuse their children would rather participate in a self-help group than receive professional counseling:

It has been our experience that most (abusive) parents judge themselves more harshly than other more objective people tend to judge them. The fear of losing their children frequently diminishes with reassurance from other members that they are not the monsters they think they are.

Generally speaking, PA members are so afraid they are going to be judged by others as harshly as they judge themselves that they are afraid to go out and seek help. Frequently our

When people help each other in self-help groups they tend to feel empowered as they are able to control important aspects of their lives. When help is given from the outside (from an expert or a professional), there is a danger that dependency may develop, which is the opposite effect of empowerment. Empowerment increases motivation, energy, personal growth, and an ability to help that goes beyond helping oneself or receiving help.

Some self-help groups (such as National Association for Retarded Citizens) raise funds and operate community programs. Many people with a personal problem use self-help groups in the same way that others use social agencies. An additional advantage

*members express fears of dealing with a professional person, seeing differences in educa-
tion, sex, or social status as basic differences that would prevent easy communication or
mutual understanding.*

*Members express feelings of gratification at finding that other parents are "in the same
boat." They contrast this with their feelings about professionals who, they often assume, have
not taken out the time from their training and current job responsibilities to raise families
of their own.*

PA emphasizes honesty and directness. In the outside world, parents who are prone to
abuse their chidlren learn to hide this problem because society finds it difficult to stomach.
In contrast, the goal in PA is to help parents admit and accept the fact that they are abusive.
The term *abuse* is used liberally at meetings. PA has found that this insistence on frankness
has a healthy effect. Parents are relieved because they've finally found a group of people
who are able to accept abusive parents for what they really are. Furthermore, only when
they are able to admit they are abusive can they begin to find ways to cope with this
problem.

During PA meetings parents are expected actually to say they are beating their child or
engaging in other forms of abuse, and the members challenge each other to find ways to
curb such activities. Members also share constructive approaches that each has found useful, and efforts are made to help each other develop specific plans for dealing with situations that have in the past resulted in abusive episodes. Members learn to recognize danger
signs and to then take necessary action to curb the potential abuse.

Leadership in the group is provided by a group member selected by the parents themselves. The leader, called a chairperson, is normally assisted by a professional sponsor who
serves as resource and backup person to the chair and the group members. The social
worker who becomes the sponsor must be prepared to perform a variety of roles including
teacher-trainer, broker of community services needed by parents, advocate, consultant, and
in some instances, behavior changer (Hull, 1978).

This description of Parents Anonymous is adapted from Charles Zastrow, "Parents Anonymous," in *Introduction to Social Welfare Institutions*, 2nd ed. (Homewood, Ill.: Dorsey Press, 1982), pp. 159–61.

---

of self-help groups is that they generally are able to
operate with a minimal budget. Hundreds of self-help
groups are now in existence. Social workers often act
as brokers in linking clients with problems to the appropriate self-help groups.

Riessman (1987, pp. ix–x) summarizes the distinctive characteristics of self-help groups as follows:

- *a noncompetitive, cooperative orientation*

- *an anti-elite, antibureaucratic focus*

- *an emphasis on the indigenous—people who
  have the problem and know a lot about it from
  the inside, from experiencing it*

- *an attitude of do what you can, one day at a time (you can't solve everything at once)*
- *a shared, often revolving leadership*
- *an attitude of being helped through helping (the helper-therapy principle) . . .*
- *an understanding that helping is not a commodity to be bought and sold*
- *a strong optimism regarding the ability to change*
- *an understanding that although small may not necessarily be beautiful, it is a place to begin and the unit to build on*
- *a critical stance toward professionalism, which is often seen as pretentious, purist, distant and mystifying. Self-helpers like simplicity and informality*
- *an emphasis on the consumer . . . The consumer is a producer of help and services*
- *an understanding that helping is at the center — knowing how to receive help, give help, and help yourself . . .*
- *an emphasis on empowerment*

Socialization Groups

The objective of socialization groups generally is to develop or change attitudes and behaviors of group members to become more socially acceptable. Social skill development, increasing self-confidence, and planning for the future are other foci. Illustrations include working with a group of predelinquent youth in group activities to curb delinquency trends, working with a youth group of diverse racial backgrounds to reduce racial tensions, working with a group of pregnant young females at a maternity home to make plans for the future, working with a group of elderly residents at a nursing home to remotivate them and get them involved in various activities, and working with a group of boys at a correctional school to help them make plans for returning to their home community. Leadership of such groups requires considerable skill and knowledge in using the group to foster individual growth and change. Leadership roles of socialization groups are frequently filled by social workers.

Therapeutic Groups

Therapy groups are generally composed of members with rather severe emotional or personal problems. Leadership of such groups generally requires considerable skill, perceptiveness, knowledge of human behavior and group dynamics, group counseling capacities, and ability to use the group to bring about behavioral changes. Among other skills, the group leader needs to be highly perceptive regarding how each member is being affected by what is being communicated. Considerable competence is needed to develop and maintain a constructive atmosphere within the group. Similar to one-to-one counseling, the goal of therapy groups is generally to have members explore their problems in depth and then to develop one or more strategies for resolving them. The group therapist generally uses one or more therapy approaches as a guide for changing attitudes and behaviors; examples of such therapy approaches include psychoanalysis, reality therapy, learning theory, rational therapy, transactional analysis, client-centered therapy, and psychodrama.

Group therapy is being used increasingly in social work. It has several advantages over one-to-one therapy. The *helper* therapy principle generally is operative, in which members interchange roles and sometimes become the helper for someone else's problems. In such roles, members receive psychological rewards for helping others. Groups also help members to put their problems into perspective as they realize others have problems as serious as their own. Groups also help members who are having interaction problems to test out new interaction approaches. Research has shown that it is generally easier to change the attitudes of an individual alone than in a group (Lewin, 1952). Research on conformity has found group pressure can have a substantial effect on changing attitudes and beliefs. Furthermore, group therapy permits the social worker to help more than one person at a time, with potential savings in the use of professional effort.

In essence a group therapist uses the principles of one-to-one counseling (discussed in Chapter 5) and of group dynamics (see Chapter 7) to work with clients to change dysfunctional attitudes and behavior. Generally

A therapy group for prison inmates

the group leader also uses the principles of certain treatment techniques (such as reality therapy, rational therapy, Parent Effectiveness Training, and assertiveness training) to help clients resolve personal and emotional problems. The selection of the techniques to use should ideally be based upon the nature of the problems presented.

Encounter Groups

Encounter groups and sensitivity training groups (these terms are used somewhat synonymously) refer to a group experience in which people relate to each other in a close interpersonal manner, and self-dis-

closure is required. The goal is to improve interpersonal awareness. Jane Howard (1970, p. 3) offers a typical description of an encounter group:

Their destination is intimacy, trust, awareness of why they behave as they do in groups; their vehicle is candor. Exhorted to "get in touch with their feelings" and to "live in the here-and-now," they sprawl on the floor of a smoky room littered with styrofoam coffee cups, half-empty Kleenex boxes, and overflowing ashtrays. As they grow tired they rest their heads on rolled-up sweaters or corners of cot mattresses or each other's laps.

An encounter group may meet for a few hours or for a longer period of time up to a few days. Once

CASE EXAMPLE

Socialization — A Rap Group
at a Runaway Center

New Horizons is a private, temporary shelter care facility for runaways in a large mid-western city. It is located in a large house that was built over eighty years ago. Youth on the run can stay for up to two weeks. State law requires that parents must be contacted and parental permission received for New Horizons to provide shelter overnight. Services provided include temporary shelter care, individual and family counseling, and a twenty-four hour hotline for youths in crisis. The facility is licensed to house up to eight youths. Since the average stay is nine days, the population is continually changing. During the stay, intensive counseling is provided the youths (and often their parents), focusing on reducing conflicts between the youths and their parents and on making future living plans. The max-imum stay at New Horizons is two weeks. This fourteen-day limit is used partially to convey to youths and their families, beginning with day one, that they must work on the reasons for leaving home.

Every evening at 7 P.M. a rap group meeting is held. All the residents and the two or three staff members on duty are expected to attend. This rap group has four main objec-tives. One is to serve as a vehicle for residents to express their satisfactions and dissatisfac-tions with the facilities and programs at New Horizons. Sometimes the rap group appears to be primarily a gripe session, but the staff make conscientious efforts to improve those as-pects where the youths' concerns are legitimate. For example, the youths may indicate that

---

increased interpersonal awareness is achieved, it is an-ticipated that attitudes and behaviors will change. In order for these changes to occur, a three-phase pro-cess generally takes place: unfreezing, change, and refreezing.

Unfreezing occurs in encounter groups through a deliberate process of interacting in nontraditional ways. Our attitudes and behavior patterns have been developed through years of social experiences. Such patterns, following years of experimentation and re-finement, have now become nearly automatic. The in-terpersonal style we develop through years of trial and error generally has considerable utility in our everyday interactions. Deep down, however, we may recognize a need for improvement but are reluctant to make the effort, partly because our present style is somewhat functional and partly because we are afraid to reveal things about ourselves. Unfreezing occurs when we decide certain patterns of our present behavior need to be changed, and we are psychologically ready to ex-plore ways to make changes.

Stewart L. Tubbs and John Baird (1976, p.48) de-scribe the unfreezing process in sensitivity groups:

Unfreezing occurs when our expectations are vio-lated. We become less sure of ourselves when tradi-

the past few days have been boring, and staff and residents then jointly plan activities for the next few days.

Another objective is to handle interaction problems that arise between residents, and between staff and residents. A wide range of problems arise: a resident may be preventing others from sleeping; some residents may refuse to do their fair share of domestic tasks; there may be squabbles about which TV program to watch; some residents may be overly aggressive; and so forth. Since most of the youths face a variety of crises associated with being on the run, many tend to be anxious and under stress. In such an emotional climate, interaction problems are apt to arise. Staff are sometimes intensely questioned by residents about their actions, decisions, and policies. For example, one of the policies at New Horizons is that each resident must agree not to use alcohol or illegal drugs while staying at this shelter, with the penalty being expulsion. Occasionally a few youths use some drugs, and are caught and expelled. Removing a youth from this facility has an immense impact on the other residents, and at the following rap meetings staff are expected to clarify and explain such decisions.

A third objective of rap meetings is for staff to present material on topics requested by residents. Examples of topics include sex; drugs; homosexuality; physical and sexual abuse (a fair number of residents are abused by family members); how to avoid being raped; how to handle anger, depression, and other unwanted emotions; legal rights of youths on the run; how to be more assertive; how to explain running away to relatives and friends; and what other human services are available to youths in the community. During such presentations, considerable discussion with residents is encouraged and generally occurs.

The final objective of rap groups is to convey information about planned daily activities and changes in the overall program at New Horizons.

---

tional ways of doing things are not followed. In the encounter group, the leader usually does not act like a leader. He or she frequently starts with a brief statement encouraging the group members to participate, to be open and honest, and to expect things to be different. Group members may begin by taking off their shoes, sitting in a circle on the floor, and holding hands with their eyes closed. The leader then encourages them to feel intensely the sensations they are experiencing, the size and texture of the hands they are holding and so forth.

Other structured exercises or experiences may be planned to help the group focus on the "here-and-

now" experience. Pairs may go for "trust walks" in which each person alternatively is led around with his eyes closed. Sitting face-to-face and conducting a hand dialogue, or a silent facial mirroring often helps to break the initial barriers to change. Other techniques may involve the "pass around" in which a person in the center of a tight circle relaxes and is physically passed around the circle. Those who have trouble feeling a part of the group are encouraged to break into or out of the circle of people whose hands are tightly held. With these experiences, most participants begin to feel more open to conversation about what they have experienced. This sharing of

Therapy Group for Spouses of Adults with Cancer

E ight years ago Linda Sonsthagen's husband was found to have cancer. Linda was a so-cial worker, and her husband was a successful life insurance agent. They had two sons in grade school. Four and one-half years ago Mr. Sonsthagen died, after having gone through a variety of treatment programs and through considerable pain. He lost weight and his hair fell out. These years were extremely difficult for the Sonsthagens. Linda had to take a larger role in raising the children and had to be the primary care giver to her husband and to the children. During these years, the Sonsthagens found that relatives and friends shied away from them — it took several months before they became aware that the reason was that friends and relatives saw cancer as being something they didn't understand and wanted to avoid. Even more difficult was dealing emotionally with not knowing the course of the disorder, going through cycles of hope and then disappointment as different treat-ment approaches were tried. As her husband became more disabled, Linda found she had to assume more of the tasks that were previously done by her husband — for example, home repairs, maintaining their two cars, being more of a disciplinarian for the children, and doing more of the daily household tasks.

After her husband's death, Linda and the two children went through several months of mourning and grief. Linda also discovered it was somewhat awkward to go to social func-tions alone initially. Fortunately she had two single female friends with whom she increas-ingly socialized. There were very difficult years for Linda. She needed over two years after her husband's death to rebuild her life in such a way that she was again comfortable.

During these years she had received some financial help from the local chapter of the American Cancer Society. She also had met through this society another woman whose hus-band was also dying of cancer. They were able to give each other emotional support and to share with each other useful ideas for handling the problems that arose.

Eighteen months ago Linda proposed to the local chapter of the American Cancer Soci-

---

experiences or self-disclosure about the here and now provides more data for the group to discuss.

The second phase of the process is change. Changes in attitudes and behavior are usually facilitated in sensi-tivity groups by spontaneous reactions or feedback to how a person "comes across" to others. In everyday interaction we almost never get spontaneous feedback and we tend to repeat ineffective interaction patterns because we lack knowledge of our effect on others. But in sensitive groups such feedback is strongly encour-aged. The following set of interactions illustrates such feedback:

CARL: All right [*in a sharp tone*], let's get this trust walk over with, and stop dilly-dallying around. I'll lead ety that she was willing to volunteer her time to start a group for spouses of those having cancer, and for spouses who are adjusting to a recent cancer death. The Cancer Society gave their approval and endorsement.

Linda initially started a group with nine members. The objectives of the group were to give emotional support, to help members handle the new responsibilities they had to take on, and to help them deal with their emotional reactions. Linda used primarily a combination of reality therapy and rational therapy (see Chapter 17 and 18). Reality therapy was used to help the group members better understand and make decisions and plans for the problems they faced—for example, how to inform and handle the reactions of friends and relatives to their spouse's having cancer; for the survivors, the focus was on making realistic decisions to rebuild their lives. Rational therapy was used to counter unwanted emotions. Such common emotions included depression, guilt, anxiety, the feeling of being overwhelmed, and anger (particularly resulting from "Why does this have to happen to me?"). Members were instructed on how to do a Rational Self-Analysis (see Chapter 18) on their unwanted emotions, and members often shared and discussed these RSAs at group meetings.

Group members stated on several occasions that the group was very helpful. They mentioned that knowing others faced similar plights was beneficial in and of itself. Seeing how others handled difficult decisions inspired them and gave them useful ideas on how to handle crises they faced. When a member suffered a serious crisis (e.g., the spouse was hospitalized for a serious operation) other members were available for telephone contact and to lend physical assistance.

After eight months the local chapter of the American Cancer Society was so encouraged by the results that they offered Linda a full-time position to run additional groups and to be available for individual counseling for people with cancer and their relatives. Linda gave up her part-time job as a counselor at the YWCA and took this position. Her first effort was to divide her group, which was growing in size, into two groups. The definition of eligible membership was also expanded: one group was for adults who have a family member with cancer, and the other for adults who are survivors. At this time Linda is leading one group of the first type, and two groups of the second type.

the first person around—who wants to be blindfolded first?

JUDY: Your statement makes me feel uncomfortable. I feel you're saying this group is a waste of your time. Also it's the third time tonight that you've ordered us around.

JIM: I feel the same way, like you're trying to tell us peons what to do. Even the tone of your voice sounds autocratic, and I get the message you're really down on this group.

CARL: I'm sorry, I didn't mean it to sound like that. I wonder if I do that outside the group too?

Such feedback provides us with new insights on how we affect others. Once problem interactions are identified, that member is encouraged to try out new response patterns in the relative safety of the group.

The third and final phase is *refreezing*. Unfortunately this term is not the most descriptive as it implies rigidity with a new set of response patterns. The goal of this phase involves the attitude of experimenting with new sets of behaviors so that the person becomes a growing, continually changing person who increasingly becomes more effective in interacting with others. In terminating a sensitivity group, the leader may alert the participants that they have to be on guard, because old behavior patterns tend to creep back in.

Sensitivity groups usually generate an outpouring of emotions that are rarely found in other groups.

The goal of sensitivity groups provides an interesting contract to that of most therapy groups (see Figure 6.1). In therapy, the goal is to have all members explore in-depth personal or emotional problems that they have, and then develop a strategy to resolve the problems. In comparison, sensitivity groups seek to foster increased personal and interpersonal awareness and then develop more effective interaction patterns. Sensitivity groups generally do not attempt directly to identify and change specific emotional or personal problems that people have (such as drinking problems, feelings of depression, sexual dysfunctions, and so on). The philosophy behind sensitivity groups is that with increased personal and interpersonal awareness, people will be better able to avoid, cope with, and/or handle specific personal problems that arise.

Sensitivity groups are being used in our society for a wide variety of purposes: to train professional counselors to be more perceptive and effective in interpersonal interactions with clients and with other professionals, to train people in management positions to be more effective in their business interactions, to help clients with overt relationship problems to become more aware of how they affect others and to help them to develop more effective interaction patterns, and to train interested citizens in becoming more aware and effective in their interactions.

Despite their popularity, sensitivity groups remain controversial. In some cases inadequately trained and incompetent individuals have become self-proclaimed leaders and have enticed people to join through sensational advertising. If handled poorly, the short duration of some groups may intensify personal problems; for

FIGURE 6.1

Contrasting Goals of Therapy versus Sensitivity Groups

Therapy Groups

Step 1
Examine problem(s) in depth.

Step 2
Develop and select from various resolution approaches, a strategy to resolve the problem.

Sensitivity Groups

Step 1
Help each person become more aware of herself and how she affects others in interpersonal interactions.

Step 2
Help a person to develop more effective interaction patterns.

example, a person's defense mechanisms may be stripped away without his developing adaptive coping patterns. Many authorities on sensitivity training disclaim the use of encounter groups as a form of psychotherapy and discourage those with serious personal problems from joining such a group. Carl Rogers (1970, pp. 40–41), in reviewing his own extensive experience as leader/participant, echoes these concerns:

Frequently the behavior changes that occur, if any, are not lasting. In addition, the individual may become deeply involved in revealing himself and then be left with problems which are not worked through. Less common, but still noteworthy, there are also very occasional accounts of an individual having a psychotic episode during or immediately following an intensive group experience. We must keep in mind that not all people are suited for groups.

In some cases the popularity of sensitivity groups has led some individuals to enter harmful groups whose leadership was poor and where normal ethical standards have been abused. Shostrom (1969, pp. 38–39) has identified some means by which those interested in encounter groups can prevent exploitation: (*a*) Never participate in a group of fewer than a half-dozen members. The necessary and valuable candor generated by an effective group cannot be dissipated, shared, or examined by too small a group, and scapegoating or purely vicious ganging up can develop. (*b*) Never join an encounter group on impulse — as a fling, binge, or surrender to the unplanned. (*c*) Never stay with a group that has a behavioral ax to grind. (*d*) Never participate in a group that lacks formal connection with a professional on whom you can check.

After reviewing the research on the outcome of sensitivity groups, Lieberman, Yalom, and Miles (1973, p. 11) provide an appropriate perspective for those interested in the intensive group experience:

Encounter groups present a clear and evident danger if they are used for radical surgery to produce a new man [person]. The danger is even greater when the leader and the participants share this misconception. If we no longer expect groups to produce magical, lasting change and if we stop seeing them as panaceas, we can regard them as useful, socially sanctioned opportunities for human beings to explore and to express themselves. Then we can begin to work on ways to improve them so that they may make a meaningful contribution toward solving human problems.

HOW TO START, LEAD, AND TERMINATE GROUPS

The remaining part of this chapter focuses on guidelines for how to start, run, and terminate groups. This section covers (a) homework, (b) session planning, (c) relaxing before a meeting, (d) cues upon entering the meeting room, (e) seating arrangements, (f) introductions, (g) role clarification, (h) agenda, (i) additional guidelines for leading a group, and (j) terminating a

group. Many students fear taking a leadership role in groups. They are uncertain what a leader does, and they fear they do not have the qualities or traits to be a leader. Amazingly, the truth is that even the most fearful and anxious students have already taken leadership roles in many groups. Every student has in the past been a member of several groups and has performed some essential tasks for these groups. As we will see in Chapter 7, performing an essential task is simultaneously an effective leadership action.

Homework

Extensive preparation is the key to a successful experience for the group members (including yourself). Even experienced leaders have to prepare carefully for each group and for each meeting.

In planning a new group, the following questions need to be answered. What are the overall purpose and general goals of the group? What are possible ways in which these general goals can be accomplished? What are the characteristics of the members? Are some members apt to have unique, individual goals and/or needs? What resources do the members need to have in order to accomplish the general goals? What should be the agenda for the first meeting? The group members should have considerable input in suggesting and deciding upon the specific goals of the group — how can this best be accomplished? When the group first meets, should an icebreaker exercise be used — if so, what? Should refreshments be provided? How should the chairs be arranged? What type of group atmosphere will best help the group accomplish its tasks? What is the best available meeting place? Why have you been selected to lead the group? What do the members expect you to do?

As you plan for the first meeting, it is very helpful to view the group as a new member would view it. Questions and concerns that a new member may have are the following. What are the goals of this group? Why am I joining? Will my personal goals be met in this group? Will I feel comfortable in this group? Will I be accepted by other members? Will the other members be radically different in terms of backgrounds and interests? If

I do not like this group, can I get out of attending meetings? Will other members respect what I have to say or will they laugh and make fun of me? Through considering such concerns, the leader can seek to plan the first meeting in a way that will help the other members feel comfortable and will clarify the members' questions about the goals and activities of the group.

It is *absolutely essential* for a group leader to identify the group's needs and expectations before the first meeting. The quickest way to fail as a leader is to try to have a group go in a direction different from what the members want. For example, I remember going to a workshop with other counselors that was entitled "Grief, Death, and Dying." The counselors expected material on how to counsel more effectively clients who were grieving about the death of a loved one. The presenter instead gave a historical review of how present-day funeral rituals had evolved since the Middle Ages. The audience was very disappointed as their expectations were unmet.

There are a variety of ways to identify what the members want. Prior to the first meeting, it may be possible to ask some members what their expectations are. If you are asked by someone to lead the group, it is essential to ask that person about the expectations for the group. The members should generally be asked at the first meeting to give their views as to what they desire to get out of the group. Another way (which needs to be done for preparatory reasons anyway) is to "scout" the following about the members:

1. How many members are expected?
2. What are their characteristics—ages, socioeconomic status, racial and ethnic backgrounds, sex mix, educational and professional backgrounds, and so on?
3. How knowledgeable and informed are the members about the topics the group will be dealing with?
4. What are apt to be the personal goals and agendas of the various members?
5. How motivated are the members to accomplish the purposes for which the group is being formed? This can partly be determined by examining how voluntary the membership is. Groups composed of involuntary members (for example, a group that is court ordered to attend because of conviction for driving while intoxicated) have little motivation,

and may perhaps even be hostile that they are being forced to attend.

6. What are apt to be the underlying value systems of the members? A group of teenagers on juvenile probation is apt to differ significantly from a group of retired priests. (However, it is important to view the members as unique persons rather than as stereotypes.)

In planning for the first (and additional meetings) it is helpful to visualize (imagine) how you, as leader, want the meeting to go. For example, at the first meeting the following may be visualized:

The members will arrive at various times. I will be there early to greet them, to introduce myself, to assist them in feeling comfortable, and to engage in small talk. Possible subjects of small talk that are apt to be of interest to these new members are _____, _____, and _____.

I will begin the meeting by introducing myself and stating the overall purpose of the group. As an icebreaker exercise I will ask the group to give me a list of four or five facts they would like to know about the other members and have the members introduce themselves and give the four or five facts about themselves. I will also tell about myself and encourage the members to ask questions about me and the group.

After the icebreaker exercise I will again briefly state the overall purpose of the group and ask if the members have questions about this. Possible questions that may arise are _____. If such questions arise, my answers will be _____.

We will then proceed to the items on the agenda (which has previously been mailed to the members). During the discussion of each of these items, the questions that may arise are _____. My answers to such questions, should they arise, are _____.

The kind of group atmosphere I will seek to create is democratic. Such an atmosphere is best suited for encouraging all members to accept the group goals and then to contribute their time and resources toward accomplishing them. I will seek to do this by arranging the chairs in a circle, by drawing out through questions those who are silent, by using humor, and by making sure that I do not dominate the conversation.

I will end the meeting by summarizing what has been covered and the decisions that have been made. We will set a time for the next meeting. I will finally ask if anyone has any additional comments or questions. Throughout the meeting I will encourage a positive atmosphere, partly by complimenting the members on the contributions they make.

If a group has met for one or more times, the leader needs to review the following kinds of questions. Have the overall goals been sufficiently decided upon and clarified? If not, what needs to be done in this clarification process? Is the group making adequate progress in accomplishing its goals? If not, what are the obstacles that are slowing down the group that need to be confronted? Has the group selected adequate courses of action to reach its goals, or are there more effective courses of action that might be considered? What items should be placed on the agenda for the next meeting? What activities should be planned? Will successful completion of these activities move the group toward accomplishing its overall goals? If not, perhaps other activities need to be selected. Does each member seem sufficiently interested and motivated to help the group accomplish its goals, or are there some members who appear disinterested? If so, why do they appear disinterested, and what might be tried to stimulate their interests?

Session Planning

In planning a session, it is essential to be fully aware of the overall goals for the group. It is also essential to identify for each session what the specific goals are for that session. It is critical to know exactly what you want to accomplish in each session and to make sure that all the items on the agenda relate to the goals you have set. The following are some suggestions.

1. Select content that is relevant. The material should be relevant not only to the specific goals for the session but also to the backgrounds and interests of the participants. For example, in a time management presentation, the time-saver tips you give to college students probably will be quite different from those for business executives. In the former the tips should probably focus on improving study habits while the latter should probably focus on improving work activities in an office setting. An excellent way to evaluate the relevance of your material is to define precisely how it will be valuable to the members of the group. Ask yourself, "If a group member asks why I should know this, can you give a valid reason?" If you are unable to come up with more than a vague answer, it may be best to consider discarding that material and selecting other, more relevant material.

2. Use a number of examples. Examples help to illustrate key concepts. They also stimulate the interests of the participants. People tend to remember examples much more than statistics. To illustrate, in a presentation on spouse abuse, a few vivid real-life stories of the drastic effects on a woman's life of continued battering by her husband will be remembered much longer than statistics on the extent of spouse abuse.

3. Present materials in a logical order. It is generally desirable to begin by summarizing the agenda items for the session. Ideally, one topic should blend into the next. If group exercises are used, they should be placed next to the related theoretical material.

4. Plan for time. Once you have the content of the session fairly well organized, estimate how long each segment will take. Accurate estimations will help you determine if you have too much or too little material planned for the allotted time. It is also a good idea to plan what you will do if the content is covered faster or slower than what you are estimating. (For example, if the material is being covered more slowly than anticipated, you will be prepared to revise your agenda when you realize that you will not have time for everything.) You should also be prepared to cover extra material when things more more quickly than you anticipated. If you are planning to use a film, or have a guest speaker for part of the time, you should have plans for appropriate substitute material in case the film projector breaks, or the guest speaker fails to appear.

5. Be prepared to be flexible with your agenda. A variety of unexpected events may make it desirable to change the agenda during a session. The material may be covered much faster than anticipated, or interpersonal conflict may erupt between some members, which may take considerable time to process. Some members may bring up subjects related to the group's overall purpose that may be more valuable for the group to focus on than the prepared agenda.

6. *Occasionally change the pace.* People will be able to pay attention for longer periods of time if there is an occasional change of pace. Long, long lectures or long discussions bore people. The pace can be changed in a variety of ways: using a group exercise, showing a film, inviting a guest speaker, taking a break, having a debate, showing slides, changing the topics, and so on. In group therapy sessions, one way to change pace is to switch from focusing on one member's problems to focusing on another's concerns. If you are presenting a lecture, you can increase attention in several ways:

- Speaking extemporaneously rather than by reading the material.
- Occasionally walking around the room, rather than standing or sitting in one place.
- Drawing out the participants through asking them questions

(An excellent way to learn how to give more stimulating presentations is to observe the nonverbal and verbal communication patterns of dynamic speakers.) When you change pace it is critical to use appropriate transitions so that the topics blend into one another rather than becoming choppy and confusing.

In changing pace, it is helpful to use a variety of methods. There are many methods of conveying information: lectures, discussions, role-plays, films, exercises, slide presentations, diagrams, and so on. In selecting methods, it is useful to be aware that people tend to remember for a longer period of time information they receive in an active way (such as through an exercise) than information they receive in a passive way (through listening).

Relaxing before a Meeting

Prior to starting a meeting, you are apt to be nervous about how the session may go. Some anxiety is helpful in order for you to be mentally alert and to facilitate your attending to what is being communicated during the meeting. Some leaders, however, have an excessively high level of anxiety, which reduces their effec-

tiveness. If your anxiety is too high, you can reduce it by engaging in activities that you find relaxing. Relaxation techniques are highly recommended and are described at some length in Chapter 22. Other suggestions include taking a walk, jogging, listening to music you find relaxing, and finding a place where you can be alone to clear your mind. Effective group leaders generally learn they can reduce their level of anxiety through using one or more of the above techniques. Through practice in leading groups, you will gradually build up your confidence so that you are an effective group leader.

Cues upon Entering the Meeting Room

It is important for you as leader to be on time, and perhaps a little early. Being early allows you to check to see that everything is arranged as you planned. By being early, you'll be able to do what needs to be done — such as checking to see that refreshments are available (if refreshments are planned), erasing the blackboard, arranging the chairs, and so on.

An early arrival will allow you to observe the moods of the members. If it is a group you have not previously met, arriving early will give you an opportunity to gain information about the interests of the participants by observing their age, gender, clothes and personal appearance, small talk, and the way they are interacting with one another. An effective leader notices such cues and generally finds a way to "join" such participants.

I was once asked to give a workshop on suicide prevention to a high school class. Upon arriving, I was informed by the teacher that one of the students in the class had recently committed suicide. Instead of beginning with my planned presentation, I acknowledged that I had just been informed about their classmate, and I began by asking each of them anonymously to write down on a sheet of paper one or two concerns or questions that they had about suicide. After they turned in their sheets, we have a lively discussion related to these. Such a discussion was probably more valuable than the formal presentation (which was never given) because it focused on their specific questions and concerns.

Seating Arrangements

Seating arrangement is important for several reasons. It can affect who talks to whom and can have an influence on who is apt to play leadership roles. As a result, it can affect group cohesion and group morale.

It is important in most groups for the members to have eye contact with one another. It is even more important for the group leader to be able to make eye contact with everyone, in order to obtain nonverbal feedback on what the members are thinking and feeling.

A circle is ideal for generating discussion, for encouraging a sense of equal status for each member, and for promoting group openness and group cohesion. The traditional classroom arrangement (with the leader in front, and everyone facing that person while sitting in rows) has the effect of placing the leader in a position of authority. It also tends to inhibit communication, as members are generally able to make eye contact with only those closest to them.

Tables have advantages and disadvantages. They provide a place to write and to put work materials. Some members feel more comfortable at a table, as it gives them something to lean on. Disadvantages of tables are that they tend to restrict movement and may serve as a barrier between people.

The leader should consider carefully whether it is desirable or undesirable to have tables. If members are to sift through papers or are expected to take notes, tables should generally be used. In therapy groups tables are seldom used as they tend to restrict movement and act as a barrier.

In many settings tables can be arranged to best meet the goals of the meeting. For example, arranging small tables in a circle tends to facilitate communication.

Tables influence the way group members interact with each other. If the table is rectangular, it is customary for the leader to sit at one end, which then is viewed as the "head" of the table. The person who is at the head of the table is often viewed as the "authority" and usually does more talking and has a greater influence on the discussion than other group members. If an equalitarian atmosphere is desired it is helpful to use a round or square table. The "head of the table" effect can also be reduced by placing two rectangular tables together to make a square.

Tables also influence interactions by where people sit. People are most apt to talk to those who are sitting at right angles to them, and next most likely to talk to those next to them. Those sitting directly across receive less communication, and those sitting anywhere else are even less likely to be talked to.

When a group meets for the first time (and often later) members are most apt to sit next to friends. If it is important for everyone in the group to interact with one another, it may be desirable to ask people to sit next to people they do not know, in order to counteract any cliquishness in the group and to encourage members to get to know each other.

Introductions

During the introduction, the leader's credentials should be summarized in such a way that members gain a sense of confidence that the leader can fulfill the expectations of the members. If the leader is being introduced by someone else, a brief and concise summary of the leader's credentials *for the expected role* is desirable. If the leader is introducing herself, the important credentials should be summarized in a nonarrogant fashion. The summary should also be delivered in a way to create the desired atmosphere—whether it be an informal or formal atmosphere, a fun or serious one, and so on. An excellent way in many groups to handle the introduction is to use an icebreaker exercise, as described in Chapter 1.

In meeting with a group, it is highly desirable to learn the members' names as quickly as possible. This requires extra attention on the leader's part. Name tags facilitate this process for everyone. Members appreciate being called by name—it helps convey to them that they have importance.

If the group is small, it is generally advantageous for each member to introduce him or herself—perhaps through using an icebreaker. It is often desirable during introductions for members to state their expectations for the group. This helps to uncover hidden agendas. If a stated expectation is beyond the scope of the group, the leader should tactfully state and discuss it in order to prevent an unrealistic expectation from becoming a source of frustration or dissatisfaction for that member.

Role Clarification

As the leader of a group you should be clear about your roles and responsibilities. If you are unclear, you may want to discuss with the group their expectations as to the appropriate roles for the leader and for the other members. One way of doing this is for the group to select goals, and then for the group to make decisions about the tasks and responsibilities that each member will have in working toward the goals of the group. In most situations it is clearly a mistake for the leader to do the majority of the work. The group will generally be most productive if all members make substantial contributions. The more members contribute to a group, the more they are apt to feel a part of the group psychologically.

Even if you are fairly clear about what you would like your role to be, the other members may be confused about what your role is, or may have different expectations of you. If there is a realistic chance that the other members are unclear about your role, you should explain carefully what you perceive your role to be. If members indicate they have somewhat different expectations, the group should take the time to make decisions about who will do what.

In explaining what you perceive your role to be it is generally desirable to be humble about your skills and resources. Generally, you will want to come across as a knowledgeable "human" rather than as an authority figure who has all the answers.

You should always be prepared to explain the reasoning behind the things you do. If you are doing an exercise, the group should generally be informed about the goals or objectives of that exercise. (If questions arise about whether the goals for the exercise are consistent with the overall goals for the group, you should be prepared to provide an explanation.)

The role that the leader should assume in a group will vary somewhat from situation to situation. For example, there are apt to be marked differences in responsibilities of the leader of a therapy group versus a Boy Scout troop.

Agenda

For most meetings, there should be an agenda. Ideally, all members of the group should have an opportunity to suggest items for the agenda. If possible, the agenda should be sent to the members several days before the meeting to give them an opportunity to prepare for the items that will be considered.

At the start of the meeting the agenda items should be briefly reviewed, prior to consideration of the first item. This review gives each member a chance to suggest additions, deletions, or other changes. In some meetings it may be appropriate for the group to discuss, and perhaps vote, on the suggested changes in the agenda.

Additional Guidelines for Leading a Group

This section briefly summarizes additional suggestions for leading a group effectively.

1. Remember that leadership is a shared responsibility. Every member at times will take on leadership roles. Designated leaders should not dominate a group, nor should they believe they are responsible for directing the group in all of its task functions and group maintenance functions. (These functions are described in Chapter 7.) In fact, productivity and group cohesion are substantially increased when everyone contributes.

2. Seek to use decision-making procedures that are best suited for the issues facing the group. (The

merits and shortcomings of decision making by consensus and by majority voting were discussed earlier in this chapter.)

3. Seek to create a cooperative group atmosphere rather than a competitive group atmosphere. (These two atmospheres are described in Chapter 7.)

4. View controversy and conflict as being natural and as being desirable for resolving issues and furthering discussion. In resolving conflicts and in handling the issues and problems facing the group, seek to use a problem-solving approach rather than a win-lose approach. (See Chapter 7.)

5. Seek to create an atmosphere of open and honest communication.

6. You need to give attention to how to end a session. A few minutes before the session is scheduled to end, or when it appears the group has exhausted a subject, you may conclude with a summarization of the key points made by you and the other members. This summary should be brief. Such a summary emphasizes the major points to be remembered and leaves the group with a sense of achievement. It also signals that this portion of the session has come to a close.

Terminating a Group

Inherent in termination is separation from the group and from group members. Separation typically involves mixed feelings that vary in intensity according to a number of factors, several of which are mentioned here. The greater a member's emotional closeness and investment in a group, the greater will be the person's feeling of loss. The greater the feeling of success of members in accomplishing their goals through the group, the greater will be the feeling of "sweet sorrow"—sweetness from feeling that they have grown and had success, and sorrow from separation from the group that has come to be an important and meaningful part in their lives. The more emotionally dependent they have become on a group, the more members are apt to feel anger, rejection, and depression over termination. The more they have experienced difficulties in

separating in the past from significant others, the more likely it will be that the separation will be experienced as difficult, as the pattern of reacting to separations is apt to be repeated.

There are several types of termination:

1. Termination of a successful group
2. Termination of an unsuccessful group
3. Dropout of a member
4. Transfer of a member
5. Departure of the leader

Each of these types is discussed briefly.

TERMINATION OF A SUCCESSFUL GROUP   A successful group is one in which the group and its members have generally accomplished their goals. Termination of such a group is apt to generate the "sweet sorrow" reaction in members. The members are apt to be delighted with their accomplishments. The accomplishments are apt to increase their levels of self-confidence and self-esteem. Members may also experience a feeling of loss (varying in intensity) because of separating from a group in which they have become emotionally invested. Such a group may desire to have dinner together or have some other ceremony to commemorate and recognize the group and its accomplishments.

In terminating a successful group it is essential that formal termination begin one or more meetings before the final one. Ideally, the date of the last meeting should be discussed and agreed upon by the members well in advance. (For some groups the final meeting is scheduled even before the group begins to meet.) Sufficient time has to be allowed in terminating a successful group so that (1) progress made in accomplishing the tasks and goals of the group and its members can be evaluated, (2) plans can be made for continued work by the members on remaining problems, (3) work can be done on unresolved, last-minute, issues that are identified by members, (4) the emotional reactions of members to terminating can be handled, and (5) the members have time to discuss whether they want to plan for a special social event for the group's ending.

While goodbyes are often sad, the negative feelings can be offset by emphasizing what members have given and received, the ways they have grown, the skills they have learned, and the accomplishments of the group. In some cases an extra session could be held to complete unfinished business items. The members may decide to have periodic "class reunions" or social get-togethers in the future.

TERMINATION OF AN UNSUCCESSFUL GROUP   An unsuccessful group is one in which most or all the goals of the group and its members are largely unmet. The reactions of members to the lack of progress may vary considerably: anger, frustration, disappointment, despair, guilt (for unproductive efforts or lack of effort), scapegoating, blaming, and apathy. In rarer cases, it is possible for an unsuccessful group to be fairly pleased and accepting of its efforts. For example, a group that is formed to write a grant (when there is limited hope of funding from the federal government) may be pleased with its efforts and with the new relationships with others that were formed; the members may be only mildly disappointed when they learn they were not funded.

The termination of an unsuccessful group is as important as the termination of a group that has achieved its goals. As with all groups, the plan for termination should have been made well in advance. The date of the last meeting should have been discussed and agreed upon by the members long before the final meeting. Sufficient time for discussion must be allowed in terminating an unsuccessful group: (1) The reasons for the lack of progress of the group need to be assessed and analyzed. (2) Discussions should be held about alternatives by which the group and its members can reach their goals. (Such alternatives may involve changing the format of the present group, referring members to other groups, and encouraging individual rather than group efforts.) (3) There must be time to handle the emotional reactions of members to terminating as well as their reactions to the lack of progress made by the group. (4) The members need time to work on unresolved, last-minute issues that are identified. (5) The members should have time to discuss whether they want to plan a special social event for the group's ending.

At times the ending of an unsuccessful group is chaotic and abrupt. A group that has been appointed to write a grant may be nearly finished when they are informed the funding organization has had a financial shortfall and is therefore withdrawing its request for funding proposals. Such a group may end abruptly in despair. Or, in a group of involuntary members (such as at a prison or at an adolescent residential treatment facility), the leader may decide that to continue the group is counterproductive because the members are continually "goofing off" and are not putting effort into achieving the group goals. In any case, the reasons for the group's ending should be fully explained and time should be given to handle the reactions of the members to the closing. If there is insufficient time at the last meeting to deal with the tasks involved in ending a group, it is sometimes advisable either to have another session or for the leader to meet individually with each member to discuss their reactions to the group's failure to meet their goals, alternatives for reaching their goals, their reactions to the group's ending, and unresolved concerns they may have. When an unsuccessful group ends abruptly, some group members may be highly critical of the leader, of other group members, or of experiences that occurred in the group. If the leader contacts members to learn their thoughts about the group, he or she needs to be prepared to respond to highly critical feedback. One way of preparing is for the leader to "visualize" possible criticisms and then to formulate a positive and realistic response to each anticipated criticism.

DROPOUT OF A MEMBER   When a member drops out, that member terminates even though the group continues on. A member may drop out for a variety of reasons. She may become disenchanted with the group and feel that neither she nor the group will accomplish the goals that have been set. The member may have a disagreement with, or dislike, another group member. The member may be a parent who must now provide child care at the time the group meets or may have begun a new job with work hours that conflict with the meeting time. There are numerous other reasons.

When a member drops out without informing the group of the reasons, the leader should contact the member to learn why she decided to terminate. In some instances it is desirable for the leader to explain that deciding to leave is a major decision that should not be made abruptly and that the leader would like the opportunity to explore the reasons that led to the decision. If the member has a conflict with another group member, perhaps the conflict can be resolved so that the member will decide to return. Likewise, for other reasons, perhaps action can be taken to enable the member to return. If child care is a problem for a parent, perhaps child care arrangements can be made. If the member decides not to return, the reasons for leaving should be explored. Perhaps the member will raise legitimate concerns that may need to be dealt with so that other members do not also become discouraged and leave. If the member drops out of a therapy group, sensitivity group, or an educational group, and he still has unresolved personal concerns, a referral to another group or to one-to-one professional help may be advisable. Whenever a member drops out, the leader needs to inform that member of his positive contributions to the group. Dropping out of a group is often viewed by that member as a personal failure, and therefore the leader needs to thank him for his positive contributions to help dispel the leaving member's sense of personal failure.

When a member drops out, the remaining members may experience a variety of emotions. Some may feel they failed this person. Some may feel guilt for what they said or did—or feel guilt for failing to do or say what they believe would have led the member to stay. Some may feel relief or joy over the member's leaving; they may view the member as unworthy of the group or as an obstacle in the group's efforts to accomplish its goals. Some may feel sadness for the member's dropping out and be concerned that something tragic has happened to that member. Some members may be angry, feeling that the person who is leaving is abandoning the group. Some may feel personally rejected. Often, when a member drops out, erroneous rumors begin to circulate about the reasons. Therefore it is essential that the group be informed of the reasons for the member's leaving. When a member leaves, it can be devastating to group morale. If other members have also recently left, the group's survival may be jeopardized.

Ideally, the member who leaves should inform the group of the reasons, either in person or in writing. If the member does not, the leader or some other group member should contact the person who leaves to ascertain the reasons for leaving, and then soon afterward inform the group.

TRANSFER OF A MEMBER   A transfer of a group member to another group or to some other type of professional services generally involves a planned arrangement between the group leader and the member. The transfer may occur for a variety of reasons. In a problem-solving group, the employing agency may decide the group member's talents and skills could be used better in some other capacity. In a therapy group, the leader and group member may jointly decide the member will be served better by receiving more specialized services in some other therapeutic format. A group member may be transferred in any kind of a group because of a conflict that cannot be resolved between the group member and other group members, especially when the conflict is severely interfering with goal accomplishment within the group. (For example, there may be a serious and insurmountable gap in mutual understanding and communication caused by differences in religious beliefs, values, or language.)

When a transfer occurs, the leader should do everything possible to keep it from being unexpected or abrupt. The member being transferred should clearly understand the reasons for the transfer and should ideally be accepting of it. In addition, the group should receive an explanation of why a member is transferring. The member should explain the reasons to the group. This would allow the other group members an opportunity to wish the member well and to gain a sense of "closure" to the member's leaving.

DEPARTURE OF THE LEADER   Sometimes a group leader must terminate her work with a group because of reassignment, change of employment, health reasons, or family crises. The termination is often difficult for both the group leader and the members. Emotional reactions may be intense, and adequate time for working through these reactions may not be available. Members who feel vulnerable and dependent upon the leader may feel devastated. Some may erroneously personalize the leader's leaving as resulting from something they said or did. Some may feel anger and betrayal over having made a commitment to the group, confiding and trusting in the leader, and then feeling rejected by the leader who leaves when their goals and the group's goals are only partially accomplished.

The leader, too, may experience intense emotions, including guilt, for not being able to follow through on the implicit commitment to lead the group until its goals are accomplished and it ends.

When a leader leaves, she should encourage the members to express their feelings. She may want to initiate this expression by explaining fully why she is leaving, giving the members positive comments about the group, and stating her feelings of sadness and guilt over leaving. Prior to leaving, the group or the leader should select a new leader. If the new leader is not a member of the group, the one who is leaving should inform (outside of a group meeting) the new leader about the goals, characteristics of members, current tasks and difficulties in the groups, and progress toward goals that the group has made. The new leader should be introduced to the group by the departing leader. A smooth transition should be the goal in shifting responsibilities from the former to the new leader.

Another essential component of group process that is closely related to termination is evaluation. Evaluation is described at considerably length in Chapter 10.

A few concluding comments follow about the personal benefits you will receive in leading groups. Through learning how effectively to lead you will become more aware of yourself, grow as a person, become more self-confident, feel good about yourself, develop highly marketable skills that employers are seeking, learn to improve interpersonal relationships, and help yourself and other members accomplish important tasks. Leaders are not born. They are trained. You have the potential to become an effective group leader. You can do it!

SUMMARY

Social group work's historical roots were in the informal recreational organizations — the YWCA and YMCA, scouting, Jewish centers, settlement houses, and 4-H Clubs. Now almost every social service agency provides some group services. Most undergraduate and graduate social work programs provide practice courses to train students to lead groups, particularly training in leading socialization, educational, and therapeutic groups. The focus of social work groups has considerable variation including recreation, recreation skill development, problem solving and decision making, self-help, socialization, therapy, and education.

With problem-solving and decision-making groups, group decision making is usually superior to individual decision making. Problem-solving groups have the danger of groupthink, which may lead a group to make ineffective and even dstructive decisions. It has also been found that making decisions by simple majority voting may alienate the minority.

Socialization groups generally have the objective of developing or changing attitudes and behaviors of group members in some socially accepted direction. Social skill development, increasing self-confidence, and planning for the future are other foci.

The goal in therapy groups is generally to have each member explore in depth personal or emotional problems and then to develop a strategy to resolve the problems. A group therapist uses principles of one-to-one intervention and of group dynamics to assist members in achieving positive changes in attitudes and behaviors. In contrast, sensitivity groups seek to foster increased personal and interpersonal awareness and to develop more effective interaction patterns.

The chapter concluded with guidelines on how to start, lead, and terminate groups. Aspects included homework, planning a session, relaxing before starting a meeting, cues upon entering the meeting room, seating arrangements, introductions, clarifying roles, agenda, and terminating a group.

EXERCISES

1. Assertiveness Training

GOAL: Demonstrate to the class how to run an educational group by illustrating how to run an assertiveness training group.

Step 1: Indicate the purpose of this exercise. Describe nonassertive, aggressive, and assertive behaviors (see Chapter 19 for descriptions).

Step 2: Distribute a handout that describes the twelve steps of assertiveness training (contained in Chapter 19). Summarize these steps.

Step 3: Ask for volunteers (two for each situation) to role-play assertively the situations that you give them, such as

a.   asking someone who is smoking next to you to put out a cigarette;
b.   asking for a date and refusing a date;
c.   indicating to an objecting father that you want to live with the person you are dating.

After a situation is role-played have the class discuss the assertiveness strategy.

Step 4: Ask students to write anonymously on a note card one or two situations involving assertiveness with which they are struggling and which they would like others in the class to role-play.

Step 5: Collect these note cards and select some situations for volunteers to role-play. After a situation is role-played, have the class discuss the assertiveness strategy.

2. The Nominal Group

GOAL: This exercise is designed to have the class learn how a nominal group is conducted.

Step 1: The steps of how to run a nominal group are described in this chapter. Ask a question for the nominal group such as "What do you see as the shortcomings of our social work program (do not mention the names of faculty members)?" Then follow the steps for conducting a nominal group as described in this chapter.

3. Trust Walk

GOAL: This exercise is designed to demonstrate an approach, the trust walk, that is frequently used in sensitivity groups. A trust walk helps students to get in touch with aspects of themselves that they are unaware of.

Step 1: Inform the class of the purpose of the exercise. Have the students form groups of two. (If a member is without a partner, the instructor can be a partner.) Have a member of each subgroup close her eyes and instruct her keep her eyes closed during the first part of this exercise. The "seeing" partner then is instructed to lead the "blind" partner down corridors, around the room, and perhaps outside. The "seeing" partner can lead the "blind" partner with verbal directions and by taking her hand. The "seeing" person has the responsibility to watch that the "blind" partner does not run into objects, fall, stumble, or hurt herself in any way. (Inform the students to be very careful going up and down stairs.)

Step 2: After eight to ten minutes have the partners reverse roles and continue the exercise for another eight to ten minutes.

Step 3: Have the students then discuss their feelings about doing this trust walk. Ask questions such as the following. Did you occasionally open your eyes when you were the "non-seeing" partner? Did you have trust in your partner? Did you feel you would run into objects and hurt yourself? Were you afraid? If yes, how did you handle these fears? Did you become aware of feelings or thoughts about yourself that you previously were unaware of? If yes, what thoughts and feelings?

7

SOCIAL WORK WITH GROUPS: CONCEPTS AND SKILLS

This chapter presents key group dynamic concepts and summarizes guidelines for leading therapeutic groups. We will begin by reviewing the following ideas that are important in understanding group process:

a. Membership and reference groups

b. Stages in group development

c. Task and maintenance roles

d. Leadership theory

e. Social power bases in groups

f. Personal goals and group goals

g. Conformity

h. Competitive and cooperative groups

i. Controversy and creativity

j. Win-lose approach versus problem-solving approach

k. Handling disruptive behavior

l. Group size

MEMBERSHIP AND REFERENCE GROUPS

A membership group is any group to which a person belongs. In a sense membership in a group is clearly defined, as a person either belongs to a group or does not belong. Membership is thus a boundary condition.

Some people are marginal members of a group. For example, everyone who is enrolled at your campus is a member of the student body, but some students are only marginal members of the student body since they do not get involved in any campus activities. Tim Kelly at this campus only attends classes. He works nearly full-time in the evening and does not live on campus. He identifies primarily with the people with whom he

Material in this chapter is adapted from Charles Zastrow, "Social Work Practice with Groups," in *Introduction to Social Welfare Institutions*, 2nd ed. (Homewood, Ill.: Dorsey Press, 1982), pp. 507–29. Grafton H. Hull, Jr. was a contributing author to this chapter.

Places of worship are reference groups . . .

works. The other students influence him very little. He comes to campus only for his classes and leaves almost immediately afterward.

Full psychological membership in a group occurs only when a person is positively attracted to being a member and is positively accepted as a member. Tim Kelly, for example, has limited psychological membership with the student body as he has only a small identification with the campus. The more a person is attracted to a group, the greater will be that person's commitment toward accomplishing the goals of the group.

Aspiring members include those who are seeking admission to a group but as yet have not been admitted. They are not members but act as if they are. For example, students who aspire to be admitted to a fraternity or a sorority will seek to act like members to

increase their chances of being admitted. Aspiring members are psychologically identifying with the group even though they are not as yet formally admitted.

There is also a difference between voluntary membership and involuntary membership. Voluntary membership occurs when an individual deliberately chooses to belong to a certain group, such as a fraternity or athletic team. In other situations a person may have little or no choice over becoming a group member. Social workers often work with groups whose membership is involuntary as in prison settings, mental hospitals, residential treatment facilities, group homes, programs for people arrested for driving while intoxicated, and school settings. Involuntary group members are apt (at least initially) to be uninterested in participating and are sometimes hostile and disruptive.

Reference groups are those groups whose influence we are willing to accept. They are the ones with which we most closely identify. In the example given earlier, Tim Kelly is a member of a student body and his work group. Since he primarily identifies with his work group, the work group is a reference group for him while the student body, for all practical purposes, is not.

The groups we use as a reference have two distinct functions. First, the behavior, attitudes, and other characteristics of the members represent standards or comparison points that we use in making judgments and evaluations. Second, reference groups have a normative function in that we seek to conform to the standards for behavior and attitudes of our reference groups.

In a given group there are only some members who are referents for us. The referents are the people who influence us and who we, in turn, seek to influence. In a large group we normally have only a small subgroup of referents. These referents make sense to us, or they seem in contact with reality, or they are people we identify with, or they have most of the power. The other members we tend to "tune out" and interact with less.

STAGES IN GROUP DEVELOPMENT

Garland, Jones, and Kolodny (1965) developed a model that identifies five stages of development in social work groups. This model seeks to describe the kinds of problems that commonly arise as groups begin to form and continue to develop. Understanding of these problems, it is theorized, enables the designated leader to anticipate and respond to the reactions of group members more effectively. The conceptualization of Garland et al. (1965) appears particularly applicable to socialization groups, therapeutic groups, and encounter groups. To a lesser extent, the model is also applicable to self-help groups, problem-solving and decision-making groups, educational groups, and recreation skill groups.

Closeness (that is, the question of how near group members will allow themselves to come to one another emotionally) is the central focus of the model. The question of closeness is reflected in *struggles* that occur at five levels of growth of the group: (*a*) preaffiliation, (*b*) power and control, (*c*) intimacy, (*d*) differentiation, and (*e*) separation.

In the first stage, preaffiliation, members are ambivalent about joining the group. Interaction is guarded. Members test out, often through approach and avoidance behavior, whether they really want to belong to the group. New situations are often frightening, and the members seek on the one hand to protect themselves from being hurt or taken advantage of in such new situations. They attempt to maintain a certain amount of distance and to get what they can from the group without risking much of themselves. Individuals are aware that group involvement will make demands that may be frustrating or even painful. On the other hand, members are also attracted to the group because they generally have had prior rewards and satisfying social experiences in other groups, and this group offers the hope of similar rewards. In the first stage the leader should seek to increase the attractions toward the group "by allowing and supporting distance, gently inviting trust, facilitating exploration of the physical and psychological milieu, and by providing activities if necessary and initiating group structure" (Garland and Frey, 1973, p. 3). The first stage gradually ends when members come to feel fairly safe and comfortable with the group and view the rewards as being worth a tentative emotional commitment.

The second stage, power and control, emerges as the characteristics of the group begin to develop. Patterns of communication within the group emerge, alliances and subgroups begin to appear, members begin to take on certain roles and responsibilities, norms and methods for handling group tasks develop, and membership questions arise. Such processes are necessary for the group to conduct its business. However, these processes lead to a struggle of the members to establish their places within the group. Each member seeks power, partly for self-protection and partly to attempt to gain greater control over the gratifications and rewards to be received from the group. In this struggle, a major source of gratification is the group leader. The leader is perceived as having the greatest power to influence the direction of the group and to give or withhold emotional and material rewards. At this point members realize that the group is becoming important to them.

The second stage is a transitional stage with certain basic issues needing to be resolved: Does the group or the leader have primary control over the group's affairs? What are the limits of the power of the leader and of the group? To what extent will the leader use her power?

This uncertainty results in anxiety among group members and considerable testing by group members to gauge the limits and establish norms for the power and the authority of both the group and the group leader. Rebellion is not uncommon at this point, and the dropout rate in groups is often highest at this stage. During this struggle the leader should (*a*) seek to help the members understand the nature of the power struggle, (*b*) give emotional support to weather the discomfort of uncertainty, and (*c*) help the group establish norms to resolve the uncertainty. It is very important that group members develop trust in the leader so that the leader will maintain a safe balance of shared power and control. When this trust is achieved, group members make a major commitment to become involved in the group.

In the third stage, intimacy, the loves and dislikes of intimate relationships are expressed. The group becomes more like a family, with sibling rivalry between members being exhibited and the leader sometimes even being referred to as a parent. Feelings about the group at this stage are more openly expressed and discussed. The group is now viewed as a place where growth and change take place. Individuals feel free to examine and make efforts to change personal attitudes, concerns, and problems. Group tasks are also worked on during this stage, and there is a feeling of "oneness" or cohesiveness within the group. Struggle or turmoil during this stage leads the members to explore and make changes in their personal lives, and to examine "what this group is all about."

During the fourth stage, differentiation, there is increased freedom for members to experiment with new and alternative behavior patterns. There is a recognition of individual rights and needs and a high level of

communication among members. At this stage the group is able to organize itself more efficiently. Leadership is more evenly shared and roles are more functional. Power problems are now minimal, and decisions are made and carried out on a less emotional and more objective basis. Garland and Frey (1973, p. 5) note:

This kind of individualized therapeutic cohesion has been achieved because the group experience has all along valued and nurtured individual integrity. . . .

The worker assists in this stage by helping the group to run itself and by encouraging it to act as a unit with other groups or in the wider community. During this time the worker exploits opportunities for evaluation by the group of its activities, feelings, and behavior.

The differentiation stage is analogous to a healthy functioning family in which the children have reached adulthood and are now becoming successful in pursuing their own lives; relationships are more between equals, members are mutually supportive, and members are able to relate to each other in ways that are more rational and objective.

The final stage is separation. The purposes of the group have been achieved, and members have learned new behavioral patterns to enable them to move on to other social experiences. Termination is not always easily accomplished. Members may be reluctant to move on and may even display regressive behavior in an effort to prolong the safety of the group. Members may also express anger over ending the group or even psychologically deny the end is near. Garland and Frey (1973, p. 6) suggest the leader's (or worker's) role should be the following:

To facilitate separation the worker must be willing to let go. Concentration upon group and individual mobility, evaluation of the experience, help with the expression of the ambivalence about termination and recognition of the progress which has been made are his major tasks. Acceptance of termination is facilitated by active guidance of members as individuals to other ongoing sources of support and assistance.

It is common for leaders just beginning their work with groups to expect a smooth transition from one stage to another and to be disappointed if this does not come about. Additionally, many new practitioners, lacking experience and trust in the group process, tend to force the group out of one stage and into another. Experience will demonstrate the futility of such efforts. Barring unforeseen circumstances, each group will move at its own pace and will eventually arrive at the same destination. Groups that skip stages or whose development is otherwise thwarted will often return to a previous stage where business is yet unfinished. The leader can best facilitate group life by recognizing this and by allowing the natural process to evolve. While groups do sometimes become mired in one stage such occurrences are less common than feared.

TASK AND MAINTENANCE ROLES

All groups (whether organized for therapeutic reasons, for problem solving, or for other objectives) rely on the performance by members of a variety of roles. The needs of a group generally require that both task roles and group-building roles be performed satisfactorily. Task roles are those that are needed to accomplish the specific goals set by the group, while maintenance roles include those that serve to strengthen social/emotional aspects of group life (Pfeiffer and Jones, 1976). Though there are a wide variety of functional (positive) task roles that might be carried out, the most common are seeking or giving information and/or opinion, coordinating, summarizing, and proposing. Frequently encountered maintenance roles include encouraging others, establishing standards, and following and expressing group feeling. In some instances roles that assist the group in accomplishing its tasks while meeting its affective needs may be played. Examples are evaluating, diagnosing or assessing, mediating, reducing tension, and testing for consensus. At a given point in the life of all groups each of the above roles may be required; it is an effective group whose members (and leader) are sensitive to these needs.

Hersey and Blanchard (1977) have developed a situational theory of leadership that serves as a guideline for when effective leaders should focus on task behaviors, when they should focus on maintenance behaviors, and when they should focus on both. In essence, the theory asserts that when members have low maturity in terms of accomplishing a specific task, the leader should engage in high-task and low-maintenance behaviors. Hersey and Blanchard refer to this situation as *telling*, as the leader's behavior is most effective when the leader defines the roles of members and tells them how, when, and where to do needed tasks. The task maturity of members increases as their experience and understanding of the task increases. For moderately mature members, the leader should engage in high-task and high-maintenance behaviors. This combination of behaviors is referred to as *selling*, as the leader should not only provide clear direction as to role and task responsibilities, but should also use maintenance behaviors to get the members psychologically to buy into the decisions that have to be made.

Also, according to Hersey and Blanchard, when group members' commitment to the task increases, so does their maturity. When members are committed to accomplishing the task and have the ability and knowledge to complete the task, the leader should engage in low-task and high-maintenance behaviors, referred to as *participating*. Finally, for groups in which members are both willing and able to take responsibility for directing their own task behavior, the leader should engage in low-task and low-maintenance behaviors, referred to as *delegating*. Delegating allows members considerable autonomy in completing the task.

LEADERSHIP THEORY

There are at least three major approaches to leadership theory: trait, style, and distributed functions. Each of these approaches is briefly summarized below:

The Trait Approach

Aristotle observed, "From the hour of their birth some are marked for subjugation, and others for command"

(Johnson and Johnson, 1987, p. 39). As implied by this comment, the trait approach to leadership has been in existence for centuries. This approach assumes that leaders have personal characteristics or traits that make them different from followers. It also implies that leaders are born, not made, and that leaders emerge naturally rather than being trained. The trait approach has also been called the *great person* theory of leadership. Research studies on leadership have found the following.

Krech, Crutchfield, and Ballachey (1962) reviewed research studies on the traits needed by a leader. The results suggest a leader needs to be perceived (*a*) as a member of the group she is attempting to lead, (*b*) as having to a special degree the norms and values that are central to the group, (*c*) as being the most qualified group member for the task to be accomplished, and (*d*) as fitting the members' expectations about how she should behave and what functions she should serve.

Research on personality traits indicate leaders, compared to followers, tend to be better adjusted, more dominant, more extroverted, and more assertive; they often have greater interpersonal sensitivity. Other traits such as intelligence, enthusiasm, self-confidence, and equalitarianism are also frequently found to characterize leaders (Hare, 1962).

Although potential leaders tend to have more of all positive attributes than any of the members in the group, they cannot be so extreme that they become deviates. In one study, for example, Davie and Hare (1956) found that B students were the campus leaders, while the more intelligent A students were considered "grinds" who occasionally were treated as outcasts for being "curve wreckers." Also, the person who does most of the talking has been found to win most of the decisions and become the leader, unless he talks so much that he antagonizes the other group members (March, 1956).

Two postulated leadership traits that have received considerable attention are charisma and Machiavellianism. We will take a brief look at each of these traits.

CHARISMA   Johnson and Johnson (1987, p. 43) have defined charisma as "an extraordinary power, as of working miracles." Johnson and Johnson (1987, p. 44) give the following definition of a charismatic leader:

The charismatic leader must have a sense of mission, a belief in the social-change movement he or she leads, and confidence in oneself as the chosen instrument to lead the movement to its destination. The leader must appear extremely self-confident in order to inspire others with the faith that the movement he or she leads will, without fail, prevail and ultimately reduce their distress.

Some charismatic leaders appear to inspire their followers to love and be fully committed to them. Other charismatic leaders offer their members the hope and promise of deliverance from distress.

Charisma has not been precisely defined and its components have not been fully identified. The qualities and characteristics that any charismatic leader has will differ somewhat from those of other charismatic leaders. The following leaders all have been referred to as charismatic, yet they differed substantially in personality characteristics: John F. Kennedy, Martin Luther King, Jr., Julius Caesar, General George Patton, Confucius, Gandhi, and Winston Churchill.

One difficulty with the charisma approach to leadership is that people who are viewed as having charisma tend to express this quality in a variety of diverse ways. A second difficulty is that many leaders do well as leaders without being viewed as having charisma. For example, many group therapists are very effective in leading groups, even though they are not viewed as charismatic.

MACHIAVELLIANISM   Niccolò Machiavelli (1469–1527) was an Italian statesman who advocated the use of cunning, craft, deceit, and duplicity by rulers as political methods for increasing their power and control. (Machiavelli was not the originator of this approach as there were earlier theorists who conceptualized leadership in terms of manipulation for self-enhancement. However, the term *Machiavellianism* has become associated with the notion that politics is amoral and that any unscrupulous means can justifiably be used in achieving political power.) Machiavellian leadership is based on the concepts that followers (*a*) are basically fallible, gullible, untrustworthy, and weak; (*b*) are impersonal objects; and (*c*) should be manipulated in order for the leader to achieve his goals.

Christie and Geis (1970) concluded that Machiavellian leaders have four characteristics: (*a*) They have little emotional involvement in interpersonal relationships, as it is emotionally easier to manipulate others when others are viewed as impersonal objects. (*b*) They are not concerned about conventional morality and they take a utilitarian view (what they can get out of it) rather than a moral view of their interactions with others. (*c*) They have a fairly accurate perception of the needs of their followers — which facilitates their capacity to manipulate them. (*d*) They have a low degree of ideological commitment, as they focus on manipulating others for personal benefit rather than for achieving long-term ideological goals.

While a few leaders may have Machiavellian characteristics, most do not. Very few groups would ever function effectively or efficiently with Machiavellian leaders.

In recent years the trait theory of leadership has declined in popularity. Studies on the importance of leadership traits have often been inconclusive. The characteristics, for example, needed to be a good leader (such as a colonel or general in the military service) differ markedly from characteristics needed in many other leadership positions, such as being a good therapy group leader. Though such qualities as high intelligence and being well adjusted may have some correlation with leadership, it is obvious that many highly intelligent persons never get top leadership positions and that some leaders (such as Adolf Hitler and certain kings) have been emotionally unstable.

Trait research has shown that characteristics of leaders have also been found in followers, and that different leadership positions may require different leadership traits. The best rule for leader selection appears to be to select those individuals who have the necessary skills and who are motivated to help the group accomplish its goals.

The Style Approach

Because research on the trait approach was turning out contradictory results, Lewin, Lippitt, and White (1939) focused on examining leadership styles. These researchers described and studied three leadership styles: authoritarian, democratic, and laissez-faire.

Authoritarian leaders have more absolute power than democratic leaders. They alone set goals and policies, dictate the activities of the members, and set major plans. They are the purveyors of rewards and punishments, and they alone know the succession of future steps in the group's activities. In contrast, democratic leaders seek maximum involvement and participation of every member in all decisions affecting the group. They seek to spread responsibility rather than to concentrate it.

Authoritarian leadership is generally efficient and decisive. One of the hazards, however, is that group members may do what they are told out of necessity and not because of any commitment to group goals. The authoritarian leader who anticipates approval from subordinates for accomplishments achieved may be surprised to find backbiting and bickering common in the group. Unsuccessful authoritarian leadership is apt to generate factionalism, behind-the-scenes jockeying and maneuvering for position among members, and lead to a decline in morale.

Democratic leadership, in contrast, is slow in decision making and sometimes confusing but frequently proves to be more effective because of strong cooperation that generally emerges with participation in decision making. With democratic leadership, interpersonal hostilities between members, dissatisfactions with the leader, and concern for personal advancement all become issues that are discussed and acted upon. The danger of democratic leadership is that the private, behind-the-scenes complaining of the authoritarian approach becomes public conflict in a democratic approach. Once this public conflict has been resolved in a democratic group, a strong personal commitment develops which motivates members to implement group decisions rather than to subvert them. The potential for sabotage in an authoritarian group is high, and therein lies the advantage of the democratic style.

The democratic leader knows that some mistakes are inevitable, and that the group will suffer from them. Yet, such mistakes require the leader's ability to stand by without interfering because to do otherwise might harm the democratic process and impede the progress of the group in developing the capacity to make decisions as a group.

In some situations authoritarian leadership is most effective, while in others democratic leadership is most effective (Hare, 1962). As in any situation, the group will be more effective when members' expectations about the behavior appropriate for that situation are met. Where group members anticipate a democratic style, as they do in educational settings, classrooms, or discussion groups, the democratic style is usually found to produce the most effective group. When members antitipate forceful leadership from their superiors, as in industry or the military service, a more authoritarian form of leadership results in a more effective group.

In the laissez-faire style there is very little participation by the leader. The group members are primarily left to function (or flounder) with little input by the designated leader. There are a few conditions where group members function best under laissez-faire style (when the members are committed to a course of action, have the resources to implement it, and need a minimum of designated leader influence to work effectively). Because different leadership styles are required in different situations (even with the same group), research interest in recent years has switched to the distributed functions approach.

The Distributed Functions Approach

With this approach leadership is defined as the performance of acts that help the group reach its goals and maintain itself in good working order (Johnson and Johnson, 1975). Leadership functions include setting group goals, selecting and implementing tasks to achieve goals, and providing resources to accomplish goals. Leadership functions also include the group maintenance tasks of improving the group's cohesion and seeking to assure that individual members are satisfied. The functional approach to leadership seeks to discover what tasks are essential to achieve group goals under various circumstances and how different group members should take part in these actions.

A state capitol: The electoral process is a legitimizing agent for the people who enact the laws in our society.

This approach disagrees with the *great person* theory of leadership. It asserts that any member of a group will at times be a leader by taking actions that serve group functions. With this approach, leadership is viewed as being specific to a particular group in a particular situation. For example, telling a joke may be a useful leadership function in certain situations if it relieves tension, but telling a joke when other members are revealing intense personal feelings in a therapy group may be counterproductive and therefore not a leadership function.

The functional approach defines leadership as occurring whenever one member in a group influences other members to help the group reach its goals. Because at times all group members influence other group members, each member in a group exerts leadership. A difference exists in most groups between being a designated leader (such as a president or chairperson) and engaging in leadership behavior. A *designated leader* has certain responsibilities (such as calling meetings and leading the discussion), while the term *leadership* means one member is influencing other group members to help the group reach its goals.

The functional approach asserts that leadership is a learned set of skills that anyone with certain minimal requirements can acquire. Responsible membership is the same thing as responsible leadership, as both involve doing what needs to be done to help the group maintain itself and accomplish its goals. This approach asserts that people can be taught the skills and behaviors that help the group accomplish its tasks and maintain good working relationships. The implications of this theory for a social work practice course is that practically everyone in the class can learn to be an effective leader.

Like any member of a group, the designated leader may be called upon or may be forced to adopt one or more of the task specialist or maintenance specialist roles that have been discussed earlier in this chapter. Indeed, the leader has a special obligation to be alert for such occasions and to assume or to assist others to assume whichever roles are timely and appropriate. The leader's contribution to the group is not limited, however, by the assumption of specified roles. Each leader is responsible for a variety of functions that range from the performing of intake to the planning for termination. The needs and developmental stage of a group may at different times require a leader who can assume any of the previously described roles as well as those that follow:

- Executive (being the top coordinator of the activities of a group).
- Policymaker (establishing group goals and policies).
- Planner (deciding the means by which the group shall achieve its goals).

- Expert (serving as the source of readily available information and skills).
- External group representative (being the official spokesman for the group).
- Controller of internal relations (controlling the structure as a way to control in-group relations).
- Purveyor of rewards and punishments (determining promotions, demotions, and assigning pleasant or unpleasant tasks).
- Arbitrator and mediator (acting as both judge and conciliator with the power to reduce or to increase factionalism within the group).
- Exemplar (serving as a model of behavior to show what the members should be and do).
- Ideologist (serving as the source of the beliefs and values of the members).
- Scapegoat (serving as the target for ventilating members' frustrations and disappointments).

SOCIAL POWER BASES IN GROUPS

French and Raven (1968) have developed a framework for understanding the extent to which one member of a group has influence power over another. Five bases of power are identified: reward, coercive, legitimate, referent, and expert. Each of these power bases will be more fully described. This framework allows leaders of groups to analyze the source of their power and also presents suggestions to leaders on when, and when not, to use their power to influence others.

Power is often erroneously viewed negatively in human interactions. But all human interactions involve power. In groups it is natural and generally desirable that every member seek to influence other members to accomplish both personal goals and group goals.

Reward power is based on the perception of B (one member) that A (another member, or the entire group) has the capacity to dispense rewards or remove negative consequences in response to B's behavior.

The power will be greater the more the group members value the reward, and the more that members believe they cannot get the reward from anyone else. Rewards include such things as promotion, pay increases, days off, and praise. Group members will usually work hard for someone who has high reward power, will usually like the person, and will communicate effectively with him. But reward power can backfire if group members feel they are being conned or bribed into going along, which can lead to dislike of the high reward person. If reward power is used by A in a conflict situation with B, B is apt to feel he is being bribed and being controlled.

Coercive power is based on B's perception that A can dispense adverse consequences or remove positive consequences. Coercive power stems from the expectation of B that he will be punished by A if he fails to conform to A's wishes. The ability to fire a worker if he falls below a given level of production is a common example. The distinction between reward and coercive power is important as French and Raven note that reward power will tend to increase the attraction of B toward A, while coercive power will decrease this attraction. If coercive power is used by A to attempt to settle a conflict, it often increases B's hostility, resentment, and anger. Threats often lead to aggression and counterthreats. Thus, coercive power may exacerbate the conflict by leading both A and B to trust each other less and to seek to retaliate against each other. Therefore, whenever possible, coercive power should not be used in a conflict situation. (Unfortunately, it often is with the result that the conflict is exacerbated. For example, military threats often increase conflict between rival countries.)

Legitimate power is based on the perception by B that A has a legitimate right to prescribe behavior for him, and that B has an obligation to accept this influence. Legitimate power is probably the most complex of the five power bases. Legitimate power is based on some internalized value or norm. There are several bases for legitimate power. Cultural values constitute one common basis for legitimate power and include such things as intelligence, age, caste, and physical characteristics. For example, in some cultures the aged are highly respected and granted the right to prescribe

behavior for others. Acceptance of a social structure is another basis for legitimate power; for example, legitimate power in a formal organization is largely a relationship between positions rather than between persons. (An illustration in a factory would be the perceived right of a supervisor to assign work.) A third basis for legitimate power is a legitimizing agent; for example, the process of electing a group leader is a common method of legitimizing a person's right to a position that already has a legitimate range of power associated with it.

The areas in which legitimate power may be used are generally specified (e.g., in a job description) along with the designation of that power. The attempted use of power outside the range of legitimate power will decrease the legitimate power of the authority figure, and decrease attractiveness of the authority figure.

Referent power is based on B's identification with A. Identification in this context means either a feeling of oneness with A or a desire for such an identity. The stronger the identification of B with A, the greater the attraction to A and the greater the referent power of A. A verbalization of referent power is "I am like A, and therefore I will believe or behave as A does," or, "I want to be like A, and I will be more like A if I believe or behave as A does." In ambiguous situations B will seek to evaluate his thoughts, beliefs, and values in terms of what A thinks, believes, and values. In ambiguous situations B is apt to adopt the thoughts, beliefs, values of the individual or group with which B identifies. French and Raven note that B is often not consciously aware of the referent power that A exerts.

Expert power is based on the perception that A has some special knowledge or expertise. Accepting a physician's advice in medical matters is a common example of expert influence. Another would be accepting directions from a service station owner when in a strange city. For expert influence to occur it is necessary for B to think that A has the right answer, and for B to trust that A is telling the truth. A client accepting a suggestion by a counselor is another example of expert power. The range of expert power is more limited than that of referent power, as the expert is seen as having superior knowledge or ability in very specific areas. French and Raven (1968) note that the attempted exertion of expert power outside the perceived range of that power will reduce it, as an undermining of confidence seems to take place.

French and Raven (1968) theorize that for all five types, the stronger the basis of power, the greater the power. Referent power is thought to have the broadest range of power. Any attempt to use power outside the prescribed range is hypothesized to reduce the power.

PERSONAL GOALS AND GROUP GOALS

A goal is an end toward which an individual or a group of people are working. It is an ideal or a desired end point that people value. A personal goal is a goal held by a member. A group goal is one held by enough members of a group that the group can be said to be working toward its achievement.

All groups have goals, and every person who joins a group has personal goals. Groups generally have both short-range and long-range goals. The short-range goals should be stepping stones to reaching the long-range goals.

There are several reasons that it is very important to set group goals. The effectiveness and efficiency of the group (and group procedures) can be measured by the extent to which goals are achieved. Goals are guides that give direction to groups and to members of groups. Goals direct the programs and efforts of the group. Conflicts of opinions between group members are often resolved by making judgments as to which opinion is most helpful in achieving group goals. Group goals are a motivating force that stimulates members to work toward achieving these goals. Once members make a commitment to achieve a certain goal, these members will psychologically feel an obligation to put forth their abilities, efforts, and resources to attain this end.

The motivation of members to work toward accomplishing group goals is increased by involving group members in setting the goals. Through involvement members will (1) have a greater chance of having their personal goals for joining the group become a component of the group goals, (2) have an increased awareness of the importance of choosing these goals, and (3) feel a greater commitment to providing their resources to achieve the goals as they have had input in selecting the goals.

The more congruence there is between the personal goals of members and the goals of the group, the more attacted to the group the members are likely to be and the more willing the members are apt to be in providing their resources and energies to achieve the goals of the group. The personal goals of group members can be heterogeneous (different) or homogeneous (alike). The more homogeneous personal goals are, the more apt members are to agree on group goals and to work together toward achieving them. They also tend to be happier with the group when personal goals are homogeneous.

When members have heterogeneous personal goals, the more likely hidden agendas are to develop. A *hidden agenda* is a personal goal held by a member that is unknown to the other group members and that interferes with the group's accomplishing its group goals. Hidden agendas, at times, can be very destructive. For example, I have participated in some groups where an individual sought to observe the comments and actions of others in order to obtain evidence to bring legal harassment charges. Usually, however, hidden agendas are less destructive. For example, a lonely person who enjoys talking may slow down a group in reaching its goals by monopolizing the "air time" with insignificant small talk.

Because hidden agendas can severely hamper a group, it is important that a group seek to set group goals that incorporate the personal goals of the members. With such a focus, hidden agendas are apt to be minimized.

Still, it should be remembered that all groups work on two levels: the surface task and the hidden needs and motivations. Although hidden agendas siphon off energy, they are a reflection of individual needs and may (or may not) even be known to the person who holds them. All members join groups with the intention of meeting their personal needs. Sometimes after initial needs are met, other, less obvious needs surface.

Such needs are not selfish but are normal and expected. The real issue is the effect these needs have on the rest of the group. The important question is whether meeting A's needs will prevent B (or the rest of the group) from satisfying their needs. The goal is to find a means to legitimize the individual's needs in ways that allow for effective problem solving.

Managing hidden agendas requires that members and the designated leader be on the lookout for them and support members who try to bring hidden agendas to the surface. One such approach might involve the leader's saying "I wonder if we've said all that we feel about this idea. Perhaps we should go around the room once more and see whether anyone has anything to add." At the same time, the leader and other members should be aware that some hidden agendas might best be left hidden. Frequently it is best not to criticize a member for having a hidden agenda, since doing so often creates defensiveness and inhibits problem solving.

CONFORMITY

There have been some classic studies that have examined conforming behavior. Sherif (1936) examined what has been called the autokinetic effect. In this experiment subjects are first placed in a darkened room and asked to judge how far a dot of light moves. Although the light appears to move (the autokinetic effect) it actually does not. Each subject sees the dot of light and makes a series of individual judgments as to how far the light moves. The subjects are then brought together in groups of about three to judge again how far the light moves. In this situation, their judgments tend to converge to a group standard. Later, when they again view the light alone, they tend to retain the group standard and give that answer. The essential finding is that when a situation is ambiguous and there is no objective way of determining the "right" answer, members rely on the group to help define reality. In real life this means membership in a group determines for individuals many of the things they will see, learn, think about, and do.

FIGURE 7.1

Cards in Asch Conformity Studies

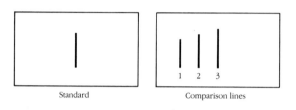

Standard   Comparison lines

Asch (1955) also examined conforming behavior. Asch investigated what happens when an individual's judgment conflicts with the judgments of other group members. The experiments were designed as follows. There were two sets of cards, such as shown in Figure 7.1. Subjects from psychology classes who volunteered for the experiment were arranged in groups of seven to nine. They were seated at a table and asked to state in turn, starting at the left, which line was closest in length to the standard. In the control groups practically all the subjects chose line two. The experimental groups, however, were the ones of greatest interest. In the experimental groups all of the group members, except for one subject, were accomplices of the experimenter. The subject was always seated at the end of the line (or near the end of the line) for giving his judgment. The accomplices all chose the same incorrect line. When it came to the subject's turn, he was then faced with relying on his individual judgment or conforming to what the group was erroneously saying. In a variety of studies similar to this, Asch found that over one third of the subjects conformed to the group judgment. Such a large conformity is amazing as there was no overt group pressure to conform, the situation was not ambiguous, and the subjects did not know each other. In addition, there was no promise of future favor or advancement, nor was there any threat of ostracism or punishment.

Conformity is the yielding to group pressure. For there to be conformity there must be conflict — conflict between the influences being exerted by the group and those forces in an individual that tend to lead a person to value, believe, and act in some other way. For a member experiencing such conflict there are two available options: announce his own independent decision, or conform by announcing agreement with the group's position. Conforming can take two forms: The expedient conformer outwardly agrees but inwardly disagrees. The true conformer both outwardly and inwardly comes to agree with the group.

A number of conclusions have arisen from conformity research (Krech et al., 1962, pp. 509–12).

1. Considerable amounts of yielding are produced by group pressure, even when the bogus group consensus to which the person conforms is obviously wrong. In one study, for example, a sample of fifty military officers were asked to indicate which of two figures, a star and a circle presented side by side, were larger in area. The circle was clearly about one third larger, but under group pressure 46 percent of the men agreed with the bogus group consensus.

2. Many people can be pressured into yielding on attitude and opinion items, even those having significant personal implications for them. For example, fifty military officers were asked privately and then later under bogus group consensus the question: "I doubt whether I would make a good leader." In private none of the officers expressed agreement, but under unanimous group pressure, 37 percent expressed agreement.

3. Yielding is far greater on difficult, subjective items than on easy, objective ones.

4. There are extremely large individual differences in yielding. A few people yield on almost all items; a few yield on none; most people yield on some and not on others.

5. When people are retested individually and privately on the same items some time later, a major part of the yielding effect disappears as the person tends to revert to his own unchanged private judgment. Yet, a small part of the yielding effect does remain, indicating group pressure does have a lasting effect on changing attitudes.

6. As a group increases in size, the pressure for yielding increases, and more yielding occurs. When a person is opposed by a single other person, there is very little yielding.

7. Yielding is markedly reduced when a person has the support of one other person (a partner) in the group. Apparently a dissident opinion has a tremendous effect in strengthening the independence of like-minded people.

In a dramatic study involving conformity Milgram (1963) demonstrated that subjects in an experimental situation would administer electric shocks of dangerous strength to another person when instructed to do so by the experimenter. (The other person unknown to the subject did not actually receive the electrical shocks.) Most of the subjects complied with the experimenter's commands, even when they were instructed to give increasingly strong shocks to the victim, in spite of the victim's protests and cries of anguish. This series of studies on obedience demonstrated that people will yield to "authoritative" commands even when the behavior is incompatible with their own moral, normal standards of conduct. Milgram suggested his studies help us understand why the German people complied with the unethical commands of Hitler. Group pressures, especially when viewed as authoritative, have a tremendous effect on a person's actions, attitudes, and beliefs.

Stanley Schacter (1959) has developed a theory of social comparison. Schacter assumed that everyone has a need to evaluate the "rightness" of his or her feelings, opinions, values, and attitudes. It was also assumed that everyone has a need to evaluate the extent of his or her abilities. Schacter then theorized and conducted studies to demonstrate that in the absence of objective, nonsocial means of evaluation, a person will rely on other people as comparison points of reference. To a large extent, the groups we belong to define social reality for us. For most of our opinions, values, beliefs, and abilities, there is no objective, nonsocial way to evaluate ourselves, so we rely on others.

Idiosyncratic Credits

Every member of a group gains credits (and rises in status) by showing competence and by conforming to the expectations applicable to her time. Eventually these credits allow a person to break norms and rules of the group without being chastised. To some extent, after credits have been accumulated, nonconformity to general procedures or expectations serves as a confirming feature of one's status. Yet there is a limit on the number of earned idiosyncratic credits. Nonconformity beyond this limit will result in a dramatic decrease in status and perhaps even rejection by the other group members (Hollander, 1958).

COMPETITIVE AND COOPERATIVE GROUPS

Groups basically have either a cooperative or a competitive group atmosphere. In a cooperative group there is open and honest communication, trust, pooling of resources, and cohesion. Research has found a number of positive consequences for a cooperative group atmosphere in problem-solving groups. Cooperation among members increases creativity, coordination of effort, division of labor, emotional involvement in group accomplishment, helping and sharing, interpersonal skills, cooperative attitudes and values, positive self-attitudes, liking among group members, positive attitudes toward the group and tasks, divergent thinking, acceptance of individual and cultural differences, and problem-solving skills (Johnson and Johnson, 1975, p. 88).

A cooperative group atmosphere results when the personal goals of group members are perceived to be compatible, identical, or complementary. An example of a highly cooperative group is a successful basketball team in which the main goal of each member is to win, and the main goal of the team is to win. In a cooperative group each member seeks to coordinate her efforts with those of other group members in order to achieve the goals of the group. In establishing a cooperative atmosphere, it is important that rewards to members be based upon the quantity and quality of group performance rather than upon individual performance.

In contrast, a competitive atmosphere in a group can be very detrimental and destructive. A competitive atmosphere exists when the members perceive their personal goals to be incompatible, different, conflicting, or mutually exclusive. In a highly competitive group, a member can achieve her goal only if the other group members fail to obtain their goals (Deutsch, 1949). An example of a group that is structured to be competitive is a group interview that is held for several applicants for a position vacancy. In a competitive group each member seeks to accomplish her goals, while seeking to block other group members from accomplishing their goals. The consequences of competition in problem-solving groups are numerous. Competition decreases creativity, coordination of effort, division of labor, helping and sharing, and cohesion. Competition promotes ineffective communication, suspicion and mistrust, high anxiety about goal accomplishments, competitive values and attitudes, negative self-attitudes, dislike among group members, and negative attitudes toward the group and its tasks. Competition encourages rejection of differences of opinion, divergent thinking, and cultural and individual differences. A competitive atmosphere leads to low effectiveness in solving complex problems (Johnson and Johnson, 1975, p. 97).

Kelly and Stahelski (1970) examined the question of what happens when a competitive person joins a group that has a cooperative atmosphere. Since cooperative groups are much more effective in problem solving than competitive groups, the question is significant. Three consequences were found to occur. The competitive behavior of the new member leads the other members to behave competitively. The competitive person views the former cooperative members as having always been competitive. The former cooperative members are generally aware their competitive behavior is largely a consequence of the new member's competitiveness. Thus, it appears that one competitive person can change a cooperative group into a competitive group. Why does a competitive person have such a strong, destructive effect? Apparently what happens is that the cooperative members realize the competitive person will, if given a chance, take advantage of their cooperativeness and use it to his own personal advantage. In many situations their only recourse to prevent exploitation is to also become competitive. Thus it appears that while cooperation is by far the most effective atmosphere in problem-solving groups, it takes only one competitive person to change the atmosphere of the group to a competitive one. If a cooperative group is to survive, it is important that new members have an orientation compatible with that of other members of the group.

CONTROVERSY AND CREATIVITY

Controversy is a debate, dispute, or discussion involving differences in beliefs, information, opinions, ideas, or assumptions. Controversy in groups is natural. If handled constructively, controversy will increase creativity, increase involvement of members, and lead to high-quality decisions. Emotional reactions to controversy may be positive (curiosity, liking for other members, excitement, exhilaration, stimulation, involvement, commitment) or negative (frustration, disgust, anger, fear, resentment, rejection, distrust, apathy, paranoia), depending on how the group handles the controversy.

Different people react differently to controversy. Some people shy away from it. Others take a difference of opinion personally and become hurt or angered. Others find controversy to be stimulating and fun; they hope to find a little each day. Still others view controversy as a way for each side to express themselves, ventilate concerns, and work out differences.

Controversy has many values for a group. When handled effectively in groups, controversy encourages inquiry, stimulates interest and curiosity, sharpens analysis, and promotes objectivity. It also increases commitment of members to the group, and improves the problem-solving processes of the group. It stimulates members to search for new and better alternatives and to synthesize suggested alternatives into higher quality decisions. Through controversy members often reassess and clarify their values and beliefs and grow as people. Through learning how to resolve interpersonal conflicts, members may also learn how to become better managers of their internal conflicts.

On the other hand, some groups do not manage controversy well. Ineffective groups tend to suppress and withdraw from controversy. They have group norms that urge members to suppress conflicts and to agree outwardly even when some members believe the group is making a serious mistake. When controversy does arise in ineffective groups, the members are apt to view the opposing positions in terms of "right versus wrong" or "we versus they."

THE WIN-LOSE APPROACH VERSUS THE PROBLEM-SOLVING APPROACH

Ineffective groups are apt to view resolutions of controversy between opposing positions as being *win-lose situations*. We live in a very competitive society where in many fields (such as sports, business, and politics) individuals or teams are pitted against each other. In groups, destructive controversies are often cast in the "win-lose" mold. Members interrupt each other to sell their positions without really listening to what the other person is saying. Power blocs are formed to support one position against proponents of another. The original goals and objectives of the group may fade into the background as seeking to win on issues becomes the objective of the warring sides.

In win-lose situations, each side denies the legitimacy of the other side's interests and concerns. Each side is concerned only about its own needs. Each side seeks to muster support and power for its position in order to defeat the other side.

In win-lose situations the group often winds up losing in terms of failing to achieve its long-range goals and objectives. The side that loses on an issue has little motivation to provide its resources to carry out the actions of the winning side. It resents the winner and may continue to seek to reverse the decision or to impede the implementation of the decision. Distrust increases among opposite sides, communication becomes more limited and inaccurate, and cohesion or togetherness of the group decreases. Often members develop unre-solved feelings (or gunnysacks full of grievances) that result in biased judgments and actions. In win-lose sit-uations members frequently refuse to vote for a good idea because they dislike the person who suggested it. Conflict in win-lose situations leads to the denial or distortion of unpleasant facts and information. It leads to blind spots in which members misinterpret the ideas and actions of members perceived as being op-ponents. It leads to disagreement being interpreted as personal rejection by some or all group members. It leads to decisions that are of low quality and often in-correct. It increases group tension.

A more effective approach to use in resolving con-flicts is the *problem-solving approach*. Effective groups generally use this approach. With a problem-solving approach members attempt to find a mutually satisfy-ing course of action. Members tend to listen to each other, to recognize the legitimacy of one another's in-terests, and to influence one another with rational ar-guments. Instead of a competitive orientation, the problem-solving approach functions in an atmosphere of cooperation among group members.

The steps in the problem-solving approach can be summarized as follows:

Step 1: The needs of each person or subgroup are identified and defined.

Step 2: Alternative solutions are generated.

Step 3: The alternative solutions are evaluated.

Step 4: A highly evaluated solution that is accept-able to practically everyone is selected.

Step 5: The solution is implemented.

Step 6: There is follow-up to evaluate how well the selected solution is working.

Adjusting win-lose situations so that the outcome is win-win is the goal of members and leaders committed to effective problem solving. It is very difficult for any one person to redirect a win-lose situation and usually a significant segment of the membership is needed to accomplish this goal. There are several means to this end. First it is important to have clear goals which all members understand and agree to. Issues that arise in a win-lose situation should be tested against the goals to determine whether they really are relevant to the

group's functioning. Being on the alert for win-lose sit-uations is important also. When a member feels that she is being attacked by others or feels herself lining up support for a particular position the likelihood is that a win-lose situation is developing.

Of course, active listening (see Chapter 22) often is effective in these situations. The listener can be empa-thic, listen to the other's reasoning (and perhaps be persuaded), and at least understand the other's posi-tion. When responding to other members' positions, it is better to suggest alternatives than say, "This is the only intelligent way to do this." As we have seen in the preceding chapter, arriving at decisions through a consensus model rather than majority-minority voting tends to be more effective and reduces the win-lose nature of some group debates. Finally, it is important to test whether compromises or consensus agreements actually are accepted by all members. This is best de-termined by polling all group members in turn, asking whether they have anything they would like to add to the discussion. The key for resolving win-lose situa-tions is to try for a solution that is best for all members rather than attempting to get one's own way.

A cooperative, problem-solving atmosphere in a group has a number of payoffs. It increases the chances of finding a high-quality solution. It increases the com-mitment of all the group members to support and im-plement the group's decisions. It increases trust and reduces hostility among group members. It increases communication and cohesion. It increases each mem-ber's satisfaction with the group. It increases the chances of the group's achieving its long-range goals and objec-tives. It leads group members to interact together with fewer inhibitions. It sets up an atmosphere in which members can freely express and work out their frustra-tions and concerns. (If such frustrations are not ex-pressed, they often fester and snowball, resulting in in-creased apathy and disengagement from the group.) The problem-solving approach keeps arguments fo-cused on the present, as past conflicts have been worked out. It improves relationships with other group members and leads to greater understanding of self and others.

A cooperative, problem-solving approach in a group promotes creativity. Creativity is a process of bringing something new into existence. Creativity results from productive controversy, as the problem is viewed from new perspectives, new alternatives are suggested, and a new synthesis of alternatives is formulated for resolving the problem.

HANDLING DISRUPTIVE BEHAVIOR

There may be hostile or disruptive members in any group, even in groups whose members come voluntarily. Hostile or noncooperative members are, however, more likely to be found in involuntary groups. Involuntary groups are those whose members are forced to come. Involuntary members often (at least at the initial meetings of the group) wish they were a thousand other places rather than in the group. They may be angry because they are forced to come and may believe the time spent in the group will be a "complete waste of time."

There are various settings where social workers encounter involuntary clients: corrections, protective services, mental health facilities, certain public school settings, group homes, residential treatment facilities, nursing homes, and hospitals. In such settings, groups may be established which unwilling clients are required to attend and social workers are expected to lead. Disruptive behavior includes aggressiveness, competing, fooling around, sympathy seeking, and failing to finish tasks on time.

There are three main ways a designated leader might handle hostile and disruptive behavior: (1) allowing members to continue to be disruptive while seeking to ignore or minimize the effects of the disruptive behavior; (2) confronting members about their disruptive behavior; and (3) having other group members besides the leader confront the disruptive members. Each of these ways will be briefly discussed. The approach chosen should be based on a judgment as to which will be most helpful to the group in handling the disruptive behavior.

1.   Allowing the member to continue to express the disruptive behavior is often effective. Such expression

has a ventilating effect, so the member may become less disruptive as time goes on. When a member is disruptive it is often helpful to tactfully ask the member to express concerns that he has. Interviewing the member and modeling good listening skills while reflecting feelings expressed by the person often helps to defuse a disruptive situation. In certain instances there may be benefit in using a role reversal in which the disrupter is asked to argue the alternate point of view with the designated leader taking the disrupter's position. Whenever possible disruption should be dealt with as a group issue, and the group may, in fact, decide to deal with at least some of the disrupter's concerns, especially those that are legitimate. Through resolution of some of these concerns, the disruptive group member may become less unhappy and begin to see that the group has some payoffs for him.

2.   The designated group leader may assertively confront the member about how his behavior is disrupting the group. This confrontation may take place with other group members present or the group leader may meet privately with the disruptive member. The choice of whether to confront privately or with other members present should be based on a judgment as to which will be most beneficial. If other members are present, they may be able to help by elaborating on the ways in which the member's behavior is proving disruptive. Also, having others present emphasizes the seriousness of the problem. A disadvantage of confronting when others are present is that the hostile member may feel ganged up on and may be more inhibited in fully expressing what he is unhappy about. In some instances simply indicating to the member in private that you are concerned about his behavior and are considering opening it up as a matter of discussion for the entire group will help the member to reconsider whether the disruptions are accomplishing the desired purpose.

3.   The third approach is to have a member other than the designated leader do the confronting. There are certain situations in which the confrontation is best handled by someone other than the leader. For example, another member may have better rapport with the disruptive member than the designated leader, and therefore the disruptive member may be more re-

sponsive if the confrontation comes from the neutral member.

Any of these approaches may prove fruitful. It is important to realize that conflict and differences in opinion are not uncommon or unnatural in groups, and may, in fact, be healthy. It is therefore in the interests of the group not to use the techniques noted above to stifle debate and differences but to reserve them for situations that threaten the effective continuation of the group.

GROUP SIZE

The size of a group has effects on members' satisfactions, interactions, and output per member. Smaller groups are often rated more favorably (Hare, 1962). Larger groups tend to create more stress, have more communication difficulties, and although successful in some tasks because of the greater number of skills available, are generally less efficient or productive. In larger groups each person has less opportunity to talk, and some people feel inhibited and reluctant to talk. In discussion groups it has been shown that as the size of the group increases, the most frequent contributor assumes an increasingly prominent role in the discussion. The bigger the group, the greater the gap in amount of participation between the most frequent contributor and other members of a group.

Slater (1958) found in one study that groups of five persons were considered most satisfactory by group members themselves. Observations of the interactions of groups of a size smaller than five indicated the members were inhibited from expressing their ideas through fear of alienating one another and thereby destroying the group. Above the size of five, members felt restrictions on participating.

Groups of two members tend to avoid expressing disagreement and antagonism. This size also has high-tension levels as each member is more "on the spot," as each is forced to react to what the other says. If a dispute arises in such a group, it becomes deadlocked as there is no majority and the group may break up.

Groups of even size tend to have higher rates of disagreement and antagonism than odd-size groups, apparently because of the possible division of the group into two subdivisions of equal size.

Groups of three members have problems of the power of the majority over the minority; that is, a two to one split leaves the minority feeling isolated.

To sum up, it appears probable that for any given task there is an optimal group size. The more complex the task, the larger the optimum size to assure the greater number of needed abilities and skills.

STARTING, LEADING, AND ENDING THERAPY GROUPS[1]

Extensive preparation is needed for leading therapeutic groups. The leader should have considerable training in (a) assessing human behavior and human problems; (b) comprehensive therapeutic intervention approaches—such as reality therapy, behavior therapy, rational therapy, transactional analysis, and client-centered therapy (see Chapters 14–19); (c) specialized therapeutic intervention techniques—such as assertiveness training and relaxation techniques (see Chapter 22); (d) interviewing and counseling; and (e) principles of group dynamics—such as cohesion, task roles, social-emotional roles, and effects of authoritarian versus democratic styles of leadership. Baccalaureate and master's programs in social work generally provide considerable material on these areas. For any therapy group, the leader also needs to study the literature on the causes of the problems that the members are experiencing, the most effective intervention strategies for these problems, the prognosis for positive changes, and expectations as to the length of time

---

[1]Material in this section is adapted from Charles Zastrow, "Starting and Leading Therapy Groups: A Beginner's Guide," *Journal of Independent Social Work*, 4, no. 4, 1990, pp. 7–26. Adapted by permission of the Haworth Press.

the intervention strategies need to be applied to induce positive changes.

This section summarizes a number of guidelines for starting, leading, and ending therapy groups. Chapter 6 has covered substantial material on the following aspects of leading groups: preparation and homework, relaxing before starting a session, cues upon entering the meeting room, seating arrangements, introductions, and clarifying roles. This material is directly applicable to therapy groups and will not be repeated here. (Students learning how to lead therapy groups should review this material.) This section will focus on building rapport, exploring problems in depth, exploring alternative solutions, ending a session, and ending a group.

Building Rapport

In group therapy, as in individual therapy, there are two types of members—voluntary and involuntary. In voluntary groups, the therapist can take a more casual, less directive approach to begin with. In such groups the therapist may begin by involving members in small talk. This preliminary chitchat may be about the weather, parking problems, baseball, something currently in the news, and so on. Such casual conversation has the advantage of letting group members become acquainted with the therapist and the other group members.

In involuntary groups, the therapist may begin by introducing herself and making a formal statement about the purpose of the group. Then members may be asked to introduce themselves. Generally, in involuntary groups, less is left up to the members themselves since they have less motivation for being there and less commitment to the group itself.

Sometimes with both voluntary and involuntary clients it is helpful (after introductions) to begin a session with providing some factual information. This can be done by a brief presentation by the group leader, or by showing a short film or videotape. For example, if the group members are involuntary clients who have been convicted of operating a motor vehicle while intoxicated, the leader may choose to show a film that vividly demonstrates that as alcohol consumption increases, reaction times slow and the chances of serious accidents occurring dramatically increases. Such factual information is designed not only to provide educational material, but to also serve as a trigger to ignite a discussion. Sometimes after factual information is presented it is useful to involve the group members in an exercise related to the factual material.

When members are forced to attend a group they do not want to attend, as is the case with involuntary clients, the group leader may begin by saying something like, "I know most of you really don't want to be here, and I wouldn't either if I were forced to come. I wonder if we might begin by talking about your anger and unhappiness about being here?" Then the group leader should attempt to convey the purposes of the group, what is going to happen, and how the members can satisfy the minimal requirements of "passing." The group leader can mention that each member can (1) choose to participate actively and get as much out of the group as possible, (2) remain silent and listen to what others have to say, (3) vent their anger and unhappiness in disruptive ways (which will probably anger and alienate others in the group), or (4) refuse to come, which will have certain consequences. The group leader can then indicate that he can in no way control their behavior, so the choice among these alternatives is up to each member. Such an approach almost always leads the involuntary clients to choose either the first or second alternative, perhaps because such an approach leads these clients to conclude that the leader is understanding of their anger—and they then focus on making the most constructive choice.

If the group has met previously, the leader may choose to begin by bringing up for discussion a topic that was not fully discussed at the last meeting. Or, if homework assignments were given to some members the leader may begin by saying, "Jim, at the last meeting you indicated you were going to do (such and such). How did that work out?"

The therapist should try to establish a nonthreatening group atmosphere in which the members feel accepted and safe enough to communicate their troubles fully. During the initial contacts, the therapist needs to "sell" herself (but not arrogantly) as a knowledgeable, understanding person who may be able to help and who wants to try. The tone of the therapist's voice should convey the message that she understands and cares about group members' feelings. The therapist should be calm and never laugh or express shock when members begin to open up about problems. Emotional outbursts, even if subtle, will lead group members to believe that the therapist is not going to understand or accept their difficulties, and so they will usually stop discussing them.

A therapist should view group members as equals. New therapists sometimes make the mistake of thinking that because someone is sharing her intimate secrets with them, they must be very important, and end up assuming a superior position vis-à-vis their clients. If members feel that they are being treated as inferiors, they will be less motivated to reveal and discuss personal issues.

The therapist should use a "shared vocabulary" with the members. This does not mean that the therapist should use the same slang and the same accent as group members. If clients perceive the therapist is mimicking their speech patterns, they may feel seriously offended. In order to communicate effectively, the therapist should use words that members understand and do not find offensive.

The therapist (and other members) need to keep what members say confidential. Unfortunately, many people have nearly irresistible urges to share "juicy secrets" with someone else. If a group member discovers that confidentiality has been violated that member's trust in the group will be quickly destroyed. It is essential that the therapist explain the importance of "what is said in the group, remains in the group."

Exploring Problems in Depth

In exploring a member's problems in depth, the therapist and group members need to examine such areas as the extent of the problem, how long the problem has existed, what the causes are, how the member feels about the problem, and what physical and mental capacities and strengths the member has to cope with the difficulty, prior to exploring alternative solutions.

A problem area is often multidimensional; that is, there are usually a number of problems that are involved. Explore all these. A good way to decide which

problem to handle first is to ask the group member which problem she perceives as most pressing. If it can be solved, start with exploring that problem in depth and together develop a solution. Success in solving one problem will increase each group member's confidence in the leader, and thereby further solidify rapport.

Therapists should convey empathy, not sympathy, and encourage group members to do so, too. Empathy is the capacity to understand and to share in another person's feelings. Sympathy also involves sharing feelings, but it results in offering pity. The difference is subtle, but empathy usually encourages problem-solving, while sympathy usually encourages group members to dwell on their problems without taking action to improve the situation. For example, if a leader offers sympathy to a person who is frustrated and angry about someone ending a romantic relationship with him, that person will keep telling his sad story over and over, each time having an emotional outpouring reinforced by the leader's sympathy, without taking any action to improve the situation. Telling the story over and over only reopens old wounds and prolongs the anger and frustration.

Therapists should "trust their guts." The most important resources that a therapist has are her own feelings and perceptions. A therapist should continually strive to place herself in members' shoes, understanding that their values and pressures may be different from her own. It probably never happens that a group leader is 100 percent on target in her appraisal of a client's pressures, problems and perspectives, but 70 to 80 percent is usually sufficient to allow the therapist to be helpful. Empathizing is very useful in helping the therapist to determine what additional areas may need to be explored, what she should say, and in figuring out possible solutions.

When a therapist believes that a client has touched upon an important area of concern, further communication can be encouraged in a number of ways. Showing interest nonverbally (by making and continuing eye contact, leaning forward, and raising eyebrows slightly) encourages further sharing. Allowing for pauses is important. New therapists usually become anxious when there is a pause and hasten to say something—anything—to have conversation continue. This is usually a mistake, especially when it leads to a change in the topic. Although a pause will often make the group member anxious, it gives him time to think about what areas of concern are most important and then usually motivates him to continue conversation in that area.

Neutral probes that do not control the direction of conversation but encourage further communication are helpful. For example, "Could you tell me more about it?" "Why do you feel that way?" and "I'm not sure I understand what you have in mind" all ask for further information, but just what kind is left up to the member. Reflecting feelings—for example, "You seem angry" or "You appear to be depressed about that"—works that same way. Summarizing what a group member is saying not only shows that you are listening but also that you have received the same message the group member sent. An example is, "During this past hour, you made a number of critical comments about your spouse; it sounds like you're fairly unhappy about certain aspects of your marriage."

Socially unacceptable topics should be approached tactfully. Tact is an essential quality of a competent therapist. Try not to ask a question in such a way that the answer will put the respondent in an embarrassing position.

When pointing out a limitation that a group member has, mention and compliment him on any assets. When a limitation is being mentioned, the person will literally feel that something is being laid bare or taken away. Therefore, compliment him in another area to give something back.

A competent therapist will generally watch for nonverbal cues and use them to identify a sensitive subject, as the client will generally display anxiety by a changing tone of voice, fidgeting, yawning, stiff posture, or a flushed face.

The therapist should be honest. An untruth always runs the risk of being discovered. If that happens, the group member's confidence in the therapist will be damaged and the relationship seriously jeopardized. But being honest goes beyond not telling lies. The therapist should always point out those shortcomings that are in the group member's best interest to correct. For example, if a father's negative comments to his son

are a factor in the son developing a negative self-concept (which is partly responsible for the son receiving failing grades at school), this should be brought to the father's attention.

Exploring Alternative Solutions

After a problem is explored in depth, the next step is for the therapist and group members to consider alternative solutions. The therapist's role is generally to begin by asking something like "Have you thought about ways to resolve this?" The merits, shortcomings, and consequences of the alternatives thought of by the member should then be tactfully and thoroughly examined. Next, the therapist should seek to involve other group members by asking them if they are aware of other alternatives that may work for this situation. Those members who do suggest alternatives temporarily assume a "helper" role. In such a role the "helper therapy" principle is operating as a member receives psychological rewards from helping others. If the therapist has additional viable alternatives to suggest, she should mention these at this time. The merits, shortcomings, and consequences of the alternatives suggested by other group members and by the therapist should then be thoroughly explored.

Group members usually have the right to self-determination, that is, to choose a course of action among possible alternatives. The therapist's role is to help each individual clarify and understand the likely consequences of each available alternative but generally not to give advice or choose the alternative for him. If the therapist were to select the alternative, there are two possible outcomes: (1) the alternative may prove to be undesirable for the group member, in which case he will probably blame the therapist for the advice and their future relationship will be seriously hampered, or (2) the alternative may prove to be desirable for the person involved. This immediate outcome is advantageous, but the danger is that the group member will then become overly dependent on the therapist, seeking the therapist's advice for nearly every decision in the future and generally being reluctant to make decisions on his own.

Group therapy is done *with* group members, not *to* or *for* them. Each member should have responsibility for doing many of the tasks necessary to improve a situation. A good rule to follow is that each member should take responsibility for those tasks that he has the capacity to carry out. Doing things *for* group members, similar to giving advice, brings with it the risk of creating a dependent relationship. Furthermore, successful accomplishments of tasks by clients leads to personal growth and better prepares them for taking on future responsibilities.

A group member's right to self-determination should be taken away only if the selected course of action has a high probability of seriously hurting the client or others. For example, if it is highly probable that a group member may attempt to take his life, the therapist should intervene (for example, making arrangements for the member to receive inpatient psychiatric care if the risk of suicide is high), even if the intervention is a course action that the group member objects to. For most situations, however, the group member should have the right to select an alternative, even when the therapist believes that another course of action is better. Frequently, a client is in a better position to know what is best for himself, and if it turns out not to be the best, he will probably learn from the mistake.

When a group member does select an alternative, he should clearly understand what the goals will be, what tasks need to be carried out, how to accomplish the tasks, and who will do them. Frequently, it is desirable to write a "contract" for future reference, with a time limit set for the accomplishment of each task.

If a group member fails to meet the terms of a contract, the therapist should not criticize him or accept excuses. Excuses let people off the hook; they provide temporary relief, but they eventually lead to more failure and to a failure identity. Simply ask, "Do you still wish to try to fulfill your commitment?" If the person answers affirmatively, another time deadline acceptable to the member should be set.

Perhaps the biggest single factor in determining whether a group member's situation will improve is his motivation to carry out essential tasks. A therapist should try to motivate apathetic group members. One way to increase a member's motivation is to clarify what will be gained by meeting a goal. When individuals meet commitments, therapists should reward them, verbally or in other ways. Never criticize members for failing. Criticism usually increases hostility and rarely leads to positive lasting change. Also, criticism serves as only a temporary means of obtaining different behavior; when a person no longer believes that he is under surveillance, he will usually return to the destructive behavior.

If a group member lacks confidence or experience, it may be helpful to role-play a task before actually attempting it. For example, if a male member wants help in telling his partner that he no longer is "in love" with her and wants to end the relationship, role-playing the situation within the group will assist the male in selecting words and developing a strategy for informing his partner. The therapist or another group member can first play the male's role and model an approach, letting the male play the partner's role. Then, the roles should be reversed so that the male practices telling his partner.

Ending a Session

Ending is not always easy. Ideally, the therapist and group members should accept the fact that the session is ending and subjects being discussed should not be left hanging in the middle. Abrupt endings are apt to be perceived by the group members as being discourteous and rejecting.

There are some useful guidelines on how to terminate a therapy session. Preparation for ending the session should be initiated at the very beginning of the session. The members should be explicitly informed the time the session will end. Unless an unusual situation develops, the leader should assertively seek to terminate at the end of the scheduled time.

When the allotted time is nearly up, the therapist may so inform the group members by saying something like "I see our time is just about up. Is there anything you'd like to add before we look at where we've come to, and where we go from here?" At the end of the session, it is often helpful to summarize what was discussed. If this session focused only on exploring problems that the members have, another one should be set up for fuller exploration and to begin looking at alternatives for resolving the problems.

It is very helpful to give members "homework" assignments between sessions. A couple who is having trouble communicating with each other might, for example, be encouraged to set aside a certain amount of time each evening to discuss their personal thoughts with each other. At the next session this "homework" assignment may then be reviewed.

Ideally, the group members should be emotionally at ease when the session ends, and therefore the therapist should not introduce emotionally charged content at the end but should reduce the intensity of emotion. Just as it is sometimes advisable to begin a session with small talk, a short social conversation at the end may provide a transition out of the session. If a group member displays a reluctance to end a session, it is sometimes helpful to confront this directly by saying, "It appears to me that you wished we had more time." The reasons for the person's reluctance can then be discussed.

At times a group session can be ended with a restatement of the way both the therapist and group agreed to proceed. Or, a more explicit summation may be made by the group leader of what was discussed, what decisions were arrived at, what questions remain to be resolved, and what actions will be taken.

A somewhat different approach is to ask each group member to state one item that was discussed or learned from the session, and/or what he now plans to do. Some therapy groups end by leaving a bad feeling and taking home a good one to be acted upon during the week.

Sometimes concerns that were alluded to but not fully discussed might be mentioned in closing as topics that will be taken up at the next session. Some members will reveal their most serious concerns for the first time at the end of a session, perhaps because they are ambivalent about whether they are ready to explore these concerns fully with the group. In these instances the therapist has to make a professional judgment about whether to extend the session beyond the allotted time, to set up an appointment to discuss these concerns privately, or to wait until the next group session.

Sometimes it is helpful to end a group session with the therapist leading the group in a relaxation exercise.

(Relaxation exercises are described in Chapter 22.) A relaxation exercise not only helps members to relax but also reduces their level of stress so that they can view their problems more objectively and work on resolving them after they leave.

Closing is especially important because what occurs during this last phase is likely to determine the members' impressions of the session as a whole. Group leaders should leave enough time for closing that the members do not feel rushed, as that might create the impression that they are being evicted.

Ending a Group

The ending phase of a group frequently offers the highest potential for powerful and important work. Group members may feel a sense of urgency as they realize there is little time left, and this can lead them to reveal their most sensitive and personal concerns. Because the work remaining to be done is usually clearly identified at this point, members can focus their efforts on completing it. However, the relationship dynamics are also heightened in this phase as the members prepare to move away from each other, and the termination of the group may evoke powerful feelings in group members.

If group members have grown emotionally close to each other, the ending of a group will be interpreted as a loss and produce a variety of emotions. Kübler-Ross's (1969) stages of emotional reactions that people display when terminally ill resemble the reactions that people have to other important losses, including the ending of a successful and cohesive group. Members may display denial through ignoring the imminent end of the group, anger and rage, or sadness and depression. They may attempt to bargain for an extension of the group in a variety of ways, such as urging that the group deal with additional problems. Ideally, members will ventilate and work through such feelings and gradually come to accept the ending of the group. (Kübler-Ross's stages are more fully described in Chapter 5.)

Other emotions may also be displayed. Some members may feel guilty because of adverse comments they made or because they believe they failed to take certain actions that would have benefited themselves or other members of the group. If a member left prematurely, some members may feel the group let him down. Members may want to share their feelings about the support system they will lose when the group ends. If certain members want the group to continue, they may interpret the ending of the group as a personal rejection. On the other hand, members who feel that the group was very successful may want to have a celebration to give recognition to the successes and to say goodbye.

In many ways the concluding sessions are the most difficult for the therapist and the group members. Strong emotions are often generated and should be ventilated and worked through. It is painful to terminate a group when members have formed relationships to share their most personal and important concerns and feelings. Our society has done little to train us to handle such separations; in fact, some segments in our society have a general norm of being "strong" and not expressing feelings.

The therapist can help members accept the ending of a group in a number of ways, and the process of terminating a group should, in fact, begin during the early stages of the group. This guideline is particularly relevant for time-limited groups. The therapist should attempt to prevent the formation of dependency relationships between the members and the therapist. The goal is independence and better functioning, and this should be reiterated whenever appropriate during group sessions.

The therapist may summarize the emotional reactions that people have to group endings, and an appropriate point for a discussion occurs when some members display denial, anger, guilt, bargaining, or sadness. When discussing these feelings, the therapist should share her personal feelings and recollections, since the ending of the group has meaning for the therapist as well. The therapist can, in effect, provide a model that may help members to express both their positive and negative concerns about the ending of the group. A problem-solving approach can be used to alleviate concerns; for example, if a group member is apprehensive about future problems, the therapist might provide the member with several other counseling resources.

The ending process should provide enough time for the therapist and the members to sort out their feelings and use the ending productively. A sudden ending will cut short necessary work and may not allow enough time to work through feelings and complete the remaining tasks. Sometimes, members will indirectly express their anger by being late, appearing apathetic, being sarcastic, or battling over minor issues. In these situations the therapist should respond directly to the indirect cues by saying something like, "I wonder if your recent critical remarks are related to your anger that this group is ending? I know you have invested a lot in this group and may dislike the idea that our meetings are coming to an end." By helping members to recognize and articulate their feelings, a therapist can help members express and work through those feelings. Once such feelings are dealt with, members will be more productive during the remaining time.

At or near the end of some groups, members may test new skills and do things independently. They may report having tackled a tough problem or dealt with an issue by themselves. The therapist should acknowledge their independence and make positive remarks about the member's ability to "go it alone."

At times, the therapist may be the person leaving the group, perhaps to take a job elsewhere. In these situations the therapist should create a smooth transition, and if appropriate, the members should be involved in selecting the new leader. At times it is helpful for the former leader and the new leader to be co-leaders for a brief period of time.

The ending of a group is always a transition to something else. The important element during the ending phase of a group is to work with all members to help them develop a game plan so that the transition will enable them to work toward higher goals. The transition should not work to stifle members but help them to progress. It may be valuable to note that life is full of transitions and passages: from early childhood to kindergarten, from kindergarten to elementary school, from childhood to puberty, from puberty to dating, from school to the work world, from being single to being married, from having responsibility only for self to becoming a parent, from working to retirement, and so on. In a transition phase we have the potential to control our future; the choices we make and the efforts we put forth will determine whether the transition will be constructive or destructive for us.

Helping each member to make productive, realistic plans for the future is a goal of the ending phase of many groups.

During the process of terminating a group it is important for the therapist to spend time obtaining feedback on how to improve future groups by having members fill out a brief evaluation at the last (or next-to-last) session. This evaluation should be done anonymously by the members. The following questions will apply to a variety of therapeutic groups. For the first seven questions use the following scale: (1) Strongly disagree, (2) Disagree, (3) Neutral or uncertain, (4) Agree, (5) Strongly agree.

1. I am very satisfied with what this group accomplished.
   1   2   3   4   5

2. My personal goals in this group have been attained.
   1   2   3   4   5

3. I truly enjoyed being a member of this group.
   1   2   3   4   5

4. The therapist has done a superb job in leading the group.
   1   2   3   4   5

5. This has been one of the most rewarding groups I have participated in.
   1   2   3   4   5

6. I have grown extensively as a person through participating in this group.
   1   2   3   4   5

7. I have made substantial progress in resolving those personal problems that led me to join this group.
   1   2   3   4   5

The next three questions are open-ended.

8. The strengths of this group are:

9. The shortcomings of this group are:

10. My suggestions for changes in this group are:

At the final session it is also desirable for the members to discuss what they got out of the group, the merits of the group, and suggestions for improving it. They should be given a chance to bring up unfinished business. In some cases an extra session may be held to complete unfinished business items.

One final important suggestion will be given. The therapist should refer an individual to another group or therapist, or at least discuss the case with another professional therapist, if (*a*) she feels that she is unable to empathize with that group member, (*b*) the therapist has extreme personal difficulty in accepting the fact that a member is choosing alternatives (such as continuing to abuse his spouse) that the therapist finds disgusting, (*c*) the member's problems are of such a nature that the therapist feels she and the group will not be able to provide therapeutic help, (*d*) a working relationship is not established with the member, and (*e*) the member is such a disruptive force in the group that he is preventing other members from constructively working on their problems. A competent therapist knows she can work with and help some people but not all, and that when she cannot, it is in the individual's and the therapist's best interests to refer the person to someone else who can.

SUMMARY

This chapter summarizes key group dynamic concepts, and presents guidelines on how to lead therapeutic groups. A membership group is one of which a person is a member, while a reference group is one whose influence a person is willing to accept.

Most social work groups have the following stages of development: preaffiliation, power and control, intimacy, differentiation, and separation. All groups have task roles and maintenance roles that need to be performed by members. Task roles are those needed to accomplish the specific goals set by the group, while maintenance roles are those that serve to strengthen social/emotional aspects of group life.

The theory of leadership that is highlighted in this chapter is distributed functions. With this approach leadership is defined as the performance of acts that help the group reach its goals and maintain itself in good working order. Leadership occurs when one member in a group influences other members to help the group reach its goals. Because all group members at times influence other group members, each member in a group exerts leadership.

French and Raven (1968) have identified the following five bases of power in which group members influence each other: reward, coercive, legitimate, referent, and expert. Each power base has different effects on those being influenced.

Personal goals and group goals should be identified soon after a group is formed. The more congruent personal goals are with group goals, the more effective the group is apt to be. Conformity studies have found that a group has considerable influence on members' opinions and attitudes.

Groups are more apt to be effective with a cooperative group atmosphere than with a competitive atmosphere. If handled constructively, conflict and contro-versy can have a number of beneficial effects on a group, including increasing creativity. The problem-solving approach is much more effective in resolving controversy than the win-lose approach. Members who usually are hostile or disruptive in a group should generally be confronted by the designated leader or by other group members.

It appears probable that for any given task there is an optimal group size. The more complex the task, the larger the optimum size to assure the greater number of needed abilities and skills.

This chapter concluded with guidelines on how to lead therapeutic groups. Aspects discussed included building rapport, exploring problems in depth, exploring alternative solutions, ending a session, and ending a group.

EXERCISES

1. *The Autokinetic Effect*

GOAL: This conformity exercise is designed to demonstrate that in ambiguous situations students will usually rely on the group to help define reality.

Step 1: Explain that this exercise is a study to measure students' capacities to judge how far a dot of light will move in the dark. Have the students sit in back of the classroom. Inform the students they will need a pen and paper to record their answers. Turn off all lights (the room has to have all lighting removed). Place a small flashlight that will produce a dot of light in front of the room in a position where it can't move. Turn the flashlight on for about thirty seconds, and then turn it off. Ask the students to record on a sheet of paper how far the light moved. Ask the students not to share their answers with others. Repeat the turning on and off of the flashlight for thirty seconds for a second and third time. Each time have the students record their answers as to how far the light moves. (Do not let the students see that the flashlight is stationary.)

Step 2: Have the students form subgroups of about four, and have them continue to sit in back of the room. Turn the classroom lights off, and turn the flashlight on for thirty seconds, and then off for three more trials. After each time the flashlight is turned off, have the subgroups discuss and record their answers as to how far the light moved.

Step 3: Indicate that for the final three trials the students will again have to record individually how far the dot of light has moved, without talking to each other. Turn the flashlight on again for thirty seconds and then off, for the final three trials, and have students record their answers.

Step 4: Ask several volunteers to write their answers to the nine trials on the blackboard. Discuss whether the results are similar to previous studies which have found that the final three judgments tend to converge to the subgroup standard in trials four, five, and six.

Step 5: Summarize the results of conformity studies described in this chapter.

2. Power Bases

GOALS: This exercise is designed to help students learn how to analyze influence efforts in terms of the bases of power identified by French and Raven (1968).

Step 1: Inform the students of the purpose of this exercise. Indicate that it is natural and desirable for group members to seek to influence each other. Briefly describe the following five power bases: reward, coercive, legitimate, expert, and referent.

Step 2: Ask the students to form subgroups of five students each. Ask each subgroup to answer the following questions. (These questions should be written on the blackboard by the instructor.)

a. What kinds of power does the instructor have in this class?
b. For each type of power that is identified, what are specific ways in which the instructor has sought to use this power?
c. How do the students feel about the instructor's use of each of these different power bases?
d. What power bases do students have in this class?

Step 3: Have the subgroups share with the class their answers to the above questions.

3. Task and Maintenance Roles

GOAL: This exercise is designed to help students identify task and maintenance roles.

Step 1: Inform the students of the purpose of the exercise. Describe task and maintenance roles, which are discussed in this chapter. Indicate for the purposes of this exercise that the class can be assumed to be a group.

Step 2: Ask the class to form subgroups of four or five students. Ask the subgroups to identify task functions and specific maintenance functions performed by the instructor and by students in this class.

Step 3: Have the subgroups share and discuss their conclusions.

4. Group Therapy in Action

GOAL: This exercise is designed to give class members an experiential awareness of being in a group therapy session.

Step 1: The leader indicates at the next class period that a simulated group therapy session will be conducted, with the purpose as stated above. Each student is given the "homework" assignment of identifying one or two personal problems that a friend or relative currently has. Students are told that they should not reveal the identity of the person having the problem and that the personal problem should be that of a friend or relative (and not their own).

Step 2: At the next class period, the leader begins by stating the following ground rules. "Today we will have a simulated group therapy session in order to give you an experiential awareness of being in group therapy. Because this is a class, I strongly request that you do not reveal any personal information about any dilemmas or difficulties you are experiencing. Instead, I ask you to describe one or two complicated personal dilemmas that a friend or relative is currently facing. For confidentiality reasons, please do not reveal the identity of the person whose problems you talk about. Remember, for reasons of confidentiality, what is said here, stays here. Are there any questions about what we are going to do, or about the ground rules?" If there are questions, seek to answer them.

Step 3: Ask students to begin sharing concerns being faced by a friend or relative. If the class is reluctant to start to share, the leader may initiate the process by specifically asking a normally vocal student to begin. When a student is sharing, the leader should encourage the other students to probe with questions in order to explore the problem further, and then should encourage the other students to suggest realistic and creative courses of action to resolve the problem. (In group therapy sessions, each member at times takes on the role of a therapist.)

Step 4: After the dilemma revealed by one student is fully discussed and problem-solved, the exercise continues by having other students share dilemmas that are currently being experienced by their friends or relatives. The exercise continues until the end of the class period, or until no one has anything further to share. At the end of the exercise, students should be asked their thoughts about the benefits and shortcomings of the exercise and their suggestions for changes in the format of the exercise when it is again used.

Comment: During the exercise, one or more of the students may begin talking about a personal problem he or she is facing. The leader at this point will have to make a judgment as to whether to let the student continue. The leader should not allow any students to divulge personal information that they are apt to regret later.

8

SOCIAL WORK
WITH FAMILIES

Often the focus of social work services is on the family. A family is an interacting interdependent system. The problems faced by any person are usually influenced by the dynamics within a family. Because a family is an interacting system, change in one member affects others. For example, it has been noted that the abused child is at times a scapegoat on whom the parents vent their anger and hostility. If the abused child is removed from such a home, another child within the family is apt to be selected to be the scapegoat (Kadushin, 1980).

Another reason for the focus on the family rather than on the individual is that the other family members are often needed in the treatment process. For example, other family members can put pressure on an alcoholic to have her or him acknowledge that a problem exists. The family members may also need counseling (or support from a self-help group) to assist them in coping with the alcoholic when she or he is drinking, and these family members may play important roles in providing emotional support for the alcoholic's efforts to stop drinking.

DIVERSITY OF FAMILY FORMS

The family is a social institution that is found in every culture. The family has been defined by Coleman and Cressey (1990, p. 125) as "a group of people related by marriage, ancestry, or adoption who live together in a common household." It should be noted such a definition does not cover a number of living arrangements in which the members consider themselves to be a family. Some of these arrangements are

- A husband and wife raising two foster children who have been in the household for several years.
- Two women, lesbians in a loving relationship, who are raising children born to one of the partners while in a heterosexual marriage that ended in divorce.

- A family unit in which one of the spouses is living away from home—perhaps because of military service in a foreign country or because of incarceration.

- A family unit in which one of the children who is severely and profoundly retarded is living in a residential treatment facility.

- A man and a woman who have been living together for years in a loving relationship but who have never legally married.

A wide diversity of family patterns exist in the world. Families in different cultures take a variety of forms. In some societies, husband and wife live in separate buildings. In others, they are expected to live apart for several years after the birth of a child. In many societies, husbands are permitted to have more than one wife. In a few countries, wives are allowed to have more than one husband. Some cultures permit (and a few encourage) premarital and extramarital intercourse.

Some societies have large communes where adults and children live together. There are communes in which the children are raised separately from adults. In some cultures without communes, surrogate parents (rather than the natural parents) raise the children. Some societies encourage certain types of homosexual relationships, and a few recognize homosexual as well as heterosexual marriages.

In many cultures, marriages are still arranged by the parents. In a few societies, an infant may be "married" before birth (if the baby is of the wrong sex, the marriage is dissolved). Some societies do not recognize the existence of romantic love. Some cultures expect older men to marry young girls. Others expect older women to marry young boys. Most societies prohibit the marriage of close relatives. Yet, a few subcultures encourage marriage between brothers and sisters or between first cousins. Some expect a man to marry his father's brother's daughter, while others insist that he marry his mother's sister's daughter. In some societies, a man, upon marrying, makes a substantial gift to the bride's father, while in others the bride's father gives a substantial gift to the new husband.

There are indeed substantial variations in family patterns. People in each of these societies generally feel strongly that their particular pattern is normal and proper, and many feel the pattern is divinely ordained. Suggested changes in their particular form are usually viewed with suspicion and defensiveness, and are often sharply criticized as being unnatural, immoral, and a threat to the survival of the family.

In spite of these variations, sociologists have noted that most family systems can be classified into two basic forms: the extended family and the nuclear family. An *extended family* consists of a number of relatives living together, such as parents, children, grandparents, great-grandparents, aunts, uncles, in-laws, and cousins. The extended family is the predominant pattern in preindustrial societies. The members divide various agricultural, domestic, and other duties among themselves.

A *nuclear family* consists of a married couple and their children living together. The nuclear family type emerged from the extended family. Extended families tend to be more functional in agricultural societies where many "hands" are needed; the nuclear family is more suited to the demands of complex, industrialized societies, as its smaller size and potential geographic mobility enable it to adapt more easily to changing conditions—such as the need to relocate to obtain a better job.

Although the nuclear family is still the predominant family form in the United States, Canada, and many other industrialized countries, it is a serious mistake for social workers and other helping professionals to use the nuclear family as the ideal model that individuals in our society should strive to form. There are many other family forms that are functioning well and are deserving of respect, such as the following:

- A married couple without children who are the primary care givers for the wife's mother who has Alzheimer's disease and who is residing with the couple.

- Two men who are gay in a committed relationship, each of whom has joint custody of two children with his former wife.

- A childless married couple who have decided not to conceive children.

- A single parent with three young children. According to Coleman and Cressey (1990, p. 141) over 25 percent of the families in the United States are single-parent families.

CASE EXAMPLE

Sex-Role Expectations Are Culturally Determined

I n the classic study *Sex and Temperament in Three Primitive Societies*, Margaret Mead demonstrated that sex-role expectations are culturally rather then biologically deter-mined. The study further showed that family socialization patterns are immensely influ-enced by the larger culture. The study was conducted in three tribes in the early 1930s in New Guinea. Mead found that many characteristics that Americans classify as typically feminine or masculine are classified differently in these tribes.

Both sexes among the Arapesh would seem feminine to us. Both men and women are gentle, nurturant, and compliant. The personalities of males and females in this society are not sharply differentiated by sex. Both girls and boys learn to be unaggressive, coopera-tive, and responsive to the needs and wants of others. Relations between husband and wife parallel the traditional mother-child relations in our society, with the Arapesh husband of-ten seeing his role as providing training to his much younger wife.

In contrast, among the Mundugamors, both sexes would seem masculine to us. Both are headhunters and cannibals, are nonnurturant and aggressive, and actively initiate sexual involvement.

The most interesting society studied was the Tchambuli. This society virtually reverses our traditional sex-role expectations and stereotypes. The men spend much more time than the women in grooming and decorating themselves. Also, the men spend much of their time in painting, carving, and practicing dance steps. In contrast, the women are efficient, impersonal, unadorned, managerial, and brisk. The women are the traders and have most of the economic power.

Source: Margaret Mead, *Sex and Temperament in Three Primitive Societies* (New York: Morrow, 1935).

- A blended family in which the husband and wife procreate children in the marriage, and each spouse has children from earlier marriages who are also living in the household.

- An unmarried young couple living together in what amounts to a "trial marriage."

In the past few decades there has been a trend in the United States for greater diversity in marital ar-rangements and family forms. There are increasing numbers of transracial marriages, marriages between spouses of diverse ages, transracial adoptions, single-parent families, and blended families. Although some social workers may personally judge a few of these types to be "wrong," it is essential that social workers not allow their personal beliefs to reduce the quality or quantity of professional services that are provided to family units that the workers view as improper.

As the above material suggests, family patterns and forms are substantially affected by the culture (larger system) in which they are located. In our culture, for example, women have traditionally been brought up to be passive, nurturing, and maternal, while males have traditionally been reared to be aggressive, competitive, outgoing, and nonexpressive.

SOCIETAL FUNCTIONS OF FAMILIES

Families in modern industrial societies perform the following essential functions that help maintain the continuity and stability of society:

- *Replacement of the population.* Every society has to have some system for replacing its members. Practically all societies consider the family as the unit in which children are to be produced. Societies have defined the rights and responsibilities of the reproductive partners within the family unit. These rights and responsibilities help maintain the stability of society, although they are defined differently from one society to another.

- *Care of the young.* Children require care and protection until at least the age of puberty. The family is a primary institution for the rearing of children. Modern societies have generally developed supportive institutions to help in caring for the young—for example, medical services, day-care centers, parent training programs, and residential treatment centers.

- *Socialization of new members.* To become productive members of society, children have to be socialized into the culture. Children are expected to acquire a language, learn social values and mores, and dress and behave within the norms of society. The family plays a major role in this socialization process. In modern societies, there are a number of other groups and resources involved in this socialization process. Schools, the mass media, peer groups, the police, movies, and books and other written material are important influences in the socialization process. (Some-

times these different influences clash by advocating opposing values and attitudes.)

- *Regulation of sexual behavior.* Failure to regulate sexual behavior would result in clashes between individuals due to jealousy and exploitation. Unregulated sexual behavior would probably result in the birth of large numbers of children outside of marriage—children whom no fathers could be held responsible for raising. Every society has rules that regulate sexual behavior within family units. Most societies, for example, have incest taboos, and most disapprove of extramarital sex.

- *Source of affection.* Spitz (1945) has demonstrated that humans need affection, emotional support, and positive recognition from others (including approval, smiles, encouragement, and reinforcement for accomplishments). Without such affection and recognition, a person's emotional, intellectual, physical, and social growth would be stunted. The family is an important source for obtaining affection and recognition, as family members generally regard each other as among the most important people in their lives and gain emotional and social satisfaction from family relationships.

PROBLEMS IN FAMILIES

An infinite number of problems may occur in families. The following is a small listing of some of the problems:

Divorce

Alcohol or drug abuse

Unwanted pregnancy

Bankruptcy

Poverty

Terminal illness

Chronic illness

Death

Desertion

Empty shell marriage

Emotional problems of one or more members

Behavioral problems of one or more members

Child abuse

Child neglect

Sexual abuse

Spouse abuse

Elder abuse

Unemployment of wage earners

Money management difficulties

Injury from serious automobile accident involving one or more members

Mental retardation of one or more members

Incarceration or institutionalization of one or more members

Compulsive gambling by one or more members

Being a crime victim

Forced retirement of a wage earner

Becoming a care giver for an elderly relative

Involvement of a child in delinquent and criminal activities

Illness of a member who acquires AIDS

A runaway teenager

Sexual dysfunctions of one or more members

Infidelity

Infertility

THE NATURE OF SOCIAL WORK WITH FAMILIES

When there are problems in a family, social services are often needed. There is extensive variation in the types and forms of services that are provided by social workers to troubled families. These services require the social worker to perform a variety of roles (for ex-

ample, broker, educator, advocate, supporter, mediator). The following examples illustrate the diverse nature of social work with families.

Ray Falk, age fifty-six, is diagnosed as having a malignant brain tumor that is inoperable. The prognosis is that Mr. Falk has only a few more months left to live. Mr. Falk leaves the hospital and moves in with his daughter and her husband. Mary Brey, medical social worker at the hospital, serves as a broker for Mr. Falk and his care givers to receive respite care, counseling, and other services from the hospice program in the community.

Mark Schwanke, age thirty-two, is diagnosed as having AIDS. Betty Seely, a social worker with the AIDS Support Network in the community, serves as a case manager in providing a variety of services to Mark, his partner, and members of Mark's family. These services include medical information and care, housing, counseling, emotional support services, and financial assistance. Because of frequent discrimination against persons with AIDS, Betty Seely often must act as an advocate on Mark's behalf to assure that he actually receives the services he needs.

Beth Roessler, age fifteen, is adjudicated to be delinquent for committing six burglaries. Steve Padek, a juvenile probation officer and a social worker, is assigned to be Beth's juvenile probation officer. Mr. Padek provides the following services to Beth and her mother who is divorced: holding weekly supervision meetings with Beth to monitor her school performance and leisure activities, linking Beth's mother with a Parents Without Partners group, and conducting several counseling sessions with Beth and her mother to mediate conflicts in their relationship.

Cindy Rogerson, age twenty-seven, has three young children. She is badly battered by her husband, and contacts the House of Hope, a shelter for battered women and their children. Sue Frank, a social worker at the shelter, assists in making arrangements for shelter for Mrs. Rogerson and her children. The oldest child is attending school, so Ms. Frank makes arrangements for him to continue attending school. Ms. Frank at the shelter provides one-to-one counseling to Ms.

Rogerson to help her explore her options and to inform her of potential resources which she may not be aware of. Ms. Frank also leads groups at the shelter for residents and nonresidents which Mrs. Rogerson is required to attend while at the center. After two and one-half weeks Mrs. Rogerson decides she is interested in returning to live with her husband. Ms. Frank convinces Mrs. Rogerson to give her husband an ultimatum prior to returning—he must receive family counseling together with her from the Family Service agency in the community and must attend a group for batterers in the community. Mrs. Rogerson reluctantly agrees. Mrs. Rogerson, at the urging of Ms. Frank, only then returns to live with her husband, with the understanding that she will leave immediately if he again hits her or if he drops out of family counseling or the group for batterers.

Luke Harder, age twelve, is failing the sixth grade and appears apathetic. He is referred for an M-team assessment. (An M-team is a multidisciplinary team that consists of a school psychologist, school nurse, speech and hearing specialist, and the social worker, Patrick Riesen.) Mr. Riesen's beginning responsibility is to do a social study of the Harder family. He arranges to meet with Mr. and Mrs. Harder at their home. When Mr. Riesen arrives at the Harders, Mrs. Harder is present and explains that her husband has chosen to go to a tavern instead of meeting with the social worker. Mrs. Harder appears depressed and intensely frustrated with her family's plight. She explains that her husband may well be an alcoholic. She is overwhelmed with anger that he is spending most of his paycheck at the bar, that he is not helping to rear their children, and that he is very disruptive when he comes home intoxicated. Mr. Riesen asks Mrs. Harder if she thinks her husband would be interested in attending some joint sessions to discuss further what might be done. Another meeting, this time at school, is arranged, but again only Mrs. Harder attends. Three additional sessions are held with Mrs. Harder to discuss various options. Mr. Riesen encourages Mrs. Harder to join Al-Anon, which she does. After some meetings at Al-Anon, Mrs. Harder gives her husband an ultimatum that he must either stop drinking and enter family counseling

with her, or she'll leave with the children. Mr. Harder stomps out in a rage. When he comes home he is physically abusive. He has been drinking again. Fortunately he passes out before causing serious physical injury. Mrs. Harder flees the house, taking the children. She spends the night with her parents. The next morning she calls Mr. Riesen, who arranges to meet her immediately. His first role is to provide emotional support to this distraught, frightened woman. Then various options are discussed. Mrs. Harder appears committed to her decision to divorce her husband. Mr. Riesen refers her to the Department of Social Services which assists her in getting financial assistance through the AFDC programs, assists her in finding an apartment, and refers her to an attorney in order to start divorce proceedings. The son, Luke, continues to fail in his courses during this family turmoil. At the end of the school year, he is required to repeat the sixth grade. During the summer Mrs. Harder and her children have time to begin adjusting to a new life. Life as a single parent for Mrs. Harder and the children is not easy, but it is a lot better than living with an abusive alcoholic. When Luke returns to school in the fall, he is more relaxed, settled, and motivated to do better academically. He does not want to repeat the sixth grade again, and therefore he works hard to raise his school performance to the "satisfactory" range.

Katy Hynek, age seventy-six, has Alzheimer's disease. She has been living alone in her house since her husband died three years ago. Her physician contacts Adult Services of the Department of Social Services and requests that an assessment of living arrangements be conducted. Linda Sutton, social worker, does an assessment, and determines that Katy Hynek can no longer live alone. Katy's son Mark and his wife Annette agree to have Katy move in with them. During the next nineteen months, Ms. Sutton has periodic contact with the Hyneks. As is common with this disease, Katy Hynek's physical and mental condition continues to deteriorate. Ms. Sutton listens to the concerns of Mark and Annette and seeks to answer their questions about the disease. She also provides suggestions to help them cope with the changes in Katy's condition. As Katy's condition deteriorates, Ms. Sutton makes arrangements for Katy to attend an adult day-care center during the daytime, partly for respite care for Mark and Annette. At the end of nineteen months, Mark and Annette request a meeting with Ms. Sutton to discuss the possibility of placing Katy in a nursing home, as her condition has so deteriorated that she now needs twenty-four hour care. (For example, she gets up in the middle of the night and gets lost in closets; she is also now incontinent.) The pros and cons of placing Katy in a nursing home are identified and discussed. Making the decision is exceedingly emotional and agonizing for Mark and Annette. With a careful discussion of the entire situation with Ms. Sutton, Mark and Annette decide they have no choice but to seek a nursing home placement. Ms. Sutton gives them the names of three nursing homes, which they visit, and then proceed to select one.

One of the many social services provided to families is family therapy (also called family counseling). A substantial amount of literature about family therapy has been developed in social work. The remainder of this chapter will focus on describing family therapy. Although social work with families involves many approaches and services in addition to family therapy, the importance of family therapy in social work practice necessitates an extended discussion of this approach.

FAMILY THERAPY IN SYSTEMS PERSPECTIVE

Family therapy: What is it? Strictly speaking, family therapy is a subset of the broader classification of group therapy that is aimed at helping families with whatever interactional, behavioral, and emotional problems that may arise in the course of everyday living. Problems include marital conflicts, parent-child interactional problems, and conflicts with grandparents or other relatives. A wide variety of problems are dealt with in family therapy, such as domestic violence, communication problems, and disagreements between family mem-

bers on drug use and abuse, curfew hours, school performance, money management, sexual values and behavior, performance of domestic tasks and methods of disciplining the children.[1]

The Whitlock family walked into the therapist's office in an orderly fashion, the oldest son looking annoyed and bored, the younger children looking scared. Mrs. Whitlock introduced the group to the therapist immediately, saying that she was sure nothing was wrong with her family, yet the youngest daughter had been crying all the time lately and had been doing very poorly in school of late; she was also obese. The mother said she was sure the daughter would grow out of these problems, but when the little girl's teacher had called and said the child was talking about suicide, the mother was persuaded to seek help for the girl. The only reason the rest of the family were here, she announced, was because the therapist had requested that everyone be present at the interview to contribute ideas as to what the trouble was with the younger daughter.

The father stood by the door while the mother was talking, and no one sat down. The therapist noted that the older daughter stood close to the father, and the younger son stood alone looking at the floor. The older son moved over to the window and looked out, whistling to himself. When the mother, holding her young daughter's hand, finished her rapid-fire introductory speech, the therapist took advantage of the moment to invite the family to be seated. She asked each person present to introduce himself or herself. She noted that the older daughter had difficulty with that request; she stuttered badly and could not utter the first sound of her name.

Fortunately, not every family is troubled as are the Whitlocks. Some parents rear their children with minimum discomfort and maximum growth for all involved. Family therapy is a practice or activity to help those other families, those families who are hurting, overtly or covertly. The reason families enter into therapy is because they are hoping to reduce their pain and increase their happiness, as individuals and as a group.

---

[1]The remainder of this chapter was especially written for this text by Carolyn Wells, Ph.D. Dr. Wells is associate professor of social work at Marquette University, Wisconsin, and is a practicing family therapist.

Family counseling

Families that hurt internally are also likely to find their standing in the community diminished because one or more of the children exhibit embarrassing behavior in public, perhaps delinquent behavior. The family self-image of happiness and tranquility is likely to be shattered by angry, rebellious, or destructive behavior within the home. Crises precipitated by the behavior of the children are likely to precipitate flare-ups of old marital stresses and arguments. People suffer, and their self-esteem and personal growth is inhibited.

Virginia Satir (1972), after years of working with troubled families, believes that four factors differentiate troubled and untroubled families: (*a*) level of felt self-worth, (*b*) pattern of communication, (*c*) type of family rules, and (*d*) the way the family members relate to people and institutions outside the family (their pattern of linkage to society). She finds that in all the troubled families she has worked with self-worth is low; communication is indirect, vague, and dishonest; rules are rigid and nonnegotiable; and the linkage to society vacillates between being fearful, placating, or blaming (Satir, 1972, pp. 3–4). By contrast, in nurturing families

self-worth is high; communication is clear, specific, and honest; rules are appropriate and flexible; and the linking to society is open.

Obviously, troubled and untroubled families stand at opposite ends of a continuum. Probably most families stand somewhere along the continuum. It takes a great deal of effort and energy to enter an activity like family therapy, and usually a family has to be far along the continuum toward the troubled end before it will make the move to seek help. Often the family is troubled for a long time before any effort is made to reach out for assistance. A particular event such as the clash of a family member, often a child, with an outside authority (such as the school or the police) may precipitate the seeking of help. Perhaps the sudden desertion of a spouse or the running away of a child brings about a great enough crisis that the family will seek professional help. At any rate, members of middle-class American culture, who have been exhorted to solve their own problems and lift themselves up by their own bootstraps, tend to enter therapy well after external intervention would have been useful. Often the

CASE EXAMPLE

School Phobia

A system inherently attempts to maintain a dynamic balance, or homeostasis, in order to maintain the particular arrangement or ordering of parts that was successful in the past and so resulted in the establishment of the system. As an example of how problematic behavior in a family member may arise to help maintain the family homeostasis (balance of the system, so that the system can continue), let us discuss a school phobia that arose in a little girl in a Jefferson County, Wisconsin, elementary school in the 1970s. The school phobia arose apparently spontaneously, but the school social worker discovered on her first home visit that the little girl was almost mute with strangers (at least with the social worker herself), and in fact ran out into the yard rather than cope with a new person. The mother would not fetch the daughter ("she's too frightened of strangers"), and offered only the most broad and general information about the child's development. On the other hand, the mother wanted to talk about herself; she listed a variety of stresses in her life unrelated to the daughter, in particular her aloof husband and her boring job. It became increasingly clear that this mother resented the time and attention her daughter was receiving; she wanted some attention herself. Yet the only reason she was receiving any attention from her husband was due to the daughter's phobia. The husband had to talk to the lonely woman fairly often because of the little girl's problematic behaviors (in the home the child would often stay in her room, or refuse her supper, and so forth). Because of the girl's school phobia, the mother got to stay home from her disliked job and to talk with her husband.

A combination of family therapy to help create a genuine relationship between the marital pair without the assistance of the daugher's problematic behaviors, plus reduction in the mother's work hours, helped reduce this family's need for a problematic daughter. At school, during the initial stages of the family therapy, the little girl was placed in a special class with an empathic and firm teacher. Father was assigned the task of taking his daughter to school. Mother was to accompany them but not take responsibility. Fortunately, father was a well-meaning person and faithfully carried out his responsibility, which strengthened his relationship with the child and thus his investment in the family system as a whole. After successfully getting the child to school, father and mother would discuss their success, strengthening their own communication and increasing their appreciation of one another. The school phobia disappeared within a few weeks.

---

family member finally to reach out will be female, since males in our society are traditionally reared to believe erroneously it is a sign of weakness to seek help for individual and family problems. Unfortunately, seeking professional help for reasons of emotional adjustment will usually be perceived by the family as an admission of dependency and failure rather than as an assertive action in the direction of constructive problem solving, an act that would be more permissible for a male.

When a family does consult the therapist for help in reducing their family pain, there is hope. The act of seeking help itself is a positive indication that the family is capable of at least one innovative act in helping itself. However, the family will usually enter therapy using an identified client as a sort of ticket for admission. Very often, in fact, the family will perceive that this identified client really is their only problem. If the therapist can only fix this person, the family will be just fine. An example of such a circumstance is the Whitlock family, described at the beginning of this section. The youngest daughter, obese and talking about suicide, is the family's identified client. At least within the first interview as described so far, there seems to be no indication from among the family members that they think anything else is wrong. The rest of the family is dutifully tagging along to the interview to contribute ideas as to what is wrong with the little girl.

The family therapist will perceive the identified client as serving an important function in the family system. Like all systems, a family has an overall purpose. In the case of the family, the purpose of the system is to provide for the physical and emotional needs of the adults and to procreate new people. The interrelated parts of this system are the family members themselves. These parts establish a certain working order, for example, communication patterns, rules, levels of self-esteem. Energy to keep the system going is supplied by food, water, housing, and so forth, plus certain empowering beliefs regarding the emotional, intellectual, social, and spiritual lives of the family members and how one fits in with another (Satir, 1972, pp. 113–19). Each family system is, like all systems, bounded, in that communication patterns within the family have special forms and a special significance and purpose (for example, continuation of the family). However, the boundary around the family is permeable to varying degrees. In a healthy family system, new information can flow into and out of the family through the boundary and the family is thus characterized as an open system. In the family that is an open system, rules are related to communication and change is considered normal. The self-worth of the members is granted higher importance than the maintenance of a fixed power structure. On the other hand, in the family that is a relatively closed system, family members cling to the familiar even when it is painful and does not foster growth. Where self-worth is low, pain is at least familiar

and thus preferable to the unknown. Self-worth is relegated to a secondary position below fixed authority, change is resisted, and relationships are regulated by force (at the whim of the person on top). Information from outside the system is resisted, as there is just one "right way."

To repeat, when a family comes to therapy, they will generally do so in order to have the therapist "fix" a particular family member so that their system can maintain itself as before, only without the stress that the particular identified client has been recently exerting on the system. The perspective of the systems-oriented family therapist is that the identified client developed problematic behavior in order to help maintain the family system in some way. Now the problematic behavior has become severe enough that the family views it as a problem. So when the referral for therapy is made by a family member or outside institution (for example, school), the therapist will insist on the involvement of all family members, even very young children. The therapist will want to determine from direct observation what function the problematic behavior of the identified client plays in maintenance of the family system, and how and why it has now become stressful.

The possbility of family therapy is ultimately limited by the family itself. As mentioned before, when a family seeks help there is hope, because the seeking of help itself indicates that the family is capable of innovative action. But the family may be willing to go only so far as to have the identified client "cured" by the therapist. At this point the therapist can explain as simply and clearly as possible the obvious advantage of working with many different sources of information to solve this important problem of the family. The therapist may be successful with this sort of persuasion. But if the family refuses, the therapist has the choice of working with the identified client alone, or of refusing service (in the latter case, the therapist should, of course, refer the patient to a different kind of agency). Most family-oriented therapists will refuse their services if the family will not participate in treatment. However, if a significant subsystem of the family will involve itself (perhaps the mother and the child), the therapist may consider beginning therapy with part of the system with the hope that the rest will enter in later. This decision is a delicate one and every therapist will gradually evolve criteria for choosing when to refer and when to start with a subsystem only. More research data on significant criteria would be helpful in making such discriminations. Therapists also have to make choices on whether they will or can work with certain families who seek their services involuntarily. Perhaps the family has been ordered to enter therapy by a court as an alternative to a jail sentence for a child, due to continual delinquent behavior of the child. In these cases the purposes and potential of family therapy must be carefully explained to the family, and their option of taking the alternative course should be made explicit.

THREE APPROACHES TO FAMILY THERAPY

Three major contemporary family therapists, Satir (1967), Haley (1976), and Minuchin and Fishman (1981) have contributed enormous amounts to the growing theory and practice of family therapy. All three begin their work with a systems-oriented framework, but within that framework they manifest differences in emphasis and approach.

Virginia Satir

Satir stresses clarification of family communication patterns in her work; hence she is considered among the school of communication theorists. Satir notes, in particular, that communication patterns among troubled families tend to be vague and indirect. In other words, rather than speaking clearly for themselves, the marital pair tends to avoid talking with one another about their needs and desires; or they talk to each other about what they want through their children. Children are thus maneuvered into the stressful position of speaking for, and therefore allying with, one parent or another, precipitating fear of loss of the other parent.

In Satir's view, indirect communication in the troubled family begins with courtship of the marital pair (if not before), due to the low self-esteem of the individuals involved. Each spouse-to-be feels worthless, but hides the feeling of worthlessness by acting confident and strong. Neither person talks about these feelings of worthlessness for fear of driving the potential mate away. So each sees in the other a strong person who will take care of him or her, and essentially marries to gain an extension of the self, but a stronger self who will be able to meet all felt needs; in other words, each marries to "get" (Satir, 1967, pp. 8–10).

Unfortunately, after marriage some of the illusions must fall away. Each spouse is forced to realize at some level that the other spouse is not just an extension of the self. One insists on using a separate toothbrush, for example, while the other wants to share the same one. Such incidents force perceptions of difference, and difference is experienced as bad because it leads to arguments. A desire for fusion and to be cared for conflicts with the other's different felt needs. Facing difference feels frightening—it might lead to arguments and that could result in the other's leaving.

Hence each frightened spouse with low self-esteem and high need for the other tries to mask differences as much as possible, attempting to please the other on one level to keep him or her, while yet fearing and resenting expressed needs from the other that may be experienced as undesirable. Since both spouses are in the same uncomfortable position of resenting differences yet needing the other, interpersonal communication gradually becomes more and more indirect. Rather than risk a clear statement such as "I'd like to get a dog," the spouse desiring a pet might state something like "Aunt Matilda likes dogs." The hope will be that the other spouse will mind-read the intended message of the speaker, and that he or she will then spontaneously agree to get a dog for the family. However, the receiver of this particular message will more likely communicate a return response dealing with Aunt Matilda, bringing disappointment to the speaker. The speaker isn't able to negotiate the desired dog with this type of communication and is left with angry feelings toward the spouse and a sense of unfulfilled needs, but this state of affairs is experienced as being preferable to risking a point-blank denial. Meanwhile, the receiver of the message may become aware of the disappointment or anger of the speaker through nonverbal channels but have no idea what caused the anger or disappointment. If the spouse is also afraid to deal with conflict, he will not ask the reason for the apparent upset. So the mis-understanding and tension builds.

Satir also notes that communicating involves far more than the literal meaning of any words used. First of all, she notes that much communication is nonverbal—gestures, facial, expressions, voice tone, posture, and the like. If nonverbal communication matches the meaning of any words used (if, for example, the words "I am sad" are accompanied by tears and a down-turned mouth), then Satir considers the communication *congruent*. The receiver is not likely to misunderstand the meaning of this message because the verbal and nonverbal components agree. However, messages sent are often *incongruent*. For example, the statement "I am sad" may be accompanied by a grin. Which message should the receiver believe: the words or the facial expression? The receiver is likely to make a mistaken interpretation unless he explicitly asks the sender to explain. But the person who feels safe only with indirect communication is not likely to ask. Moreover, the sender who becomes skilled at sending incongruent communication for self-protection may even be unaware of the action and will be unable to explain if asked. Satir believes that incongruent communication can lead to misunderstanding in troubled families. Mother, for example, may say to her spouse in words, "I am angry with you." However, since she fears rejection if she sends this message too forcefully, she smiles sweetly as she says it. The spouse may then choose to believe the smile, not to take his spouse's words seriously, and continue the very behavior that made her use the word *angry*. This is likely to make her angrier, but she may not feel safe enough to express the feeling more congruently, and the communication driving the spouses apart goes on.

While incongruent communication is one example of a double message, another type of double message may place the receiver in a *double bind*, where no matter how one responds, the sender will criticize. This type of situation can occur in a family where father says, on the one hand, that all good children should keep their toys picked up, and yet on the other tells his son that all "real" boys are messy. The boy who receives both these messages will be unable to please father whether he keeps his toys neat or messy. He may solve the problem by refusing to listen at all. At the ex-treme, he may pull away from reality to such a degree that he may develop a severe emotional disturbance.

Satir's therapeutic goals and techniques are based on her assumption that people have the inherent ability (even drive) to grow and to mature. She feels that people can choose to take responsibility for their own lives and actions and that the mature person will

a. *Manifest himself clearly to others.*

b. *Be in touch with signals from his internal self, thus letting himself know openly what he thinks and feels.*

c. *Be able to see and hear what is outside himself as differentiated from himself and as different from anything else.*

d. *Behave toward another person as someone who is separate and unique.*

e. *Treat the presence of differentness as an opportunity to learn and explore rather than as a threat or signal of conflict. (Satir, 1967, p. 92)*

To help the members of a troubled family differentiate from one another and learn to own their special unique beings, Satir patiently teaches each person to speak for himself and to send "I-messages."[2] She serves as an active, directive, loving role model. She teaches that differentness is normal and should be viewed as a catalyst for growth. She points out incongruent messages and double binds, and teaches family members to send clear, congruent messages instead. She uses touch and other nonverbal means, such as family sculpturing, to help illustrate to families the unverbalized assumptions they operate by, and in this way takes the burden of labeling off the identified client and reveals his symptomatic behavior as a product of the family system as a whole. She analyzes rules in the family and helps clarify them in the context that some rules may be bad, but the people setting the rules or bound by them are not. She teaches that bad rules can be changed and has the family members negotiate new ones as she insists that each member be heard in her presence, thus teaching respect for each person and point of view.

Clearly, then, Satir views the family as a system and works with the family as a whole as the means of reliev-

---

[2]"I-messages" are described in Chapter 22.

ing the distress of the identified client, or of the family itself due to the previous dysfunctional behavior of the identified client. Her major emphasis in intervention with the family as a system is to clarify the family communication patterns and to help them become direct and congruent. Basically, Satir's therapeutic goal of improving methods of communication involves three outcomes: (1) Each member should be able to report congruently, completely, and obviously on what he or she sees and hears, feels and thinks about himself or herself and others. (2) Each person should be related to his or her uniqueness so that decisions are made in terms of exploration and negotiation rather than in terms of power. (3) Differentness should be openly acknowledged and used for growth (Okun and Rappaport, 1980, p. 93).

Salvador Minuchin

Like Satir, Minuchin and Fishman (1981) operate from a systems perspective in their work with families. In short, this means that if a particular person is referred for therapy due to certain undesirable symptoms, Minuchin will assume that this behavior is generated and maintained by needs of the family as a whole, so that intervention with the family will be necessary for effective alleviation of the problems of the identified client.

Unlike Satir, however, Minuchin's major emphasis in therapy is not clarification of communication patterns per se but in restructuring the major subsystems within the family (spouse, parental, sibling) so that each may accomplish its appropriate functions. Because of this emphasis, Minuchin is considered a member of the *structural* school of family therapists. In restructuring the family, Minuchin may certainly work with communication patterns in the family, just as in clarifying communication patterns, Satir may restructure the family subsystems into a more functional relationship. However, the theoretical perspective on the importance of clear, direct communication versus a functional family structure is clearly different for the two therapists. Minuchin, for example, may actually choose to bypass direct cognitive understanding by a family of its communication patterns in order to re-

structure the family subsystems; for example, he may use a paradoxical suggestion in working with a resistant family. He chooses to do so only in highly selected circumstances where direct explorations and clarifications of family communication patterns and behavior in therapy have failed to change the dysfunctional aspects. An illustration of a systemic paradox is described by Minuchin:

A systemic paradox is used in treatment of the Allen family, in which an eight-year-old boy is failing in school. The therapist determines that the symptom serves the function of keeping the mother's disappointment focused on her son, Billy, rather than her husband. The husband is failing in business and, rather than redoubling his efforts, is sinking into apathy, leaving the mother to shoulder much of the financial burden. He gives off signals that he would collapse if confronted openly with this issue and the mother collaborates in protecting him. Whenever she becomes angry at his lack of ambition, she nags Billy to straighten out and make something of himself, do his homework, practice his violin, or clean up his room. The mother and Billy end up fighting, and the father retires to the den to watch television. Both parents deny there is a marital problem, the wife stating, "My husband doesn't like to fight and I've accepted this."

The therapist tells the mother it is important for her to continue to express her disappointment in Billy, because otherwise she might begin to express her dissatisfaction with her husband. This would be risky, as her husband might become depressed, and since Billy is younger and more resilient than her husband, he can take it better. Billy is advised to continue to protect his father by keeping the mother's disappointment focused on him, and the father is commended for his cooperation. The mother has an immediate recoil, saying, "You're suggesting I fight with my eight-year-old son instead of my husband, a grown man? Why should I damage my son to protect my husband?" thus defining her own predicament. The husband supports the therapist, saying he thinks her suggestion is a good one "because Billy bounces right back. With him it doesn't last for a long period of time, and he doesn't get depressed as I do. Besides, we

*can't know for sure if it's doing him any damage."
The mother is outraged at her husband and proceeds
to fight with him. The conflict is refocused onto the
parents, and Billy is released from his middle position. Defining and prescribing their system in a way
that is both accurate and unacceptable makes it impossible for them to continue it. (Minuchin and Fishman, 1981, p. 247)*

In this example, by the use of paradoxical suggestion Minuchin has clarified the boundaries around the
spouse subsystem in such a way that the son is appropriately excluded. Solving the problems of the spouse
subsystem has now been squarely placed back within
the boundaries of the spouse subsystem. The wife's disappointment with her husband is not "cured" nor is
the apathetic behavior of the husband toward his failing business, but the wife's dissatisfaction with her
spouse is now appropriately expressed within the
boundaries of the spouse dyad, where it can be dealt
with directly. Prior to the use of this therapeutic technique, eight-year-old Billy was being pulled in between the spouses in order to divert them from fighting. Billy's inappropriate inclusion by the parents in
their spouse subsystem might temporarily work to
keep the family together for a longer period of time,
but the cost to Billy is unacceptable. In the long run,
using Billy this way will not work for the spouses either, for their problems obviously cannot be solved by
Billy's failing in school.

In Minuchin's structural perspective, every family
contains multiple interacting systems, including each
particular individual and the various dyads, but three
major subsystems are of particular importance in families with children. These are the spouse, the parental,
and the sibling subsystems. Each has different major
functions that must be fulfilled if the family is to survive
as a healthy unit. The spouse subsystem must be able to
protect itself as a unique entity with clear boundaries if
the spouses' long-term psychological needs are to be
met. This will involve certain rules of interaction with
other significant subsystems, such as in-laws or children, that reinforce rather than interfere with the
rights and needs of the spouses to interact as spouses.
Once children are born, a parental subsystem then
comes into being. The parental subsystem is likely to

interfere with the spouse subsystem, because when
one parent bonds so closely with a newborn child then
the primacy of the relationship with the other spouse is
threatened. Moreover, in-laws may demand parental
rights that conflict with the wants and needs of the biological parents. Later on, older children may be asked
to take on parental functions that interfere with their
own needs to be nurtured and protected as they learn
and grow. Finally, the sibling subsystem is of particular
importance because this is the context in which children first learn what the world is all about for them:
initially, how to interact and deal with peers and hierarchies. Minuchin points out that families continue to
develop and change as children are added, grow, leave
home—so that constant adaptational changes are required for every family. The family has both to maintain
itself and to change with the changing conditions.
Sometimes professional intervention is required to
help troubled families to cope successfully.

In working with a given family, Minuchin analyzes
its structure to determine whether the boundaries of
the major subsystems are clear and defined, or whether
they are too enmeshed (too close, as when a parent
and a child are emotionally closer than the two members of the spouse subsystem) and/or too disengaged
(as when two spouses communicate with each other
only through their children). Minuchin may draw a hypothetical structural diagram of the family, noting positions and types of boundaries as they exist when the
family is referred. He may then rediagram the subsystem boundaries as new information emerges or as
they change throughout the therapeutic process. His
goal is to restructure the family so that there is (1) a
functioning spouse subsystem with a clear boundary
differentiating it from other subsystems; (2) a parental
subsystem with clear executive functions that may or
may not involve other persons besides the spouses, but
where at any rate the channels of authority are clear;
and (3) a sibling subsystem that is free from enmesh-
ment with both the spouse and the parental subsystems so that the siblings may develop and grow under
the protection, guidance, and appropriate authority of
the parents.

To achieve these objectives, Minuchin has developed a creative variety of techniques ranging from direct education of the family members all the way to the

occasional use of paradoxical suggestion, where the family interactional patterns are restructured within appropriate subsystem boundaries without the members' conscious understanding as to how it happened. Minuchin uses himself actively and directively within the therapy sessions according to his assessment of the requirements of the situation. He may move people physically around his office or out of the office, and move himself physically as well to demonstrate and enact appropriate and inappropriate subsystem boundaries.

Minuchin cautions against preoccupation with therapeutic techniques — he believes that they should be studied with care and then consciously forgotten, so that the educated practitioner can spontaneously meet the requirements of each unique therapeutic situation. He describes his own restructuring techniques in family therapy as belonging to three major categories: (1) boundary making, (2) unbalancing the current dysfunctional family structure, and (3) complementarity (changing perceptions of hierarchical relationships within the family) (Minuchin and Fishman, 1981, p. 145).

Jay Haley

Like Satir, Jay Haley, a leading advocate for the approach generally known as *strategic*, was an early student of communication theory. He actively participated in the research that developed the concept of the *double bind* in interpersonal communication theory, described earlier in this section on Satir (Bateson, Jackson, Haley, and Weakland, 1956). Like both Satir and Minuchin, Haley is an adherent of the family systems approach. Rather than search for intrapsychic causes for behavioral symptoms, he looks instead for interpersonal meanings of symptomatic behavior. For example, Haley views symptoms (such as certain illnesses, alcoholism, or phobias) as creative means for the sufferer to exert control in a relationship. Such unhealthy means for control would surely arise as a last resort and outside of the consciousness of the sufferer. Nevertheless, these symptoms constitute important interpersonal tactics for control in a relationship; the sufferers would not be able to give them up without meeting the need for control in some other way.

For example, a woman whose husband is engaging in a series of affairs may develop a severe physical illness that eludes exact diagnosis, but which serves the function of forcing the husband to come home at night to take care of her physical needs. The philandering husband's time is now required for shopping, housecleaning, and meal preparation. He no longer has enough time to conduct his extramarital affairs. The wife thus is able to regain control in her marital relationship. The cost to her is her health, a price she may be more than willing to pay to reclaim her husband. However, both she and her husband will be puzzled about the nature of the illness and concerned that she does not seem to be getting well. Doctors may call her a hypochondriac.

While Haley, in his strategic model of therapy, is interested in family communication patterns, his particular interest involves communication specifically in the present. How does current communication, both verbal and nonverbal, maintain the status quo (homeostasis) in the family? Haley consciously focuses narrowly on the presenting problem as it is brought to him by the family. He feels that this is the most powerful point of entry for family therapy. He works actively with the whole family to help them define the presenting problem clearly and distinctly. Then, he develops a specific plan to change the particular behavior that has been described as problematic. He uses directives or tasks to get the family to move beyond the present functioning that is maintaining the problem behavior. For example, one family's presenting problem was bedwetting by a young daughter. Father sided with the daughter against the mother — he felt that the mother should be more understanding. Father was assigned by the therapist the task of washing the sheets every time his daughter wet the bed (Haley, 1963, p. 60).

Many systems-oriented therapists argue against "just curing a symptom" in family therapy. They argue that after one symptom is cured, another will crop up to fill the same function (maintaining the family homeostasis, or status quo) that the first symptom served. Haley's point of view, however, is that if the therapist can get a family to experience positive change, the family members will learn from the results of their actions. The learning can then be applied to further systems change. For example, in the case above, Haley's immediate strategy was to end the bedwetting. But the reason Haley believed the intervention would work involved a structural perspective. According to Haley's observation of the current interactions within this family, father and daughter formed a subsystem that was "tighter" than either the parental subsystem (father and mother) or the spousal subsystem (husband and wife). By assigning father the task of washing wet sheets, Haley assumed that father would soon tire of the daughter's symptomatic behavior and would join with the mother in defeating it. To do so, father would have to disengage from the daughter. This disengagement could then become the basis for further work, in which different tasks could be assigned to help father and mother strengthen their own subsystems (parental and spousal). Work with the marital pair could then remove the need for the development of further symptomatic behavior by the daughter.

Even more than Minuchin's structural model, Haley's strategic therapy utilizes paradoxical directives in helping families change symptomatic behavior. The paradoxical approach is normally used only with families who consciously wish to change but who resist control by the therapist. They resist because unconsciously, the change they think they want is threatening to them in some way. Yet they have contracted for help. The therapist might find, for example, that for some apparently inexplicable reason a given family does not carry out the therapist's directives as assigned. In such a circumstance, Haley might experiment with paradoxical directives. Supposing, in the case above, father forgets that his task is to wash his daughter's wet sheets, or mother forgets that father is supposed to do it and does the washing herself before he gets the chance. Haley might then *reframe* the bedwetting to the family as something the daughter is doing to help the parents in some way. Reframing is a therapeutic technique in which the meaning of problem behavior may be redefined as somehow good for the family system as a whole. (Reframing changes the conceptual and/or emotional setting or viewpoint in relation to which a situation is experienced and places it in another frame that fits the "facts" of the same concrete situation equally well, or even better, and thereby changes its entire meaning.)

In the case above, the therapist might suggest that the daughter be encouraged to wet her bed because the bedwetting might just be the most important thing the couple has to talk about with each other at the end of the day. The therapist might even tactfully suggest that if the girl were cured, the couple might grow bored with each other and split apart. This would be a terrible thing, and so the parents should be advised not to do anything to change the bedwetting behavior.

According to the theory behind paradoxical interventions such as these (actually, this is double-bind theory applied to the therapeutic intervention itself), if the family were to follow Haley's instructions as given, the bedwetting would continue; yet the parents cannot consciously consent to this directive. The parents cannot consciously let themselves think that the daughter's bedwetting is important to the preservation of their marriage. But to continue to resist the therapist's directives, as they have been doing so far, the parents have to cure the bedwetting! When the bedwetting is cured, the therapist must act puzzled and complimentary, saying that he doesn't know how the family has managed to bring about this important change. (This helps stabilize the results.)

PROBLEM-SOLVING STAGES

Family therapy can be viewed as a process of problem solving in a systems context, and from this perspective can be seen to consist of different stages, although in the actual interview session these stages may not appear to be distinct and may actually take place at the same time. However, for the best cognitive understanding of the process, distinguishing the stages is helpful. The stages of the problem-solving process can be conceptualized as follows:

a. Initial information gathering and assessment.

b. Defining the problem.

c. Developing a working contract between therapist and client system.

d. Further data gathering and assessment for the purpose of formulating alternative plans for intervention.

e. Choosing a plan for intervention.

f. Intervening for problem alleviation.

g. Stabilizing the results of the change effort.

h. Evaluating.

i. Terminating.

At the initial interview, the anxious family may spill out the entire problem as they see it; or, at the opposite extreme, they may be unable to speak coherently at all. The initial session may be spent largely in helping the family feel comfortable in this new environment so that they can function more or less in their own normal manner. Of primary importance is building a relationship between therapist and family that will involve essential trust and goodwill. The therapist can help by making sure that the physical office and furnishings are comfortable and pleasing to the eye, eliminating frightening barriers such as the huge desk that some professionals seem to feel safer thrusting between themselves and their clients. A desk, if needed, can be pushed into a corner and chairs can be placed so that other physical objects do not come between them (unless used for the therapeutic purposes, for example, to demonstrate visibly the invisible barriers that may separate family members). The therapist can also help build a trusting relationship by modeling a reachable, personal, and informal style of communication. The beginning part of the initial interview is usually a social session in which all participants get a feel for each other. An atmosphere of hope and goodwill can make the therapy session much less threatening. Virginia Satir (1967) has suggesting taking a structured family history during the initial interview or interviews. Since questions on a family history are reasonably predictable, this procedure may help the family members feel safer and more in control, while at the same time they reveal important information about themselves. For example, Satir asks couples how and when they met, and how and why they decided to marry each other in particular. She asks each spouse what his/her family of origin was like, including parents, siblings, and lifestyle. She asks what each spouse expected to get from marriage, and what early married life was actually like. She asks each spouse how their expectations of marriage, gleaned from their respective families of origin,

affected their present marriage in its early stages. Satir continues to question each spouse about his or her significant experiences in marriage up to the present, so that a smooth transition to present problems is usually possible (Satir, 1967, p. 135). Tactics for building trusting relationships are not fixed, and different therapists develop their own techniques over time.

As explained previously, when the therapist feels that the family is ready to enter into the problem-solving process, he will ask for initial information regarding the family's perception of the problem and why they have come for help. It is likely that the family will then talk about their concern for or frustration with a particular family member, the identified client. The therapist with a systems orientation will recognize that the problematic behavior of an identified client manifest strains involved in the effort to maintain the family system as it exists. Since maintaining the family system as it exists requires at least one of the members to develop behavioral problems, the therapist can consider theories and guess that "fixing the patient" alone won't work. Rather, the family interactional system itself, which has led to the development of the identified client's problem, should be the real target of any change effort. Family therapists have argued for years whether it is legitimate to contract with the client system to work on reducing the problems of the identified client. Since the therapist knows that the problems of the identified client cannot be modified for any significant period of time without change in the interaction and communication patterns of the entire family system, some family therapists argue that it is not legitimate to make an initial contract with a family to work on the problems of the identified client alone. Rather, these therapists believe that the family must be convinced to include their entire family pattern of interaction as a target for therapy from the very beginning.

Social workers as a profession, however, have taken the point of view historically that the most effective problem-solving interventive efforts can be achieved by "starting where the client is." If the family states that its problem is the identified client alone and wants help in problem reduction, a legitimate initial contract between family and therapist is working on the reduction of the client's problems. In order to accomplish problem reduction, change in the family system will have to be implemented anyway; and in order to maintain problem reduction, the change in the interaction patterns among members of the family system will have to be maintained. However, developing a family's understanding of its interactional patterns as a system takes time and demonstration, so that the working out of a sophisticated contract between therapist and family in the initial stages of therapy would probably be unwise anyway. The family would be unlikely to understand what they had agreed upon and might submit to a contract involving change in family interactional patterns only under the influence of the therapist's authority, which they might then resent. It is legitimate to develop a limited initial contract involving problem reduction in an identified client as long as the family will agree that the entire family will take part in the therapy sessions, as sources of information, helpers, spectators, or whatever role initially appeals to the family members to get them there. When the family is together and trying to help solve the presenting problem, the therapist can begin to observe the family system at work and can begin to identify and understand the factors that led to the development of the problematic behavior in the identified client.

Regardless of content of the therapeutic contract, it is important to take time to discuss and establish a contract in the problem-solving process. The contract specifies the respective roles of the participants in therapy and is an initial working agreement, which can be renegotiated later as new facts shed light on a need for new contract terms. The contract specifies the "problem for work" as well as more mundane agreements such as fees, frequency, and place of interviews, and so forth. The role of the therapist in any therapeutic contract is that of change agent. Skill will be essential in locating and manifesting the strains in the maintenance of the family system and in working out ways to teach and demonstrate to the family members the maladaptive elements in their communication patterns and new, healthier patterns. The therapist must be particularly careful not to get "sucked into" the family system, becoming in fact another member of the family who contributes to the maintenance of the pain-producing system (Minuchin and Fishman, 1981, pp. 161–62).

It may become apparent with time that other persons besides nuclear family members need to be in-

cluded in some of the therapy sessions. A divorced spouse or a grandparent may wield strong influence not understood at the beginning of the family interviews. As described before, the family therapist will strongly attempt to have all family members included in the sessions, although very young children, approximately three years of age or younger, may not be included by some therapists except at the initial sessions and then on occasion later. Any disruptive behavior exhibited by the children during the family sessions provides valuable on-the-spot clues as to family rules, patterns of communication, and respective levels of self-esteem. Family interviews in the home setting can be extremely important in terms of understanding the meaning of certain patterns of family communication and behavior.

Beginning the Counseling Process

Let us return to the Whitlocks. Due to nonverbal cues of spatial position in the office, the family therapist has already formulated some initial hunches about family alliances. These hunches are based on visual data and hence are worth investigating, although only some will prove true. For example, the physical separation of husband and wife, with husband barely within the office, and the wife well inside, might tend to indicate an emotional distance between the two and indicate the relative positions of the marital pair with the family, one at the center and one on the way out, so to speak. The location of the older daughter (Pat, fourteen) close to the father and also near the door, might indicate that they form a coalition of some sort. The mother's holding of the younger daughter's hand (Susan, ten) might indicate a similar close bond. Both sons maintain positions alone, and each further separates himself from family contact in a physical way—the younger son, George, seven, by staring at the floor and the older son, Lacey, sixteen, by looking out of the window and whistling. These cues also signal to the therapist the presence of family pain, felt in different ways and probably to different degrees by each member. It is likely that this family does not experience much closeness among its members as a total group; however, it is also possible that anxiety relating to this interview alone is precipitating the separation of various members of this family group.

It must be remembered that an initial interview for family therapy is not a normal situation for the family, and hence their behaviors will not be normal; most likely "company manners" or anxiety will tend to be exhibited.

When the therapist seats the family and asks the family members to introduce themselves, even though the mother has already taken charge and done so for everyone, the therapist is structuring a new communication style that is important in family therapy in order to break old and unsatisfying patterns. Each family member needs to be permitted and needs to learn how to speak for himself/herself so as to minimize the amount of mind reading the other family members must do (so often inaccurately), and also to reduce the tendency of the family communication system to relegate a family member to a fixed position in the family structure that is not necessarily the one he or she wants.

When Pat Whitlock attempted to introduce herself, she found "p" a difficult sound to pronounce. After a second or two of stuttering by Pat, Mother broke in. "Now Pat, take a deep breath and speak slowly or you'll never learn to stop stuttering," Mother said in a loud, impatient voice. She turned to the therapist and explained: "Pat doesn't need to stutter. She never stutters when she takes a deep breath first and slows down. She just tries to say everything too fast." "Now let's come back to Pat when she's ready," the therapist commented. "Pat, you tell me when you are ready," the therapist continued. And then the therapist went around to each member of the family and asked for names. The therapist checked with Pat visually and learned that Pat was not yet ready to speak. She had a hunch that Pat needed to feel safe in order to use her tongue effectively. The therapist then turned to Mr. Whitlock. "Mr. Whitlock, I'm wondering what it is that you hope will change for you and your family." The statement by the therapist contains an embedded question that assumes that the father has hopes for change, which may not necessarily be the same as the mother's. The question is aimed intentionally at Mr. Whitlock because all too

often in the American family, the male is excluded from important family transactions, partly because his primary work is considered to take place outside of the home. So much of virtually any American father's actual time is in fact spent outside of the home that his sporadic presence may actually be experienced as uncomfortable by other family members. Systematic adjustments will be made to maintain the normal interactional system as if father were in fact still absent, which socially erases father. However, a wife and an absent husband do not form an intact marital pair, and the stability of the family system is endangered. The family may fall apart unless primary contact between the marital pair can in some way be reestablished. There is real danger that the father will actually continue his drift out of the mainstream of the family system until he formalizes the reality with desertion, divorce papers, perhaps even alcoholism; or, in some instances, "accidental" death.

Mr. Whitlock responded that the problem as he saw it was out of the province of the therapist to help. His daughter was having problems in school like his wife said, but he knew that she was an intelligent girl and she was just a little lazy this year. Lots of children go through periods of being lazy. That was the same reason she was fat—she just lacked self-discipline. She'd outgrow it. He wasn't really very concerned. What did bother him was his health. His stomach constantly bothered him. But, he repeated, he certainly didn't expect a family therapist to be much help with that. Moreover, he hated his job, and the therapist couldn't do anything about that either. These children all had to get to college, and the first one would start in two years. Time was passing too fast, and the savings account looked pretty inadequate to put four children through college. However, if his wife thought that therapy was important for Susan, and the agency said he had to come too, he wouldn't object. But he sure was upset about the cost. (Mr. Whitlock was already demonstrating potential for change—he was unhappy, he knew it, and when given an opportunity to express himself, words came out like a flood. But his attitude, while overtly cooperative, came across like that of a self-perceived martyr, who was good enough to sacrifice himself but who would let his family know subtly that he was being wronged.)

"Now Daddy," interrupted Mother, "you know you're just being a hypochondriac about your stomach. The doctor says there's nothing wrong with you. And you've got a good job. We can afford whatever is important. You just always find something wrong with your boss, no matter who he is. And we're lucky all our children are bright and college material."

Mr. Whitlock spills out his words when elicited, the therapist notes, but Mrs. Whitlock has just cut him off. Is this by coincidence, or is it an ongoing pattern? This is something to check out over time.

The therapist now asks the oldest son what he experiences as a problem in the family. "The family's OK," he responds, "only Dad's always afraid I'm going to screw my girl friend, and Mom doesn't like her because of her religion . . ."

"And," interrupts Mother, "she is skinny as a beanpole and she'll grow up to look worse, you can tell by what her own mother looks like. I can't imagine marrying a woman like that — that's why I keep my figure, so that the boys who date my girls can see that I'm . . ."

"But Mother," interrupts the son, "Who says that I'm going to marry her?"

"It's not a matter of wanting to marry her," Mother responds. "She just isn't the kind of girl that wouldn't try to trap you, just trap you — you're too young to understand . . ."

"I understand exactly what you mean," Lacey replies angrily. "You think she's going to seduce me. That's crazy. Anything I do I'll do of my own choosing."

"Well," says mother, looking vacant. Silence ensues.

Older son can stop mother, the therapist notes. Father is silent and fidgeting.

Both parents are apparently worried about their older son's sexuality. How satisfactory is their own sexual relationship?

"How do you feel about Susan's problem?" the therapist asks Lacey. "She's OK, just a little too fat," he replies. "She'll be a knockout someday," "Anything else?" probes the therapist. "No, not particularly," responds Lacey.

The therapist turns to Pat and asks how she feels about the family situation. Pat begins to respond, "Susan isn't v-very happy when k-k-kids t-tease her. K-kids are mean, and I tr-try to k-k- . . ."

"Now Pat, take a deep breath . . ." says Mother.

The therapist intervenes, "Let's let Pat keep going. I'm interested in what she has to say. You find that kids are mean sometimes, Pat, and what do you try to do about it?" "Tr-try to k-k-keep to myself a lot. The gym t-t-teacher lets me run on th-the t-track by m-m-myself whenever I want t-t-to, and I run alone during study halls and by m-myself a lot after school. I hate school." Pat has said that she hates school clearly and effectively.

"You hate school, but you stay there when school is out in the afternoon?"

"Well, M-M-Mom w-w-won't let us stay in the house . . ."

Mother breaks in. "She just drives me crazy when she's home. All she does is sit in her room with the door closed and the radio blaring. Children need fresh air to stay healthy. I make her go out in the afternoon for her own good. All of the children have to keep out of the house to get their air after school. That's my job, to keep them healthy until they know better. They'll thank me someday. A woman's place is in the home."

"I see," responds the therapist. "But I don't believe that Pat is finished. Pat, let's continue.

"W-W-Well" says Pat, "th-th-that's ab-b-bout i-i-it."

Pat has been effectively silenced by Mother, notes the therapist. And she seems to stutter a little worse after each interruption.

"George," says the therapist, "Please feel free to share with us what you think hurts in your family."

"Aw," says George looking at his toes, and then he starts to cry. "George," says Father, "don't act like a baby." George drops his head and shoulders further.

Father has not scolded Pat, his apparent ally, for her stuttering; Mother has. But Father has ordered his youngest son to hide his feelings, just as Mother has ordered father to hide his own feelings. It is possible that Father tries to maintain his self-esteem by putting down his youngest son?

"He-he-he-he's n-n-not acting l-l-l-like a b-baby," says Pat. Interesting. Pat, although apparently part of a coalition with the father, is now allying herself with George, with considerable personal effort.

George stops crying, but continues to look at his toes with an almost theatrically tragic look on his face. Even with encouragement by the therapist, he will not say a word. He does look up at the therapist once or twice with big moist eyes, a pathetic, almost doglike expression warping his features.

"Susan," asks the therapist, "what makes you feel unhappy at times? I understand that sometimes you talk about being very unhappy, and that is why the family came here tonight." "Oh, not at home," gasps Susan. "I never say anything at home. My teacher told on me. I thought she wouldn't tell; she said she wouldn't ever get me in trouble with Mom. And then she went and called Mom and she must have told her everything I said. I'm not going to talk to anybody anymore. People can't keep a secret. Nothing's the matter with me except I wish I weren't so fat. Even Mom says sometimes she's so upset she might as well commit suicide, and nobody cares."

At this point Mother begins to cry loudly and insistently. "Now everybody's going to blame me for everything," she sobs, "and I'm only trying to help as best I know how. Here I work hard trying to get everybody in here for this appointment, and nobody here has even asked me what I think the problem is even though I tried to explain right when I got here. And now everybody's going to think everything is all my fault. Just listen to her, saying that I've threatened to commit suicide, like it was all my idea. Susan, you know I never meant it, and you are a very naughty child for talking about that here." (Session overtaken by several minutes of loud sobbing by Mother. Therapist gets a box of tissues.)

Mother has now effectively shut off Susan, as she has shut off Father, George, and Pat. Only Lacey has been able to gain the upper hand with her in this session, but Lacey's life is clearly far from his own. Now is not the time to bring this communication pattern to the attention of Mother and the family. Mother, although she is effectively manipulating (controlling everyone's attention and silencing others) is genuinely hurting. She will not be able to assimilate at this time any information the therapist has already learned about the functioning of this family system and the roles the various members are playing which help maintain rather than alleviate family pain. The communication pattern within this family system, which inhibits the growth of most of its members, will need to be demonstrated

over time by a therapist who can remain outside of its control. The family will have to be taught how to change its pattern of communication and personal interaction, with opportunities for concrete practice of the new patterns.

The usual introductory social phase of an initial interview has been virtually omitted in this particular session, because Mother immediately attempted to control the input of information to the therapist. The therapist has had to intervene immediately to model and elicit new communication patterns, asking for information from each family member directly rather than permitting that information to come through Mother. However, the phase of problem exploration and family interaction has yielded rich data for the therapist. Since, on this occasion, the therapist estimates that the family has already undergone as much stress as is a good idea in the initial interview (for the family may choose not to return to therapy if more fearful than hopeful), she will utilize the break in communication precipitated by Mother's crying to decrease the situational stress. The therapist's goal at this point, in recognizing a genuinely troubled family, is to enable the family to make a decision to return. Kleenex tissues, and reassurance of the mother that she is demonstrably capable, having produced four admirable children, will mollify Mother and reestablish her position of family dominance, which will return the family to its normal homeostasis. In future interviews the task will be instead to upset this same homeostasis, since it manifestly inhibits self-expression and personal growth in every member of the family. The therapeutic goal for the future will be to restructure the rules and interactional patterns of the family system into a more satisfying and growth-enhancing system, with higher rather than low morale or self-esteem among the members.

The basic purpose of an initial session is beginning problem definition, at least to the stage of the presenting problem; basic fact finding related to the presenting problems, which one hopes will reveal clues as to contributing underlying systemic factors; and helping the family to begin to trust the therapist. Therapist and family also need to work out a tentative initial contract, defining the initial "problem for work," the respective roles of therapists and family, specification of who will be included in the interviews, fees, places of meeting, frequency and time of appointments, and so forth.

In the latter part of the above initial interview, the therapist will help reduce the family's (particularly the Mother's) fear of family therapy by helping them see her (the therapist's) role as that of helper rather than judge. She can reassure the family that when there is pain present, it is reasonable and normal to seek outside consultation in order to gain relief. Many families have indeed been able to benefit by working on their problems together, she will point out, and she (the therapist) has noted many families strengths that make their particular situation look hopeful as far as potential for improvement is concerned. The therapist will list these strengths: intelligence, caring, ability to work hard, sense of responsibility, ability to present thoughts verbally (and the clear potential for those less comfortable with speaking, Pat and George, to develop the ability to do so).

The therapist will then help the family develop an initial commitment to therapy. Is the family willing to invest the time and effort necessary to make their family circumstances better? Can the family afford the fee (perhaps a sliding scale is available to alleviate worries about cost). If the family is willing to enter into a contract to meet with the therapist for general improvement of family functioning, this is a useful and open-ended agreement. If the family is willing to meet with the therapist only on the more limited problem of learning how to help Sue, this is a valid contract also. If the entire family will agree to meet together regarding how to help Sue, then Sue becomes the key to working with the family. Later, the therapist may recontract with the parents: for example, "It is becoming clearer that Sue's unhappiness has something to do with the fact that you, Mr. Whitlock, and you, Mrs. Whitlock, are not very happy yourselves, and that you sometimes are not happy about certain things concerning each other. I think it would be a good idea to talk about you and your relationship together. How about it?" When Mr. and Mrs. Whitlock have come to trust the therapist and her concern for them, they will more likely be willing to admit that they have a problem between themselves.

The Whitlocks clearly have the capacity for change, but there are indications that change will be difficult. For one thing, commitment to therapy is low. Mr. Whitlock indicates feelings of hopelessness and he believes the important things that are stressing his life (the pain in his stomach, the endless need to earn money, his dissatisfaction with his job) cannot possibly be changed through family therapy. He believes therapy can only cause him more pain (it costs money). Mr. Whitlock has said that he isn't worried about Sue. From his point of view at the commencement of therapy, therapy is only an unnecessary new financial pressure.

Mrs. Whitlock is threatened by therapy, because already in the first interview her preferred patterns of family communication have been disturbed. She is the controlling member of the family. Yet she has felt a bigger threat from outside. That threat is her fear of loss of social standing if one of her products (her child, Sue) should be labeled defective by a highly visible outside institution, the school. So Mrs. Whitlock's commitment to therapy does not initially involve a desire to bring about any change in herself or her lifestyle; rather, she wants to have her daughter straightened out.

Continuing the Counseling Process

In order for the therapist to work effectively with the Whitlock family (or any family), she will have to create a safe setting for interaction, a setting in which all members will be able to reduce their fearfulness and will recognize that their attempts at communication will be received empathetically and nonjudgmentally. Reducing fear reduces need for defensiveness. The therapist will need to structure the interviews with certain rules that will help decrease threat for all members, from very basic ones such as "no hitting," to more complex ones such as "each person here speaks for himself." The therapist needs to demonstrate for the family that difficult material will be treated with care, and that privacy, when any family member feels the need, will be respected. This means that some counseling sessions may be held with only certain family members or subsystems present, if there is a clear need and purpose. The therapist needs to know how to ask for information in such a way that the person is enabled to answer. Questions that a family member may not feel safe to answer early in therapy may be necessary and possible later when trust is firmer. Techniques such as the use of embedded questions, which clearly verbalize the therapist's question without demanding or otherwise putting the client "on the spot," are helpful as are questions that ask for a description or clarification rather than a simple yes or no answer (although the simple yes or no question can be very helpful with fearful clients before rapport is established, because these questions require less energy, and generally clients feel they are safer to answer).

A feeling of safety in the therapeutic setting can also be enhanced by the therapist's demonstrating that she is not afraid of discussing or observing issues that are emotion laden and by offering support to family members as they experience the fears, stresses, and strains of life itself and of the experience of therapy. The therapist must also be able to demonstrate that she will not be sucked into the family system with its destructive operational patterns. Use of a cotherapist on occasion can be very helpful in avoiding the pitfall of becoming too intimate a part of the family system rather than a change agent for the system. Also useful is a one-way mirror through which a consultant may watch the session as it happens. The interview can be taped or videotaped so that the therapist, the family, or both can study it later.

Family interactional patterns and rules will resist change. This is the nature of systems, as discussed earlier in this chapter. Merely "diagnosing" the nonfunctional behavior patterns and communication systems and telling the family members about them will not be sufficient to create change. The family needs more than an intellectual grasp of their respective roles in maintaining dysfunctional family patterns. However, it is necessary for the therapist to understand the patterns and rules of the ongoing family system if she is to select appropriate intervention techniques to change the system. Hence the therapist will need to observe how the family interacts, so she will insist that the family members talk with each other rather than to her in the sessions. Where an identified client or scapegoat is present, the therapist will try to understand the function of that individual in maintaining the system.

Often, the term *scapegoat* is used in a more limited sense than the term *identified client*. A child identified as a scapegoat is usually a child *blamed* by the family for a series of misdemeanors that make the family angry at him or her: bad behavior, instigating family arguments, and so forth. The term *identified client* includes the scapegoat, but may also include children whom the family do not apparently blame for creating problems for anybody except themselves. They merely see the child as having embarrassing or self-destructive problems, such as obesity, suicidal tendencies, and anorexia nervosa.

In the Whitlock family, Susan is clearly the identified client, but why Susan, and what function does she play? There are other persons in the family who seemingly could have been presented as the identified client: Pat, for one, because of her stuttering and extreme social discomfort, and Father, for another, because of his feelings of hopelessness and his physical problems, which appear to be psychosomatic in origin (that is, largely caused by stress). It is probable that Sue became the identified client in this case because she is manifesting Mother's own fantasies, "committing suicide."

If the model used for therapy with this family were purely strategic as in Jay Haley's approach, in the first session Susan's symptoms would have been highlighted more specifically as the immediate problem for work. Susan's presenting symptomatic behaviors would have been more deeply explored and outlined in detail: staying at home during many school days, doing poor work at school, overeating, and talking about suicide. A specific plan to change these behaviors would have been developed. For example, the therapist might have directed Susan to stay home from school every day for the first week between sessions; Susan might have been directed to talk about suicide with Mother every day, but only between the hours of 9 and 10 in the morning. The therapist would be acting on the theory that this would allow Susan to stay home. Then, as a part of expected behavior, she would be practicing obedience. The fearful pull of suicide would be reduced by getting that topic right out into the open, yet discussion of suicide would be confined to one hour per day. Mother, as a responsible parent, would feel constrained to tell Susan that she herself had no intention of committing suicide; Mother would come up with all sorts of reasons to persuade Susan why Mother would not really do such a thing, and why

Susan should not consider doing such a thing either. Under close scrutiny, the "pull" of suicide as a means of problem-solving (gaining attention) would be exposed as inadequate (the perpetrators wouldn't be around to enjoy the attention they would receive).

Under the strategy therapy model, how the task was carried out (and the results) would be discussed in detail at the next family therapy session. Further tasks would then be assigned as needed to interrupt Susan's symptomatic behaviors. The therapist would hope that this type of work would lead into therapy with the marital couple, Mr. and Mrs. Whitlock.

The Whitlocks' therapist does not utilize a purely strategic model, however. This counselor chooses to begin with a structural approach combined with techniques derived from the communication model. The therapist chooses to study patterns of interaction within the family as a whole to determine what factors are helping to maintain Susan's symptomatic behavior. Further interviews reveal that mother feels very stressed and unappreciated within the family, even though she clearly occupies the position of dominant parent, and in that role is the key to the family pain. Mother can make the decisions in this family. But what factors led to this situation?

Mother, the only child of elderly parents, learned when she was young that she could get anything she wanted by making enough noise about it. When a direct request was often ignored—because her parents tended to be tired or involved in community issues—asking, insisting, tears, and finally temper tantrums always worked if carried on long enough. Hence Mother learned to get the attention she needed by demanding it, and her demands were effective for her in that setting. Father, on the other hand, was a middle child in a large family controlled by a very dominant male parent. Father wasn't able to get what he wanted, either materially or in terms of affection, no matter what he did, and so he tended to withdraw and feel hopeless during much of his childhood. He made the most gains with his own father when he was visibly obedient, so father tended to repeat the role of the good child within his family of procreation because they worked best for him as a child. But it didn't meet his needs very well in either situation, and as an adult he still feels helpless and hopeless.

The combination of a demanding, blaming wife and a withdrawn, compliant, and placating husband developed into an increasingly rigid system within the Whitlock family. Mrs. Whitlock kept right on demanding, and on the surface of things, she got everything she wanted; Mr. Whitlock did her bidding. He was able to send effective messages to his wife, however, that he did not appreciate how he was treated, that he did not deserve how he was treated, and that he did not like Mrs. Whitlock very much because of how she treated him. Mr. Whitlock felt used and unappreciated; but Mrs. Whitlock felt lonely and misunderstood. A new family system developed in which everyone's self-esteem remained low and rules were rigid (set by the mother). In the family rules for communication that developed, everything had to go through the mother and be approved by her before communication was considered valid. This type of system tended to feminize all the members of the family (speaking in terms of feminine sex-role training as culturally tending to be in the direction of impulse control, inhibition, passivity, and dependence upon the parents, in this case the mother). All males in the Whitlock family, at the time of entrance to therapy, were responding by withdrawing in one way or another, and, in fact, Pat was also. Only Susan was emotionally bonded with Mrs. Whitlock.

It is interesting to note how the cultural norms for expected male and female gender role behaviors and means for achieving personal happiness have affected the life and emotions of the Whitlocks, helping produce some of the unhappiness and confusion of various family members. Mother is not happy but she cannot openly admit her unhappiness to herself and thus examine the causes, because she is doing exactly what she has been taught she should want to do: to be a wife and a mother. Mother has also had exactly the number of children she thought she wanted (two more than her husband wanted). A bright woman, she has read most of the literature circulated among her generation of mothers, which extolled the virtues of bright young women bearing large families, to maintain the quality of the population. The children she produced are all bright and physically attractive. She thinks she ought to feel happy, and spends a lot of energy telling herself and everybody else how happy she is and what a fine family she has. Happiness and a fine family are important status symbols to Mother because her culture says that these products are her means of achieving personal importance. However, when the children or husband try to defy Mother's strong will at times, she feels desperate and deserted and breaks into tears, threatening to commit suicide because "nobody cares about me around here." Since four children and one husband add up to five against one, even with Mother the very dominant and controlling personality she is, incidents of defiance do occur with reasonable regularity. However, Mother's tears, angry words, and accusations usually bring her the desired results. She wins each battle at the price of standing alone — nobody dares to get emotionally near to her. All defend themselves against her. Mother's closest emotional bond is with her ten-year-old daughter, Sue, who feels her mother's loneliness. Sue becomes fearful of leaving mother (does poorly in school, stays home from school a lot), talks about suicide with her teacher when she does attend school (the environment in which she consciously feels the most stressed), and overeats. Sue's problem then has the function of manifesting Mother's unhappiness as well as her own. Moreover, Sue does not feel especially wanted by her father. She does not think her father likes her very much and knows her existence is a financial burden to him.

Sue's problems are the ones recognized within the family quite simply because Mother is the parent with the power to recognize them. She is the dominant parent and thus can make the decision to take Sue to therapy when virtually nobody else wants to go. Mother will want to help Sue because she feels a bond with Sue. She will not necessarily recognize that Sue's problems reveal her own distress, although this realization comes very close to the surface in the first interview.

Further interviews reveal that Mr. Whitlock consciously feels alienated from and angry with his wife. He feels she has put him in an impossible position. He hates his work but knows he has to work to support his family. Society teaches him that monetary support of the family is up to him, or he is a failure. He feels responsible to support his children now that they are born, but he wishes they hadn't been born, particularly Sue and George, because he felt overburdened already after the birth of the first two. He feels stuck, and because Mrs. Whitlock made him have a large family, everything is her fault. To do his duty to his family he will have to continue to do work he dislikes forever. He is extremely resentful about it, toward his wife and the children too. He cannot express his resentment toward his wife overtly because she is too powerful — she verbally puts him down whenever he tries to express his resentment, or she bursts into tears and threatens suicide. Besides, she can make him feel very guilty about his wish to have had fewer children. How can he not want George and Sue? Sometimes Mr. Whitlock expresses his resentment toward his children in subtle ways — by criticizing Lacey's relationship with his girlfriend, or George's hypersensitivity. Mr. Whitlock is also developing somatic problems — taking out on his own body what he cannot express against the significant others in his life. This happens because his constant tension affects his body chemistry.

Continued therapy sessions reveal clear coalitions or subsystems within the family: Father and the oldest daughter Pat; Mother and Susan; Mother and Lacey (not as strong); Pat and George, which occasionally conflicts with Pat and Father. Father has little or no relationship with Lacey, because of competition for influence with the mother. Lacey can get his way with Mother more than Father can. Mother respects Lacey more than Father as Lacey is a successful leader at school and a social success, although she disapproves of all the girls he dates. Father avoids George and Susan; he feels too tired to play with them when he comes home from work, and they are still little enough that at times they ask for his attention. Mother has little or no relationship with Pat, except to criticize her social awkwardness, her stuttering, and her appearance. Mother does not think Pat is a very good family showpiece. She is obviously awkward.

The normal *natural* subsystems do not manifest themselves in this family. The husband-wife, or spouse, subsystem exists only minimally — father brings home the income and mother takes care of the housework and the children. Emotionally they do not satisfy each other's basic needs, and each feels resentful about what he/she is not getting (appreciation, love, and so forth). However, Mr. and Mrs. Whitlock are also both fearful of completely losing each other, the only scrap of adult sustenance they have. Once Mother did run off with

Sue to her father's home, terrifying Mr. Whitlock that he would be left having to hire a baby-sitter to take care of George. She came home, however, and no one spoke of the incident thereafter until it finally came up in therapy. Mrs. Whitlock had hoped that her leaving would make Mr. Whitlock more attentive, but after the first stir, nothing changed. Mr. Whitlock felt he was already doing more than could be reasonably expected of him in terms of holding up his end of the family bargain. Only fear of the unknown on the part of Mr. Whitlock and his strong conservative values kept him from leaving his family. He felt he did not love Mrs. Whitlock any longer, although he didn't admit it to her. He had not attempted a sexual relationship for years; she demeaned him as being impotent. In fact, anger and fear of another pregnancy created Mr. Whitlock's main sexual problem. Being ignored sexually, of course, effectively communicated to Mrs. Whitlock her husband's displeasure with her.

The children do not form a normal subsystem, either. Only Pat and George have even a minimal bond between them, and this is actually a substitute parent bond. Neither Mr. nor Mrs. Whitlock feels close to George—each has other favorites. George is alone except for Pat; their relationship has to be parental in nature as Pat is seven years older. However, she cannot provide George with much protection, since no one can stand up to Mother's anger except Lacey. The isolation is frightening for the little boy, and when he began therapy he was effectively speechless. Mother's dominance had, in fact, kept all the children separate. She would not permit the children to have any sort of conflict in her presence, which developed an emotional separation among all the children. Rather than help the children solve problems of conflict together, so that they could learn how to communicate and to resolve their differences constructively, she separated them and punished them individually for taking part in a quarrel. She also would not permit the children to stay inside the house during the day except to do chores, because they irritated her. The children actually did not have much time together. Mr. Whitlock, although he often disapproved of his wife's parenting when he was present to observe it, rarely offered any parenting of his own, corrective or otherwise. Lacey had no

strong relationship with any sibling, nor did Susan. It was every child for himself or herself.

Restructuring the Family System

In this household full of relatively isolated individuals, the family subsystems need restructuring. The husband-wife bonds needs to be strengthened and made primary in order to provide the protection and nurturance the children need. The lopsided dominance relationship between Mr. and Mrs. Whitlock needs to be more of a relationship of equals. While the cultural mores call for the male to be dominant, and Mr. Whitlock's suffering in his subordinate position in this family is only increased due to the perceived gap in what he sees as his reality and the cultural ideal, the family need is not male dominance. What is needed is a relationship in which the needs of both parents are more nearly equally met. By apparently meeting all the dominance needs of Mrs. Whitlock and none of those of the father, both parents are isolated and both are suffering, along with the children. Mr. Whitlock's essential feelings of suffering revolve around hopelessness and helplessness and being stuck as an overburdened economic provider. Mrs. Whitlock's essential feelings of suffering revolve around loneliness and the sense of not being loved or appreciated.

The parent subsystem has been truncated in this family so that it effectively consists of mother only. Father has withdrawn into his depression and somatic complaints. The parent subsystem needs restructuring and strengthening so it includes both parents.

Moreover, the boundary between the spouse subsystem and the sibling subsystem is enmeshed. Mrs. Whitlock and Lacey, and Mr. Whitlock and Pat, are more involved emotionally than the two spouses themselves are with each other. Such a lack of boundary between the spouse subsystem and the sibling subsystem can only be frightening and confusing to the children and to the marital pair as well.

The children could benefit by a strengthening of their subsystem as well. If the bonds among the chil-

[handwritten marginal note: Done on the move about child abuse.]

dren were stronger, or their bonds with peers outside the family were stronger, their dependence on the emotional situation between their parents would not be so profound.

Restructuring a family system is a difficult task. Certain techniques can help a family prepare for change, however. Family members can watch themselves interact on videotape, which can sensitize them to how they come across to other people. Even an audiotape recording can be very helpful for this purpose. Virginia Satir (1972) suggests the use of problem-solving vignettes are relatively nonthreatening because they describe the problems of other people, and each family member is asked to choose a solution independently. Then the family members must compare their responses and come to an agreement on a group approach. In this way family coalitions are revealed but the family also has the opportunity to observe their own coalitions explicitly and can learn how to compromise effectively in a situation where nobody is going to lose anything perceived as vital.

Family members can also be separated from the rest of the family and allowed to observe family interaction patterns from behind a one-way mirror. Or, a subgroup can sit behind the rest of the family as they interact, in the role of observers. At the end of the specified interaction, the persons in the subgroup can provide feedback to the family on the communication patterns they observe.

The therapist can have various members of the family group reenact conflicts through role-play. Role-play brings the conflicts right into the therapy room. But in role-play situations, there is opportunity to reconstruct the scenes. The therapist may choose to model more constructive ways of handling conflict, or may instruct the family members to reenact the scene but perform different or reversed roles. The therapist may have a child play the role of a parent in instances where discipline is an issue, may have the respective parent play the child, and so forth. Role-play offers the possibility of practicing new and more constructive methods of conflict resolution and of developing empathy for the other person's point of view.

In the therapy sessions, the therapist may choose to escalate stress in order to break a nonproductive stalemate in a family conflict. Escalation of stress can temporarily break an unhealthy pattern of interaction. For example, in the Whitlock family situation, the therapist can choose to side with father on every issue until mother explodes; the therapist can then deal with the function of tears and threats, and discuss and demonstrate other means of conflict resolution. The therapist may choose to side with the mother on every issue until the father is goaded into changing his habitual pattern of being the placater and martyr and will finally become angry enough to defend himself. The therapist can then observe his method of expressing angry feelings and will be able to learn why they are normally so ineffective in this particular family. New methods of self-assertion may be discussed, demonstrated, and practiced (Minuchin and Fishman, 1981, p. 179).

The therapist may take on an educator's role with the family, explaining how apparent success at dominating and getting what a person wants in the short run can rob him or her of the goodwill of significant others, eventually resulting in isolation (no one left to dominate), as was happening between Mr. and Mrs. Whitlock. However, to fortify the intellectual understanding, simulation and role-play games can be utilized.

Virginia Satir (1972), for example, uses family structuring and communication games in which she has appropriate members of the family model the stance and nonverbal gestures of the placater, the blamer, the computer, and the distractor (Satir, 1972, pp. 59–79). With the Whitlock family, Mrs. Whitlock would initially be assigned the role of the blamer. The therapist would help her to position her body so that the nonverbal symbols of blaming would be highlighted and magnified—the pointed finger, twisted face, and so forth. Mr. Whitlock would be arranged as the placater, kneeling, open hand upward, and so forth. Lacey could be assigned the role of distractor, looking off in an irrelevant direction, whistling, and so on, and Pat the computer (stiff body, upright spine). The next step is to act out the corresponding roles. Satir suggests role-playing the communication stereotypes in triads, keeping sessions to approximately five minutes in length. The family is to choose the problem to communicate about, but each role-player must stick to his or her role in a given role-play situation. The blamer must blame, physically and verbally. The placater must apologize for anything and everything and agree with the blamer that he or she is unworthy of living. The distractor must toss in irrelevant words and gestures. The computer must mouth logical positions irrelevant to the emotional components of the situation. After five minutes, roles should be shifted. The game should continue until every family member has played all the roles. This may take hours, depending on family size, but Satir feels that this is an excellent and intensive way of demonstrating to family members how the various roles feel, how to shift to a new method of interaction, and what that feels like.

The very humor of some of the games, and the surprises revealed through observing themselves on audiotape or videotape can help loosen the rigid defenses of the individual family members and can break up the rigidity of the old communication patterns. For example, among the Whitlocks, a communication pattern existed in which Mrs. Whitlock played blamer, Mr. Whitlock placater, and the children shifted between the placater and the distractor roles in the real family situation. Through practice and demonstration, they were able to loosen these patterns toward the more ideal interaction pattern that Satir calls "leveling" or "telling like it is."

In the case of the Whitlock family, Mother also created a typical double-bind situation for all family members. She told them that people shouldn't speak unless they had something pleasant to say. She also told them people worth their salt were honest and should be frank, like herself. If she then asked a family member to express an opinion on something she had done (which she often did: "Look at the new dress I made; what do you think of it?") in order to get some needed attention, she placed the person she addressed in a double bind if that person did not like the dress. If the person lied and said the dress was lovely, then that person was worthless. If the person was frank, Mother would feel unappreciated and would become angry. It was a "damned if you do, damned if you don't" communication system.

Because Mrs. Whitlock so often placed the other family members in a double-bind situation, the other family members had learned to avoid attempting real communication with her. They became experts at eva-

siveness ("I'm sure you must have worked hard on it, Mother"), or at disappearing, either through silence, stuttering, or through activities away from home. Lacey generally chose the latter by remaining as uninvolved as possible. The toll was great, even on Lacey, because he lost the nurturance and protection a family should provide. Moreover, Mother was openly critical of all his friends, and Lacey couldn't silence her all the time. Mother recognized that Lacey preferred the friends to herself.

The toll was also great on Mother. Nobody leveled with her and she knew it, driving her to distress. She had no idea she created double binds and thus had no idea of her own role in driving her family away. She could learn to identify the setup, however, through the use of audiotapes, videotapes, and role-play, and she could then decide which she really wanted most — a real relationship with her family or placation and rote obedience. Mother will need courage and persistence to break her patterns of relationship. It is hard to change, and besides, a dominant role provides a lot of immediate rewards.

The therapist was also able to identify a destructive family communication "loop" involving Mother. Mother usually had to initiate verbal exchange if she wanted verbal communication, due to the various types of withdrawal of the rest of the family system. But then when Mother succeeded in eliciting a response, she would criticize it, precipitating a new withdrawal response. The new withdrawal response would anger Mother, and she would further criticize, usually couched in language of "I'm only telling you this because I love you." Her words were of love, but her voice tone and facial expression were of anger. Family members generally believed the visual communication cues rather than the verbal, and responded as if attacked: Lacey by attacking in return, the others by further withdrawal, precipitating a new destructive communication loop, with Mother forcing a new response to try to maintain contact, being displeased with the response, and criticizing it. Pat and George effectively solved this problem by being unable to speak in their own various ways, so it was harder for Mother to "hook" them. Not surprisingly, Mother felt closer to Lacey and Susan.

To break the loop, all family members had to recognize it intellectually. Then they had to practice new patterns of communication, using techniques of role-play and modeling by the therapist. Mrs. Whitlock's control of the communication process had to be blocked. The process took a great deal of energy and commitment from the family. The person for whom new self-assertion was hardest was Mr. Whitlock, because he honestly felt he was being "a good guy" by letting Mrs. Whitlock run her show the way she thought she wanted it. He had to understand that she was in pain too before he could permit himself to alter his placater role. Moreover, he had never successfully attempted any other role in his life. He had to begin to believe that his own feelings were important, that he wasn't being a good guy, but rather dishonest and lazy by withdrawing from the household, and that he wasn't totally stuck with his unsatisfactory life. He could make a change. (He had to learn emotionally to understand that Mrs. Whitlock's control over him was not as truly invincible as his father's had been when he was a small boy.)

The therapist assigned tasks to Mr. Whitlock and Mrs. Whitlock that they were to do together without the children, so as to strengthen their marital bond. Lacey was old enough to baby-sit, so the parents were instructed to go away together on several different weekends, all by themselves, leaving Lacey in charge.

The therapist was able to engage the couple in a discussion of their lengthy sexual abstinence, and brought the factor of fear of pregnancy out into the open. Fear of pregnancy was discussed early in the therapeutic process, and Mr. and Mrs. Whitlock were able to agree on sharing responsibility for birth control. Fortunately they did not have to cope with negative religious values in this area. Some sexual activity resumed. Later in the therapeutic process, as part of discussions of the functions of sex in the marriage as a means of communicating approval or disapproval, Mr. Whitlock was able to realize that he was equally responsible with his wife for procreating four children. Gradually he was able to let go of most of his resentment toward his wife for "insisting" on having the children. In fact, Mr. Whitlock had chosen to go along with her desires and could instead have exerted the energy to refuse to participate in conception. In the case of the Whitlocks, the wife had never deliberately deceived her husband through, for example, "forgetting" to use

her means of contraception and "accidentally" conceiving children. She had been emotionally powerful enough to secure her husband's voluntary (if grudging) cooperation. It was later on that Mr. Whitlock's growing resentment manifested itself in sexual abstinence. (In family therapy, some therapy sessions may be scheduled with particular family subsystems if there is a special purpose. Most of Mr. and Mrs. Whitlock's therapeutic sessions surrounding their sexual lives together were conducted with the husband-wife subsystem.)

Lacey's baby-sitting responsibilities involved him more closely with the sibling system without bringing him in competition with Mrs. Whitlock. Attention from Lacey was pleasing to all the children and helped strengthen the sibling system. Another related task the therapist assigned was for Mrs. Whitlock to take time outside of her family system without her children, leaving Mr. Whitlock in charge, strengthening his bond with the children and weakening her total dependence on child rearing as her only meaning in life. The therapist also met with Sue and her teacher (as soon as possible after the commencement of the family counseling) to discuss means for overcoming her fear of school. A "big sister," who also acted as a tutor, was found for her.

The family as a whole discussed with the therapist their various future hopes for themselves. It became clear that Pat in particular was not excited about going to college but would prefer to work in a music store for awhile. She thought she might want to go to college someday but was willing to save some money in advance for it. However, she had been certain her parents would insist on college attendance right after high school and hence resented rather than appreciated her parents' real financial sacrifice in her behalf as they tried to save ahead for her college expenses. George and Sue were too young to know what they thought about college, but Mr. and Mrs. Whitlock were able to recognize that their preoccupation with college for their children was more their own expectation (reflecting a societal status symbol) than a necessity. Lacey did want to go to college right after high school but was willing to pay some of his own expenses. He enjoyed the idea of contributing to his own support. He hadn't wanted his father to pay for his college expenses anyway, even before coming to therapy, because he had felt so alienated from his father, whom he perceived as an unhappy and ineffective man. However, Lacey hadn't been able to tell anybody about these feelings before. Now that the children could talk about their feelings in a safe place, and could work out ways of dealing with them, they could release themselves from their restrictive and rigid roles in their destructive family myth—that everybody had to do what was expected, from saying the right things on command to going to college when and where expected.

It was learned that none of the children wanted Father to continue working at a job he hated so much. They felt responsible for his misery and helpless to change it. Mother was also able to recognize that Father's unhappiness more than canceled out the benefits of his reliable and adequate income. Moreover, Mrs. Whitlock was able to recognize that she did not enjoy being in the home all day herself, that maybe her place wasn't totally in the home, and that perhaps she could better utilize her time and energy by helping provide part of the family income. Once Mrs. Whitlock could recognize her irritation with child rearing without guilt, the family could make some shifts in its linkage with the economic market. Mr. Whitlock changed to a lesser paying job that allowed him more freedom and personal creativity, which he craved. Mrs. Whitlock took on a part-time job, which both demanded and provided emotional energy, thus reducing her demands on her children to supply her meaning in life. She was also able to help reduce the financial pressures in the family through producing her own income. The children began to understand that seemingly hopeless circumstances could indeed be changed and that they could influence their own futures. They began to take themselves seriously, and the family began to pull together.

Maintenance of Gains and Termination of Counseling

While family therapy can often be effectively completed in a few weeks, the problems of the Whitlocks required a longer time to resolve. Therapy for the family continued for approximately a year, until Mr. Whit-

lock was established in a new job and Mrs. Whitlock was working part-time and able to release her rigid control on the family system. Important changes had taken place and were being maintained. Lacey was working part-time, saving for college, and Pat was seriously visiting music stores with an eye toward future employment. She still stuttered somewhat but was no longer being reprimanded for it. Susan was attending school regularly, doing average work scholastically, and no longer talking of suicide. George was talking, at least occasionally. Mr. and Mrs. Whitlock regularly took time to do things as a couple, and while they still disagreed with each other frequently, they could talk with each other about their feelings and work out compromise solutions. At this point, termination of therapy became appropriate.

Termination itself requires preparation, so that the family system will not revert to its old patterns of interaction, brought on by distress precipitated by the withdrawal of the person (the therapist) who has been actively intervening to restructure the system. Discussion of termination must begin well in advance of its actual occurrence. Mutual evaluations by the family members of where they came from at the beginning of therapy, where they are now, and where they would like to be ideally can be helpful. Assurance by the therapist of continued availability should the family feel the need is also helpful. A gradual tapering off of interview sessions—for example, from once a week to once every two weeks, with a final meeting a month or so later may help reduce regression. (For further information on termination and evaluation, see Chapters 6, 7, and 10.)

SUMMARY

This chapter describes social work practice with families. A wide diversity of family patterns exist in the world. Although the nuclear family is still the predominant family form in our society, it is a serious mistake for social workers to use the nuclear family as the ideal model that individuals in our society should strive to form. There are many other family forms that are functioning well and are deserving of respect.

Family patterns and forms are substantially affected by the culture (larger system) in which they are located. Families in our society perform the following functions that help maintain the continuity and stability of society: replacement of the population, care of the young, socialization of new members, regulation of sexual behavior, and source of affection.

An infinite number of problems may occur in families. When there are problems in a family, social services are often needed. There is extensive variation in the types and forms of services that are provided by social workers to troubled families.

One of the many social services provided to families is family therapy. In this chapter family therapy is defined. Characteristics of open and closed family systems are described. Coalitions and alliances between subsystems and members of subsystems are discussed, as well as ideas of how and why certain subsystems are formed and how behaviors of particular subsystems affect behaviors in others. The role of the identified client and/or scapegoat in helping maintain unhealthy family homeostases and in serving as somewhat socially acceptable tickets of admission to therapy is explored and discussed in detail.

Three approaches to family therapy are described and compared: those of Satir, Haley, and Minuchin. Satir stresses clarification of family communication patterns. Satir points out incongruent messages and double-binds to family members and teaches family members to send clear, congruent messages instead. She analyzes rules in the family and helps clarify them in the context that rules may be bad but the people setting or bound by them are not. She teaches family members how to change bad rules and insists each member be heard in her presence, thus teaching respect for each person and each point of view. She emphasizes that differentness between family members should be openly acknowledged and used for growth.

Haley's approach involves clear definition and description of the presenting problem and the assigning of specific tasks or directives to solve the presenting problem. With resistive families, paradoxical directives may be used, with the therapist choosing to act "puzzled" when the presenting problem is alleviated.

Minuchin's major emphasis in therapy is restructuring the major subsystems (spouse, parental, and sibling) within the family so that each may accomplish its appropriate functions. Minuchin is considered a member of the *structural* approach to family therapy. According to Minuchin, the parental, the spouse, and the sibling subsystems have different major functions that must be fulfilled if the family is to survive as a healthy unit. In restructuring the family Minuchin may seek to have members consciously understand and improve communication patterns. Or, he may bypass direct cognitive understanding by a family of its communication patterns and instead use a paradoxical suggestion.

The chapter also examines the role of the social worker as change agent in the guise of family counselor or therapist, utilizing the perspective of family counseling and therapy as a particular example of the problem-solving process in the systems perspective.

EXERCISE

*The Application of Systems Theory Concepts to a Family's Interaction**

Description: This activity is designed to illustrate systems theory principles in a meaningful manner. Student volunteers are asked to assume specific roles in a family. The family is

---

*This exercise was written by Karen K. Kirst-Ashman, Ph.D., professor in the social work department, University of Wisconsin — Whitewater.

presented with various situations after which family members are asked to describe their reactions. Following each situation in a brief total class discussion focusing on the identification of various systems concepts to describe family interactions.

Objectives: On completion of this exercise, students will be able to

A. Describe some systems theory concepts and apply them to a family's interactions.
B. Examine the effects of various problem and crisis situations upon families.

Step 1: Name and define for the class the following family systems concepts:

System: a set of elements so arranged and so interrelated that change in any one of the parts of the system activates reaction and change in all the other parts.

Homeostasis: the dynamic balance and particular ordering of parts that was successful in the past for maintaining the system and that the system strives to maintain.

Boundaries: the repeatedly occurring patterns of behavior that characterize the relationships within a system and give that system a particular identity.

Open system: a system that tends to exchange new information relatively easily across the system's boundaries and can develop a new homeostasis that incorporates new information.

Closed system: a system that tends to inhibit any flow of new information across the system's boundaries. A closed system tends to become rigid and atrophy.

Subsystem: a secondary or subordinate system within the larger system.

Step 2: Describe the following family roles to the entire class and solicit volunteers to play each role:

ROB: husband and father
         age forty-one
         calm, level-headed
         makes most of the family's decisions
         works as an accountant
         makes an upper-middle-class income

LAURA: wife and mother
         age thirty-five
         pleasant, attractive, warm
         typically follows Rob's lead
         does not work outside the home

BENJI: fifteen-year-old son
         quiet, private, likes to spend time alone
         has a few friends who tend to have a history of minor delinquencies
         maintains a B− average in school

SUSIE: ten-year-old daughter
         outgoing, personable
         has numerous friends and interests
         maintains an A average in school

Step 3: Have the volunteer family assemble in a group before the class. Tell them that you will be presenting to them three different situations that will happen to the family. Ask them each to discuss their personal reactions to each situation. After the family's reactions, ask the class to discuss which system's concepts apply to the family.

Step 4: Present the following situation, ask for family member's reactions, and ask the class to discuss how the family system might be affected:

Situation: Rob loses his job and the family is in serious financial difficulty.

Family members' reactions: The following are some potential reactions of family members:

a. Stress due to economic conditions may cause Rob and Laura to have marital conflict. The spouse subsystem may be weakened.
b. Benji and Susie may be confused and worried about the future.
c. All family members might be angry at the lack of funds for personal use.

Systems theory applications: The class may focus on the following possible applications of systems concepts.

a. Homeostasis within the system is disrupted.
b. Change affecting Rob affects the entire family system.
c. The system may change from being an open system with easy interchange of information across system boundaries to a closed system under stress. New information and input may no longer be easily assimilated.

Step 5: Using the procedure described above, present the following situation:

Situation: Rob finds another comparable job. However, Laura also has found a full-time job as a receptionist at a law firm. She decides she likes the additional income and the feeling of competence and independence that the job provides.

Family members' reactions: The following are some potential reactions of family members:

a. Rob may resent Laura's new found sense of independence. The spouse subsystem may be further disrupted.
b. The children may resent not having a mother doing things for them at home more regularly.
c. All family members may feel more pressure to participate in household tasks when they are at home.

Systems theory applications: The class may focus on the following potential applications of system concepts.

a. The parental subsystem may be disturbed as a result of the change in roles.
b. Boundaries within the system may change. Rob, Benji, and Susie may form a new subsystem in reaction to Laura's absence.

Step 6: Once again, using the same procedure, present the following situation:

Situation: The school vice-principal calls and complains that Benji was found falling asleep in his class several times, and that a bottle of Southern Comfort was found in his school locker.

Family members' reactions: Family members may have the following reactions:

a. Rob and Laura are shocked and worried about what to do.
b. Benji may feel isolated and become even more withdrawn.
c. Susie may become very worried about Benji and approach him to offer any help she can give.

Systems theory applications: The following applications to systems theory may be discussed:

a. Homeostasis within the family system has been disturbed.
b. The parental subsystem may be strengthened to combat this newly defined problem.
c. The sibling subsystem may be strengthened if Benji and Susie form an alliance.
d. The entire family system may have to become a more open system to work with outside resources in order to solve the problem. The school, a counselor or therapist, or Alcoholics Anonymous may become involved in problem solving.

9

SOCIAL WORK COMMUNITY PRACTICE

In the words of one of the pioneers of social work, Bertha Reynolds, social work's unique place is "between client and community" (Hartman, 1989). Throughout the range of fields of practice and agencies in which social workers are employed, social workers are more effective when they have the knowledge and skills of *community practice*.

The great majority of social work students envision themselves working with individuals and/or with groups when they graduate — working as juvenile probation officers, as adult protective service workers, or as social workers in nursing homes, for example. They do not see themselves as being integrally involved in community practice, and the topic may seem to be as irrelevant as other unpopular course areas, like research or biology.

In a sense, they are correct. Especially for B.S.W. graduates, most will not be working exclusively in macropractice. In the undergraduate social work program in which I teach, only a handful of the 100-plus graduates in the last two years are working totally in this area.

Yet the functions and roles of macropractice are ones that all social workers can be involved in, either as part of the employing agency's tasks or in one's role as a citizen and professional concerned about how societal institutions treat people. To be more effective, social workers who are providing one-on-one service have been urged recently to expand their repertoire of skills and techniques; among the roles suggested are those of advocate, program developer, and organization reformer (Weissman, Epstein, and Savage, 1987).

These suggestions mirror the realities of the ways in which social workers are involved in their communities. The following examples illustrate the ways social workers are involved in macropractice:

Workers in an agency serving people with developmental disabilities learn how to communicate effectively with politicians and residents to obtain community support for group homes being located in residential neighborhoods and get around the NIMBY (Not In My Back Yard) Syndrome (Hogan, 1986).

This chapter was especially written for this text by James Winship, M.S.W., D.P.A. Dr. Winship is an assistant professor in the social work department at the University of Wisconsin — Whitewater.

Macro practice seeks to benefit the community at large. Above, representatives from social service agencies lobby for more funds at a public hearing.

Foster care and adoption workers work with black churches, civic, and social organizations to promote the "community ownership" of children in foster care, and thereby dramatically increase the number of black foster parents and adoptive parents in these communities (Washington, 1987).

A mental health center worker, aware of the lack of services for Vietnam War veterans in his area, arranges for space and publicity and helps start a support group for Vietnam vets dealing with post-traumatic stress syndrome.

Social workers and other professionals have become concerned about the loneliness, fearfulness, and boredom of latchkey children, who are home alone in the afternoon after school until a parent or parents come home from work. "Warmlines" have been established in a number of communities, where volunteers provide contact with children who need information, support, or assistance (Nichols and Schilit, 1988).

A foster care worker in a rural community is concerned because payments to foster parents do not cover some expenses that the foster parents incur — school fees and eyeglasses, for example. With the help of a local civic club, fund-raising events are organized to set up a fund to pay for those kinds of expenses.

A social worker working in a community support program for individuals with schizophrenia who have been deinstitutionalized helps organize a local group of Recovery Inc., a self-help group for former mental patients.

A social worker in an agency that serves people with physical disabilities hears a number of horror stories about how physically inaccessible the community is. She meets with a group of individuals with disabilities and works with them to publicize their case through the local media, to lobby the city council for sidewalk curb cuts, and to persuade local restaurants and theaters to make their facilities accessible.

These examples involve various kinds of activities — fund-raising, group skills, publicity, lobbying, political skills, communication, and more. What they have in common is that they involve more than an individual or a family; in a sense, *the community is the client*. The focus is not just on helping an individual or a relatively few individuals through group therapy but to benefit the community. If the workers in these scenarios are successful in their endeavors, not only individuals but also the community would benefit. A community that offers more opportunities for people with developmental disabilities to live in the community, that provides a greater number of options for people who need support or self-help groups, and that works actively to recruit foster parents and other care givers is, by the standards of the social work profession, a better community.

A commonality in these examples is that the workers involved are all people whose jobs are not primarily in macropractice, but who are willing to become active on that level when the need arises.

PERSONAL PROBLEMS AND COMMUNITY PROBLEMS

Some of the problems that the clients of social workers face are almost as old as the sibling rivalry of Cain and Abel; others are ones that a decade ago were not considered problems. For emerging issues such as AIDS and homelessness, the newness of the problem means that many communities have not put into place services, benefits, or programs for people confronted with this difficulty. Consequently, the social worker whose client has a "new problem" may be dealing with both the personal problem of the client and the broader problem of inadequate community response or support for those needing help in this area.

Because of the limited involvement in the 1980s of the federal government in the AIDS crisis, local communities have had to take leadership roles in response to the problems caused by AIDS. In rural areas, social workers can be active in creating an AIDS task force, in educating the community, and developing an AIDS services network (Rounds, 1988).

The homeless, who number between one and three million, have problems difficult for the social worker and community to address. How do you provide for continuity of schooling for children of homeless parents when there is a limited amount of time (often three to six weeks) that families can stay in one shelter before they have to move? How can you help individuals find low-income housing in areas where the low-income housing stock is dwindling? (There are twice as many low-income families as housing units available.) How do you help a community develop more affordable housing or supports for low-income families seeking the "American Dream" of home ownership? The difficulties of the emerging problems facing the "new American poor" have prompted one book's authors to describe their efforts as "working under the safety net" (Burghardt and Fabricant, 1987).

GENERALIST SKILLS AND MACROPRACTICE

The differences between *macro-* (large-scale) practice, *micro-* (one-on-one), and *mezzo-* (group) practice will become evident in this chapter. Macropractice is an integral part of social work practice, and many of the skills and much of the training for micro- and mezzopractice are also applicable to macropractice.

Working on a scale larger than one-on-one or group still involves working with people, and the interpersonal/communication skills are indispensable in this area. Especially in rural areas, the ability of a social worker to communicate effectively with others and be accepted as a person may be as significant in getting approval or cooperation for a project as the worth of the project itself (Davenport and Davenport, 1982; Falck, 1966). Showing empathy and respect are not confined to counseling sessions.

In their article on planning in social work, Googins et al. also stressed the importance of the interactive aspects of planning as well as the analytic or cognitive dimensions. The ability of the social worker to utilize herself is crucial in being more effective in facilitating and integrating the efforts of all the people involved in the planning process (Googins, Capoccia, and Kaufman, 1983).

Problem-solving skills are also as appropriate on the macro level as they are at the micro and mezzo levels. The ability to help people clarify issues and problems, decide which of these are the most important to work on, set feasible goals, evaluate the options for action, decide on the most appropriate actions, implement the plan, and then evaluate it are as important in working with citizen groups and community projects as in individual work.

It is the author's experience that well over half the attempts by groups of people to address community problems (for example, a group of people concerned over the lack of recreational facilities for youth) are not successful. In many of these cases, people who come to meetings with an interest in doing something are stymied by unorganized discussions or fragmented planning. Thirty-three people may come to the first meeting, nineteen to the second, and only five to the third. These five complain to each other about the apathy in the community, unaware that if someone had served as a facilitator in the meetings, the group might have made the kind of progress that would have kept people's interest.

Related to this is the need for skills in working with groups. In working to help people form a self-help group, the social worker will use group work skills, including the skills of being an enabler and catalyst for the individuals interested in the group. At the beginning, to attract potential members the social worker may use information networks as well as the media. As the group becomes established, the role becomes more of working with process-oriented issues to help

group members express themselves, work out differences, question the movement of the group, and so on (King and Meyers, 1981).

The skills of relationship formation and communication, problem solving, and working with groups are as important in macropractice as they are in working with individuals and groups. However, just as there are specific intervention techniques and knowledge appropriate for these levels, there are also specific skills and knowledge useful in macropractice. The following sections summarize material on the importance to social workers of knowing their community as well as information on essential macropractice skills.

KNOWLEDGE OF THE COMMUNITY

Given the agency and client base of the worker, it is useful to know not only "the community" but also the community as perceived by newcomers to the area, by members of minority groups, by those with differing sexual orientations, and so on. Different groups have preference for the kinds of help they would seek or use. Farm families, according to one study, are more likely to go to clergy, family, or friends than to social service agencies when problems arise (Martinez-Brawley and Blundall, 1989). Pregnant teenagers in one urban area also demonstrated a preference for their informal supports (families and friends) over formal organizations (Bergman, 1989).

Too often social work educators talk about how social services and financial assistance programs meet human needs in general terms—for example, "home health care services can be started in communities, which will be useful in helping the elderly stay in their homes." While the statement is an accurate reflection of the worth of that service, it also leaves the impression that all communities are essentially alike—what will work in Midland, Texas, will work in Midland, Michigan. In actuality, many characteristics of regions and communities will work for or against the success of a project. For this reason, it is essential to be aware of the services, governmental structure, the values, and other characteristics of the community.

How does a citizen's local government, or a department of it, work now? Who is to blame when it seems not to work? What are the long-range problems? Which are short term? Does the failure to resolve these problems result from the lack of money and capable people? Is the failure because of conflicting or overlapping responsibilities? Is the problem one that can't be handled by the city but needs to be treated regionally, or by the neighborhood? Is the system itself set up wrong? Does it not work because of the kinds of people in charge, or from not having enough people, or from poor management?

The average citizen (if unable to get help with a problem) may in frustration want to change the system. But he can't make much of a start unless he knows something about "the system," or at least about the part he wants changed. A little digging may show that it isn't the system but the people in charge who are at fault. Or he may find that the local government wants to do certain things but can't—because the state constitution or the state legislature won't let it raise the money or provide the services.

A citizen who wants to bring about change in the government of a community should first analyze how the existing apparatus is meant to work, what limits there are on the department that concerns him and who imposes them, and how each part fits into the rest of the system.

Beyond the correction of particular problems, social workers and other citizens have a tremendous stake in finding workable solutions to the ever-increasing demands on governments. Future problems as well as current ones need to be taken into account. If people are to make intelligent proposals for change they first need to analyze their present government, its structure, its functions, what it can do now, and what it is unable to do. They should also analyze neighborhood governments and the more comprehensive systems of which their local government is a part, as the actions of these systems will affect their local community.

The questionnaire presented in Figure 9.1 (page 228) is a useful tool in obtaining the kind of specific information that is invaluable in planning for services (or just functioning as a social worker in the community).

KNOWLEDGE OF ORGANIZATIONS

The social worker who is getting involved in macropractice will need information on how organizations function in general, and specific knowledge on the social worker's employing organizations. For example, if a social worker in protective services is interested in helping to start a Parents Anonymous group for unwed mothers, one important issue is that of permission and approval. Does the supervisor approve of this involvement? Does this approval extend to the worker's being involved in this undertaking on agency time? Is the worker acting as a representative for the agency or just as an individual? Does the supervisor (or other administrators) see any potential conflicts as a result of this activity? These questions are best answered before the worker becomes too involved. Otherwise, she could find herself in the position of the Saturday morning cartoon character who is walking out on a tree limb and hears the sound of a saw.

I was once employed by a private social service agency in a midwestern city. Not long after I was hired, the director asked me to represent the director at a meeting of people interested in expanding mental health services in the area. After the meeting, I enthusiastically reported to the director that I was serving on one of the task forces. The director became irate, informing me that my purpose was to go and observe and not to become involved in a project about which he had reservations. What I didn't know how to do at that time was to get clarification on my purpose and ask what behaviors would be supported.

Another important concept is that of organizational memory. Individually, each of us may have positive or negative associations with a particular object or event because of past memories. A friend of mine does not eat bananas because he once was violently ill with intestinal flu after eating them. While he knows cognitively that the bananas did not cause the flu, the association is such that bananas are not palatable.

Similarly, some organizations or governing bodies may be unwilling to become active in certain areas if similar efforts in the past were unsuccessful. If the worker and others are interested in starting a program

FIGURE 9.1

Your Community — Its Background*

A. Community characteristics

1. What are the major population characteristics; for example, what percentage is white? Foreign-born? Black? Mexican-American? Chinese? Indian? Puerto Rican? What are the principal ethnic and religious groups? What is the age composition? How do the population characteristics compare to state/national averages?

2. What are the principal economic characteristics of the community? Principal types of employment? Major industries? What other sources of wealth are there? Have there been recent changes in the economic life? (Moving in or out of industry? Substantial industrial or other expansions? Diversification?)

3. What is the unemployment rate? Its characteristics; that is, largely black, Chicano, young people, and so on? Have there been recent changes in this rate? If so, to what can the changes be attributed? Are there sections of your community where the rate is appreciably higher than the average?

    What is the median family income? If only average per capita income figures are available, assess in terms of these questions: Is the average skewed because of large numbers of wealthy people? Large numbers of poor? How does it compare to the national average? (Caution: even if lower, or higher, it may not reflect, in either case, wide variations or a skewed range in your community.)

4. What are the housing patterns: Percentage of residential property that is high cost, moderate, low? Condition of housing; for example, mostly new? Well-kept or maintained? Deteriorating? What is the pattern of rental property; that is, range of rents? Availability of moderate and low-cost housing? Is the community dependent on a large metropolitan area for employment? For housing of those who work in your community?

5. To what degree are "outsiders" accepted by the "insiders" who have always lived there? To what degree do "newcomers" and "old-timers" use the same services and facilities?

6. What are the norms regarding the role of the church in helping? Do the churches help out their own members who are having difficulties or are in need? Do they help other community members who are not church members? If so, what kinds of persons are aided?

7. What are the norms regarding conformity to community values regarding individual conduct? Which norms seem to be strongest? How are people treated who violate these norms?

B. Community life

1. How many newspapers are there? (If more than one, are they independently owned?) Radio stations? Television stations? Are radio and/or television stations owned by newspapers? Is news of your community carried on a regular basis in a metropolitan newspaper? What are the principal out-of-town media influences? How does one learn about local governmental activities? Hearings? Meetings? About community cultural activities?

2. What are the voluntary welfare organizations? Is there a community welfare council? Joint fund-raising, such as United Way? If more than one overall fund-raising effort, why?

3. What are principal communitywide civic and service organizations? Fraternal groups? Labor organizations? Business organizations? Cultural groups? Do they work together on communitywide problems? Are there coalitions among these groups on common interests? Ad hoc? Of longer standing? Which groups are more likely to be aligned? On what kinds of issues? Are there neighborhood groups? If so, around what are they organized — cultural, school, political interests, other?

4. How successful is the community in resolving disputes between various groups or over issues such as schools and zoning? Is there high participation in local decision making (as measured by voter turnout?) Are the elected officials and local leaders committed to long-term local services, or are they "training" for statewide office?

---

*This guide was adapted from League of Women Voters, *Know Your Community*. Copyright 1972, pp. 6, 7, 35–37. Adapted by permission of League of Women Voters of the United States.

FIGURE 9.1

━━━━━━━

(Continued)

Public welfare/Social services

A. Administration
   1. What governmental agencies (town, county, state, federal) are involved in administration of public welfare/social services in your community?
   2. Is there a public welfare board? If so, what is its composition? How are members selected? Are there legal requirements for their selection? What are terms of office? Salaries? Duties?
   3. What employees are engaged in public welfare/social service activities? How selected? What qualifications are required? What are the salaries? Are any jobs available in public welfare/social service functions for those on public assistance?

   Interagency cooperation
   1. What cooperative programs exist between public welfare agencies and the juvenile court, probation officers, schools, day-care centers, nursing homes, public health, other agencies?
   2. What cooperation is there with private social service agencies, if any exist? If there are any, what are they? Is there exchange of information? Joint planning?

B. Programs and facilities
   Noninstitutional care
   1. What agency or agencies administer services for children — neglected, abandoned children without parents or relatives to care for them? Are foster homes used? What is the rate of pay to foster homes? How are such homes chosen? Supervised?
   2. What money is available for aid to families with dependent children? General assistance? How much comes from state? Federal government? Local sources? What is the average amount available for each child? What is the caseload per worker? What type of care is provided? Are there efforts to help parents find jobs? If so, what kind? Are there adequate day-care centers?
   3. Is there an adoption service?

Other public assistance programs
   1. What programs are there for needy blind persons? Permanently disabled? Partially disabled? Elderly who don't qualify for social security?
   2. What other assistance programs exist? Temporary assistance, special and corrective needs, exceptional needs (fares, emergencies, and so on), employment services, legal services, others? What money is available for such assistance? From what sources is it available? How do individuals apply for such assistance? How is information about such special assistance made available to the people?
   3. Are special assistance programs administered by a public department? If so, what agency or agencies?

Institutional care
   1. Are there public institutions for individuals with a physical or mental disability? The aged? Orphaned? Delinquent? Emotionally disturbed? Needy persons? If private institutions are used, how? On a contracting-for-services basis? Cost sharing? Are county, regional, or state institutions used? If so, on what basis?
   2. How are public institutions administered? What are the procedures and requirements for admission?
   3. What kind of services (educational, recreational, training, and so on) are provided in each public institution? Do any community groups or individuals provide services? If so, what kinds?
   4. What is the cost per resident per day? What is the average stay? Do any of the users pay? On what basis? Do these institutions operate on a budget or a given amount per day per patient?
   5. Are there standards for public institutions — inspections, licensing, state supervision, and so on?
   6. How many persons from your community are in state institutions? What is the cost to your local government per patient? What is the procedure for admission? Average length of stay by case type?
   7. Do any of the local institutions provide outpatient services? What kinds?

that would provide jobs and/or training for teenagers, it is important to know whether anything in this area has been attempted before. It may be that five years ago a program was funded but was poorly supervised. Youths were paid for standing around and in some instances, even when they weren't there. Armed with this knowledge, the worker would realize that many people would have reservations about any youth employment program and would be careful in talking with people to point out the specific ways that the proposed program is different from the failed effort.

The worker also needs to be cognizant about the realities of organizational change. As Robert Pruger (1978, p. 161) points out, much of the discussion of organizational change is not applicable or relevant to the situation of most social workers:

Organizational change is an attractive subject to many students and faculty. Consequently, it is likely to come up in classroom discussions even where the formal curriculum seems to allow no place for any consideration of bureaucratic phenomena. The problem here is that most treatments are not helpful. They are ideological in character, rather than oriented to skill building. In class, as in the literature, the matter is too often addressed as if the central problem of change is to convince people to be for it. Though it is difficult to identify anyone who has directly opposed change, somehow there is an endless supply of able advocates seeking opportunities to cross swords with this invisible enemy. The results of these efforts are as morally satisfying as they are intellectually dulling. Through them, audiences regularly experience an invigorating, personal commitment to change. Unfortunately, such vicarious experience is no substitute for the patient observation, hard-headed analyses, and consistent behavior required to effect real change.

For the social worker interested in changing his or her employing organization or others in the community, the following organizational characteristics are relevant:

1. All organizations change. Just as an individual is not the same person she was a year ago, neither is an organization. Changes in funding or funding priorities, changes in societal values or trends, occurrences within the community, and changes in personnel all affect an organization's actions and policies.

2. The perceived risks and benefits of the proposed change to the organization need to be assessed and communicated to others in the organization as part of the change strategy. Identifying these can lead to understanding the sources of support and resistance to a proposed change (Frey, 1990).

3. The social worker who realizes that change within an organization is a continuous process can be prepared to attempt to influence organizational policies and politics when the opportunity arises. The juvenile probation worker who believes that his agency in general does an inadequate job of working with clients who are ethnic minority members can develop documentation to support this. If the present director and staff do not share the concern, the case can then be made if a new director is hired, or new training funds become available, or if other changes in the organization or community occur that allow the issue to be raised again. To the organized go the spoils.

4. As change occurs slowly in organizations and communities, individuals who "stick around" in organizations and communities are more likely to be able to contribute to change than persons who "parachute" into a community and then leave a year or two later. The image of a community organizer that many people have is that of a Saul Alinsky-type (see the section, "Models of Macropractice" later in this chapter) who comes into a community, helps people right wrongs, and then rides off like the Lone Ranger. While outside resource people, like Alinsky-trained organizers, can be useful in winning battles, wars are won and lost by the people who have staying power in organizations and communities.

KNOWLEDGE OF FUNDING SOURCES AND FUNDING CYCLES

As was stated earlier in this chapter, social workers often become involved in helping people or groups to organize in order to develop services for unmet community needs. In some cases, such as self-help groups, money may not be needed. In many other cases, funds will be needed to put the ideas or plans into operation.

Three questions are important in this area:

1. *Where is the money?* One interpretation of the golden rule is "the person that has the gold, rules."

Many times organizations and communities are able to do only what the state or federal government is funding at that time. A knowledge of those funding sources is important, but also is awareness of other sources of funding. In many states where funding has been decentralized, county governments make most of the decisions on how mental health, mental retardation, and juvenile corrections services will be provided.

Additionally, there are local foundations in some areas that will provide "seed" money for services or organizations in their first year or two of operation. United Way or United Givers may be another source of funds for new or expanded services.

Another option for securing money is fundraising, which will be covered later in the chapter.

2. *What is the funding cycle of the governmental unit or organization with the money?* Every level of government — city, county, state, federal — and every formal organization has a defined fiscal year. For the federal government, it is October 1 — September 30. For many state and local governments, it is July 1 — June 30. Some organizations use the July 1 — June 30 fiscal year, and some use the standard calendar year. Depending on the fiscal year used, decisions on how money will be spent are made at different times by different governmental bodies. For example, a county government that would be able to fund a Youth Diversion Project (which would treat youthful offenders in their home community) may be on a July 1 — June 30 calendar. Budget hearings and deliberations are generally held in March and April for the coming year. By June 1 at the latest, all funding decisions for the coming year will have been made. If a community group approached the county on that date, the county's reply would most likely be "wait until next year."

3. *How "real" is the money?* At times there is an announcement of a new source of funds that gets people excited about the prospect of doing something about unmet needs. Often, it turns out that the "new program" is simply a relabeling of an already existing program that supports service programs, and no additional money is available. I was working in Georgia in 1976 when Title XX funding for social services was introduced. Public hearings were held all over the state to help the state government decide how the $300 million plus was to be spent. Hundreds of people came to hearings in rural counties, advocating their interest. (In reality, the hearings probably measured the effectiveness of individual agencies' transportation systems in busing their clients to the meetings rather than measuring community opinion.) What people discovered at the hearings was that there would be no additional money, and if they wanted funding for new services, this would require reduced funding for the day-care centers, senior citizen programs, and so on, that had been funded in the past years.

Social work students generally learn about governments and the mechanisms by which they fund programs in social welfare policy courses. While the information may seem dry and somewhat irrelevant at that time, it becomes useful when they are working in a community with unmet needs.

SKILLS FOR MACROPRACTICE — GROUP DECISION-MAKING SKILLS

In addition to specific information and knowledge that are applicable to macropractice, there are also a number of skills and techniques that are useful in certain situations. Some of these, like the decision-making techniques described below, are also used in group work. Others, such as fund-raising and community awareness, are used primarily in macropractice.

Brainstorming

One excellent technique for use in groups that are looking for ways to accomplish a goal is brainstorming (Maier, 1970; Osborn, 1963). One common definition of *brainstorming* involves generating ideas about an issue. However, the term also denotes a *specific technique* for generating ideas, possibilities, or alternate courses of action. In using brainstorming, one tries to identify as many different ways of achieving a goal as possible. Brainstorming was developed by Alex Osborn (1963) who outlined the following ground rules:

1. Brainstorming can last anywhere from about one minute to half an hour.

2. The session continues as long as ideas are being generated.

3. Each session is to be freewheeling and open.

4. The quantity of ideas counts, not quality. A greater number of ideas will increase the likelihood that usable ideas will be suggested.

5. Members are encouraged to build on the ideas of other members whenever possible, so that thoughts are expanded and new combinations of ideas are formulated.

6. The focus is on a single issue or problem. Members should not skip from problem to problem, or try to brainstorm a multiproblem situation.

7. A relaxed, congenial, cooperative atmosphere should be promoted.

8. All members (no matter how shy and reluctant to participate) should be encouraged to contribute.

9. It is often advisable to limit members to one idea at a time so that less vocal individuals feel encouraged to say their ideas.

10. For new members unfamiliar with brainstorming, the rationale and rules for brainstorming should be explained.

11. If groups are being formed specifically for brainstorming, it is helpful to seek members having some diversity of opinion and background.

12. After the brainstorming session is over, the group then selects the best ideas (or a synthesis of these ideas) related to the issue or problem.

Brainstorming has a number of advantages:

1. It increases involvement and participation by all members.

2. It reduces dependence on a single authority figure.

3. It provides a procedure for obtaining a large number of ideas in a relatively short period of time.

4. It reduces the pressure to say the "right things" in order to impress others in the group.

5. It makes the meeting more interesting, fun, and stimulating.

6. It encourages an open sharing of ideas.

7. It helps to create a nonevaluative climate.

8. The ideas of one member can build upon those of others so that creative and unique combinations are suggested.

There are some shortcomings of brainstorming that should be noted. For many people brainstorming is a strange experience and it may lead to an initial sense of discomfort. To a restricted, self-conscious group, brainstorming may actually hinder participation as it forces members into new patterns of behavior.

Conversely, in some situations it is possible to use brainstorming as an icebreaker to open up a stuffy and inhibited group. Whether brainstorming will have an inhibiting effect or an opening-up effect will depend partially on the leader's skills and timing in using the approach.

One example of a situation in which brainstorming was useful is that of a group of residents in a part of a town where there were no recreational facilities for children. A group of the residents negotiated with the city to turn a city-owned lot in the area into a park. The city council agreed to let the residents use the area indefinitely as a park and that city maintenance personnel would keep the area mowed. However, the residents would have to raise the money for the playground equipment.

A social worker met with the group and acted as facilitator for a brainstorming session. The twenty-three neighborhood residents were initially skeptical about the process, but "got into it" as the ideas started rolling in. A total of forty-six ideas were generated, which were then categorized. The two major categories were fund-raising and looking for playground equipment not presently being used. After some discussion, the residents decided to hold a carnival on the proposed site and to use that as a focus for the fund-raising effort. A group of residents volunteered to work on that project. Another small group then volunteered to make inquiries as to the possibilities of locating unused playground equipment.

Nominal Group Technique

The process for using this technique has been explained in Chapter 6. It can be a useful approach in helping groups attempt to reach consensus, or at least give the group members information on the thoughts of the other members.

Several years ago I was asked by an interagency council in a medium-sized southern county to help them define their priorities. The interagency council was well attended by representatives of health and social service agencies in that county, and the council leadership believed that the group could influence both the United Way and the county commission if they were to speak with one voice. The problem, as always with service providers, was that each member tended to think that his area of concern (the aging, juveniles, people with developmental disabilities, and so on) was most deserving of support.

I met with forty or more human service professionals representative of all the service providers in a one-day planning session. By using the nominal group technique (and asking the participants at each step to identify *two* groups that they considered to be especially in need of services and at a later stage of the process to list *two* specific kinds of services that should be started or strengthened), the individual biases of the participants toward their own services canceled out. By the end of the day, the participants had agreed on two specific service areas that they later proposed to the funding bodies.

As this example indicates, nominal group techniques can provide members of a task force or planning group with information about their own priorities. As such, it can also be considered a needs assessment technique. This concept is explained in the next section.

Needs Assessment

Needs assessment (NA) is a term that has acquired wide usage and a variety of meanings. It has been used in referring to a statewide comprehensive appraisal of problems and needs. It has also been used on a smaller scale to refer to assessment of a community of its needs or assessment by an agency in a community of the needs of its clients. For example, a youth service agency in a community may conduct a needs assessment of its clientele. On a large or small scale, needs assessment refers to efforts of acquiring and making sense out of information so that it can be used as an aid in making decisions.

Social workers involved in macropractice can find themselves in situations where they have no information on which to make decisions, or at other times they may have an overabundance of data and have difficulty sorting out the pertinent information from the rest. When a needs assessment study is being designed, the following questions help in sharpening the focus of the NA.

WHY DO WE WANT THE INFORMATION?   An NA may be conducted for various reasons. A sponsoring group may be aware of the existence of a need, but without documentation it is difficult to convince decision makers and others of the necessity for action. In the same vein, an NA can serve to increase the visibility of an issue, condition, or subpopulation (Center for Social Research and Development, 1974).

An agency or organization may conduct an NA to determine whether its efforts are addressing the needs that are most critical. Especially when new money is involved, an NA is a procedure that can be used to gain information about various problem areas in order to determine which area most needs attention.

Another impetus for conducting an NA is that it is frequently required by a funding agency. Various governmental and private funding organizations have policies that include a needs assessment as part of the proposal development process.

Needs assessment can also be used as a consciousness-raising device. Based on the work of Paolo Freire, who combined adult literacy with politicization in working with the poor in Latin American countries, needs assessments can be designed with low-income community members so that the needs assessment is a vehicle for discussion of empowerment and community

FIGURE 9.2

Types of Information Used in Needs Assessments

A. *Profile of community characteristics.* A profile gives an overview of the demographic characteristics of a community; for example, age structure, ethnic and racial composition, length of residence, and so on.

B. *Profiles of domains of living.* These profiles provide data on the incidence of a problem and the social patterns of the population. This can include the following:
1. Economic data, including income levels, expenditure analysis, money management, and credit patterns.
2. Employment data, including occupational levels, work history, occupational aspiration levels, and vocational needs.
3. Family patterns, such as parent-child relationships, adjustment problems of children, marriage problems, and divorce rate.
4. Educational patterns, including educational attainment and needs of adults, school adjustment of children, school dropout rate, and educational attainment.
5. Housing, such as density, condition of dwelling units, and overcrowding.
6. Physical and mental health, including long-term disability, causes of death, incidence of diseases, and environment conditions.
7. Home management, including housekeeping problems, nutrition, home maintenance, and child care.
8. Recreational patterns, including leisure activities, sports and athletics, and cultural activities.
9. Criminal justice, including adult crime and juvenile delinquency rates, fear of crimes, and so on.
10. Life satisfaction, such as community solidarity and self-appraisal.

C. *Knowledge and utilization of services.* Persons needing a service often are unaware of existing services or resources. Before making decisions, it is important to discover whether this lack of knowledge among those needing services is one cause of the problem's persistence.

D. *Barriers to service utilization.* Individuals who need services may be aware of them and still not use the services because of barriers to utilization. The following types of barriers can be identified in a needs assessment:
1. Physical barriers, such as inadequate transportation or distance of the agency from target population.
2. Negative attitudes of the staff, as perceived by the clients or potential clients.
3. Feelings that a social stigma is attached to service usage.
4. Fee for usage, which is beyond the means of those needing services.
5. Actual or perceived restrictive eligibility criteria.

E. *Existing community information system.* Before a service can be utilized, the potential service recipients must be aware of its existence. A needs assessment can identify the formal and informal channels by which a given group is most likely to be reached.

F. *Resource assessment.* Identification of existing and potential resources available for utilization should occur before planning or allocating decisions are made.

G. *Political resources assessment.* The potential mobilization of political and community leaders and the population at large is necessary, since decisions are generally made in the political arena.

---

needs as well as a data collection and analysis technique (Marti-Costa and Serrano-Garcia, 1987).

One general rule is that if you cannot clearly answer the "why" question, you are probably better off not conducting an NA at this time. Information that is collected without a clear purpose rarely is used.

WHO WILL BE THE USERS OF THE DATA?   In the early stages of drawing up an NA, it is essential to identify and involve the decision makers who will eventually use the data. Allowing the potential consumers of the data to define the scope, focus, and content of the needs assessment is required if the findings are to have an impact on their concerns (Center for Social Research and Development, 1974, p. 58).

WHAT KIND OF INFORMATION DO WE WANT?   There are many different types of information that may be appropriate for a given local needs assessment. Figure 9.2

summarizes some of the types of information used in needs assessments.

WHERE DO WE GET THE DATA?   There are two broad categories of data used in NAs. One is already existent information and the other is information that needs to be generated.

Among the sources of existent information for every community are census records, state labor department and health department statistics, and agency records and reports. These data can serve as statistical indicators of the extent of problems or conditions. Another potential source of existent information might be studies conducted at some previous time for a different purpose.

One good source of information may be the regional planning commission that serves the given geographical area. In addition to possessing certain statistical information, individuals at a planning commission may be helpful in directing one to other sources. In areas where there are city and county planning units, these can be valuable sources of information.

There are times when information that is not presently available will need to be generated. This can be done in many ways. A community forum is one way of obtaining information. Interviews with selected individuals, the community leaders, frontline workers, or clients can yield valuable data.

One commonly used approach in generating data is the survey. Three techniques used in surveys to gather information are (1) the telephone interview; (2) the mailed questionnaire; and (3) the person-to-person interview.

A survey of a number of people can yield useful information that cannot be obtained in other ways. The obvious advantage of using a survey is that information directly relevant to the problem under consideration is collected.

The drawbacks to using a survey are that it requires substantial time, substantial effort, survey research expertise, and usually money. The way in which a survey is designed and conducted will influence the results. While the question "When did you stop beating your wife?" is laughable, there are questions in surveys that produce results almost as slanted.

It is a good idea to bring in someone with expertise or special knowledge about surveys to assist with the preparation or implementation. Potential sources of expertise might be found in the state office of human service departments, local colleges or the business community.

WHO ELSE NEEDS TO BE INVOLVED?   As well as involving the potential users of the data, it may also be appropriate to enlist the cooperation of other organizations, agencies, and prominent individuals in the needs assessment planning. This involvement may be advisable because the NA may indicate problem areas that the sponsoring agency may not be involved in. Also, if other agencies are involved in the collection and preparation of information, they are more likely to use it in their planning and decision making. A further reason for involving others is that at times the information will be more favorably received in a community if certain key individuals are involved in the NA process.

WHAT INFORMATION IS NECESSARY ON AN ONGOING BASIS? Some of the information yielded in an NA becomes obsolete within a short time. One thing that agencies may discover in conducting an NA is that certain types of information need to be collected or updated periodically to be useful. Also, a process of needs assessment often indicates what information is not available; this in itself, is an important finding.

A needs assessment may involve a long, complex, and costly process, or it may be a relatively simple procedure. The process should mirror the need assessment's purpose — designed to yield most fully the information needed by those making decisions.

PUBLIC RELATIONS SKILLS/ COMMUNICATING WITH THE PUBLIC

Social workers are aware of the lack of knowledge and the amount of misinformation that the public has about human services and those that use them. They also know the powerful influence that the media have. Yet, as a profession, we are ill prepared to use the media to get our message across. Skills in public education and public relations are not generally a part of social work curricula.

Brawley (1983, p. 13) believes that there are a number of barriers to effective use of the media:

Many of the barriers that exist to the achievement of positive media treatment of human service topics are primarily psychological in nature. We think that the media are entirely out of sympathy with or disinterested in our causes; we think that prevailing "news values" that stress conflict, immediacy, sensationalism, personalities, and the like present hopeless obstacles to the proper understanding and reporting of human service issues; or we view the domain of radio, television, and newspapers as alien territory that we enter only at considerable risk.

Other barriers are more concrete. The typical human service practitioner simply does not know enough about the workings of the news media to know what opportunities exist for positive action and does not possess the tools needed to undertake activities in this area with confidence that his or her efforts will be productive.

For the social worker who wants to use the media, either to publicize a new service on a one-time basis or to spotlight a community problem as part of a larger change process, it is necessary to develop relationships with the media and to acquire the skills to utilize them.

RELATIONSHIPS WITH MEDIA REPRESENTATIVES

The first step in getting coverage for your program is to get to know, personally, those who report the news in your community. Introduce yourself to the editor of a county weekly paper or the reporter for a daily paper that would cover your story. The person(s) in charge of

news at local radio and television stations are also important to know. When working with the media you should follow some basic rules.

1. Be honest at all times. This includes not only being truthful but also not leaving out important facts about a situation or issue. Representatives of the media will forgive mistakes if they trust you, so don't do anything that would damage the trust.

2. Know the deadlines of newspapers and those of the radio or television news show. Nothing is as irritating for an editor as someone walking in with a news article two hours after the deadline, or five minutes before the deadline.

3. Know the orientation of the newspaper. Are they pro-social services or do they have axes to grind?

4. Know the staff of the newspaper. To whom do you address your story?

5. Do not complain about a story unless a serious error has been made, and then first call the reporter who handled the story. Do not go to her boss unless it is absolutely necessary.

6. Do not heckle newspeople by constantly asking them why a story you submitted was not used. It is all right to ask your contact if there was something wrong that you can correct next time. But there are many reasons why your story might have been thrown out at the last minute to make room for something the editor considered more newsworthy.

7. Do not forget to say "thank you." It pays big dividends to let members of the press know you appreciate their efforts. When someone does a particularly good job of reporting about your program (on one occasion or over the space of several months), a short, simple note saying "thank you" will always be appreciated and remembered. And if you are thanking a reporter, write to the editor with a copy to the reporter.

8. Every newspaper is run differently. It is important to remember that general rules of how newspapers operate are just that, general. To know the specifics of each paper you should ask for a copy of its *style sheet*. This is a list of news article rules that editors usually give to beginning reporters. If a small newspaper does not have a style sheet, the

editor will probably refer you to a sample article or articles as a guide to how articles should be written.

9. There are distinct differences in the editorial content of a daily versus a weekly newspaper. Although a daily typically has a larger audience, a weekly places more stress on local issues and is therefore more closely targeted to the immediate needs of the readers. This is especially true in a rural area. Dailies usually have larger staffs than weeklies, so weekly editors may have a need for well-written news stories for their papers.

SKILLS FOR MEDIA UTILIZATION

Familiarization with the rules of the media is one step toward getting good coverage, but this doesn't automatically get your story in print or on the air. The social worker who doesn't have the skills to write newspaper articles or public service announcements (PSA) for the radio can follow one of several approaches:

1. Find out whether the media will do the actual work. Some newspapers do all of their own writing. If you want a feature on a client who has established a self-help program for others, a feature writer will come out and do the story. Similarly, some radio and television stations have people on staff who will develop public service information.

2. Find community volunteers to do publicity. People enjoy doing what they do well. In all communities, there are people with expertise in drawing, writing, design and layout, and so on. Some of these people will be interested in helping your agency, either for one project or on an ongoing basis. Journalism and public relations classes at nearby colleges and universities are also a good resource.

3. Develop the skills. There are a number of excellent books on using the media that have detailed explanations on writing news articles, getting your message on television, and so forth (Brawley, 1983; Church, 1980; MacShane, 1979). Writing or designing community awareness materials is a skill. Like riding a

bicycle or interviewing, you get better at it the more you do it.

FUND-RAISING

People who are involved in helping others are aware of the limitations of governmental funding. For some programs, it's just not enough money. The money can only be used for certain purposes and not for others. Regulations on how dollars are to be spent are designed to prevent waste and target the money, but they also restrict flexibility on how program dollars can be spent.

For new or small agencies and community groups, it may be difficult to get any or sufficient governmental help. There may not be any "new" money available, or the agency or group may not have the expertise or time to write a complicated, 250-page grant proposal. In all these cases, fund-raising may be an answer.

In addition to the obvious benefit of having the money when you do fund-raising, there are other advantages:

1. You gain credibility when you can show that local people support you.

When Kate Bradley was raising money for the Petros, Tennessee, health clinic, she learned the railroad was going to sell the land around its unused tracks. She wrote the president of the railroad and asked for the first option to buy the land for the clinic building. Then the politicians in Morgan County learned the land was for sale and tried to outbid her. It was clear they could double or triple her offer. Coal companies in Tennessee are used to getting their own way by using county and state politicians. Kate drove 175 miles to Nashville to meet with the railroad president and the representatives of the coal companies. When she walked into the meeting she was the only woman in the room.

The president said, "You must be Mrs. Bradley."

"I am," she said, looking him straight in the eye. Without waiting to be asked, Kate Bradley spoke her piece to the older man:

"Sir, I know you are going to honor your letter giving the health clinic the right to buy your land in Petros. I know these politicians can give you a lot more money. But I just want you to know that our money comes from cupcakes. We've had a rummage sale every Saturday, and held dinners and bake sales. Everyone in the community has given me a quilt, or a jar of beans, or put up some preserves to sell for the clinic. That's where my bid comes from."

The railroad president sold her the land, and adjourned the meeting (Flanagan, 1977, pp. 16–17).

2. It looks good to other funding sources if you have raised a significant amount of money. A women's center raised $2,500 its first year of operation through a raffle and solicitation of donations. They were able to use this as a demonstration of public support when they went to a United Way for support.

3. It creates favorable publicity for the agency or group. When people buy tickets for a raffle, attend a benefit concert, or buy a cupcake, they have some contact with the sponsoring organization. This can be a time for informing the public, one at a time, about the organization.

METHODS OF FUND-RAISING

There are a number of excellent books and pamphlets that explain the "how-to's" of fund-raising (Clifton and Dahms, 1980, chap. 3; Flanagan, 1977; Grubb and Zwick, 1976; Leibert and Sheldon, 1972). In deciding what to do and carrying it out, the following principles can be useful:

1. Be creative. One shelter for abused women in Wisconsin created and copyrighted a logo with the phrase "Women — You Can't Beat Them." They sell T-shirts, bags, and other items with that logo locally and nationally, and support most of their activities with the proceeds.

2. Work on your fears, and the fears of those working with you, of asking people for money.

Money is like sex. Everyone thinks about it, but no one is supposed to discuss it in polite company. Everyone has a lot of inhibitions about money, especially asking for money; think of all the cartoons of the office worker afraid to ask for a raise. In our society fears about money are normal.

Most people are afraid to ask someone else for money. They are afraid they will fail and afraid they will lose face. A few admit they are afraid, but others will give a lot of excuses: I can't make calls at the office; I don't know anyone rich; I can't get a baby-sitter. Or they postpone forever: I can't do it until after the kids are back in school, the holidays, the election, the tennis season, the vacation, the promotion. Volunteers often make asking for money sound like a bothersome chore, like taking out the garbage. It is not a chore; it is a challenge. Asking for money is like going out to beat up a bear. The larger the amount, the more frightening it becomes because you have to beat up a bigger bear.

One of the jobs of a good fund-raiser is to teach volunteers how to conquer their fear of the unknown. The first step is understanding that each person comes complete with his or her own set of fears and hang-ups, and the package of inhibitions usually includes a fear of asking for money. The second step is realizing this is normal and nothing to be ashamed of. The third step is working with the volunteers so they can get control of their own fears.

It is imperative that you understand and appreciate your volunteer's real feelings, because when members succeed at fund-raising they do more than bring in money for the organization. They have also overcome their own fear. When they raise money, they have won a personal victory, they have conquered the bear. When people can raise money, they can do anything. (Flanagan, 1977, p. 38)

3. Make the fund-raising activity appropriate for your community. A benefit concert may not work in a

small town where few people go out at night to hear music. Some churches have admonitions against gambling, which includes raffles. In a community where many people attend such churches, a raffle may not work.

4. Make it fun. When people work together on a project, they can develop camaraderie and develop or strengthen friendships. An atmosphere that allows the social as well as the work aspect of a fund-raising project (coffee, doughnuts, and fruit at work meetings, for example) helps people to feel good about what they're doing. After a fund-raising effort is finished, a get-together allows the participants a chance to celebrate what they have accomplished.

POLITICAL ACTIVITY AND LOBBYING

Chauncey Alexander states that "the social work profession, from its inception, has had a love-hate relationship with politics" (1982, p. 15). Partly because their interests and much of their interaction is on a one-to-one basis, and partly because of a lack of skills in the area, social workers have shied away from the political arena. Yet, because of their work "in the trenches," social workers have a greater knowledge of inequities and inadequate legislation than do most people.

Recently, in the social work profession there has been a growing understanding of the need to understand the political process and to work with it. Social workers are active in issues that affect the profession—such as lobbying—and issues that affect clients.

The whole arena of social work and politics is too large to cover in this chapter. Examples of the way social workers can be politically active include writing and introducing legislation, guiding it through the legislative process, and helping elect candidates. At various times, social workers will be involved in these activities. On a regular basis, however, social workers and human service agencies can attempt to influence local, state, and federal elected officials.

Attempting to influence elected officials, or lobbying, is an activity that we usually associate with high-

powered, high-paid lobbyists in expensive suits. Yet, it is something that all social workers can do effectively. The following principles are useful:

1. Get to know your legislators. Agencies can invite elected officials to meet with staff to share information and concerns at a time when the legislature is not in session. My experience has been that breakfast is a good time for this. It's before the elected official's schedule is too busy, and it can be more relaxed than a meeting sandwiched between other appointments. Often, legislators don't know much about the nuts and bolts of what social workers and human service agencies do, and they appreciate the knowledge.

2. Contact your legislators not only when you want them to do something but also when you approve of what they've done. Elected officials don't get a lot of fan mail. They appreciate it and will remember it.

3. Never write anyone off. A lobbyist that I know says, "There are no permanent friends or permanent enemies, only permanent issues." People who oppose your position one year may change in the future, especially if you don't treat them as if they are the enemy. The social work values of treating people as individuals worthy of respect is applicable to people in public life as well as clients.

COMMUNITY PRACTICE — A PROBLEM-SOLVING PROCESS

One of the dilemmas of teaching social work practice is that reality is not always as sequential as we make it out to be. For example, in micropractice we talk of problem identification, followed by problem assessment or clarification, followed by goal setting. What may happen in working with a client is that the client discovers for himself or reveals during goal setting that there are more urgent concerns.

Similarly, in macropractice, things do not often go as smoothly as the following process indicates. Yet, a knowledge of the ideal is helpful. In the following section, a description of how the problem-solving process can be used in macropractice is presented.[1]

Planning, according to Meryl Ruoss (1970), is organized foresight. From the time a problem or opportunity arises until some action is taken, the persons involved in the decision making will in some manner gather information, look at alternatives, and make a decision. This may be done in an organized fashion or the principals may just be "muddling through."

Many efforts, such as involving citizens in an advisory committee or designing a telephone reassurance system, seem overwhelmingly large at first sight. A man once was invited to dinner, and when he arrived, was seated at a table where an immense elephant, cooked in its entirety, was laid out before him. When he confusedly asked how he was supposed to eat something so big, the host calmly replied, "One bite at a time."

In this section, the planning process is presented one bite at a time. The various steps are grouped into three stages:

Preplanning: Questions to ask	Why is the planning being done? Who is the sponsor? Who is to do the planning? Are varying points of view included?
Planning: Plans to make	Problem assessment Problem clarification Goal setting Objective setting Examination and decision among alternatives Determination of strategy
Impact: Steps to take	Implementation of strategy Monitoring Evaluation

This sequence is intended to serve as a guide for those involved in a planning process. The process in-

cludes ten steps, each of which needs to be considered. The amount of time and effort spent on each step will vary depending on the situation.

The agency setting, the time frame, the resources to be utilized, and other factors will determine (and should determine) how much effort is expended in each step. You don't call the Army Corps of Engineers to build a sandbox. Similarly, an extensive needs assessment or prolonged search for all the alternatives may be unnecessary if the outcome of the planning process will be a relatively minor program change.

Preplanning: The Questions to Ask

The first of the three stages is that of preplanning. This includes all the activities that go on before a decision is made to confront actively a problem or opportunity.

The question "Why is the planning being done?" must be answered first. Generally, planning is done because someone perceives a problem or an opportunity.

The existence of a problem or an opportunity is not in itself sufficient reason to begin planning. In the case of a problem, John DeBoer (1970, p. 75) lists four questions that persons should ask themselves before beginning to plan, in order to check the validity of the problem and the assumptions on which it is based. They are the following:

1. Is this concern *our* concern, or some other individual's or group's concern?

2. Is this concern our concern *alone*, or should it be shared with by others?

3. Is this a concern that is important to us *now*, or would be better to postpone consideration to a later time?

4. Is the apparent concern the *real concern*, or a symptom of a deeper underlying problem — or of a different but related problem?

Sometimes the "why" question is answered for you. Legislation or administrative mandates may indicate that you begin planning in order to comply with legislation or administrative policy by a certain date. While there may be some latitude in these instances,

---

[1]This section is adapted from James R. Shimkus and James P. Winship, *Human Service Development: Working Together in the Community*, Athens, Ga.: University of Georgia Printing Department, 1977, pp. 8–17. Adapted by permission of the copyright owners.

thorough examination of these questions is important before moving on to the next step.

From the beginning, the agency or organization sponsoring the human service development effort must be clearly identified. The organizational base often influences the nature of the effort. For example, a task force composed of professionals from many agencies and cities looking at the needs of youth will likely come up with a plan that is different from one developed by a single agency.

Another reason for clarifying sponsorship of an effort is to sanction those working on the effort. Planning on the local level is linked to service delivery, and if the agency involved is to deliver the service, the administrator may be the person doing the planning. If the administrator is not the chief planner, the person who is the planning manager still needs to have the active support of the administrator in order to conduct the planning and to ensure that the results are implemented.

There may be times in a planning process when the administrator is the appropriate person to initiate contacts; if the administrator is not "on board" with the process and is not willing to take appropriate actions, it may falter. At times, the administrator may also need to have the sanction of his division or board before tackling a project.

The other component of the "who" question deals with the composition of the group doing the planning. A "planner" formulating a "plan" in an office separated from an agency's activities will produce a far different outcome from that of a task force composed of staff, representatives from other agencies, consumers, and other interested citizens.

Preplanning includes persuasion; the project should be formulated with regard to the known philosophies of those who must approve what is to be done. Involving key persons who may have differences at an early stage affords them the opportunity to voice their ideas, and the final product is less likely to be rejected by those who participated in it.

At times, influential individuals will register initial opposition to an effort and refuse to participate in it. In these situations it is important that when the planning group formulates its strategy, they do so in a way that recognizes and adjusts to the expected opposition.

Planning: Plans to Make

The first step in the planning sequence is the problem assessment. As used here, problem assessment includes needs assessment, problem identification, problem causal analysis, and resource assessment.

Needs assessment involves the gathering, ordering, and analyzing of information pertinent to the problem.

George Bernanos (1970) once stated that "the worst, the most corrupting of lies, are problems poorly stated." Problem identification is concerned with ascertaining whether the problem under consideration is the appropriate problem, and how well the problem is stated.

The difficulty in problem identification lies in the subjective nature of "problems" — a problem is what somebody or something perceives as a problem. The nature of the problem is determined by the manner in which it is perceived (Cartwright, 1973).

The perceptions of what the problem is are shaped by data, attitudes, and value judgments. A merchant and a juvenile court worker may interpret the same data on juvenile delinquency quite differently.

Because of the difficulty in defining a problem, determining who is to do the planning is very important. If the problem under consideration is a controversial one, such as juvenile delinquency, it is inevitable that at some point there will be conflict about what the problem is and what the solution should be. If the planning process is carried out by relatively few people, when the results are released or the program is to be implemented, there likely will be considerable conflict. The proposed program may be rejected, or be so embroiled in controversy that it is not fully effective.

This may be because the omission of certain persons in the planning process has caused the planning group to overlook vital information about conditions, resources, or attitudes.

Whenever the problem under consideration is controversial or will affect a large number of people, conflict will arise. It can be postponed but not avoided. What can be done is to attempt to involve the principals in the planning process, starting with problem identification. If persons can agree on the problem, there is more likelihood that they will be able to agree on goals, objectives, alternatives, and strategies. If a number of people are involved, they are more likely to advocate the action or plan in the larger community.

As the dimensions of the problem are revealed, the next move is to clarify them. Three measures that are helpful in this process relate to the problem's identity (exactly what is it?), its location, (where is the problem under consideration?), and its magnitude (what is the extent of the problem?). For example, a group working on housing might define the problem as deteriorating housing (what) in a fourteen-block neighborhood, south of the downtown area (where), which has 37 percent substandard housing according to the last census, compared to 23 percent in the previous census (to what extent).

In clarifying a problem, it also helps to identify what is *not* the problem. In the previous example, the problem is not defined as the sidewalks, the streets, or the storm sewers.

After identifying the problem, the next component of problem assessment is to attempt to analyze the causes of the problem. In doing this, it is necessary to look at the forces that contribute to the problems — economic factors, political pressures, institutionalized values, and attitudes.

Another reason for conducting a causal analysis is that the analysis may reveal that the problem under consideration was not the "real problem," and it is necessary to backtrack and redefine the problem. For example, several decades ago it was thought that people who committed crimes did so because they were mentally retarded. This theory led to the notion that the crime problem could be solved by developing approaches to prevent and treat mental retardation. However, intelligence testing of prison inmates found that most inmates were of normal intelligence. The mental retardation theory of criminal behavior was then discarded. Discarding this theory forced criminologists to change their conceptualizations of criminal behavior.

An integral part of problem assessment is resource assessment. This involves cataloging all actual and potential resources for dealing with the problem. It may include a compilation of agencies and community groups involved in or sympathetic to the problem, a listing of potential funding sources, and a determination of the amount of advocacy around this problem present in the community. In the case of funding

sources, it is important to ascertain the limitations under which the money may be spent. In many instances, "form follows financing."

The next step in the planning process is that of establishing goals. Goals are the long-term aims of the project and may be expressed in general terms. They are statements about a desired condition, and they may not be attainable. In the example of the neighborhood housing, the goal of the project might be to bring every housing unit in the neighborhood up to code-enforcement standards.

In writing goals, it is helpful to express them in terms of generally accepted standards whenever possible. In the above example, the state or local housing code regulations serve as a standard. In describing adequate or satisfactory conditions in other areas, such as child-care or homemaker services, state agencies or private accrediting groups will have standards against which to measure the adequacy of a program.

After establishing the goals, the next step is to set specific objectives. These should relate directly to the goals, but they are different in that they describe outcomes that the planners realistically expect to meet instead of expressing an ideal condition.

Objectives are quantifiable. An objective is measurable both in relation to what is to be done and within what time period it is to be done. The use of the standards and measures in the objectives should also reflect the quality desired.

In the housing example, specific objectives might be the following:

1. Conducting a housing inspection of every house in the neighborhood within the first three months.

2. Rehabilitating twenty housing units in the first year that are structurally sound but do not presently meet code regulations.

3. Beginning proceedings to condemn and demolish all vacant houses judged not structurally sound.

There are two types of objectives. There will be some objectives that must be reached if the project is to be a success. Other objectives are desirable but not essential. The three objectives mentioned above would be essential objectives. In this case, an example of a desirable objective might be:

4.   The planting of trees along four residential streets.

Clear, specific objectives are necessary for several reasons. The consideration of alternatives and the selection of the strategy are based on the objectives. As computer operators say, "GIGO—Garbage In, Garbage Out."

Furthermore, it is extremely difficult to evaluate a program if it does not have quantifiable objectives. Without good objectives, one can evaluate a program only by personal biases.

In the sport of archery there is one sure way for beginners to hit the bull's-eye on the side of the barn every time—paint the bull's-eye after the arrow has landed. A program that is launched without a clear statement of goals is like such an arrow; though wide of the mark intended by its launchers long ago, it may be dubbed on target by anyone who can paint a convincing bull's-eye (DeBoer, 1970, p. 108).

After the objectives are set, the next step is to examine and choose among various alternative approaches. In most cases there will be more than one way to meet the objectives.

The bases on which the alternatives are judged will vary with the circumstances. In selecting among alternative approaches, factors such as cost resources, technical feasibility, and political feasibility will be considered. The length of time in which a program has to prove itself is a consideration. If it is funded for only one year and then must find alternative sources of support, an approach that will give short-term results must be chosen.

When selecting among alternatives, one must guard against the practice of selecting the approach that seems most manageable or more interesting or convenient for the staff rather than the one that best meets the objectives.

When the approach that best meets the objectives has been selected, the next step is to determine strategy. The process of identifying the problem, setting the goals and objectives, and choosing among alternatives has indicated *what* needs to be done. In determining the course of action, the question of *how* it is to be done and *who* will do it are addressed.

In this step, one is packaging the plan of action. Parts of the strategy will have become apparent in the previous steps, but one can easily ignore some important factors unless a thorough examination of the proposed course of action is undertaken.

Realism is imperative at this point. Further refinements of the selected approach may be necessary. When considering who is to implement the plan and how it is to be done, the participants may discover that there are not sufficient resources to implement the approach fully; and some hard decisions about modifying the approach will need to be made.

In setting the strategy, it is also necessary to build in procedures that will facilitate implementation, monitoring, and evaluation. If money is to be secured for a new program, and if there are civil service or state merit systems to work with, preparing the positions should be done before the money is received in order to cut down on the start-up time. Similarly, one can begin informally to look for staff before the hiring process can officially begin.

The mechanisms for monitoring and evaluation need to be decided upon at this time. If an evaluation of the effects of the actions on a target population is desired, then data on that population's characteristics need to be gathered before the program is implemented.

Impact: Steps to Take

The final stage of the planning process is the impact stage, which covers implementing the strategy, monitoring it, and evaluating it. In all these steps, especially implementation, the actual situation will determine what actions need to be taken.

The last two steps are too often left out. Planning is done, a program is launched, and then there is an inclination to neglect monitoring (that is, the process of continually gaining information about the program's performance) and evaluation until such time as a review is called for.

The procedures and instruments for monitoring activities might include reporting forms for fiscal transactions, personnel, training, and participant intake in a program; site visits by the appropriate persons; and mechanisms for permitting client feedback.

Monitoring serves many important purposes. It provides information for guidance while the program is in operation. If the administrator receives up-to-date information, she can make ajustments and correct program flaws before they become major.

Monitoring will also provide information for periodic evaluations. Two requisites for effective evaluation are clear objectives against which to measure performance and accurate data that reflect the performance.

The importance of evaluation cannot be overstated. In the planning process itself, the participants should continually check to see whether the objectives meet the problem and whether the strategy addresses the problem and objectives. The participants should also concern themselves with periodically evaluating how well they are working together.

VALUES AND MACROPRACTICE

In Chapter 2, the topic of values in social work practice was discussed. In this section, the application of values to macropractice will be addressed. Figure 9.3 illustrates the importance of recognizing and adhering to community values.

The vignette in Figure 9.3 was designed to illustrate the barriers to social workers' utilizing natural helping networks; in this case, the attitudes of Sally and Jim hinder the effective involvement of Mrs. Worthington in meeting community needs. It also shows how disregard for community values can thwart the efforts of social workers to secure or improve services for their clients. Because Sally Meanwell acquired a reputation as being a violator of community values, she received a negative reception from the board when she advocated expanded services. (Incidentally, the authors state that although the dialogue is exaggerated, they have either committed or observed every ill-considered action in the account.)

Social workers in macropractice are also confronted with other value issues. One of these goes back to my assertion at the start of the chapter that the client is the community, and that the community benefits if human needs are met better than they were before. This assertion is a value statement that is not shared by

everyone. Some people believe that social welfare benefits and services should be eliminated or severely curtailed, either because they believe that people should "make it on their own" or because they do not want to support governmental helping programs with their taxes. Others may not share these values when it comes to particular actions or programs. Public or community education efforts in sex education are opposed by some people because they believe that information on sexuality will lead to increased promiscuity among teenagers. Within their value framework, the community would not be better off, but rather worse off if such community education efforts were carried out.

Another value issue that can be raised is whether social work and social welfare institutions are "part of the problem or part of the solution." Galper states that "conventional social work community organization practice is as likely to serve a co-optive role, or to function as a commonly-based approach to social control, as it is to operate as a vehicle for progressive change" (1980, p. 151). From the perspective of Galper and other radicals, much of what is advocated in community organization and other macropractice approaches have two basic aims. One is to give people who participate in planned change activities a sense of belonging, of not being powerless or isolated from society. In their opinion, the sense of power may not reflect reality. A second goal is to make minor changes in programs or practices that do not have an impact on the major societal forces that oppress the poor, persons of color, and others (Galper, 1975).

All social workers in practice must question the goals of any effort they are involved in. They must also question the means they are using, especially in working with people who are culturally or ethnically different. It may be that what you envision as feasible may not seem so to the people you are working with.

A number of the activities previously discussed (lobbying, publicity, fund-raising, group decision making) may not be within the range of behaviors of many people. For example, many Asian-Americans come from a culture in which one does not question authority, so pressuring a local official is not an activity in which many Asian-Americans feel comfortable. It has been my experience that Appalachian whites do not participate easily in community meetings in which a

FIGURE 9.3

Sally Meanwell and Jim Goodheart* *(As you read this, seek to identify which community values are being violated by Sally and Jim)*

Sally and Jim are employed by a small human service agency in Gusty, Wyoming, a ranching-farming community about fifty miles from Cultureville, a city of 100,000. Sally was unable to find a job in her native Chicago and accepted employment in Gusty a little over one year ago. Jim, a native of New York, plans to return to the East but views his present employment as a "good experience," akin to the Peace Corps or Vista. He has been in Gusty for two years. It is Friday afternoon and they are taking a coffee break.

Jim slumps back in his chair and exclaims, "What a week; I'll sure be glad to get into Cultureville!"

"What have you got planned?" asks Sally.

"Oh," Jim replies, "I think I'll take in a play at the University, but first I better get my hair cut and styled. It's getting pretty long again and a few people have made comments. And I sure don't want Johnson to butcher it again. These locals don't keep up with anything. Anyway, last time I was in there, I started talking about a beef boycott to protest high beef prices, and he and a couple of ranchers in there really got into it with me. I think one of them even tore my Kennedy sticker off when he left."

"I know what you mean," said Sally. "Johnson wouldn't even let me put up a family planning poster in there. He's a Mormon and you know how they are. Guess I'll be glad to escape Gusty, too. I need to pick up some groceries at the new mall. They have a better selection than Bick's [the local grocer]. Anyway, I don't feel like supporting Bick. He butchers deer for hunters and I think hunting should be outlawed. At the very least, they should let the poor deer grow up to be elk."

"By the way," Jim interjected, "Worthington wants you to call her before five. I think it's about the O'Connell family."

"Oh, yeah," responded Sally, "the O'Connell kid has cancer and the family can't afford all the expenses. Mrs. Worthington has been trying to help them. She means well, but I think she's getting too involved."

"She doesn't have any education or training in helping people, does she?"

Sally shook her head, "No, she's done some volunteer work for us, but she didn't seem very sure of herself. Anyway, she's talking about getting some community groups to help the O'Connells. It sounds good, but I'm not sure she can pull it off.

I'm willing to help if I can, but I don't know much about organizing."

"Neither do I," replied Jim. "My background is all clinical. I did have a course in C.O., but it was dry as hell and I cut it a lot. Say, wouldn't confidentiality be a problem here? You just can't tell the whole community a lot of personal stuff about the family."

"That is a problem," nodded Sally. "Perhaps I should tactfully discourage Mrs. Worthington."

"I meant to ask you," said Jim, "how did your board meeting go?"

"You would ask!" said Sally, with a negative countenance. "It was the pits. I had the new budget request all ready and I was ready to answer any possible questions. But most of them didn't seem to be all that interested in expanded services. Baldwin really gave me a rough time."

"Isn't Baldwin the guy with all the sheep?"

"Yeah," replied Sally, "I think he found out I signed that 'Save the Coyotes' petition. He claims they killed thirty-seven of his sheep in one day, but everyone knows they only kill for food. Hell, the coyotes were here first."

"Sure," said Jim, "anyway, people eat too much meat for their own good. Why don't you suggest that Baldwin go on a macrobiotic diet?"

"Don't kid, Jim. I was halfway joking once when I suggested a Marxist perspective on county problems. He's had it in for me ever since."

"Well, what about Reverend Gebhart? Wasn't he really pushing for extra services?"

"He sure was," said Sally, "but he's been a little cool lately. You know, he lives down the street from you, and he must know we sometimes spend the night together. He sure knows that neither one of us goes to any church. He was lukewarm toward the new budget, and the board voted to table the request until further study. I'm not too optimistic about it."

"Too bad," said Jim; "it's a hell of a note when people don't separate our personal lives from professional ones. Not much we can do about that, though. It's a good excuse to have a few drinks in Cultureville, though."

"Sounds good, Jim. Why don't we take off now. I can call Mrs. Worthington Monday."

*This vignette is adapted from Judith Davenport and Joseph Davenport, III, "Utilizing the Social Network in Rural Communities," *Social Casework*, February 1982, pp. 109–10. Permission to use this material has been received from the publisher, Family Service America.

variety of persons are present. There are cultural values that discourage "opening up," especially in front of strangers.

What the social worker needs to do, in Saul Alinsky's words, is to "never go outside the experience of your people. When an action or tactic is outside the experience of the people, the result is—confusion, fear, and . . . a collapse of communication" (1972, p. 127).

The social worker can look for culturally sensitive or culturally acceptable methods of achieving goals. For example, one traditional Native American ritual, the Talking Circle, has been used with a number of Northwest tribes in the United States as a means for group decision making and communication with which tribal members feel comfortable (Stephenson, 1983).

MODELS OF COMMUNITY PRACTICE

Up to this point, this chapter has discussed macropractice from the perspective of the worker who is involved with it as a part of his job duties or personal conviction, not from the perspective of the full-time macropractice social worker. In this section, that aspect will be explored, largely relying on the work of Jack Rothman.

Rothman (1979) states that there are three major orientations or models to planned or deliberate change in contemporary American communities. These he identifies as locality development, social planning, and social action. In this conceptual framework, he refers to community efforts of a continuing nature with paid staff who are responsible for sustained actions or involvement.

Model A, the *locality development approach* (also called *community development*), asserts that community change can best be brought about through broad participation of a wide spectrum of people at the local community level. The model seeks to involve a broad cross section of people (including the disadvantaged sector and the power structure) in identifying and solving their problems. Some themes emphasized in this

model are democratic procedures, a consensus approach, voluntary cooperation, development of indigenous leadership, and self-help.

The roles of the community practitioner in this approach include enabler, catalyst, coordinator, and teacher of problem-solving skills and ethical values. The approach assumes that conflicts that result between various interest groups can be creatively and constructively handled. It encourages people to express their differences freely, but assumes people will put aside their self-interests in order to further the interests of their community. The approach assumes people will put aside their self-interests through appeals to altruism. The basic theme of this approach is "Together we can figure out what to do and do it." The approach seeks to use discussion and communication between different factions to reach consensus about the problems to focus on and the strategies or actions to resolve these problems. An example of locality development is the Peace Corps in village-level work in overseas community development programs. Peace Corps workers seek to bring together residents in a village to identify and then work on solving their most urgent community needs.

Model B, the *social planning approach*, emphasizes a technical process of problem solving. The approach assumes that community change in a complex industrial environment requires highly trained and skilled planners who can guide complex change processes. The role of the expert is stressed in this approach to identifying and resolving social problems. The expert or planner is generally employed by a segment of the power structure, such as an area planning agency, city or county planning department, mental health center, United Way board, community welfare council, and so on. Because the social planner is employed by a segment of the power structure, there is a tendency for the planner to serve the interests of the power structure. Building community capacity or facilitating radical social change is generally not an emphasis in this approach.

The planner's roles in this approach include gathering facts, analyzing data, and serving as program designer, implementer, and facilitator. Community participation may vary from little to substantial with this approach, depending on the community's attitudes to-

FIGURE 9.4

Social Action Tactics Should Be Enjoyable to the People in the Movement

Saul Alinsky, one of our country's most noted organizers, describes a tactic used by students at a private college to change the college's restrictive policies on social activities:

> I was lecturing at a college run by a very conservative, almost fundamentalist Protestant denomination. Afterward some of the students came to my motel to talk to me. Their problem was that they couldn't have any fun on campus. They weren't permitted to dance or smoke or have a can of beer. I had been talking about the strategy of effecting change in a society and they wanted to know what tactics they could use to change their situation. I reminded them that a tactic is doing what you can with what you've got. "Now, what have you got?" I asked. "What do they permit you to do?" "Practically nothing," they said, "except—you know—we can chew gum." I said, "Fine. Gum becomes the weapon. You get 200 or 300 students to get two packs of gum each, which is quite a wad. Then you have them drop it on the campus walks. This will cause absolute chaos. Why, with 500 wads of gum I could paralyze Chicago, stop all the traffic in the Loop." They looked at me as though I was some kind of a nut. But about two weeks later I got an ecstatic letter saying, "It worked! It worked! Now we can do just about anything so long as we don't chew gum."

Source: Saul Alinsky, *Rules for Radicals* (New York: Random House, 1972), pp. 145–46.

ward the problems being addressed. For example, an effort to design and obtain funding for a community center for the elderly may or may not result in substantial involvement by interested community groups, depending on the politics surrounding such a center. Much of the focus of the social planning approach is on identifying needs and on arranging and delivering goods and services to people who need them. The

change focus of this approach is "Let's get the facts and take the next rational steps" (Rothman, 1979, p. 33).

Model C, the *social action approach*, assumes there is a disadvantaged (often oppressed) segment of the population that needs to be organized, perhaps in alliance with others, in order to pressure the power structure for increased resources or for treatment more in accordance with democracy or social justice. Social action approaches at times seek basic changes in major institutions or in basic policies of formal organizations. Such approaches often seek redistribution of power and resources. Unlike the vision of a unified community held by locality developers, the power structure or opposition is the target of action. Perhaps the best-known social activist was Saul Alinsky (1972, p. 130) who advised, "Pick the target, freeze it, personalize it, and polarize it." An example of his approach is illustrated in Figure 9.4.

The roles of the community practitioner in this approach include advocate, agitator, activist, partisan, broker, and negotiator. Tactics used in social action projects include protests, boycotts, confrontation, and negotiation. The change strategy is one of "Let's organize to overpower our oppressor" (Rothman, 1979, p. 34). The client population is viewed as being a "victim" of the oppressive power structure. Examples of the social action approach include boycotts during the civil rights movement during the 1960s, strikes by unions, protests by antiabortion groups, and protests by black and Native American groups.

The social action model is not widely used by social workers at present. Many workers find that being involved in social action activities may lead their employing agencies to penalize them with unpleasant work assignments, low merit increases, and refusal to grant promotions. Many agencies will accept minor and moderate changes in their service delivery systems but are threatened by the prospect of radical changes that are often advocated by the social action approach.

The chart in Table 9.1 (page 248) illustrates the similarities and differences in the three approaches of locality development, social planning, and social action.

One role that social workers may perform that is not covered by the Rothman model is that of broker. A broker links individuals and groups who need help (and do not know where help is available) with

TABLE 9.1

Three Models of Community Organization Practice According to Selected Practice Variables*

	Model A (locality development)	Model B (social planning)	Model C (social action)
1. Goal categories of community action	Self-help; community capacity and integration (process goals)	Problem solving with regard to substantive community problems (task goals)	Shifting of power relationships and resources; basic institutional change (task or process goals)
2. Assumptions concerning community structure and problem conditions	Community eclipsed, anomie; lack of relationships and democratic problem-solving capacities; static traditional community	Substantive social problems; mental and physical health, housing, recreation	Disadvantaged populations, social injustice, deprivation, inequity
3. Basic change strategy	Broad cross section of people involved in determining and solving their own problems	Fact gathering about problems and decisions on the most rational course of action	Crystallization of issues and organization of people to take action against enemy targets
4. Characteristic change tactics and techniques	Consensus: communication among community groups and interests; group discussion	Consensus or conflict	Conflict or contest: confrontation, direct action, negotiation
5. Salient practitioner roles	Enabler-catalyst, coordinator; teacher of problem-solving skills and ethical values	Fact gatherer and analyst, program implementer, facilitator	Activist-advocate: agitator, broker, negotiator, partisan

community services. Today even moderate-sized communities have 200 or 300 social service agencies/organizations providing community services. Even human resource professionals are frequently only partially aware of the total service network in their community. As in the fields of finance and real estate, social service brokers serve the function of negotiating, for their cli-

ents, a complex network of social institutions about which clients are uninformed and with which they are inexperienced in dealing. Grosser (1973, p. 176) describes this role:

Like his commercial counterparts, the social broker is primarily committed to "consummating the deal"; his

TABLE 9.1

(Continued)

	Model A (locality development)	Model B (social planning)	Model C (social action)
6. Medium of change	Manipulation of small task-oriented groups	Manipulation of formal organizations and of data	Manipulation of mass organizations and political processes
7. Orientation toward power structure(s)	Members of power structure as collaborators in a common venture	Power structure as employers and sponsors	Power structure as external target of action: oppressors to be coerced or overturned
8. Boundary definition of the community client system or constituency	Total geographic community	Total community or community segment (including "functional" community)	Community segment
9. Assumptions regarding interests of community subparts	Common interests or reconcilable differences	Interests reconcilable or in conflict	Conflicting interests which are not easily reconcilable; scarce resources
10. Conception of the public interest	Rationalist-unitary	Idealist-unitary	Realist-individualist
11. Conception of the client population or constituency	Citizens	Consumers	Victims
12. Conception of client role	Participants in an interactional problem-solving process	Consumers or recipients	Employers, constituents, members

---

*This chart is reprinted from J. Rothman, "Three Models of Community Organization Practice," in *Social Work Practice* (New York: Columbia University Press, 1968), pp. 24–25. Reprinted with permission from *Social Work Practice*, published for the National Conference on Social Welfare by Columbia University Press.

function is not fulfilled unless the social-service institution is in fact providing service to the beneficiary. The broker works directly neither for the recipient nor for the service institution; in a sense, his client is the transaction itself. And it is on behalf of the transaction that he expends his energies and develops his strategies. Community obstacles to the transaction have to be removed or circumvented; policies of the service institution that inhibit the transaction have to be altered; attitudes or misinformation that prevent the recipient from completing the transaction have to be dealt with. The broker is "kept honest," however, by the fact that he must keep the parties to the potential transaction in a common relationship. Because his *commitment is to the deal, he enjoys a neutrality that enables both the beneficiary and the institution to relate to him with special confidence. Each party can accept his actions in that they favor neither side; he is committed merely to effecting an exchange of service.*

Often all that is required to perform this linkage function is to provide information that puts people in contact with resources. However, if difficulties arise, collective action (a community organization effort) may be needed to effect the exchange. (For example, a broker may suggest to welfare recipients that needed benefits may be provided if they *collectively* request the local public assistance department to reexamine certain of its eligibility policies.) Through such brokerage activity, changes in policies may occur that affect whole classes of persons.

A few agencies (such as some mental health clinics, neighborhood centers, community action agencies, agencies serving the elderly) employ "community outreach workers" whose function is to inform residents about available services, identify individuals and families with problems, and link such families with available services.

A number of governmental agencies (particularly in human services, education, health, and housing) now employ one or more staff persons to work parttime or full-time with citizens, educating citizens to the problems the agency is dealing with and eliciting citizens' ideas to make changes in the delivery system to better serve consumers. This broker function acts as a consciousness-raising device to show people what the system is really like, and also to make the system more responsive to the needs of consumers.

SUMMARY

Community practice (also called macropractice) is a term that describes social work activities in which the client is the community, where the focus of the change effort is larger than an individual, family, or therapy group. Practitioners are usually involved in this as one part of their work and lives.

There are similarities between community practice and work with individuals, families, and groups. Skills in communicating and forming relationships, skills in working with groups, and problem-solving skills are as applicable in this realm of practice as in the others.

To be effective, however, it is necessary for the social worker to have knowledge of communities and organizations in general, and of the specific community and organization(s) for which he works. For some efforts, knowledge of funding sources and funding cycles is essential.

Depending on the kind of macro effort in which the social worker is involved, the following techniques can be utilized: group decision-making techniques, community awareness or publicity approaches, fundraising techniques, and lobbying strategies.

The problem-solving model can be used in addressing community problems. The various steps in a community problem-solving model were summarized in the following three stages:

Preplanning: Questions to ask	Why is the planning being done? Who is the sponsor? Who is doing the planning? Are varying points of view included?
Planning: Plans to make	Problem assessment Problem clarification Goal setting Objective setting Examination and decision among alternatives Determination of strategy
Impact: Steps to take	Implementation of strategy Monitoring Evaluation

In using this or other macro approaches, value issues such as community values, the role of social welfare in society, and ethnic/cultural sensitivity have to be considered.

Models of macropractice include community development, or locality developments, social planning, social action, and community brokering.

EXERCISES

1. Community Assessment

GOAL: This exercise is designed to instruct the class in how to conduct a community assessment.

Step 1: State the purpose of the exercise. Ask the students to form subgroups of about five. Inform the subgroups that one of the major class assignments will be for them to conduct a needs assessment on a community. Inform the subgroups they need first to select a community, and then use the questions in Figure 9.1 as a basis for conducting the community assessment.

Step 2: As the course moves along, periodically allow class time to discuss questions and obstacles that the subgroups encounter.

Step 3: Grade the completed assessments and return them to students. Have the students discuss what they learned from this exercise.

Note: As an alternative approach to this exercise, the entire class may assess one community, with subgroups focusing on different subtopics to assess. Or, as another alternative, each student may be assigned individually to choose and assess a community.

2. Needs Assessment and Proposal Development

GOAL: The purpose of this exercise is to give students experience in conducting a needs assessment and in developing proposals to meet the needs that are identified.

Step 1: Explain the purpose of this exercise. Instruct the students to form subgroups of five or six. Inform the subgroups their tasks are to conduct a needs assessment of an issue on the campus or in the surrounding community and then to develop a proposal to meet the needs that are identified. (Background material on how to conduct a needs assessment is contained in this chapter.)

Note: This assignment may be a major course assignment. Or, as an alternative, the subgroups may be instructed to make as much progress as they can in a class period to conduct a needs assessment and develop a program proposal. For example, if the latter approach is used the subgroups may be asked to arrive at answers to the following questions:

a. What are the most urgent, unmet needs of our social work program?
b. What evidence or documentation is there that these are urgent, unmet needs?
c. What additional information needs to be sought in order to determine fully whether these needs are urgent and unmet?
d. What specific, realistic proposals do you have for meeting the needs that have been identified?

Step 2: Have the subgroups present their needs assessments and proposals in verbal or written form. Provide feedback to the subgroups.

3. *Identifying Violations of Community Values*

GOAL: This exercise is designed to help the class recognize violations of community values.

Step 1: Explain the purpose of the exercise. Ask for a volunteer to read a vignette with you. (If you are a female, ask for a male volunteer to read a male's part. If you are a male, ask for a female volunteer.) Inform the class the two of you will read a vignette and that the task of each student is to identify the specific attitudes and specific behaviors that are apt to be violations of the values in a rural community in Wyoming.

Step 2: Together with the volunteer, read the Sally Meanwell and Jim Goodheart vignette presented in Figure 9.3.

Step 3: Ask the students to state the violations of community values that they have identified. End the exercise by stating the importance of identifying community values, and discuss with students whether they are willing to make possible adjustments in their personal lives in order to live up to community expectations. Indicate that a balance sometimes has to be found between living the way you want to live, and meeting community expectations in order to maintain credibility.

4. *Identifying Community Values*

GOAL: This exercise is designed to help students examine the values of their home communities.

Step 1: Indicate that community values influence the types of services that are publicly available and supported by a community. Instruct the class to form subgroups of 3 or 4. Ask students in each subgroup to discuss their home communities' reactions to the following community activities. (These activities can either be written on a blackboard or read from this text.)

a. High school students seek to establish a clinic in their school that dispenses contraceptive materials.
b. An avowedly lesbian woman launches a campaign to seek election to a local political office (such as to the city council).
c. A group of working parents requests the local school system to establish an all-day kindergarten, partially to meet the needs of working parents.
d. An AIDS support group seeks authorization to use the public meeting room of the library for its weekly meetings.
e. A local organization seeks the establishment of an additional (or the first) shelter for the homeless.

Step 2: Ask a representative from each subgroup to summarize to the class what was discussed. The instructor may choose to end the exercise by making some summary statements about community values that underlie community reactions (that were discussed) to these activities.

10

EVALUATING SOCIAL WORK PRACTICE

T o this point, you've learned about social work with individuals, families, groups, and communities. You've studied systems analysis, and you will study psychoanalysis (Chapter 13) and transactional analysis (Chapter 16), and will read about half a dozen other therapies. You're probably eager to try out your new knowledge, confident that you can be of help to your prospective clients. But wait! How will you know if your choice of therapy is working?

As a professional social worker, you'll want to be accountable to your clients and to yourself. You'll want to know whether your clients achieve their goals and, if so, whether it is because of your interventions. In short, you'll want to evaluate your practice. That is what this chapter is all about.

Although most social workers evaluate their practice implicitly, few approach evaluation as systematically as they might. Systematic evaluation of your practice will provide you with reliable information about the achievements of your clients and may lead to improved practice. Good evaluation will also help you avoid jumping to unwarranted conclusions about your work.

WHAT IS EVALUATION?

Evaluation, as we shall use the term here, refers to the use of research techniques to assess the outcome of social work interventions. As Thomas (1984) has suggested, there are two types of evaluation, outcome evaluation and evaluative research. As we shall see, these two types of evaluation address different but related objectives.

Outcome evaluation asks whether the intended outcome was achieved. Simply put, was the goal

This chapter was especially written for this text by Wallace J. Gingerich, MSW, Ph.D. Dr. Gingerich is a professor in the Mandel School of Applied Social Sciences at Case Western Reserve University, Cleveland, Ohio.

achieved? Since outcome evaluation has a limited objective, it is relatively easy to do. It requires minimal methodological know-how, and it doesn't impose rigid requirements on practice. Outcome evaluation should be a part of normal practice. However, outcome evaluation does not provide a sound basis on which to conclude whether the intervention was effective.

Evaluative research also asks whether the outcome was achieved, but in addition it seeks to determine if the outcome can be attributed to your intervention. In other words, was treatment effective? Evaluative research is like traditional experimental research in that causal relationships are the focus of study. You might think of evaluative research as research applied to questions of practice effectiveness. While it is relatively easy to determine whether the intended outcome was achieved (outcome evaluation), inferring that it was due to the intervention is considerably more difficult. Evaluating the effectiveness of interventions is important. If we know that it was our intervention that produced the outcome, we will want to continue using it. On the other hand, if we know the intervention had little or no impact, we should stop using it and look for something better.

Although both types of evaluation are important for social work practice, the main focus of this chapter is outcome evaluation. Outcome evaluation has become an essential part of ordinary practice; you and your client will always want to know if the desired outcome was achieved. Outcome evaluation does not interfere with practice, but may enhance and improve it (Gingerich, 1983b). On the other hand, rigorous evaluative research is not a requirement of ordinary practice (Gingerich, 1990b). The additional controls and measurements needed to conduct evaluative research may conflict with service objectives (Thomas, 1978). We are required as a profession to conduct scientific research to improve our knowledge about practice effectiveness; however, in many instances evaluative research is best left to trained researchers who can implement the rigorous controls and measurements required for inferring causality.

Just as social work practice may be carried out at various levels of intervention (individuals, groups, families, and communities), evaluation is also carried out at different levels. Evaluation at the level of individuals and groups has sometimes been referred to as *clinical evaluation*, while evaluation at the level of program development and community practice has been called *program evaluation*. The main focus of this chapter is on evaluation at the level of individuals and groups. As we shall see, many of the concepts and methods underlying clinical evaluation apply to program evaluation as well.

Until recently, evaluating practice usually meant that one would use some form of an experimental control group research design (Bloom, 1983). Such designs assign subjects randomly to two groups: one group gets the intervention and the other does not (or gets a different intervention). After intervention, the groups are compared on some measure of the desired outcome. Assuming all else was equal, differences between the two groups are attributed to the intervention the experimental group received. Although experimental control group designs are a useful research strategy, they are often not practical for evaluating day-to-day social work practice.

During the 1970s a new approach to evaluating practice began to emerge, based on the earlier work of clinical psychologists who were trained in research (Bloom, 1983). This approach, known as *single-subject* or *single-system* research, took a rather different approach to evaluation, an approach that was much more compatible with clinical practice. Instead of comparing randomly assigned groups of clients on some outcome measure after intervention, the single-system approach observes a single client (or client system) repeatedly before, during, and after intervention, and notes changes in the outcome measure that coincide with the intervention. In this way it is possible to determine whether the outcome was achieved and, perhaps, whether the change was due to the intervention.

While single-system designs are not as rigorous methodologically as classical control group designs, they are much more compatible with most social work practice. Further, they are adequate in most instances for purposes of outcome evaluation. Thus, the single-system approach to evaluation is the one taken here.

THE SINGLE-SYSTEM EVALUATION APPROACH

Much has been written about how to evaluate practice (Jayaratne and Levy, 1979; Bloom and Fischer, 1982; Barlow, Hayes, and Nelson, 1984; Barlow and Hersen, 1984). As a result, the procedures for evaluating practice are well defined. They may be described generally as follows:

1. Specify the goal.
2. Select a suitable measure(s).
3. Record baseline data.
4. Implement intervention and continue monitoring.
5. Assess change.
6. Infer effectiveness.

If these steps sound familiar, that is because they parallel very closely the steps one follows in social work practice (Jayaratne and Levy, 1979). Evaluation is based on the problem-solving process, just as social work practice is. The difference is one of emphasis, and it is a slight difference at that. While the main purpose of practice is to produce a desired outcome, the main purpose of evaluation is to assess whether in fact the outcome was achieved.

Specify the Goal

The first step in single-system evaluation is to specify the goal of your work with your client. The goal should reflect the information obtained in the social work assessment and should state in concrete terms what will be different at the end of treatment. Usually the goal involves a change in behaviors, thoughts, or feelings, or perhaps a change in social relationships or the environment. The goal should reflect the needs and wishes of your client and what is realistic to achieve, but it also must be an outcome that can be defined specifically and measured.

Select a Suitable Measure(s)

Evaluation requires that the desired outcome be measurable in some reliable way. Measurement means that the outcome must be quantifiable. At a minimum you must be able to tell whether it has occurred or not; but you may also be able to rate the level of the outcome using a scale or some other procedure.

Although some outcomes may seem to defy measurement, it would be irresponsible to intervene if one has no way to know if the outcome has occurred (Hudson, 1978). Neither you nor your client could tell if things were getting better. When practitioners say they cannot measure their clients' outcomes, they usually mean the outcomes are difficult to measure directly, or they are too complicated and multifaceted to measure quantitatively. Numerous advances have been made in the field of measurement in recent years and there are many available measuring instruments and procedures.

Measurement Methods

There are three main methods for measuring client outcomes: direct observation, self-anchored rating scales, and standardized measure (Bloom and Fischer, 1982).

DIRECT OBSERVATION   Many client outcomes are behavioral. Simply put, clients want to *do* something different. When the outcome can be stated in behavioral terms, direct observation by the client or someone else is usually the measurement method of choice. Direct observation requires a clear and objective definition of the behavior. *Clear* means that two people using the definition agree on occurrences of the behavior. *Objective* means that the behavior is directly observable; that is, it requires little or no inference by the observer.

Examples of typical behavioral outcomes are playing cooperatively, completing assigned homework, having fewer headaches, and discussing disagreements calmly. Even some seemingly nonbehavioral outcomes such as improved self-esteem or reduced depression can be stated in behavioral terms. Clients can often give specific behavioral indicators of internal states when asked; for example, when asked what they will be doing (or not doing) when they have improved self-esteem, clients may indicate such behaviors as initiating conversations, making positive self-statements, or working more productively. Although it is not always possible to specify outcomes in behavioral terms, it is useful to attempt to do so. From a therapeutic standpoint, the client (and you) will have a more concrete idea of the actual desired outcome. From an evaluation standpoint, direct observation is generally considered the most reliable and direct measurement method. By the way, specifying behavioral outcomes does not imply that you must, or even should, use behaviorally based interventions. It simply means that the outcome you and the client are interested in is behavioral.

Behaviors may be observed and counted using a variety of methods (Barlow, Hayes, and Nelson, 1984). The most common method is a *frequency count*. Here, you simply record the number of times the behavior occurs during a specified time interval. For example, you might record the number of temper tantrums a child has each day, or the number of problems a child solves correctly during math class. Frequency counts work well for discrete behaviors (behaviors that have clear beginnings and endings) that do not occur too frequently to make counting impractical.

A related method of observation is counting *discriminated operants*. These are behaviors that occur only in the presence of clearly specified antecedents. For example, a child can comply only when the parent makes a request, or a husband and wife can resolve differences only when they have a disagreement. In such cases, rather than report the absolute frequency of occurrence, you would report the percentage of times the desired behavior occurred following the antecedent.

Continuous behaviors (no clear beginnings or endings) or high-frequency behaviors can be observed using *time-sampling* methods. In time-sampling the observation period is divided into short intervals (usually five to fifteen seconds) during which you record the behavior as occuring or not. Usually this is done on an all-or-none basis, with the results presented as a

percentage. For example, you might observe whether a psychiatric patient attends to the therapy group discussion during a ten-minute period using fifteen-second intervals. If the patient was observed to attend for thirty-five of the forty intervals you would report that she or he attended 88 percent of the time. Because of its nature, time-sampling is almost always done by someone other than the client, usually a staff member or perhaps a parent.

Several other observational methods are sometimes used. *Latency* measures the elapsed time between a particular event and the behavior, for example, the times it takes a child to get into bed after being told to do so. *Duration* measures how long the behavior lasts, such as how many minutes the child spends doing homework, or how long a headache lasts.

General procedures for observing behaviors, as well as specific definitions, codes, and recording systems for observing many predetermined behaviors are described in detail by Bellack and Hersen (1988) and Ciminero, Calhoun, and Adams (1986).

SELF-ANCHORED RATING SCALES   Not all desired outcomes can be stated in behavioral terms. Sometimes the outcome is a change in an internal state (e.g., thought, feeling, belief) such as becoming more self-confident, less anxious, or less depressed. In such cases it would not make sense to try to define the outcome behaviorally if the client truly views the problem as an internal state. Accordingly, when the desired outcome is an internal state, the most direct method of measurement is of necessity some form of self-report.

One of the best methods of measuring internal states is to develop a self-anchored rating scale (Bloom, 1975). A self-anchored scale is a rating scale you and your client develop specifically to measure your client's outcome (Gingerich, 1979). To construct a self-anchored scale, begin with a five- or seven-point rating scale (see Figure 10.1). Give the scale the name of the outcome you and your client have agreed upon; for example, you might call it a "feeling good" scale.

Next, you will develop anchors for the low end of the scale by having your client imagine a recent time when she did not feel good at all. After she has begun to visualize the situation, ask her to recall (1) what she

FIGURE 10.1

Self-Anchored Scale

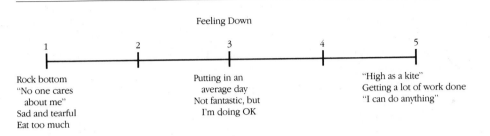

Feeling Down

| 1 | 2 | 3 | 4 | 5 |

Rock bottom
"No one cares
about me"
Sad and tearful
Eat too much

Putting in an
average day
Not fantastic, but
I'm doing OK

"High as a kite"
Getting a lot of work done
"I can do anything"

was doing, (2) any recurrent thoughts she was having, and (3) what she was feeling. Behaviors sometimes occur along with internal states; for example, your client may stay in bed all day, not answer the phone, cry frequently, and overeat on a bad day. Your client may also experience recurrent thoughts or self-statements such as "no one likes me," "I am ugly," or "life is not worth living." Feelings are more difficult to elicit but often are expressed best in word pictures such as "feeling blue," "my stomach is tied up in knots," or "I'm down in the dumps." In any case, the behaviors, thoughts, and feelings the client experiences when at the low point on the scale become the anchors for that point.

Once you have anchored the low point, ask your client to imagine a recent time when she was feeling very good. This time you will elicit anchors for the high end of the scale. You should proceed to develop anchors for other points of the scale as well; ideally at least alternate points of the scale should be anchored.

If you have developed the anchors carefully, the completed scale should be a sensitive measure of your client's outcome as she uniquely experiences it. Since self-anchored scales are client-specific, you must develop a new one for each new client and each new outcome.

Because self-anchored scales are subjective (they measure the internal states of clients) they have sometimes been criticized on methodological grounds. Their reliability cannot be assessed directly, and they

are always potentially reactive (more about these measurement issues later). On the other hand, self-report measures are the most direct measure of internal states, and there is little evidence that self-reports are any less adequate methodologically than many other types of measures (Bloom and Fischer, 1982). For purposes of outcome evaluation, self-anchored scales are often useful, and sometimes they are the only direct measure of the outcome.

STANDARDIZED MEASURES   In most cases the preferred method of measuring client outcomes is direct observation of behavior or self-anchored ratings of internal states. That is because these methods are likely to provide the most direct and sensitive measures of outcome. Occasionally, however, standardized measures may exist that would provide a suitable measure of outcome. Further, it is often a good idea to use standardized measures, in addition to behavioral and self-report measures, to provide a basis of comparison with known groups, or to be sure that you are measuring what you think.

Standardized measures include tests, questionnaires, rating scales, inventories, and checklists, which have three characteristics. First, they have uniform procedures for administration and scoring so that everyone who uses the instrument uses it in the same way. Second, standardized measures must meet minimal standards of methodological adequacy (i.e., reliability and validity). Third, most standardized measures have established norms; that is, they have guidelines for interpreting test scores based on the scores of known groups who have completed the measure or some independent standard of performance.

Standardized measures fall into two broad categories, published and unpublished. Published measures (commercially published) are described in the *Ninth Mental Measurements Yearbook* (Mitchell, 1985). Published measures have met accepted standards of reliability and validity, so you can use them with assurance that they will in fact measure what you think they will. The publishers of these measures require a fee, however, and some of them are available only to psychologists or other qualified professionals.

Unpublished measures are those measures that have been developed and used in research and practice situations but are not published commercially. There is no one source or listing of unpublished measures; however, several collections have particular value for social work practice. Hudson (1982) has developed a package of nine scales designed for use in social work practice. Sample scales include self-esteem, marital satisfaction, child's attitudes toward parents, and generalized contentment. All of these scales are scored and interpreted in the same way, making them easy to use in daily practice. A computer-administered version of Hudson's clinical measurement package is also available which permits the client to complete the scale on the computer, with the computer scoring the scale and graphing the results.

Corcoran and Fischer (1987) have compiled a collection of over 125 measures that they refer to as *rapid assessment instruments*. Instruments are included for children, adults, and couples, and cover a broad range of psychological, behavioral, and interpersonal problems. The sourcebook includes a description of each measure, its norms and scoring procedures, and reliability and validity data. In addition, each measure is reproduced in the book so you can decide for yourself whether it would be suitable for your clinical application.

In addition to these two collections, a wide range of standardized measures may be found in Bellack and Hersen (1988); Ciminero, Calhoun, and Adams (1986); Freedman and Sherman (1987); Gibson and Otten-

bacher (1988); Grotevant and Carlson (1987); Hersen and Bellack (1988), and Touliatos, Perlmutter, and Straus (1990).

GENERAL ISSUES IN MEASUREMENT

At times we have referred to the reliability and validity of measurement. These are terms that describe the methodological adequacy of measures. *Validity* refers to what the measure measures and *reliability* refers to how well it measures it. If a measure is not reliable, it will not give consistent and accurate readings. Thus, when observing behavior, for example, it is important that the description of the behavior be clear and objective so that the observer will record it consistently from day to day. If a measure is not valid, it will not measure what you think it measures. That is why, when developing self-anchored scales, for example, you should be sure that the anchors the client gives are real indicators of the outcome for each scale point.

In addition to reliability and validity, you also want a measure to be *sensitive* to the changes you expect a client to make. Direct observation of client behavior and self-anchored rating scales are sensitive measures of most client outcomes. On the other hand, standardized scales frequently are not since they have been developed to measure personality traits which, by definition, are relatively fixed and are not likely to change significantly during intervention.

Another requirement of measurement in single-case evaluation is that the measure be suitable for *repeated use* (at least weekly) during treatment. This is true for most behavioral observation measures and self-anchored scales but is often not true for standardized scales. The scales described by Hudson (1982) and Corcoran and Fischer (1987) are exceptions.

Finally, it is important to consider the *reactivity* of your measure. Since in most instances clients will be recording their own behavior, the measurement process itself will likely have some impact on the behavior it is reporting. For example, if you ask a mother who complains of her child's temper tantrums to count the tantrums, it is likely that she will notice some new things about her child's behavior as well as her own, and her behavior and that of her child may change as a result.

Because reactivity influences the behavior the measure is meant to measure, it is difficult to sort out how much behavior change is due to the intervention and how much is due to reactivity. Researchers generally try to minimize this problem by using unobtrusive measures (having someone else observe the client, for example), so they can be more sure of the exact impact on the intervention. However, from a practice point of view, reactivity may actually benefit the client. This is especially true if you are helping someone learn problem-solving strategies in which observing and altering one's own behavior are explicit goals of treatment.

Reactivity is a very complex process and its effect is difficult to gauge. Generally, however, you should have your clients record *positive* behaviors or internal states rather than negative ones, since the effect of reactivity (all else being equal) is apt to increase response rates rather than decrease them. For example, rather than recording an unwanted behavior such as eating snacks between meals, you could have your client record the number of times he thought of snacking but refrained. Koop (1988) provides an excellent discussion of the factors involved in estimating the reactivity of self-monitoring and how you can use it for your client's benefit.

Measurement of client outcomes is a crucial step in evaluating practice. Conclusions about whether the outcome has been achieved will be valid and trustworthy only if appropriate measures are used, so care and thoughtfulness are advised. You have also probably noticed the parallels between measurement as we have talked about it here and assessment as it has been discussed in Chapter 3. We have been talking about the same process from different perspectives: in the present discussion of measurement the emphasis has been on *how* to assess, whereas in the previous chapter the emphasis has been on *what* to assess. Clearly, you will want to pay careful attention to both aspects of assessment in your practice.

Record Baseline Data

After the selection of the measure or measures, the next step is to collect the data for a period of time before you implement intervention. This is called *baselining*, meaning that you are establishing the base rate of the outcome measure before intervention occurs and the expected change takes place. The main purpose for baselining is to provide a basis of comparison for the data collected during and after treatment. If the treatment data show a different level or pattern from the baseline data, you may reasonably conclude there has been a change. If you collected data only after treatment, you would have no way of knowing whether there had been a change.

Since you may not implement treatment during the baseline period, an important question is: How long should you baseline? Barlow, Hayes, and Nelson (1984) make several recommendations. First, you should collect baseline data for a *minimum of three data points*. At least three points are required to begin to assess the level, trend, and stability of the data. (More about these properties later when we discuss assessing change.) Although three data points constitute a minimum, in normal practice baselines are often taken for a week or more. Some statistical aids for assessing change require a minimum of ten baseline observations. Second, you should continue baselining until the data form a *stable pattern*. Frequently there is some fluctuation or trend in evidence during baseline, for example, there may be four or five tantrums one day and none the next, or the number of tantrums may seem to be decreasing. The idea is to baseline long enough that the pattern of behaviors becomes clear and consistent and (ideally) there is no upward or downward trend.

In order to be able to see the patterns contained in your data, you should always graph the data (see Figure 10.2 on page 260). Not only is this helpful for you, but graphs are a very effective way to provide feedback to your clients (and others such as parents and third-party funders). Using lined graph paper, begin by drawing a vertical line on the left side and a horizontal line at the bottom. The vertical axis is always used to represent the outcome, and the horizontal dimension represents

FIGURE 10.2

___

A Simple Graph

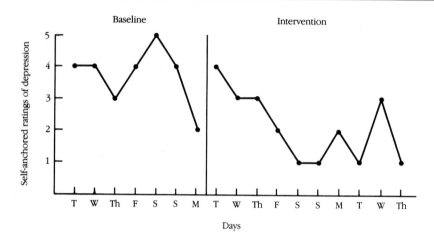

___

time units. Thus, you might record self-anchored ratings of "feeling good" on the vertical axis and days on the horizontal axis. Drawn in this way, the pattern of the client outcome over time can be readily seen. Other considerations in graphing are discussed in more detail in Bloom and Fischer (1982) and Parsonson and Baer (1978).

Conceptually, baselining parallels the assessment phase of treatment when the worker gathers information about the level of the client's problem, and when and where it happens. Seen in this way, baselining usually does not require you to delay the start of intervention any longer than you normally would. From a practice standpoint, it is unwise to begin intervening until you have a clear description of the problem or desired outcome and have reliable information about its current level. Occasionally, however, there will be situations (crises, for example) when it will be impossible to baseline before intervening. In such situations you may be able to reconstruct a baseline from archival data, or ask the client to estimate how often the identified outcome occurred during the previous week.

Without any baseline data whatsoever you will be severely hampered later on in determining whether there has been change in the outcome.

Implement Intervention and Continue Monitoring

___

Once you have established a baseline it is time to implement the intervention. The most important consideration from the point of view of evaluating practice is to specify and describe clearly just what the intervention consists of. Assuming your client improves, you will want to know what you did so you can do it again and can describe it to other professionals as well.

While this step sounds easy, it is perhaps the most difficult aspect of evaluation. In fact, there is ongoing debate in the literature regarding the extent to which interventions can be described and replicated (Frank, 1973). The helping process is a complex, multifaceted activity that can probably never be described completely. The practical goal, however, is to describe the intervention with sufficient clarity and completeness that someone else can replicate it and obtain similar results (Blythe and Tripodi, 1989). Further, it is assumed that although your actions from the start may be generally therapeutic, you will implement a *specific intervention* at the conclusion of baseline.

In addition to describing your intervention, you should verify that you have actually implemented it. Planning to do something does not necessarily mean it will happen. Occasionally, research studies on practice effectiveness have failed to produce positive results but on closer examination reveal that the intervention was never implemented as planned. This is important to know since it prevents you from mistakenly concluding that the intervention was unsuccessful when in fact it was never implemented.

Once you have implemented intervention, you should continue the same measurement procedure established during baseline (Figure 10.2). It is important that there be no changes in the definitions, times of measurement, or measurement procedures because such changes could affect the data you obtain. If you keep the measurement procedure exactly the same as baseline, changes in the data during treatment will reflect changes in the outcome itself, not the measurement procedure.

Assess Change

After you have collected data on your outcome measure during the baseline and treatment phases, the next step is to assess whether there has been any change. Actually, the issue is whether any significant change has occurred from a statistical or clinical standpoint (Kazdin, 1977). Statistical or *experimental* change refers to actual change in outcome between phases. It is assessed on purely statistical and logical grounds. Clinical or *applied* change refers to change that is sufficient, desirable, or meaningful from a clinical or practical standpoint.

The first task is to determine whether there has been experimental change; that is, whether there has been any real change in the outcome during interven-

tion. This task is sometimes made difficult because of some of the unique characteristics of time-series data (Jones, Vaught, and Weinrott, 1977; Kratochwill, 1978). Time-series data may be characterized by their level, trend, variability, and autocorrelation. *Level* refers to the central tendency or location of a set of data. When there is no trend, level is equivalent to the mean of observations in the baseline or treatment phase. *Trend* refers to a deterministic change in the level of the data over time; that is, a continuing upward and downward trend. *Variability* refers to the extent to which the data vary around the trend line. The more fluctuation around the trend line, the greater the variability of the data. Finally, *autocorrelation* refers to the possibility that the value of one observation may be related to previous observations. This is a complicated statistical phenomenon which in practical terms means that most of the usual statistical techniques (which assume independence of observations) may not be suitable for assessing change in time-series data.

There are two general approaches for assessing change in time-series data: visual analysis and statistical analysis. We shall place most emphasis on visual analysis since it is fairly straightforward and easy, and it is one procedure you should do routinely. The following discussion of visual analysis is based heavily on the work of Parsonson and Baer (1978).

Visual analysis simply means that you look at the graphed data and, applying rules of analysis, conclude whether there has been change in the client outcome from phase to phase. The standard of significance for visual analysis is "clearly evident and reliable"; that is, the change must be clear and unmistakable (Parsonson and Baer, 1978, p. 112).

The first step in visual analysis is to graph the baseline and treatment data following the suggestions noted earlier. The data within phases should be connected by a solid line, and the phases should be divided by a vertical line.

Ideally, in visual analysis, you would want to see little or no overlap between phases, with no clear trend in the data (see Figure 10.3a on page 262). In such cases it is clear there has been a change. Also, the more immediate the change and the greater its magnitude, the easier it is to conclude there has been real change.

FIGURE 10.3

Visual Analysis of Graphed Data

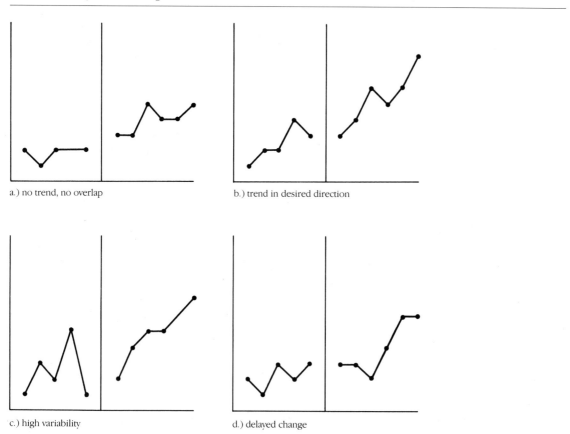

a.) no trend, no overlap

b.) trend in desired direction

c.) high variability

d.) delayed change

Sometimes the baseline data may contain a trend; that is, the outcome measure seems to be on a continuing increase or decrease. When this happens, you should make every effort to extend the period of baseline to see whether the trend will taper off and stabilize around a constant level. If not, you must analyze change cautiously. If the trend is in the opposite direction of desired change, then it will have little impact on assessing change. However, if the trend is in the desired direction, assessment of change will be ambiguous (Figure 10.3b). From a practice standpoint, it may

be wise not to intervene in such cases since the desired change appears to be happening already. If you must intervene, and if intervention produces a large and immediate increase in outcome or a change in slope, you might cautiously conclude there has been change. However, in most situations where there is a trend in the desired direction it will be difficult if not impossible to conclude reliably that there has been change.

On occasion the baseline data may be highly variable such that they overlap with the treatment data (Figure 10.3c). Again, your first strategy should be to try to reduce the variability by extending the baseline period or observing extraneous events affecting your client's responses that can be controlled. If not, it will be difficult to conclude unequivocally there has been change. On rare occasions the goal of intervention may be to increase or decrease the variability of a client's behavior (for example, to help a person with mood swings maintain a steadier state). Unfortunately, there are no readily available techniques for assessing change in variability of time-series data.

It is not uncommon in social work practice for client change to be delayed or gradual (Figure 10.3d). Since the change is not immediate and there is overlap between phases, it is difficult to reach a reliable conclusion (Gibson and Offenbacher, 1988). In such cases the best thing to do is continue the intervention and continue observing to see whether the behavior eventually stabilizes around a new level. If so, you can be relatively confident there has been change in the outcome.

Ideally, our interventions would be so effective that visual analysis of graphed data would be sufficient to reach reliable conclusions about change. Of course, we know that this doesn't always happen. Sometimes there appears to be some change, but the change doesn't strictly meet the criteria of "clearly evident and reliable." What then? Some writers have suggested that if change is not clearly evident the intervention is simply not potent enough to be of interest, so we should abandon it altogether rather than try to sort out whether there was significant change. This argument is very persuasive from a practical standpoint. On the other hand, some of the outcomes we are interested in change slowly, and change may not be very immediate or dramatic. Further, when developing new interventions it may be important to know whether there is even a small change, so we can improve and refine the intervention to the point that it may be of practical value. In cases such as these statistical and quasi-statistical techniques may be needed to determine whether there has been a reliable change in outcome. Although such techniques are beyond the scope of this chapter, good discussions are available in Bloom and Fischer (1982) and Gingerich (1983b).

In contrast to experimental significance, applied (clinical) significance compares the amount of change that has occurred with the amount of change thought necessary or desirable. This is often a difficult judgment to make since individuals disagree on what is necessary or desirable.

Kazdin (1977) discusses a number of approaches for assessing applied significance. One of these, the *aim-star technique*, simply places an *aim-star* on the graph at the level and day that represent the desired outcome. You then graph the treatment data to see if they are moving in the direction of the aim-star. If the data coincide with the aim-star you have achieved applied significance. *Goal attainment scaling* offers a similar approach conceptually (Kiresuk and Lund, 1978). Both procedures are admittedly subjective, although they probably reflect what our clients consider significant change better than does experimental significance.

Kazdin discusses several additional ways to evaluate applied significance. One of these, *social comparison*, compares the client's performance in the target area with that of "normal" peers. For example, you might decide what a reasonable standard of cooperative play is by observing "normal" children in the natural setting. Another approach for assessing applied significance is called *subjective evaluation*. Here you would poll qualified individuals such as teachers, social workers, or probation officers to determine what a reasonable standard of performance would be. For a more detailed discussion of applied significance see the articles by Kazdin (1977) and Gingerich (1983b).

In practice, you should always attempt to assess change using both experimental and applied criteria. At the minimim, you should perform visual analysis of graphed data, and perhaps use some of the statistical techniques available if visual analysis is ambiguous. In addition, you should always specify before intervention what the goal of intervention is. You may express this verbally or graphically using the aim-star technique.

The above five steps constitute the necessary steps for carrying out outcome evaluation as defined earlier. Your measure should indicate in quantitative terms what the desired outcome is; data should show what the baseline level was and whether there was change during intervention; and finally your analysis should tell you whether the change was significant. As we said earlier, practice evaluation should be a regular part of normal social work practice.

CASE EXAMPLE

Treatment of Obsessive-Compulsive Disorder

The following case example is based on a study by Cooper (1990) in which she used behavioral interventions to help a client reduce her ritualizing behavior. Improvement was also noted in depression and anxiety.

1. Specify the Goal

This study involved a woman in her late twenties who displayed at intake pervasive ritualistic behavior, social isolation, depression, and anxiety. She had been in psychotherapy for the previous five years. The specific goals for this study were to reduce three behaviors: (1) ritualistic opening and shutting of her makeup case, (2) excessive rinsing in the shower, and (3) ritualistic counting of belongings.

2. Selecting a Suitable Measure(s)

The measure used was client self-monitoring of the three behaviors on a 3 × 5 note card. The client recorded the number of times she opened and closed her makeup case, the minutes spent rinsing after soaping in the shower, and the percentage of times she counted her belongings when carrying them. In addition to these target behaviors, Cooper also asked her client to complete the Spielberger State-Trait Anxiety Inventory and the Beck Depression Inventory.

3. Record Baseline Data

Cooper implemented a modified form of the multiple baseline design in which each behavior was recorded for a variable period prior to the start of treatment. Baselines ranged from thirteen days for opening and closing the makeup case to six weeks for counting belongings while carrying them.

4. Implement Intervention and Continue Monitoring

The intervention consisted of behavior modification techniques (including modeling and response prevention). It was directed first toward the makeup case ritual, then the excessive rinsing, and finally the counting of belongings. The order of target behaviors was determined by client ratings of each on an anxiety hierarchy. Cooper continued to monitor each target behavior during the intervention period.

5. Assess Change

Each target behavior was monitored during intervention (just as in baseline) and placed on a time-series graph. The results for the opening and closing of the makeup case are shown in the graph below. It is clear from visual analysis that there was significant change during intervention — there was no overlap across phases and behavior changed abruptly when treatment was started. Cooper did a celeration line test that confirmed her visual analysis. The other two target behaviors showed similar reductions. Pre and post measures on the

Source: Marlene Cooper, "Treatment of a Client with Obsessive-Compulsive Disorder," *Social Work Research and Abstracts, 26* (1990), pp. 26–32.

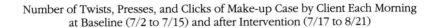

Number of Twists, Presses, and Clicks of Make-up Case by Client Each Morning
at Baseline (7/2 to 7/15) and after Intervention (7/17 to 8/21)

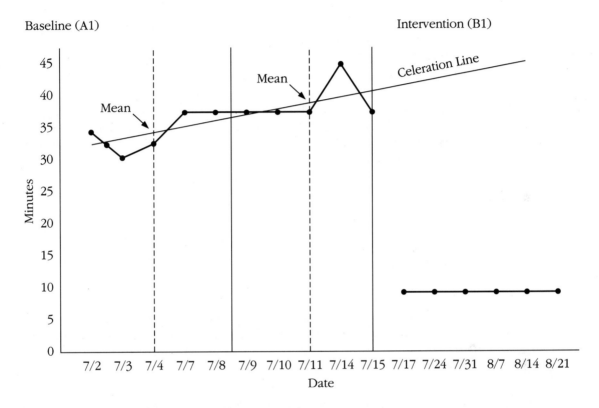

State-Trait Anxiety Inventory and the Beck Depression Inventory showed no significant change. Anxiety scores began high and continued high, and depression scores began low and remained so throughout. Cooper did three-month and six-month follow-ups, which verified that changes the client made during treatment continued.

6. Infer effectiveness

This study used a modified multiple baseline design to evaluate the impact of behavioral intervention on three ritualistic behaviors. In each case, introduction of treatment was followed immediately by a reduction in the target behavior. These results were confirmed using the celeration line. The fact that treatment was begun at different points in time for the three different target behaviors and was followed by immediate change lends credibility to the hypothesis that treatment produced the change, not historical events, maturation, and some other factor. Thus, we can be fairly safe in concluding that the intervention produced the observed changes in target behaviors. Intervention did not appear to influence general anxiety or depression.

Continued

CASE EXAMPLE   *Continued*

This study is a good example of the extent to which one can implement a fairly rigorous single-subject evaluation design in direct practice. It used clear, concrete measures of the target behaviors. The modified multiple baseline design is able to rule out most competing explanations for the observed change in target behavior. Although realities of the practice situation did not permit an exact implementation of the multiple baseline design, it could be closely approximated, which adds considerably to the therapist's ability to infer the effectiveness of the intervention. Even if the multiple baseline design could not have been implemented, a simple AB design (baseline-intervention) on any one of the target behaviors would have provided valuable information about change.

You may notice, however, that we have said almost nothing up to now about intervention effectiveness — that is, whether the intervention was responsible for producing the change. The question of effectiveness leads us into evaluation research per se in which we must use research designs to develop a logical and empirical basis for making inferences about treatment effectiveness. Although it is not the goal of this chapter to make you a skilled researcher, a brief review of research designs and design issues will help you begin to think about effectiveness and, perhaps more important, deter you from making assertions about effectiveness that go beyond your data.

Infer Effectiveness

In order to infer that your intervention was effective, you must show logically and empirically that the intervention is the only plausible explanation for the observed change in client outcome. To put it a bit differently, you must rule out other possible explanations for the observed change.

The primary criterion for inferring causality is *concomitant variation*; that is, the observed change in client outcome must occur at (or soon after) the time the intervention is implemented. If change begins before intervention, logically we would have to conclude that something other than the intervention was responsible for the change. Likewise, if change occurs too long af-

ter intervention, then other possible explanations take on more credence.

Threats to Validity

Concomitant variation alone is not sufficient to establish causality; it is only suggestive of a causal relationship. We must also rule out other possible (and plausible) explanations for why the client changed. These competing explanations fall into several categories, which have been called threats to validity (Cook and Campbell, 1979). Validity, as the term is used here, refers to the best available approximation of truth regarding the cause of client change. The following discussion includes several of the more important threats to validity.

HISTORY   History refers to any event that may have occurred during the time the intervention was implemented that could also account for the change. Examples are events such as getting a promotion, getting a new classroom teacher, or having a birthday. Observed improvements in the client's functioning may result from such historical events rather than the intervention. Simple baseline-intervention designs (AB designs) do not permit us to rule out the effects of history. Other more advanced designs are needed.

MATURATION   Maturation includes any processes within the client that operate as a function of the passage of time, such as growing up, becoming senile, or becoming tired. Maturation generally becomes more of a threat the longer it takes for the intervention to have an impact.

STATISTICAL REGRESSION   Usually clients come to social workers for help when things have gotten worse; that is, they are in an extreme state. However, chances are good that things will look better at the next observation simply because of the random fluctuations of the behavior. This threat to validity is called statistical regression. The best way to control statistical regression is to take an adequate baseline. If the baseline shows an upward or downward trend, or an unusual amount of variability, you should continue to baseline to see whether the data stablize or the pattern of normal variability becomes clear. The point is to not mistake normal variation in your client's behavior for a real change in behavior.

MULTIPLE INTERVENTION INTERFERENCE   When a client receives more than one intervention at a time, there is no empirical basis for knowing which intervention produced the change. This is a common problem, particularly in institutional settings where clients may participate in a variety of groups, receive individual therapy, and perhaps take medication. Again, simple AB designs are inadequate to control for this threat. Other designs, such as multiple baseline designs, are useful in ruling out multiple intervention interference.

Although these are the most common and obvious threats to the validity of single-system evaluation, others are discussed by Cook and Campbell (1979) and Kratochwill (1978).

SINGLE-SYSTEM DESIGNS

The Basic AB Design

Up to now we have discussed only the simplest of single-system designs, the baseline-intervention, or AB

design. It is the most basic design because it provides the information necessary for determining that there has been change, and it suggests the possibility that the intervention produced the change. Since AB designs are not able to control for many of the threats to validity mentioned above, however, they are generally not adequate for inferring causality or intervention effectiveness. More advanced single-system designs are needed to control for such threats.

Withdrawal Designs

Withdrawal designs are characterized by repeated occasions in which the intervention is implemented and then withdrawn. The rationale underlying withdrawal designs is that the causal inference is stronger when there are more occasions on which client outcome can be shown to vary concomitantly with intervention. Common examples are the ABA and ABAB designs (see Figure 10.4 on page 268). In the former, treatment is withdrawn after it has been implemented, and in the latter treatment is implemented again. Withdrawal designs are useful for controlling threats due to history, maturation, and statistical regression, among others. Withdrawal designs are often difficult to implement in day-to-day practice, however, because they require withdrawal of intervention, even when it appears to be working. This is one example in which the goals of research (demonstrating causality) may conflict with the goals of service (providing effective treatment).

It is important to be careful to distinguish between withdrawal phases and follow-ups. In withdrawal designs the objective is for the client outcome to return to the pretreatment level in order to demonstrate repeatedly that it is under the control of the intervention. In follow-ups, however, the objective is to show that change is permanent and that it lasts even after treatment has been discontinued. You should be clear in your own mind about which objective you are addressing so you will know how to interpret the data.

MULTIPLE BASELINE DESIGNS   In multiple baseline designs several outcomes of interest are identified and baselined simultaneously. The intervention is then implemented on each outcome at staggered intervals

FIGURE 10.4

Withdrawal Design

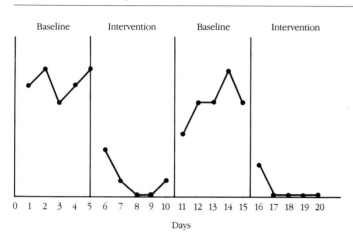

(Figure 10.5). This type of design is stronger than simple AB designs because it provides for several occasions on which outcome can vary concomitantly with intervention. Further, it avoids the practical and ethical problems of withdrawing treatment as in ABA and ABAB designs.

There are still other advanced single-system designs that should be considered if the objective is to infer causality. The texts by Jayaratne and Levy (1979), Bloom and Fischer (1982), and Barlow and Hersen (1984) offer a more detailed discussion of single-system research designs.

EVALUATING PROGRAMS

Most of the discussion up to now has assumed that we are evaluating social work practice with individuals, groups, and families. There is nothing inherent in the single-system approach that limits it to clinical evaluation, however. Some of the first applications of single-system designs were to evaluate the impact of policy, such as a change in speed limits or a change in monetary policy. Single-system designs can easily be applied to the evaluation of policy and program interventions. The basic designs are the same; the primary differences are the conceptualization of the intervention and outcome, and the selection of suitable measures.

In program evaluation, the policy or program becomes the intervention. Such interventions include providing incentives for able-bodied welfare recipients to obtain employment, instituting a token economy to reward good behavior in a group home, or starting a new procedure whereby staff ignore the obnoxious noises of children but give positive attention for appropriate talk.

Likewise, in program evaluation the desired outcome has to do with the behavior of the targets of the policy or program change, usually a group of people.

FIGURE 10.5

Multiple Baseline Design

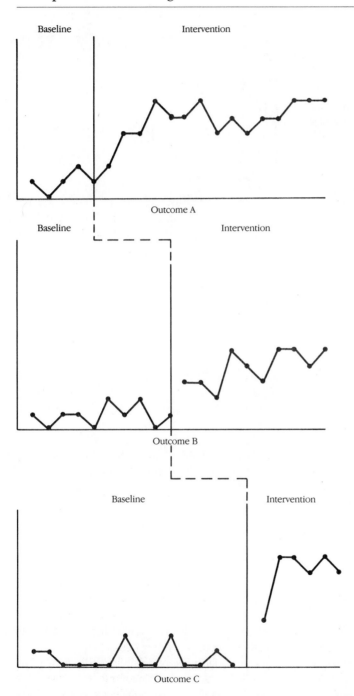

Accordingly, the measures must be ones that are suitable for all individuals. This usually rules out client-specific measures such as self-anchored scales. Frequently, the desired outcomes are observable behaviors, such as getting a job, cooperative play in the cottage, or appropriate table conversation. In program evaluation you must be careful to define outcomes in sufficiently general terms so that the definitions will be relevant for all individuals in the target group. When the desired outcome is an internal state, you may need to use some of the standardized measures or rapid assessment instruments mentioned above.

Program evaluation, then, is no different conceptually from clinical evaluation. The main difference is that the intervention is a policy or program rather than a therapeutic technique, and the outcome is reflected in the behaviors of a target group of individuals rather than a single individual or therapy group.

The single-system approach to evaluation has much to recommend it. Single-system designs are compatible with most of social work practice, and they provide a beginning basis for inferring that our interventions are effective. Single-system designs, including the more advanced designs, are not always sufficient, however. Single-system designs cannot always rule out all threats to validity. Some social work interventions, particularly policy and program changes, cannot be implemented abruptly, and other interventions sometimes have a delayed effect on outcome. In both cases it is difficult empirically to relate changes in outcome to the intervention. In such cases, traditional group designs may be justified.

The requirements of group designs—random assignment to groups, relatively large numbers of clients, and uniform treatment of all subjects within groups—make them costly and difficult to implement in normal practice settings. Frequently, the potential benefits of doing a group evaluation do not justify the costs involved. There are times, however, when group designs are warranted, particularly when single-system evaluation has provided cumulative evidence of effectiveness and a more rigorous test is desired. Group evaluation is a rather technical undertaking for which research expertise is advised. Texts by Weiss (1972), Rossi, Freeman, and Wright (1979), Posavac and Carey (1980), and Kaufman and Thomas (1980) are recommended for further reading in this area.

COMPUTER APPLICATIONS IN SOCIAL WORK PRACTICE

At several points in our discussion of evaluation, the use of computers was mentioned. Computers have been used for some time in evaluation and research, and they are beginning to have an impact on many other aspects of social work practice as well. This brief summary introduces some of those applications and suggests how you may be using computers in your practice in the near future.

The rapid development of computer technology in the last several decades has been due to advances in miniaturization of computers and tremendous strides in the economics of production. Today it is possible to obtain in a desktop computer (costing about a thousand dollars) the computing capacity of the large mainframe computers of a decade or two ago (which cost hundreds of thousands of dollars). These trends are expected to continue. Comparable computing capacity will likely be available soon in machines the size of hand-held calculators costing perhaps only hundreds of dollars.

What does all this mean for social work practice? Well, for one thing, it means that the capacity to process large amounts of data at high speed with little or no error will be widely available. Consequently, the computer will be called upon more and more to do the repetitive data processing tasks that until recently had to be done by people. Advances in the design of computing machines will make it possible for computers to handle symbolic processing tasks such as understanding human language and simulating human vision. With developments occurring so rapidly it is impossible to predict just how computing technology will be

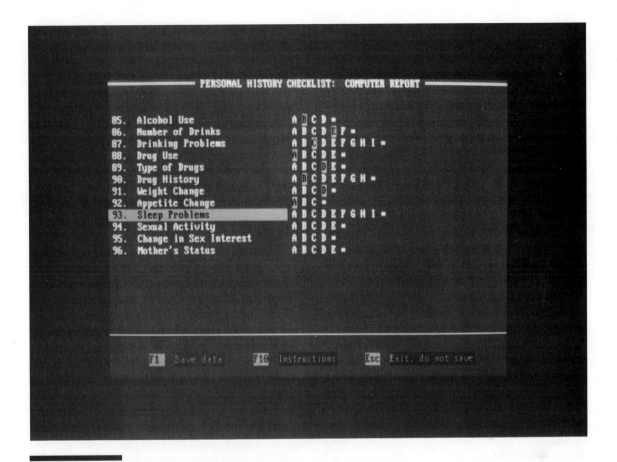

A computer-administered version of psychological assessment.

applied even several decades from now, but it is certain to change significantly the ways in which social workers will do their work.

Computers come in all sizes, from small lap-top computers the size of notebooks to large mainframe computers that fill entire rooms. Today, social workers are most likely to use personal computers, computers that fit on a desk, cost from one to five thousand dollars, are easy to use, and have a wide range of software available. In "computerese," *hardware* refers to the machine itself and the related peripheral equipment such as printers and monitors, and *software* refers to the programs the machines use to do tasks.

Typical software programs include word processing programs, which allow you to use your computer much like an electronic typewriter; database programs, which turn your computer into an electronic filing system; and spreadsheets, which instruct your computer to function like an accountant's ledger for use in budgeting and accounting. There are many additional types of software for computers, with new applications being added every day. One of the best ways to become familiar with the new computing technology is to read some of the magazines available on newsstands or the books available in the computer section of your local bookstore.

Computer-based psychological assessment.

Office Management

The most common computer applications in social work fall into the following areas:

The two most common office management applications are word processing and accounting. Word processing is used for routine correspondence, case notes, and reports: but it is most useful for repetitive tasks such as individualized form letters, or documents that are composed of standard subsections. Most word processing software includes the capability to manage mailing lists—useful for maintaining lists of clients, volunteers, contributors, and staff. The day will soon come when no office, even small human service agencies, will be able to justify being without word processing capabilities.

The other common office management function is accounting. Many social work agencies already use computers for keeping the general ledgers, accounts receivable, accounts payable, and payroll. Sometimes these functions are performed on the agency's own equipment, and sometimes they are contracted out to firms that specialize in providing such services.

Client Information Systems

Client information systems are computerized database systems that contain information about each client, the services received, and outcomes achieved. Comprehensive systems may also include appointment scheduling, commmunity resource directories, and billing functions. The primary function of client information systems is to generate routine reports on the clients served and the services provided. Frequently client information systems focus mainly on serving the needs of agency managers.

Decision Support

If client information systems are designed properly, they can also be used to monitor client progress in treatment, to guide case managers and line workers in the design and implementation of treatment, and to evaluate the impact of agency services. For example, the system may be able to identify those clients who are making satisfactory progress toward their goals and should be preparing for termination. Likewise, clients who are not making progress can be identified so the treatment team can reassess and revise treatment as needed. Finally, well-designed systems permit analysis of which interventions seem to work best with which kinds of problems. These are referred to as decision support functions because the information generated by the computer is used to assist decision makers as they do their work.

Another important decision support function is provided by spreadsheet programs. These popular programs, which are electronic versions of the account's spreadsheet, permit "what if" analysis of alternative courses of action. When used effectively, spreadsheets can help managers analyze cash flow, determine optimal agency fees, analyze patterns in intakes, or plan the most effective use of agency resources.

Clinical Assessment

One of the earliest uses of computers in mental health settings (along with computerized client records) was clinical assessment. Initially, this consisted of putting standardized psychological tests on the computer so the computer could administer and perhaps score the test. Recently, assessment applications have expanded to having the computer administer social history interviews and write up narrative reports, or conduct diagnostic interviews of clients.

One of the newest applications of computers in social work practice is *expert systems* (Gingerich, 1990a). An expert system is a computer program that contains the facts and rules of thumb a human expert uses to solve a given problem. For example, expert systems are being developed to advise social workers on the risk of child abuse, or which intervention to use in family therapy. Expert systems have the potential to make scarce and highly specialized expertise widely available to practicing professionals at negligible costs.

Direct Intervention

Computers are just beginning to be used to actually deliver interventions. Programs have been developed to teach relaxation techniques, modify depression, and treat sexual problems of couples. In some cases, computer-delivered intervention appears to be as effective as intervention delivered by human therapists. Because of the importance of human involvement in social work practice, however, computers are not expected to have a large impact on direct intervention in the near future.

Electronic Networking

Computers can be connected to the telephone system and in this way access any other computer in the world. This capability is opening up many new possibilities for computer use in social work. The most common application of telecommunications to date is electronic mail—sending and receiving messages electronically. *E-mail*, as it is called, provides the capability for social workers to send messages, documents, and reports almost instantaneously at very low cost. Some agencies use electronic networking to maintain up-to-date listings of available resources. The Computer Use in Social

Services Network (see Resources at end of chapter) maintains an electronic network to provide information and computer-related assistance to human service professionals.

Education and Training

Computers are also beginning to be used in the education and training of social workers. Some schools offer computer simulations of social work situations as a learning experience. Simulations may involve problems, such as managing a waiting list or developing a budget, or how to handle a variety of interviewing situations. In one agency the computer was combined with videodisc technology to provide training to new staff on how to determine eligibility for services. It was found in this case that the computer-delivered training took half the time of the usual classroom training, and the results appeared to be superior.

Research and Information Retrieval

One of the oldest applications of computers in social work is to analyze data for research purposes. Computers are accurate and very fast when it comes to numerical computations. It is now possible to do routinely computations such as factor analyses, which previously required weeks for a human to do. On a more practical level, computers can be used to do some of the statistical analyses described above for assessing change in client outcomes or even graphing the client's behavior. Graphs can be printed out and made a part of the client's record.

A related application of computers is to access large databases such as bibliographic services. It is now possible, and economically feasible in many cases, to dial up some of the social work–related bibliographic services to obtain a listing of professional publications that deal with a particular topic. (*Social Work Research and Abstracts* is available on line through several bibliographic services, and is also available on CD ROM.) You might ask for references on group homes for the

hearing impaired, or treatment approaches for agoraphobia, for example.

Issues in Computer Applications

Computer applications such as these have raised some important questions that you should consider carefully before using this new and glamorous technology. For example, does the lack of a human interacting with the client reduce or limit the impact of services? How does being interviewed by a computer affect the client? What are the threats to maintaining confidentiality? What functions can the computer serve best? What functions should the computer not do? There are no clear answers to many of these questions. Initial research does indicate, however, that some clients prefer to be interviewed by the computer, especially when personal information such as illegal or sexual behavior is discussed. In some cases, clients actually give more accurate and complete information to the computer! When using computers, however, it is essential that we be sensitive to our clients' reactions to the computer and use computers only when it clearly seems to improve services to the client. Additional resource materials on computer applications to social work practice are listed at the end of this chapter.

SUMMARY

Outcome evaluation asks whether the desired client outcome was achieved, and evaluative research asks whether the observed change was due to the intervention. Because it is an inherent part of the problem-solving approach to interventions, outcome evaluation should be done with all clients. Evaluative research requires more rigorous controls, and therefore it is more difficult to carry out and often requires research expertise.

The single-system approach to evaluation consists of the following six steps. First, you must specify the outcome you and your client are interested in. Second, you must select a suitable measure of the outcome, one that is adequate methodologically and is sensitive to the changes you expect your client to make. Third, you should record baseline data on the outcome measure until the pattern of behavior before intervention is clear. Fourth, implement your intervention and continue to monitor the outcome. Fifth, you must analyze your data to decide whether there is significant change in the outcome. Sixth, if you have used an appropriate research design, you may be able to infer whether your intervention produced the change.

Although it uses research techniques to assess change and infer treatment effectiveness, the single-system approach to evaluation is compatible with most social work practice. In treatment you ordinarily make informal judgments about whether your client is getting better and whether your intervention is working.

Evaluation simply makes the process more systematic and rigorous with a view to improving your information and making your conclusions more reliable. The goal of evaluation is to improve our information about outcomes and thereby improve our practice. Further, several studies show that clients may actually prefer to work with practitioners who evaluate their practice (Campbell, 1988, 1990).

The chapter concludes with a summary of computer applications in social work practice. Not only have computers been used in evaluation and research, but they are beginning to have an impact on many other aspects of social work practice as well. The most common computer applications in social work fall into the following areas: office management, client information systems, decision support, clinical assessment, direct intervention, electronic networking, education and training, and research and information retrieval.

EXERCISES

1. *Selecting a Suitable Outcome Measure*

GOAL: This exercise is designed to help students consider alternative ways of measuring client outcomes and become aware of the advantages and disadvantages of each.

Step 1: Describe the purpose of this exercise. Explain that client outcomes may be expressed in observable behaviors, or in internal feelings or thoughts. Sometimes even though the outcome is an internal event, such as feeling depressed, it may be preferable to define constructive change in terms of observable behaviors such as socializing with friends, going to work, or expressing one's feelings directly. Review the three major measurement strategies: direct observation, self-anchored rating scales, and standardized measures.

Step 2: Ask students to form groups of three or four. Then ask each group to recruit one of its members voluntarily to identify an outcome that will become the focus for this exercise. The outcome should be a real one that would be desirable for the student, although it need not be a personal one. For example, a student may identify "improving study habits," "feeling more confident in my field placement," or "settling disagreements with my roommate" as possible outcomes.

Step 3: Ask the other students in each group to interview the volunteer to find out more about the desired outcome. How would the volunteer like things to be? What will he be doing differently when the outcome is achieved?

Step 4: Now ask the students to identify at least two possible measurement strategies to measure the outcome. For the sake of this exercise, encourage them to use direct observation and a self-anchored scale. They may also want to select a standardized measure with which they are familiar. Students should describe each measure in detail. What would the anchors on the self-anchored scale be, for example? Or what specific behavior would they observe or ask their volunteer to observe?

Step 5: Have the students ask the volunteer to estimate what data he would have collected during the past week had they used each measure. What would the data be like when the problem has been solved?

Step 6: Next, ask each group to discuss the pros and cons of each measure they developed. They should consider these questions: (1) How reliable (accurate and consistent) would the measurement data be? (2) How valid would the data be—that is, would the behavior counts or self-ratings be good indicators of the outcome the volunteer is hoping to achieve? (3) Will the measure be sensitive to changes the volunteer would like to see? Do you really expect to see changes in the measures you have selected? (4) Which measure does your volunteer think is best? Why?

Step 7: Ask each group to discuss the practical value of identifying outcomes and measuring them. How do they think this will benefit their work with their clients? How could it interfere? If they do not plan to collect measurement data, how will they know if there is any change?

Step 8: Ask each group to report briefly to the entire class what outcome their group worked with, the measures they developed, and what they concluded in their discussion.

2. Threats to Inferring Causality

GOALS: This exercise is designed to make students aware of the problems involved in inferring causality and to help them avoid making assertions about treatment effectiveness that cannot be supported by data.

Step 1: Describe the purpose of this exercise. Review briefly the concept of concomitant variation as the primary empirical basis for inferring causality. Then summarize the threats to validity (categories of other explanations for why the client might have changed): history, maturation, statistical regression, and multiple intervention interference. Mention that the purpose of a research design is to provide a logical and empirical basis for inferring that the intervention, not something else, produced the change in outcome.

Step 2: Ask students to imagine they have conducted the following evaluation of their work. Your client, a mother of two children (ages five and eight), comes in complaining that her eight-year-old, Joey, clings to her too much and doesn't play with other children his age. You and she agree that the desired outcome is for Joey to play with neighbor children his own age. Mother agrees to record the number of fifteen-minute periods each evening after supper and before bedtime that Joey plays nicely with his peers. Mother dutifully collects baseline information as shown below.

After a week of baselining, you instruct the mother to invite a neighbor child over to play with Joey each evening and to get the children started in an activity appropriate to their age level. Once the activity has started, mother is to give specific praise to the children for their play and to continue to praise every five or ten minutes as it seems appropriate. Also, mother is instructed to ignore Joey when he clings to her dress and whines. After role-playing some situations in your office, you are convinced that mother understands the intervention and is able to carry it out. Mother returns the next week for her appointment during which you review the data, and refine and rehearse again the intervention. The next week mother reports the following data:

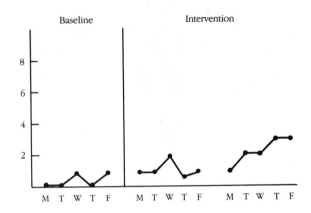

During the interview, mother reports the following additional information. She has begun to think that Joey is a nice kid after all. Last week when she took him to the park to play they had a really good time. Joey seemed to get along well with the other children on the playground, too. Mother also mentioned that Joey seemed to enjoy his last two weekend visits with his dad. In general, Joey seems to be getting back to his good old self.

Step 3: Now ask students to decide first whether they agree with mother that there has been a change in Joey's behavior. Is the standard of "clearly evident and reliable" met? What are their doubts about whether the change is experimentally or clinically significant?

Step 4: Next, ask students to enumerate all the other possible explanations for why Joey's behavior has changed. What is the likelihood of each other explanation? Does the simple AB design used allow you to rule out these explanations?

Step 5: Based on the discussion in steps three and four, ask the students whether they think their intervention was successful. How confident are they of the conclusion? If they are not completely convinced, does the intervention seem promising enough to continue using it and observing the results?

Resource Materials on Computer Applications to Social Work Practice

Administration in Social Work 5, nos. 3–4. Fall/Winter 1981. Special issue devoted to computer applications in social work administration.

Computer Use in Social Services Network, Dick Schoech, Co-ordinator. University of Texas at Arlington, P.O. Box 19129, Arlington, TX 76019. (quarterly newsletter, $10.00/year — $5.00 for students)

Computers in Human Services. New York: Haworth Press. A new journal devoted exclusively to computer applications in the human services.

Deitel, Harry M., and Barbara Deitel, 1985. *Computers and Data Processing.* Orlando, Fla.: Academic Press.

Geiss, Gunther R., and Narayan Viswanathan, eds. 1986. *The Human Edge: Information Technology and Helping People.* New York: Haworth Press.

NASW Practice Digest 6, no. 3. Winter 1983. Special issue devoted to computers in social work practice.

Schoech, Richard J. 1982. *Computer Use in Human Services.* New York: Human Science Press.

Schwartz, Marc D., ed. 1984. *Using Computers in Clinical Practice.* New York: Haworth Press.

For more information on the computer programs in this chapter write the author:

Wallace J. Gingerich
Mandel School of Applied Social Sciences
Case Western Reserve University
11235 Bellflower Road
Cleveland, Ohio 44106

11

SOCIAL WORK PRACTICE WITH DIVERSE GROUPS

The social work profession has long prided itself on its recognition of the importance of ethnic, cultural, racial, and sexual differences. Social workers were involved in early efforts to establish the National Association for the Advancement of Colored People (NAACP) and the National Urban League (Garvin and Cox, 1987, p. 36). The social work *Code of Ethics* specifically prohibits discrimination against others based on race, color, sex, sexual orientation, age, religion, national origin, marital status, political belief, and other factors (see Appendix A). More recently, the 1990 Delegate Assembly adopted a resolution calling upon the Council on Social Work Education to strengthen its standards on sexual orientation. On the basis of public pronouncements at least, one would expect that social workers would perform admirably when working with people from among the groups listed above. Unfortunately, this benign view is not necessarily accurate. Mizio (1972, p. 82) has noted that "all Americans are products of a racist system," the influence of which is inescapable. Romero (1977, p. 217) claims that "implicit and explicit biases have been incorporated in the foundation of the recognized knowledge and competence of the profession." Gilligan's (1982) work on women has underscored that much of what we have assumed about human development is marred by a male perpsective. Clearly, there is evidence that social workers face a difficult task understanding and working with clients whose background differs from that of the practitioner.

In this chapter we will review some of the barriers inherent in worker-client differences and attempt to point out some of the reasons for the problematic nature of cross-cultural relationships. In the second section we will identify some of the conditions that facilitate more effective relationships, discussing in particular self-knowledge and knowledge of the client group to be served. In the final section some specific techniques and approaches to be used (or avoided) will be suggested focusing on social work practice with

This chapter was specially written for this text by Grafton H. Hull, Jr., Ed.D. Dr. Hull is chairperson of the social work department at the University of Wisconsin—Eau Claire.

Native Americans, African-Americans, Latinos, women, gays and lesbians, and rural clients. While much of this chapter is written from the perspective of a white male (the author), many of the examples and points raised are applicable to other workers as well.

PROBLEMS AND BARRIERS

Clearly the social work profession needs to recognize the reality of practice in a culturally diverse environment. A variety of studies have demonstrated that social workers and other helping persons do share many of the prejudices and misperceptions of the general society. Brown and Hellinger (1975), for example, found that social workers in general lag behind psychiatric nurses in holding contemporary attitudes toward women; and male workers, in particular, tend to hold relatively traditional views of females when compared to their sister therapists. Rauch (1978) cites multiple examples of sexism in the social work knowledge base. It has been asserted that "unless the therapists are . . . sensitive to feminist issues or committed to feminism, a certain amount of bias will exist in their therapy no matter how humanistic they view themselves" (Thomas, 1977, p. 450). Romero (1977) argues that sex biases are often in operation in the practice of social casework. If "male counselors share cultural values, for instance, that consider women to be less effective and more likely to have difficulty coping with life situations," the effectiveness of the worker is definitely compromised (Hook, 1979, p. 63). For example, males working with depressed women may simply recreate old relationships between the dependent woman and the controlling male, relationships counter to the goals of intervention.

The tendency to use one's own cultural, social, or economic values as the norm poses additional dangers for the well-meaning practitioner. The ease with which many workers confuse a healthy adaptation to a sick environment with pathology points up the difficulty. Both the habit of misreading strengths as deficits and

the assumption that African-Americans and other minorities are culturally deprived arise from the use of norms derived from the dominant white middle class (Thomas and Sillen, 1972). Medina and Reyes (1976, p. 515), viewing Latino counselors working with other Latinos, add that Spanish-speaking counselors "are subject to the same cultural characteristics as are their clients." The problematic nature of cross-cultural counseling does not, however, preclude its effectiveness. Some white workers, for instance, can establish viable working relationships with minority clients, while in other instances, minority workers are less effective with others of the same race or culture (Williams et al., 1985; Logan, 1990). The following excerpt illustrates this point quite well.

In answering the question of whether a white middle-class psychiatrist can treat a black family, I cannot help but think back over my own experiences. When I first came to New York and decided to go into psychotherapy I had two main thoughts: (1) that my problems were culturally determined, and (2) that they were related to my Catholic upbringing. I had grown up in an environment in which the Catholic Church had tremendous influence. With these factors in mind, I began to think in terms of the kind of therapist I could best relate to. In addition to being warm and sensitive, he had to be black and Catholic. Needless to say, that was like looking for a needle in a haystack. But after inquiring around, I was finally referred to a black Catholic psychiatrist.

Without going into too much detail, let me say that he turned out to be not so sensitive and not so warm. I terminated my treatment with him and began to see another therapist who was warm, friendly, sensitive, understanding and very much involved with me. Interestingly enough, he was neither black, nor Catholic. As a result of that personal experience, I have come to believe that it is not so much a question of whether the therapist is black or white but whether he is competent, warm, and understanding. Feelings, after all, are neither black nor white. (Sager, Brayboy, and Waxenberg, 1970, pp. 210–11)

Though this view may seem somewhat sanguine given the vast differences which sometimes separate client and worker, there is every reason to believe that the perception is accurate. Logan (1990, p. 33) concludes that "ethnicity and class are important variables in service delivery and should not serve as barriers to effective client-worker relationships." Despite rather disparate backgrounds and experiences, many social workers and clients do develop productive relationships. This is not to say there are not difficulties in intercultural relationships. Lewis and Ho (1975, p. 382) recognize this when they note "it is impossible for a social worker always to know precisely how to respond to a . . . given client or group." The problem becomes increasingly complex when we focus on some of the major barriers to effective cross-cultural social work practice. The next section will review selected characteristics of a sample of diverse groups with whom a social worker is likely to interact and will identify some of the potential dangers facing the unwary helper. These issues are intended only to sensitize the social worker to the upcoming task and are not designed to cover all possible situations. They should be viewed accordingly.

Native American Clients

A social worker working with a Native American client could readily assume that the quietness of the client indicates either an uncooperative attitude or, conversely, that the worker and client are on the same wavelength (Locklear, 1972). Unfortunately it is possible that neither assumption is appropriate. As a general rule, a Native American will not correct or challenge a worker who is off the track because to do so would be to violate a basic tenet of Native American culture: noninterference (Good Tracks, 1973). Noninterference in practice is similar, but not identical, to the social work value of self-determination. It requires the the Native American meet unwanted attempts at intervention or intrusion with withdrawal—emotional, physical, or both. In other cases, this may take the form of changing the subject or pretending not to hear the offending words. Even the most well-intentioned worker may be perceived as a coercive authority figure whose efforts are resisted passively but firmly. As Ferris and Ferris

(1976, p. 388) note, "The aggressive probings of many contemporary methodologies conflict with such tribal values as nonverbal passivity, decision making by consensus and noninterference." The Native American as a consequence is perhaps less likely to assert himself to obtain his due than might be true of members of other protected classes. This assumption that feedback will be given if the worker is off target is only one of several beliefs the worker must unlearn to practice effectively in a cross-cultural environment.

Another response pattern of social work practitioners that frequently proves counterproductive is the attempt to maintain direct eye contact. Such face-to-face eye contact is considered rude and intimidating by many Native Americans (Lewis and Ho, 1975). Kadushin (1990) notes that ethnic differences in eye contact have been acknowledged by other writers and that Native Americans in particular find eye contact disrespectful. Avoiding eye contact is a way of showing deference in this culture. Obviously, a white worker who plans to practice in a Native American community needs to be cognizant of these factors if he is not to exacerbate the already tenuous relationship that exists between cultures. Lacking a thorough knowledge of Native American culture often results in a failure to recognize its complexity and a worker does this at his own peril.

African-American Clients

With African-American clients the picture is somewhat similar; workers frequently misread the meaning of client behavior with resultant deleterious consequences. For example, the adaptive behavior of many African-Americans which includes "guardedness or assuming a strong sense of identity" may be seen by whites as threatening or rejecting the worker (Pinderhughes, 1979). Grier and Cobbs (1968) suggest that a certain level of cultural paranoia on the part of the African-American client may intrude on the client-white worker relationship and Gilbert (1974) adds that African-American youths in particular lack trust in traditional social service agencies. With these factors in mind it is easy to understand why some writers and

A cross-cultural relationship: Black worker and white clients

others feel that only a worker from the client's cultural background can effectively work with minority clients. At times a non–African-American worker may attempt to overcompensate for these differences by unrealistic empathicness. This reaction is understandable since, as Mizio (1972, p. 84) notes, "working with minority clients arouses acute anxiety" for some whites. To counter this, some workers ascribe all the emotional and social difficulties experienced by the African-American client to a racist society. This, in effect, denies the client his humanity and his similarities with other human beings, a result which is, of course, unintended.

Language differences may also serve as barriers to communication. Wofford (1979) estimates that 80 percent of African-Americans use what he terms *Ebonics*. Ebonics is a verbal communication system that includes not only rate and rhythm, but also syntax, word choice, and nonverbal communication. The result is that words may have different meanings to the speaker and the listener. Wright and Isenstein (1975, p. 13) cite an example of this communication when they note that "I don't know what page you are on" means "I don't understand what you are saying." The result of these language differences may affect both oral communication and performance on psychological tests and pose difficulties for the novice social worker.

Latino Clients

As noted earlier, even workers who share common characteristics with minority clients sometimes experience comparable difficulties to those described above. Bilingual white practitioners, for example, who work in a predominantly Latino community do not necessarily possess the requisite skills to understand all aspects of the language. The special language of the barrio in particular is not easily understood unless one has some shared experience with the actual culture. Both the meanings of words and their usage differ, sometimes significantly (Norton, 1978). As a consequence the worker who does speak Spanish must be acutely sensitive to the possibility that the words he hears may have other meanings. Enhancement of one's ability to perceive accurately the intended "communication is fostered by a knowledge of the range of lifestyles or circumstances of the group with which one is working" (Norton, 1978, p. 21). Aguilar (1972, p. 66) adds that "each minority group has its own problems and personality derived from long existing cultural and moral values, language, patterns of behavior, socioeconomic conditions, ethnic background, and many other factors." While bilingualism may not be a sufficient condition for successful practice with Latinos, it must be recognized as necessary in many instances.

Lest one become discouraged at this point about the difficulties inherent in cross-cultural social work, we should note that even counselors of the same race are not guaranteed freedom from problems. Medina and Reyes (1976) note that even Chicano counselors may actually be hindered by the culturally supported bias regarding women that undermines the client's confidence in a female therapist's ability.

Gays and Lesbians

It has been estimated that approximately 10 percent of the adult population is primarily homosexual (Berger,

1987, p. 797). This fact, combined with the usual family constellation suggests that a large number of people will be directly affected by the issue of homosexuality. Humphreys (1983, p. 60) has estimated that the lives of almost half of all Americans will be touched by homosexuality. Berger (1987, p. 797) has concluded that "virtually everyone, whether self-identified as homosexual or heterosexual, has a close relationship with a gay man." Woodman (1987) suggests that the actual incidence of homosexuality may be greater than estimates.

Unfortunately, homosexuality traditionally has been viewed variously as deviant, criminal, an illness, an emotional disturbance, and among some groups, a sin. The result has been an irrational fear of homosexuality often called homophobia that has become as serious a problem as other forms of prejudice, such as sexism and racism.

As noted before, helping professionals are as likely to be affected by these prejudices as the general public. Lack of knowledge, acceptance of stereotypes, and fear of the unknown are not limited to the layperson. While many social work practitioners may have been exposed to minority group members, the stigma associated with gay and lesbian lifestyles has kept a large number of homosexuals from sharing this information with others. As a result, social workers who come in contact with gay and lesbian clients are often no better prepared to help these groups than is the general public. The tendency to stereotype homosexual clients flies in the face of what is known about the differences and similarities among human beings. Loewenstein (1980, p. 31) has argued, for example, that "lesbian women are extremely diverse in personality, family constellation, and developmental experiences, and categorizing them as a group becomes as meaningless as categorizing all heterosexual women." The same can likely be said for gay men.

The social worker who works with gay and lesbian clients can start with the information on diversity and yet still recognize common difficulties experienced by homosexuals in our society. The barriers and discrimination encountered by gays and lesbians should be acknowledged for their impact on the client's life as well as for their effect on the relationship between helper and client.

As a beginning, it is helpful to recognize that debate over causation of homosexuality is irrelevant to efforts to help. A focus on etiology does not assist the client with present functioning and tends to obscure the multiple problems resulting from societal reaction to gays and lesbians. Attempts to focus on cause have not been beneficial in coping with stereotypes and in fact have led to homosexuals' being mistreated in order to correct for some presumed deficit in early life experiences. Social workers should also be aware that few gays and lesbians can be identified either by appearance or mannerisms. This, coupled with the risks in coming out (publicly identifying oneself as homosexual), has resulted in a lack of attention to the needs of gay and lesbian clients. As Berger notes, "This has especially been true of older homosexuals who have been all but ignored by the social work profession" (1982, p. 236). Later in this chapter we will suggest several means by which social workers can be of assistance to lesbian and gay clients by recognizing and dealing with the specialized needs of this group.

Rural Settings

Like practitioners in a biracial environment, social workers who work predominantly with clients of their own race or ethnic group may not be spared the necessity of adjusting their practice style. For example, the worker who is practicing in a basically rural environment must also be aware of a multiplicity of factors that impinge on effectiveness. The case below illustrates the risks inherent in ignoring the norms of a rural area.

The Vistas packed their belongings the next day, after being asked to move. Before they left, they asked the man from whom they had purchased groceries if he had heard anything said about them.

He told them that a woman customer had told him that Mary Newman had told her the Vistas had "dirty picture magazines" and "loads of beer cans" lying around the house. Mary Newman had said that the Vistas "hadn't shown proper respect for her dead mother by treating her house this way."

The Vistas did recall a single copy of Playboy *and one occasion when two empty beer cans were left on the table for two days. (Council on Social Work Education, 1968, p. 13)*

The episode above suggests the greater visibility experienced by the rural worker and, of course, the consequences of failing to be sensitive to community expectations.

Such seemingly innocuous factors as style of dress and model of car may set the social worker in a rural community apart (Buxton, 1976). In addition, the worker in a rural area may discover that events of the past still affect the behavior of residents today. For example, long-standing family and church conflicts may exist and create barriers to getting community members together to work on a problem or issue. The fact that many rural social workers lack exposure to the rural environment prior to beginning their practice can create additional difficulties. The worker's attitude and ideas regarding rural communities may be outdated or even quite negative. This attitude may affect her interaction with residents just as strongly as would racial bias in a minority community. The struggle to survive in a rural setting under these conditions may explain the relatively common problem of burnout experienced by the in-migrant practitioner.

Feminist Social Work

Increasing sensitivity to the impact of gender on the development, definition, and amelioration of social and personal problems has helped identify another barrier to effective social work practice—sexism. There is greater recognition today that many of the difficulties experienced by both men and women in society are related to gender inequality, specifically in the areas of privileges, power, and access to resources. The enormous role played by gender provides some limitations to social work practice and suggests ways in which the worker's own sex may become a contributing problem. Van Den Bergh and Cooper, (1986, pp.

610–18) identify some of the situations, for example, where a male worker may be less appropriate than a woman practitioner: "(1) all-female groups, which may reinforce stereotypic dependencies or set up competition for male attention; (2) women who are hostile to men unless they work as a cotherapist in the therapeutic process; (3) women who relate to male therapists primarily in a seductive manner; (4) extremely dependent, inhibited women who equate femaleness with passivity and docility; (5) women who are in the midst of a divorce crisis and who may, as a result of intense transference feelings, see the male therapist as a surrogate spouse."

As will be shown later, these limitations do not mean that gender always must be a delimiting factor in social work practice. They do mean, however, that both male and female social workers must be aware of ways in which gender can have a major impact on a client's problems and the ways in which help can and should be provided. The significant consideration is the extent to which gender-related oppression encompasses all aspects of society — economic, social, religious, and political — and the fact that gender itself plays no less a role in social work practice than is true for race, sexual preference, and location. The difficulty in overcoming the bondage of sexism provides a challenge as great as dealing with the pressures that perpetuate racism and homophobia. Some methods of providing effective intervention within the context of nonsexist practice will be described later.

Other Examples

There are many elements that can potentially separate worker and client and undermine the empathic quality of the relationship. We have identified some of the cultural, racial, and sexual differences that create this gulf. Kadushin (1990) describes additional worker-client characteristics that may affect the outcome of the relationship. The age difference between a younger worker and an older client, for instance, may prove a barrier because of differences in values, perceptions or physiological factors. At the same time, workers attempting to establish relationships with children will find that as adults they are potentially contaminated by their association with parents, a state of affairs that may have to be overcome if the child is to develop trust in the counselor.

Even something as individual to the counselor as a "preference for brief or short-term treatment may be antagonistic to the needs of minority clients or others whose situational conditions are nonsupportive and whose problems will be chronic until structural conditions are changed" (Norton, 1978, p. 22).

Clearly the role of a social worker can be complex. The critical and fundamental issues affecting the counselor's practice, however, are generally categorized into four areas: (*a*) ignorance of the culture or characteristics of those with whom one is working; (*b*) retention of stereotypic perceptions of the target group; (*c*) lack of self-knowledge; and (*d*) reliance on standard counseling techniques and approaches without regard to their implications for the client group. Each of these areas can be overcome, providing the worker is willing and able to make the necessary adaptations. The task is not necessarily an easy one since, as Montiel (1973) notes, much of the research available to the interested social worker paints an inaccurate picture of minority groups, misjudging such salient areas as family structure and lifestyle characteristics.

Part of the problem experienced in gathering factual data, of course, is that much of the research is based on the perceptions of white middle-class investigators. Despite this handicap, the worker who has a significant intercultural practice must seek appropriate information on the groups with which he intends to interact. Such knowledge represents, however, only a beginning since cross-cultural social work demands a high degree of self-knowledge and self-awareness on the part of the worker. Unlike sociological, psychological, and anthropological data, which is obtained with reasonable ease, self-knowledge is perhaps the most difficult to obtain since it can be anxiety-producing for the worker. "An individual may deny his racist feelings because they conflict with his self-image as a humanitarian and a liberal. However, even if he does admit his prejudices and tries to work them through, it is impossible to reverse them completely" (Mizio, 1972, p. 82). And therein lies the dilemma. The worker must expect to practice in a somewhat prejudiced world as a result, though this does not prevent effective intervention.

KNOWLEDGE OF SELF

There is no substitute for self-awareness on the part of the social work practitioner. The ability to be responsive to one's own senses, feelings, behavior, and thoughts is considered a prime requisite for effective practice in the helping professions. This includes a thorough recognition, knowledge, and acceptance of one's value system. "It is especially crucial for the social worker to . . . possess . . . an understanding of the extent that his professional behavior contributes to the oppression or freedom of" minorities in general (Gilbert, 1974, p. 94).

In some cases, workers' feelings about racism and the plight of minorities or other groups suffering from discrimination may effectively block their functioning by generating guilt, depression, or a sense of being overwhelmed. This process can be averted by recognition of the likelihood of growing up prejudiced and by a willingness "to be more ready to listen, less ready to come to conclusions, more open to guidance and correction of . . . presuppositions" (Kadushin, 1983, p. 304) which have arisen as a function of growing up in a racist society. The ability to correct one's own tendencies toward racist thinking obviously requires a sensitive worker willing to put forth the effort. "A white social worker cannot help a minority client unless he can accept the ugliness of racism without being overwhelmed by guilt" (Mizio, 1972, p. 84). To do so requires workers to be willing to make fundamental changes in their thinking patterns, attitudes, and behavior. Still, such growth in self-knowledge (of and by itself) is insufficient without a concomitant growth in one's awareness of the uniqueness of the client group with whom one will work.

KNOWLEDGE OF DIFFERENCES

It has long been asserted that similar needs exist in all cultures but that the molding and shaping of those needs is culturally relative. Thus, while a basic acceptance of the worth and dignity of each human being is required, the worker intending to practice with any of a variety of diverse groups must enhance this acceptance with hard facts. While we believe ourselves to be grounded in reality, our reality is nevertheless only a function of our perception of the real world. An individual who comes to a counseling situation from a different cultural background, especially one who has experienced the racist or sexist behavior of others, may have a reality potentially different from others. Therefore the worker must be cognizant of the ways in which cultural and other background factors affect perceptions and feelings and the expression of these qualities. For example, Rauch (1978, p. 391) argues that many of the problems experienced by female clients are actually biopsychosocial in origin. "Teenage and unwanted pregnancy, postpartum depression, and sexual dysfunction . . . vulnerability to wife abuse and rape . . . the empty nest syndrome," incest, and displaced homemaker status are simply a sample of the specific gender-related problems which may be experienced by the woman. As Kravetz (1982, p. 46) has pointed out, "Women's personal concerns, experiences, and problems are intricately related to their social, economic, legal, and political condition." The institutionalized prejudice against women presents the worker with additional problems. Thus, the profeminist worker must be aware of the unique difficulties to which women are especially vulnerable, the absence of coping resources experienced by many women, and the stereotypist tendencies of much of society.

Also beneficial is some knowledge of the history and language of the group to be worked with. A familiarization with common phrases or vocabulary would be helpful even if the worker is not bilingual. This background should also include a solid knowledge base in minority lifestyles so that the client's strengths and ability to adapt are not ignored or branded as abnormal behavior. For example, the minority client who appears hostile or suspicious of a white worker may well be expressing a quite reasonable reaction based on past experiences with well-meaning professionals or other representatives of "helping" agencies.

The growing incidence of ethnoviolence (conflict and violence motivated by prejudice) experienced in the United States over the past ten years is testimony to the continued difficulties experienced by members of minority groups (Weiss, 1990). It has also helped underscore the earlier observation of Thomas and Sillen (1972, p. 63) that "in order to judge what is healthy or morbid in an individual's psychological functioning, one must be aware of what is appropriate within his cultural mileau." Living with racism, prejudice, discrimination, and violence are going to have important consequences for one's feelings, thoughts, and behaviors. Workers cannot ignore this reality.

Even the same behavior may carry a variety of meanings to persons from different cultures. The ability to understand and "work constructively with norms, family patterns, leadership patterns, community organizations and other cultural patterns of minority groups" is essential, yet more uncommon than common (Turner, 1972, p. 115). The knowledge of how a given group responds to authority, to stress, and to dependency is invaluable since a worker may easily mistake a given reaction as inappropriate without a sound grasp of the culture. This grounding could ideally come from living in a minority area, taking part in community activities, such as council meetings, powwows, and neighborhood get-togethers. Certainly, these activities should be pursued by any social worker serving a given population. Obviously a background of direct experience with minorities would perhaps be ideal, but most social workers who begin practice do not have this base. As a result it behooves the worker to take advantage of some of the excellent bibliographic material available on the subject, some of which is listed at the end of this text in the bibliography. A worker, for example, who intends to work with Native Americans should plan to study carefully the unique cultural heritage of this group. There are many Native American cultures, and each tribe has its own history, traditions, customs, and environment. This makes it a bit more difficult to generalize from tribal group to tribal group. However, there are some important similarities. For example, the fact that the Native American father plays a stronger disciplinarian role in the family may suggest to the unknowing worker that child abuse is occurring, when in fact the Native American family is perhaps less dependent on corporal punishment than the average non–Native American family. The failure to recognize cultural factors such as this will inevitably result in misunderstanding and frustrations for the erring worker. Awareness of the principal values of the Native American and an understanding of the cultural context in which the Native American exists will lessen this possibility.

The Native American tradition of sharing is another area which serves to confuse white workers unaccustomed to this kind of hospitality. Though resources be meager, the Native American is willing to allow other family and friends to partake of what there is. While this may appear to be nonfunctional to many whites, the value is intrinsic to the Native American heritage. To do otherwise would be to ignore part of a value system which has helped the culture survive over 400 years of racism.

Even the Native American use of time can be a subject of confusion to the non–Native American, as the following account suggests (Hall, 1959, pp. 21–22):

I can still remember a Christmas dance I attended some twenty-five years ago at one of the pueblos near the Rio Grande. I had to travel over bumpy roads for forty-five miles to get there. At seven thousand feet, the ordeal of winter cold at one o'clock in the morning is almost unbearable. Shivering in the still darkness of the pueblo, I kept searching for a clue as to when the dance would begin.

Outside everything was impenetrably quiet. Occasionally there was the muffled beat of a deep pueblo drum, the opening of a door, or the piercing of the night's darkness with a shaft of light. In the church where the dance was to take place, a few white townsfolk were huddled together on a balcony, groping for some clue which would suggest how much longer they were going to suffer. "Last year I heard they started at ten o'clock." "They can't start until the priest comes." "There is no way of telling when they will start." All this punctuated by chattering teeth and the stamping of feet to keep up circulation.

Suddenly an Indian opened the door, entered and poked up the fire in the stove. Everyone nudged his neighbor: "Maybe they are going to begin now." Another hour passed. Another Indian came in from outside, walked across the nave of the church, and disappeared through another door. "Certainly now they will begin. After all, it's almost two o'clock." Someone guessed that they were just being ornery in the hope that the white man would go away. Another had a friend in the pueblo and went to his house to ask when the dance would begin. Nobody knew. Suddenly, when the whites were almost exhausted, there burst upon the night the deep sounds of the drums, rattles, and low male voices singing. Without warning the dance had begun.

Though some might suggest otherwise, Native Americans are not unaware of time, but rather do not allow themselves to become captive to its tyranny the way many whites have done. Punctuality is not the preeminent concern with Native Americans that it is with non–Native Americans, a fact that confounds many time-conscious helping professionals. The time-bound worker may also misperceive the related Native American value of patience as evidence of laziness or lack of motivation. Respect for and appreciation of the Native American culture is essential if the worker is not to become an obstacle to an effective relationship.

Similarly, the Latino experience will be sufficiently new to most workers that a dedicated effort must be made to replace ignorance with knowledge. As in the case of Native Americans, the family unit of Latinos is more likely to be characterized as extended. This expanded family network is another indication of the adaptability of Latinos. The worker therefore needs to be alert for the boundaries of the family system so as not to exclude or overlook pertinent members. The fact that the elderly have an important role to play and must be included in planning places a special burden

on the practitioner, but one that cannot be ignored. The significance of religion in Latino life is more commonly known to most non–Latinos, as is the importance of the male role. Although there is some evidence that the cross-cultural differences in these areas may be exaggerated in the literature, the worker needs to be aware of the significance of these factors in Latino life. The worker "must be bicultural enough to be able to perceive, model and encourage behaviors that are not only more psychologically adaptive but are more suitable to the client's particular type of barrio [neighborhood] and familia [family]" (Boulette, 1975, p. 404).

The diversity of cultural backgrounds found within the Native American culture is duplicated within Latino culture. The tendency to see any culture as unidimensional fails to recognize the diversity within cultures. For instance, the term *Latino* encompasses Mexican-Americans, Puerto Ricans, Colombians, Brazilians, and others whose ancestry can be traced to Spanish or Portuguese beginnings. The term also masks the degree of mixed-racial background found among, for example, Puerto Ricans, a situation that has created "intragroup divisiveness" (Soloman, 1987, p. 859).

Though the client group and community may not be ethnically or racially different from that of the worker, the practitioner who works in a rural environment also must possess a certain knowledge base to be effective. The social worker in a rural setting must be aware of the network of nontraditional services often available in these areas. Service clubs and church groups, for instance, may assume greater import than in larger, more metropolitan communities. Likewise, the existence of natural support systems can be a real asset but must be known to workers before they can use them effectively. Knowledge of the local power structure is perhaps more crucial than for the urban worker since the worker's effectiveness may be seriously impaired without the necessary sanction and cooperation. As in the case of other diverse groups, ignorance of values, beliefs, and attitudes of the rural client system is inexcusable and likely to be counterproductive. If this need to be alert to, and operate within, local norms is seen as onerous by the worker, then she should consider moving elsewhere.

As discussed earlier, age differences between worker and client may also affect the worker's practice. Kadushin (1983) suggests, for example, that the worker must be aware of the effect that the physical condition of the elderly can have on the interview. Among other factors, lack of energy and hearing difficulties may impair the aged client's ability to participate in the relationship. The competent worker, thus, must have a firm foundation in human behavior and development as well as sensitivity to the nuances of communication within a helping relationship.

APPLICATION OF KNOWLEDGE — TECHNIQUES OF INTERVENTION

Once a sufficient knowledge base is acquired, workers must incorporate this into practice in such a manner as to increase the effectiveness of their interventive activities. In this section we will review some specific approaches and techniques of intervention designed to enhance the worker's capabilities. The material presented is not intended to be exhaustive, and obviously there is not substitute for direct experience. The worker whose practice encompasses any of these areas must do more extensive reading (and, it is hoped, receive formal training) than is presented here.

Basic to any relationship, according to Truax and Mitchell (1971), is empathy, clearly communicated to the client, plus warmth and genuineness. Workers in a bicultural relationship must pay special heed to this advice since authenticity is even more crucial when differences are greater between client and helper. Moreover, workers must use their own patterns of communication and avoid the temptation to adopt the client's vocabulary and speech. A worker who does not follow this stricture may find clients either withdrawing from the relationship or attacking the helper for lack of sincerity. In many cross-cultural relationships there is a greater need on the part of the client to know the

worker as a person (Kadushin, 1983). A helper who is uncomfortable stepping outside the professional role probably should avoid either working with many minority clients or practicing in a rural environment since a greater informality is expected in both settings.

To prevent the reader from getting the wrong impression from the above comments, we should acknowledge that there are clear limits to the time and place for informality in intercultural counseling. Generally the kind of informality which marks the effective relationship does not occur immediately. For example, in the initial interview, Kadushin (1983) recommends using all the formalities associated with culturally prescribed displays of respect. This should include use of the client's proper full name, title (Mr., Miss, Mrs., Ms.), greeting with a handshake, and the other courtesies usually extended. It is also important that workers be upfront with clients about the reasons for their presence. For example, if the contact was worker-initiated, it is appropriate for workers to give their identification, state the reasons for the meeting, and avoid placing the client in the position of having to guess the purpose.

It is important to keep in mind that "the helping relationship is in itself a power relationship in which the dynamics of power and lack of power are operating. The expertise of the worker and the neediness of the client place them in positions of power and lack of power, respectively. The cross-racial and cross-ethnic helping encounter compounds the consequences of this power differential. Power issues related to differences in ethnicity, class, sex, age, and other social markers may exaggerate the power inherent in the helping role in a way that causes the worker to misperceive the client" (Pinderhughes, 1979, p. 315). Workers in an empathic relationship must be alert to the power Gestalt engendered by race and other differences and strive to reduce or eliminate this differential. The use of proper protocol is an aid in this effort.

Awareness of these differences and a degree of sensitivity to the subtle impact of racial prejudice should help the counselor avoid the related trap of color blindness that often serves to confuse the novice helper. In an effort to avoid appearing prejudiced the new worker may decide to adopt the strategy of color blindness and ignore the race or ethnic background of the client. While well-intended, color blindness is ineffective as a strategy for social workers because of the tendency it creates for separating "the black person's internal problems from his color" (Burgest, 1973, p. 23). Color blindness ceases to be a "virtue if it means denial of differences in the experience, culture and psychology of black Americans and other Americans" (Thomas and Sillen, 1972, p. 58). "To gloss over race in a racist society may in itself be a capitulation to racism" (Thomas and Sillen, 1972, p. 143). It is understandable if upon occasion the worker's feelings about racism get in the way of the relationship; guilt, depression, or a sense of being overwhelmed are not uncommon reactions, yet the helper must reject sympathy when empathy is required. Conversely, while some impact of racism may almost always exist, its impact on the presenting problem may be greater or less. It may be a contributing factor in the client's problem, the cause of the problem, or unrelated entirely to the issues at hand. The worker should not automatically attribute all difficulties to racism.

Like the culturally sensitive worker, an agency can be equally dedicated to providing services to different client groups. The agency's responsiveness can be demonstrated through relatively simple measures such as establishing hours that coincide with the needs of the groups to be served. This may include evening hours to avoid the need for some clients, already economically marginal, to lose time from the job, and it could extend to weekend hours and walk-in arrangements such as Kadushin (1983) suggests. The fact that the poor are frequently afflicted by crises requires that there be more flexible means of dealing with immediate client needs and greater accessibility to services for the here and now, present-oriented client. Logically, the immediacy of the situation coupled with the economic and political existence of many minority clients suggest that first-level needs must be attended to on a priority basis. This orientation is basic to the social work principle of starting where the client is. It is most unlikely that the client whose housing needs are imminent will tolerate a worker who insists on focusing on the dynamics of the marital interactions. Clients from all cultures reject an incompetent and insensitive social worker.

Within the relationship the counselor will have to judge the need to be more or less active. As we shall see later, a high level of intervention on the part of the worker dealing with a Native American family may well prove less productive than with a client from another cultural or racial group. Kadushin (1983) recommends that the focus in the relationship be on specific problems and behaviors while other authors state that "particularly inadequate is the school of psychology called behaviorism which de-emphasizes the very patterns that distinguish ethnic strategies while publicizing merely obvious behaviors" (Southwestern Cooperative Educational Laboratory, 1968, p. 157). This issue likely cannot be resolved for all cases and the social worker must therefore adopt the approach that fits most naturally with her helping style. Certainly, attempting to utilize a method of intervention in which one is uncomfortable or only marginally competent would be a serious error.

African-American Client — White Worker

Most of the guides to practice discussed above are directly applicable to the relationship between the non–African-American worker and the African-American client. In addition, however, Hopkins (1973) has stressed the need to avoid placing the African-American client in a position of dependency. The power discrepancy described earlier in this chapter is often the result when this is neglected. Both workers and agencies serving the African-American client, according to Hopkins (1973), must recognize the value of supporting African-American manhood as well as efforts aimed at maintaining the male's role in the family. This may require that the agency arrange to have male social workers available in situations where a sex differential would be counterproductive to the goal of supporting African-American males as males. While same-sex workers are by no means required in all cases, the agency should be sensitive to the possibility that individual cases may necessitate the utilization of a worker of the client's gender.

In the area of group services to minority clients Davis (1979) recommends that membership be selected in such a manner that no one race vastly outnumber the others represented and that biracial leadership may have a benign effect if members tend to be more open with workers of the same race. As always, if the worker is alert and responsive to the client's feelings and reactions, needed adjustments in the intervention approach can be made and the use of standard formulas for success can be tempered by the practitioner's judgment.

Since the client's exposure to and experience with professional therapeutic relationships may be very limited, Kadushin (1983) points out that there may be a need to educate the client about the processes of counseling. The use of unambiguous jargon is the best means for conveying this information and, in fact, should be the rule for most worker-client interaction. Also suggested is the promotion of concrete activities by worker and client, including greater use of role-playing, gaming, and simulations to supplant or supplement, as appropriate, more verbal techniques. Clients from lower socioeconomic backgrounds may both understand better, and appreciate more, direct action on the part of the worker.

Latino Client — Non-Latino Worker

With Latino clients, as with other groups, the verbal tradition of social work may need to be supplemented by other means of communication. The worker must bear direct responsibility for communicating when language difficulties compound the situation and the need for an interpreter is apparent. Lest the worker err by commission, however, certain rules apply to the use of such individuals. First, "bilingual children of the family are not suitable interpreters" (Norton, 1978, p. 22). Respect for the individual and for the family relationships dictate that children maintain their culturally established place. Serving as conduits for sensitive family information is not an acceptable role for children to play and places an unfair and unpleasant burden on the child. In addition, children often lack an adult's knowledge base, in fact that further reduces their value as interpreters. This prohibition on the use of children applies equally to other ethnic groups including Asian-Americans. Described below is a situation in which a probation officer has ignored some of the basic caveats of relationship building with unfortunate consequences for the client.

The purposes in mind for this first interview were accomplished, to meet Mr. and Mrs. X personally and to establish a comfortable relationship that would lead to a partnership once they were able to share their problems with the social worker. The next step would be to share a common purpose, in this case, helping Freddy.

Mr. X was included in the helping process from the beginning. Had he been left out, it would have meant that Mrs. X was assuming an improper role, that Mr. X was being put down by her, and that his role as head of the household plus his macho role were being jeopardized.

The following day Mr. and Mrs. X came a little late to the meeting and were reluctant to talk about their conference with the probation officer. Mr. X just kept silent, looking down. Mrs. X, red-eyed, finally said, "I am very ashamed. You should have heard what the probation officer said about us. He blamed us for all the troubles with Freddy and said that if we were not able to speak English we should go back to Mexico. Perhaps worst of all, our daughter heard all of this because she had to translate for us."

It was suggested that they arrange to meet with the probation officer the next time at the center; there the social worker could translate for them and make the necessary interpretations. Thus the harmful effect of the probation officer's prejudices against them would be minimized. Mr. and Mrs. X were assured that they had certain legal and moral rights that had to be respected — among them the right to be treated as human beings. Major differences between the systems of law in the United States and Mexico were explained, as were the functions of the probation department and the role of its officers.

Mr. and Mrs. X then seemed somewhat relieved

and looked less tense and fearful. Mrs. X thanked the social worker and, looking at her husband, said: "We are not ignorant and dumb. We just did not understand anything about what was happening." (Aguilar, 1972, p. 70)

A second guide to the use of interpreters is equally important. The worker must at all times relate and talk to the client and not to the interpreter. To address the translator diverts attention from the client and places him in the position of bystander to, rather than central figure in, the relationship. The opportunity to enhance the personal dignity and individual autonomy of the client should be pursued with vigor since the same goal of helping the client to help himself is applicable both between and within cultures. Whether termed "empowerment, liberation or consumerism" (Norton, 1978, p. 23), or self-determination, the effect is similar.

Workers beginning a relationship with Latino clients should be prepared for a longer assessment period, and be more leisurely, warm, personal and informal, and more low key than otherwise might be the case (Aguilar, 1972). Directness is considered rude and should not be utilized in these situations if possible. Boulette (1975) suggests that a behavioral approach would be an appropriate methodology to employ in working with Mexican-Americans from a low-income background, coinciding with Kadushin's (1983) belief. Aguilar (1972) notes that obstacles faced by Mexican-American families include prejudice, ignorance, fear of formal social and legal systems, and a reluctance to deal with them. This would suggest some areas to which workers could direct their attention during the early stages of the relationship. It has also been noted that Mexican-Americans often make decisions more quickly than is typical of Anglo clients. Once alternatives have been explored the worker should be prepared for a decisive response from the client.

Successful intervention with Latino families, however, requires greater knowledge of the culture of this ethnic group. Ghali (1982) has provided some helpful guidance in this matter, focusing on the Puerto Rican culture. Ghali notes that close family ties exist in this culture, and stresses that these ties are a source of pride. Anglo culture, on the other hand, values independence from the family. She also points out that

practices that are frowned upon in American society are more readily accepted among many Puerto Ricans. Examples include common-law marriages among the low income, bearing a child by a teenager which often accords the mother the status of adulthood, and the relatively supreme position of the father in the family. She acknowledges that many Puerto Rican values need to be changed to reflect the reality of living among the dominant culture, pointing to the subservient role of the woman as an example.

Ghali (1982) correctly identifies the special dilemma of Puerto Ricans who have two countries, two languages, and two cultures. The role confusion that this can entail, the resultant family problems, and the value conflicts inherent in this duality must be recognized. Ghali suggests that the worker keep these in mind during the interview. Other suggestions include the following:

1. Determine how important her ethnic values are to the client, and whether the values are a source of conflict. (This could be ascertained by asking which, if any, of the old traditions are still observed; that is, holidays.)

2. Focus on the short-term benefits and on strengthening the worker-client relationship.

3. Recognize that some measure of client dependence is likely.

4. Demonstrate competence, respect, and warmth toward the client.

5. Engage in sharing of some personal experience.

6. Respect the role of the father in the family.

7. Ask "What do you see as the problem here?" rather than "How do you feel about this?"

8. Be alert to nonverbal cues to feelings such as facial expressions and tone.

9. Be prepared to explain the therapeutic process to the client.

10. Begin and end the session with a handshake (the man extends his hand to the woman first).

11. Use formal greetings to convey respect.

12. Accept food or drink offered in the client's home (not to do so may offend the host).

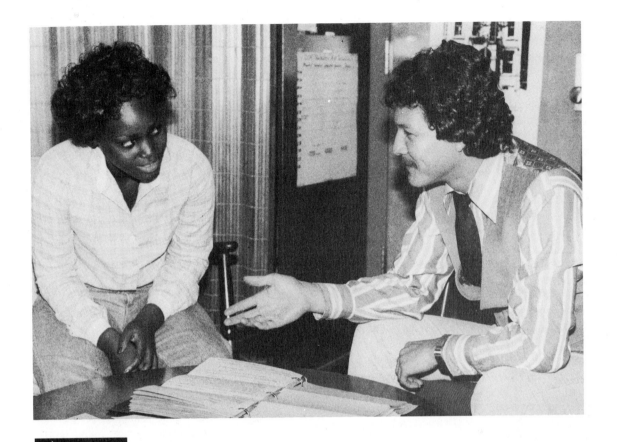

One-to-one counseling by a campus Hispanic counselor.

13. Recognize that the client may verbally agree with the worker to show respect for authority but may not follow through.

14. Remember that the Puerto Rican culture does not look favorably upon laughing at oneself so humor must not be of the self-depreciatory type.

15. Remember that touching little girls even to be friendly is not done by strangers.

16. Place signs in one's agency in both Spanish and English.

Ghali's recommendations are very appropriate and should serve as a model for practice with Puerto Rican families.

Delgado and Humm-Delgado (1982) suggest other ways of providing assistance to Latino families. The use of natural support systems is one of their recommendations. Natural support systems include family and friendship groups, local informal care givers, volunteer service groups, and mutual or self-help groups (Baker, 1977). Delgado and Humm-Delgado (1982, pp. 83–84) identify four types of such resource systems important for Latino clients: extended family, folk healers, religious institutions, and merchants' and social clubs. Included in the category of extended family are the family of origin, nuclear family members, others related by marriage or blood or custom including "adopted relatives" and *"como familia"* (non-family members who are considered to be like family)

(Delgado and Humm-Delgado, 1982, p. 84). God-parents also become an important resource for Latino children in the event that anything befalls the natural parents.

Folk healers also include a variety of individuals including spiritists and *santeros* who focus on emotional and interpersonal problems, herbalists and *santiguadors* who deal primarily with physical ailments, and the *curanderos* whose interventions include both emotional and physical realism. In Mexican-American, Cuban, and Puerto Rican communities any one of the five, or a combination, may exist. The *santero* is more common in the Cuban community, while the *curandero* is found frequently in Mexican-American communities (Delgado and Humm-Delgado, 1982, pp. 84–85). Some of the folk healers use treatments that blend natural healing methods with spiritual or religious beliefs. The latter is not surprising given the importance of religion, particularly Roman Catholicism in Latino life.

Religious institutions that serve as a resource include the Roman Catholic church as well as such denominations as the Jehovah's Witness, Seventh-Day Adventist, and Pentecostal. Among the services offered are pastoral counseling, housing and job-locating assistance, emergency money, and specialized programs in areas such as drug abuse (Delgado and Humm-Delgado, 1982, p. 85).

Finally, the merchants' and social clubs provide such items as herbs and native foods, credit and information, referrals to other resources, recreation, prayer books, and the services of healers. Table 11.1 identifies the types of needs served by these various resource systems in the Latino community.

Natural support systems are highly significant. They ensure "maintenance of the Hispanic tradition and language," provide "warm, personal helping relationships," and include acceptance of those who are emotionally disturbed without stigmatizing the person (Delgado and Humm-Delgado, 1982, pp. 85–87). Formal agencies that provide services to Latinos should benefit from the availability of these additional community resources. The reluctance of some clients to come to the formal agency could be reduced if the agency staff made greater use of the natural support system and made increased attempts at reaching the targeted population. Outreach can be done at the merchants' and social clubs, at churches, through radio and newspaper ads or public service announcements, and through notices on barrio grocery bulletin boards (Watkins and Gonzales, 1982, pp. 68–73). Agencies should consider developing community resource directories in both English and Spanish and including nontraditional resources within the directory.

The worker who chooses to work in the Latino community must be much more alert to the unique resources available as well as to the many cultural issues that impinge on social work practice with what has become the fastest growing minority group in the United States.

Native American Client — Non–Native American Worker

"Any kind of intervention is contrary to the Indian's strict adherence to the principle of self-determination" (Good Tracks, 1973, p. 30). With this statement in mind, the well-meaning worker might respond "Well, how can I help if I can't intervene?" The difficulty of this dilemma is at the heart of the problems faced by many non–Native American social workers. Native Americans will request intervention only infrequently and the white worker must develop patience and wait for the necessary acceptance. How long this will take remains an unknown. During this period the non–Native American should be available and may offer assistance as long as there is no hint of coercion accompanying the offer. Once help is accepted, the competence of the worker will be tested, and, if found wanting, the word will spread. Conversely, the ability of the worker to do what he says he can or will do will spread equally fast. The results of the former will be a cessation of clients; in the latter case, just the opposite is true. The situation described below indicates noninterference with a Native American family:

The Redthunder family was brought to the school social worker's attention when teachers reported that both children had been tardy and absent frequently in the past weeks. Since the worker lived near Mr.

TABLE 11.1

Needs Served by Latino Natural Support Systems

	Natural Support Systems			
Needs Served	Extended Family	Folk Healers	Religious Institutions	Merchants' and Social Clubs
1. Accessibility to community	X	X	X	X
2. Communication in Spanish	X	X	X	X
3. Continuation of cultural traditions	X	X	X	X
4. Crisis intervention	X	X	X	X
5. Emotional support for interpersonal problems	X	X	X	X
6. Friendship, companionship, trust	X	X	X	X
7. Identification with Hispanic role models, leaders, or experts	X	X	X	X
8. Information and referral	X	X	X	X
9. Care and treatment of the disabled or aged	X	X	X	
10. Financial aid or credit	X		X	
11. Medical care and pharmaceutical products	X	X		X
12. Recreation	X		X	X
13. Translation or interpretation	X		X	
14. Advocacy	X		X	
15. Physical and emotional rehabilitation		X	X	
16. Religious or spiritual affiliation		X	X	
17. Baby-sitting, day care, respite care, foster care, or adoption	X			
18. Child rearing and parent education	X			
19. Educational alternative to public school			X	
20. Housing	X			

Source: Reprinted from Melvin Delgado and Denise Humm-Delgado, "Natural Support Systems: Source of Strength in Hispanic Communities," *Social Work*, 27, no. 1 (January 1982), Table 1, p. 87. Copyright 1982, National Association of Social Workers, Inc. Reprinted with permission.

Redthunder's neighborhood, she volunteered to transport the children back and forth to school. Through this regular but informal arrangement, the worker became acquainted with the entire family, especially with Mrs. Redthunder, who expressed her gratitude to the worker by sharing her homegrown vegetables.

The worker sensed that there was much family discomfort and that a tumultuous relationship existed between Mr. and Mrs. Redthunder. Instead of probing into their personal and marital affairs, the worker let Mrs. Redthunder know that she was willing to listen should the woman need someone to talk to. After a few gifts of homegrown vegetables and Native American handicrafts, Mrs. Redthunder broke into tears one day and told the worker about her husband's problem of alcoholism and their deteriorating marital relationship.

Realizing Mr. Redthunder's position of respect in the family and his resistance to outside interference, the social worker advised Mrs. Redthunder to take her family to visit the minister, a man whom Mr. Redthunder admired. The Littleaxe family, who were mutual friends of the worker and the Redthunder family, agreed to take the initiative in visiting the Redthunders more often. Through such frequent but informal family visits, Mr. Redthunder finally obtained a job, with the recommendation of Mr. Littleaxe, as recordkeeper in a storeroom. Mr. Redthunder enjoyed his work so much that he drank less and spent more time with his family. (Lewis and Ho, 1975, p. 381)

White workers who are working with Native Americans can expect that the interview will also be a new experience. Periods of silence at the start of the interview, for example, are not uncommon. Neither is the practice of some clients of switching from English to the native tongue and back as they address other members of the family. The use of the Native American language is not necessarily meant to keep the message from the worker but rather indicates that this is the easiest way to translate a particular idea.

The establishment of intervention objectives should also be consistent with the environment of the Native American client, as must the specific techniques

to be used. Approaches that are culturally repugnant will not succeed regardless of the good intentions of the worker. Transactional analysis is an example of one approach that will likely prove ineffective since it ignores "differences in culture and background between client and worker" (Lewis and Ho, 1975, p. 381). Any type of manipulation is likely to fail also, though the provision of alternative choices from which the Native American client may choose is generally acceptable. Lewis and Ho (1975, p. 380) emphasize that "techniques based on restating, clarifying, summarizing, reflecting and empathizing" are more likely to be successful with Native Americans. Certainly, a low-key, nondirective, permissive, and nonthreatening relationship can be both effective and gratifying for both client and worker (Palmer and Pablo, 1978). Though the holistic nature of Gestalt therapy is consonant with the traditional Native American recognition that we are one with the world, the intrusive style with which Fritz Perls imbued this approach will also not be acceptable in most situations.

The use of group approaches for treating Native Americans is discussed by Lewis and Ho (1975) who feel it is a natural one, though group composition needs to be more racially homogeneous than might be true for many other groups, notably Latinos (Boulette, 1975). The use of both indirect and extra group means of influence is particularly recommended. For example, the careful planning and implementation of program activities is to be preferred to the use of more direct and unwelcome techniques. The use of group pressure on an individual would be one such tactic to avoid if the worker and setting are not to appear coercive. Also recommended are self-help groups and other family support networks that are group based and are consistent with the values and culture of Native American clients.

Female Client — Male Worker

Though it is generally conceded that a difference in gender between client and worker is not an insurmountable barrier to an effective relationship, there are some points to be considered when such differences do exist. According to Davenport and Reims (1978, p. 308), a clinician's sex has a decided influence on attitudes toward women's roles and, as a result, "anyone preferring a therapist with contemporary attitudes toward women would more likely be successful with a female therapist." Kravetz (1983, p. 44) has argued that most social workers hold "traditional and stereotypic views of women" and that such views have detrimental effects on the health of women and their treatment by the systems of our society. Certainly, counselors of the same sex may be more of an aid in modeling new behaviors or when client identification with the worker is a major part of the change effort (Hook, 1979). Some authors feel that a female social worker engages in more modeling for women clients and is more likely to take the client's problems seriously. Some topics may be more comfortably discussed with a counselor of the same sex, and workers and agencies must not overlook this possibility. However, as in many other situations where dissimilarities between client and worker exist, the relationship can usually transcend the differences.

Since the sexist nature of much of society has in part contributed to the problems experienced by women, Thomas (1977) and Berlin (1976) have provided a useful set of guides for those whose practice includes women clients. First, the nature of the relationship between males and females in our society tends to be characterized by the same sort of power disparity noted in cross-cultural relationships; therefore reduction of this power differential should be one goal of the therapeutic process. The suggestions discussed earlier in regard to this issue are equally applicable here. Second, the worker who can comfortably engage in greater levels of self-disclosure and use of self and of one's own experience should aid in the process of reducing this power differential. Third, the use of contracts with specified goals assists in involving the client in her own treatment effort. Fourth, a greater emphasis on problem solving and action should assist in achieving a degree of self-mastery for which the client can feel justifiably proud. Fifth, the assessment period should involve a thorough analysis of the client's "strengths, frustrations, wants and satisfactions" (Berlin, 1976, p. 493). This requires separating the client's

needs, feelings, and beliefs from those of significant others, such as parents and husband. This may be accomplished through the use of a journal detailing the day's significant events, as illustrated in the following example:

Since early childhood, Jill had tried hard to be what she thought people wanted her to be. Despite her efforts to be sweet and compliant, the stored-up resentment and anger sometimes emerged. Her parents strongly objected to these outbursts and shamed her for them. To be "good" in the eyes of her parents — and later her male friends — Jill suppressed her "selfishness," her own thoughts, views, and feelings, until she felt like a nonentity. When she came in for counseling, Jill said that she no longer knew what she liked and didn't like or who she was. She was living with a boyfriend but felt distant from him. At the age of twenty-four, her life had already taken on a bland, weary quality.

At her counselor's suggestion, Jill began keeping a journal in which she recorded the events of her day and her different responses to them. During each counseling session these details were reviewed to reveal that Jill did indeed have specific likes and dislikes, she liked gardening; she liked being alone in the house; she liked to read, draw, and visit with a particular friend. She didn't like the routine nature of her job. Particularly, although she was afraid of standing up for herself, she didn't like herself to be closed or passive with her boyfriend, other friends, and her mother. She disliked not having a room of her own and resented it when her boyfriend pursued his own interests without telling her when he would be away. Jill found that there was a whole range of thoughts, talents, and behaviors that made her an identifiable and specific person. Moreover, she learned to pinpoint which of these aspects she wanted to capitalize on. Eventually, Jill decided to move into her own apartment. She left her job and got a new one in a plant nursery. She began practicing more assertive, honest responses to the people in her life. (Berlin, 1976, pp. 493–94)

Sixth, the client should be assisted to recognize alternatives and to choose among them rather than feel limited or constrained unnecessarily. The following case example illustrates this guideline:

Ellen had lived through an almost unendurable number of personal crises—the death of two children, the subsequent divorce from her husband, a second brutal marriage, financial problems, the loss of custody of her third child, and a second divorce. Her reaction to all these events was flight, the abuse of amphetamines, and just plain helplessness.

As a girl, Ellen had been brought up to sparkle and to make others laugh. It was assumed that she would find a clear-headed, stable man who could make the hard decisions and manage the details of living. Ellen didn't know how to take care of herself and didn't think she could. Her solution to loneliness—spending binges, reckless driving, instant intimacy with strangers—only brought more problems and more guilt. Each time she was called on to take a stand and protect herself, Ellen would capitulate. The situations were too much for her and she felt victimized by them.

The counselor's approach to this situation was a relatively simple and basic one. She tried to help Ellen perceive different alternatives—to see that there were some things she could do differently if she wanted to. In addition to realizing that she had some choices, Ellen needed to decide what she wanted to do and to acquire the skills and confidence to do it. She had to be made aware that she didn't lose control, but that she stopped exercising it; that she wasn't being punished for being a bad person, but that she associated with people who were disrespectful and abusive. Ellen is now finding what she can do to make her life less frantic and destructive. She wants to continue her education, to clear up her debts, and to achieve equality in her relationships with other people. (Berlin, 1976, p. 494)

The worker should encourage action on the options that are available and can aid the client by posing questions such as "What choices do you see yourself as having?" "Do you know what you like about this particular alternative?"

Seventh, the use of behavioral rehearsal and practice in decision making can be extremely effective in building the necessary skills essential for choosing and implementing choices. The following client illustrates this guideline:

Cynthia came for counseling in a state of panic because the woman she loved and was living with was considering ending the relationship. Although there was little she could do to persuade her partner to stay, Cynthia did have considerable latitude in deciding how she wanted to behave and the way in which she could influence other facets of the terminating relationship.

Realizing that she still had considerable choice was a partial antidote to Cynthia's sense of helplessness. Instead of waiting silently and miserably for her friend to leave, Cynthia practiced certain responses with the counselor until she felt able to cope with the reality of the situation. She explained to her partner her feelings regarding the relationship—that she valued it, was aware that both of them needed to make some specific changes in order for it to stay viable, and that she herself was willing to make certain accommodations. She acknowledged that her friend would be the one to decide whether to stay or leave, but Cynthia wanted the decision made within the week—she didn't want to be tortured by uncertainty. To this extent, Cynthia ceased to be the victim. She felt strengthened by her new position of influence and control over her circumstances. (Berlin, 1976, p. 495)

Eighth, a client who exhibits fears and a poor self-concept needs to be helped to evaluate these perceptions realistically. The worker must press the client for concrete examples the client believes exemplifies the perceived self-worthlessness and expose them to a rigorous objective analysis. The likelihood is that under this sort of scrutiny the client's behavior will indicate more evidence of self-worth than the client has been led (or had led herself) to believe.

The counselor who maintains a focus on assisting the client increase her control over her own life can be "profoundly helpful to . . . women by encouraging them to value their own ideas and interests, by helping them decide what they want, by urging them to develop the necessary skills and by letting them know they are not alone in their efforts" (Berlin, 1976,

p. 497). Kravetz (1982, p. 46) has suggested additional guidelines that seem appropriate:

1. *Problem assessment and goals must not be based on culturally prescribed sex-role behaviors. Alternative lifestyles, lesbianism, and other behaviors that do not meet cultural expectations should not be viewed as pathological or deviant.*

2. *It is growth-producing for women to understand the influence of social factors on their personal lives. Therefore work with women should incorporate a sex-role analysis, encouraging women to evaluate the ways in which social roles and norms and structural realities influence their personal experience, and to explore solutions that transcend traditional ones.*

3. *Women's lack of social power can generate passivity, dependence, and submissiveness. Therefore intervening should encouarge female clients to be assertive, autonomous, and self-directed.*

Profeminist social work can be practiced by both men and women. It does require a commitment to challenging the oppression that pervades much of our society and to empowering clients to act in their own behalf. It means being willing to alter everything from the client-worker relationship to the larger institutions of society. On a one-to-one basis it includes reducing client-worker distance and power differentials and encouraging clients to redefine experiences to recognize oppression they have encountered. It also means recognizing sexist assumptions regarding appropriate gender behavior; encouraging assertive, independent client behavior; building upon client strengths; encouraging woman-to-woman bonding rather than competition between women; and advocating equalitarian rights for women. While this stance does not necessarily mean that a worker must develop an entire new intervention model, it does require a recognition that some traditional approaches are inconsistent with a profeminist stance. Psychoanalytic social work is largely inappropriate because of its focus on the intrapsychic and its failure to take into account environmental influences. Humanistic practice approaches, problem-solving interventions, and systems perspectives are largely functional if used by a worker who also

recognizes that many problems develop precisely because of the systemic inequities structured within society (Van Den Bergh and Cooper, 1986, pp. 613–14).

In summary, a profeminist worker will be more sensitive to ecological factors in the etiology of problems, oriented to prevention whenever possible and supportive of client empowerment strategies. This approach is consistent with good social work practice, in keeping with the values of the profession, and will help ensure that the worker does not perpetuate gender-based oppression of women.

Gay and Lesbian Clients

The role of social work in providing assistance to gay and lesbian clients is clear. The worker's responsibility is to help clients meet their basic human needs and provide linkages with resources that further these goals. The problems of homosexual clients are often similar to those of heterosexuals. In other situations the problems are unique to gays and lesbians. For younger homosexuals the stress associated with identity confusion regarding their sexuality may be a source of difficulty requiring intervention. The worker can assist here by "making the client aware of the incongruence between ways of acting, thinking, and feeling and the client's self-image" (Berger, 1983, p. 134). The goal of such help is self-acceptance by the client. The worker can also help with finding peer support if the client has decided to adopt or maintain his or her identity as a homosexual. Such a decision may also necessitate dealing with parents, employers, and friends of the gay/lesbian. Here again, the social worker can be of help. These significant others can be worked with individually or in groups to assist them in dealing with their own feelings and reactions.

For older gays and lesbians, the tasks and problems may be considerably different. Berger (1982) has identified four problem areas facing the elderly homosexual: institutional, legal, emotional, and medical. The older gay may find that institutional rules prohibit visits to a hospitalized patient by anyone but a member of the immediate family, thus excluding a lover of many years. Similarly, medical decisions in cases of emergency often require consent by next of kin, thus ignoring the gay or lesbian partner completely. While services to the grieving spouse are common, there are almost no efforts made to provide similar help to the partner of the deceased homosexual. The need for companionship and dealing with loneliness in old age are also problems confronting many gays and lesbians that can be ameliorated by professional assistance. The worker can help clients prepare relationship contracts and encourage them to make other arrangements, such as wills.

The difficulties of the older gay may differ somewhat from those of younger homosexuals. For instance, the task of coming out may be easier when one is older because the most common problem of dealing with one's parents often no longer exists. At the same time, older gays may prefer not to address the issue of sexual orientation directly and the worker would be advised to follow suit. This requires a worker who is open to the client's needs but who feels no compulsion to press the client into coming out or openly communicating his or her sexuality.

For some homosexual clients, homophobia may indeed be a problem requiring assistance. The stigma associated with sexual orientation of gays and lesbians sometimes creates self-loathing among homosexuals themselves. Such a reaction is at odds with the goal of self-acceptance and can be dealt with accordingly. Social workers should be aware of local support groups for gays and lesbians and should encourage the development of such organizations when absent. Likewise, agencies that provide specialized services to gays or that are especially sensitive to their needs can be supported by referrals and by other means.

On another level there are equally concrete activities in which the social worker can engage. Support for legislation to decriminalize same sex acts would help to reduce the psychological risks of being gay or lesbian, and civil rights protection would help ensure that discrimination in employment and housing would be avoided. Currently, many cities and states have adopted such laws removing yet another unnecessary burden to those whose sexual orientation is gay or lesbian.

Adequate sex education in schools, churches, and within the family can also be encouraged (Gramick, 1983). In-service training for agency staff on the topic of homosexuality and multi-agency efforts to combat prejudice and discrimination toward gays and lesbians can also be undertaken. Gramick (1983) has also suggested refusing to accept homophobic behavior from colleagues and argues that such actions should be pointed out as a violation of the NASW Code of Ethics.

Certainly, to be of help to gay and lesbian clients we must become more comfortable with the topic of homosexuality and begin to deal with our own homophobic tendencies. Just as in other areas of practice, ignorance and confusion about sexual orientation must be dealt with directly and openly.

Rural Settings

Social workers who elect to practice in a rural setting are likely to discover that a multiplicity of differences exists in the way they conduct business. For example, the social worker who comfortably assumes the role of advocate in a nonrural setting will quickly find that this is more difficult now. A rural advocate risks losing the trust of the community which she nurtured so carefully in such other roles as broker, mediator, and problem solver. The fact that workers become more a part of the area they serve means that there is a greater informality and less professional detachment than would be true in an urban setting. The need to have relationships with and the support of community power sources makes it more difficult to pursue changes that threaten those interests. Workers, especially in-migrant practitioners, are often perceived as outsiders and it takes time for the community to develop trust and confidence in the worker's competence. Thus, to advocate strongly for anything under these conditions is not recommended if other equally effective alternatives can be pursued. The greater autonomy of the rural worker is an asset but it also carries with it additional responsibilities. The worker needs to develop the ability to form relationships quickly because the geographical distance to be covered means less time can be devoted to long-term projects. Making each contact with a client count is essential since those contacts are more infrequent than would otherwise be the case. Knowledge of natural and informal rather than formal support systems is crucial, as is the ability to work with other professionals and nonprofessionals in achieving change. The rural worker must also be patient, however, since changes, when they come, can be exceedingly slow. Any "attempt to change beliefs or practices can cause dislocations, anxiety, and resistance against the change agent" (Buxton, 1976, p. 37). As we described earlier, the worker must be knowledgeable about local norms and especially conscious of local etiquette. Moreover this awareness must be matched by "greater conformity with conventional norms" (Southern Regional Education Board, 1976, p. 42). Workers may need to adjust their personal lifestyles to the community and to the job to be done, and clearly not every social worker will be willing or able to accomplish this. It follows from what we have indicated previously that any existing cultural or ethnic differences may complicate understanding of, and practice in, the rural community.

Social workers new to rural areas and small towns sometimes ignore the many ways their private actions affect the way they are seen as professionals. For example, workers finding higher prices in smaller communities have often resorted to shopping in nearby communities that are larger. Purchases of groceries, automobiles, clothes, and other items are often made without regard to how this affects the local community. While this pattern of shopping may result in a lower price paid for goods and services, the net result may be that the worker is not seen as a member of the community. Shopping in the community where one practices helps link the worker with that community, supports the local economy, and gives the practitioner an opportunity to talk regularly with business people and leaders in the area. This entree makes it easier to approach community leaders later on when the worker is pursuing a change opportunity.

Similarly, participating in local community activities helps ensure that the worker is seen as a member of the community. Workers who work in a community and do not live there, shop there, or participate in community activities will have greatly diminished ability to exert influence within that setting. In smaller

communities, becoming part of the community is key to influencing local events. Workers are encouraged to attend the local chicken dinners sponsored by church or civic groups, participate in the volunteer fire department fund-raising effort, serve on the centennial committee, and accept membership in local service organizations. Other ways of becoming involved include volunteering to work on special projects (such as the historical museum renovations, tree planting, and community beautification efforts). In the long run, the worker who is seen as part of the community will be better able to influence the course of events within that community.

Other Differences Affecting Practice

A variety of potential and actual differences between client and worker can impinge on the relationship and affect the outcome of interventive efforts. Age differences, as mentioned earlier, will dictate certain adaptations to the usual style of the worker. When working with older clients, for example, the worker should exercise greater patience and understanding of the problems of the aged, and if feasible, elect to conduct the interview out of the office, in a location more suitable to the client. Home interviews are suggested when possible.

Similar care should be utilized when the worker is engaged in a practice with young children. The worker, as an adult, may need to place some distance between herself and the child's parents in order to gain the youngster's confidence. While children are more open in many ways, they are also quick to tune out questions, thus reducing the worker's reliance on standard verbal techniques. The child's medium is play, and the worker would be advised to utilize such activities in the helping process. While adult rules of conversation are more strict, an interview with a child may appear both random and disorganized (Kadushin, 1983). This places a special responsibility on the practitioner to be sensitive to the unspoken aspects of the interview and to stay attuned to the bits and pieces of information that are generated in these situations. Though the process will be somewhat disjointed, in the author's view the rewards are substantial.

SOME GENERAL OBSERVATIONS

This chapter has focused extensively on the unique differences among various groups, such as racial minorities, women, and gay and lesbian individuals. While the emphasis has been on characteristics that help to differentiate these groups and social work practice as it relates to the groups, it is important to realize that there are some important commonalities that affect our efforts to help. In this section we will attempt to highlight some of these similarities.

Any intervention effort that is ethnic sensitive should take into account those individuals affected by the problem. Social workers, for example, who plan to work with minority families should be certain they understand "who the appropriate actors are" (Devore and Schlesinger, 1981, p. 179). This might include nuclear family members as well as other relatives and friends who are "like family" members. Most minorities of color evidence a sound respect for elders and seek their advice and opinion. In addition, most are also tolerant of other ethnic groups to a degree not found among the dominant majority. While the religious orientations and spiritual beliefs of each group may differ markedly, each is likely to be characterized by some degree of religiosity or belief in a supreme being (Burgest, 1983).

People of color also share their commonality of color, their oppression, and their victimization by white society. Most have experienced conflict with this society ranging from colonization to slavery to economic bondage (Burgest, 1983). The result of this conflict has been a distrust of traditional social service institutions, a pride of and reliance on one's own kind, and a sense of impotence when dealing with the typical governmental agency.

To provide competent social services within the framework outlined above the worker must attend to a variety of issues. First, it is helpful to keep in mind that feelings, emotions, and thoughts are all shared. Differences most often lie in how we choose to express them. Our own culture influences us to the extent that some say we are culture bound. As a result, feelings, thoughts, and ideas we felt were firmly under control or previously resolved may become aroused in us during one-on-one encounters with those of a different race. It is healthier to recognize this possibility than to be surprised at an inopportune time. Our attempts to provide sensitive and effective social work intervention can be enhanced by observing the following guidelines:

1. Avoid color blindness — this issue was addressed earlier.
2. Avoid jargon and clichés, such as referring to clients as culturally deprived.
3. Concentrate on building the relationship first and showing sensitivity to the client's culture and difficulty.
4. Consider client behavior as functional/dysfunctional rather than normal/abnormal based on an a priori standard.
5. Recognize and accept that client distrust is likely to be the norm.
6. Accept the limits of your own knowledge.
7. Acquire some familiarity with clients' language whenever possible.
8. Recognize that culture is fluid, not static.
9. Acquire and maintain a sound working knowledge of programs, services, agencies, and workers providing specialized assistance to diverse groups.
10. Keep abreast of new rules and laws affecting diverse groups.
11. Support training and education for agency staff related to diverse groups.
12. Take active steps to combat discrimination within your own agency and programs.
13. Place greater emphasis in your practice on developing community-based alternatives to reduce the discriminatory reliance on institutional placements for people of color.

SUMMARY

This chapter reviews some of the barriers inherent in worker-client differences and discusses some of the factors that are obstacles in workers' forming relationships with clients who differ in terms of race, culture, age, gender, or sexual orientation. The chapter also provides information on how such obstacles and barriers can be overcome. The final section provides specific techniques and approaches that can be used (or should be avoided) in social work practice with Native Americans, African-Americans, Latinos, women, gays and lesbians, children, and rural clients.

Generally the difficulties that workers experience can be attributable to four fundamental issues: (1) ignorance of the culture or characteristics of those with whom one is working; (2) retention of stereotypic perceptions of the target group; (3) insufficient knowledge of self; and (4) a tendency to rely on standard interventive techniques without regard to their appropriateness for the client group.

The existence of these barriers may give the reader the impression that client and worker differences present obstacles that only superhuman effort on the part of the helper can overcome. In actuality, the similarities between helper and client often outweigh the dissimilarities. Workers can deemphasize some of the differences that do exist through those mechanisms that are important to all relationships. A belief in (and practice consistent with) respect for the worth and dignity of the client is significant. A worker who is genuinely interested in the problems and situation of the client and who gives hope for improvement will assuage much of the division caused by racial, ethnic, cultural, or sexual orientation differences. Adhering to the values of the profession, while not a panacea, increases the likelihood that the worker in these situations will be accepted and accorded the status of a competent and sensitive professional. When coupled with a thorough knowledge of the client group, a depth of self-understanding, and a repertoire of culturally relevant techniques, the applied values of the profession provide an effective means to this end.

EXERCISES

1. Diversity Self-Assessment

GOAL: This exercise is designed to encourage students to recognize and understand their attitudes toward various diverse groups.

Step 1: Provide each student with a copy of the diversity checklist.

Step 2: Explain the purpose of the exercise and allow about ten minutes for completion.

Step 3: When all students have completed the checklist, provide each with two copies of the self-assessment guide and allow another ten minutes or so for completing these sheets. The sheets are to be completed in duplicate. The student's name should be placed on only one of the two copies, leaving one without a name.

Step 4: The class should be broken into small groups of six to eight persons to discuss the exercise, focusing on things each student learned about herself while completing the exercise. At the same time the instructor should collect one copy of the self-assessment guide (without any identifying information), and should use the small group time to prepare a profile of the class that can be placed on the board.

Step 5: The class should be reassembled and asked to share their reactions to the small-group sessions. The instructor should review the class profile and ask students to react to the profile and discuss the implications of their own self-assessment for their ability to work with diverse groups. Finally students are asked to consider ways in which they might deal with prejudices and attitudes that interfere with their ability to be effective social workers.

Diversity Self-Assessment Checklist

Below are listed a number of individuals with whom you may come in contact in your role as a social worker. In addition there are questions listed that should be answered with reference to each of the individuals mentioned. Please keep in mind that the exercise will work best if you are as honest in your answers as you can be. Your individual responses will not be revealed to anyone else.

Instructions

a. Answer only one question at a time. When you have answered the question about the first individual, go on to the second individual. Continue through the list until you have answered the first question for each individual listed. Then proceed to question two and so on.
b. Place an X in the correct column for any individual for whom you answered no. Also place an X if you have to hesitate before answering yes.

Question 1: Would I be able to greet this person in a warm and sincere manner?

Question 2: Would I be sufficiently comfortable interviewing this person to be able to listen to his/her problems?

Question 3: Would I feel comfortable trying to help this person deal with the problems that brought him/her to me?

Individuals	Question number		
	1	2	3
1. Asian-American			
2. Mexican-American			
3. Jew			
4. Gay male			
5. Native American			
6. Senile senior citizen			
7. Ku Klux Klan member			
8. Prostitute			
9. Blind person			
10. Alcoholic			
11. Drug pusher			
12. Farmer			
13. African-American			

(continued)

Individuals (continued)	Question number		
	1	2	3
14. Lesbian			
15. Puerto Rican			
16. Person in a wheelchair			
17. Cerebral palsied person			
18. Jehovah's Witness			
19. Pimp			
20. Person with a badly disfigured face			

Diversity Self-Assessment Guide

The purpose of this guide is to help you recognize areas of potential difficulty when working with various diverse groups. The individuals listed on the checklist can be divided into subgroups: ethnic or racial, religious/spiritual, mental/physical disability, political, and lifestyle.

You should be alert to any concentration of Xs under any of these categories since they may indicate potential barriers to your efforts to work with certain diverse groups. Transpose your answers from the Diversity Self-Assessment Checklist to this Guide.

Categories	Question		
	1	2	3
Ethnic/racial			
1. Asian-American			
2. Mexican-American			
5. Native American			
13. African-American			
15. Puerto Rican			
Lifestyle			
8. Prostitute			
4. Gay male			
10. Alcoholic			
11. Drug pusher			
12. Farmer			
14. Lesbian			
19. Pimp			
Religious/spiritual			
3. Jew			
18. Jehovah's Witness			

(continued)

Categories (continued)	Question		
	1	2	3
Mental/physical disability			
6. Senile senior citizen			
9. Blind person			
16. Person in a wheelchair			
17. Cerebral palsied person			
20. Person with a badly disfigured face			
Political			
7. Ku Klux Klan member			

2. The Billy Martin Case

GOAL: This exercise is designed to help students clarify their values toward homosexuality
and foster care.

Step 1: State the purpose of this exercise. Have the students form subgroups of about five
persons. Read the following vignette to the subgroups:

Billy Martin has been in foster care for the past three years. At age fourteen he was
thought too old to be adopted and his worker expected he would remain with Julie and
Ed Saunders until he turned eighteen. A typical teenager, Billy has begun to act up and
assert his independence, challenging the Saunders on almost every issue. Mrs. Saunders is
having a difficult time coping with Billy, but is willing to try since Billy really has no other
alternative.

Last week, Billy's older brother, Glenn, who is twenty-four and works as a repairman
for the telephone company, offered to take Billy to live with him. Glenn is now living with
another man and is active in the movement to have the city adopt an ordinance prohibiting
discrimination against gays and lesbians. He is also involved with the Gay Task Force and a
strong advocate for rights for homosexuals. Billy would miss the Saunderses, but wants to
live with his big brother. Glenn is economically able to care for Billy, but the case manager,
Mr. Walton, has some strong reservations.

Step 2: Instruct the subgroups to arrive at answers to the following questions (these questions should be written on the blackboard).

1. Would you let Billy live with his brother? Why or why not?
2. Should Billy be moved to another foster home if the Saunders are no longer able to
    handle him?
3. How much should the sexual preference of a person affect decisions on such issues as
    suitability for raising children?

Step 3: Reform the class. Have the subgroups share and discuss their answers to these
questions.

3. *The Mary Mills Case*

GOAL: This exercise is designed to help students clarify their values toward the roles of women and men in our society.

Step 1: State the purpose of the exercise. Have the students form subgroups of about five persons. Read the following vignette to the subgroups:

Mary Mills is angry. Her husband has been arguing with her about the time her new job takes and the fact that she is not home to vacuum and clean like she was before. The Mills have been married for seven years and have no children. During the first years of marriage, Mary remained at home because her husband felt he should be the breadwinner. After she become bored with this routine, Mary decided to get a part-time job working as a clerk in the local supermarket. While they do not need the money, Mary enjoys the chance to meet people and do something different. After six months on the job, the manager offered Mary a chance to become her assistant. The new job is full-time and Mary was very excited about the possibility of this position. Mr. Mills is opposed to her taking the position. Her best friend, a social worker named Allison Goetz, suggested she should not take the job because it would cause more difficulty in the Mills marriage. Instead, she suggested Mary begin to do some volunteer work at the local hospital. This would give her a chance to get out of the house and would not be opposed by her husband.

Step 2: Instruct the subgroups to arrive at answers to the following questions (these questions should be written on the blackboard).

1. Is Mary better off to stay at home and not risk her marriage?
2. Is Allison right in her opinion that Mary should quit her job and do volunteer work of which her husband approves?
3. Does it make any sense for Mary to take a full-time job with important responsibilities if her husband objects so strongly?
4. If you had been Allison, what would you have recommended?

Step 3: Reform the class. Have the subgroups share and discuss their answers to these questions.

The focus of this chapter is on how to survive and enjoy a career in social work. First, guidelines are presented on how to handle common concerns of students receiving professional training in social work. Sections that follow then present material on how to avoid burnout, how to survive in a bureaucracy, and how to enjoy social work and life.

12

SURVIVING AND ENJOYING SOCIAL WORK

COMMON CONCERNS OF STUDENTS

One of the surprises I found in teaching social work students is that although students have a number of common concerns, they believe their concerns are so unique and "secret" that they are reluctant to share and discuss these concerns with others. In this section a number of these concerns are presented and some suggestions given for resolving them.

Will I Be Able to Make It in Field Placement?

Associated with this concern are a number of more specific concerns. Will I be accepted and liked by the agency staff? Will I be accepted and liked by clients that are assigned? Will I be able to help clients? Will the clothes I wear be acceptable? Will my shortcomings do me in? (*Every* student perceives a number of personal shortcomings — such as unusual tone of voice, inability to speak clearly, low level of interviewing skills, questionable personal appearance, inability to start and maintain a conversation, and so on; students by far are their own harshest critics.) Am I emotionally stable enough to handle field placement? Will I be able to speak on the telephone and be able to dictate? Will I be able to learn to do all the paperwork? Will I be attacked by clients? Will my car hold up, or will I be able to get where I'm supposed to be? Will I become too anxious and get stage fright when I'm assigned certain tasks?

In twenty years of supervising students in field placement, I have heard these and many similar concerns from practically every student. The students I worry about in arranging field placements are those who deny having such concerns, as I have found they generally are not perceptive about themselves. If a person is not perceptive about personal concerns and emotions, it generally means he or she will not be perceptive about the thoughts and emotions of clients and therefore will not make a skillful counselor.

Practically every student will be anxious prior to field placement and during at least the first few weeks at placement. This anxiety is to be expected. Students will find in field placement that their moderate level of anxiety will drain their energy, and most will be exhausted when they leave in the evening.

Although such anxiety and concerns are normal, there are ways of reducing some of the concerns.

a. In many social work programs students have considerable input in choosing their field placement setting. If you have a voice in selecting a placement, you should use this opportunity to visit the agency you are considering for a placement. You can meet with agency staff, receive a description of the agency's programs, and also discuss the expected tasks for student interns. Certain other concerns, such as expected dress code, can also be discussed. If after the visit you have serious reservations about taking a placement at that agency, your reservations should be discussed with faculty at school who coordinate field placements. If your concerns are not reduced after such a discussion, many programs allow you to visit another agency to explore doing a field placement there.

b. Ask other students currently in field placement, or who have completed field placement, to share and discuss their experiences and concerns. Such discussion will give you a better idea of what placement is like and also may provide you with answers to some of your concerns. It is particularly useful to talk with students who have had a field placement at the agency where you desire to go.

c. Discuss your concerns with faculty who coordinate field placements at your school. They will be able to answer some of these concerns, and also provide

you with additional information about the agency where you want to be placed.

d. Volunteer in your classes to role-play simulated counseling situations. Particularly useful is to have these role-playings videotaped and played back to you. Such role-playing will enable you to assess and further develop your interviewing skills. Zastrow and Navarre (1979) have found that videotaped role-playing of counseling situations also develops students' confidence in their counseling capacities.

e. It should be noted that the above suggestions will reduce some, but certainly not all, of your concerns about whether you will make it in field placement. Therefore, it is normal for you to be anxious when you begin your placement. As the weeks pass in field placement, the vast majority of students receive feedback they are doing well and become more and more relaxed.

While at your placement it is highly recommended that you express your concerns to your agency supervisor and ask questions that you have about agency procedures and policies, and expectations for student interns. Also, if you are confused about how to carry out tasks that are assigned or have other questions related to your placement, talk to your agency supervisor. Open communication between you and your agency supervisor is an important key to making it in field placement.

Will I Conduct a Satisfactory Interview with My First Client?

Students have a number of specific concerns related to this question. How will I know what to say? How will I keep the conversation going? If I say the wrong thing, won't it be a calamity for the client? How will I introduce myself? Will the client discover that I am only a student and therefore feel he is being used as a guinea pig to train me? What if I become tongue-tied and am unable to say anything? Am I really ready to assume the awesome responsibility of counseling others? I've got personal problems that are unresolved—how can I possibly help others?

Some students become so concerned prior to seeing their first client that they are unable to sleep well the night before; others may develop a tension headache. A few have told me they have had such visceral reactions as being unable to eat, or developing diarrhea, or regurgitating. It happens. If you have such severe reactions, you are not alone. Furthermore, it is highly unlikely that you will "bomb" during your first interview, as most anxious students report once the interview began they relaxed and the interview went fairly well.

Some suggestions follow for reducing some of the concerns:

a. Role-play simulated counseling situations, ideally playing the roles of both counselor and client. Videotaping and reviewing the tape is particularly helpful. Such role-playing will give you practice in counseling.

b. Before the interview prepare for it by identifying what your objectives are, and by thinking about the kinds of questions you will need to ask to accomplish these objectives. Also helpful is to review the material in Chapters 4 and 5 on how to begin and end interviews, on how to build a relationship, and on how to begin to explore the client's problems.

c. Clients are much less fragile than beginning counselors believe they are. If you fail to cover something, you can probably do that at some future interview. If you fail to phrase a question properly, you won't cause a calamity in the client's life. It is irrational to expect that if you make some mistakes in this first interview that you will cause a disaster for the client—no one has that kind of power. Clients have been exposed to much more trauma and chaotic situations than talking to you; they survived those experiences, so they will definitely survive talking to you.

d. Review the interview with your agency supervisor or your faculty supervisor to identify the aspects you did well, and the aspects you need to improve. It is irrational to expect perfection in your first interview, or for that matter in any interview. Everyone is fallible, so mistakes will be made. In addition, the main purpose of field placement is *training*—helping you to test out

and further develop your social work skills and techniques. Therefore, agency staff expect you will learn and grow and make some mistakes. Students who generally do best in placement are those who seek to test out and develop their social work skills. It is a serious mistake to "hang back" in field placement for fear of making mistakes. Focusing on making few errors to get a high grade usually leads the student intern to "hang back"—which then tends to result in a lower grade.

e. If you have specific questions prior to this first interview, ask your agency supervisor. For example, you may wonder whether you should inform the client that you are a student. Different agencies handle this question differently. In field placement your agency supervisor wants to hear your questions and concerns. Only through hearing your questions can your agency supervisor determine "where you are" and how to be most helpful to you. Agency supervisors were once in training themselves. They are aware of the pressures and anxieties of being in field placement and are committed to helping you. Many have told me that the questions students ask frequently add a fresh, new perspective to their practice, which leads them to make improvements in their counseling and interviewing approaches.

I'm Really Depressed, Because My Supervisor Is Able to Handle an Interview Much Better Than I — Will I Ever Be Able to Do That Well?

When student interns observe the interviewing and counseling skills of their agency or faculty supervisor, many student interns become depressed because they realize their skills are not as highly developed. They tend to "awfulize" and erroneously conclude they never will do well at interviewing and counseling. It is simply irrational for a student to expect that his or her skills should be as highly developed as the supervisor's; the supervisor has had many more years of training and experience. With additional years of training and experience, most beginning counselors eventually develop skill levels that are comparable to those of their supervisors. "Rome was not built in a day." Rather than thinking negatively and "self-downing" oneself, it is much better for student interns to think positively and use their supervisors as role models in developing interviewing and counseling skills.

How Should I Separate the Role of Counselor from That of Friend?

Students generally have a small caseload in field placement, which allows them to spend considerable time with clients. It is not uncommon for clients to begin to become attracted to their worker as the sharing of personal concerns fosters an attachment. Students are also generally young and physically attractive, which also fosters an attachment. A frequent question that students in field placement have is, "Is this client beginning to see me as someone he wants to get socially involved with—and if so, how do I handle this?" There are a number of related questions. "This client has invited me to her home—should I go?" "This client has suggested we go have a soda (or a cup of coffee, or dinner) together—should I go?" "This client has suggested we go to a park (or play golf, or go to a bar, or play cards)—should I go?"

There are no yes or no answers to these questions. Most agencies frown upon, and some prohibit, fraternizing with clients. For example, if a probation officer were to socialize extensively with a probationee, problems might arise. The probationee might violate some conditions of probation and then try to use the friendship with the probation officer to avoid diverse consequences of the violations. In addition, other probationees and parolees are apt to become aware of the friendship relationship, and conclude they no longer have to rigidly adhere to the conditions of probation or of parole as the probation officer is "a nice guy" and "a soft-touch." In addition, administrative officials are apt to see the friendship relationship as leading to a possible conflict of interest situation and may disapprove highly of such a relationship.

In addition, if you become socially involved with a client, it is often more difficult to counsel that person effectively. The client, for example, may no longer be willing to accept suggestions from you as he may misinterpret the suggestions as being "put-downs." Counseling someone you are socially involved with brings forth the same personality clashes as when you try to teach a close member of your family how to drive a car.

On the other hand, attraction of a client to a counselor can be a component of a helping relationship. This attraction can occasionally be used positively. For example, I've seen elderly, apathetic, depressed male clients in nursing homes become attracted to female student interns. These interns have then been able to use this attraction to motivate these elderly men to become involved in programs at the nursing homes (such as hobbies and craft activities). Once involved in such programs, they usually start to enjoy them, and as a result become more energetic, happier, and more active.

How then should a counselor decide whether to accept an invitation from a client to do something together? The guideline is simple. If the counselor believes doing something with a client will help develop a working relationship and be constructive for the client, then do it. For example, for some clients, going to a park and talking will help them to relax and develop the kind of atmosphere where they will feel free to share and discuss their secret personal concerns. On the other hand, if the counselor believes accepting an invitation has the potential for being destructive to the helping process, then don't do it. For example, if the counselor believes going to a park will lead the client to interpret that the counselor wants to become involved in a "dating" relationship, then it is best to tactfully decline the invitation.

It may be useful for beginning workers to be aware of the essential difference between a friendship and a professional relationship. Friendship is both for *giving* and *receiving*; while a professional relationship involves the helping person *giving* and the client *receiving*.

As discussed above, beginning counselors often wonder how, in practice, to separate the role of counselor from that of a friend. With experience, this problem gradually disappears. Apparently experienced counselors become more perceptive in determining the intent behind invitations from clients and more skillful in conveying the boundaries of the professional relationship. Experienced counselors also have more cases, which often reduces the amount of time spent per client, which reduces socializing opportunities.

How Can I Avoid Becoming Too Emotionally Involved with Clients' Problems?

Every counselor has, at one time or another, become overly emotionally involved in some cases.

I recently was a faculty supervisor for a student in a child welfare unit at a public welfare department. One of the cases assigned to this student was a fourteen-year-old girl who had been in a series of foster homes. The student, Linda H., became fairly attached to the girl, partly because she sympathized with the girl for having been placed in a series of foster homes since she was three. This fourteen-year-old girl became interested in dating, which her conservative foster parents could not accept. Considerable friction developed, and the foster parents suggested to the agency that it would be best if the girl was placed in a different foster home. Linda H. arranged a meeting between the foster parents and the fourteen-year-old to try to work out a compromise, particularly because the girl was feeling rejected. The meeting didn't resolve any concerns. So Linda H., after considerable effort, found another foster home, and a trial visit was attempted. Linda H. indicated in describing this visit, "I felt like a nervous mother" about this visit. (Right away this statement led me to believe the student was becoming overly involved.) The trial visit went fairly well, but after a day of reflecting, these foster parents decided they did not want to take a foster child at this time. The girl felt rejected, unloved, and depressed. Linda H., being too emotionally involved, became so depressed that she had to take two days off from her placement. She sympathized, rather than empathized with the girl. Fortunately she realized she was too emotionally involved at this point to search for another foster family. (She

did ask the foster parents to keep the youth for a few more days until a new placement could be found, which they consented to do.)

As the above case example indicates, when counselors become too emotionally involved, they have a reduced capacity to help clients discuss their problems, and a reduced capacity to explore alternative solutions objectively with clients.

There appear to be several types of irrational thinking that lead to overinvolvement. Figure 12.1 lists these types of irrational thinking and presents rational self-challenges to counter them.

Beginning counselors are much more apt to become overly involved than experienced counselors, because with experience, counselors increasingly learn that clients own their problems, that clients are the primary problem solvers, and that to be of optimal assistance counselors need to remain objective rather than exaggerating the consequences of resolution approaches that don't work out. (The main reason counselors are less successful in counseling close friends and relatives is because they are too involved to be objective.)

Yet, even experienced counselors at times become too involved. I speak from experience. A few years ago I was asked by a high state official to provide counseling help for a number of personal problems she faced—including burnout, grief over death of husband, drinking problems, insomnia, depression, and lack of meaning in work or in living. This state official was highly respected. I realized I was giving myself the following irrational thinking that was leading to overinvolvement: "I must solve her problems. If she resigns her position this will be tragic, as several thousand people in the state will be adversely affected. If this person resigns, it will be awful." Through countering such irrational thinking with rational self-challenges, I was better able to help the person explore her problems, one at a time, and develop strategies to handle each.

Suggestions to counter emotional overinvolvement include the following:

a. When you feel emotionally involved in a case (for example, taking it home with you by thinking about it for several hours), discuss it with others, particularly your supervisor. Other people are often able

FIGURE 12.1

Irrational Thinking Leads to Emotional Overinvolvement, Which Can Be Changed by Rational Self-Challenges

Irrational Thinking of the Worker	Rational Self-Challenges
1. "This client has shared his problems, and therefore I must help this client resolve these problems." (Such thinking leads to taking on ownership of the client's problems.)	1. "Clients own their problems, and have the responsibility for resolving them. I do not have the power to resolve them. All I can do is help clients explore their problems, explore alternative solutions, and encourage clients to select a resolution approach."
2. "If things (events) don't work out for clients, I have failed. I am at fault for their problems. I am a failure."	2. "Everyone has ups and downs. We are all fallible, and will have problems. If one resolution approach does not work out for a client, it only means that approach failed. It in no way means I am a failure. What the client and I need to do is to examine why that approach did not work out, explore other alternatives, select one, and try that."
3. "If things don't work out for clients it is *awful, terrible, overwhelming, unbearable.*"	3. "As Ellis and Harper (1977b) point out, it is irrational to conclude that a problem is either awful, overwhelming, or unbearable. Events are sometimes inconvenient, and a problem, but assigning labels such as awful only leads to unwanted emotions. Instead of viewing problems as being overwhelming, I need to take each problem one at a time, and in a step-by-step fashion develop strategies to deal with each."
4. "If I don't solve the client's problems, the consequences for the client, the client's family, and others close to the client will be tragic, unbearable." (Overly involved counselors often view the consequences as being more tragic than the clients themselves view the consequences.)	4. "Clients own their problems, and have the responsibility to resolve them. I am not God, as I have no miracle power to resolve problems. All I can ever do is 'give it my best shot' in counseling. It is irrational and counterproductive to overexaggerate consequences. If the selected approach doesn't work, the client needs to select and try another."
5. "I've tried the only approach that there is, and that failed. There is no hope. Things are certainly bleak for this client. I feel overwhelmed—I give up!"	5. "There is always hope. Even though I am unaware of other alternatives, there may well be others. I need to talk to an authority in this area to learn about other alternatives."

to offer suggestions on alternatives and may be able to suggest ways to become more objective and less emotionally involved.

b. Do a rational self-analysis (described in Chapter 18) on your unwanted emotions about a case. A rational self-analysis will enable you to identify your irrational thinking and to counter it with rational self-challenges.

c. If you are intensely emotionally involved with a case, seriously consider transferring it to another worker. It is irrational to expect you will be able to handle all cases optimally. You will be able to handle some cases better than your fellow workers, while your fellow workers will be able to handle other cases better than you. If you become intensely emotionally involved over a long period of time, this strongly suggests you will have difficulty in being objective and therefore transfer is indicated.

Do I Really Want to Have a Career in Social Work?

Related specific concerns of students to this question are the following: Do I have the capacities to be a competent social worker? What area of social work (for example, mental health, corrections) should I pursue? Will a career in social work pay me enough money to live the way I want to live? What do I really want to do with my life? What will my parents, friends, and relatives think of me if I become a social worker? Is there a profession/vocation that I would find more enjoyable and gratifying?

Most of these questions only you can answer. As far as the money question goes, faculty members in your social work department will be able to tell you what the average starting salary is in your area for graduates of baccalaureate and master's programs in social work. Starting salaries vary considerably in different regions, and in different positions. Pay increases are largely determined by you — your skills, your efforts to obtain advanced degrees, and your efforts to seek administrative and supervisory positions that generally pay more than direct services. Some successful psychotherapists in private practice (who have an M.S.W. degree and two or more years of counseling experience) are now earning over $80,000 per year. Skills at grant writing, consultation, public speaking, and developing new programs are also often financially rewarded.

But how do you determine whether social work is the right career for you, and which area of social work to pursue? Only you can make such decisions. The following are some suggestions:

a. Relax, don't be in a hurry to make a final career decision. Some social work students think they must make such decisions within a few weeks. They become so anxious over thinking about the pros and cons that they literally become overwhelmed and are unable to make any rational decision. In one sense you've got most of the rest of your life to make such career decisions. Many people have successfully started new careers in their forties, fifties, sixties, and even seventies.

b. Actively pursue a trial and error approach. If you try an area of social work that you find unsatisfying, try another. Skills learned in one area usually transfer to another. Perhaps you will find one area fulfilling for awhile, and then gradually find the position becoming more and more mundane, routine, and uninspiring. If that occurs, you may well want to try another area. If you really don't think you want a career in social work, fine; try something else — you may like it. Perhaps some day you'll change your mind and want to try social work again. No problem. You can take refresher or continuing education courses, or attend workshops to polish your skills, and to learn about newer techniques and revised procedures. We have students in our undergraduate courses in their 40s, 50s, and 60s who are now pursuing a career in social work, and securing a position upon graduation. It is a mistake to think that you have to make a *final* career decision. Times change, agencies change, and our interests and values change. With such changes we may find it to our advantage at some point in future years to make career changes.

Now, I'm not suggesting that you should idly sit back and wait for some unknown force to make career decisions for you. That's the ostrich head in the sand approach, which is totally unproductive. What is being recommended is that you use a *trial and error* approach, trying those career opportunities you feel might be fulfilling, and moving on to other opportunities when you become disenchanted.

BURNOUT

Ron Pakenham is ten days behind in his paperwork. He has been a juvenile probation and parole officer for the past three and one-half years. Both the agency director and the juvenile judge are putting pressure on him to do his paperwork. Mr. Pakenham is also having problems at home. His mother has emphysema, and he and his wife are going through a divorce. While working on his paperwork he receives a call from a house-parent at a group home for adolescent youths, inquiring when high school is starting in fall. (Mr. Pakenham is supervising two teenage boys at this home.) Mr. Pakenham replies, "Hey, I don't know. You'll have to call the school system. I'm not your errand boy. Don't you know I have more important things to do than to hunt information for you." After hanging up the phone, Mr. Pakenham considers his aggressive response. He also thinks about his family problems, and about being behind in his work. Mr. Pakenham realizes he is nearing burnout.

Definitions and Symptoms of Burnout

Burnout is increasingly being recognized as a serious problem affecting many people, particularly professionals employed in human services. Pines and Aronson (1981, p. 3) define burnout as being

a state of mind . . . accompanied by an array of symptoms that indicate a general malaise: emotional, physical, and psychological fatigue; feelings of helplessness, hopelessness, and a lack of enthusiasm about work and even about life in general.

Maslach and Pines have studied burnout extensively among the following professionals: social workers, psychiatrists, psychologists, prison personnel, psychiatric nurses, legal aid attorneys, physicians, child care workers, teachers, ministers, and counselors. Maslach and Pines (1977, pp. 100–01) define burnout and summarize a number of symptoms:

Burnout involves the loss of concern for the people with whom one is working. In addition to physical exhaustion (and sometimes even illness), burnout is characterized by an emotional exhaustion in which the professional no longer has any positive feelings, sympathy, or respect for clients or patients. A very cynical and dehumanized perception of these people often develops, in which they are labeled in derogatory ways and treated accordingly. As a result of this de-

humanizing process, these people are viewed as somehow deserving of their problems and are blamed for their own victimization, and thus there is a deterioration of the quality of care or service that they receive. The professional who burns out is unable to deal successfully with the overwhelming emotional stresses of the job, and this failure to cope can be manifested in a number of ways, ranging from impaired performance and absenteeism to various types of personal problems (such as alcohol and drug abuse, marital conflict, and mental illness). People who burn out often quit their jobs or even change professions, while some seek psychiatric treatment for what they believe to be their personal failings.

Freudenberger (1977, pp. 90–91) describes the symptoms of burnout as follows:

Briefly described, burnout includes such symptoms as cynicism and negativism and a tendency to be inflexible and almost rigid in thinking, which often leads to a closed mind about change or innovation. The worker may begin to discuss the client in intellectual and jargon terms and thereby distance himself from any emotional involvement. Along with this, a form of paranoia may set in whereby the worker feels that his peers and administration are out to make life more difficult.

Burnout Is One of the Reactions to High Stress

The term *burnout* has been applied to many different situations. A student who has been writing a term paper for three hours may feel burned out with writing, but yet have plenty of energy to do something else. Individuals who abuse their spouse or children may attempt to explain their actions by claiming that they are under considerable stress and just burned out. People who become apathetic and cynical about a frustrating job may claim they are burned out. Some sport coaches (at the college and professional levels) claim the pressure to win is so extensive that after several seasons they feel burned out. A person in an unhappy romantic relationship may feel burned out.

TABLE 12.1

Conceptualizing Stressors, Stress, and Stress-Related Illnesses

Stressor
{
Events or experiences: (For example, backing into another car in a parking lot)
↓
Certain kinds of thinking: (For example, "What have I done! I'll probably get a ticket and maybe even get kicked out of my insurance company. What a hassle this is going to be!")
↓
Emotional reactions: (Such as tenseness, anxiety, worry, alarm)
↓

Stress
{
Physiological reactions: (Alarm stage of General Adaptation Syndrome)
The body prepares for fight or flight. Adrenaline and other hormones increase heartbeat and rate of breathing, increase perspiration, raise blood sugar levels, dilate the pupils, and slow digestion. The process results in greater muscular strength, a huge burst of energy, and better vision and hearing. If the body remains at a high level of stress for a prolonged time period, a stress-related disorder is apt to develop, such as an ulcer, insomnia, heart problem, or digestive problem.

The term *burned out* is closely related to, and has not been adequately differentiated from, the following terms: *alienated, indifferent, apathetic, cynical, discouraged, mentally or physically exhausted*, and *overwhelmed by stress*.

In order to understand better the nature of burnout, it is useful to conceptualize burnout as being one of the reactions to high levels of stress. The advantage of this conceptualization is that it suggests that stress management strategies can be used to prevent burnout and to treat burnout when it does occur.

Stress is a contributing causal factor in most illnesses, including heart attacks, migraine headaches, diabetes, allergies, colds, cancer, arthritis, insomnia, emphysema, hypertension, and alcoholism (McQuade and Aikman, 1974). Stress is also a contributing factor in numerous emotional and behavioral difficulties, including depression, anxiety, suicide attempts, spouse abuse, child abuse, physical assaults, irritability, and stuttering (Greenberg, 1980). Becoming skillful in reducing stress is now recognized as an effective way to prevent emotional and physical disorders, and is also an effective adjunct to treatment for emotional and physical disorders if they do develop (Pelletier, 1977).

Stress can be defined as the emotional and physiological reactions to stressors. A stressor is a demand, situation, or circumstance that disrupts a person's equilibrium and initiates the stress response. There are an infinite number of possible stressors: crowding, noise, death of a friend, excessive cold, loss of a job, toxic substances, arguments, and so on.

Hans Selye (1956), one of the foremost authorities on stress, has found that the body has a three-stage reaction to stress: (*a*) the alarm stage, (*b*) the resistance stage, and (*c*) the exhaustion stage. Selye called this three-stage response the General Adaptation Syndrome.

In the alarm stage the body recognizes the stressor, such as an argument. The body reacts to the stressor by preparing for fight or flight. The body's reactions are complex and numerous, and will be summarized only briefly here.[1] The body sends messages from the brain (hypothalamus) to the pituitary gland to release its hormones. These hormones trigger the adrenal glands to

---

[1]For an extended discussion of the physiological reactions involved in the stress reaction, see Greenberg (1980).

TABLE 12.2

Burnout Is One of the Reactions to High Levels of Stress

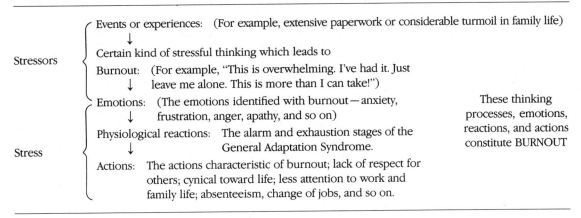

Stressors {

Events or experiences: (For example, extensive paperwork or considerable turmoil in family life)
↓
Certain kind of stressful thinking which leads to
Burnout: (For example, "This is overwhelming. I've had it. Just
↓   leave me alone. This is more than I can take!")

Stress {

Emotions: (The emotions identified with burnout — anxiety,
↓   frustration, anger, apathy, and so on)
Physiological reactions: The alarm and exhaustion stages of the
↓   General Adaptation Syndrome.
Actions: The actions characteristic of burnout; lack of respect for
others; cynical toward life; less attention to work and
family life; absenteeism, change of jobs, and so on.

These thinking processes, emotions, reactions, and actions constitute BURNOUT

release adrenaline. Adrenaline increases the rate of breathing and heartbeat, increases perspiration, raises blood sugar level, dilates the pupils, and slows digestion. The process results in a huge burst of energy, better hearing and vision, and greater muscular strength — all reactions that increase a person's capability to fight or flee.

In the second stage of resistance the body seeks to return to homeostasis. During this stage the body repairs any damage caused during the alarm stage. Most stressors cause the body to go through only the stages of alarm and repair. During a lifetime a person goes through these two stages thousands of times. Much stress is beneficial. Stress increases concentration and enhances capacities to accomplish physical tasks. A life without stress would be boring, and is in fact impossible as even dreaming produces some stress.

The type of stress that causes long-term damage results when the body remains in a state of high stress for an extended period of time. When this happens the body is unable to repair the damage and eventually the third stage of exhaustion occurs. If exhaustion continues, a person is apt to develop one or more diseases of stress, such as ulcers, hypertension, or arthritis.

A number of authorities on stress have noted there are two components of a stressor: (*a*) events or experiences that are encountered, and (*b*) a person's thoughts and perceptions about these events. Table 12.1 presents a conceptualization of stressors, stress, and stress-related illnesses.

The conceptualization in Table 12.1 suggests that there are two general approaches for reducing stress. People under stress can reduce stress either by changing the distressing events or by changing their thoughts and perceptions about the events.

As indicated earlier, burnout can be conceptualized as being one of the reactions to high-stress levels. Table 12.2 summarizes this conceptualization.

This conceptualization views burnout as being one of a number of possible reactions to high levels of continued stress. As suggested in Table 12.2, *burnout is caused primarily by what people tell themselves about events or experiences they encounter*. Examples of this kind of thinking are "I've had it." "What's the use, whatever I try won't work." "I'm going to give up — am no longer going to make an effort." It should be noted that *other people encountering the same events will not burn out if they do not give themselves the self-defeating thoughts characteristic of those who burn out. Conceptualized in this fashion, it follows that burnout will occur only when people give themselves the kind of self-defeating thoughts described above.*

Structural Causes of Stress That May Lead to Burnout

As indicated in Table 12.2, burnout is one of the possible reactions to or consequences of high stress levels. It therefore follows that those events or structural factors that are contributing causes of high-stress levels are also contributing factors to burnout.

Edelwich (1980) has identified a number of structural factors associated with work that contribute to high stress levels and may lead to burnout:

Too many work hours

Career dead end

Too much paperwork

Not sufficiently trained for job

Not appreciated by clients

Not appreciated by supervisor

Not paid enough money

No support for important decisions

Powerlessness

System not responsive to clients' needs

Bad office politics

Sexism

Too much travel

Isolation from peers

No social life

Edelwich adds that people who seek a career in the helping professions are particularly vulnerable to burnout as many enter this field with unrealistic expectations. Such expectations include the beliefs that (*a*) the services they provide will decisively improve the lives of practically all their clients, (*b*) they will be highly appreciated by the employing agency and practically all clients, (*c*) they will be able to substantially change bureaucracies to be more responsive to client's needs, and (*d*) there will be many opportunities for rapid advancement and high status. The frustrations experienced at work and the gradual recognition that many of these expectations are unrealistic are contributing factors to stress and to burnout.

Maslach (1976, p. 19) has found high caseloads in the helping professions are a major cause of stress and may lead to burnout:

Burnout often becomes inevitable when the professional is forced to provide care for too many people. As the ratio increases, the result is higher and higher emotional overload until, like a wire that has too much electricity flowing through it, the worker just burns out and emotionally disconnects.

A lack of approved *time-outs* at work is another source of stress and may be a factor in leading to burnout. Time-outs are not merely short coffee breaks from work, but are also opportunities for professionals when they are having a stressful day to switch to less stressful tasks. Time-outs are possible in large agencies that have shared work responsibilities.

Additional causes of burnout include poor time management, inability to work effectively with other people, lack of purpose or undefined goals in life, and inability to handle effectively emergencies that arise (Pines and Aronson, 1981).

Clients are also a factor in determining staff burnout (Maslach, 1978). Certain types of clients are more apt to cause high levels of stress, particularly those whose problems are depressing or emotionally draining (such as terminally ill clients, belligerent clients, suicidal clients, obnoxious clients, incest cases, and severe abuse cases). Working with chronic clients who show no improvement (such as an alcoholic family in which the problem drinker denies a drinking problem) is also more apt to lead to frustration and high stress levels. Working with clients who remind workers of personal difficulties they are presently facing is also emotionally draining, such as providing marriage counseling services when workers are having marital difficulties at home.

Another important contributing factor to high stress and burnout at work is having extensive family responsibilities, such as taking care of a terminally ill parent. Extensive home responsibilities can drain the

Extensive paperwork may lead to burnout

energy of a person and may lead to burnout at home and at work.

In the helping professions another cause is taking on "ownership" of client's problems. When people tell a worker their innermost secrets and problems, there is a tendency to want to rescue and save that person. Helping professionals, especially in their early years of practice, are apt to fall victim to the rescue or savior fantasy. This fantasy involves the helping professional erroneously believing she has the power to make clients' lives better. When this fails, the helping professional is apt to feel emotionally drained and burned out. Realistically, clients are the chief problem solvers, and are the ones who decide whether they will put forth the effort to improve their lives.

Approaches to Manage Stress and Prevent Burnout

The following is a list and brief description of a number of approaches that have been useful for reducing stress and preventing burnout. In a sense this list is a "smorgasbord" as a wide variety of approaches are covered. It is up to each person to select the ones he believes are most needed and he is most motivated to use. These approaches are similar to healthy diet plans — they *will* work for those who put forth effort to make them work. (The references provide expanded reading of these approaches.)

Goal Setting and Time Management

It is highly distressing and depressing to be uncertain of what you want out of life — for example, what career you want to pursue. Many people muddle through life without ever setting goals — and thereby generally feel unfulfilled, frustrated, bored, and dissatisfied. Realistic goal setting leads to increased self-confidence, improved decision making, a greater sense of purpose, and an improved sense of security. Have you set goals in your life, or are you a muddler?

Considerable stress also comes from the feeling of having "too much to do in too little time." Time is life. To waste time is to waste life.

Time management approaches help people to set goals and to use their time effectively in reaching their short-term and lifetime goals. Time management has users first set lifetime and short-term goals (Lakein, 1973). (Admittedly this is often a lengthy process. But failure to set such goals is almost a certain guarantee for feelings of being unfulfilled and dissatisfied.) For the high-priority goals (both short-term and lifetime goals), users write down tasks for accomplishing these goals. The tasks are then prioritized according to what is most important to do to accomplish each goal. Users are then instructed to do the high-priority tasks first, and urged to generally ignore doing the low-priority (low payoff) tasks. Low-priority tasks can bog down a person's time, and interfere with a high-priority task.

Positive Thinking

Everyone has a choice to take either a negative view of events that occur or to take a positive view. People who

are prone to burnout tend to take a negative view and to tell themselves such things as "I've had it. I'm no longer going to try. I'm just going to go through the motions. I'm giving in." With such an attitude, one becomes cynical, apathetic, uncaring and unproductive.

The positive thinking philosophy asserts that taking a positive view and positive action will lead to others' liking you, your being appreciated, your feelings worthwhile about yourself, your liking yourself, your being productive and creative, your having a pleasant disposition, and good things happening to you. (Positive thinking is discussed more fully later in this chapter.)

Closely related to positive thinking is having a philosophy of life that allows you to travel through life at a relaxed cruising speed. This philosophy also allows you to look at the scenery with enjoyment, to remain calm during crises and emergencies, to approach work thoughtfully so as to increase creativity, and to enjoy leisure so as to develop more fully as a person.

Changing the Thoughts That Produce Burnout

As indicated earlier, burnout is largely caused by a certain kind of thinking. Typical thinking processes that produce burnout are "I'm not going to try anymore. I've had it. I give up. I've failed so many times in the past. From now on I'm going to do as little as possible to get by."

Rational therapy (Chapter 18) has demonstrated that the primary cause of all our emotions and our actions is what we tell ourselves about our experiences. The emotions and actions associated with burnout are also primarily determined by our thinking processes.

Although we often cannot change events that happen to us, we always have the power to think rationally and positively, and thereby change *all* of our unwanted emotions and unproductive actions, including the emotions and actions associated with burnout. For example, burnout-producing thoughts can be challenged and changed by telling ourselves instead: "I'm not going to give up. To give up will only hurt me and other people. I've handled challenges in the past and I can and will be able to handle this. Instead of thinking negatively, I've got to work on things constructively, one step at a time. When the going gets tough, I get going."

The keys to changing burnout-producing thoughts are to (*a*) recognize when you are thinking burnout-producing thoughts, (*b*) select the kinds of positive thoughts that will challenge the burnout-producing thoughts, and (*c*) everytime you start thinking the burnout-producing thoughts, replace them by telling yourself the positive thoughts.

Relaxation Techniques

People who burn out tend to maintain at high levels of stress for prolonged time periods. They have not learned to relax. Therefore, learning to relax is very helpful in preventing burnout. There are a number of relaxation techniques that induce the relaxation response: deep breathing relaxation, imagery relaxation, progressive muscle relaxation, meditation, self-hypnosis, and biofeedback. (These relaxations techniques are described in Chapter 22.)

Exercise

Regular exercise will also help reduce stress and prevent burnout. An exercise program we enjoy (perhaps running, tennis, dancing, swimming, walking, softball, or golf) helps in a variety of ways. It helps keep us in physical shape, which makes us feel good about ourselves, and also gives us increased energy to meet crises and emergencies. It helps take our mind off negative aspects of our job and home life. A final advantage of exercising is that it directly reduces stress. As mentioned earlier, under stress the body prepares us to engage in large muscle activity, including fighting or fleeing. Through exercising we use up fuel in the blood, reduce our heart rate and blood pressure, and set off other physiological changes that reduce stress and induce the relaxation response (Greenberg, 1980).

In addition to exercising, there are several other components to taking care of our physical self: having a nutritious diet, getting sufficient sleep, and taking appropriate medical care of ourselves. Being in good physical condition helps us to handle stresses and emergencies better and thereby decreases the chances of burnout.

Outside Activities

Getting involved in hobbies and attending entertainment events (concerts, movies, sporting events) will also help switch our thinking away from the negative aspects of our work and home life. Instead, we will be thinking positive thoughts about the outside activities we enjoy, thereby reducing stress and helping to prevent burnout.

Research (Schafer, 1978) indicates that "stress reduces stress"; that is, an appropriate amount of stressful activities in one area helps reduce excessive stress in others. Outside activies stop our negative thinking about our day-to-day concerns. (The key to reducing stress is to relax — we always will relax when we stop thinking negatively about our day-to-day concerns.)

Pleasurable Goodies

"Goodies" make us feel good; they change our pace and relieve stress; they are personal therapies. They add spice to life and serve as reminders that we have worth. Personal goodies vary among people. Possible goodies include traveling, listening to music, laughing, being hugged, shopping, sitting in a tub of warm water, and having an exotic drink. Personal goodies help to "recharge our batteries."

Goodies can also be used as rewards to ourselves for tasks done well. Most of us would not hesitate to compliment others for jobs done well; equally we should reward ourselves for successfully accomplishing tasks we take pride in.

Taking a mental health day is a goody that should not be overlooked. When under extended stress, take a day off and do only the things you want to do. (Some agencies now allow employees to take a certain number of mental health days with pay.) Mental health days help people who are wearing down from high stress to recharge their batteries.

Learning to relax can be helpful in preventing burnout.

Social Support Systems

Developing trusting and mutually caring relationships at work will result in a "lifeline" support system, particularly during intense, exhausting days. Maslach (1976, p. 19) notes:

Our findings show that burnout rates are lower for those professionals who actively express, analyze and share their personal feelings with their colleagues. Not only do they consciously get things off their chest, but they have an opportunity to receive constructive feedback from other people and to develop new perspectives of their relationship with patients/clients. This process is greatly enhanced if the institution sets up some social outlets such as support groups, special staff meetings or workshops.

Social support groups (at work or outside work) allow people to let their hair down, to "kid around," to share their lives, to keep in touch, and to have a source of security and help when crises arise. There are a variety of possible support groups: coworkers, friends, sport or hobby groups, one's family, church groups, and community organizations such as Parents without Partners. Support groups have several essential features: (*a*) the group meets regularly, (*b*) the same people attend, (*c*) a feeling of closeness has developed, and (*d*) there is an opportunity for spontaneity and informality (Greenberg, 1980).

Variety at Work

Doing the same thing, such as paperwork, for long periods of time becomes exhausting and mundane. Particularly important is to recognize that emotionally draining work (such as suicide counseling or hospice work) can be done only for time-limited periods or burnout will occur. Therefore it is important to attempt to structure a job to have a variety of job tasks during the week. "Variety is the spice of life." A useful way of adding variety, and also helping us grow as people, is to participate in workshops, conferences, continuing education courses, and in-service training programs.

Humor

Humor relaxes us, makes work more enjoyable, and takes the edge off intense emotional situations. Recognizing and using humor in our work and at home relieves stress and helps to prevent burnout.

Changing or Adapting to Distressing Events

There are an infinite number of distressing events: an unfulfilling job, death of someone close, the end of a romantic relationship, unresolved religious questions, an unwanted pregnancy, and so on. When distressing events arise it is important to confront them head-on to attempt to improve the situation.

For example, if you feel you are beginning to burn out at work, it is important to identify what you find frustrating and exhausting at work and then attempt to develop new approaches for handling these responsibilities. One worker, for instance, may find incest cases particularly exhausting, while another at the same agency may find working with the terminally ill to be more draining—perhaps they can exchange these cases.

If a worker is frustrated because program objectives and job expectations are unclear, these need to be discussed with the worker's supervisor and efforts made to clarify such objectives and expectations.

Most distressing events can be improved by confronting them head-on and then taking positive action to change the event. Some events or situations cannot be changed. For example, you may not be able to change certain distasteful aspects of your job. If you cannot change these, the only constructive remaining alternative is to "bite the bullet" and accept them. It is counterproductive to get upset and to spend time complaining about a situation you cannot change.

SURVIVING IN A BUREAUCRACY

There are basic structural conflicts between helping professionals and the bureaucratic systems in which they work. Helping professionals place a high value on creativeness and changing the system to serve clients. Bureaucracies resist change and are most efficient when no one is "rocking the boat." Helping professionals seek to personalize services by conveying to each client that "you count as a person." Bureaucracies and highly depersonalized, emotionally detached systems that view every employee and every client as being a tiny component of a large system. In a large bureaucracy employees *don't* count as "persons," but only as functional parts of a system. Figure 12.2 (page 325) lists additional conflicting value orientations between a helping professional and bureaucratic systems.

Any of these differences in value orientations can become an arena of conflict between helping professionals and the bureaucracies in which they work. Knopf (1979, pp. 21–22) has concisely summarized the potential areas of conflict between bureaucracies and helping professionals:

The trademarks of a BS (bureaucratic system) are power, hierarchy, and specialization; that is, rules and roles. In essence, the result is depersonalization. The system itself is neither "good" nor "bad"; it is a system. I believe it to be amoral. It is efficient and effective, but in order to be so it must be impersonal in all of its functionings. This then is the location of the stress. The hallmark of the helping professional is a highly individualized, democratic, humanized, relationship-oriented service aimed at self-motivation. The hallmark of a bureaucratic system is a highly impersonalized, valueless (amoral), emotionally detached, hierarchical structure of organization. The dilemma of the HP (helping person) is how to give a personalized service to a client through a delivery system that is not set up in any way to do that.

A number of helping professionals respond to these orientation conflicts by erroneously projecting a "personality" onto the bureaucracy. The bureaucracy is viewed as being "red tape," "officialism," "uncaring," "cruel," "the enemy." A negative personality is sometimes also projected onto officials of a bureaucracy who may be viewed as being "paper shufflers," "rigid," "deadwood," "inefficient," and "unproductive." Knopf (1979, p. 25) states:

The HP (helping person) . . . may deal with the impersonal nature of the system by projecting values onto it and thereby give the BS (bureaucratic system) a "personality." In this way, we fool ourselves into thinking that we can deal with it in a personal way. Unfortunately, projection is almost always negative and reflects the dark or negative aspects of ourselves. The BS then becomes a screen onto which we vent our anger, sadness, or fright, and while a lot of energy is generated, very little is accomplished. Since the BS is amoral, it is unproductive to place a personality on it.

A bureaucratic system is neither good nor bad. It has neither a personality nor a value system of its own. It is simply a structure developed to carry out various tasks.

A helping person may have various emotional reactions to these conflicts in orientation with bureaucratic systems.[2] Common reactions are anger at the system, self-blame ("It's all my fault"), sadness and depression ("Poor me"; "Nobody appreciates all I've done"), and fright and paranoia ("They're out to get me"; "If I mess up I'm gone").

Knopf (1979) has identified several types of behavior patterns that helping professionals choose in dealing with bureaucracies. The *warrior* leads open campaigns to destroy and malign the system. A warrior discounts the value of the system and often enters into a win/lose conflict. The warrior generally loses and is dismissed.

The *gossip* is a covert warrior who complains to others (including clients, politicians, and the news media) how terrible the system is. A gossip frequently singles out a few officials to focus criticism upon. Bureaucratic systems often make life very difficult for the gossip by assigning distasteful tasks, refusing to promote, giving very low salary increases, and perhaps even dismissing.

The *complainer* resembles a gossip, but confines complaints to other helping persons, to inhouse staff, and to family members. A complainer wants people to agree in order to find comfort in shared misery. Complainers desire to stay with the system, and generally do.

The *dancer* is skillful at ignoring rules and procedures. Dancers are frequently lonely, often reprimanded for incorrectly filling out forms, and have low investment in the system or in helping clients.

The *defender* is scared, dislikes conflict, and therefore defends the rules, the system, and bureaucratic officials. Defenders are often supervisors, and are viewed by others as being "bureaucrats."

---

[2]This description highlights a number of the negatives about bureaucratic systems, particularly their impersonalization. In fairness, it should be noted that an advantage of being part of a large bureaucracy is that the potential is there for changing a powerful system to the advantage of clients. In tiny or nonbureaucratic systems the social worker may have lots of freedom but little opportunity or power to influence large systems or mobilize extensive resources on behalf of clients.

FIGURE 12.2

Value Conflicts between a Helping Professional and Bureaucracies

Orientations of a Helping Professional	Orientations of Bureaucratic Systems
Desires democratic system for decision making.	Most decisions are made autocratically.
Desires that power be distributed equally among employees (horizontal structure).	Power is distributed vertically.
Desires that clients have considerable power in the system.	Power is held primarily by top executives.
Desires a flexible, changing system.	System is rigid and stable.
Desires that creativity and growth be emphasized.	Emphasis is on structure and the status quo.
Desires that focus be client oriented.	System is organization centered.
Desires that communication be on a personalized level from person to person.	Communication is from level to level.
Desires shared decision making and shared responsibility structure.	A hierarchical decision-making structure and a hierarchical responsibility structure are characteristic.
Desires that decisions be made by those having the most knowledge.	Decisions are made in term of the decision-making authority assigned to each position in the hierarchy.
Desires shared leadership.	System uses autocratic leadership.
Believes feelings of clients and employees should be highly valued by the system.	Procedures and processes are highly valued.

The *machine* is a "bureaucrat" who takes on the orientation of the bureaucracy. Often a machine has not been involved in providing direct services for years. Machines are frequently named to head study committees and policy groups and to chair boards.

The *executioner* attacks persons within an organization with enthusiasm and vigor. An executioner usually has a high energy level and is impulsive. An executioner abuses power by indiscriminately attacking and dismissing not only employees but also services and programs. Executioners have power and are angry (although the anger is disguised, denied). They have commitment to neither the value orientation of helping professionals or to the bureaucracy.

Knopf (1979) lists sixty-six tips on how to survive in a bureaucracy. A number of the most useful suggestions are summarized here:

1. Whenever your needs, or the needs of your clients, are not met by the bureaucracy, use the following problem-solving approach: (*a*) Precisely identify your needs (or the needs of clients) that are in conflict with the bureaucracy; this step is defining the problem. (*b*) Generate a list of possible solutions. Be creative in generating a wide range of solutions. (*c*) Evaluate the merits and shortcomings of the possible solutions. (*d*) Select a solution. (e) Implement the solution. (*f*) Evaluate the solution.

2. Obtain a knowledge of how your bureaucracy is structured and how it functions. Such knowledge will reduce fear of the unknown, make the system more predictable, and help in identifying rational ways to best meet your needs and those of your clients.

3. Remember that bureaucrats are people, too, who have feelings. Communication gaps are often most effectively reduced if you treat them with as much respect and interest as you treat clients.

4. If you are at war with the bureaucracy, declare a truce. The system will find a way to dismiss you if you remain at war. With a truce, you can identify and use the strengths of the bureaucracy as an ally, rather than having the strengths being used against you as an enemy.

5. Know your work contract and job expectations. If the expectations are unclear, seek clarity.

6. Continue to develop your knowledge and awareness of specific helping skills. Take advantage of continuing education opportunities (for example, workshops, conferences, courses). Among other advantages, your continued professional development will assist you in being able to contract from a position of competency and skill.

7. Seek to identify your professional strengths and limitations. Knowing your limitations will increase your ability to avoid undertaking responsibilities that are beyond your competencies.

8. Be aware that you can't change everything, so stop trying. In a bureaucracy, focus your change efforts on those aspects that most need change and which you also have a fair chance of changing. Stop thinking and complaining about those aspects you cannot change. It is irrational to complain about things that you cannot change or to complain about those things that you do not intend to make an effort to change.

9. Learn how to control your emotions in your interactions with the bureaucracy. Emotions that are counterproductive (such as most angry outbursts) particularly need to be controlled. Doing rational self-analysis on unwanted emotions (see Chapter 18) is one way of gaining control of your unwanted emotions. Learning how to respond to stress in your personal life will also prepare you to handle stress at work better.

10. Develop and use a sense of humor. Humor takes the edge off adverse conditions and reduces negative feelings.

11. Learn to accept your mistakes and perhaps even to laugh at some of them. No one is perfect.

12. Take time to enjoy and develop a support system with the people you work with.

13. Acknowledge your mistakes and give in sometimes on minor matters. You may not be right, and giving in sometimes allows other people to do the same.

14. Keep yourself physically fit and mentally alert. Learn to use approaches that will reduce stress and prevent burnout (a number of these approaches were discussed in the section on burnout in this chapter).

15. Leave your work at the office. If you have urgent unfinished bureaucratic business, do it before leaving work or don't leave.

16. Occasionally take your supervisor and other administrators to lunch. Socializing prevents isolation and facilitates your involvement with and understanding of the system.

17. Do not seek self-actualization or ego-satisfaction from the bureaucracy. A depersonalized system is incapable of providing this. Only you can satisfy your ego and become self-actualized.

18. Make speeches to community groups that accentuate the positives about your agency. Do not hesitate to ask after speeches that a thank-you letter be sent to your supervisor or agency director.

19. If you have a problem involving the bureaucracy, discuss it with other employees, with the focus being on problem solving rather than on complaining. Groups are much more powerful and productive than an individual working alone to make changes in a system.

20. No matter how high you rise in a hierarchy, maintain direct service contact. Direct contact keeps

you abreast of changing client needs, prevents you from getting stale, and keeps you attuned to the concerns of employees in lower levels of the hierarchy.

21. Do not try to change everything in the system at once. Attacking too much will overextend you and lead to burnout. Start small and be selective and specific. Double-check your facts to make certain they accurately prove your position before confronting bureaucratic officials.

22. Identify your career goals and determine whether they can be met in this system. If the answer is no, then (*a*) change your goals, (*b*) change the bureaucracy, or (*c*) seek a position elsewhere in which your goals can be met.

ENJOYING SOCIAL WORK AND YOUR LIFE

To gather material to write this section, I asked some friends who have practiced social work for several years to summarize their satisfactions and frustrations about pursuing a career in social work. Attached is one of the replies that was received.

It is difficult to find the right words to describe my satisfaction with having made a decision to be a social worker. I have worked in a protective services unit of a public welfare department for two years, as a probation and parole officer for three years, and now am a director of a group home for teenage males who have conflicts with their parents.

One of the satisfying aspects of social work is that there are a wide variety of areas where a person can work. When I found myself becoming stale as a probation officer, it was inspiring to look forward to moving on to something else. If this job becomes routine and no longer something I would look forward to doing, I would again move on to some other social work position.

I truly find it gratifying to work with people. If you don't like working with people, then certainly this

is the wrong job to have. I know this sounds "naive," but when I feel I've been of some help in assisting someone to better handle a personal or social problem, it really makes me feel good. It should be noted I'm no longer as idealistic as I was when I was going to college and thought I would be able to help the vast majority of my clients. I've learned that most clients simply aren't sufficiently motivated to put forth the time and effort needed to improve their lives—it's like exercising; we all know exercising will improve our health and keep us trim, but only a few people are willing to put forth the time and effort.

Social work is a challenging profession. Every client's problem is unique. For that matter every client's personality is unique. Interacting with new people, and working out somewhat different treatment strategies with each client is a challenge. Through helping clients I also grow as a person, and learn more about myself. Also challenging, and often learning experiences, are speaking to groups in the community, and seeking to develop new services when a need arises. Also educational (and a way of seeing old friends) are in-service training sessions that are held at the agencies I've worked at.

I don't want to give an ever-glowing picture of social work. There are also frustrations. At every agency there seem to be occasional personality conflicts between staff. (Such conflicts are furthered by staff members being pitted against each other for merit increases, for desired task assignments, and for who will get to go to conferences.)

Another frustration is the amount of paperwork. At the three agencies I've worked at, ten to fifteen hours per week are spent on paperwork.

Some social workers complain this profession doesn't pay enough. I've found that in social work there are some jobs that pay a lot more than others. When I first started out, my annual salary was pretty low, but now that I'm a director of this group home I have no complaints.

Another thing that is frustrating is being aware that there are a few workers who are cynical, who always look at the negative side of things, and who really appear to be only interested in drawing their paycheck, rather than helping people. With their negative attitude, I frankly don't see how they can ever help anyone. If I was a client of theirs I would become even more discourated and apathetic. To me, these social workers are "deadwood" and are on "welfare" themselves as they are drawing a check without doing anything productive. These people either burned out years ago, or were never "encouraging" persons who were motivated to help others.

All in all I really am delighted I chose a career in social work. I enjoy working with most clients (certainly not all of my clients as some I do find obnoxious) and with most of the other staff. I hope this information will be useful to you, and if you ever want someone to speak in your classes, give me a "jingle."

(Since this is only one social worker's response, the views expressed may or may not be representative of most social workers.)

One of the factors identified by the above social worker is the importance of being an "encouraging" person. Chapter 5 noted this as a crucial characteristic of counselors if they are to motivate clients. Closely related to being an "encouraging" person is to be a positive thinker. Positive thinking is important not only in working with clients but also in being able to enjoy life.

The remainder of this chapter elaborates on three specific approaches for learning to enjoy social work and your life: (1) becoming a positive thinker, (2) developing a identity, and (3) using rational challenges to develop a success identity.

Becoming a Positive Thinker

In the following quotation from *A Treasury of Success Unlimited*, W. Clement Stone (1966, pp. 9–10) presents some of the basic principles of positive thinking:

Your most precious, valued possessions and your greatest powers are invisible and intangible. No one can take them. You, and you alone, can give them. You will receive abundance for your giving. The more you give—the more you will have!

Give a smile to everyone you meet (smile with your eyes)—and you'll smile and receive smiles. . . .

Give a kind word (with a kindly thought behind the word)—you will be kind and receive kind words. . . .

Give appreciation (warmth from the heart)—you will appreciate and be appreciated. . . .

Give honor, credit and applause (the victor's wreath)—you will be honorable and receive credit and applause. . . .

Give time for a worthy cause (with eagerness)—you will be worthy and richly rewarded. . . .

Give hope (the magic ingredient for success)—you will have hope and be made hopeful. . . .

Give happiness (a most treasured state of mind)—you will be happy and be made happy. . . .

Give cheer (the verbal sunshine)—you'll be cheerful and cheered. . . .

Give encouragement (the incentive to action)—you'll be cheerful and cheered. . . .

Give a pleasant response (the neutralizer of irritants)—you will be pleasant and receive pleasant responses. . . .

Give good thoughts (nature's character builder)—you will be good and the world will have good thoughts for you. . . .

Few living Americans can write or speak on the power of positive thinking with more authority than W. Clement Stone. Beginning as a newsboy on the streets of Chicago, Mr. Stone applied the principles of positive thinking to amass, and share with others, a fortune that is in excess of $160 million (Mandino, 1967).

Harold Sherman (1966, pp. 111–13) in "The Surest Way in the World to Attract Success—or Failure" further elaborates on positive thinking:

"You might know this would happen to me!" Is this a comment you have made, not once, but many times, when things have gone wrong? . . . Certainly—you knew it was going to happen—and it did. Your faith in "things going wrong" caused the "power of TNT"

[thinking negative thoughts] within you to work against you instead of for you. There is a great law of mind by which your thinking and your conduct should always be guided: "Like attracts like."

Think good thoughts; you will eventually attract good things. Think bad thoughts, you will ultimately attract bad things.

Simple — easy to remember — but also easy to forget. . . .

Get this point clearly in mind: you supply the material (by the nature of your thoughts) out of which your creative power builds your future. If the material is inferior, comprised of mental pictures of failure, despair, defeat and the like, you can readily see that only unhappy results can be materialized from them. . . .

Whatever conditions you are facing at the moment are the result of your past thinking — good and bad. These conditions cannot change until you have first changed your thinking. . . .

Things first happen in your mind before they can happen in this outer world. What are you picturing? Do you want it to happen? If not, you are the only one who can prevent it. Your future success or failure is in your hands — where it should be.

There are a number of books on positive thinking philosophy (for example *Looking Out for #1* by Robert Ringer, 1977, and *Move Ahead with Possibility Thinking* by Robert Schuller, 1973). Positive thinking certainly has considerable merit. However, there is a potential danger. Every accomplishment requires certain abilities. For those who set goals above their capacities, positive thinking could create a false sense of hope. When people fail to achieve what they are seeking (particularly people suffering from emotional problems like anxiety or depression), they are going to realize what they have been taught doesn't work for them. After an initial period of hope, they are apt to become even more depressed.

On the other hand, positive thinking will usually get people started on a project. And, since many people do not realize their own potential, a bright outlook and positive action can help them achieve their goals as it enables them to use their capacities to the fullest.

You have the choice. You can think and act negatively about events that happen to you — which usually leads you to experience unwanted emotions and increases the chances that negative events will occur in the future. Or, you can think and act positively about events that happen to you — which usually leads you to experience pleasant emotions and increases the chances that positive events will occur in the future.

Positive thinking is an important aspect of enjoying your career (whatever it is) and your life. Another important part of enjoying life is knowing who you are and what you want out of life.

Developing an Identity[3]

What kind of a person are you? What do you want out of life? What kind of person do you want to be? Who are you? These questions are probably the most important you will have to face. Without answers, you will not be prepared to make such major decisions as selecting a career; deciding whether, when, or whom to marry; deciding whether to have children; deciding where to live; and deciding what to do with your leisure time. Unfortunately, many people muddle through life and never arrive at answers to these questions. Those who do not find answers may be depressed, indecisive, anxious, and unfulfilled. All too often, their lives are carbon copies of Stan Sinclair's.

At age eighteen, Stan graduated from high school. Unable to find a job, he enlisted in the army for a three-year hitch. At twenty, he started dating Julia Johnson while he was stationed in Illinois. He liked Julia. She became pregnant and they decided to get married. Money was tight and Julia wanted to live near her relatives. Two months after his discharge, Stan became a father. Needing a job in the area, he became a gas station attendant since it was the only employment he could find. Two and one-half years later, an opening

---

[3]This section is adapted from Charles Zastrow, "Who Am I? The Quest for Identity," in *The Personal Problem Solver*, edited by Charles Zastrow and Dae H. Chang, © 1977, pp. 365–70. Adapted by permission of Prentice-Hall, Inc., Englewood Cliffs, New Jersey.

occurred in an auto assembly plant. The pay was better, so Stan applied and was hired. The job was relatively easy but monotonous. Stan faithfully attached mufflers to new cars, over and over for forty hours a week. During the next eight years, Stan and Julia had three more children. The pay and fringe benefits, combined with his family and financial responsibilities, locked Sam into this assembly line job until he retired at age sixty-five. The morning after he retired, he looked into the mirror and began asking, finally, the key questions. Was it all worth it? Why did he feel empty and unfulfilled? What did he want out of the future? Never having in the past figured out what he wanted out of life, his only answer was a frown.

Identity is having a sense of who we are, a knowledge and a feeling of the ways in which we are separate, distinct persons.

IDENTITY DEVELOPMENT   Identity development is a lifelong process, and there are gradual changes in one's identity throughout one's lifetime. During the early years our sense of who we are is largely determined by the reactions of others. Cooley (1902) a long time ago coined this labeling process as resulting in the *looking-glass self*; that is, persons develop their self-concept (who and what they are) in terms of how others relate to them. For example, if a neighborhood identifies a male youth as being a "troublemaker" (a delinquent), the neighbors are apt to relate to the youth as if he were not to be trusted, may accuse him of delinquent acts, and will label his semidelinquent and aggressive behaviors as being *delinquent*. This labeling process, the youth begins to realize, also results in a type of prestige and status, at least from his peers. In the absence of objective ways to gauge whether he is, in fact, a delinquent, the youth will rely on the subjective evaluations of others. Thus, gradually, as the youth is related to as a delinquent, he is apt to begin to perceive himself in that way and will begin to enact the delinquent role.

Fortunately, since identity development is a lifetime process, positive changes are probable even for those who have a negative self-concept. In identify formation, a key principle to remember is that *although we cannot change the past, what we want out of the future, along with our motivation to achieve what we want, is more important (than our past experiences) in determining what our future will be.*

HOW TO DETERMINE WHO YOU ARE   Forming an identity essentially involves *thinking* about, and arriving at, answers to the following questions: (1) What do I want out of life? (2) What kind of person am I? (3) What kind of person do I want to be? (4) Who am I?

The most important decisions you make in your life may well be in arriving at answers to these questions. In answering them you are literally developing beliefs and attitudes about how you are and what you want out of life.

Answers to these questions are not easy to arrive at. They require considerable contemplation and trial and error. But if you are to lead a gratifying, fulfilling life, it is imperative to arrive at answers to give direction to your life and to help you have a chance of living the kind of life you find meaningful. Without answers, you are apt, like Stan Sinclair, to muddle through life by being a passive responder to situations that arise, rather than a continual achiever of your life's goals.

To determine who you are, you need to arrive at answers to the following more specific questions:

1. What do I find satisfying/meaningful/enjoyable? (Only after you identify what is meaningful and gratifying will you be able to consciously seek involvement in activities that will make your life fulfilling, and avoid those activities that are meaningless or stifling.)

2. What is my moral code? (One possible code is to seek to fulfill your needs and to seek to do what you find enjoyable, doing so in a way that does not deprive others of the ability to fulfill their needs.)

3. What are my religious beliefs?

4. What kind of a career do I desire? (Ideally, you should seek a career in which you find the work stimulating and satisfying, that you are skilled at, and that earns you enough money to support the lifestyle you want.)

5. What are my sexual mores? (All of us should develop a consistent code that we are comfortable with and that helps us to meet our needs without

exploiting others. There is no one right code—what works for one may not work for another, because of differences in lifestyles, life goals, and personal values.)

6. Do I desire to marry? (If yes, to what type of person and when; how consistent are your answers here with your other life goals?)

7. Do I desire to have children? (If yes, how many, when, and how consistent are your answers here with your other life goals?)

8. What area of the country/world do I desire to live in? (Variables to be considered are climate, geography, type of dwelling, rural or urban setting, closeness to relatives or friends, and characteristics of the neighborhood.)

9. What do I enjoy doing with my leisure time?

10. What kind of image do I want to project to others? (Your image will be composed of your dressing style and grooming habits, your emotions, personality, degree of assertiveness, capacity to communicate, material possessions, moral code, physical features, and voice patterns. You need to assess your strengths and shortcomings honestly in this area, and seek to make improvements.)

11. What type of people do I enjoy being with and why?

12. Do I desire to improve the quality of my life and that of others? (If yes, in what ways, and how do you hope to achieve these goals?)

13. What types of relationships do I desire to have with relatives, friends, neighbors, with people I meet for the first time?

14. What are my thoughts about death and dying?

15. What are my plans for achieving these goals in these time periods? What do I hope to be doing five years from now, ten years, twenty years?

To have a fairly well-developed sense of identity, you need to have answers to most, but not all, of these questions. Very few persons are able to arrive at rational, consistent answers to all the questions. Having answers to most of them will provide a reference for developing your views to the yet unanswered areas.

Honest, well-thought-out answers to these questions will go a long way toward defining who you are.

Again, what you want out of life, along with your motivation to achieve these goals, will primarily determine your identity. The above questions are simple to state, but arriving at answers is a complicated, ongoing process. In addition, expect some changes in your life goals as times goes on. Environmental influences change (for example, changes in working conditions). Also, as personal growth occurs, changes are apt to occur in activities that you find enjoyable and also in your beliefs, attitudes, and values. Accept such changes, and if you have a fairly good idea of who you are, you will be prepared to make changes in your life goals so that you will be able to give continued direction to your life.

Your life is shaped by different events that are the results of decisions you make and decisions that are made for you. Without a sense of identity, you will not know what decisions are best for you, and your life will be unfulfilled. With a sense of identity, you will be able to direct your life toward goals you select and find personally meaningful.

Using Rational Challenges to Develop a Success Identity

While some people are muddling through life without a clear sense of what they want or who they are, a number of people wallow through life in self-pity, seeing themselves as failures. In another publication (Zastrow, 1979, pp. 92–93) I compare people who have a success identity with those who have a failure identity:

Success identities are characterized by the following kinds of self-talk. "I have accomplished many of the things I have tried in the past." "I am a competent, worthwhile person." "I, similar to other people, have certain special talents." "Trying something new is challenging and stimulating." "I look forward to trying something more complicated that has the opportunity for substantial payoffs, and which will test and further develop my special talents." "Trying new things helps me grow as a person, and helps provide meaning to living." "I look forward to each new day with its opportunities for involvement in activities that will be gratifying and fulfilling."

Developing a Positive Self-Concept

S ince her early teenage years this individual had viewed herself as a failure. Her sense of being a failure was temporarily alleviated during her junior and senior years in high school when she steadily dated and became overly dependent upon Tom.* However, her failure concept soon returned shortly after Tom left to attend the Air Force Academy. In this case example the student describes her deep sense of being a failure, and how she used rational self-challenges to develop a more positive self-concept.

An excerpt from my journal, August 10, 1975:

Breakfast at the airport appeared cheerful enough. His parents, full of optimistic talk of his future, kept the conversation light and promising. And I, my real feelings hidden by a facade of carefully planned cheerfulness, made attempts at bright small talk which seemed to add to the somehow phony color and splendor of the day.

At that point, after all of the months of waiting and preparation, all was ready. Every last detail had been checked and it was time. Tom was ready to embark on a new and challenging life style—without me!

Later, as I recall that first painful goodbye, our words edged with emotion, full of promises for the future, and yet our every thought charged with the upcoming agony of being apart from one another, I do not once remember thinking of how I was going to adjust to his absence. Tom was the most significant person in my life to that date, and yet I had not realized the powerful effect our new "separateness" would take in relation to my life from there on.

The sequence(s) of events and emotions that followed seemed to me to be normal, or what I thought as being normal reactions for a person to feel when a loved one is away for a prolonged period of time. That is when I began my "Poor Me" syndrome!

It was summer and I was very lonely and didn't have enough to keep me busy. I worked at a local restaurant as much as I possibly could to pass the time, but it didn't seem to be enough—I still had those lonely nights to myself.

"Poor me," I'd say to myself. "I'm alone and no one cares enough to spend time with me, I must be worthless, boring, etc." This became repetitious with me to the point that whenever I felt a bit depressed, I would reinforce those feelings with other intense feelings of worthlessness. I could really bring myself down, you see, because I truly felt that I could never be happy, feel my personal worth, expand myself unless Tom was with me. I guess that was a rather natural feeling for me to have because while he was home, I allowed myself to be dependent upon him to fill my every need and whim. And gladly, he filled them. Call it "ego" or whatever, but it somehow filled a need in him to have me need him so desperately. It seemed to be a very workable arrangement while he was home with me. My belief was that we were "in love" and it was a very positive point to "need" someone I loved. What I hadn't considered was how my dependency upon him was, in fact, setting me up for a lifetime of unhappiness. Time progressed and I felt myself more and more alone. I walled myself off from my "helpful friends," people who did in fact care for me and who wanted to include

---

*Names and other identifying information in this case example have been changed.

me in their activities. I did join them on occasion, but generally if I did, I'd begin to feel sorry for myself and bring out my tale of woe. Of course they listened, but one can listen to the same negative thoughts only so many times. I remember having feelings of bitterness and hostility toward these friends, people who had things going their way. I was jealous.

It seemed as though everything was going wrong. I began to drink more and to experience the effects of drugs. At times this seemed to be a haven for me, an escape from what seemed to be insurmountable problems.

I took an apartment with an acquaintance who was pregnant. (It created many problems.) I overextended myself financially, knowing full well that I was. I was enrolled in classes but had neither the motivation nor goal to attend all of them.

All around I began to see myself as a failure. Whenever I'd receive a poor grade on a test, paper, or quiz, I'd tell myself that I was stupid. If it came time to pay the bills and I did not have the money, I'd tell myself that I was poor at supporting myself. Then, to pay those same bills for which I spent the money on extravagances, I'd have to work doubly hard.

Well, eventually I became tired of feeling negative all the time. After all, if I could feel good about myself when I was with Tom, then somehow I should be able to feel good about myself at other times. I had to — either that, suicide, or stay miserable. Neither of the latter two sounded too appealing, so I decided to make the best of it, and give my life a positive try. Many times, over tears on the telephone, I would explain to Tom my fears and anxieties and it would hurt him some, as he felt a bit responsible. He is a person whom I genuinely care for and I began to have my doubts as to what I should and shouldn't tell him. After all, I really don't intend to make those I care for feel responsible for my feelings and actions. I'm responsible for myself.

Fortunately, it was at this point in my life that I enrolled in a course on counseling, which exposed me to the concepts of rational therapy, and I proceeded to write the following rational self-analysis (RSA) on my personal concerns.

A Event	D[1] Camera check
In August of 1975 my boyfriend left for the Air Force Academy. At his leave-taking the two of us promised to wait until the end of his education and then to marry. I had little confidence in myself as a person to begin with. When he left I became less confident and began to discount myself as a person having no worth or value. As time progressed, I began to do poorly in several aspects of my life: poor grades, too much financial responsibility (too many extravagances), poor organization of my life's plans (work or school, which has priority?), hostile attitude toward friends, etc. I generally felt worthless and sad because Tom left.	This is all factual.

Continued

CASE EXAMPLE   *Continued*

B Self-Talk	D² Rational Self-Challenges to the Self-Talk in Section B
1. "I am able to be happy only if Tom is with me." (bad)	1. False. If I hope to be a self-sufficient and satisfied person in my lifetime, I know that I must do it alone—for myself. Others may make it easier for me, but essentially, I have to make myself happy.
2. "I'm dependent upon Tom in all ways if I allow his leaving to affect me this way." (bad)	2. True. But I'm not allowing myself my own rights as a person. I realize that I could never mold my life around another's wants and likes. I've got to have my own identity.
3. "I'm a failure in my studies." (bad)	3. False. I'm not a failure and never have been. At my lowest point, I still received C's for grades. I received those C's with a minimal amount of effort; so if I really tried, I could do better.
4. "I'm worthless." (bad)	4. False. Every person has some worth. I do too. At times when I'm depressed I may like to tell myself I'm worthless, but I really know that I'm not. Every human being has some worth. I'm as valuable as any other person, just because I'm human.
5. "My friends won't like me if I react to them in a hostile manner." (bad)	5. True. My friends don't like to spend time with me when I react to them in a negative, hostile way. It doesn't do much for the friendship, which was built of positive, mutual concern to begin with. I really don't like to treat them in this way and from now on I will make a conscious effort to be more pleasant.
6. "I can't support myself sufficiently. I buy extravagant items." (bad)	6. False. In the past I've done quite well. It is when I take trips to visit Tom, or buy a new wardrobe that I feel depleted financially. At other times I manage quite well, and even if I over-extend myself—I still work to pay for my expenses.
7. "Because Tom has left me, all things go wrong in my life." (bad)	7. False. Things do not go wrong because Tom left me, but because of circumstances or something I do to allow things to go wrong. Tom is away; there is no possible way he can control what happens to me here.
8. "The only thing I can look forward to is becoming Tom's wife and then I will hopefully feel better." (bad)	8. False. I intend to become a counselor if I really put forth an effort. If I do decide to become Tom's wife that will be a major event to

B Self-Talk	D² Rational Self-Challenges to the Self-Talk in Section B
	look forward to — a life together, but that is not all I'm looking forward to. For two and a half years I've struggled with college — certainly not for nothing!
9. "Tom is responsible for my feeling so rotten. It's all his fault!" (bad)	9. False. Tom is away and has no control over my life. He never did. In the past I felt the way I wanted to, did what I liked because that is the power that I have as a person. When Tom left it was an unfortunate circumstance. I allowed myself to blame him for all the "wrongs" and unhappiness in my life when actually he had nothing to do with it. I'm the person living my life — choosing my own feelings, situations, etc., of which Tom has no control.

C My Emotions	E Emotional and Behavioral goals
Depression, sadness, insecurity, inferiority, and loneliness. I had nine "bad." That doesn't say much for my ability to adjust well to a given situation.	In the future I'd like to try to build my self-image so that I will be capable of accepting and utilizing change in my life in a positive way. A way in which I can do this is through my self-talk — what I tell myself about occurrences. The given (A) situation is a continuing occurrence — it happens at least once every summer. Having worked on the problem since September, I've begun to realize what I need to do in this situation to make myself happy. I need to see myself happy. I need to see myself as a strong, self-sufficient, happily functioning person — with a "separate" life and identity from Tom. Since these qualities (strength, independence, self-sufficiency, etc.) have been hidden in me for some time, I've yet to cultivate them totally, but instead I'm working on them slowly. This, I expect, will make me a more satisfied person, and for others more pleasant and satisfying to be with.

Continued

CASE EXAMPLE *Continued*

(This young woman also wrote the following summary of the usefulness of this approach.)

I used Rational Therapy with the belief that I really did have the power to control my emotions and then, in turn, to control my life. I have always been a person of a negative nature—I had too much to say about all the "bads" and "wrongs" in my life that happened, and too little to say of the good.

I saw myself as a worthless, weak, submissive, and stupid person who really didn't matter in the course of this big world. There was one person who made me feel valuable, and when he left I allowed myself to feel useless again. This was followed by a succession of negative thoughts about myself, and fears.

A strong point of doing an RSA is what I found to be my ability to look at myself objectively on paper. What is written on paper looks factual and truthful. I found myself debating those facts and truths and actually finding out more of how I really felt inside. I had an outsider's view of myself on the objective side. This allowed me to weigh the pros and cons of my behavior, emotions, etc., and to take positive, realistic means to change what I didn't like.

Also doing a Rational Self-Analysis helped me to become, through my problem, more rational and realistic in regard to living my everday life. In a world that is so disproportionate in itself, I find it easy to stretch many aspects of my personal life out of proportion. A rational self-analysis doesn't allow one to do that. A person must face the facts, debate the arguments of his behavior and emotions, and determine what he chooses to feel from there on. A rational self-analysis allows only honesty and a willingness to change those feelings that one is not comfortable with. A person who does his rational self-analysis dishonestly will get nowhere.

Ultimately, Rational Therapy taught me the power of control. A human person is a complex, highly intelligent organism. Then why should he not have the power of controlling what could turn out to be his own destiny in life?

An excerpt from my journal, December 1, 1977:

Inside myself, I guess that I'm really satisfied with the person I'm becoming. Sure, it can be a long, hard struggle at times, and often frustrating, but it is a part of my life. That is how things become important and significant in life—through the living of such experiences. Sometimes I'm amazed when I think that I was born a person in my own right, with potential emotional growth, strength, and abilities to become what I choose to become.

This case example is reprinted from Charles Zastrow, *Talk to Yourself: Using the Power of Self-Talk*, © 1979, pp. 99–105. Reprinted by permission of Prentice-Hall, Inc., Englewood Cliffs, New Jersey.

Do you give yourself these types of positive self-talk, or do you give yourself the following negative kinds of self-talk, which are characteristic of those with a "failure identity"?: "I can't accomplish anything I try." "I'm inferior to other people." "Why can't I be as competent, capable, or attractive as others?" "I'm a failure." "I can't afford to risk trying anything new as it will reveal my weaknesses to others." "I wish people would stop picking on me, and making cutting comments about my shortcomings." "I've got a number of personal problems that are overwhelming me, and draining my energy." "There just is no hope for a brighter tomorrow." "My problems are certainly more confusing and unresolvable than those that other people have." "Life is certainly the 'pits' and really not worth living." "I wish I was someone else." "I wonder why such and such hurt me so badly—I just can't stop thinking about it." "What did I do wrong to deserve all this misery?"

Such self-talk by people with failure orientations generates a variety of negative emotions, including excessive worry, fatigue, anxiety, boredom, depression, loneliness, and/or general feelings of misery.

Merlin Manley (1977, p. 38) also notes:

A sense of failure becomes a further problem since it limits the amount of risk-taking behavior in which we are willing to engage. If we feel that we are failures, we will feel threatened by any new behavior patterns that we perceive as risky. Accordingly, we will be very reluctant to try any such behaviors. This means that we will continue to operate as we have in the past, thereby creating somewhat of a "rut." To the degree that we follow this practice, we are precluded from growing psychologically or expanding our behavioral responses. We are stultifying ourselves from greater use of our potential and becoming a more complete individual. We learn and grow by our experiences. If we limit ourselves to only the "tried and true" modes of behavior, we are putting disabling constraints on ourselves and seriously limiting our growth potential.

In order to be an "encouraging" person in working with clients, and to feel good about yourself, it is essential to have a positive, success self-concept. There is a very simple formula for improving the lives of people who view themselves as failures; they need to shift their thinking from focusing on negative items to focusing on positive items.

One way of changing a failure identity into a success identity is to identify the failure self-talk, and then challenge this with rational self-talk (see Chapter 18 for how to write a rational self-analysis). A feeling of being a failure is an emotion. Similar to any other emotion, the feeling of being a failure results mainly from a certain kind of self-talk, and the emotion can be changed by rational self-challenges.

SUMMARY

This chapter presents material on how to survive and enjoy social work and in a broader sense, on how to enjoy living.

Although social work students have a number of common concerns, they often are reluctant to share these concerns with others. The following concerns are discussed, with suggestions given for resolving them: Will I be able to make it in field placement? Will I be able to handle my first interview with my first client? I'm really depressed as my supervisor is able to handle an interview much better than I—I doubt whether I'll ever be able to do that well. How should I separate the role of being a counselor from that of being a friend? How can I avoid becoming too emotionally involved with clients' problems? Do I really want to pursue a career in social work?

Burnout is increasingly being recognized as a major problem encountered by professionals, particularly by professionals employed in human services. The symptoms and causes of burnout are discussed and suggestions given for reducing stress at work and preventing burnout.

There are basic structural conflicts between helping professionals and the bureaucratic systems in which they work. Helping professionals want bureaucratic systems to individualize interactions with clients and employees, to be humanized, to be democratic in decision making, to be relationship-oriented, and to quickly change to meet emerging needs. On the other hand, bureaucratic systems are generally depersonalized, autocratic, procedures- and process-oriented, emotionally detached, and resistive of change. Such differences in orientations have the potential of becoming arenas of conflict between helping professionals and the systems they work in. A number of suggestions are given on how to survive in a bureaucracy.

The chapter ends with providing tips on how to enjoy social work and life. The value of positive thinking is described. Also, the importance of developing a sense of who you are and what you want out of life is discussed and suggestions are given for developing such an indentity. Having a failure identity is contrasted with having a success identity, and a Rational Self-Analysis is presented as one approach that is useful in challenging and changing a failure identity.

EXERCISES

1. *Common Concerns of Social Work Students*

GOALS: Practically every student has concerns about field placement and about pursuing social work as a career. This exercise is designed to help students realize their concerns are common and to help students become more comfortable with their concerns.

Step 1: Describe the purposes of this exercise. Briefly indicate common concerns of students including the following:

a. Will I be able to make it in field placement?
b. I really wonder if I will be able to handle my first interview with my first client adequately.
c. I'm really depressed as my supervisor is able to handle an interview much better than I—I doubt whether I'll ever be able to do that well.
d. How should I separate the role of being a counselor from that of being a friend?
e. How can I avoid becoming too emotionally involved with clients' problems?
f. Do I really want to have a career in social work?

Indicate that while students think their concerns are unique, these concerns are generally common to practically all students. Through analyzing and discussing concerns, information can generally be provided that will help students become more comfortable with them.

Step 2: Ask students to write on a note card or a sheet of paper a few concerns they have about field placement or about pursuing social work as a career. Indicate to students they should not place their names on what they write.

Step 3: Anonymously collect these concerns. Read each concern, and together with the class, seek to provide information that will provide at least partial answers to each concern. (Partial answers to a number of concerns are provided in the first section of this chapter.)

2. Reducing Stress and Preventing Burnout

GOAL: This exercise is designed to help students reduce stress and prevent burnout.

Step 1: Describe the purpose of this exercise. Using the material in this chapter, define stress and burnout. Indicate that burnout is one reaction to high stress levels. Also summarize a variety of strategies to reduce stress and prevent burnout. (These strategies are outlined in this chapter. It may be helpful to prepare and distribute a handout that identifies these strategies.)

Step 2: Ask students to write answers to the following questions on a sheet of paper:

a.   A few students that are presently causing high levels of stress in my life are:
b.   My current ways of handling these high levels of stress are:
c.   Ways in which I could better handle these situations and become more relaxed are:

Step 3: Ask students to form subgroups of three and have them share what they wrote. Indicate that the subgroups may be able to offer additional suggestions on how to handle the stress-producing situations and on how to relax. Also indicate that each student has a right to privacy and is not expected to self-disclose what he wants to keep private.

Step 4: After the subgroups have concluded their discussions, ask whether there are questions or comments about what was discussed in the subgroups.

3. Establishing a Sense of Identity

GOAL: This exercise is designed to help students establish a better sense of self and to help them determine what they want out of life.

Step 1: Describe the purpose of this exercise. Indicate forming a sense of "who we are" is probably the most important psychological need we face. Indicate that while we cannot change the past, what we want out of the future, along with our motivation to achieve what we want, is more important (than our past experiences) in determining what our future will be.

Step 2: Indicate that one way to find out who we are and what we want out of life is to arrive at answers to the fifteen questions listed on identity formation in this chapter. Distribute a questionnaire which lists these questions and which has space for students to write their answers.

Step 3: Give the students twenty-five to thirty minutes to write down their answers. After this is completed have the students form subgroups of three in which they are asked to share the questions they do not have answers to. Indicate that the subgroups may be able to offer additional ideas on how to arrive at answers to the unanswered questions. Also indicate that each student has a right to privacy and is not expected to share what he wants to keep private.

Step 4: After the subgroups have concluded their discussions, ask whether there are any questions or comments.

4. Positive and Negative Thinking Become Self-Fulfilling Prophecies

GOAL: This exercise is designed to help students become aware that positive and negative thinking often become self-fulfilling prophecies.

Step 1: Indicate the purpose of the exercise. Indicate that we always have a choice of thinking either positively or negatively about events that happen to us. Also indicate that both positive and negative thinking frequently become self-fulfilling prophecies. For example, if we go for a job interview and think we have a good chance to get the job, we will be more relaxed and probably better able to sell ourselves. If we think negatively, we will be more anxious and probably less able to present ourselves with confidence. Additional examples may be given.

Step 2: Ask the students to write on a sheet of paper a situation in which positive thinking led to a self-fulfilling prophecy for themselves or for someone close to them. Also ask the students to write a situation in which negative thinking led to a self-fulfilling prophecy for themselves or for someone close to them.

Step 3: Ask for volunteers to share what they wrote. Also ask the class if they are aware of any situations where (*a*) positive thinking led to undesirable results, and (*b*) negative thinking resulted in desirable consequences.

III

CONTEMPORARY

THEORIES

OF

COUNSELING

13

PSYCHOANALYSIS

An effective social worker needs to have a knowledge of comprehensive counseling theories[1] and specialized treatment techniques to be able to diagnose precisely what problems exist and how to intervene effectively. There are a number of contemporary comprehensive counseling approaches, including psychoanalysis, client-centered therapy, rational therapy, behavior modification, Gestalt therapy, reality therapy, and transactional analysis. These therapy approaches generally present theoretical material on (*a*) personality theory, or how normal psychosocial development occurs; (*b*) behavior pathology, or how emotional problems arise; and (*c*) therapy, or how to change disturbed behavior.

An effective counselor generally knows several treatment approaches and, depending on the unique set of problems being presented by the client, is able to pick and choose from a "bag of tricks" the intervention strategy apt to have the highest probability of success. In addition to comprehensive counseling approaches, there are a number of specialized treatment techniques for specific problems: assertiveness training for people who are shy or overly aggressive; muscle relaxation training for people under stress or suffering from a variety of psychosomatic problems; and parent effectiveness training for parent-child relationship difficulties. An effective worker strives to gain a working knowledge of a wide variety of treatment techniques in order to increase the likelihood of being able to help clients.

This chapter and the next several chapters summarize contemporary approaches to counseling and illustrate with case examples how each is used. It is practically impossible for a social worker to acquire a working knowledge of all the comprehensive and specialized intervention approaches that are available. These chapters present an overview of the most widely used approaches. As indicated in Chapter 1, instructors (in conjunction with the other program faculty) are urged to select and cover those intervention theories that are most useful for students in their geographic area to learn.

---

[1]A comprehensive counseling theory is a counseling approach that the theorist proposes as being applicable in treating practically all personal problems.

ery personality theorist's hypotheses (and definitely Freud's) are partially related to societal concerns and to internal concerns. Freud's emphasis on sexuality is a reflection of Europe's sexual oppression at this time and also of some of Freud's personal struggles.

Freud graduated from the medical school of Vienna, was married, and had six children. He conducted a searching self-analysis that began in the 1890s and continued throughout his life, had personal conflicts with his parents, and suffered in his later years from cancer of the jaw. Freud had considerable charisma that enabled him to "market" and gain adherents to his views. He also had trouble in interacting with colleagues who questioned aspects of his theories, interactions that often resulted in intense disagreements and a discontinuance of further communication.

A number of authorities have recognized Freud as being one of the greatest contributors to humanity in the twentieth century. Although adherence to psychoanalysis is now waning, between 1920 and 1950 social workers, psychiatrists, and certain psychologists largely believed and adopted his approach to therapy.

Sigmund Freud (1856–1939)

SIGMUND FREUD

The father of psychoanalysis was Sigmund Freud (1924). His theories have had an immense impact on the helping professions, including psychiatry, psychology, and social work.

Freud was born in Moravia, May 6, 1856, and died in London on September 23, 1939. For over seventy years, however, he lived in Vienna and left that city only when the Nazis overran Austria. He developed his theories primarily between 1895–1925, which was the end of the Victorian age (an era of sexual oppression). Ev-

THE MIND

Freud's (1924) conception of the mind was two-dimensional, as indicated in Figure 13.1 (page 344). One dimension of the mind consisted of the *conscious*, the *preconscious*, and the *unconscious*. The second dimension consisted of the *id*, the *superego*, and the *ego*.

Emphasis on the Unconscious

Freud thought that the mind was composed of thoughts (ideas), feelings, instincts, drives, conflicts, and motives. Most of these elements in the mind were thought to be located in the unconscious or preconscious. Elements in the preconscious area had a fair chance of becoming conscious, while elements in the unconscious were unlikely to arise to a person's conscious

FIGURE 13.1

Freud's Conception of the Mind

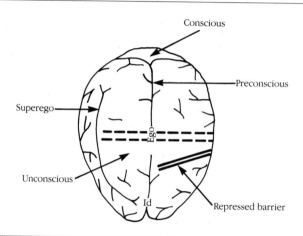

mind. The small "conscious cap" at the top of this diagram indicates Freud's theory that a person was aware of only a fraction of the total thoughts, drives, conflicts, motives, and feelings in the mind.

The "repressed" area was a barrier under which disturbing material (primarily thoughts and feelings) had been placed by the defense mechanism of repression. Repression was thought by Freud to be the defense mechanism that psychologically caused the most problems. Repression is a process in which unacceptable desires, memories, and thoughts are excluded from consciousness by sending the material into the unconscious under the "repressed" barrier. Once material has been repressed, Freud thought that material has energy and acts as an unconscious irritant, producing unwanted emotions and bizarre behavior, such as anger, nightmares, hallucinations, and enuresis.

The Id, Superego, and Ego

The *id* is the primitive psychic force in the unconscious. At birth a child's mind is thought to be entirely composed of the id. As the child grows older, the ego and superego develop out of, and become differentiated from, the id. The id contains biological instincts. Many of these instincts are viewed as immoral or asocial and need to be controlled by the individual and by the larger society. The id is governed by the pleasure principle; that is, the instincts within the id seek to be expressed regardless of the consequences.

The *superego* normally develops sometime between the ages of three and five, and consists of the traditional values and mores of society that are interpreted to a child by the parents. The superego's main function is to decide whether something is right or wrong. The superego is considered to contain a person's conscience and also his self-ideal (what that person wants to become). When an instinctual demand strives for expression of which the superego disapproves, the superego sends a signal of anxiety to the ego as a warning to prevent the expression of the instinct. The emotion of guilt is said to originate from the superego.

The *ego* begins to develop from the id through experience shortly after birth. The ego acts as the coordinator of the personality, with its major function being to

Definitions of Common Defense Mechanisms Postulated by Psychoanalytic Theory

Defense mechanism   Any *unconscious* attempt to adjust to conditions that are painful; conditions such as anxiety, frustration, and guilt. Defense mechanisms are measures through which a person preserves self-esteem and softens the blow of failure, deprivation, or feelings of guilt.

Compensation   Making up for a real or fancied defect or inferiority by creating a real or fancied achievement or superiority. A common example is an effort to achieve success in one field after failure in another.

Repression   Mechanism through which unacceptable desires, feelings, memories, and thoughts are excluded from consciousness by being sent down deep into the unconscious.

Sublimation   Mechanism whereby consciously unacceptable instinctual demands are channeled into acceptable forms for gratification. For example, aggression can be converted into athletic activity.

Denial   Mechanism whereby a person escapes psychic pain associated with reality by unconsciously rejecting reality. For example, a mother may persistently deny that her child has died.

Identification   Mechanism through which a person takes on the attitudes, behavior, or personal attributes of another person whom he has idealized (parent, relative, popular hero, etc.).

Reaction formation   Development of socially acceptable behavior or attitudes that are the opposite of one's repressed unconscious impulses. Reaction formation is apparent in individuals who turn anal impulses into scrupulous cleanliness.

Regression   Acting in a more childish fashion. This mechanism involves a person's falling back to an earlier phase of development in which he felt secure. Some adults when ill, for example, will act more childish and demanding with the unconscious goal of having others around them give them more care and attention.

Projection   Mechanism through which a person unconsciously attributes his own unacceptable ideas or impulses to another. For example, a person who has an urge to hurt others may turn it around and consciously feel that others are trying to hurt him.

Rationalization   Mechanism by which an individual, faced with frustrations or with criticism of his actions, finds justification for them by disguising from himself (as he hopes to disguise from others) his true motivations. Often this is accomplished by a series of excuses that are believed by the person. For example, a student who fails an exam may blame it on poor teaching, having to work, and so on, rather than consciously acknowledging the real reasons.

Undoing   Mechanism whereby when a person feels guilty about some act or wish, he acts or speaks in a manner reflecting the reverse of some act or wish. For example, a spouse who has been unfaithful may react by being overly attentive to his mate.

Isolation   The separation of an object (idea, experience, or memory) from the emotions associated with it, resulting in showing no emotion to the object. This mechanism makes it possible for a person to avoid the pain of anxiety, shame, or guilt. For example, a person uses this mechanism when he is able to discuss a violent act he has committed without showing any emotion.

Fantasy formation   Involves using fantasy to dull the pain of reality. For example, an unhappy child in an adopted family may fantasize that his natural parents are exalted, loving people who will one day rescue him.

find the least painful balance between meeting the desires/demands of the id, the superego, and the outside world. It operates on the basis of the reality principle, which is to achieve a balance between id instincts, the demands of the superego, and the demands of society.

An example may help to illustrate how the id, superego, and ego function. Suppose a sex instinct seeks expression from the id of a teenager. The superego will note the instinct is seeking to be expressed and will send a signal of anxiety to the ego to inform it that an "evil" instinct is seeking expression. This will alert the ego that such expression will lead to condemnation from the superego. The ego is then in a crisis and usually functions defensively to handle the instinct. On one hand the ego has severe pressure from the id to allow the instinct to be expressed; on the other it is aware that a direct expression will lead to condemnation from the superego and probably also from the outside world. The ego has to choose between various options. These options include letting the instinct be directly expressed (for example, through intercourse or self-stimulation), which will probably lead to condemnation from the superego and society. Another option is for the ego to do nothing; the result is that the energy from the sexual instinct (which in this case is not allowed to be expressed) is then transformed into anxiety. (Freud thought anxious people were generally sexually frustrated.) A third option is to use a defense mechanism. For example, sublimation might be used by the ego. *Sublimination* is the mechanism whereby consciously unacceptable instinctual demands are channeled into acceptable forms for gratification — in this case the sexual instinct might be expressed by channeling the energy of the sexual instinct into athletic activity. Or, the mechanism of repression might be used whereby the sexual instinct is sent down deep into the unconscious under the "repressed" barrier.

THE LIBIDO   The energy of the biological instincts is called the *libido*. This energy is conceived as being primarily sexual energy. The libido is the unit that gives energy to a person's personality. In various writings Freud vacillated between locating the libido in the ego and locating it in the id. For Freud, the location of the libido was a vexing dilemma: if he claimed the libido was located in the ego, he could not explain where the id obtained its energy, and vice versa.

EROS AND THANATOS   In his early writings Freud thought that humans primarily had only sexual instincts (also called Eros). Unable to explain sadism (pleasure from hurting others) and masochism (pleasure from being hurt), Freud in his later writings identified a second type of instinct (Thanatos), which he indicated was the death instinct. He was then able to explain masochistic and sadistic behavior in terms of fulfilling the death instinct's focus on seeking to return to an inorganic state, either by hurting oneself or by seeing others hurt.

EMPHASIS ON SEXUALITY   Partly because of the oppression of sexual expression in Freud's time, Freud came to realize that many people had sexual conflicts. He made sexuality a focus of his theories and defined most emotions and behaviors as being primarily sexual in nature. Freud thought sexuality included physical love, affectionate impulses, self-love, love for parents and children, and friendship associations. Freud believed sexual excitement originates from diverse sources: stimulation of an erogenous zone (an erogenous zone could be located on any part of the body — an example would be "tingling sensations" on an ear), expression of an impulse (e.g., laughing), muscular activity (e.g., running), emotional excitements (e.g., fear or happiness), and intellectual work. (As can be seen from these examples, Freud had an exceedingly broad definition of the components of human sexuality.)

PSYCHOSEXUAL DEVELOPMENT (PESONALITY DEVELOPMENT)

1. Oral Stage

This phase extends from birth to approximately eighteen months. This stage is called *oral* because the primary activities of a child are centered around feeding and the organs (mouth, lips, and tongue) connected with that function. Feeding is considered to be an important area of conflict, and a child's attention is focused on receiving and taking. People fixated at this stage are thought to have the most severe personality disorders, such as schizophrenia or psychotic depression. (By the term *fixated* Freud meant that a person's personality development is largely, though not completely, halted at the stage that is specified.)

2. Anal Stage

Between ages eighteen months to three years a child's activities are mainly focused on giving and withholding, primarily connected with retaining and passing feces. Bowel training is an important area of conflict. People fixated at this stage have such character traits as messiness, stubbornness, rebelliousness; or they may have a *reaction formation* and have such opposite traits as being meticulously clean and excessively punctual.

3. Phallic Stage

From the third through the fifth year the child's attention shifts to the genitals. Prominent activities of the child are pleasurable sensations from genital stimulation, showing off one's body, and looking at the bodies of others. Also, a child's personality becomes more complex during this stage. Although still self-centered, the child wants to possess those who give him pleasure. He becomes more curious, wants to love and be loved, and seeks to be admired. Character traits that are apt to develop from fixation at this stage are pride, promiscuity, and self-hatred.

Boys and girls experience separate complexes during this stage. Boys encounter an Oedipus complex. (Freud took many of his terms from Greek mythology. *Oedipus Rex* was a Greek drama in which Oedipus, who had been raised by foster parents, unwittingly kills his father, marries his mother, and then undergoes severe psychological trauma when he discovers what he's done.)

The *Oedipus complex* refers to the dilemma faced by every son at this stage when he falls sexually in love with his mother and has antagonism toward his father,

whom he views as a rival for her affections. As the intensity of these relationships mounts, the son increasingly suffers from castration anxiety; that is, he fears his father is going to discover his "affair" with his mother and then remove his genitals. Successful resolution of the Oedipus complex occurs through defense mechanisms. A typical resolution is for the son to first *repress* his feelings of love for his mother and his hostile feelings toward his father. Next, the son has a *reaction formation* in which he stops viewing his father negatively, but now turns this around and has positive feelings toward his father. The final step is for the son to *identify* with his father, and thereby seek to take on the attitudes, values, and behavior patterns of his father. Freud also asserted that the resolution of this complex results in the formation of the superego. (Precisely how the resolution of this complex results in the formation of the superego has not been clarified.)

Girls undergo an *Electra complex* during this phallic stage. (Freud, as you will see, would not be very popular with the feminist movement if he were advancing his theories at the present time.) The name *Electra* was taken from a Greek drama. Electra assisted her brother in avenging their father's death by slaying their mother — this mother had conspired with her lover to murder her husband.

Freud believed girls fall sexually in love with their father during this stage and also view their mother with antagonism. Because of these relationships, girls also suffer from castration anxiety, but the nature of this anxiety is different from that for boys. Castration anxiety in a girl results from the awareness that she lacks a penis. She then concludes she was castrated in infancy and blames her mother for this. Freud went on to theorize that because girls believe they have been castrated they come to regard themselves as inferior to boys (have penis envy). From this point on they perceive their role in life to be submissive and supportive of males. Freud did not identify the precise processes for resolution of the Electra complex in girls.

4. Latency Stage

This stage usually begins at the time when the Oedipus/Electra complexes are resolved, and ends with puberty.

The sexual instinct is relatively unaroused during this stage. The child can now be socialized and becomes involved in the educational process and in learning skills.

5. Genital Stage

This stage occurs from puberty to death. It involves mature sexuality and the person reaching this stage is fully able to love and to work. Again, we see Freud's emphasis on sexuality and on the work ethic, which was part of the "Protestant Ethic" and highly valued in Freud's era.

PSYCHOPATHOLOGICAL DEVELOPMENT (DEVELOPMENT OF EMOTIONAL AND BEHAVIORAL PROBLEMS)

Freud theorized that disturbances can arise from several sources. One source is traumatic experiences that a person's ego is not able to cope with directly and thereby strives to resolve using such defense mechanisms as repression. The problem with using repression is that there is energy associated with the repressed material that then unconsciously acts as an irritant. Breuer and Freud (1895) provide an example of a woman named Anna O. who developed a psychosomatic paralysis of her right arm. Anna O. was sitting by her father's bedside (her father was gravely ill) when she dozed off and had a nightmare that a big black snake was attacking her father. She awoke terrified and hastily repressed her thoughts and feelings about this nightmare for fear of alarming her father. During the time she was asleep her right arm was resting over the back of a chair and became "numb." Freud theorized that the energy connected with the repressed material then took over physiological control of her arm, and a psychological paralysis resulted.

In addition to unresolved traumatic events, Freud thought that internal unconscious processes could also cause disturbances. There is a range of possible sources. An unresolved Electra or Oedipal complex could lead to a malformed superego; it could also lead a person to have a variety of sexual problems — such as frigidity, promiscuity, sexual dysfunctions, excessive sexual fantasies, and nightmares with sexual content. Unresolved internal conflicts (e.g., an unconscious liking and hatred of one's parents) may be another source that causes such behavioral problems as hostile and aggressive behavior and such emotional problems as temper tantrums. Fixations at early stages of development are additional sources that largely prevent development at later stages and lead the person to display such undesirable personality traits as messiness or stubbornness. (It should be noted Freud thought that traumatic experiences are important contributing factors in leading to internal conflicts and fixations.)

As indicated earlier, the main source of anxiety is thought to be sexual frustration. Freud thought that anxiety arises when a sexual instinct seeks expression, but the ego blocks its expression. If the instinct is not then diverted through defense mechanisms, the energy connected with sexual instincts is transformed into anxiety.

Obsessions (a recurring thought such as a song repeatedly on one's mind) and compulsions (such as an urge to step on every crack of a sidewalk) are thought to be mechanisms through which a person works off energy connected with disturbing unconscious material.

For all types of mental disorders, unconscious processes (including fixations, internal conflicts, and defense mechanisms) are thought to be the causes. These disturbing unconscious processes are almost always connected with traumatic experiences, particularly traumatic experiences during childhood that are repressed.

PSYCHOANALYSIS (THEORY OF THERAPY)

The goal of psychoanalysis is to discover the disturbing unconscious processes and bring them into the conscious part of the patient's mind so that the unconscious emotion (or energy) can be expressed (and thereby dissipated) and the disturbing unconscious ideas (now conscious) can be "worked through" (dealt with). Often, Freud thought, emotional disturbances are the result of pent-up, undischarged emotional tension connected with the repressed memory of a traumatic childhood sexual experience.

Psychoanalysis is a long process, generally because a chain of traumatic events stemming deep into the past is believed to be the determinant of each symptom. To treat a patient it is necessary to bring the memory of these traumatic experiences to the conscious part of the patient's mind to bring about an emotional catharsis (release of pent-up energy) and to allow the person to consciously handle the disturbing ideas connected with the trauma. For example, in the case of Anna O. (cited earlier), Freud (Breuer and Freud, 1895) asserted that her arm became psychologically paralyzed due to the repression of the nightmare of a snake attacking her father. The paralyzed right arm was viewed as a *symptom* of unconscious processes that stemmed deep into Anna O.'s past. Freud asserted that the paralysis of the right arm disappeared when Anna, through psychoanalysis, remembered the nightmare, had an emotional catharsis, and was able to then consciously deal with having such a nightmare. However, Freud asserted only the symptom (paralyzed arm) of her emotional disturbance was treated by remembering this event. Freud believed Anna was still rather severely disturbed as the underlying unconscious processes that had caused this symptom still remained. Therefore the aim of psychoanalysis is to treat not only the symptoms but also the unconscious processes that are viewed as causing the symptoms. These disturbing, unconscious processes generally stem from traumatic experiences that occurred far back in a person's past. The goal with Anna O., as with other patients, is to bring the unconscious memory of each of these traumatic events to a person's conscious mind so that an emotional catharsis can occur, and through such an awareness or insight, a person can consciously handle the disturbing ideas. In Anna's case, Freud believed that Anna's nightmare of a snake indicated an unresolved Electra complex. Freud believed that snakes in dreams are a symbol for the male sex organ. Anna's

nightmare involving a snake suggested to Freud that Anna had sexual conflicts, probably stemming from repressed childhood sexual traumas. Freud thus sought with all his patients to have them become aware of (gain insight into) these traumatic experiences.

To discover such unconscious processes, Freud (1924) used four main techniques: hypnosis, free association, dream analysis, and transference.

Hypnosis

An early technique that he used was *hypnosis*. However, he soon discarded this technique because many of his patients could not be hypnotized. Also, for even those patients that could be hypnotized, Freud usually did not know the exact date and time a traumatic event had occurred so he did not know where to direct a patient's attention. (Hypnosis is further described in Chapter 22.)

Free Association

A second technique that Freud used was *free association*. In free association a patient is instructed to say whatever comes to mind, no matter how trivial the thought or association may seem. It is thought that if patients can let their minds associate while relaxed, their defenses will also be relaxed; therefore, disturbing unconscious material will have a much greater chance of coming into a person's conscious mind. To facilitate this relaxed state, patients usually lie on a couch without looking at the analyst. Patients then make free associations with dreams, traumatic experiences, thoughts, feelings, fantasies, anything that comes to mind. At times patients remember traumatic events that occurred far back in their past, have an emotional cartharsis, and together with the analyst "work through" the disturbing ideas. Usually after about forty-five minutes of associating, and occasionally during associating, the analyst helps the patient gain insight into the meaning of some associations by attempting to interpret the psychological significance in terms of the pychoanalytic framework of what was being

CASE EXAMPLE

Sybil

Perhaps the most widely known case treated by psychoanalysis in recent years was that of Sybil Dorsett (Schreiber, 1973). (Sybil's name is a pseudonym.) Sybil was a young woman living in New York City who exhibited sixteen different personalities, most of whom were unaware the other personalities existed. The main personality was Sybil, who was fairly depressed, quiet, nonassertive and plain-looking in appearance. Fifteen other personalities were occasionally exhibited. Only a few will be mentioned. Vicky was a self-assured, sophisticated, attractive blonde. Peggy Lou was an assertive, enthusiastic, and often angry pixie with a pug nose and a Dutch haircut. Vanessa was a very attractive redhead who was intensely dramatic. Mike was one of Sybil's two male selves, who had dark hair and who was a builder and carpenter. Clara was intensely religious and highly critical of Sybil.

The reason that Sybil developed these multiple personalities was explained as being the only way she could give expression during her childhood years to different aspects of herself. Also, the analyst states that Sybil would probably have become mentally ill had she not developed these different personalities.

Sybil had a very traumatic childhood. She was born and raised in a small midwestern town and had parents who were prominent and wealthy. Her father was described as religious, weak, and nonassertive. The main source of Sybil's problems stemmed from her mother, Hattie. In outward appearance Hattie presented an image of being deeply religious and proper. But her private life and her interactions with Sybil were startling. A few of Hattie's bizarre actions in Sybil's childhood years will be mentioned. Hattie, on some summer evenings, would take Sybil for a walk, and occasionally Hattie would defecate with perverse pleasure on the lawns, behind bushes, of other wealthy people. She occasionally baby-sat for children in the neighborhood. With some of the girls she played "horsey" and put her finger in their vaginas while yelling "Giddyap." With some of the young boys she held and moved them between her hips stimulating her genitals. She was at times very abusive to Sybil. She forced objects such as a flashlight and a dinner knife into Sybil's genitals. She filled her rectum at times with water, and pressed a hot flat iron on Sybil's hand. At times she put Sybil in a trunk in an attic, closed the lid, and let her lie there for awhile in

said—for example, pointing out that dreaming of clambering out of water is a symbol for the birth process (Freud, 1924, p. 160). The analyst, during the association, listens to the patient and unobtrusively observes emotional reactions such as signs of distress or resistance to the treatment.

Dream Analysis

A third technique was *dream analysis*. Freud believed the focus of dreams centered around unfilled wishes. (If you got a grade on an exam that you were satisfied with, you would not be apt to dream about it; but if you order to show her what it was like to be dead. At another time she threatened to put Sybil's hand in a meat grinder. A favorite ritual of Hattie was to tie up Sybil, suspend her from the ceiling, and then fill her urethra and bladder with cold water. Hattie abused her in many other ways, for example by not allowing her to go to the bathroom and then beating her when she soiled herself. Another time she tied a scarf around Sybil's neck until she gasped for breath. There were other times when she stuffed a damp wash rag down Sybil's throat and put cotton in her nose until Sybil lost consciousness. At other times Hattie was warm and loving toward Sybil, and gave the neighbors the impression she was a model mother. Many times Hattie preached to Sybil and admonished her to behave in a prudish and puritanical manner. In such an environment it was hypothesized that Sybil developed multiple personalities as a way of coping with these abuses, as a way of giving expression to her wishes and desires and to different aspects of herself, as a way of developing and growing, and as a way to avoid becoming mentally ill.

Sybil was in analysis for eleven years. The analyst used hypnosis, dream analysis, free assocation, and transference to assist Sybil in recollecting these traumatic experiences that had been repressed into her unconscious. Also used was sodium pentothal, a barbituate drug, which helped enable Sybil to remember the experiences. The aim of analysis was to help Sybil relive these traumas. Reliving each of these experiences released the energy or emotion of these painful experiences and also led to increased insights. Delving into the past in this manner enabled the analyst, Dr. Cornelia Wilbur, to understand the reasons that each of these personalities emerged. The process of integrating all these personalities into one integrated personality (the new Sybil) was largely accomplished through hypnosis. Dr. Wilbur first gradually suggested to each of the personalities, individually, that they were growing older and older until each became thirty-seven years old (Sybil's age at that time). Then Sybil was placed in a deep hypnotic sleep, and each of the different personalities (over several months) were introduced to her and she was given the suggestion that she would remember each and that each would become part of her. The reintegration into one personality was fraught with resistances from some of the personalities and required a few more years of analysis. Gradually a new, integrated Sybil emerged. After the integration of her personalities, Sybil continued her education, graduated from college, and eventually secured a college teaching position.

---

strongly desired a higher grade, you would tend to dream about it.) Freud thought dreams are a royal road to the unconscious, as a person's defenses against allowing unconscious material into the conscious part of the mind are relaxed while dreaming. Freud believed there are two distinct types of content in dreams: manifest content and latent content. The dream as remembered upon awakening is the manifest content. Psychologically, the manifest content is not the significant portion of the dream, since in the process of becoming conscious, it has undergone considerable distortion in order to make it more acceptable to the dreamer's conscious self. The latent or hidden content is much more important and must be discovered by searching deep below the surface of the manifest content.

This depth analysis is accomplished in two ways. The first way is to have the patient free associate around elements within the dream. Presumably the elements have some hidden significance that may be uncovered by the patient as she free associates about her thoughts and feelings related to these elements.

The second method for discovering the latent content is symbol analysis. Since the meaning of many symbols in dreams varies from individual to individual, the meaning of symbols must be determined in relation to the psyche of the individual dreamer. Yet there are certain symbols that have similar meanings for nearly everyone. The majority of symbols in dreams are sexual. Parents appear in dreams as king and queen, or as other exalted personages. Clothes and uniforms stand for nakedness. The male sex organ appears in the form of poles, sticks, steeples, snakes, or some other pointed object. The female genitals are symbolized as trunks, caves, enclosed places, and pocketbooks. Children and sisters and brothers are symbolized by little animals or vermin. Dying is indicated by setting out on a journey or traveling by train (Freud, 1924).

Transference

Another approach that Freud used to discover disturbing unconscious processes was *transference*. In psychoanalysis an analyst seeks to be an unobtrusive, neutral person who does not reveal herself. Freud noted that when a patient is in analysis, he will transfer to the analyst feelings and thoughts relating to significant people (usually parent figures) of an earlier period of life. The patient, for example, may react as if he is a small child and the analyst is his father. Transference came to be recognized as an important area of insight as the analyst would observe the transfer and gain an awareness of the patient's unconscious feelings and thoughts about significant people in the patient's past. This insight would then be interpreted to the patient, and further discussed.

Freud believed dreams were a road to the unconscious. Above, The Sleep of Reason Produces Monsters, *an etching by the Spanish artist Francisco Goya.*

When the analyst gains insight into the traumatic events, unconscious conflicts, and fixations of the patient, the process of "working through" begins. Working through involves interpretation to the patient of his difficulties, and is a long process involving repetition, elaboration, and amplification. One or two experiences of insight into the nature of one's conflicts are usually not sufficient to bring about changes. The analysis is continued many times and in many different ways so that the patient increasingly gains insight into the disturbing unconscious. Once insight is achieved it is expected that the patient will be better able to function.

EVALUATION

Freud is to be credited as the person who was most instrumental in developing a worldwide recognition that people who have emotional problems are in need of psychological help. Prior to Freud's time many disturbed people were looked upon as "malingerers" and given little support or understanding. Freud also formulated a theory of personality development that is fairly comprehensive and is still being widely used in assessing human behavior. When Freud began formulating his theories, there was little interest or support for psychological understanding and help for people with personal problems. Freud is to be credited for demonstrating the importance of helping people through "talk" therapy and for inspiring a wide range of other theorists to develop counseling techniques to help people.

There are, however, a number of shortcomings in his theories:

1. Most of his concepts are difficult to operationalize (test out) so his hypotheses are difficult to prove or disprove. For example, there is no way to determine scientifically whether the following hypothesized concepts ever exist: the death instinct, Oedipal complex, penis envy, castration anxiety, Electra complex, superego, libido, fixation at the phallic stage of development, and an unconscious conflict.

2. Research has shown that patients undergoing psychoanalysis have a *lower* rate of improving than people with comparable problems who receive no treatment (Eysenck, 1965)! This startling result has been found in a number of reviews on outcome studies on psychoanalysis (Stuart, 1970; Arlow, 1989). The reason for these discouraging results may be that when a person has a problem, such as being depressed, undergoing psychoanalysis may not focus the person's attention on how to handle the personal problem better but instead may lead a person to become more disturbed by worrying about having some of the mystical problems implied by psychoanalysis, such as an anal fixation, an unresolved Electra complex, castration anxiety, a death instinct, or an unconscious desire to retaliate against one's parents (Stuart, 1970).

3. Little attention is given by Freud to personality development beyond puberty. Other authorities have noted that personality development and changes occur throughout life (Hall and Lindzey, 1957). In another area, other theorists have noted conscience development occurs throughout life, rather than occurring as Freud suggests between the third and fifth year of life (Maddi, 1968).

4. Psychoanalytic theory is somewhat culture bound, particularly Freud's emphasis on sexuality. Freud lived in an era of sexual oppression, a time when many people had sexual concerns. Other theorists have noted that factors in addition to sexual instincts are driving forces in personality development. Rogers (1951), for example, discusses a self-actualization motive that strives to develop one's capacities to the fullest. Glasser (1972) indicates that the need to form an identity is a primary factor in personality development.

5. Psychoanalysis is time-consuming and expensive. A complete analysis takes several years with the patient seeing the analyst once or twice a week. Who can afford the time and the money (usually over $120 per hour) to see an analyst?

A few final comments will be made about the case of Sybil.[2] Multiple personality cases are very rare. Sybil's life was indeed startling, and the book and the TV movie that followed were engrossing. The psychoanalytic interpretation was indeed fascinating. But is it accurate? And is it the only interpretation of the case that can be made? Certainly other intepretations are possible. Sybil was in analysis for eleven years, a very long time. This writer can only raise some questions. Being in analysis for such a long time certainly gave Sybil considerable emotional support for her concerns. This writer wonders whether Sybil did not develop at least some of her different personalities to

---

[2]The author is presenting this alternative explanation of Sybil's problematic behavior to convey that the same facts can often be explained in very different ways. Which explanation is more accurate—the psychoanalytic or the author's—is unknown. In fact, other explanations could probably be presented. Research is needed on counseling theories to determine which framework is more accurate. As will be seen in this case example, different explanations suggest radically different intervention approaches by therapists.

attempt to keep her analyst interested and to continue the therapy she was receiving. In reading the book, I wondered whether Sybil was not in fact aware of the other personalities, but played these different *roles* to get attention and to try to meet certain psychological needs that she had. (This writer has worked with a number of people who developed elaborate contrived stories—and if they received positive responses from enacting these roles, they continued to play these roles.) Also, if Sybil was truly unaware of the other personalities within her, would not a more effective treatment approach have been to videotape the different personalities and then play this back to her? Such an approach would have confronted her directly with the other personalities. Also it might have been helpful to videotape the transformations from one personality to another (changing hairdos, clothes, and makeup takes time). This videotape could be played back to her and discussed. It would have been useful, it would seem, to get her thoughts on why she was switching to another personality, and to get her views on when one personality loses recognition and another is emerging.

It is very difficult to believe that Sybil was not aware of the other personalities within her. Some had long hair, while others had short hair. Some were blonde, some were redheads, and some had dark hair. Each personality dressed differently. Sybil must have had an apartment full of different clothes and wigs. How could she not be aware there were other personalities when she could see all these clothes and wigs? A more logical interpretation would seem to be that Sybil intentionally played different roles, and knew exactly what she was doing.

In reviewing this case I question whether Sybil had a loss of memory of her other personalities. I remember supervising a student for a field placement in a probation and parole setting who was assigned a woman arrested for theft. The woman claimed to be a "kleptomaniac" who had no memory of taking things. The student asked for advice on how to handle this case. I suggested the woman's so-called loss of memory might be a "con act" to have people feel sorry for her. My suggestion was to inform this woman that if she claimed she didn't remember taking things, the judge would probably find her "mentally ill" and send her to a mental hospital for an indefinite period of time. The student intern tried this and the woman's memory of taking the stolen items dramatically returned.

SUMMARY

Psychoanalysis was developed primarily by Sigmund Freud. Freud theorized that we pass through the following psychosexual development stages: oral, anal, phallic, latency, and genital.

For all types of mental disorders he thought that unconscious processes (including fixations, internal conflicts, and defense mechanisms) were the causes. These disturbing unconscious processes were almost always connected with traumatic experiences, particularly traumatic experiences during childhood that were repressed.

The goal of psychoanalysis is to discover the disturbing unconscious processes and bring them into the conscious part of the patient's mind so that the unconscious emotion (or energy) can be expressed and so that the disturbing unconscious ideas (now conscious) can be dealt with or worked through by the patient.

Psychoanalysis is a long process, as generally a chain of traumatic events stemming far back into the past is believed to be the determinant of each symptom. To treat a patient it is necessary to bring the memory of these traumatic experiences to the conscious part of the patient's mind, to bring about an emotional catharsis, and to allow the person consciously to work through the disturbing thoughts connected with the trauma. In order to bring such unconscious material to the conscious part of the mind, psychoanalysis uses the following treatment techniques: hypnosis, free association, dream analysis, and transference.

Freud played a major role in developing a worldwide recognition that people who have emotional problems are in need of psychological help. While Freud's concepts and theories about human behavior are still frequently used by social workers in assessing human behavior, very few social workers now use psychoanalysis in counseling clients.

EXERCISES

1. Analyzing Unusual Behavior

GOAL: This exercise is designed to help students analyze unusual human behavior in terms of psychoanalytic concepts.

Step 1: Instruct the students to read this chapter and indicate the purpose of this exercise. Assign a book to read or have the students watch a TV program (such as *Sybil*) that seeks to explain why someone does something unusual.

One possible assignment is to have the students read newsmagazines in order to psychoanalyze why John W. Hinckley shot President Ronald Reagan on March 30, 1981. At the next class session have the students present their psychoanalytic interpretations as to why the selected character did something unusual.

Step 2: Ask the students to suggest alternative explanations for why this selected character did something unusual. If the students are unable to present alternative explanations, the instructor may suggest one or more. End the exercise by asking the students their thoughts on the merits and shortcomings of using psychoanalytic theory to assess human behavior.

2. Word Association

GOAL: This exercise is designed to demonstrate word association, which is a form of free association.

Step 1: Ask for a volunteer to say the first word that comes to mind to a variety of words that you will say.

Step 2: State a word, and then have the volunteer respond with the first word that comes to mind. Below are examples of words you might use:

chair	pepper	salt
room	spoon	fork
grave	love	mountain
blue	red	romance
window	fire	sky
book	lamp	table
sex	relationship	pencil
green	death	money
picture	vacation	stress
gift	college	plant
mother	grief	car
brother	grandmother	summer
marriage	sister	winter

(In saying these words, seek to interchange neutral words, such as "chair," with words that are more apt to have emotional connections, such as "death.")

Step 3: Explain that psychoanalysis uses word association to identify possible areas that a person may have conflicts about. Indicate that psychoanalysis believes possible conflicts are suggested if (*a*) the respondent takes a longer than usual time to respond to a word, (*b*) the respondent gives an unusual response, such as responding with "death" to the word "vacation," and (*c*) the respondent signals with nonverbal cues that a sensitive area may have been touched on. After the word association game is over, indicate that a psychoanalyst would then seek to probe further into possible areas of conflict with the patient.

Step 4: Do not seek to psychoanalyze the volunteer's responses, but in a positive fashion discuss with the students their thoughts about word association.

14

CLIENT-CENTERED THERAPY

T he founder of client-centered therapy is Carl Rogers.[1] Born in Oak Park, Illinois, in 1902, Carl Rogers was the fourth of six children. During most of his childhood years he lived on a farm in Wisconsin. He received a doctorate in clinical psychology from Columbia University (New York City) in 1931 in a highly Freudian atmosphere. Following graduation he was employed for twelve years in a community guidance clinic in Rochester, New York. His work was to diagnose and plan for the delinquent and underprivileged children who were referred by the courts and agencies. During these years Rogers was exposed to a variety of therapy approaches, including psychoanalysis and Otto Rank's functional approach. In 1940 he was offered a full professorship at Ohio State University where he remained for five years. During this time he realized he had developed a distinctive point of view in psychotherapy. In 1942 he published *Counseling and Psychotherapy*, which brought the term *nondirective* (later replaced by *client-centered*) into use. He later published a number of other books, and taught at other campuses, including the University of Chicago and the University of Wisconsin. In 1968 Rogers and some colleagues established their own Center for the Studies of the Person in La Jolla, California. Rogers died in 1987.

Rogers's views have found their way into psychiatry, psychology, social work, and guidance counseling. His contributions to psychotherapy are perhaps most noteworthy in delineating the type of relationship between therapist and client that is conducive to positive therapeutic changes. His emphasis on such concepts as "empathy," "nonjudgmental attitude," "acceptance," and "nonthreatening atmosphere" is prevalent in social work literature.

Rogers was a world figure in humanistic approaches to therapy. (*Humanism* is a philosophy that emphasizes the dignity and worth of people and their capacity for self-realization through reason.) Rogers also became highly involved in trying to inspire humanistic changes in business, education, and marriage.

---

[1] Rogers and his colleagues now prefer the term *person-centered* therapy to *client-centered*, as they believe this term describes more adequately the human values their way of working incorporates.

CARL ROGERS: CENTRAL CONCEPTS

The central hypothesis of client-centered therapy as stated by Meador and Rogers (1979, p. 131) is that

the growth potential of any individual will tend to be released in a relationship in which the helping person is experiencing and communicating realness, caring, and a deeply sensitive nonjudgmental understanding.

Meador and Rogers (1979, p. 131) further add:

The basic theory of person-centered therapy can be stated simply in the form of an "if-then" hypothesis. If certain conditions are present in the attitudes of the person designated "therapist" in a relationship, namely, congruence, positive regard, and empathetic understanding, then growthful change will take place in the person designated "client."

To understand client-centered therapy it is essential to have an understanding of certain terms used by Rogers. Client-centered therapy squarely rests on the assumption that everyone has a *self-actualization motive*. This motive is defined as the inherent tendency of every person (and all organisms) to develop her capacities in ways that serve to maintain or enhance the person (Rogers, 1959). If this assumed motive does not exist, then client-centered therapy's main focus on being *nondirective* would be called into question. Rogers belived a therapist should not make suggestions or interpretations in therapy as he believed the actualizing motive will best guide a client. If this motive does not exist, then there is no rationale for a therapist to be nondirective.

In contrast to Freud, who viewed the basic nature of humans as being "evil" (having immoral, asocial instincts), Rogers viewed the basic nature of humans as being inherently good. Rogers further believed that if a person remains relatively free of influence attempts from others, that person's self-actualization motive will lead him to become a sociable, cooperative, creative, and self-directed person.

The following are definitions of other key concepts in client-centered therapy:

Self concept — One's conception of who one is.

Ideal self — The self-concept that one would like to possess; what one would like to be.

Incongruence between self and experience — A discrepancy that exists between one's self-concept and what one experiences. Example — an individual may perceive herself as outgoing, attractive, and sociable, but when together with others may generally feel ignored. When such a discrepancy exists, a person will feel tension, internal confusion, and anxiety.

Psychological maladjustment — Condition in which a person denies or distorts to awareness, significant experiences. A psychologically maladjusted person is one who has an incongruence between self and experience.

Congruence, congruence of self and experience — Condition in which one's concept of self is consistent with what one experiences.

Need for positive regard — Need to be valued and held in esteem by others.

Need for self-regard — Need to value oneself.

Conditions of worth — Conditions of worth result from the introjection of those values of others that are inconsistent with one's self-actualization motive. A person has conditions of worth when she feels her worth as a person is judged conditionally upon certain behaviors. Those behaviors which she feels valued low on will be avoided. The result is that some behaviors, which are not actually experienced as satisfying, are regarded positively while other behaviors, which are not actually experienced as unsatisfying, are regarded negatively.

Empathy — The capacity to perceive the internal frame of reference of another with accuracy *as if* one were the other person. Example — to sense the hurt or the pleasure of another as that person senses it. Also involved in empathy is the capacity to convey to the other person that you are sensing what that person is feeling.

Unconditional positive regard — To feel unconditional positive regard toward another; to "prize" her. This means to value another, irrespective of the differential values that one might place on her specific behaviors. In therapy this attitude comes in part from the therapist's belief in the inner wisdom of the self-actualization motive, which asserts that the client is best able to decide what courses of action are most advantageous. Showing unconditional positive regard means to communicate respect, warmth, acceptance, liking, caring, and concern for a client, all of which are *not* conditional on what the client says or does.

Genuineness or congruence of therapist — A therapist's being his own self in the therapeutic relationship. To be genuine or congruent the therapist has to read his own inner experiencing and to allow the quality of this inner experiencing to be apparent in the therapeutic relationship. Meador and Rogers (1979, p. 153) state:

Congruence in the therapist's own inner self is his sensing of and reporting his own felt experiencing as he interacts in the relationship. The therapist trusts his own organismic responses in the situation and conveys those feelings of his that he intuitively believes have relevance in the relationship.

Being genuine or congruent is being "real" in a relationship; it is the absence of phoniness and defensiveness. Being genuine means the therapist does not put up a professional front or personal facade.

THEORY OF PERSONALITY DEVELOPMENT AND PSYCHOPATHOLOGY

Developing a theory of personality has not been a primary focus of client-centered theorists. Rogers was more interested in investigating the manner in which personality *changes* come about than in identifying the *causes* of present personality characteristics.

The driving force in personality development is seen by client-centered theorists as the "self-actualiza-

tion motive," which seeks to develop optimally a person's capacities. As an infant grows, the infant's "self-concept" begins to be formed. The development of the self-concept is highly dependent on the individual's *perceptions* of his experiences. The person's perceptions of experiences is influenced by the "need for positive regard" (to be valued by others). The need for positive regard is seen as a universal need in every person (Rogers, 1959). Out of the variety of experiences of frustration or satisfaction of the need for positive regard, the person develops a "sense of self-regard" — that is, a learned sense of self that is based on the perception of the regard he has received from others.

Emotional and behavioral problems develop when the child *introjects* (takes on) those values of others that are inconsistent with his self-actualizing motive. Introjecting values inconsistent with one's self-actualizing motive results in "conditions of worth." For example, a child may introject values from his parents that sex is dirty, or that dancing is bad. Rogers added that a child is apt to be influenced by others because of the need for positive regard.

When a person has conditions of worth the result is that some behaviors are regarded positively (e.g., avoiding all sexual activity) by the person even when they are not internally experienced as unsatisfying. Meador and Rogers (1979, p. 144) then state:

What happens to the actualizing tendency as conditions of worth develop in the self-regard system? The actualizing tendency remains the basic motivation for the individual. However, a conflict develops between his organismic needs and his self-regard needs, now containing conditions of worth. The individual, in effect, is faced with the choice between acting in accord with his organismic sense or censoring the organismic urging and acting in accord with the condition of worth he has learned.

Such conditions of worth lead to an "incongruence between self and experience." For example, a person may feel morally righteous and view himself as being a value setter for refusing to dance or date; however, his peers may consider him a prude with archaic values. When a discrepancy exists between one's self-concept and one's experiences, that person will feel tension, anxiety, and internal confusion.

A person then responds to this "incongruence" in a variety of ways. One way is to use various defense mechanisms. A person may *deny* that experiences are in conflict with his self-concept. Or the person may *distort* or *rationalize* the experiences so that they are then perceived as being consistent with his self-concept. If a person is unable to reduce the inconsistency through such defense mechanisms, the person is forced to face the fact directly that incongruences exist between self and experiences, which will lead the person to feel unwanted emotions (such as anxiety, tension, depression, guilt, or shame.)

If a person has a large or significant degree of incongruence between self and experiences with which the defense mechanisms cannot cope, "disorganization of self" generally occurs (e.g., a "psychotic" breakdown).

THEORY OF THERAPY

Client-centered therapy asserts that the following three therapist attitudes are necessary and sufficient conditions to effect positive change in the client: empathy, positive regard, and genuineness or congruence. It is theorized that whenever a therapist displays these three attitudes toward a client, the actualizing potential of the client will begin to change and grow.

Empathy is the capacity of the therapist to "put herself in the shoes" of the client so that the therapist is able to understand what the client is thinking and feeling. Empathy also involves communicating this understanding to the client.

Unconditional positive regard means that the therapist fully accepts the client and conveys a genuine caring for the client. Involved in positive regard is a nonjudgmental attitude. Also, the therapist does not express approval or disapproval, does not make interpretations, and does not probe unnecessarily. The therapist conveys that he fully trusts the client's resources for increased self-understanding and positive change. With this attitude the client concludes (Meador and Rogers, 1979, p. 152): "Here is someone who re-

peatedly tells me in one way or another that he believes in my ability to find my way in the process of growth. Perhaps I can begin to believe in myself."

Genuineness or congruence is the capacity of the therapist to "trust his own gut reactions," and then convey those feelings or reactions that the therapist believes have relevance in the relationship. This willingness of the therapist to be real and to express what he is thinking and feeling provides the client with a reality base that the client can trust. It also takes away some of the risk of sharing hidden secrets with another.

For Rogers the *nature* of the relationship between client and therapist is seen as *the* key variable in producing positive changes. Rogers (1961, p. 32) states:

The more the therapist is perceived by the client as being genuine, as having an empathetic understanding, and an unconditional regard for him, the greater will be the degree of constructive personality change in the client.

Rogers indicates that two conditions are necessary before therapy can occur. First, the client needs to be uncomfortable or anxious because of incongruences between self and experiences. (Client-centered therapy will not work well with clients who deny that a problem exists or who are unmotivated to change.) Second, a therapist must create a nonthreatening atmosphere in which the client feels she is being fully accepted and understood, and that the therapist genuinely cares for the client.

In such a relationship a client feels free (perhaps for the first time) to explore her incongruences between self and experiences. (For example, a client begins to examine the inconsistency between believing that sex is sinful while organismically her experiences do not agree.) The client then comes face to face with the awareness that there is this incongruence. The client begins to examine this incongruence and begins to think about what it would mean if other values were held (for example, having a value that responsible sexual experiences are desirable). During this process the client usually experiences feelings that have in the past been denied, repressed, or otherwise kept from consciousness. (Similar to Freud, Rogers believed the person in therapy should become aware of unconscious feelings and ideas, and deal with them in the conscious part of the mind.) If and when the above occurs, the concept of self becomes reorganized to include those experiences that in the past have been kept from consciousness. In addition, one's concept of self becomes increasingly congruent with one's experiences, and also more consistent with the self-actualizing processes.

The role of the therapist is best characterized as being *nondirective*. The therapist's role is to create a permissive, nonthreatening psychological atmosphere in which the client feels accepted by the therapist and feels free to explore her defenses and the incongruencies between self and experiences. If growth of the individual is to occur, it is postulated that it is necessary for each person to assume responsibility for her actions, decisions, and behavior. Change that is significant and enduring, Rogers postulated, must be self-initiated. Therefore, complete responsibility for the direction of treatment sessions rests with the client. A client-centered therapist does *not* bring up subjects to discuss, give advice, make interpretations, or provide suggestions. It is postulated that a person's self-actualization motive best knows what courses of action a person should take, and therefore the focus of client-centered therapy is to help the client gain insight into values that are inconsistent with this motive, and then to allow the self-actualizing processes to make decisions and determine future directions.

During therapy, a client-centered therapist seeks to help the client clarify personal thoughts and feelings. Three types of statements are primarily, and continually, used in the interview:

1. Clarification, or Reflection of Feeling

For example, if a client begins an interview by making critical statements about his boss, his wife, and the weather, the therapist might help the client better understand what he is feeling by saying something like "you seem angry today" or "you're really upset about something today."

It should be noted that when client-centered therapists reflect feelings, they at times add to the reflection by expressing their own feelings at the moment, as indicated in the following excerpt (Meador and Rogers, 1979, p. 157):

CLIENT: I think I'm beyond help.

THERAPIST: Huh? Feel as though you're beyond help. I know. You feel just completely hopeless about yourself. I can understand that. I don't feel hopeless, but I can realize that you do. Just feel as though nobody can help you and you're really beyond help.

The focus of a therapist in reflecting feelings is not simply to repeat the feelings expressed by the client but to reflect their intensity and meanings (that is, how the client feels) about the feelings he or she is expressing.

2. Restatement of Content

For example, if a wife goes on a twenty-minute outburst about how her husband is not supporting the family, nor being affectionate, and is frequently coming home intoxicated, the therapist might say, "You're pretty unhappy with the way your husband is treating you and the children"—which is designed to help the wife take an overall look at her marriage. The focus of a therapist in restating content is to express to the client the therapist's view of the meanings of the content being expressed by the client.

3. Simple Acceptance

For example, the therapist might respond with "I see" or "M-hm" to something the client has said, with the therapist's words being said in a tone that conveys that the therapist understands and fully accepts what the client has said.

The theoretical objective of therapy is for the client to become fully functioning. A fully functioning person is a mature individual who has achieved complete congruence, hence, is psychologically adjusted. This individual is not in a static state, but is a person in process, a person who is continually changing (Rogers, 1959). Therapy frees clients of their faulty learning so that

CASE EXAMPLE

Gloria

I n 1964, Carl Rogers interviewed for thirty minutes a client named "Gloria" for a film series, *Three Approaches to Psychotherapy*. This film is available for purchase or rental
(Rogers, 1965). Rogers believes this film is an excellent example of client-centered therapy.
Meador and Rogers (1979, p. 180) state: "The quality of this interview is like a piece of music, which begins on a thin persistent note and gradually adds dimension and levels until
the whole orchestra is playing."

Gloria is a thirty-year-old divorcee. Her presenting problem involves how she recently
responded to her nine-year-old daughter, Pammy, when Pammy asked whether she had
made love with any man since her divorce. She indicated to Rogers she lied by telling her
daughter no. She feels guilty about this as she feels she has always been honest with
Pammy. She also wonders whether she should tell Pammy the truth — that she lied. Furthermore she wonders how she should respond in the future if Pammy again raises this question, and wonders whether the truth will affect Pammy adversely.

At the beginning of this interview Gloria asks, "I want you to tell me if it would affect
her wrong if I told her the truth, or what?" On two later occasions, Gloria directly asks for
Rogers's opinion to this question. On all three occasions Rogers's responses convey that he
understands her dilemma, and that Rogers feels that is a question that she can best answer
by herself. At one point Gloria shows her frustration in not getting an opinion by saying:
"You're just going to sit there and let me stew in it, and I want more." Rogers replies, "No, I
don't want to let you just stew in your feelings, but on the other hand, I also feel this is the
kind of very private thing that I couldn't possibly answer for you. But I sure as anything
will try to help you work toward your own answer."

---

they can be what they are innately meant to be. That is
not to say that therapy will produce an optimally adjusted person, but the therapeutic experience can help
to start the development of a new pattern of adjustment.

The fully functioning person represents an ideal
that Rogers does not expect to be achieved at least as
the immediate consequence of therapy. The main characteristics of a fully functioning person are these:

a.   Is open to all experiences.

b.   Does not use defenses to distort or deny ex-
     periences.

c.   Has a self-concept congruent with experiences.

d.   Has her own locus of evaluation; that is, the person
     determines for herself what choices are best, and
     these decisions are based on her judgments of
     what is desirable or undesirable, rather than on
     what others say.

e.   Has unconditional positive regard for herself.

f.   Enjoys others because of the reciprocal positive
     regard.

g.   Generally is socially effective and approved by sig-
     nificant others.

Throughout the interview Rogers primarily uses the three types of statements mentioned earlier: clarification or reflection of feeling, restatement of content, and simple acceptance. Rogers, in the interview, conveys empathy, positive regard, and congruence. The main focus of the interview is to help Gloria examine the dilemma of what to tell her daughter, while conveying that *she* has the resources to decide what to do, and then to carry out her decisions. After awhile Gloria realizes Rogers is not going to give his opinion or give suggestions on how to handle this. She further realizes that Rogers believes she has the ability to find the answer within herself. Gloria goes on to discuss some other concerns, including the fact that she has never felt very close to her father.

Rogers is able to form a very close relationship to Gloria in this interview. Near the end Gloria says,

All of a sudden while I was talking to you, I thought, Gee, how nice I can talk to you and I want you to approve of me and I respect you, but I miss that my father couldn't talk to me like you are. I mean, I'd like to say, Gee, I'd like you for my father. I don't even know why that came to me.

Rogers responded:

You look to me like a pretty nice daughter. But you really do miss that fact that you couldn't be open with your own father.

Since the making of this film Rogers (1984) noted that Gloria continued to write to him, once or twice a year for fifteen years until her untimely death. Rogers (1984, pp. 423–25) added:

I am awed by the fact that this fifteen-year association grew out of the quality of the relationship we formed in one thirty-minute period in which we truly met as persons. It is good to know that even one half-hour can make a difference in a life.

EVALUATION

Rogers can be praised for the outstanding contributions he has made in articulating the components of a therapeutic relationship. He has emphasized the importance of the following concepts in building a helping relationship: *nonthreatening atmosphere, nonjudgmental attitude, empathy, genuineness, unconditional positive regard*, and *client as problem solver*. Rogers has also developed techniques involving the therapist's responses that have facilitated the development of a constructive relationship: *clarification or reflection of feeling, restatement of content*, and *simple acceptance*. The relationship between the social worker and the client, partly due to Rogers's emphasis, has become recognized as the keystone of social work practice (Simon, 1970).

Fischer (1978) reviews a large number of studies conducted on the three attitudes hypothesized by Rogers as being necessary and sufficient conditions for producing positive changes in clients—the three attitudes of empathy, genuineness, and positive regard or warmth. Fischer (1978, p. 207) concludes:

The findings from these studies have been remarkably consistent. Taken together, this research strongly supports the view that the level of therapist or helper empathy, warmth, and genuineness and associated interpersonal skills is related to positive change in client personal and social functioning. Practitioners who are relatively high on these core conditions of interpersonal helping tend to be effective practitioners. These findings hold with a wide variety of types of practitioners regardless of training, background, or theoretical orientation.

These findings dramatically suggeest that regardless of the theoretical orientation of a counselor, a successful outcome of counseling is highly dependent on a counselor's conveying empathy, warmth, and genuineness!

Rogers is also to be credited for emphasizing the importance of evaluation studies. Client-centered therapy is one of the most extensively researched approaches to counseling in existence (Prochaska, 1979).

In spite of these strengths there are some limitations of client-centered therapy.

1. Eysenck (1965) has reviewed outcome studies conducted on the effectiveness of contemporary psychotherapy approaches, including that of client-centered therapy. The results are not encouraging for client-centered therapy as the studies of this approach *fail* to demonstrate that clients receiving client-centered therapy will improve at a higher rate than control groups of people with similar problems. Although the results are complex and subject to different interpretations, studies generally show that about two thirds of clients receiving "insight" counseling improve, which is the same rate of improvement for people with personal problems who receive no counseling. (Client-centered therapy is an "insight" approach to counseling. Insight approaches seek to increase the client's awareness and understanding of his problems, without focusing on ways to resolve those problems. See Chapter 23.)

Why these rather discouraging results? It would seem that while developing a helping relationship and helping clients to gain insight into their problems are an essential part of counseling, these elements do not constitute the total counseling process. As indicated in Chapter 5, clients not only need to gain an understanding of the nature and causes of their problems; they also need to be made aware that there are various courses of action that they can take to resolve the problem. Client-centered therapists do not inform clients of available resolution strategies, as they believe it is the responsibility of clients to figure this out for themselves. Many other therapists, such as Glasser (1965), have pointed out the importance of having the counselor suggest various alternatives, of helping clients explore the merits and consequences of these alternatives, and then having clients make commitments (contracts) to try one of these alternatives.

Examples of the importance of exploring alternatives are easily listed. People who are depressed may understand why they are depressed (for example, a broken romance) but may not know how to resolve the depression. A person who knows he has a drinking problem, or is addicted to narcotic drugs, or is a chain smoker, may be unaware of the various programs and approaches to resolve these addictions. A mother who is aware she is an ineffective parent may be unaware of what she can do to be more effective. A person who knows he is shy or aggressive may be uninformed about specific assertiveness training techniques that he can use to express himself more effectively. A person who has a phobia (for example, high test anxiety) knows a problem exists but is often unaware of how to resolve the fear and anxiety. Gloria, the client in the film discussed earlier, was in a dilemma about what to tell her daughter when asked if she had made love since her divorce—and was given no specific strategies for responding to such a question.

In the session with Gloria, for example, the therapist may have suggested that the next time her daughter asks if she has ever made love with another man, Gloria might respond with something like, "Let's sit down and talk. What is it exactly that you're interesting in knowing?" The nine-year-old daughter could be concerned about a variety of things. She may want to ask questions about the facts of life. She may be wondering if her mother is intending to remarry soon. She may be concerned that she will have to establish a relationship with a male friend of her mother. Hopefully, such suggestions will provide a useful alternative for Gloria in handling her dilemma.

While empathy, warmth, and genuineness may well be an essential part of counseling, Prochaska (1979, p. 137) notes that Rogers "seems to have gone too far and concluded that what may be necessary conditions for therapy to proceed are also sufficient conditions for therapy to succeed."

2. Rogers claims to be nondirective. He indicates that a therapist should not bring up topics to discuss, nor make suggestions, nor make interpretations. The direction that an interview takes should be the sole responsibility of the client. Truax (1966) has, however, shown that client-centered therapists in fact do subtly direct clients with nonverbal communication (for example, by showing greater interest in certain topics) and by selectively choosing which topics to respond to (for example, discouraging further communication by not saying anything when a client talks about his job, and encouraging further communication by reflecting feelings when a client talks about how he feels about his spouse).

3. Client-centered therapy does not provide much useful material on personality development, or on how emotional and behavioral problems arise. For example, the theory does not help very much in explaining why depression, grief, and shyness occur, or why an individual may display such behavioral problems as enuresis, problem drinking, aggressive behavior, and acts of crime and violence.

4. Rogers assumes with his emphasis on therapists being "genuine" with clients, that therapists will like all their clients. (It would not be very therapeutic for a therapist to say, "You know, I really don't like you.") In reality, it is highly unlikely that a therapist will like all clients, as practically every person knows at least a few people that she dislikes.

5. Prochaska (1979) provides an intriguing interpretation of client-centered therapy from a learning theory perspective. He asserts that whatever positive effects occur from this therapy occur due to extinction—that is, by gradually reducing the client's concerns through having the client repeatedly talk about his concerns in an environment free of positive or negative consequences. Prochaska (1979, p. 136) notes:

Beneath all the rhetoric, Rogers is advocating a treatment that is apparently based on a fuzzy form of extinction. Theoretically, troubled responses are assumed to have been conditioned by the contingent love and regard of parents. The therapist is supposed to reverse the process by establishing a social learning environment in which there are no contingencies, no conditions for positive regard. The client is allowed to talk on and on about troubled behavior without being reinforced or punished. Eventually the absence of contingencies leads to an extinction of talking about troubles. Of course, we cannot determine from this verbal extinction paradigm alone whether the client's troubled behavior itself has changed or whether the client has just quit talking about such problems.

But why rely on extinction when it is unnecessarily lengthy and can lead to complications such as the spontaneous recovery of the extinguished responses? Furthermore, when only extinction is used, there is no way of telling which new behaviors will be learned in place of the maladaptive responses that are being extinguished.

SUMMARY

Client-centered therapy was formulated primarily by Carl Rogers. The approach postulates that every person has a self-actualization motive. The focus of this therapy approach is to help clients become aware of incongruencies between their self-concept and their experiences. Once this insight is achieved, the self-actualizing motive fosters a reorganization of the self-concept to be more congruent with experiences. Because of this self-actualizing motive, client-centered therapists are nondirective. They do not even suggest possible resolution approaches to clients.

Client-centered therapy assists that the following three therapist attitudes are necessary and sufficient conditions to effect positive changes in clients: empathy, positive regard, and genuineness or congruence. It is theorized that whenever a therapist displays these three attitudes toward a client, the actualizing potential of the client will begin to change and grow. During therapy, a client-centered therapist seeks to help the client clarify his thoughts and feelings by using primarily three types of statements: clarification or reflection of feeling, restatement of content, and simple acceptance.

Client-centered therapy has made outstanding contributions in identifying the components of a therapeutic relationship. A shortcoming of the approach appears to be that client-centered therapists do not suggest viable alternatives when clients are unaware of strategies to resolve their difficulties.

EXERCISE

GOAL: This exercise is designed to help students understand the merits and shortcomings of client-centered therapy.

Step 1: Prior to explaining client-centered therapy, ask for two volunteers to come up with a contrived problem that they jointly have (e.g., a "wife" wants to become a surrogate mother, and her "husband" doesn't want her to.) Ask for two students to volunteer to be counselors. Instruct the "clients" to go out in the hallway to select and develop their contrived problem. While the "clients" are out in the hallway, inform the counselors they can only use statements that (*a*) clarify or reflect feelings, (*b*) restate content, or (*c*) convey simple acceptance. Briefly give examples of these statements. Inform the "counselors" that they should not ask questions, make interpretations, or provide suggestions. Indicate that in theory, client-centered therapist use only the above three types of statements.

Step 2: Ask the "clients" to return, and have the "counselors" then counsel the "clients."

Step 3: After the counseling is completed, ask the "counselors" to discuss their feelings about being limited to these three types of statements. Ask the "clients" and the other students in class to discuss their thoughts about this type of counseling.

Step 4: Explain the principles of client-centered therapy.

15

GESTALT THERAPY

T he founder of Gestalt therapy was Frederich (Fritz) Perls (1893–1970). Born and reared in Berlin, Germany, his early therpeutic career was heavily influenced by his studies of psychoanalysis. After receiving an M.D. in Berlin, he studied at the Institutes of Psychoanalysis in Berlin and in Vienna. Perls said (1969b) he probably would have spent his professional career doing psychoanalysis if it had not been for Hitler.

Anticipating the horrors of Hitler, he left Germany in 1934 to go to Johannesburg, South Africa, where he established a psychoanalytic practice and also founded the South African Institute for Psychoanalysis. While in South Africa he began to revise Freud's theories. These revisions gradually became more distant from psychoanalytic theory. After a few years it became obvious he was developing a new approach to psychotherapy.

With the rise of apartheid in South Africa, Perls decided to leave, and came to the United States in 1946. With his wife Laura, he began the New York Institute of Gestalt Therapy. Many therapists attended Gestalt workshops at this institute and were deeply impressed by Perl's charisma and Gestalt exercises. They came away from these encounters with Perls feeling inspried and more alive, and began to spread the word about the merits of Gestalt therapy.

In 1951 Perls, together with Ralph Hefferline and Paul Goodman, published *Gestalt Therapy: Excitement and Growth in Personality*, which further popularized Gestalt therapy. In the 1960s Perls went to California to hold workshops at Esalen in Big Sur, California, where many people flocked to attend encounter groups with Perls. In 1970 Perls wanted to build a Gestalt Training Center and Community in British Columbia, Canada, where he moved shortly before his death.

Perls was very impressed with J. L. Moreno's (1946) psychodrama and, having come from a theatrical background, incorporated many psychodramatic techniques into Gestalt therapy. Perls has been a dominant force in developing a therapy approach that emphasizes feelings and deemphasizes thinking. Gestalt therapy has had a prominent effect on the direction taken by encounter groups, marathon groups, and sensitivity groups. The therapy developed by Perls is an experiential, existential approach. In his writings, Perls throws

FIGURE 15.1

The Reversible Staircase

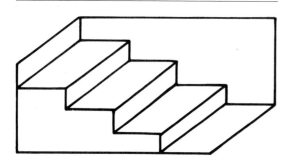

Focus on this figure, and after a few moments the staircase will appear to be "upside down."

FIGURE 15.2

Test Your Awareness

First read the sentence enclosed in the box below

> FINISHED FILES ARE THE RESULT
> OF YEARS OF SCIENTIFIC STUDY
> COMBINED WITH THE EXPERI-
> ENCE OF MANY YEARS.

Now count the Fs in the sentence. Count them only once and do not go back and count them again. (See correct answer at bottom of this page.)

out a lot of ideas, while giving little attention to tying his theories together and making them consistent (Prochaska, 1979).

FRITZ PERLS: GESTALT PSYCHOLOGY

Gestalt therapy is related to Gestalt psychology. The main idea of Gestalt psychology is that the "whole" is more than, or something else than, the summation of the parts. The theory is antireductionistic in nature. Most other scientific approaches try to determine how something functions by breaking the unit into components and then examining the parts. Gestalt psychology asserts this is a mistake. Gestalt psychologists say, for example, that water has characteristics that could never be observed by looking at its gaseous components of hydrogen and oxygen. Another example would be a

person's mind—by looking at the individual parts of a human there is no way that the parts would suggest that a person can think and experience such emotions as fear and happiness.

A simple definition of the word *gestalt* is *whole*. A more formal definition (*Webster's Ninth New Collegiate Dictionary*, 1983) is "a structure, configuration, or pattern of physical, biological, or psychological phenomena so integrated as to constitute a functional unit with properties not derivable by summation of its parts."

An area that Gestalt psychology has done considerable research in is perception, particularly studying the contributions made by the viewer as to what is perceived. Figures 15.1 and 15.2 are two examples. These figures show that the perceiver makes substantial contributions to what is perceived.

Answer: There are six Fs. Most of us count three or four because we are trained to read fast and give little attention to prepositions such as of—there are three *ofs* above.

THEORY
OF PERSONALITY AND
OF PSYCHOPATHOLOGY

Perls, similar to Carl Rogers, theorizes that all organisms (including humans) have a self-actualization motive that is an inherent drive toward growth and need satisfaction. If there is no interference with this motive, people will trust their own nature and seek to become themselves rather than striving toward becoming someone they are not. Perls (1969a, p. 31) states:

Every individual, every plant, every animal has only one inborn goal — to actualize itself as it is. A rose is a rose is a rose. A rose is not intent to actualize itself as a kangaroo. An elephant is not intent to actualize itself as a bird.

Homeostasis (that is, the tendency toward balance) is an important concept in Gestalt therapy. Any imbalance is experienced as a need to correct this imbalance. Our life is basically nothing but an infinite number of unfinished situations; for example, at any one point in time each of us has a variety of needs — hunger, shelter, bathing, visiting friends, studying, sleeping, recreation, sex, going to the bathroom, calling relatives, arranging future social events, exercise, going to the dentist, and so on. At any one point in time, we have hundreds of unfinished situations inside us. Through *awareness*, we discover that which is not in balance. The reason we do not become completely confused about which unfinished situation to focus our attention on is because we have internal organismic self-regulation (that is, a self-actualization motive), which, if unhampered, is best able to focus attention upon the most urgent unfinished situation.

Awareness is a crucial concept for Perls (1969a, pp. 16–17).

I believe that this is the great thing to understand: that awareness per se — by and of itself — can be curative. Because with full awareness you become aware of this organismic self-regulation, you can let the organism take over without interfering, without interrupting, we can rely on the wisdom of the organism.

Perls believes control from the outside (for example, parental pressures and attempts to influence) interferes with internal organismic self-regulation. Perls also deemphasizes intellect and thinking, and instead emphasizes feelings, awareness, and sensitivity. The organism knows all, our intellect knows very little. For example, a woman may be able to sleep through loud rock music, but if her child whimpers a little, the organism will waken the person as the organism knows an emergency exists. Perls disesteems thinking because he feels there is a danger that a thinking person will become preoccupied with concepts and will lose a sense of her real nature.

Perls believes healthy development involves a natural process in which we develop from children dependent on environmental support into self-supporting adults. In early childhood we are dependent on others, primarily our parents for support — for shelter, food, clothing, protection. As a healthy child grows, he gradually learns to be his unique self. A mature person is being what one is. Prochaska (1979, p. 145) describes such mature people:

as healthy adults we also are aware that other maturing organisms are equally able to respond for themselves, and the maturation process includes shedding responsibility for anyone else. We give up our childish feelings of omnipotence and omniscience and accept that others know themselves better than we can ever know them and can better direct their own lives than we can direct them. We allow others to be self-supporting and we give up our need to interfere in the lives of others. Others do not exist to live up to our expectations, nor do we exist to live up to the expectations of others.

The definition of a mature person as being "I am what I am" is highlighted in the Gestalt prayer (Perls, 1969a, p. 4)

I do my thing, and you do your thing.
I am not in this world to live up to your expectations
And you are not in this world to live up to mine.
You are you and I am I,
And if by chance we find each other, it's beautiful.
If not, it can't be helped.

Perls presents a variety of ways in which emotional and behavioral problems arise. One way is by playing social roles. Perls indicates that healthy personalities do not become preoccupied with playing social roles, since such roles are nothing more than a set of social expectations that we and others have for ourselves. Social roles interfere with the time and energy that we should be expending to meet our organismic, or natural, needs. As we play social roles, the roles gradually become habits and rigid behavioral patterns that we erroneously interpret as the essence of our character. As these roles (for example, that of a therapist, or student, or engineer) become more fixed, we transform our basic natural existence into a pseudosocial existence. Much of our thinking becomes preoccupied with practicing how we can better enact our roles and manipulate the environment. As social roles become more fixed, our organismic self-regulation gradually loses awareness of our most urgent unfinished situations. As a result, we do not respond by organismic awareness to situations but according to others' expectations of how we ought to play that particular social role.

Playing roles is one way that a person may become sidetracked from the natural process of growth or maturation. Another way is by being spoiled by overindulgent parents. Perls believes many parents want to give their children the things they never had. There is a danger in this as children may prefer to remain spoiled and let their parents do everything. In such situations, children get stuck in the maturational process and therefore seek environmental support, rather than growing to become self-supported.

Withdrawing environmental support before children have developed the capacity for inner support is another way in which pathology can arise. Such a child is in an *impasse*, as the child can no longer rely on the safe, environmental support nor rely on self-support. Forcing a child to try to walk before the child's muscles and balance are adequately developed is one example of such an impasse.

Perls (1969a) presents a number of other examples of how pathological personalities may become "stuck." One way this may happen is by having unacceptable thoughts or feelings toward something or someone. If we have such thoughts and feelings, we are tempted to deny or disown them. But denying that an unhappy marriage is not working or failing to acknowledge a problematic job is not in our best interests. When we disown thoughts and feelings, we do not allow ourselves to be totally ourselves. In such cases our energy and power are drained; we become rigid and fail to actualize ourselves.

If organismic self-regulation is interfered with, a number of "polarities," or splits, may arise. Therapy often focuses on these polarities. A healthy personality attempts to find wholeness in life by accepting and expressing the opposite poles in life. An unhealthy personality generally gives attention to one aspect of the polarity while ignoring the other.

Perhaps the best known and most frequently encountered split is the Topdog versus Underdog polarity. Topdog versus Underdog results from a faulty socialization process, according to Simkin (1979, p. 283):

During the process of socialization, many children are miseducated and forced to introject (swallow whole) ideas and behavior that do not suit them. This results in an enforced morality rather than an organismically compatible morality. As a result, the person frequently feels guilty when he behaves in accordance with his wants as opposed to his shoulds.

To counteract the dictates of the topdog, a person will develop an underdog to placate his shoulds. The underdog makes promises, New Year's resolutions, and is a built-in sabotage mechanism. In some people, an enormous amount of energy is invested in maintaining the topdog-underdog split, the resolution of which would require a recognition of one's own suitable morality as opposed to an introjected one.

Topdog is often experienced as an overrighteous conscience that attempts to control us by commanding, insisting, scolding, and demanding. Underdog acts as a passive resistance to deal with the "shoulds" of Topdog that are inconsistent with the self-actualization motive. It acts lazy, stupid, and inept as a passive way to keep from successfully completing the commands of Topdog.

In regard to such polarities Prochaska (1979, p. 149) notes, "As long as people avoid accepting that they are also the opposite of what they pretend to be, that they are strong as well as weak, cruel as well as kind, and master as well as slave, they are unable to complete the gestalt of life, to experience the whole of life."

THEORY OF THERAPY

The basic concept of therapy is that *awareness in the here and now* is therapeutic. Awareness of the present moment is theorized to be curative as it allows clients to work on the Gestalt principle that organismic self-regulation will then be able to give attention to the most important unfinished situation that will always emerge into consciousness.

Awareness is defined as being in touch with one's existence. It is the ability to focus on what exists in the now. In therapy, clients are often asked to report what they are aware of at the moment. What a person is aware of is what exists for that person.

Yontef and Simkin (1989, p. 323) note:

Gestalt therapy focuses more on process (what is happening) than content (what is being discussed). The emphasis is on what is being done, thought, and felt at the moment rather than on what was, might be, could be, or should be.

The goal of Gestalt therapy is to have a client mature, to grow up. Children are often more mature than adults, as they are more open to their feelings. An adult is usually someone who plays the role of an adult, and the more he plays the role, the less organismically he is aware of feelings and the more immature he becomes. Maturing is the transcendance from environmental support to self-support. The aim of therapy is to make the client not depend on others but become independent. Most other therapies try to adjust the person to society, while the goal of Gestalt therapy is to have a person actualize himself (a rose is a rose is a rose). Being grounded in one's self is the highest state a person can achieve.

Gestalt therapists do not delve deeply into the past. What is important to focus attention on in therapy will emerge from the client because of organismic self-regulation as soon as the client achieves awareness in the here and now. The therapist seeks to frustrate a person, again and again, until the client is face-to-face with his inhibitions. For example, the therapist is likely to frustrate a client by asking such questions as "Do you often wiggle your foot like that?" and "Are you reluctant to look directly at me?" Clients' awareness of being stuck, and the awareness of how they are stuck, makes them recover. Gestalt therapists do not make interpretations, as the focus is on fostering clients' awareness and helping them to sort things out for themselves.

Gestalt therapy may be conducted individually with clients or in a group. When in a group, Perls's therapy is really an individual therapy occurring in a group setting because the interaction primarily is between the therapist and a client, with first one member and then another becoming the client.

Gestalt therapy uses a wide variety of exercises to help clients become more aware in the here and now. The exercises that can be used to stimulate awareness are limited only by the creativity of the therapist. Gestalt therapists do not use a predetermined pattern of exercises. Exercises are selected while therapy is occurring based on the therapist's judgment as to what will be most useful at that point for each client so that she can experience her own blocks in awareness. A few of these exercises will be presented to give the reader a flavor for them.

The exercises that are most involved in consciousness raising have been summarized by Prochaska (1979, p. 153):

1. *Games of dialogue*, in which patients carry on a dialogue between polarities of their personality, such as a repressed masculine polarity confronting a dominant feminine polarity.

2. *I take responsibility*, in which clients are asked to end every statement about themselves with "and I take responsibility for it."

3. *Playing the projection*, in which clients play the role of the person involved in any of their projections, such as playing their parents when they blame their parents.

4. *Reversals*, in which patients are to act out the very opposite of the way they usually are in order to experience some hidden polarity of themselves.

*A young woman experiences an entire range of emotion
in a single session with a Gestalt therapist.*

5. *Rehearsals,* in which patients reveal to the group the thinking or rehearsal they most commonly do in preparation for playing social roles, including the role of the patient.

6. *Marriage counseling games,* in which spouses take turns revealing their most positive and negative feelings about each other to each other.

7. *May I feed you a sentence,* in which the therapist asks patients to repeat and try on for size a statement about them that the therapist feels is particularly significant for the patient.

A frequent technique that is used in groups is the "hot seat." The hot seat involves a group member volunteering to deal with a particular problem. The focus of the interaction is between this client and the group leader, as the client works on the problem. Levitsky and Simkin (1972, p. 140) further expand on the hot seat technique:

As therapist and patient work together, occasions arise in which the patient is asked to carry out some particular exercise, for example, "Could you repeat what you just said, but this time with your legs uncrossed?" or "Could you look directly at me and say this?" The attitude with which these exercises are carried out is an important element. The patient is gradually educated and encouraged to undertake these exercises in the spirit of experiment. One cannot really know the outcome beforehand even though a specific hunch is being tested. The spirit of experiment is taken seriously and the question raised, "What did you discover?" The discovery is the most potent form of learning.

The following is a brief excerpt from a client on the hot seat (Perls, 1969a, pp. 245–51):

CLAIRE: I want to get—

FRITZ: "I want"; get out of this seat. You want. I don't want any wanters. There are two great lies: "I want" and "I try."

CLAIRE: I am fat . . . this is my existence. (*whimpering*) I don't like it. And I constantly bug me with this fact. And that is always with me . . . and I'm tired of crying about it. . . . Do you want me to get off this seat?

FRITZ: No.

CLAIRE: Don't you want me to get off?

FRITZ: No.

CLAIRE: Yes?

FRITZ: No. . . . I neither want you to get off nor do I don't want you to get off.

CLAIRE: Are you going to sit here, Claire, or are you going to try and do something about what you're doing (sigh) you just want to sit here and stay fat . . . (the interaction continues for several minutes)

CLAIRE: So I'm back to the same thing. I'm the one that has to give *me* the answer how to get out of the impasse.

FRITZ: No, answers can't help.

CLAIRE: Well what the fuck does? . . . What does help?

FRITZ: Another question. Come on, come on.

CLAIRE: The answer is, you just stop eating if you don't want to eat.

FRITZ: Here are all the typical symptoms of the impasse. The merry-go-round everybody sees the obvious except the patient. She drives you crazy. She is stuck. She is in despair. Mobilizes whatever gimmicks and tricks she has to get out of the impasse. I feel that you started out with some kind of feeling inside, that you are dead. Or you call it bored. Bored and empty. You have to fill yourself . . .

CLAIRE: Yes. I do eat when I am bored and empty. (The interaction continues for several more minutes as the client increasingly realizes and acknowledges she eats compulsively when she feels bored and empty.)

Dreams are also used in Gestalt therapy because they are seen as the most spontaneous part of a person. Dreams are viewed as a way in which people can express all parts of themselves, especially the parts that have been disowned in efforts to succeed in social roles. In therapy, clients do not just talk about their dreams but are encouraged to become each detail of a dream in order to give expression to the disowned aspects of their personality. When clients become as spontaneous as their dreams, they then become healthy and whole again. The following is a brief excerpt from a dreamwork seminar (Perls, 1969a, pp. 82–83).

CASE EXAMPLE

Impotence

Prochaska (1979) presents a case of a middle-aged adult whom he treated for sexual impotence using Gestalt therapy. From age seventeen to twenty-seven Howard had been sexually active, and relating sexually was stated by him to be the most significant activity in his life. He prided himself on being a great lover. The onset of impotence was described as being sudden, with Howard making a number of unsuccessful attempts over a series of months. As could be expected Howard continued to become more anxious and depressed over this difficulty.

Prochaska first began therapy using a type of sensate focus developed by Masters and Johnson (Belliveau and Richter, 1970). Howard had a close female friend who was understanding and who participated in the sensate focus with Howard. (Sensate focus involves touching experiences between two people, which are described in Chapter 20.) The results were discouraging. Prochaska next tried systematic desensitization to reduce the anxiety over failing. With this technique Howard was able to progress to the point of imagining sexual intercourse without anxiety, but the results did not generalize to the actual event of sexual relations. (Systematic desensitization is described in Chapter 19.) Prochaska (1979, p. 142) then describes his efforts using a Gestalt approach.

Finally I decided to resort to a gestalt exercise to help Howard discover the special significance of the intense pressure he was having over his sexual drive. I asked Howard to imagine as vividly as he could that he was his penis and that his penis had something to say. As he got into the fantasy, I encouraged him to just let the mouth of his penus say whatever it spontaneously desired, and here is what came out: "You're asking too much of me, Howard. You've been asking me to carry the whole meaning of your life on my back and that's just too big a load for any one penis to carry. I'm bound to bend under such weight."

Prochaska unfortunately does not discuss the outcome of this exercise.

LIZ: I dream of tarantulas and spiders crawling on me. And it's pretty consistent.

FRITZ: Okay. Can you imagine I am Liz and you are the spider? Can you crawl on me now? How would you do this?

LIZ: Up your leg and . . .

FRITZ: *Do* it, *do* it . . . (*laughter*)

LIZ: I don't like spiders.

FRITZ: You are a spider now. It's your dream. You produced this dream . . .

Liz then goes on to talk about a variety of topics, including that the spider is aggressive and she is not, that she feels she is a perfectionist, and that she desires to be a good girl although she feels being bad is more fun.

Another technique used by Gestalt therapists is to focus on the nonverbal expressions of clients, their posture, the quality of their voices, their eyes, and their movements, as indicated in the following example (Levitsky and Perls, 1970, p.143):

T: What are you aware of now?

P: Now I am aware of talking to you. I see the others in the room. I'm aware of John squirming. I can feel the tension in my shoulders. I'm aware that I get anxious as I say this.

T: How do you experience the anxiety?

P: I hear my voice quiver. My mouth feels dry. I talk in a very halting way.

T: Are you aware of what your eyes are doing?

P: Well, now I realize that my eyes keep looking away—

T: Can you take responsibility for that?

P: —that I keep looking away from you.

T: Can you be your eyes now? Write the dialogue for them.

P: I am Mary's eyes. I find it hard to gaze steadily. I keep jumping and darting about . . .

EVALUATION

The goal of Gestalt therapy provides an intriguing contrast to most therapy approaches. In most therapy approaches, the goal is to have clients explore emotional or behavioral problems that they have, and to then develop or select courses of action to resolve these problems. In comparison, Gestalt therapy seeks to develop increased personal and interpersonal awareness. Gestalt therapy generally does not directly attempt to identify and change specific emotional or behavioral problems that people have (such as drinking problems, feelings of depression, and sexual dysfunctions). *The philosophy behind Gestalt therapy is that with increased personal and interpersonal awareness, people will be better able to avoid, cope with, and/or handle specific personal problems that arise.*

Gestalt therapists have generally shown little interest in conducting controlled outcome studies. Since their focus is on increased awareness rather than on alleviating specific emotional and behavioral problems, traditional outcome approaches are generally viewed as not being applicable because they do not measure changes in self-awareness. Simkin (1979, p. 288) presents another reason that Gestalt therapists have shunned experimental testing of their approach:

Most Gestalt therapists would argue that their approach is experimental: that each session is seen as an existential encounter in which both the therapist and the patient engage in calculated risk taking (experiments) involving a willingness to explore heretofore unknown or forbidden territories.

Gestalt therapy predicts that clients will show increased self-awareness, increased self-actualization, and increased personal growth. Prochaska (1979, p. 168) reviews the studies (only a few have been conducted) that have investigated whether Gestalt therapy does lead to these predicted changes and concludes, "The result of the studies on the growth-oriented effectiveness of Gestalt therapy are at best mixed."

It should be noted that clients who participate in Gestalt therapy, and related encounter and sensitivity groups, generally report that such approaches lead to increased awareness and have a significant positive effect on their lives.

Yontef and Simkin (1989, pp. 355–56) provide a summary of the present status of Gestalt therapy:

In 1987 there were scores of training institutes, hundreds of psychotherapists who had been trained in Gestalt therapy, and many hundreds of nontrained or poorly trained persons who called themselves "Gestaltists." Thousands of people have experienced Gestalt therapy—many with quite favorable results—others with questionable or poor outcomes.

Because of the unwillingness of Gestalt therapists to set rigid standards, there is a wide range of criteria for the selection and training of Gestalt therapists. Some people, having experienced a weekend workshop, consider themselves amply equipped to do Gestalt therapy. Other psychotherapists spend months and years in training as Gestalt therapists and have an enormous respect for the simplicity and infinite innovativeness and creativity that Gestalt therapy requires and engenders.

There are some criticisms that can be made of Gestalt therapy.

1. Gestalt therapy is reminiscent of psychological hedonism—the doctrine that pleasure is the sole or chief good in life and that moral duty is fulfilled in the gratification of pleasure. The notion of Gestalt therapy that "You do your thing and I do my thing" may sound romantic to some, but if widely adopted would lead to societal chaos and anarchy. A few examples underscore this point. What would happen if parents of young children would follow their desires of not wanting to change diapers? If married individuals followed every sexual temptation, what would be the effect on their marriages? Some people desire to rape others, or "punch out" others—what would happen if society did not restrict such behavior? Like it or not, social expectations and social rules are essential for enabling people to live together with one another. People who have undergone Gestalt therapy have primarily been "normal" individuals who previously have successfully gone through a socialization process. One wonders what would be the results of encouraging people convicted of crimes of violence (e.g., Charles Manson) "to do their own thing"! Should people who threaten to take their own lives be encouraged to do what they desire? And what about exhibitionists, drug users, voyeurs, parents who abuse their children, check forgers, burglars?

2. Perls criticizes playing social roles. He urges that people be their "natural" selves (whatever that is) rather than playing roles. Yet, role theorists present a strong case that learning to play certain roles is crucially important for a person's well-being. A few examples will be given. In interviewing for a job or a position a person needs to present herself in a way that is most likely to obtain a job offer—which includes playing a role in which the person dresses in a certain fashion and says the kinds of things that will best present herself. Being a parent, or a social worker, or a doctor requires playing a certain role—would you, for example, consent to surgery by a physician who was unkempt and seldom bathed? People who are involuntarily committed for a mental illness need to learn to play the "sane" role in order to be released; that is, they need to learn to present themselves in a manner in which they stop displaying irrational behavior. Would ministers or teachers be effective and have the support of the people they interact with if they wanted to be their "real" selves by, for example, getting high on drugs and slurring their words at nearly every meeting they attended? There has to be a balance between your "real" self and playing social roles—some occasions

are appropriate for giving expression to your thoughts and feelings while there are other occasions that require playing a social role. In a correctional setting, for example, much of the efforts of probation and parole officers are geared to helping clients become better socialized, often through teaching clients how to play roles (for example, interviewing for a job and learning to accept such job expectations as being punctual).

3. Perls urges people to act on the basis of their feelings rather than their intellect. Unwanted emotions (such as grief, depression, anxiety, anger, hostility) are often irrational. Perls does not provide techniques for helping people to resolve such unwanted emotions. In contrast, as will be discussed in Chapter 18, Ellis and Harper (1977b) have demonstrated that all emotions, including unwanted emotions, are determined by our thoughts and can be changed by changing our thinking.

In regard to Perls's deemphasizing the importance of intellectual processes, Prochaska (1979, p. 169) notes: "Perls's disesteeming of thinking encourages an irrational anti-intellectualism that could result in empty-headed organisms."

4. Most clients seen by people in the helping professions have specific problems that they need help with—a drinking problem, severe depression or anxiety, being suicidal, having a spouse who is abusive, being pregnant and single, being severely in debt, needing a job, having a terminal illness. Perls's theories provide very little usable information on (*a*) how such problems arise, (*b*) how such problems are perpetuated, and (*c*) how to treat such specific problems. Therefore, Gestalt therapy is generally inappropriate to use when clients need to develop resolution strategies for urgent specific problems they face.

SUMMARY

Fritz Perls founded Gestalt therapy. Gestalt therapy assumes everyone has a self-actualization motive. Balance is an important concept. Our life is basically an infinite number of unfinished situations. Through awareness we discover that most urgent unfinished situations. The reason we do not become confused about which unfinished situations to attend to is because we have internal organismic self-regulation which, if unhampered, is best able to determine the most urgent unfinished situations.

Perls presents a variety of ways in which personal problems may arise. An important way is by playing social roles, which interferes with the time and energy we should be expending to meet our organismic needs. Personal problems may also arise from being spoiled by overindulgent parents, by parents' withdrawing environmental support before children have developed the capacity for inner support, and by a person's disowning unacceptable thoughts or feelings, which results in the person's disowning valuable parts of herself.

The basic concept of Gestalt therapy is that *awareness* in the *here and now* is therapeutic. Awareness allows the organismic self-regulation within clients to give attention to the most important unfinished situations. The goal of Gestalt therapy is to have a person actualize herself. Gestalt therapy uses a wide range of experiential exercises (for example, psychodrama and the "hot seat") to help clients become more aware in the here and now.

Gestalt therapy has had a major influence in the growth of encounter groups, sensitivity groups, and marathon groups. The approach, however, is reminiscent of psychological hedonism and provides little usable information on how to treat specific problems of clients.

EXERCISE

1. *Awareness*

GOAL: The purpose of this exercise is to demonstrate how Gestalt therapy can be used in a group.

Step 1: The instructor should state the purpose of the exercise. Explain that the basic concept of Gestalt therapy is that awareness in the here and now is therapeutic. Also indicate that a Gestalt therapist seeks to frustrate a client, again and again, until the client is face-to-face with his inhibitions.

Step 2: Have the students form a circle with their chairs, with one chair next to the instructor left empty. The instructor should indicate that he will take the role of the group leader and will work progressively with different members of the group. Ask one member to sit in the empty chair next to the instructor. The instructor then focuses on this person by asking questions and making statements similar to the following which are largely based on the nonverbal communication of the "client."

"Tell me what you are now aware of."

"Are you aware you're tapping your feet?"

"Are you feeling anxious?"

"Are you aware of your smile?"

"Are you aware when you speak that you talk with your hands?"

"Are you aware that you're blushing?"

"Your fingers are tapping."

"Tell me what you're experiencing now."

"Are you feeling frustrated?"

Step 3: After working with one member for awhile, end it and then ask another member to come and sit next to you. Ask questions similar to those indicated in Step 2. Continue the exercise until the instructor has worked with four or five students following the procedures outlined above.

Step 4: Have the "clients" and other students discuss the merits and shortcomings of this approach. Ask the "clients" to discuss how they felt about being asked these types of questions. Ask the "clients" if they believe this type of therapy would lead to increased self-awareness.

2. Practicing Being a Gestalt Therapist

GOAL: This exercise is intended to demonstrate how to use Gestalt therapy.

Step 1: Show a film or videotape of Fritz Perls (or some other Gestalt therapist) counseling a client. (An alternative to a film is having the instructor use the techniques of Gestalt therapy with a student in the class who volunteers to be a "client.")

Step 2: Explain the principles of Gestalt therapy and summarize the techniques that are used. (These are described in this chapter.)

Step 3: Ask for a student to volunteer to role-play being a Gestalt therapist, and another student to volunteer being a "client." Have these two students role-play a Gestalt therapy session.

Step 4: Have the student who role-plays being a Gestalt therapist summarize his thoughts and feelings about this experience. Have the "client" and the other students in the class discuss the role-playing.

Step 5: As an additional, optional step, the role-playing may be repeated (and discussed by the class) by having two additional students volunteer to role-play—with one being a "Gestalt therapist" and the other being a "client."

16

TRANSACTIONAL
ANALYSIS

The founder of transactional analysis was Eric Berne (1910–1970). Like many other psychotherapy innovaters, Berne was formally trained in classical psychoanalysis. He received his M.D. at McGill University in 1935 and did his psychiatric residency at Yale from 1936 to 1941. He then began his training as a psychoanalytic candidate in New York, but his training was interrupted by service in the army during World War II from 1943 to 1946. In the army he became excited about using group therapy and began moving away from the strict one-to-one format of psychoanalysis.

After the war he settled in Carmel, California, and resumed his psychoanalytic studies. In 1956 he applied for membership in the Psychoanalytic Institute. He was turned down on the basis that he was not doing orthodox analysis. Berne agreed with this reason and disassociated himself from psychoanalysis. A year later he presented his first paper on transactional analysis (TA). Although this marked the formal beginning of TA, Berne had been developing his system several years prior to this time. Beginning in the early 1950s, he formed a seminar group in Carmel in which he began presenting his emerging theory and having it critiqued by professionals who attended.

In 1964 he published *Games People Play*, which was written primarily for professionals who were interested in TA. The book became a national best-seller. The popularity of TA grew dramatically. Several other books, written by other TA authors, such as *I'm Ok — You're OK* (Harris, 1969) have also become best-sellers.

Prochaska (1979) notes that Berne was an unlikely person to establish and market a new psychotherapy system. He was rather shy and lacking in the charisma that tends to characterize many leaders. However, he was highly creative, articulate, and hard working. His personal life was sacrificed for his professional life as he spent most of his time writing, doing therapy, consulting, or conducting seminars.

ERIC BERNE: THEORY OF PERSONALITY DEVELOPMENT

Personality Structure

The basic premise of transactional analysis is that human personality is structured into three separate ego states—Parent, Adult, and Child. The definition of these ego states varies somewhat among TA authorities—this text will present Dusay and Dusay's (1979) definitions, which appear to be the most consistent and understandable. TA authorities assert that these ego states are not theoretical constructs but are actual realities that are steadily identified by anyone trained in TA concepts.

The Parent ego state is basically composed of attitudes and behaviors that are copied through identification with parents and other authority figures. While much of the Parent is learned during childhood, it can be modified throughout life as the person copies new authority figures. The Parent is the limit setting, controlling, and rigid rule maker of the personality. It expresses one's morals, value systems, and beliefs. The Parent uses such words as *ought*, *should*, *must*, and *you'll be sorry*. Certain gestures, like pointing a finger, also characterize the Parent. The Parent's attitudes and behaviors may promote growth in others as well as being critical and controlling. The Parent may be judgmental and opinionated as well as protective and nurturing.

The *Parent* ego state has two forms: the *Critical Parent* and the *Nurturing Parent*. The Critical Parent is the part of one's personality that finds fault and criticizes. It also is directing, assertive, sets rules, enforces one's value system, and stands up for one's rights. Too much Critical Parent is dictatorial. The Nurturing Parent is empathic, acts out of genuine concern for others, is warm, supportive, and protective. It usually promotes growth in others, but too much Nurturing Parent leads to overprotection, overinvolvement, and may be smothering. A classic example of a Nurturing Parent is a warm, friendly, fatherly, yet firm police officer.

A male dressed as a female nurse on Halloween. Halloween is one of many occasions that encourage adults to enter the child ego state.

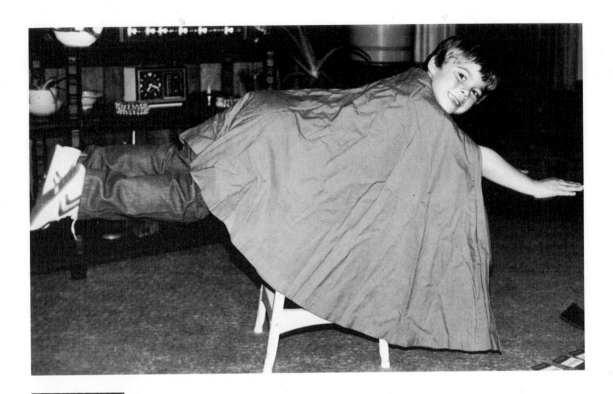

Berne and many other therapists encourage creativity.

The *Child* ego state is considered to be the best part of the personality as it is the only part that can truly enjoy life. People in the Child state speak, stand, think, perceive, and feel as they did in childhood. Behavior of the Child is impulsive rather than delayed by reason. Some typical expressions of the Child include daydreaming, fantasizing, throwing temper tantrums, being irrational or irresponsible, having fun, and being creative.

The Child has two types: *Free Child* and *Adapted Child*. The Free Child is impulsive, creative, curious, playful, fun-loving, free, and eager. Too much Free Child leads to a person's being uncontrollable. The Adapted Child is compromising, conforming, adapting, compliant, and easy to get along with. A person with too much Adapted Child may display a variety of personal problems: being depressed, guilty, robotlike, or prone to temper tantrums.

The *Adult* ego state is factual, nonemotional, precise, nonjudgmental, and accurate. The Adult essentially acts like a computer, an unfeeling aspect of the personality that gathers and processes information for making predictions and decisions. The Adult not only accurately evaluates the environment but also assesses the demands and emotions of the Parent and of the Child.

Each of these three ego states (Parent, Child, and Adult) have adaptive functions — when used in the appropriate situation.[1] The Parent is ideally suited when control is needed, for example, disciplining children. The Child is best when creative solutions to problems that appear unresolvable arise. The Child is also most adaptive for parties, celebrations, and other fun situations. The Adult is best suited for making important decisions, for example, making a career decision or deciding whether to marry. The well-adapted personality, then, switches from one ego state to another depending upon the circumstances.

Harris (1969, p. 39) describes "a great moment in psychotherapy" involving a client in therapy which was significant in leading Berne to conclude the existence of the Parent, Adult, and Child ego states:

A thirty-five-year-old lawyer, whom he was treating said, "I'm not really a lawyer, I'm just a little boy." Away from the psychiatrist's office he was, in fact, a successful lawyer, but in treatment he felt and acted like a little boy. Sometimes during the hour he would ask, "Are you talking to the lawyer or to the little boy?" Both Berne and his patient became intrigued at the existence and appearance of these two real people, or states of being, and began talking about them as "the adult" and "the child." Treatment centered around separating the two. Later another state began to become apparent as a state distinct from "adult" and "child." This was "the parent" and was identified by behavior which was a reproduction of what the patient saw and heard his parents do when he was a little boy.

Psychosocial Drives

While ego states provide the structure of the personality, the motivation for behaving comes from fulfilling basic human needs (food, shelter, sex) and from psychosocial drives. Berne (1966) identifies the following psychosocial drives: stimulus hunger, recognition hunger, structure hunger, and excitement hunger.

Stimulus hunger is the need to be stimulated. Stimulus deprivation studies have demonstrated that human beings will become highly disturbed when they are deprived of adequate amounts of physical stimulation (Hebb, Held, Riesen, and Teuber, 1961; Solomon, Kubzansky, Leiderman, Menderson, Trumbull, and Wexler, 1961; Spitz, 1945). One of the most important forms of stimulation is by receiving "strokes." The basic motivating force for all human social behavior is one's lifelong hunger for human recognition, which TA terms as seeking "strokes." In young children Spitz (1945) has demonstrated that stroking needs to be in the form of direct physical contact that comes from being cuddled, held, and soothed. Without such direct physical contact, the emotional and physical development of children will be severely stunted. While direct physical contact is the most nourishing form of stimulation, adults generally are able to fulfill their *recognition hunger* by being recognized or attended to by others. Positive recognition through such strokes as greetings, smiles, approval, cheers, and applause is highly valued. However, if such strokes are not received, negative strokes are then sought as they are considered better than no strokes. Such negative strokes include cold looks, disapproval, criticism, and frowns. Dusay and Dusay (1979, p. 388) note: "Habitual criminals with high recidivism rates illustrate that negative strokes are better than no strokes at all." This principle is also illustrated by those battered women who choose to continue to live with their abusive husbands rather than living alone and receiving no strokes. As can be seen by this discussion, stimulus hunger is closely related to recognition hunger. Stimulus hunger is a broader term thta encompasses recognition hunger. It is possible to receive stimulation from the environment (e.g., being in a thunderstorm) that is not a form of recognition.

Structural hunger is the need to structure time, and develops out of the dilemma of what to do with 24 hours a day, 168 hours per week, 8,760 hours per year. This dilemma is heightened in societies such as ours in which people have surplus time. Preferred ways of structuring times are those that are most exciting.

---

[1]The reader will note that Berne appears to have been influenced by Freud in developing his Child, Adult, and Parent ego states. The Child has similarities to Freud's "Id." The Adult has similarities to Freud's "Ego." The Parent has similarities to Freud's "Superego."

Excitement hunger is the desire to avoid boredom and to have interesting and exciting things to do. Among the most interesting ways of structuring time are those involved in getting strokes from others and those involved in exchanging strokes with others.

Types of Transactions

A transaction is a unit of social intercourse. A transaction is composed of a transactional stimulus (verbal and nonverbal messages sent by one individual) and a transactional response (verbal and nonverbal messages by another individual who is reacting to a transactional stimulus). The following is an example of a transaction:

HUSBAND: What are we going to have for dinner tonight?

WIFE: I don't know—whatever you'd like to make.

Structure hunger, excitement hunger, and recognition hunger motivate humans to participate in transactions. TA identifies five types of transactions:

1. Ritual.   The safest form of interaction is a ritual, which is a stereotyped transaction programmed by external social forces. Informal rituals include greetings such as "Hi, how are you?" "Fine, thank you." Examples of formal rituals include weddings and funerals, which are highly structured and predictable. Rituals are basically signs of mutual recognition and convey very little information.

2. Activity.   Activities structure time. Common activities include studying for exams, doing the dishes, mowing the lawn, building a house, and doing projects at work. Activities may be satisfying in and of themselves or they may lead to satisfactions in the future through receiving strokes. During the time of the activity there may, or may not be, involvement with another person. Some people use their work activity to avoid intimate involvement with others. (Critics of TA have questioned whether activities are transactions.)

3. Pastime.   Pastimes are semiritualistic and are usually shared with people having mutual interests— for example, a softball team, ham radio operators, poker players. Pastimes allow people to structure their

time in fairly interesting ways but are also structured to minimize the possibility of incidents that are threatening or too emotional. Small talk at social gatherings is a typical example of a pastime.

4. Intimacy.   Interactions that are entirely spontaneous and direct are intimate transactions. Such transactions may be exciting but also may be threatening and overwhelming. Such free and unstructured exchanges are generally avoided in favor of some structured and safer interactions.

5. Game.   A game is a set of transactions with a gimmick (that is, a hidden scheme for attaining an end). In a game one or more participants are consciously or unconsciously striving to achieve an ulterior outcome by using a hidden scheme.

There are two levels of communication involved in games: social and psychological. The social level is the overt or manifest; the psychological level is the covert or latent.

Prochaska (1979, pp. 237–38) gives an example of these two levels of communication in a game:

For example, if a woman asks a man, "Why don't you come by my place to see my collection of sculpture?" and the man responds "I'd love to. I'm really interested in art," they may be having a simple, candid interchange between two adults beginning to share a pastime. In a game, however, both players are also communicating a message at a different level, such as Child-to-Child messages like "Boy, I'd really like to get you alone in my apartment" and "I'd sure love to look at your curves."

This game is diagrammed in Figure 16.1 (page 384).

For a game to progress, at least one of the participants has to pull a switch, as further described in the above example by Prochaska (1979, p. 238):

For the payoff to occur, one of the players has to pull a switch. In this case, after fixing drinks and sitting close on the couch examining a reproduction of Rodin's The Kiss, *the woman still seems to be sending a seductive communication. The man's vanity convinces him to proceed, and he puts his hand on her leg, only to be rebuffed by a slap on the face and an irate "What kind of woman do you think I am?"*

FIGURE 16.1

A Game Diagram*

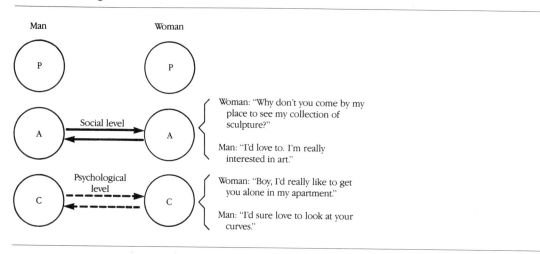

*The ego states of Parent, Adult, and Child are indicated by P, A, C.

The couple has just completed a heavy hand of RAPO.[2] Besides gaining mutual recognition, excitement, and some structured time together, there is also a strong emotional payoff for each. The woman is able to proudly affirm her position in life that she is OK, while feeling angry toward men for not being OK, just as her mother always said. The payoff for the man is to feel depressed and thereby reaffirm his conviction that he is not OK.

People who are attempting to achieve a hidden outcome may or may not be aware of their intentions—or aware of the gimmick they are using. For instance, a husband who has a vague fear his wife may desert him may not be aware he is playing a game when he says to her, "Honey, why don't you quit work and stay home to take care of the house. I can earn enough to support both of us."

Although some games may lead to substantial financial loss or mental anguish for some participants, not all games are necessarily undesirable. For instance, an individual having a strong need for social approval may perform many "altruistic" and "charitable" deeds.

A game may also be repeated over and over. A few people, for instance, continually play "One Up." For some, playing a certain game may become so much a part of their personality that it can aptly be called their style of life. A male alcoholic who denies to himself and to others he has a drinking problem is an example of this. (The alcoholic's payoffs for denying his drinking problem are the rewards he receives from drinking—such as feeling high and as a way to temporarily escape facing his problems.)

The "alcoholic" game also illustrates another aspect of games—several people may be involved. In the traditional alcoholic game described by Berne (1964) there may be a nagging, masochistic wife who literally drives her husband to drink in order that he will abuse her when inebriated. This wife receives two sets of payoffs. The abuse received is a form of recognition or attention. The second reward the wife receives is that the day after a drunken episode the wife has ammunition to belittle and berate her husband and to get him

---

*The ego states of Parent, Adult, and Child are indicated by P, A, C.
[2]Berne (1964) defines RAPO as being "Kiss Off" or "indignation."

to do things for her to atone for his behavior. The alcoholic is also apt to have companions who frequently invite him to "Let's go have a drink—a drink will be good for you." Their payoff is the fun and partying they have. Then there may also be a sympathetic listener to the alcoholic—perhaps a bartender who listens in order to get the alcoholic to spend his money.

Some people are involved in playing games that have destructive outcomes for themselves and for others. Often, people are unaware a destructive game is being played. For example, family members of an alcoholic may make elaborate efforts to keep the drinking problem hidden from others without realizing they are continuing to make it possible for the alcoholic to drink.

Common Games

Eric Berne lists a large number of psychological games in *Games People Play* (1964). People tend to have a repertoire of favorite games they play, and many people base their social relationships upon finding suitable partners to play the corresponding opposite roles. The following are common games played by people.

In the game "Why Don't You? Yes, but . . . ," a person consistently asks for suggestions or advice and then consistently rejects any that is offered. The other participants in this game assume that the principal player is attempting to solve a real problem in a concrete manner so they offer suggestions. The principal player in this game is able to get at least two payoffs—one is attention from other people and the other is a payoff that comes from being able to put others down by implying "That's really a dumb suggestion." The other participants may get a payoff through telling themselves "I must be a warm, caring person as this person respects and trusts me enough to share this problem with me."

In the "One Up" game one person seeks to top whatever someone else says. If the conversation is about big fish, the One Upper always has a story about how he caught this mammoth fish. If the topic is about bad grades received, the One Upper seeks to amaze everyone with how bad her grades are. If jokes are being told, the One Upper begins by saying, "I've got one that'll top that. Have you heard about . . ."

"Wooden Leg" is a game in which people attempt to manipulate others not to expect too much from them because of such wooden legs as having a physical handicap, being raised in a ghetto, having had a tragic romance, and having emotional problems such as being depressed. Closely related, "If it weren't for . . ." is a cop-out game in which players seek to rationalize not succeeding at a variety of tasks and goals.

A person who plays "Poor Me" is seeking sympathy and may at times try to get others to do things for him. Closely related is someone who plays "Ain't It Awful" through taking a negative view of events. Such a person is usually seeking attention and sympathy. In the game, "There I Go Again," the player seeks to excuse away his ineffective behavior without taking responsibility.

Some clients enjoy playing "Confession" when they seek to tell all their personal and interpersonal troubles in the hopes of receiving recognition and help from others. Some unhappily married men get together and enjoy discussing "Wives Are a Pain" as a way of ventilating their unhappiness. Some unhappily married wives enjoy discussing "Men Aren't Worth It" as a way of ventilating their frustrations. Parents enjoy discussing "Look How Hard I've Tried" when a home situation is particularly uproarious and hostile as a way to relieve their frustrations that the goals for their family have not been achieved. Many people seek to avoid assuming responsibility for their failures and shortcomings by playing "It's All Them."

Some individuals who have received few positive strokes end up seeking a lot of negative strokes, which to them is better than receiving no strokes. One game that is played to receive negative strokes is "Kick Me" in which the player seeks to do things that will elicit negative reactions from others.

People who enjoy creating trouble for others are apt to play "Let's You and Him Fight."

People who receive psychological rewards in analyzing others and in giving advice often play "Psychiatry." A person who seeks to see how many different sexual relationships he can have often seeks to play "Love 'Em and Leave 'Em." Men are socialized in our society to play "Mr. Macho" and women are socialized to play "Miss America."

"Monday Morning Quarterbacks" seek to make themselves feel important by telling you what you should have done differently *after* things have not turned out well for you.

The number of different games that can be played is best described as infinite.

Life Scripts

Every person has life scripts (plans) that are formed during childhood and are based on early beliefs about oneself and others. These plans are developed from early interactions with parents and others and largely determined by the pattern of strokes that are received.

Scripts (as in a play in a theater) are plans we learn and then carry around in our heads. These scripts enable us to conceptualize where we are in our activities, and are plans for directing what we need to do to complete our activities and to accomplish our goals. Scripts are also devices for helping us to remember what we have done in the past.

Many details of a life script are supplied by parental opinions, suggestions, and encouragements: Examples include: "She's such a cute girl, everyone loves her," "He's stupid and will never amount to much," "He'll be famous some day," "He's sure nutty," "All the girls will want to date him." Fairy tales, myths, TV shows, early life experiences, and children's stories are also important sources of life scripts. While parental influences and fairy tales are important contributing factors, the life script is still the creation of a young child. One's life script may be either winning or losing, being a success or a failure, exciting or banal. Each script also includes specific roles, such as heroes and heroines, villains, persecutors, innocent bystanders, and victims.

Harris (1969) has identified four general life scripts that a person chooses involving how a person views herself in comparison with others. These four positions are (1) I'm OK—You're OK; (2) I'm OK—You're not OK; (3) I'm not OK—You're OK; and (4) I'm not OK—You're not OK.

People who decide "I"m OK—You're OK" tend to be productive, law-abiding people who are successful and who have positive, meaningful relationships with others.

People who decide "I'm OK—You're not OK" predispose themselves to exploit others, cheat others, rob others, or succeed at the expense of others. This type of person may be a criminal, a ruthless business executive, or a destructive lover who loves them and leaves them.

People who decide "I'm not OK—You're OK" feel inferior in the presence of those they judge as superior. Such a life script frequently leads to withdrawal from others as a way to avoid being reminded of not being OK. Withdrawal is not the only alternative. The person can write a counterscript based on lines borrowed from early authority figures: "You can be OK if . . ." The person is then driven to achieve the "if" contingencies. Examples of such contingencies include making huge sums of money, being submissive, being entertaining through making others laugh, and so on. Such a person then strives to meet these contingencies in order to receive strokes and approval from others.

People who decide "I'm not OK—You're not OK" tend to be the most unhappy and disturbed. Prochaska (1979, p. 241) states:

The extreme withdrawal of schizophrenia or psychotic depression is their most common fate. They may regress at an infantile state in the primitive hope that they may once again receive the strokes of being held and fed. Without intervention from caring others, these individuals will live out a self-destructive life of institutionalization, irreversible alcoholism, senseless homicide, or suicide.

Decisions about life scripts are generally made early in childhood. James and Jongeward (1971, p. 35) provide an incident in the life of a forty-three-year-old client that led her to conclude "I'm not OK and men are not OK either."

My father was a brutal alcoholic. When he was drunk he would hit me and scream at me. I would try to hide. One day when he came home, the door flew open and he was drunker than usual. He picked up a butcher knife and started running through the house. I hid in a coat closet. I was almost four years old. I was so scared in the closet. It was dark and spooky, and things kept hitting me in the face. That day I decided who men were—beasts, who would

Popular culture often reinforces traditional sex role expectations. On the situation comedy Leave It To Beaver, *June Cleaver was the perfect wife and mother — domestic, conforming, and in the end forever deferring to husband Ward, whose highly moral, fatherly lectures always seemed to rescue the Beaver just before fade-out.*

only try to hurt me. I was a large child and I remember thinking, "If I were smaller, he'd love me" or "If I were prettier, he'd love me." I always thought I wasn't worth anything.

Based on this script, she married an alcoholic at age twenty-three, and for the next twenty years had been living her life drama of feeling worthless and living with a "beast."

One of the areas where our behavior is largely guided by scripts is sexual behavior. Sexual scripts result from elaborate prior learning in which we acquire an etiquette of sexual behavior. Scripts tell us who are appropriate sexual partners, what sexual activity is expected, where and when the sexual activity should occur, and what should be the sequence of the different sexual behaviors.

Scripts vary greatly from one culture to another. Powdermaker (1933, p. 241) provides the following description of a script about female masturbation which is generally held by the Lesu of the South Pacific:

A woman will masturbate if she is sexually excited and there is no man to satisfy her. A couple may be having intercourse in the same house, or near enough for her to see them, and she may thus become aroused. She then sits down and bends her right leg so that her heel presses against her genitalia. Even young girls of about six years may do this quite casually as they sit on the ground. The women and men talk about it freely, and there is no shame attached to it. It is a customary position for women to take, and they learn it in childhood. They never use their hands for manipulation.

A life script and a theatrical script have many similarities. Each has a cast of characters, dialogue, themes and plots, acts and scenes; generally both move toward a climax. Often, however, a person is unaware or only vaguely aware of the life scripts he is acting out. Public stages on which people act out their scripts include home, social gatherings, church, school, office, and factory. As Shakespeare has noted, "All the world's a stage."

Most life scripts are learned at an early age. As children grow they learn to play roles — villains, law enforcers, heroes, heroines, victims, and rescuers — and seek others to play complementary roles. Through playing roles, children integrate new themes and parts into their roles and gradually develop their life scripts. The particular scripts that are developed are substantially influenced by the reactions they receive from significant people in their lives.

Individuals follow scripts, and so do families and cultures. Cultural scripts are expected patterns of behavior within a society. In our culture, for example, only men are expected to fight in military conflict while in Israel both sexes are expected to fight wars. In regard to cultural scripts, James and Jongeward (1971, p. 70) note:

Script themes differ from one culture to another. The script can contain themes of suffering, persecution, and hardship (historically the Jews); it can contain themes of building empires and making conquests (as the Romans once did). Throughout history some nations have acted from a "top-dog" position of the conqueror; some from an "under-dog" position of the conquered. In early America, where people came to escape oppression, to exploit the situation, and to explore the unknown, a basic theme was "struggling for survival." In many cases this struggle was acted out by pioneering and settling.

Historically, women are socialized in our society to have life scripts different from those of men. American women traditionally are expected to be affectionate, passive, conforming, sensitive, intuitive, dependent, and "sugar and spice and everything nice." They are supposed to be concerned primarily with domestic life, to be nurturing, to instinctively love to care for babies and young children, to be deeply concerned about their personal appearance, and to be self-sacrificing for their family. They should not appear to be ambitious, aggressive, competitive, or more intelligent than men. They are expected to be ignorant and uninterested in sports, economics, or politics. In relationships with men they should not initiate forming a relationship, and are expected to be tender, feminine, emotional, and appreciative.

There are also a number of traditional sex-role expectations for males in our society. A male is expected to be tough, fearless, logical, self-reliant, independent, and aggressive. He should have definite opinions on the major issues of the day, and is expected to make authoritative decisions at work and at home. He is expected to be strong, to be a sturdy oak, never to be depressed, vulnerable, or anxious. He is not supposed to be "sissy" or feminine. He is expected not to cry or openly display so-called feminine emotions. He is expected to be the provider, the breadwinner, to be competent in all situations. He is supposed to be physically strong, self-reliant, athletic; to have a manly air of confidence and toughness; to be daring and aggressive; to be brave and forceful; always to be in a position to dominate any situation; to be a Clint Eastwood. He is supposed to initiate relationships with women and is expected to be dominant in relationships with them. (The women's movement is now making changes in these sex-role scripts.)

In our society (as well as in other large and complex societies) there are a number of subcultures, and each subculture has its own scripts. Street gangs, Chicanos, Texans, Presbyterians, Jews, professional baseball players, dentists, farmers, and college students each have their own subcultural scripts. For example, common aspects of scripts for college students include cramming at the last moment for exams, procrastination, partying, idealism, shortage of money, and expectation of success and happiness following graduation.

Families also have scripts. These scripts provide a set of directions for family members. Examples include the following:

We Winships have always been pillars of the community.

We Navarres have always been rowdy.

The men in our family have always held political offices in our community and the women have always been active in the church.

We Hubbards have always been in trouble with the police.

We Schomakers have always been gamblers.

We Collinses have always taken a long vacation each year.

We Hepps have never had to ask for a handout from anyone.

We Watsons have all gone to college.

We Rices have always been Democrats.

The men in our family have all been coal miners who are active in union activities.

If a family member does not live up to the script expectation, he is often viewed as a "deviant" or as a "black sheep."

The importance of scripts in determining human behavior is emphasized by Berne (1966, p. 310):

Nearly all human activity is programmed by an ongoing script dating from early childhood, so that the feeling of autonomy is nearly always an illusion — an illusion which is the greatest affliction of the human race because it makes awareness, honesty, creativity, and intimacy possible for only a few fortunate individuals. For the rest of humanity, other people are seen mainly as objects to be manipulated. They must be invited, persuaded, seduced, bribed or forced into playing the proper roles to reinforce the protagonist's position and fulfill his script.

The number of script themes is infinite. A few of the more common themes are the following:

I must be loved by everyone.

I've got to be perfect.

I've got to be the best at what I do.

My purpose in life is to save sinners.

When people tell me their problems, I have to rescue them.

I will take my life some day.

To be noticed I must play tricks on people.

People will only love me if I make them laugh.

I'll also be a victim.

I'm a martyr.

I can always get what I want by being pushy.

I'll eventually go crazy.

My life will always be one big party.

I'm cut out to be a leader.

I'm a failure and always will be.

I'll never get anywhere.

I've got to save for a rainy day.

If I acquire a lot of money, I'll be popular.

I'm always the life of a party.

I'm always miserable.

Life has always shortchanged me.

I should always be silent as it is wrong to rock the boat.

Men are assholes.

I will never let anyone get the best of me.

I'm headed for fame and fortune.

James and Jongeward (1971, pp. 84–85) provide the following example of how a life script is played:

A woman who had taken the position, "Men are bums," marries a sequence of "bums." Part of her script is based on "Men are not OK." She fulfills her own prophecy by nagging, pushing, complaining, and generally making life miserable for her husband (who has his part to play). Eventually, she manipulates him into leaving. Then she can say, "See, I told you. Men are bums who leave you when the going gets rough."

Often people play games as part of their life scripts. A person who has a script of being a Casanova plays the game "Love 'em and leave 'em." A person who has a script of "I won't let anyone get the best of me" is apt to play "One-Up." A person who has a script of being an advisor to others is apt to play "Monday Morning Quarterback." A person who has a script of "I'll always find a way to seduce people into helping me" is apt to play "Poor Me."

THEORY OF PSYCHOPATHOLOGY

TA believes personal problems involve either problems within the personality or between personalities, or both.

Intrapsychic problems may result from several sources. One source that already has been described is having a self-defeating life script, such as "I'm a failure" or "I'm not OK and neither are you."

Another intrapsychic problem is rigidly holding to one ego state and shutting out the other two. As indicated earlier, having a balance of the three ego states is healthy. A "workaholic" is someone who spends too much time in the Adult ego state and thereby is unable to enjoy his family and to have fun. I've known athletes (jocks) who have spent their years in college playing games and partying, giving little attention to anything else. When their four years of eligibility for athletic competition were gone, they were far from graduating and untrained for any skilled employment. During their college years they had been in their "Child" at the expense of the other two states. I've also known people

FIGURE 16.2

Two Examples of Complementary Transaction

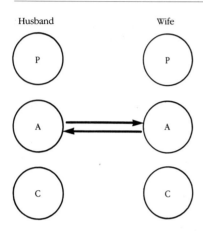

Husband: "Do you know where my cuff
    links are?"
Wife: "Yes, they're in my jewelry box."

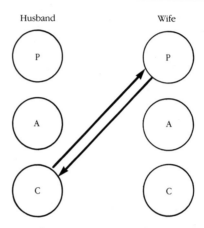

Husband: "I feel terrible today. Could you
    call the office and tell them I can't make it,
    and also get me two aspirin."
Wife: "I surely will. You just stay in bed. I'll
    call in sick also so that I can get whatever
    you need today."

who were too much "Parent" in romantic relationships by constantly giving advice and by smothering the other person through trying to do things for, rather than with, the other person.

Another intrapsychic problem is being in an inappropriate ego state for what the circumstances warrant—for example, clowning around (being in the Child) when a person should be studying for an exam or completing an urgent project at work.

TA has a unique approach to describing and understanding interpersonal problems. It focuses attention on how different individuals tend to communicate (both verbally and nonverbally) with one another. There are three rules of communication.

The first rule of communication is, Communication will proceed smoothly as long as transactions are *complementary*. Complementary transactions are those in which the arrows are complementary, some examples of which we illustrated in Figure 16.2.

The second rule of communication is, Communication on the specific topic ceases immediately whenever a crossed transaction occurs. A *crossed transac-*

FIGURE 16.3

Two Examples of Crossed Transactions

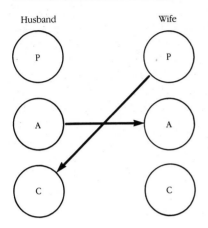

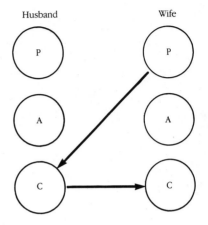

Husband: "Do you know where my cuff links are?"
Wife: "When are you ever going to learn to take care of your things—you lose everything."

Husband: "Let's call in sick to work today, and go fishing."
Wife: "You're so irresponsible. You know it isn't right to do that."

tion is one in which the arrows are not parallel as illustrated in Figure 16.3.

The third rule of communication applies to *psychological games*. The rule is, Behavior cannot be predicted by attention to the social message alone; the psychological message is key to understanding the meaning and to predicting behavior. Examples of games are presented in Figure 16.4 (page 392).

Psychological games may be constructive or destructive. If the payoffs in games help people, then they are constructive. For example, people who volunteer to give their time and resources at social service agencies usually are volunteering for some hidden personal reasons and usually receive such payoffs as feeling worthwhile and good about themselves. In some cases boredom and loneliness are also curbed. At the same time such volunteers perform useful services to others. Other games, because of the payoff, tend to be undesirable. Some people continually play "One-Upmanship," where they are overly competitive, even to the point of continually disparaging others and trying to stop every story that others tell them.

FIGURE 16.4

Two Examples of Psychological Games

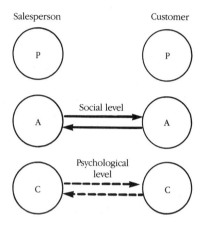

Social level
Salesperson: "This is a better product but I
    don't think you can afford it."
Customer: "I'll take it!"

Psychological level
Salesperson: "I'll motivate this person to buy
    the expensive item."
Customer: "I'll show this salesperson I'm as
    good as anyone else."

Social level
Male: "That dress really looks attractive on
    you."
Female: "Well, thank you. I like people who
    notice positive things about me."

Psychological level
Male: "If I say something nice maybe I'll find
    out if she's interested in getting something
    going between us."
Female: "This fellow appears interested in
    me and I'll show him that I'm interested
    in him."

THEORY OF THERAPY

Simply stated, therapy seeks to have clients first become aware of the intrapsychic and/or interpersonal
problems they face. In the process of helping clients
gain insight into their problems, clients are educated
in using the terms of TA. This instruction occurs in therapy (either one-to-one or in groups) and by giving clients reading such as *Games People Play* (Berne, 1964),
I'm OK — You're OK (1969), and *Born to Win* (James

and Jongeward, 1971). Early in this instructional process clients are taught *structural analysis*, that is, how
to identify their Parent, Adult, and Child ego states.
They also learn how to analyze problematic transactions through diagramming the transactions and learn
the concepts of analyzing games and life scripts. If TA
classes are offered in the client's community, clients
may be urged to take a course in TA prior to or during
therapy. As clients become educated in the TA approach and more aware of their own ego states, they
often are able to teach others how to analyze them-

selves. Prochaska (1979, p. 243) states: "The client's work is usually a pattern of going from student to self-analyzer to teacher of others."

To encourage clients to analyze their communications in terms of the TA format, the therapist frequently asks, "Which ego state is talking now?" If clients are confused or disagree with the therapist's or group's analysis of their ego states, the therapist may audiotape or videotape the clients' interactions and then play the tape back to let them see and hear how they are interacting.

The problems of clients are then analyzed in terms of TA concepts so that clients gain insight into their personal problems. Such problems include those discussed in the prior section: being in an appropriate ego state for the situation, playing destructive games, having a destructive life script, and interpersonal difficulties created by crossed transactions. Much of the work of the therapist is involved in helping clients to become aware, often through confronting them, of the ways in which they are contributing to their intrapsychic and interpersonal problems. For example, clients may be confronted with how they are playing certain destructive games, including demonstrating the payoffs in such games.

Game Analysis

Two treatment techniques that are increasingly being used in transactional analysis are game analysis and script analysis. *Game analysis* can be defined as a treatment technique in which a therapist enables a client to gain insight into some of his interactions through the use of game concepts. The kinds of games that are the main focus of game analysis are those that lead to undesirable outcomes for the client or for others.

The therapist has several roles in analyzing games: (1) Teach clients the terminology of game analysis. This perhaps can best be accomplished at the first occasion in which a therapist helps a client to gain insight into a game. (2) Point out to the clients that playing games is not necessarily undesirable. This may be therapeutically valuable as some clients may feel it is wrong to play

games because games have an exploitative connotation. Such a feeling may cause resistances to examining games. These resistances may be reduced by informing clients that everyone plays games; some games have beneficial outcomes while others have undesirable outcomes. (3) Help clients to recognize those games that are destructive for them or for other players, and also enable them to gain insight into how these games are being played. (4) Encourage clients to explore new ways of responding after they are aware of how their role in a game leads to undesirable consequences. (5) Help clients to specifically assign names to those undesirable games they are playing. Using colloquial names for games is often acceptable and advantageous as they may be more precise and have more meaning for clients. (6) Teach people the kind of games they need to play in order to achieve their goals. Some people have goals considered beneficial for themselves and society but do not know what they have to do to achieve these goals. Often such people can be instructed on what to do, using game concepts. For example, a person seeking a job may need to learn how to play "How to Get an Interview" and "How to Sell Yourself in an Interview." Or, a couple who is frequently feuding may need to learn "How to Fight Fairly" and "How to Give in a Relationship to Get What You Want."

There appear to be three reasons that game analysis appears to be a useful therapeutic approach: (1) One of the important functional values of naming something (in this case a certain kind of game) is that it increases clients' capacities to recognize similar transactions when they occur in the future. Once clients recognize and have insight into a game that is causing them difficulty, they are in a better position to cease their destructive behavior and to explore alternative modes of behavior. (2) Analyzing behavior in terms of games is apt to be intriguing to clients and, therefore, may lead to greater personal involvement in therapy and increase their motivation to resolve their difficulties. (3) Game analysis provides clients with a method of analyzing certain problematic interactions. After learning how to analyze such interactions, clients should be better able to analyze other problematic games beyond those specifically discussed in counseling.

CASE EXAMPLE

Game Analysis and Script Analysis

J ames and Jongeward (1971) indicate that three common life scripts or roles played by people are Persecutor, Victim, and Rescuer. Often a person will play a variety of games in conjunction with one of these life scripts. A person who plays a Victim role may also be persecuting those around her, and occasionally there is a direct shift to the Persecutor role. James and Jongeward (1971, p. 89) provide the following example showing how transactions between a married couple can be analyzed in terms of games and life script concepts:

Ted and Mary came into counseling complaining about the failure of their second honeymoon. Each claimed to have been victimized by the other. He shouted, "You had the gall to take your mother along. She even shared our motel room." She retorted, "And you were very rude and embarrassed me." After a number of hostile exchanges, they were asked to tell about their first honeymoon. Ted challenged, "What does that have to do with us now?" Mary retorted, "I'll tell you what. You took your parents along on our honeymoon fifteen years ago. You said, 'They never get a chance to go anywhere.' You've been taking advantage of me ever since."

Mary had assumed the role of Victim all these years. She had played the games of "Poor Me" and "See How Hard I Tried," and finally got even by assuming the role of Persecutor herself. Her favorite game became "Now I've Got You, You S.O.B." For fifteen years the theme of their marriage drama had been "Getting Even."

Script Analysis

Script Analysis can be defined as a treatment technique in which a therapist enables clients to gain insight into the scripts they are acting out through the use of script concepts. The types of scripts that are the primary focus of script analysis are those that lead to undesirable outcomes for clients or for others.

The therapist has the following role in analyzing scripts: (1) Teach clients the terminology of script analysis. (2) Point out to clients that everyone is playing a variety of scripts, and that scripts largely determine human behavior. Indicate that some scripts have benefi-

cial outcomes while others have undesirable outcomes. (3) Help clients to recognize those scripts that have undesirable outcomes. (4) Help clients to assign names to the scripts they are playing so that they can be more readily identified when they are being acted out in the future. (5) Help clients to develop new, desirable scripts to act out, and to encourage and teach clients more effective ways of responding in the future.

Within transactional analysis, game analysis and script analysis can be used with families and with small-sized groups as well as with individuals.

TA therapists emphasize personal responsibility. They believe, as does Ellis (1962), that clients are responsible for their emotions, their thoughts, and their behaviors (this concept will be more fully described in Chapter 18). If a client says "I can't think today" the TA therapist will confront him with "You mean you have decided not to think today." Or, if a client says "She makes me feel bad," the TA therapist will say "You know that you are choosing to feel bad — in response to her." Or, if a client says "He made me steal," the therapist will say "You mean you chose to steal."

After clients become aware of their personal problems and how they are contributing to their problems, various courses of action to resolve the problems are explored. Each client then usually makes a contract specifying what the client will do (and perhaps also what the therapist will do) to attempt to resolve the problem. A workaholic, for example, might make a contract limiting the number of hours per day he will spend on work and also be given homework assignments to become involved in fun activities (e.g., joining a social group, going to movies, gardening).

The types of TA therapy may differ widely. Berne originally used TA as an adjunct to psychoanalysis. Some TA therapists combine TA approaches with Gestalt exercises (James and Jongeward, 1971). TA has also been combined with reality therapy and rational therapy. Other TA therapists restrict their practice to primarily using the TA approach. TA is used individually, with groups, with families, with couples, in marathons, in prison, in outpatient and inpatient wards, and in business and industry settings.

In group therapy a variety of techniques may be used to help clients gain an awareness of their destructive transactions. One approach in game analysis involves psychodrama, which was originally developed by Moreno (1946). Dusay and Dusay (1979) describe using psychodrama by having the client play the director. In this role the client-director instructs other group members in how he is playing a destructive game. Dusay and Dusay (1979, p. 403) note:

By using this type of psychodrama, the client is able to step outside of his own game system; in this view he can view, think and direct his own part in the game. . . . Through these maneuvers, the client will gain a new awareness and experiment with corrective procedures. (Psychodrama is further described in Chapter 22.)

EVALUATION

TA has grown remarkably in acceptance and popularity since its formulation by Eric Berne in the 1950s. Dusay and Dusay (1989, p. 448) provide reasons for its popularity:

Because of its easily understood vocabulary and because of the willingness of therapists to share ideas with clients, TA rapidly became a popular psychotherapy. As such, TA has been used not only by psychiatrists, psychologists, social workers, and other traditional therapists, but also by paraprofessionals who found that the theoretical aspects of TA were easy to learn and had direct applicability to their concerns. Indeed, street workers and prison inmates have become outstanding TA therapists. Effort for the TA therapist is in practical applications rather than in decoding mystical jargon.

The popularity of such books as *Games People Play* (Berne, 1964), *Scripts People Live* (Steiner, 1974), and *I'm OK—You're OK* (Harris, 1969) suggests that readers find such concepts as the following to be helpful in resolving personal problems: game analysis, life script analysis, complementary transactions and crossed transactions, seeking strokes, and personal responsibility for emotions and actions.

Another positive feature of TA is to borrow techniques (such as Gestalt exercises and psychodrama) from other therapy approaches that are useful in producing therapeutic change. TA is an "open" therapeutic approach that actively encourages experimentation with new techniques.

In contrast to most other therapy approaches, TA is perhaps more enjoyable to participate in for both clients and therapists. The approach uses a number of experimental exercises, such as psychodrama. In addition, analyzing personal problems in terms of games and life scripts has a game mystique that facilitates interest.

There are also some criticisms that can be made about TA:

1. There have been very few studies on the outcome of transactional analysis. In a review of TA, Merkel (1975) was able to locate only two studies and the results were inconclusive regarding whether TA is effective. Prochaska (1979, p. 258) is quite critical of the lack of outcome research:

Twenty years after TA was first practiced, it has yet to be evaluated for its clinical effectiveness. The best evidence that Holland could provide in 1973 was that Berne's patients had traveled further to get to therapy than did the patients of any other therapist in the Carmel area, an average of twelve miles. What a terrific criterion for the effectiveness of a therapy!

In a review of research conducted on TA, Dusay and Dusay (1989, pp. 438–39) cite only a few outcome studies — none of which provides convincing evidence that TA is effective.

2. The concepts of TA explain some aspects of human behavior but certainly not all. For example, what causes grief, depression, anger, love, happiness, and other emotions? How are such emotions perpetuated? What causes burglaries, alcoholism, crimes of violence, or such positive action as helping others in need? Game analysis and script analysis may provide some of the reasons but not all of them.

3. There is a danger in analyzing the personality into the three separate ego states of Parent, Adult, and Child. Most authorities on human behavior emphasize the importance of the personality's functioning as an integrated "whole." The danger of a triparite personality approach is that it may encourage clients to function in separate roles as a Parent, Adult, and Child rather than as an integrated individual. For example, TA indicates the Adult ego state is best suited for work activities. But being a rational computer at work will lead a person to miss out on the "fun" activities at work and probably lead to ostracism by fellow employees who will find an Adult to be boring, especially during slack

times. Even when things are hectic, humor is often useful in relieving some of the tension.

4. I have participated in some transactional groups and have found it difficult at times to determine which ego state a transaction is coming from. I have asked leaders of groups to identify the ego state producing certain communications and have gotten different answers. One question is, "If a male student intern in field placement decides to greet his first client as his father greets a stranger, and the father is very effective in interacting with people, which ego state is such a transaction coming from?" TA group leaders have given me three different answers to this question — Parent, Adult, and Child. My concern is that the counseling process can get bogged down in a long, fruitless discussion of which ego state is the source of a transaction rather than focusing on exploring and resolving personal problems of clients.

In raising this concern I am aware that Thompson (1972) found in a study that ego states are observable, that trained TA experts have a high degree of agreement in rating which ego state is in operation in a given client, and that naive observers can be trained to correctly identify ego states (Thompson is an advocate of TA).

Part of my concern results from the observation that there are *substantial* differences among TA authorities in defining the PAC ego states. Berne (1964) states the Parent ego state has two forms, Direct Parent and Indirect Parent, while the Child has two forms, the Adapted Child and the Natural Child. Dusay and Dusay (1979) state that the Parent ego state has two forms, the Critical Parent and the Nurturing Parent, while the Child's two forms are Adapted Child and Free Child. James and Jongeward (1971) state the two Parent forms are the Nurturing Parent and the Prejudicial Parent, while the Child ego state has three forms: Natural Child, Adapted Child, and Little Professor.

While Berne (1964) divided the PAC ego states into five different forms (Direct Parent, Indirect Parent, Adapted Child, Natural Child, Adult), Steiner (1974) has divided the PAC states into twenty-seven forms!

I also find the distinction between Berne's Indirect Parent and his Adapted Child to be confusing. Berne (1964, p. 26) defines the Indirect Parent as follows:

When it is an indirect influence, he responds the way they wanted him to respond.

Berne (1964, p. 26) defines the Adapted Child as

The Adapted Child is the one who modifies his behavior under the Parental influence. He behaves as father (or mother) wanted him to behave.

It appears to me these two definitions are practically identical.

The considerable variation among TA authorities on how the PAC ego states are defined adds to the confusion of trying to identify the ego state in which a specific transaction is originating.

SUMMARY

Eric Berne was the primary developer of transactional analysis. The basic premise of transactional analysis is that the human personality is structured into three separate ego states—Parent, Adult, and Child. Basic human needs and psychosocial drives (for example, recognition hunger) are motivational forces. Intrapsychic problems arise from a variety of sources, including adopting self-defeating life scripts, rigidly holding to one ego state while shutting out the other two, and being in an inappropriate ego state for the circumstances.

Interpersonal problems also arise from a variety of sources, including playing destructive psychological games and cross transactions while communicating.

TA seeks to have clients become aware of the intrapsychic and interpersonal problems they have. These problems are then analyzed and interpreted to clients in terms of TA concepts. Once their problems are analyzed, clients make a contract to take specific courses of action to resolve them. TA emphasizes the importance of clients' taking personal responsibility for their thoughts, emotions, and actions. TA also uses a number of experiential techniques (e.g., psychodrama and Gestalt exercise) to help clients understand and work out their problems. Two treatment techniques that are increasingly being used in TA are game analysis and script analysis.

A number of concepts developed by TA appear useful in helping clients to resolve personal problems: game analysis, script analysis, complementary transactions and crossed transactions, seeking strokes, and personal responsibility for emotions and actions. There is a need for TA theorists to work toward increased consistency in defining the Parent, Adult, and Child ego states. There is also a need for researchers to conduct outcome studies on the effectiveness of TA.

EXERCISES

1. Life Script Analysis

GOAL: This exercise is designed to help students identify and describe destructive life scripts and to examine how to change such scripts.

Step 1: Describe the purpose of this exercise. Define what life scripts are and summarize several examples of common life scripts (see the material in this chapter).

Step 2: Ask each student to write on a sheet of paper as fully as possible a destructive life script. Read the following example to illustrate the kind of description that is desired.

Mrs. H has been married for twenty-two years. She was brought up to believe that a woman's role was to be supportive of her husband and to do the domestic tasks involved in raising children. She and her husband, Paul, have two children. The oldest, Kelly, is a senior in college, and Jason is a freshman. Both children are no longer living at home.

The first several years of their marriage were fairly happy but a financial struggle. Paul was a life insurance salesman, so it took several years to get a large enough number of clients to make a decent standard of living. Mrs. H helped out by doing paperwork and answering the phone at home.

After they became more financially secure, they were able to take an occasional vacation and to travel some. About seven years ago, Mrs. H discovered her husband had for the previous five years been occasionally having extramarital affairs. When Mrs. H confronted her husband, there was considerable conflict. Mrs. H considered a divorce, but she did not know how she would be able to support herself and the children, particularly because she had few job skills. She decided to stay with her husband, particularly after he apologized and stated he would never "stray" again.

Paul, as Mrs. H discovered eighteen months later, did not live up to his word. He has continued to have occasional affairs. Mrs. H has continued to remain married and has tried to make the best of it. She has not been sexually involved with her husband since the time she first discovered he was being unfaithful. Their marriage has become an empty shell marriage. The children have now left home, and Mrs. H has very little to do. She is becoming increasingly depressed. She has in recent years felt considerable tension. Her husband and her doctor have stated her medical concerns border on hypochondria. Her role of raising children has been completed. Her life plans of having a satisfying, happy marriage have long since disappeared. Her husband is now earning enough that if she stays in the marriage financially she can live comfortably. But she is increasingly depressed about her circumstances. Having few job skills she believes living independently from her husband would be very difficult. Being a strict Catholic she is morally opposed to a divorce. She is in a severe dilemma about what she should do.

Step 3: Have the students form subgroups of three and share the scripts they wrote. After a member reads a script, have the other members discuss what might be done to help the person who is playing this destructive life script.

Step 4: Form a circle and ask the students if anyone has questions about how to change any of the life scripts that were discussed. End the exercise by having the students discuss the merits and shortcomings of analyzing problematic interactions in terms of script analysis.

2. Game Analysis

GOALS: This exercise is designed to help students identify and describe destructive games and to examine how to stop such games from being replayed.

Step 1: Begin by stating the goal of this exercise. Then define what a game is and give examples of commonly played games. (This chapter identifies a number of games that can be used as examples.)

Step 2: Ask each student to describe on a sheet of paper one or more destructive games that he has played or that he has seen friends or relatives play.

Step 3: Have the class form subgroups of three and have the students share what they have written. (Inform the students that they have a right to privacy, and therefore they can, if they desire, choose not to share what they have written.) After a member shares what he has written, ask the subgroups to discuss what might be done to stop the destructive games from being replayed.

Step 4: Have the class form a circle and ask whether the students have questions about how to stop any of the destructive games they discussed. End the exercise by asking students to discuss the merits and shortcomings of analyzing interpersonal difficulties in terms of game concepts.

17

REALITY THERAPY

The founder of reality therapy is William Glasser (1925–). Glasser is a psychiatrist who graduated from Western Reserve Medical School in Cleveland, Ohio, in 1953. In 1956 he became a consulting psychiatrist to the Ventura School for Girls, a California state institution for the treatment of delinquent girls.

Glasser had become skeptical of the value of orthodox psychoanalysis in which he had received training, and at the Ventura School for Girls he set up a treatment program based on the principles of a new approach which he developed and named *reality therapy*. In developing this approach he had been highly influenced by Dr. Helmuth Kaiser, an existential psychologist, and by Dr. G. L. Harrington, a psychiatrist who was his supervisor when Glasser did his psychiatric residency at the University of California at Los Angeles. The reality therapy approach showed promise at Ventura, as the girls began to enjoy and express enthusiasm for the program at this correctional school.

Glasser also applied this new approach in his work at a private outpatient clinic with patients having a variety of problems. In 1962 Dr. Harrington was placed in charge of a ward for psychotic patients at a Veterans Hospital in Los Angeles. Following a consultation with Glasser, Harrington successfully applied the reality therapy approach at this hospital, which led to dramatic increases in the discharge rate (Glasser and Zunin, 1979).

These successes led to the publication of this new approach, *Reality Therapy* (Glasser, 1965). In 1966 Glasser began consulting in the California school system and applied the concepts of reality therapy to education. His emphasis on the need for education to highlight involvement, relevance, and thinking is having a profound impact in changing the educational system. In 1969 he published *Schools without Failure*, which presents suggestions for making education relevant for students, emphasizes developing the thinking capacities of students, and provides suggestions for getting students more involved and interested in getting a quality education.

In 1969 the Institute of Reality Therapy was formed, with Glasser as its first director. The basic principles of reality therapy are increasingly being adopted by counselors and therapists and are being used with clients having a wide variety of problems.

WILLIAM GLASSER: THEORIES OF PERSONALITY DEVELOPMENT AND PSYCHOPATHOLOGY

Glasser has developed two different theories of personality development and psychopathology—an identity theory, which he developed in the 1960s, and a control theory which he developed in the 1980s. Both are summarized here, as each has considerable merit in conceptualizing human behavior. We begin with the more recent theory.

Control Theory

Glasser (1984) has developed a control theory explanation of human behavior. A major thrust of the theory is that we have pictures in our heads of what reality is like and pictures of how we would like the world to be. Glasser (1984, p. 32) asserts, "All our behavior is our constant attempt to reduce the difference between what we want (the pictures in our heads) and what we have (the way we see situations in the world)."

Some examples may help to illustrate what Glasser is theorizing. Each of us has pictures in our head of the physical and personality characteristics of the kind of person we would like to date or form a relationship with; when we find someone that closely matches those characteristics, we seek to form a relationship. Each of us has pictures in our head of our favorite foods; when we are hungry we select one of those pictures and seek to obtain that food. Each of us has pictures in our head of what we like to do with our leisure time; when we have leisure time we select one of those pictures and seek to get involved in the activity we select.

How do we develop the pictures in our head that we believe will satisfy our needs? Glasser asserts that we begin to create our picture albums at an early age (perhaps even before birth) and that we spend our whole life enlarging these albums. Essentially, whenever what we do gets us something that satisfies a need, we store the picture of what satisfied us in our personal picture albums. Glasser (1984, p. 19) gives the following example of this process by describing how a hungry child added chocolate-chip cookies to his picture album:

Suppose you had a grandson and your daughter left you in charge while he was taking a nap. She said she would be right back, because he would be ravenous when he awoke and she knew you had no idea what to feed an eleven-month-old child. She was right. As soon as she left, he awoke screaming his head off, obviously starved. You tried a bottle, but he rejected it— he had something more substantial in mind. But what? Being unused to a howling baby, and desperate, you tried a chocolate-chip cookie and it worked wonders. At first, he did not seem to know what it was, but he was a quick learner. He quickly polished off three cookies. She returned and almost polished you off for being so stupid as to give a baby chocolate. "Now," she said, "he will be yelling all day for those cookies." She was right. If he is like most of us, he will probably have chocolate on his mind for the rest of his life.

When this child learned how satisfying chocolate chip cookies are, he placed the picture of these cookies in his personal picture album.

Glasser notes by the term *pictures*, he means *perceptions* from the five senses of sight, hearing, touch, smell, and taste. When we get hungry, or thirsty, or have some other needs or wants, we select one or more pictures from our albums and then seek to obtain what that picture represents. For example, if we are really hungry we may select a picture of a prime rib dinner (or lobster, or two hamburgers) from our album and then seek to obtain what our picture represents.

The pictures in our albums do not have to be rational. Anorexics have a picture that they are too fat and starve themselves to come closer to their irrational picture of unhealthy thinness. Alcoholics have a picture of themselves satisfying many of their needs through alcohol. Child molesters have pictures of satisfying their sexual needs through sexual activities with young children. Rapists have pictures of satisfying their power needs and perhaps sexual needs through sexual assault. To change a picture, we have to replace it with another that will at least reasonably satisfy the need in question. People who are unable to replace a picture may endure a lifetime of misery. Some battered women, for example, will endure brutal beatings and humiliations in marriage because they do not believe they can replace their husbands in their albums.

Glasser notes that whenever there is a diference between the picture we now see and the picture we want, a *signal* is generated by this difference which leads us to behave in a way to obtain the picture we want. In order to obtain what we want, we examine our behavioral systems and select from those behaviors one or more that we judge as being the best available behaviors to reduce this difference. These behaviors not only include straightforward problem-solving efforts, but also such manipulative strategies as becoming angry, pouting, and trying to make others feel guilty. People who are acting irresponsibly or ineffectually have either failed to select responsible behaviors that they have in their behavioral repertoires or as yet have not learned responsible courses of action for the particular situation they are facing.

Glasser believes humans are driven by five basic, innate needs. As soon as one need is satisfied, another need (or perhaps more than one acting together) pushes for satisfaction. The first basic need is *to survive and reproduce*. Included in this need are such vital functions as breathing, digesting food, sweating, regulating blood pressure, and meeting the demands of hunger, thirst, and sex.

A second need is *to belong—to love, share, and cooperate*. This need is generally met through family, friends, pets, plants, and material possessions such as a beloved car or boat.

A third need is *power*. Glasser says this need involves getting others to obey us and to then receive the esteem and recognition that accompanies power. The drive for power is sometimes in conflict with the need to belong. For example, two people in a relationship may struggle to take control of the relationship, rather than seeking an equalitarian relationship.

A fourth need is *freedom*. People want the freedom to choose how they live their lives, to express themselves, to read and write what they choose, to associate with whom they select, and to worship or not worship as they believe.

A fifth need is *fun*. Glasser believes learning is often fun, which then is a great incentive to assimilate what we need to satisfy our needs. Classes without fun (those that are grim and boring) are major failings of our educational system. Laughing and humor help fulfill our needs for fun. Fun is such a vital part of living that most of us have trouble conceiving how life would be without it.

Glasser adds there may be other (yet unidentified) needs in addition to these basic five. He also notes that there are differences among individuals in the intensity of each of these needs. Few people, for example, have such an intense need for power as Adolph Hitler, who wanted to control the world.

Glasser asserts that any theory that contends our behavior is solely a response to outside stimuli or events is wrong. He rejects behaviorism's stimulus-response (S-R) system. He asserts that people are in control of what they do. When a person is thirsty and seeks water (because a glass of water is a thirst-quenching picture in his or her head), the person's behavior is that of a well-functioning control system. An S-R theory, in contrast, he asserts, would suggest a person would keep drinking water (perhaps drinking himself to death) every time he was handed a glass of water.

Identity Theory

Glasser's earlier theory of personality development and psychopathology has been called identity theory. Reality therapy is based on the premise that there is a single basic psychological need faced by everyone: the need for an identity. Glasser and Zunin (1979, p. 302) define the need for an identity as

the need to feel that each of us is somehow separate and distinct from every other living being on the face of this earth and that no other person thinks, looks, acts, and talks exactly as we do.

Although identity can be viewed from several viewpoints, Glasser believes from a therapeutic vantage point it is most useful to conceptualize identity in terms of people who develop a *success identity* versus those who develop a *failure identity*.

People who develop a success identity do so through the pathways of *love* and *worth*. People who view themselves as a success must feel that at least one other person loves them, and that they also love at least one other person. They must also feel that at least one other person feels they are worthwhile, and they must feel they (themselves) are worthwhile.

In order to develop a success identity a person must experience both love and worth. Glasser and Zunin (1979, p. 312) state:

In reality therapy, we see worth *and* love *as two very different elements; consider, for example, the extreme case of the "spoiled" child. One may fantasize that a child, if showered with "pure love," whose parents' "goal" was never to frustrate or stress or strain this child in any way, and when he was faced with a task or difficulty always had his parents to perform this task for him, this child always relieved of responsibility would develop into an individual who would feel loved but would not experience worth. Worth comes through accomplishing tasks and achieving success in the accomplishment of those tasks.*

A person can also feel worthwhile through accomplishing tasks (for example, a successful business person), but believe he is unloved because he cannot name someone who "I love and who loves me." Experiencing only one of these elements (worth or love) without the other can lead to a failure identity.

A failure identity is likely to develop when a child has received inadequate love or been made to feel worthless. People with failure identities express their sense of failure by becoming mentally ill, by delinquency, or by withdrawal. Almost everyone with a failure identity is lonely.

Why do some people become "mentally ill"? Glasser indicates that people who are labeled mentally ill are those who deny or distort reality. They change the world in their minds in order to feel important, significant, and meaningful. Having a failure identity is experienced by a person as being intensely discom-

forting, and changing reality through fantasizing is one way of dealing with this discomfort. Glasser and Zunin (1979, p. 313) further elaborate:

The person who is mentally ill has distorted the real world in his own fantasy to make himself feel more comfortable. He denies reality to protect himself from facing the feeling of being meaningless and insignificant in the world around him. For example, both the grandiose delusion and the persecutory delusion of the so-called schizophrenic provide support or solace for him.

Glasser (1976, pp. 19–20) describes the *choice* aspect of those who decide to become "crazy":

Crazy, psychotic, nuts, loony, bonkers, schizophrenic. There are a dozen popular, as well as pseudoscientific, words for this condition. I happen to prefer "crazy" because it is understandable; it doesn't have the pseudoscientific connotation of schizophrenia, it is not technical, and it emphasizes much better than any of the other terms the choice aspect *of this category. Schizophrenia sounds so much like a disease that prominent scientists delude themselves into searching for its cure, when the "cure" is within each crazy person who has chosen it. If he can find love or worth he will give up the choice readily—a big "if," I will admit, but hundreds do each day as they are discharged from good hospitals and clinics. With adequate treatment they learn to become strong enough to stop choosing to be crazy. Becoming crazy is actually a fairly sensible choice of the weak because no one expects a crazy person to fulfill his needs in the real world for the obvious reason that he is no longer in it. He now lives in the world of his mind, and there within his own mind, crazy as it may be, he tries to find, and to some extent usually succeeds in finding, a substitute for the adequacy he can't find in reality. Within his own mind, within his own imagination, out of his own thought processes, he may be able to reduce the pain of his failure and find a little relief. For inadequacy he provides delusions of grandeur; for loneliness, hallucinations to keep him company. He may have a delusion that everybody loves him or that he is an overwhelmingly omnipotent person, which does relieve his pain. Every mental hospital has*

*one or two Jesus Christs, the acme of omnipotence
and power. When all of this is created within a person's own mind we call it crazy, but it makes sense to
him because it doesn't hurt as much as being lucid
but miserably inadequate.*

Other individuals seek to handle the discomfort of
a failure identity through withdrawal. Still others seek
to handle the discomfort by ignoring reality, even
though they are aware of the real world. Glasser and
Zunin (1979, p. 313) describe these people:

*These individuals are referred to as delinquents,
criminals, "sociopaths," "personality disorders," and
so on. They are basically the anti-social individuals
who choose to break the rules and regulations of society on a regular basis, thereby ignoring reality.*

A success identity or a failure identity is not measured by finances or labels but rather in terms of how a
person perceives herself. It is possible for individuals
to regard themselves as failures while others view
them as being successful. Formation of a failure identity usually begins during the years when children first
enroll in school. It is at about this age (five or six) that
children develop the social and verbal skills and the
thinking capacities to define themselves as being either
successful or unsuccessful. Children, as they grow
older, then tend to associate with others having a similar identity; those with failure identities associate with
others having a failure identity, and success identities
associate with other successful people. As the years
pass the two groups associate less and less with each
other. Glasser and Zunin (1979, p. 312) note:

*For example, it is indeed rare for a person with a suc-
cess identity to have, as a close and personal friend,
someone who is a known criminal, felon, heroin addict, and so forth.*

People with success identities tend to compete constructively, meeting and seeking new challenges. Also,
they tend to reinforce one another's successes. On the
other hand, people with failure identities find facing
the real world to be uncomfortable and anxiety producing, and therefore choose either to withdraw, to
distort reality, or to ignore reality.

THEORY OF THERAPY

In counseling clients, reality therapy advances the following fourteen principles:

1. Encourage Responsible Behavior

The main goal of reality therapy is to help clients reject
irresponsible behavior and to learn improved ways of
functioning. A responsible person is defined as one
who has the ability to fulfill personal needs and to do
so in a way that does not deprive others of the ability to
fulfill their needs. (Glasser indicates that the above description of a responsible person is also an excellent
guide to use in determining whether actions are moral
or immoral.)

One of the therapist's tasks is to confront clients
with their cop-outs. Reality therapists do not excuse clients' irresponsible behavior through theoretical interpretations that blame personal problems on the past
actions of parents or on other excuses. Responsibility is
emphasized because in order for clients to feel worthwhile they must feel they are maintaining a satisfactory
standard of behavior.

2. Recognize Mental Illness Labels as Destructive

Glasser agrees with Szasz (1961) that mental illness is a
myth. This concept will be further described in Chapter 23. Glasser (1965, pp. 15–16) presents his view.

*In consonance with our emphasis on responsibility
and irresponsibility, we who practice reality therapy
advocate dispensing with the common psychiatric labels, such as neurosis and psychosis, which tend to
categorize and stereotype people. Limiting our descriptions to the behavior which the patient manifests,
we would, for example, describe a man who believes
that he is President Johnson as irresponsible, followed
by a brief description of his unrealistic behavior and
thinking. Calling him psychotic or schizophrenic im-*

mediately places him in a mental illness category which separates him from most of us, the label thereby serving to compound his problem. Through our description it can immediately be understood that he is unsuccessful in fulfilling his needs. He has given up trying to do so as John Jones and is now trying as President Johnson, a logical delusion for a man who feels isolated and inadequate. The description irresponsible *is much more precise, indicating our job is to help him to become more responsible so that he will be able to satisfy his needs as himself.*

Glasser urges that the word *irresponsible* be used in place of medical model labels of neurotic, psychotic, schizophrenic, and so on.

Glasser raises the question, If we relate to people who have emotional problems as if they are insane and lock them up in a mental institution, how can we expect them to learn to be responsible and productive? Those who adjust to the routine in a mental hospital are in no way learning how to make it in the real world, as a mental institution is an artificial environment in which dysfunctional behavior is expected and excused. Glasser asserts that labeling people as mentally ill sidetracks them onto dwelling on the erroneous notion that they have a "disease of the mind," which no one as yet knows how to treat. Instead, Glasser asserts it would be far better to relate to people with emotional and behavioral problems as being people who have an excellent potential (like everyone) to improve and resolve their personal problems. It is well known that the way people are treated is the way they come to perceive themselves. If people are treated as mentally ill, they are apt to perceive themselves as being mentally ill, and they are apt to play that role (perhaps for the rest of their life). On the other hand, if people with emotional problems are related to as being sane, with a high potential to solve their problems, they are much more likely to become responsible and productive.

3. Foster Involved Relationships

The identity we develop is largely dependent on our involvement with others. In therapy it is important for the therapist to help a client clarify and understand herself, including her beliefs, values, opinions, and self-concepts.

For a therapist to become involved is also important, as every person at all times must have at least one person who cares about her. Cool detachment and aloofness are not considered helpful. Reality therapists seek to become involved through conveying warmth, understanding, and concern.

Reality therapists are *personal* in therapy; that is, they seek to present themselves as real people. They do not project an image of omnipotence but reveal themselves, including their strengths and frailties. When doing so is appropriate and constructive, reality therapists will personalize the counseling by self-disclosing their own experiences.

Glasser and Zunin (1979, p. 317) further elaborate on being personal and involved:

The purpose of becoming personal in reality therapy is to help people become involved with someone who can help them understand that there is more to life than focusing on misery or symptoms or irresponsible behavior. However, it is an important part of the caring relationship to define the limits of involvement. It is not possible for a therapist to become deeply involved with everyone who comes for help. He becomes involved only within the context of the office. The therapist must be honest about this. . . .

The therapist must define the situation so the patient understands exactly what the relationship is, where it is, and where it is going.

4. Focus on Present and Future

Reality therapists believe that what we want now and in the future, along with our motivation to achieve what we want, is more important than our past experiences in determining what our future will be. The past is fixed; it cannot be changed. All that can be changed is the present and the future. Past experiences brought us to the present but in no way should be used as justification for irresponsible behavior now and in the future. Permitting a person to dwell on the past is a waste of time. If the past is discussed it is always related to current behavior. For example, if a person describes a broken romance that occurred several years ago, the therapist will ask how that event is related to the client's present behavior.

5. Focus on Behavior Rather Than on Feelings

Feelings and actions are considered to be interrelated and mutually reinforcing. Reality therapists assume that humans have only limited control over their feelings. Changing actions of clients is considered to be the most productive way to help clients feel better. Glasser and Zunin (1979, p. 317) note:

We cannot order ourselves to feel *better but we can always order ourselves to* do *better, and so* doing better *makes us* feel better.

Reality therapists believe it is important for clients to become aware of what they are doing that is leading them into difficulty. If a client states, "I have really felt sad and miserable the last few weeks," a reality therapist will say, "What are you doing to make yourself depressed?" Or if a client indicates at some length that he is unhappily married, the reality therapist will ask such questions as "What are you doing that contributes to the unhappiness?" and "What are you planning to do about your unhappiness?"

6. Encourage Value Judgments

Reality therapists believe people need to learn to evaluate their own behavior and assess what they are doing to contribute to their failures before they can be assisted. This therapy is persistent in guiding clients to explore their actions for signs of irresponsible behavior. Therapists repeatedly ask clients what their current behavior is accomplishing and whether it is meeting their needs. Reality therapists believe people do not change irresponsible behavior unless they first understand what they are doing.

A major task for reality therapists is to help clients face the morality of their behavior. Reality therapists seek to help clients judge whether their behavior is irresponsible. Clients are assisted in seeing that their behavior is irresponsible whenever they are hurting themselves or hurting others — and this judgment is to be made by clients. Therapists generally do not make value judgments for clients as this would relieve them of the responsibility for their behavior.

By questioning *what* the person is doing now and *what* he can do differently, the therapist conveys a belief in the person's ability to behave responsibly.

7. Encourage Planning

Reality therapists seek to explore problems in depth with clients and then to explore alternative solutions and their consequences. If a client cannot develop a personal plan for future action, the therapist will help develop one. Once the plan is worked out, a contract is drawn up and signed by the client and the therapist. The plan is usually a realistic plan for behaving differently in matters in which the client admits to acting irresponsibly. If the contract is broken, a new one is designed and agreed upon. Plans are also generally made for the contract to be reviewed periodically.

Commitment is a keystone in reality therapy. It is only from making and following through with plans that people gain a sense of self-worth and maturity.

8. Reject Excuses

Glasser is aware that not all plans and commitments made by clients will be achieved. But he does not encourage searching for reasons to justify irresponsible behavior; to do so would support a belief that clients have acceptable reasons for not doing what they have agreed was within their capabilities. Excuses let people off the hook; they provide temporary relief, but they eventually lead to more failure and to a failure identity.

When a client fails to meet a commitment, the therapist simply asks, "Are you planning to meet your commitment?" If the answer is in the affirmative, the therapist asks, "When?" Or the therapist may suggest working together to develop a new contract.

In not accepting excuses, the therapist does not seek to depecate or demean the client for failing, but seeks to convey that a reasonable plan for improvement is always possible.

9. Eliminate Punishment

Punishing persons when they fail to meet a commitment reinforces a failure identity. It also usually leads to more hostility without producing positive, lasting changes. It serves as only a temporary means of forcing different behavior. When the client no longer believes he is under surveillance, he will usually return to exhibiting irresponsible behavior.

Eliminating punishment is quite different, according to Glasser, from following through on the natural consequences of behavior involved in contractual planning.[1] For example, if a runaway youth contracts to receive shelter at a runaway center on the condition that he will remain drug free and then is caught smoking pot, the center must follow through on the consequences spelled out in the contract, which may include removal from the shelter. Not following through on such consequences would only reinforce the irresponsible behavior.

10. Do Not Offer Sympathy

Sympathy does little more than convey the therapist's lack of confidence in the client's ability to act more responsibly. Listening to long, sad stories about the client's past or sympathizing with a person's misery will do nothing to improve that person's ability to lead a responsible life.

---

[1] Glasser has a minor conceptual problem in this area as learning theory defines following through on consequences as being a form of punishment.

11. Rarely Ask Why

Asking a client the reasons for irresponsible actions implies that such explanations make a difference. The reality therapist believes that irresponsible behavior is just that, regardless of the reasons. Listening to explanations for irresponsible behavior is not only time-consuming but may also be counterproductive as it may lead the client to conclude that the irresponsible behavior can continue if he continues to offer (often contrived) explanations. By giving little attention to such explanations, the reality therapist conveys that responsible behavior is expected.

12. Praise Responsible Behavior

People need recognition for their positive accomplishments and for their positive efforts in *trying* to accomplish something even though they may not succeed. Such responsible behavior is reinforced and praised by reality therapists.

Reality therapists also seek to convey that they believe people are capable of changing their irresponsible behavior. It is easier to do things well when others are encouraging and realistically optimistic.

13. Question Traditional Case Histories

Traditional case histories emphasize the failures, shortcomings, problems, and traumas that the client has to cope with. Such case histories are often tragic and notorious misrepresentations. They usually tell more about the theoretical orientation of the writer than about the client, as they try to reinterpret clients' behaviors and feelings in terms of diagnostic labels. Rarely do case histories provide an assessment of the person's successes and personality strengths, which are at least as important in understanding a person as that person's shortcomings and failures.

CASE EXAMPLE

Developing a Therapy Group

Several years ago when I was employed as a social worker at a maximum security hospital for the criminally insane, my supervisor requested that I develop and be a leader for a therapy group. When I asked such questions as "What should be the objectives of such a group?" and "Who shall be selected to join?" my supervisor indicated those decisions would be mine. He added that no one else was doing any group therapy at this hospital, and the hospital administration thought it would be desirable for accountability reasons for group therapy programs to be developed.

Being newly employed at the hospital and wary because I had never been a leader for a group before, I asked myself, "Who is in the greatest need of group therapy?" and "If the group members do not improve, or if they deteriorate, how will I be able to explain this, that is, cover my tracks?" I concluded that I should select those identified as being the "sickest" (those labeled as chronic schizophrenic) to invite to be members of the group. Those labeled as chronic schizophrenic are generally expected to show little improvement. With such an expectation, if they did not improve, I felt I would not be blamed. However, if they did improve, I thought it would be viewed as a substantial accomplishment. Having been trained in reality therapy in graduate school, I decided to use this approach primarily with this group.

I first read the case records of all the residents (eleven) who were diagnosed as chronic schizophrenic. I then met individually with each of the residents to invite them to join the group. (To my surprise, each of the residents appeared to be very different from the impressions I received from reading the case records.) I explained the purpose of the group and the probable topics that would be covered. I then invited them to join; eight of the eleven who were contacted decided to join. Some of the eight frankly stated they would join mainly because it would look good on their record and increase their chances for an early release.

At the first meeting the purpose and the focus of the group was again presented and described. It was explained that the purpose was not to review their past but to help them make their present life more enjoyable and meaningful and to help them to make plans for the future. Various topics, it was explained, would be covered including how to convince the hospital staff they no longer needed to be hospitalized; how to prepare themselves for returning to their home community (e.g., learning an employable skill while at the institution); what to do when they felt depressed or had some other unwanted emotion; and, following their release, what they should do if and when they had an urge to do something that would get them into trouble again. It was further explained that occasional films covering some of these topics would be shown and then discussed, and it was indicated that the group would meet for about an hour each week for the next twelve weeks (until the fall when I had to return to school).

This focus on improving their current circumstances stimulated their interest, but soon they found it uncomfortable and anxiety producing to examine what the future might hold for them. The fact that they were informed they had some responsibility and some control of that future also created anxiety. They reacted to this discomfort by stating they were labeled mentally ill and therefore had some internal condition that was causing their strange behavior. Since a cure for schizophrenia had not yet been found, they stated they could do little to improve their situation.

They were informed their excuses were "garbage" (stronger terms were used), and we spent a few sessions getting them to understand that the label "chronic schizophrenic" was a meaningless label. I spent considerable time in explaining that mental illness was a myth (that is, people do not have a "disease of the mind," even though they may have emotional problems). I went on to explain that what had gotten them locked up was their deviant behavior. I added that they held the key for getting released—that key was simply to act "sane."

The next set of excuses they tried was that their broken homes, or ghetto schools, or broken romances, or something else in their past had "messed them up," and therefore they could do little about their situation. They were informed such excuses were also "garbage." True, their past experiences were important in their being here. But it was emphasized that what they wanted out of the future, along with their motivation to do something about achieving their goals, was more important than their past experiences in determining what the future would hold for them.

Finally, after we had worked through a number of excuses we were able to focus on how they could better handle specific problems, such as how to handle being depressed; how to stop exhibiting behavior considered "strange," how to present themselves as being "sane" in order to increase their chances of an early release, how they would feel and adjust to returning to their home communities, what kind of work or career they desired upon their release, and how they could prepare themselves by learning a skill or trade while at this institution. Another focus was to help them examine what they wanted out of the future and the specific steps they would have to take to achieve their goals.

The results of this approach were very encouraging. Instead of idly spending much of the time brooding about their situation, they became motivated to improve it. At the end of the twelve weeks (when I had to return to school) the eight members of the group spontaneously stated that the meetings were making a positive change in their lives and requested that another social worker from the hospital be assigned to continue the group. This was arranged. Three years later on a return visit to the hospital I was informed that five of the eight group members had been released to their home communities; two of the others were considered to have shown improvement; while the final group member's condition was described as "unchanged."

This case example is adapted from an illustration of a therapy group presented in Charles Zastrow, *Introduction to Social Welfare Institutions*, 2nd ed. (Homewood, Ill.: Dorsey Press, 1982), pp. 512–16.

FIGURE 17.1

Psychoanalysis versus Reality Therapy

Psychoanalysis	Reality Therapy
1. Mental illness exists.	1. Concept of mental illness not accepted.
2. Therapist probes deep into client's past life.	2. Focus is on the present and the future.
3. Therapist should relate to patients as a neutral figure to further transference.	3. Therapist should relate as a genuine, real person.
4. Unconscious processes and conflicts are emphasized.	4. Unconscious processes and conflicts are deemphasized.
5. Patients are not responsible for their deviant behaviors, which are caused by unconscious motivations and/or mental illness.	5. Clients are responsible for their actions.
6. Patients will spontaneously learn better behavior through insight into the historical and unconscious sources of their problems.	6. Insight into problems will not of itself produce change; clients need to learn to act more responsibly.

14. Foster Success Experiences

In helping clients to develop plans to improve their circumstances, the reality therapist strives to help clients achieve *realistic* goals and helps them to understand and master the tasks (means) involved in accomplishing these goals. To counteract failure identities, clients need to begin to take risks and experience successes. Gradually such successes lead clients to perceive themselves more positively.

EVALUATION

Reality therapy is a commonsense approach to therapy that is sensible and rational. It affirms a firm belief in the dignity of humans and their ability to improve their situations. The concept of personal responsibility for one's own behavior has broad applications. It is through a sense of individual responsibility that meaningful personal growth occurs. The goal of therapy is to help clients identify their irresponsible behavior and then learn to be more responsible. This goal provides a very useful focus for counseling people. Compared to other therapy approaches, the concepts of this approach are relatively simple to learn and apply, which is a distinct advantage.

Reality therapy differs substantially from psychoanalysis. Glasser (1965) has discussed these differences, which are briefly summarized in Figure 17.1.

Research studies have found reality therapy to be substantially more effective than psychoanalysis in producing positive therapeutic changes (Eysenck, 1965; Stuart, 1970).

Reality therapy has been successfully applied in a variety of settings, including corrections, mental health, education, unemployment, public welfare, and in treating delinquency.

There are some criticisms that can also be made about reality therapy:

1. Glasser asserts that the way to change unwanted emotions (e.g., depression, guilt) is by first changing the actions of clients. Although getting involved in meaningful activity may be one way of alleviating unwanted emotions, it is not the only way. Ellis (1962) has demonstrated that all emotions, including unwanted emotions, are primarily caused by what people are thinking. Ellis has shown that changing clients' thoughts in a direction that is more positive and rational is also a very useful approach to alleviating unwanted emotions. (This concept will be further expanded in the next chapter when *rational therapy* is described.)

2. Glasser asserts that having a failure identity is a major determinant of having emotional problems and of becoming involved in irresponsible behavior. Yet, his theory fails to provide explanations as to why some people become depressed while others become highly anxious, or explode in anger, or are shy, or experience guilt and shame. Also, his theory does not explain why some people behave irresponsibly by becoming involved in burglary while others commit murder, or rape, or extortion, or white-collar crimes, or neglect their children, and so on. Reality therapy, at best, provides only a partial explanation for the causes of emotional problems and irresponsible behavior.

3. At the present time Glasser has advanced two theories of personality development and psychopathology. He first advanced an identity theory and in recent years has advanced a control theory. Glasser has not as yet specified how these two theories relate to each other. It is unclear whether Glasser is currently rejecting all or parts of his identity theory. If he now rejects the identity theory, it is unclear how such a rejection would effect reality therapy, as reality therapy was originally based on identity theory. One hopes that Glasser will address these issues in the near future.

SUMMARY

The primary developer of reality therapy is William Glasser. Glasser has developed two theories of personality development and psychopathology—a control theory and an identity theory. Control theory asserts that all human behavior is an attempt to reduce the differences between the pictures in our head of what we want and the way we perceive situations in the world.

Identity theory asserts that the single, basic need that everyone has is the need for identity. People who develop a success identity do so through the pathways of love and worth. A failure identity is apt to develop when a child has received inadequate love or been made to feel worthless. People with failure identities express their discomfort in facing reality by distorting reality (becoming "mentally ill"), by withdrawal, or by ignoring reality (becoming involved in antisocial activities).

The main goal of reality therapy is to help clients reject irresponsible behavior and to learn improved ways of functioning. Principles of reality therapy include the following: (*a*) mental illness is a myth; (*b*) the therapy; (*c*) the focus in therapy should be on the present and the future, as the past cannot be changed; (*d*) the focus in therapy should be on behavior rather than on feelings; (*e*) clients should make value judgments about what they are doing that contributes to their failures; (*f*) clients are assisted in developing a plan to alter their irresponsible behavior; (*g*) excuses are not accepted when a client fails to meet a commitment; (*h*) the therapist does not punish a client for failing to meet a commitment; and (*i*) the therapist praises responsible behavior and seeks to help clients achieve realistic goals.

Reality therapy is increasingly being used by social workers in a wide variety of settings. It is a commonsense approach to therapy, which research has found to be effective.

EXERCISE

Counseling with Reality Therapy

GOAL: This exercise is designed to have students practice using the concepts of reality therapy in counseling situations.

Step 1: Describe the purpose of this exercise. Summarize the fourteen principles of reality therapy described in this chapter. Indicate that in summary form the basic format of reality therapy involves three phases:

1. Developing a relationship with clients.
2. Exploring problems in depth.
3. Exploring alternatives for resolving these problems.

(There is overlap among these three phases.)

Step 2: Have two volunteers make up a contrived problem that they jointly have. (For example, a husband wants to have children and to have his wife stay home to raise them, while the wife wants a career and does not want to have children.) Ask for two more volunteers to be "counselors" and to use the principles of reality therapy. Have the "counselors" counsel the "clients."

Step 3: Have the class discuss the merits of the counseling that was given and how well the "counselors" used the principles of reality therapy.

18

RATIONAL THERAPY

The founder of rational therapy is Albert Ellis (1913–). Ellis received a Ph.D. in clinical psychology at Columbia University in 1947, where he received training in psychoanalysis. During the later 1940s and early 1950s he practiced psychoanalytic approaches to therapy but became disenchanted with the results and the approach. Ellis observed that even when patients achieved incredible insight into their childhood and unconscious processes, they continued to retain their emotional difficulties.

Ellis then began developing a new approach, which he named *rational therapy* (also called *rational-emotive therapy*), which seeks to treat clients by challenging and changing their irrational beliefs. Ellis first presented this new approach in 1957 at the annual convention of the American Psychological Association. Shortly afterward Ellis (1957) was able to demonstrate significantly greater effectiveness with this new approach than with using psychoanalytic approaches.

In 1959 Ellis established the Institute for Rational Living in New York City, which provides adult education courses in rational living and a moderate-cost clinic for clients. In 1968 Ellis founded the Institute for Advanced Study in Rational Pychotherapy, which provides helping professionals with extensive training in rational therapy and also provides seminars and workshops throughout the country. Ellis is also recognized nationally as an authority on sexuality. In addition to running workshops and seminars and being a practicing psychotherapist, he has written nearly 40 books and 400 articles!

Considering its relative newness in the field of psychotherapy, rational therapy has made an enormous impact on both professionals and the public in recent years. Well over a hundred books have been published (see Ellis, 1979, for a review) by various authors applying the principles of rational therapy to such areas as assertiveness training, sexuality, adolescence, law and criminality, religion, executive leadership, children's literature, music, feminism, philosophy, personal problems, alcoholism, marriage and the family, and sex adjustment and therapy.

Recent writers on rational therapy (Dyer, 1976; Lembo, 1974; Maultsby, 1975; Zastrow, 1979) have made some modifications in Ellis's theories of personality development, psychopathology, and therapy. Since these modifications make the approach easier to understand and easier to apply in therapy, this presentation of rational therapy will incorporate these revisions.

ALBERT ELLIS: THEORY OF PERSONALITY DEVELOPMENT AND PSYCHOPATHOLOGY

Self-Talk Determines Our Feelings and Actions

Most people believe erroneously that our emotions and our actions are determined primarily by our experiences (that is, by events that happen to us). On the contrary, rational therapy asserts and has demonstrated (Ellis, 1979) that the primary cause of all our emotions and actions is what we tell ourselves about events that happen to us.

All feelings and actions occur according to the following format:

Events: (Or experiences)
↓
Self-talk: (Self-talk is the set of evaluating thoughts
             we give ourself about facts and events that
             happen to us.)
Emotions: (May include remaining calm.)
↓
Actions:

This basic principle is not new. The stoic philosopher Epictetus wrote in *The Enchiridion* in the 1st century A.D., "Men are disturbed not by things, but by the view which they take of them" (Ellis, 1979).

An example will illustrate the above process:

Event: A husband unexpectedly arrives home
             early and upon walking into his living
             room sees an acquaintance and his wife
             embracing.
Self-talk: "My wife and this guy are having an affair —
             this is awful."
             "This guy is threatening my personal life."
             "This is morally wrong — the worst thing
             that could happen to me."
             "This guy is violating my rights — I've got to
             forcefully protect my rights."
Emotion: Anger, rage, and a vengeful feeling.
↓
Action: Running at the acquaintance and physically
             getting into a fight.

If, on the other hand, the husband remembers that his wife and the acquaintance are preparing to put on a romantic play at a nearby college, the following may occur:

Event: A husband unexpectedly arrives home
             early and upon walking into his living
             room sees an acquaintance and his wife
             embracing.
Self-talk: "Well, apparently they'e only practicing for
             the play."
             "I'll watch closely, but I don't think there is
             anything romantic occurring."
             "There is no reason for me to get upset and
             make a fool of myself."
Emotion: More emotionally relaxed and calm, al-
↓   though somewhat wary and jealous.
Action: Casually making small talk with his wife
             and the acquaintance, while observing
             their interactions.

The most important point about the above process is that our self-talk determines how we feel and act; by changing our self-talk, we can change how we feel and act. Generally we cannot control events that happen to us, but we have the power to think rationally and thereby change *all* of our unwanted emotions and ineffective actions.

Maultsby (1977) indicates thinking and behavior is rational if it *a.* Is based on objective reality (that is, fits the facts).

b. Helps us to protect our lives.

c. Helps us to achieve our short- and long-term goals most quickly.

d. Helps us to avoid significant trouble with other people.

e. Helps us to feel the emotions we want to feel.

If our thoughts or our actions conflict with one or more of these criteria, they are considered to be irrational.

Frequently we do not have the power to control the events we encounter. However, we always have the capacity to tell ourselves rational thoughts about each of our experiences. John Lembo (1974, p. 9) notes:

We can think rationally or irrationally about the things that will happen to us *and insist that we will not be a failure if our boss fires us or that we will be a worthless no-account if we are dismissed from our job; that nothing catastrophic will happen if our parents die or that it will be horrible and unbearable if they do die.*

Since we determine our feelings and our behaviors via self-talk, we are literally in control of our lives. If we are unhappy, unfulfilled, unsatisfied, frustrated, depressed, grief-stricken, or whatever, it is primarily our doing. Lembo (1974, p. 10) notes, "We have the ability to create a satisfying life for ourselves, and we will succeed in doing so if we rationally manage the thoughts we tell ourselves."

Personality Development and Self-Concept Formations.[1]

Webster's Ninth New Collegiate Dictionary (1983) defines personality as "the totality of an individual's behavioral and emotional characteristics."

According to this definition, our personality is composed of our emotions and our behaviors. Accepting such a definition leads to the conclusion that it is our self-talk that primarily controls our personality, as we have earlier seen that our self-talk determines our emotions and our behaviors.

Most personality theorists have focused on outside events in describing how our personality develops. Sigmund Freud, for example, focused on early traumatic childhood experiences, and on the nature of the relationships between parents and the child. Relatively few personality theorists have focused on the development of our thinking processes, which we have seen primarily determine our emotions and behaviors.

Our sense of identity (our sense of who and what we are) refers to the general, ongoing sets of self-talk related to the kind of person each of us is. (Other writers have referred to the sense of identity as being our self-concept, or our self-image.) Our sense of identity is *the* key element of our personality and refers to the usual sets of self-talk that control perhaps 90 percent of our emotions and actions.

The question of how our personality develops essentially involves how our self-concept develops. Identity development is a lifetime process. It begins during the early years and continues to change throughout our lifetime. During the early years, our sense of identity is largely determined by the reactions of others.

A long time ago, Cooley (1902) discussed this early labeling process as resulting in the "looking-glass self"; that is, persons develop their self-concept (sense of who and what they are) in terms of how others relate to them. For example, if a neighborhood identifies a young boy as being a "troublemaker," a "delinquent," the neighbors are apt to relate to the youth as if he were not to be trusted, many accuse him of delinquent acts, and will label his semidelinquent and aggressive behavior as being "delinquent." This labeling process, the youth begins to realize, also results in a type of prestige and status, at least from his peers. In the absence of objective ways to gauge whether he is, in fact, a "delinquent," the youth will rely on the subjective evaluations of others. Thus, gradually, as the youth is related to as being a "delinquent," he is apt to begin to perceive himself in that way and will begin to enact the delinquent role.

---

[1]This section is adapted from Charles Zastrow, *Talk to Yourself: Using the Power of Self-Talk,* © 1979, pp. 85–88. Adapted by permission of Prentice-Hall, Inc., Englewood Cliffs, New Jersey.

FIGURE 18.1

Formation of Our Self-Concept and Our Personality

Events (experiences)
↓
Self-talk ──────────→ Ongoing, repeated sets of self-talk become ──────→ Self-talk (which is based on our attitudes, beliefs,
↓　　　　　　　　　　　attitudes, values, and beliefs. (Beliefs about　　　　and needs) about our experiences determines
Immediate emotions　　who and what we are form our self-concept.)　　all of our emotions and behaviors (i.e., our
↓　　　　　　　　　　　　　　　　　　　　　　　　　　　　　　　　　　personality, which is composed of our
Immediate actions　　　　　　　　　　　　　　　　　　　　　　　　emotions and behaviors).

The labeling process undoubtedly has a substantial influence in shaping behavior. Yet, it fails to explain why children may be treated essentially the same and yet engage in very different behavior as well as develop substantially different self-concepts. We have all heard stories about children, raised essentially the same (in a ghetto or in an upper-class suburb) who develop vastly different lifestyles, with one becoming involved in a life of crime, while another becomes a law abiding, productive community leader. Why?

The following theory of self-concept development is adapted from the work of the Soviet psychologists Luria (1961) and Vygotsky (1962).

PHASE I:　Initially a child's behavior is determined by internal physical needs (e.g., hunger) and outside events (e.g., parental actions).

PHASE II:　The child begins to learn to control his (her) behavior in line with the verbal instructions and reactions of external agents (e.g., parents).

PHASE III:　The verbal instructions and reactions of external people lead to the development of elementary beliefs. Based on these elementary beliefs, the child begins to regulate some of his own actions through self-talk.

PHASE IV:　Future behavior patterns are then developed through an interaction of events and self-talk about those events. Repeated sets of self-talk become covert (i.e., go "underground," to use Vygotsky's term) and become attitudes, beliefs, and values.

PHASE V:　These attitudes, beliefs, and values form our sense of who and what we are. Our self-talk (based on our beliefs, attitudes, and values) about events that happen to us then largely controls our emotions and actions.

The diagram in Figure 18.1 shows how events and self-talk interact to form our self-concepts and our personalities.

Given the above theoretical material, let us return to the question of why, when two children have essentially the same experiences, they may develop very different personalities (that is, emotions and behaviors). The reason is that their self-talk about their experiences may vary.

For example, if an eight-year-old child is caught for shoplifting candy and is spanked by his parents, a wide range of self-talk is possible. If the child says, "I have done wrong. Stealing is wrong. Somehow I have got to restore my parent's trust in me," the child's inclinations to steal will be sharply reduced. However, if the child says the following to himself, shoplifting attempts are apt to continue: "Shoplifting is exciting. It's a way for me to get what I want. This is the first time I've been caught. Guess I was careless. I'll have to be more careful the next time." In a given situation, the self-talk of different people will vary because (*a*) the values, beliefs, attitudes, and desires upon which self-talk is based will vary among individuals; and (*b*) each person has thousands of different values and beliefs, and in a particular situation, each person will somewhat haphazardly select only a few of these beliefs and values to base his self-talk on.

In summary, there are two components that largely determine the personality of any individual: (1) the experiences that a person has, and (2) the self-talk that a person gives himself about the experiences. Of these two components, self-talk is the key element in developing and perpetuating everyone's personality.

Additional Aspects of Self-Talk

With repeated occurrences of an event, a person's emotional reactions to that event become nearly automatic because the person rapidly gives himself a set of self-talk gradually acquired through past experiences. For example, a few years ago I counseled a woman who became intensely emotionally upset every time her husband (who had a drinking problem) came home intoxicated. In examining this situation it became clear that because of repeated occurrences she would immediately give herself the following extensive set of self-talk upon seeing him inebriated:

Self-talk: "He's foolishly spending the money we desperately need in this family."
"He is making a fool of himself and me in that condition."
"He's setting a terrible example for our children."
"One of these days while drunk he's going to get into a serious accident, become incapacitated, and then what will we do?"
"He loves drinking more than he loves me!"

Emotional reaction: Anger, frustration, some depression, general unhappiness.

A person may be aware, or unaware, of the self-talk that he is giving himself about a fact or event. If a person is having a discomforting emotion and is unaware of the underlying self-talk, then the focus of counseling initially needs to be on discovering this self-talk. Several years ago I counseled a married woman who expressed a strong desire to want to continue having extramarital affairs but was afraid her husband would discover the affairs and end the marriage. Although she was fully aware of the emotional desire for having affairs, she was unaware of the self-talk generating this feeling. I probed into this area and got her to take a look (undoubtedly for the first time in her life) at the self-talk that was generating the emotional desire to have extramarital sex. Upon focusing her attention on this she gradually expressed and became aware of the following underlying self-talk, "I enjoy the feeling of being able to seduce someone to whom I am attracted," "The people I seduce then feel somewhat obligated to me," and "The conquest of someone who is very attractive is three quarters of the thrill."

Another aspect of self-talk has been labeled as *layering* in which the emotional reaction (*C*) becomes a new event (*A*) by a person's giving himself additional self-talk (*B*) about having the initial emotional reaction. Ellis (1973, p. 178) describes layering as follows:

Once the individual becomes emotionally upset — or, rather, upsets himself! — another startling human thing frequently occurs. Most of the time, he knows that he is anxious, depressed, enraged, or otherwise agitated; and he also generally knows that his symptoms are undesirable and (in our culture) socially disapproved. For who approves or respects highly agitated or "crazy" people? He therefore makes his emotional Consequence (C) or symptom into another Activating Event (A).

Thus, he originally starts with something like "(A) I did poorly on my job today; (B) Isn't that horrible! What a worm I am for failing!" and he winds up with (C) feelings of anxiety, worthlessness, and depression. He now starts all over: "(A) I feel anxious and depressed, and worthless. (B) Isn't that horrible! What a worm I am for feeling anxious, depressed, and worthless!" Now he winds up with (C) even greater feelings of anxiety, worthlessness, and depression. Or, in other words, once he becomes anxious, quently makes himself anxious about being anxious. Once he becomes depressed, he makes himself depressed about being depressed. Et cetera! He now has two Consequences or symptoms for the price of one; and he often goes around and around, in a vicious cycle of (1) condemning himself for doing poorly at some task; (2) feeling guilty or depressed because of his self-condemnation; (3) condemning himself for his feelings of guilt and depression; (4) condemning himself for condemning himself; (5) condemning himself for seeing that he condemns himself and for still not stopping condemning himself; (6) condemning himself for going for psychotherapeutic help and still not getting better; (7) condemning himself for being more disturbed than other individuals; (8) concluding that he is indubitably hopelessly disturbed and that nothing can be done about it; and so on, and so forth.

Self-talk is related to attitudes, beliefs, and values. Although self-talk is often based on our attitudes, beliefs, and values, self-talk is distinct from these terms. Self-talk has a "here and now" quality as it represents those thoughts that we are giving ourselves at the present time. At any one point in time we hold thousands of beliefs, attitudes, and values, but our self-talk is based on only a fraction of our total set of attitudes and beliefs whenever we think about a fact or event. Our self-talk may also be generated by our needs, wants, desires, drives, and motives.

Understanding Deviant Behavior

Rational therapy maintains that *the reasons for any deviant act (including crime) can be determined by examining what the offender was telling herself prior to and during the time when the act was being committed.*

The Charles Manson case will be used to illustrate this concept:

On August 9, 1969, actress Sharon Tate was slain in her home, along with four other people. The next night Leno LaBianca (a wealthy president of a grocery chain) and his wife were brutally stabbed to death. In the weeks that followed, Charles Manson and several of his followers were arrested and later convicted of these murders. Charles Manson was head of a commune, "The Family," that lived in Death Valley, California.

Why did Manson and his followers commit these bizarre murders? The prosecuting attorney for the state of California, Vincent Bugliosi, was able to document the following reasons (Bugliosi and Gentry, 1974). Manson hoped that these brutal murders of the prominent and wealthy would create fear and panic among white people. Manson thought that whites, unable to determine who actually did the killing, would conclude these murders were committed by blacks. He theorized that, out of fear, whites would go into the ghettos and start killing black people, causing a race war. Such a war, it was thought, would also lead to a split between liberals and conservatives, who would then begin killing each other. During this time Manson thought the "true black race" (at various times identified by Manson as the "Black Panthers" or the "Black Muslims"[2]) would go into hiding and would be unaffected. After almost all whites had perished, the "true black race" would come out and kill the remaining whites, except for Manson and his followers who would be in hiding in Death Valley. Manson further thought the remaining blacks would not have the capacities to govern the nation, and that after failing to govern they would turn to him to be the leader of the nation.

Thus, it appears this unrealistic belief system led Manson and his followers to murder seven people. Having an unrealistic belief system does not make a person "crazy." All the defendants in this case were judged by the court to be "sane." While living together in isolation in a commune, the members apparently gave mutual support to each other for the accurateness of Manson's beliefs, probably partly because objective evidence was unavailable to refute Manson's inter-

---

[2]The Black Panthers and Black Muslims were black organizations that were active in the civil rights movement in the 1960s and 1970s. Sometimes these organizations advocated the use of physical force to achieve racial equality.

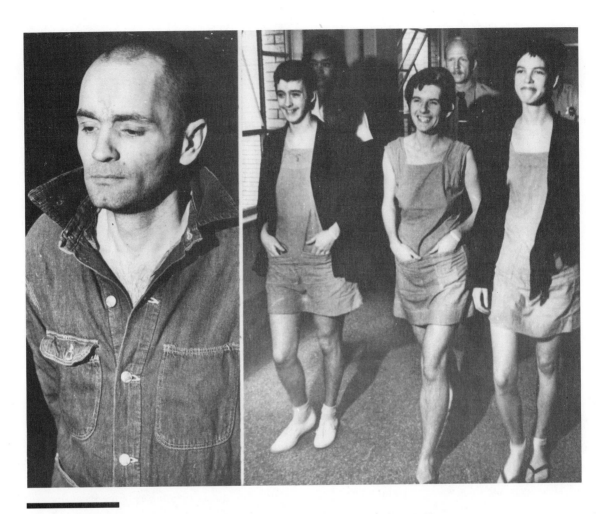

Charles Manson and members of "The Family" following their conviction in the Tate–LaBianca murder trials.

pretations. (Throughout history various erroneous beliefs have been held at one time or another: the earth was believed to be flat until Columbus's voyage, bloodletting was thought to be therapeutic, thunder was thought to be a god with supernatural powers, people who committed bizarre or criminal acts were thought to be possessed by "demons." Probably all of us presently hold certain beliefs that will one day be found to be erroneous.)

THEORY OF THERAPY

The initial focus of therapy is to help clients become aware of the irrational and negative self-talk that is the primary source of their unwanted emotions and irresponsible behaviors. (Unwanted emotions for defined as those that clients desire to change.) After clients become aware of their irrational self-talk they are instructed and encouraged to challenge such irrational self-talk with a different set of self-talk that is more rational and positive. Developing rational self-challenges to irrational self-talk is done by the client, either through discussions with the therapist or by writing out a "Rational Self-Analysis."

Rational Self-Analysis[3]

Maultsby (1977) developed an approach entitled *Rational Self-Analysis* (RSA) that is very useful in alleviating any undesirable emotion. An RSA has six parts as shown in Figure 18.2.

The goal in doing an RSA is to change unwanted emotions (such as anger, guilt, depression, and shyness). An RSA is done by recording the event and self-talk on paper.

Under Part A (facts and events) simply state the facts or events that occurred.

Under Part B (self-talk) write all of your thoughts about A. Number each statement in order (1, 2, 3, 4, and so on). Also write either "good," "bad," or "neutral" after each self-talk statement to show yourself how you believed each B section statement reflected on you as a person. (The RSA example that soon follows illustrates the mechanics of this, and other components, of doing an RSA.)

Under Part C (emotional consequences) write simple statements describing your gut reactions/emotions stemming from your self-talk in B.

Part D(a) is to be written *only* after you have written sections A, B, and C, and *only* after you have reviewed the five questions for rational thinking (described earlier in this chapter). Part D(a) is a "camera check" of the A section. Reread the A section and ask yourself, "If I had taken a moving picture of what I wrote was happening, would the camera verify what I have written as facts?" A moving picture would probably have recorded the facts but not personal beliefs or

[3]This description of Rational Self-Analysis is adapted from Charles Zastrow, *Talk to Yourself: Using the Power of Self-Talk*, © 1979, pp. 32–36. Adapted by permission of Prentice-Hall, Inc., Englewood Cliffs, New Jersey.

FIGURE 18.2

Format for RSA

A	D(a)
Facts and Events	Camera Check of A
B	D(b)
Self-Talk	Rational Debate of B
1. _____	1. _____
2. _____	2. _____
etc.	etc.
C	E
Emotional Consequences of B	Emotional Goals and Behavioral Goals for Similar Future Events

opinions. Personal beliefs or opinions belong in the B section. A common example of a personal opinion mistaken as a fact is, "Karen made me look like a fool when she laughed at me while I was trying to make a serious point." Under D(a) (camera check of A) correct the opinion part of this statement by only writing the factual part: "I was attempting to make a serious point when Karen began laughing at what I was saying." Then add the personal opinion part of the statement to B (that is, "Karen made me look like a fool.").

Part D(b) is the section designed to challenge and change negative and irrational thinking. Take each B statement separately. Read B–1 first and ask yourself whether it is inconsistent with any of the five questions for rational thinking. It will be irrational if it does one or more of the following:

1. Not based on objective reality.

2. Hampers you in protecting your life.

3. Hampers you in achieving your short- and long-term goals.

4. Causes significant trouble with other people.

5. Leads you to feel emotions that you do not want to feel.

If the self-talk statement is consistent with the five questions for rational thinking, merely write "that's rational." If, on the other hand, the self-talk statement meets one or more of the guidelines for irrational thinking, then think of an alternative "self-talk" to that B statement. This new self-talk statement is of crucial importance in changing your undesirable emotion, and needs to (*a*) be rational and (*b*) be a self-talk statement you are willing to accept as a new opinion for yourself. After writing down this D(b–1) self-talk in the D(b) section, then consider B–2, B–3, and so on in the same way.

Under Part E write down the new emotions you want to have in similar future A situations. In writing these new emotions that you desire, keep in mind that they will follow from your self-talk statements in your D(b) section. This section may also contain a description of certain actions you intend to take to help you achieve your emotional goals when you encounter future As.

Since irresponsible behavior (such as overeating, overdrinking, committing crimes, sexual deviance) is also largely determined by our irrational thinking, rational self-challenges (including doing an RSA) can be effectively used to change irresponsible actions (Lembo, 1974; Maultsby, 1978; Zastrow, 1979). *It should be emphasized that rational self-challenges will work only if the client actively practices using the rational self-challenges he develops.* They work best when they are used by the client every time he starts to give himself the original negative and irrational self-talk.

Therapy Is an Educational Process

Learning how to think rationally and to counter irrational and negative self-talk is seen as an educational process. Clients can learn how to analyze and change irrational self-talk in a variety of ways: instruction by the therapist; viewing videotapes and films on rational therapy; reading books and pamphlets on rational therapy and attending workshops or seminars on rational therapy. Ellis has demonstrated that the basic principles of how to analyze irrational self-talk and to

think rationally can be successfully taught to elementary and secondary school students.

In therapy, the role of the therapist is to instruct clients on how to analyze the irrational self-talk underlying their unwanted emotions and irresponsible behavior. The therapist uses probes, confrontation, explanations, interpretations, humor, and suggestions to help clients discover their irrational thinking. Once clients become aware of their irrational self-talk, a rational therapist uses a variety of techniques to help clients change their unwanted emotions and irresponsible behavior.

An Eclectic Approach

For changing unwanted emotions, rational self-challenges (including writing an RSA) are often used. For certain unwanted emotions, such as depression, rational therapists may attempt to get clients involved in meaningful/enjoyable activity (for example, playing golf, joining a social club). (Reality therapists, as described earlier, use this approach to change unwanted emotions.) Rational therapists theorize that getting clients involved in enjoyable activities works because it switches their negative thinking (which is causing their unwanted emotions) to positive thoughts about the enjoyable activity, which then changes their emotions.

For people who are shy or prone to temper outbursts, rational therapists are apt to use assertiveness training techniques (described in Chapter 19). For clients who have drinking problems, rational therapists may supplement therapy by getting clients involved in Alcoholics Anonymous. For clients with sexual dysfunctions, rational therapists are apt to use such techniques as sensate focus and other techniques (see Chapter 20) developed by Masters and Johnson (Belliveau and Richter, 1970). Rational therapists use whatever approaches hold promise of helping to change irrational self-talk. Ellis (1979, p. 186) notes:

The rational therapist uses role-playing, assertion training, desensitization, humor, operant conditioning, suggestion, support, and a whole bag of other "tricks."

CASE EXAMPLE

Rational Self-Analysis

A twenty-year-old coed sought counseling a year after she had had an abortion. (She was one of a small minority who continue to have feelings of depression and guilt after having an abortion.) After discussing her feelings in some depth with her, the counselor (myself) instructed her in how to counter such undesirable emotions by doing an RSA. The following RSA was written by this coed:

Remorse after an Abortion

A (Facts and Events)	D(a) (Camera Check of A)
Thirteen months ago I discovered I was pregnant. As soon as I informed my boyfriend he moved out of state to get away from all his problems. He had been All-Conference in football, baseball, and basketball. However, he had an accident and lost his left hand. After the accident Ken and I started dating. I had always idolized him. But I soon found out he was quite dependent, and I guess I began "mothering" him. We made love a few times and I became pregnant. At this time I was a freshman in college and wanted very much to complete college. My parents always respected me, and I didn't want to hurt them by informing them. I felt I couldn't have the baby and still continue in college. When Ken left I felt the only alternative was to have an abortion, which I then had. Since that time the abortion has been making me feel depressed and guilty.	All of this is factual, except for the last sentence. Having had the abortion is not making me feel depressed and guilty. Instead, it is my self-talk about having had the abortion that is making me feel depressed and guilty.

B (Self-Talk)	D(b) (Your Rational Debate of B)
B–1　I've killed a person. (bad)	D(b–1)　I believe life does not begin until birth. Similar to other women who take birth control pills, I simply prevented having an unwanted baby.
B–2　Having an abortion makes me an immoral person. (bad)	D(b–2)　Preventing having an unwanted baby is desirable, not immoral. When I was pregnant I had to make decisions in which there was no one right answer. Even if having an abortion is viewed as immoral by some people, having

B (Self-Talk)	D(b) (Your Rational Debate of B)
	made one decision that may or may not be viewed as immoral in no way makes me an immoral person. Almost all my actions and decisions are consistent with my set of moral values; therefore, I am not an immoral person.
B–3 Having an abortion makes me an irresponsible person. (bad)	D(b–3) My decision to have an abortion was responsible as I was in no position to raise a child. Ken could not have faced a continuance of the pregnancy, and I did not needlessly create problems for my parents. Perhaps I was irresponsible when I made love without taking precautions, but after becoming pregnant I made a decision that was legitimate. And again, one irresponsible action (making love without using birth control) does not make me an irresponsible person.
B–4 If I hadn't gotten pregnant, Ken would not have left me, and I would not now feel so lonely. (bad)	D(b–4) I guess I still feel attracted to Ken. I might just as well acknowledge that. However, at the present time it is obvious Ken is not able to get into an ongoing relationship, and it's better finding this out now rather than later. Loneliness is another uncomfortable emotion I now have, and I think I will write another RSA on my feelings of loneliness.
B–5 I've always wanted to have a baby and raise a family. (bad)	D(b–5) What I really want is to marry, have a career, and also raise a family. If I had had this baby I would have had to drop out of college, and perhaps I would also have had more difficulty in marrying someone having the characteristics I'm seeking.
B–6 I don't have the right to play God and decide life and death questions. (bad)	D(b–6) Again, I believe life does not begin until birth. I'm certainly not God, but I do have a right to make decisions that are in my best interests.

C (My Emotions)	E (My Emotional and Behavior Goals)
Depressed, guilty, and somewhat lonely.	To stop feeling depressed and guilty about having had an abortion, to start dating other men, and to focus my thoughts on the present and the future.

CASE EXAMPLE

Using Rational Therapy to Change Irresponsible Behavior

Dan Barber, age four and one-half, was taken to the emergency room of St. Mary's Hospital in a midwestern city. He was unconscious, severely bruised, and had a broken arm. Dan was brought in by neighbors after Mr. Barber had telephoned them. Dan had a concussion, sustained from what appeared to be several blows. Seven weeks earlier Dan had been rushed to the hospital for a broken leg. That time Mr. Barber stated Dan had fallen down a stairway. Protective services were contacted by the hospital and in the initial interview Mr. Barber acknowledged that he had beaten Dan on both of these occasions. Why? The following is Mr. Barber's account of the thinking process (self-talk) that led him to abuse his son.

Dan is my only son. I was married for nearly seven years, but got a divorce eight months ago. I'm an accountant and up until about a year ago I really thought I had it made. Mary was very attractive and we got along well. We had a nice house, and I had a good income—many days I worked eleven or twelve hours, getting overtime pay. Mary primarily took care of our son.

One day I arrived home and there was a note from my wife saying she was leaving me. I was shocked and couldn't believe it. A few weeks later I received papers indicating she had gotten a divorce in Mexico. Shortly afterward I heard she married a person from the same church I used to go to. I really don't understand how she could leave both Dan and me, without even talking about it. I guess I've been so involved with my work that I didn't realize how she felt.

As time went by after she left I discussed my problems with some of our neighbors. A few indicated that several men over the years visited with my wife during the day when I was at work. Apparently she has been having affairs for a long time.

My mother moved in after Mary left, to help take care of Dan.

In the past few months I have been wondering if Dan is really my own son. (At this point Mr. Barber was asked to indicate what he was thinking during the last time he abused Dan. The events and self-talk are put into the format presented earlier.)

Event:	*That evening I came home from work feeling exhausted. I wanted just to relax and have a peaceful evening. My mother went grocery shopping, and I guess I was feeling sorry for myself. Dan was quite noisy, and I told him to stop making so much noise. But he continued.*
Self-talk:	*"I can't take anymore of this."*
	"Here I have to take care of a kid that may not even by my own."
	"This kid reminds me of the hurt that Mary has caused me. I have a right to even the score."
	"This kid is willfully disobeying me—I've got to teach him a lesson."
	"I can't stand this! I've got to shut this brat up!"
	"My father beat me when I did wrong—that's the best way to show kids who's the boss."
Emotion:	*Anger, revenge, hostility, frustration.*
Actions:	*Hitting Dan with his hands, knocking him down several times. (Mr. Barber added, "Once I starting hitting Dan, I thought I was evening the score with Mary, and didn't want to stop.")*

At first, Mr. Barber indicated he could not understand how he could lose emotional control and abuse his son. He appeared to be remorseful and desirous of changing his actions. It was gradually explained and demonstrated that he (his thinking processes) controlled his emotions and actions and that he could change his unwanted emotions and actions by changing his self-talk. He realized he had severely hurt his son in the past and that he might lose his son if the abuse was not curbed.

Since Mr. Barber was concerned whether he really was Dan's father, blood tests were taken. It was explained to Mr. Barber that the blood tests if different would indicate that he was not the father, and if there was a match it would indicate that he probably was Dan's genetic father. The types matched, so Mr. Barber's concerns in this area were alleviated. Through rational therapy Mr. Barber learned how to challenge and change the self-talk that was leading to emotional outbursts of anger directed at Dan. Mr. Barber was also instructed to leave Dan in the care of his mother whenever he felt an urge to abuse Dan again. If an occasion arose when his mother was not available, Mr. Barber agreed to call the protective service worker to ventilate his feelings over the phone, rather than at Dan. Mr. Barber also received counseling about his feelings toward his wife and about the importance of focusing his thoughts and energies on the present and future, rather than wallowing in self-pity and dwelling on what happened in the past.

Homework assignments are frequently given to clients. Shy clients, for example, might be given an assignment to try out assertive approaches that are practiced in therapy through role-playing. Shy clients may also be given a homework assignment of writing an RSA in which they identify and challenge the negative and irrational self-talk that is leading them to feel shy. If a male client states he cannot stand to be rejected by the opposite sex, he might be assigned to ask three different females out on dates to test the hypothesis that he can indeed stand being rejected. A common homework assignment is to instruct clients to read books on rational therapy to help them learn and apply the basic concepts.

Rational therapists are willing to self-disclose some of their own foibles in order to dispute the client's irrational belief that anyone, even a therapist, can be more than human.

Common Irrational Beliefs

Rational therapy frequently seeks to refute irrational beliefs held by clients. In therapy, clients are confronted with their irrational beliefs, with the therapist asking questions such as "Show me where it is written that you must succeed at everything you try in order to feel good about yourself?" or "What evidence do you have that your girl friend *must* treat you fairly?"

Several writers (Criddle, 1974; Ellis, 1958; Ellis and Harper, 1977b; Hauck, 1972; Raimy, 1977; Zastrow, 1979) have identified common erroneous beliefs that frequently generate negative or irrational self-talk. In counseling it is frequently found that such self-talk based on erroneous beliefs lead to unwanted emotions and ineffective actions. A number of these erroneous beliefs are summarized briefly below.

1. The belief that it is a dire necessity to be loved or approved by everyone for everything you do. A more rational idea is to seek to do the things you want to do as long as you do not hinder others. No matter how hard you try, you will never get everyone to like you, since what will please one may displease another. Your opinion of yourself is much more important than others' views of you.

2. The belief that you should be thoroughly competent, skilled, and achieving in all possible respects if you are to consider yourself worthwhile. This idea represents a demand for perfection that is simply impossible to achieve. All humans are fallible. We all make mistakes. Achieving something does not make you a "better person." We all have intrinsic worth because we exist. If you fail at something, it does not make you a failure but only a person who has failed at something.

3. The belief that it is awful and catastrophic when things are not the way you would like them to be. In actuality, nothing is awful. Awful connotes that certain circumstances are more than "100 percent" negative. Events or circumstances are at times inconvenient, but they never are "awful." By telling ourselves that certain inconvenient events (such as a broken engagement) are awful, we are causing ourselves to overreact emotionally. In actuality we have only limited control over events that happen to us. You can try to change reality, but you better stop *demanding* that it be as you say — there is a great deal of evidence that neither you nor I runs the world. Rational therapy seeks to "deawfulize" thinking.

4. The belief that there will be justice in the world and in interpersonal relationships. Since humans are fallible, injustices can be expected to occur. To expect justice in all interactions is unrealistic and will lead you to react with anger or frustration when an injustice occurs. Justice does not exist and it never did. A more rational philosophy is to seek to change conditions so that they become more fair, but if you come to realize that it is impossible to change an "unfair" situation, you had better become resigned to its existence and stop telling yourself how awful it is.

5. The belief that human unhappiness (and happiness) is externally caused, and that you have little or no ability to control your unwanted emotions. The external environment can only cause you physical pain, never emotional pain. You cause all your emotions by your self-talk and thereby can control and relieve any uncomfortable emotion by changing your negative or irrational self-talk.

6. The belief that if something is or may be dangerous or fearsome, you should be terribly concerned about it and should keep dwelling on the possibility of its occurring. Worriers frequently believe the act of worrying has a "magical" value of preventing the worst from occurring. Of course, worrying has no magical power. Chronic worrying seldom achieves the results that calm deliberation and careful study do. Excessive worry often incapacitates a person to the point that the feared event is not avoided but often brought about. If you are a chronic worrier, analyze your self-talk to discover what is rational fear and what is irrational fear. Worriers will find most of their fears are irrational, and can be countered with rational self-challenges.

7. The belief that you should be dependent on others and that you need someone stronger than yourself on whom to rely. Any time you enter into a dependent relationship, you become vulnerable to the whims of the person you are dependent on. It is usually far better to stand on your own feet and gain faith in yourself by doing what you can do for yourself and for others. There is no guarantee that someone else's judgment is right—in fact, all humans are fallible. The only way you become efficient at acting on your own judgment is to practice risking it.

8. The belief that your past is an all-important determinant of your present behavior and that because something once strongly affected your life, it will indefinitely have a similar effect. In actuality, what you want out of life, now and in the future (along with your motivation to achieve what you want), is a much stronger determinant of what your life will be.

9. The belief that what other people do is vitally important to your existence and that you should make great efforts to change them in the direction you would like them to be. Forcing others to behave in a certain way frequently makes them rebel. In actuality, you have a right to live the way you want to as long as you do not hinder others in living the way they want to. You own your life and others own theirs, and you should respect their right to live the way they want to.

10. The belief that other people's problems are also yours and that you should become quite emotionally involved in other people's problems. You can do very little in controlling the emotions and behaviors of others, although you can do a great deal about controlling your own. When other people have problems, they *own* them; you don't. Becoming emotionally in-

volved by psychologically taking on joint ownership usually is more destructive than helpful. The best way to help others is to recognize their problems are theirs and be an emotionally calm person who is available to help arrive at a sensible attack on the problems.

11. The belief that people with a stereotyped label (for example, ex-convict, mentally ill, mentally retarded, whore, juvenile delinquent, welfare mother) are somehow categorically different from "normal" people and should be viewed with suspicion and avoided. In actuality, such a label (at best) refers to only a small proportion of their past or present behavior. Every person is unique. Stereotypes that are based on labels are frequently myths without a factual base. We will get to know other people much more realistically if we interact with them as "unique persons" rather than in tems of expectations based on labels. The same approach is applicable to interacting with people having labels with more positive stereotypes, for example, priests, professors, executive directors, police officers, counselors, school principals, judges.

12. The belief that human happiness can be achieved by inaction. There is no magical way in which happiness is suddenly going to happen to you. We get out of life what we put into it. If you are bored or unhappy, there are two ways of counteracting these problems: challenging the irrational self-talk, or getting involved in meaningful activities. People are the happiest when they are fully absorbed in satisfying activities.

13. The belief that what you *want* are needs that *must* be fulfilled. In actuality, you have very few *needs*—you need food, water, and shelter to exist. The consequences of thinking in terms of needs are often self-defeating. Thinking in terms of needs implies life-and-death consequences. Faced with such consequences, you will tend to panic and think and behave irrationally, and thus self-defeatingly. Ellis (1973) has coined the term *musterbation* for people who behave irrationally because they erroneously perceive their wants to be needs that *must* be fulfilled.

14. The belief that people and life *should* always be pleasing, and if they are not, they are awful and unbearable. This erroneous belief is operating when you give yourself the following self-talk about an unpleasant experience: "I *should* be treated in a totally

satisfying way; it is *awful* when I'm not." But where is the evidence that people and life *should* treat anyone in a perfectly gratifying way? Everything in life is imperfect. Nothing completely lasts or fully satisfies. All people are fallible. Demanding "I should be treated in a certain way" requires that others act and events unfold according to your private wishes. You have neither the control over others, nor are you (or for that matter, anyone) such a superspecial person that the world *should* revolve around you.

Thinking psychologically in terms of "needs," "shoulds," "musts," "awful," and "unbearable" is a distortion of reality, and frequently leads us to overact. Instead of using "shoulds" and "musts" in our interactions with others, a more rational philosophy is "I would like to be treated reasonably well by people and life."

EVALUATION

Since its formation in the 1950s, rational therapy has become one of the most widely used therapy approaches. DeGuiseppe, Miller, and Trexler (1977) summarized a wide number of outcome studies conducted on rational therapy and found over 90 percent of these studies have supported its claims. Ellis (1989, p. 223) notes:

More than 200 outcome studies have been published, showing that RET [rational-emotive therapy] is effective in changing the thoughts, feelings, and behaviors of groups of individuals with various kinds of disturbances.

(Few other psychotherapy approaches have this kind of successful documentation.)

Rational therapy has been successfully used to treat clients with a wide range of problems including unwanted emotions (depression, anxiety, fears and phobias, guilt, shame), sexual problems and sexual dysfunctions, worrying, marital problems, interaction problems, alcoholism, shyness, and such irresponsible actions as committing crimes, procrastination, and jealous actions. Its major hypotheses are also useful in

child rearing, education, executive management, and social and political affairs.

By asserting that we primarily cause our unwanted emotions and irresponsible behaviors by what we think, the approach squarely puts the responsibility on us for improving our lives. We are in charge of our lives and have the power to alleviate unwanted emotions and change ineffective actions.

Zastrow (1979) theorizes that our self-talk has immense effects on our lives that we only now are beginning to understand. Self-talk, for example, plays a major part in leading people to experience chronic stress; and chronic stress causes a wide range of psychosomatic problems including ulcers, migraine headaches, insomnia, diarrhea, heart problems, digestive problems, cancer, hypertension, and obesity. Zastrow suggests that changing the underlying irrational self-talk is a key to treating such problems. It is also hypothesized that success at any competitive game is substantially determined by the kind of self-talk we give ourselves.

Rational therapy has made a substantial contribution to psychotherapy. Yet there are some important unanswered questions:

1. Physiology of self-talk and emotions. As yet we do not precisely know the physiological components of thinking or of emotions. Our brain, of course, is important in enabling us to think. But what precisely takes place in the brain that leads us to conceptualize every thought that we have? Are there other parts of the body involved in thinking? Thinking is related to memory. But what precisely is memory, and how do we "store" and "recall" experiences that we have? And how are memory and thinking physiologically related?

Rational therapy theorizes that our self-talk primarily causes our emotions. But, again, a number of physiological questions arise: What are the physiological processes involved in self-talk resulting in an emotion? What different physiological processes occur for such varied emotions as love, depression, grief, happiness, anger, frustration, sorrow, relaxation, hostility, fear, and so on? And, how, physiologically, do certain types of self-talk and certain kinds of emotional states influence our health? In a general fashion we know certain kinds of self-talk lead to the stress reaction and that prolonged stress can cause psychosomatic illnesses. But what are the specific physiological processes involved?

2. Separating the effects of self-talk from the effects of physiological factors.   For people with injuries or abnormal conditions in the brain it is at times extremely difficult to separate the effects of their medical conditions from the effects of self-talk on their emotions and behaviors. Injuries of different areas of the brain will at times cause a change in the person's emotions and behaviors (White and Watt, 1973). Abnormal conditions of the brain can result from a wide range of factors, including brain tumors, disorders such as cerebral palsy, chronic alcoholic intoxication, Alzheimer's disease, general paresis, AIDS, and cerebral arteriosclerosis. Such medical conditions are a factor in causing confusion, incoherence, clouding of consciousness, loss of recent or past memory, reduction in reasoning capacities, listlessness, apathy, reduction in intellectual capacities, and sometimes perceptual changes. People with such medical conditions are at times fairly alert and at other times they are confused.

While the above conditions tend to have permanent or long-lasting effects on thinking patterns and emotional reactions, they are also factors that can lead to temporary changes in mental activity — such as high fever, toxins or poisons, and the intake of drugs and alcohol.

Even with the presence of any of these factors, the self-talk that a person gives herself about these conditions will also affect that person's emotions and behaviors. Separating which effects result from these other factors and which result from self-talk often is difficult.

3. Nature versus nurture.   Nurture can be defined as the sum of the influences modifying the expression of the genetic potentialities of a person. The theory of human behavior presented in this chapter focuses on nurture determinants, as it states human behavior is determined by events and self-talk. This theory fails to include genetic factors, which obviously have some influence in determining human behavior.

4. The importance of experiences or events themselves.   Some critics of rational therapy assert that experiences or events that happen to a person are as important (and perhaps even more important) in determining behavior than is the self-talk that people give themselves about such experiences. These critics point out that such events as poverty, discrimination, child abuse, overprotective parents, inadequate educa-

tion, and being victimized by crime are major determinants of human behavior.

5. Boundaries of self-talk   Rational therapy theorizes that self-talk has immense effects on our lives, and many of these effects have been summarized in this chapter. But what are the limits of the effects of self-talk? In reference to this question in another publication I (Zastrow, 1979, pp. 327–28) presented the following example, which highlights the unknown limits of the effects of self-talk:

A college student recently asked if her mother's long-time concern about giving birth to a child with a "dwarf" arm might have led to her youngest being born with a malformed arm.

The student mentioned that her mother had been mildly concerned for a number of years that she would give birth to a child with a malformed arm. This young woman and her older brother were born without having such a malformation. However, shortly after the mother became pregnant the third time, a neighbor woman gave birth to a child with a malformed arm. This led the mother to have intense concerns that the child she was carrying would be born with a "dwarf" arm. When the child was born, it in fact was born with a "dwarf" arm.

After I had given several lectures on the effects of self-talk in one of my classes, the student asked whether I thought this malformation was partly caused by self-talk or was just a matter of coincidence.

In truth, I answered I didn't know — and I still don't know. We know certain drugs (such as thalidomide and excessive drinking) can cause malformations. So can having certain illnesses, such as German measles, during the time when the mother is pregnant. There is also speculation that the mother's emotional state while pregnant can influence the emotional and physiological development of the unborn child (Ainsworth, 1966; Dunn, 1977). Is it possible that this mother's thoughts and fears about having a malformed child might have been a factor in the child's being born with a malformed arm? . . .

Daily I become aware of new ways in which my life, and that of others, is being influenced by self-talk. And, as I discuss the concept with others, the discussion usually ignites their relating to me specific incidents in which their self-talk has had a powerful effect on them.

At this point I frankly do not know what the boundaries are for the effects of self-talk. It may well be that we are only at the "tip of the iceberg" in understanding all its effects.

SUMMARY

Albert Ellis is acknowledged as the primary developer of rational therapy. Rational therapy asserts that the primary cause of all our emotions and actions is not our experiences but rather what we tell ourselves about events that happen to us. Generally we cannot control events that occur, but we have the power to think rationally and thereby change all of our unwanted emotions and dysfunctional actions. Self-talk has a "here and now" quality as it represents those thoughts we are giving ourselves at the present time. Our self-talk is frequently based on our attitudes, beliefs, values, wants, needs, drives, and motives.

Rational therapy maintains that the reasons for any deviant act (including crime) can be determined by examining what the offender was telling herself prior to and during the time the act was being committed.

The initial focus of therapy is to help clients become aware of the irrational and negative self-talk that is the primary source of their unwanted emotions and dysfunctional actions. Once the irrational self-talk is identified, a wide range of techniques is used to change the irrational self-talk, thereby alleviating unwanted emotions and changing irresponsible actions. A frequently used technique is to have the client develop (*and practice using*) rational self-challenges to counter the irrational self-talk. Often clients are asked to write out a rational self-analysis.

Learning how to think rationally and how to counter irrational and negative self-talk is seen as an educational process. Rational therapy has a wide variety of applications in addition to changing unwanted emotions and dysfunctional actions. It can be used to reduce stress, change negative self-concepts, improve negative aspects of personalities, help clients become more assertive, and to treat sexual dysfunctions. Some unanswered questions still remain about rational therapy, including how does self-talk physiologically lead to emotions, and what are the limits of the effects of self-talk?

EXERCISES

1. Changing Unwanted Emotions

GOALS: This exercise is designed to illustrate many of the principles of rational therapy and to demonstrate to students how to change unwanted emotions.

Step 1: Begin by asking students to think about the last time they were "sad" or "angry." Ask what made them sad or angry. List three or four responses on the blackboard under each heading of "sad" and "angry." The students in all probability will give you "events" as being the source of these emotions.

Step 2: Indicate to the students that what they told you was *not* the primary source of their emotions. Indicate instead that emotions are determined primarily by self-talk rather than events. For each "event" response given by a student, seek to have the student tell you about personal self-talk that led to the emotion, or seek to guess what the self-talk is. For example, if a student says, "I became sad because I received a speeding ticket," you might suggest the self-talk that led to being sad was something like "This is awful. I sure am stupid for driving so fast. Now my insurance rates will go up. Woe is me. I don't have enough money to pay for tickets and increased insurance payments. I'm a bad person for getting a ticket."

Step 3: The principles of rational therapy can be further demonstrated by asking the students, "What would be your self-talk if the person you were dating for the past four years informed you that she no longer wanted to date you?" Write this event on the blackboard. Ask students what would be their self-talk, and ask what would be the resulting emotions from each self-talk statement. Write these self-talk statements on the blackboard and also the resulting emotions. Using the five criteria for determining rational thinking, ask the students to identify which of the self-talk statements are irrational and to give the reasons they are irrational. For each irrational self-talk statement, ask the class to come up with rational self-challenges to challenge and change the irrational self-talk statement.

Step 4: Explain to students how to write a rational self-analysis. (Show them examples from this chapter or distribute a handout of an RSA that has been written.)

Step 5: Indicate to students that there are only three constructive ways to change an unwanted emotion:

a. Challenging negative and irrational thinking with rational self-challenges.
b. Getting involved in meaningful and enjoyable activities, which stops a person from thinking negatively and irrationally.
c. Changing the distressing event(s).

Step 6: As a homework assignment you may ask students to write a rational self-analysis on an unwanted emotion they have. Ask students their thoughts on the merits and shortcomings of rational therapy.

2. Positive Affirmations

GOAL: This exercise is designed to provide students with another approach to change negative and irrational thinking.

Step 1: Indicate that some people find writing a rational self-analysis too time-consuming and cumbersome. An alternative is to use positive affirmations. A positive affirmation is a positive assertion that helps in achieving emotional and behavioral goals. The process of writing a positive affirmation also enables a person to identify negative and irrational thinking that she may be unaware of.

Step 2: Instruct the students in the following process of writing a positive affirmation. Have each student select a realistic emotional or behavioral personal goal that he or she is currently struggling with. The following are examples:

"I believe I am a person of worth."

"I will no longer be depressed about _____."

"I will no longer get angry and aggressive when _____ occurs."

"I will lose fifteen pounds in two months."

"I will stop smoking today."

"I will limit my drinking of alcoholic beverages to two drinks when I go out."

"I will no longer feel guilty about _____."

"I believe I am an attractive person."

"I will assertively express myself when _____ occurs."

Step 3: Have each student start writing on a sheet of paper the selected positive affirmation. When negative thoughts enter their minds, have them record those thoughts and then continue writing the positive affirmation according to the following format:

Positive Affirmation	Negative Thoughts
"I will lose fifteen pounds in two months."	
"I will lose fifteen pounds in two months."	
"I will lose fifteen pounds in two months."	"I overeat when I'm bored, depressed or lonely."
"I will lose fifteen pounds in two months."	
"I will lose fifteen pounds in two months."	"I will need to develop an exercise program, which I hate to do."
"I will lose fifteen pounds in two months."	"One reason I'm fat is because I snack between meals."
"I will lose fifteen pounds in two months."	"I will have to limit the number of beers that I have when I go out—beer is putting a lot of weight on me."
I will lose fifteen pounds in two months."	"I wonder if I really want to make all the changes that I will have to make to lose fifteen pounds."
"I will lose fifteen pounds in two months."	
"I will lose fifteen pounds in two months."	
"I will lose fifteen pounds in two months."	

Step 4: Allow the students to write for ten to fifteen minutes. Ask for volunteers to share what they wrote. Have the class discuss the merits and shortcomings of writing positive affirmations. One advantage of repeated writing of the affirmation is that it trains the mind to accept the positive affirmation more readily.

19

BEHAVIOR THERAPY

No one person is credited with the development of behavioral approaches to psychotherapy. Behavior therapists vary considerably in both theory and technique. The main assumption of this therapy system is that maladaptive behaviors are acquired primarily through learning and can be modified through additional learning.

FOUNDERS

Historically, learning theory has been the philosophical foundation for behavior therapy even though there has never been agreement as to which learning theory is the core of behavior therapy. A number of authorities have advanced somewhat different theories of how people learn. Pavlov, a Russian who lived between 1849 and 1936, was one of the earliest. Other prominent learning theorists include Edward Thorndike (1913), E. R. Guthrie (1935), C. L. Hull (1943), E. C. Tolman (1932), and B. F. Skinner (1938).

A large number of behavior therapists have achieved international recognition for developing therapy approaches based on learning principles. Some of these therapists are R. E. Alberti and M. L. Emmons (1970), A. Bandura (1969), B. F. Skinner (1948), J. B. Watson and R. Rayner (1920), and J. Wolpe (1958).

In spite of the wide variation in behavioral therapy approaches and techniques, there are some common emphases. One is that the maladaptive behavior (such as bed-wetting) is the problem and needs to be changed. This approach is in sharp contrast to the psychoanalytic approach that views the problematic behavior as being a *symptom* of some underlying, unconscious causes. While psychoanalysts assert the underlying causes must be treated to prevent the substitution of new symptoms or the return of old symptoms, behavior therapists assert that treating the problematic behavior will not result in symptom substitution.

Another common emphasis of behavior therapists is the assertion that therapy approaches must be tested and validated by rigorous experimental procedures.

Such a focus requires that the goals of therapy be articulated in behavioral terms that can be measured. Baseline levels of problematic behaviors are established prior to therapy in order to measure whether the therapy approach is producing the desired change in the rate or intensity of responding.

The use of behavior therapy approaches in counseling has increased dramatically in the past thirty years. Behavior therapy intervention techniques are now among the most widely used techniques in counseling and psychotherapy (Wilson, 1989).

Among behavior therapists little attention has been devoted to the development of a behavioral model of personality. Behaviorists generally believe that environmental conditions or experiences are of much greater influence in controlling behavior than are internal personality traits. Consequently, we shall omit the section on personality development. Because of the wide range of behavioral therapy techniques, the focus of this chapter is on describing the best known and most used approaches.

TYPES OF LEARNING PROCESSES

Before these behavioral approaches are presented, the three major types of learning processes — operant conditioning, respondent conditioning, and modeling — postulated by learning theory will be briefly described.

Operant Conditioning

Much of human behavior, according to learning theory, is determined by positive and negative reinforcers. A *positive reinforcer* is any stimulus that, when applied following a behavior, increases or strengthens that behavior. Common examples of such stimuli are food, water, sex, attention, affection, and approval. The list of positive reinforcers is inexhaustible and highly individualized. Praise, for example, is a positive reinforcer when, and only when, it maintains or increases the be-

havior with which it is associated (for example, efforts to improve one's writing skills).

A synonym for negative reinforcer is aversive stimulus. A *negative reinforcer* (or aversive stimulus) is any stimulus that a person will terminate or avoid if given the opportunity. Common examples of negative reinforcers are frowns, electric shock, and criticism. (It should be noted that the same stimulus — for example, the smell of Limburger cheese — can be a positive reinforcer for one person while it may be a negative reinforcer for another.)

There are four basic learning principles involving positive reinforcers and aversive stimuli:

1. If a positive reinforcer (for example, food) is presented to a person following a response, the result is positive reinforcement. With positive reinforcement the occurrence of a given behavior is strengthened or increased.

2. If a positive reinforcer is withdrawn following a person's response, the result is punishment.

3. If an aversive stimulus (for example, an electric shock) is presented to a person following a response, the result is punishment. (As can be seen there are two types of punishment.)

4. If an aversive stimulus is withdrawn following a person's response, the result is negative reinforcement. In negative reinforcement, a response (behavior) is increased through removing an aversive stimulus (for example, fastening one's seat belt to turn off the obnoxiously loud and annoying buzzer).

In sum, positive and negative reinforcements increase behavior, and punishment decreases behavior. Principles of operant conditioning are used in several behavioral techniques that are described in this chapter (assertiveness training, token economies, contingency contracting, and aversive techniques).

Respondent Conditioning

Respondent learning has also been called classical or Pavlovian conditioning. A wide range of everyday behaviors are considered to be respondent behaviors — perspiring, salivating, and more important, many anxieties, fears, and phobias. A key concept in respondent learning is "pairing"; that is, behaviors are learned by being consistently paired over time with other behaviors or events. In order to explain respondent conditioning, we will begin by defining the following key terms:

Neutral stimulus (NS): A stimulus that elicits little or no response.

Unconditioned stimulus (UCS): A stimulus that elicits an unlearned or innate response.

Unlearned or innate response (UR): A response that is innate, for example, the response of salivating to having food in the mouth.

Conditioned response (CR): A new response that has been learned.

Conditioned stimulus (CS): An original neutral stimulus which through pairing with an unconditioned stimulus now begins to elicit a conditioned response.

Respondent learning asserts that when a neutral stimulus *(NS)* is paired with an unconditioned stimulus *(UCS)*, the neutral stimulus will also come to elicit a response similar to that being elicited by the UCS. That new response is called a *conditioned response (CR)* because it has been learned; the originally neutral stimulus, once it begins to elicit the response, becomes the conditioned stimulus *(CS)*. Thus, it is possible for an event that originally elicited no fear whatsoever (for example, being in the dark) to come to elicit fear when it is paired with a stimulus that does elicit fear (for example, horrifying stories about being in the dark). This learning process is indicated in the following paradigm:

a. *UCS* (horrifying stories about being in the dark) → elicits *UR* (fear)

b. *NS* (being in the dark)
↓
(paired with)
UCS → elicits → *CR* (fear)

c. *NS* becomes *CS* → elicits *CR* (fear)

The *CS → CR* bond can be broken by *respondent extinction* or by *counterconditioning*. Respondent extinction involves continuing presentation of the conditioned stimulus without any further pairing with the unconditioned stimulus. Respondent extinction gradually weakens, and eventually eliminates, the CS-CR blond. *Implosive therapy*, soon to be discussed, is based on this principle.

Counterconditioning is based on the principle that the CS-CR bond can be broken by using new responses that are stronger than and incompatible with old responses that are elicited by the same stimulus. For example, it is possible to teach a person to relax (new response) instead of becoming anxious (old response) when confronted with a particular stimulus (for example, the prospect of flying in a small plane). *Systematic desensitization* and *in vivo desensitization* (to be discussed later in this chapter) are based on counterconditioning. Another technique to be discussed, *covert sensitization*, is based on establishing new CS-CR connections to eliminate problematic behavior.

Modeling

Modeling refers to a change in behavior as a result of the observation of another's behavior, that is, learning by vicarious experience or imitation. Much of everyday learning is thought to take place through modeling — using both live models and symbolic models (such as films). Modeling has been used in behavior modification to develop new behaviors that are not in a person's repertoire, for example, showing a youngster how to swing a bat. Modeling has also been used to eliminate anxieties and fears, for example, through using a model in assertiveness training. Anxieties and fears are reduced or eliminated through modeling by exposing fearful observers to modeled events in which the model performs feared activity without experiencing any adverse effects and even enjoys the process.

THEORY
OF PSYCHOTHERAPY

Behavior therapy is based on the assumption that all behavior occurs in response to stimulation, internal or external. The first task of the behavior therapist is to identify the probable stimulus-response (S-R) connections that are occurring for the client. This part of the therapy process is called the behavioral or functional analysis. The following is an illustration of an S-R connection: For a person who has a fear of heights the stimulus (S) of flying in a small plane would have the response (R) of intense anxiety and seeking to avoid the stimulus.

Prior to and during the time the therapist is doing the behavioral analysis, the therapist is also attempting to establish a working relationship. (The characteristics of a working relationship have been described in Chapter 5.) In regard to this emphasis on establishing a working relationship, Chambless and Goldstein (1979, p. 243) state:

Although behaviorists are often portrayed as cold and mechanical, a study of recordings of therapy sessions yields a different picture. When measured on variables used in the study of client-centered therapy, behavior therapists showed high warmth and positive regard for their clients (equal to other psychotherapists in the study) and higher empathy and self-congruence than the other therapists (Sloane, Staples, Cristol, Yorkston, and Whipple, 1975).

During the behavioral analysis the therapist attempts to determine the stimuli that are associated with the maladaptive responses. Through this analysis both the client and the therapist arrive at an understanding of the problem and generally how it developed. This insight, although it does not treat the problem, is useful because it reduces some of the client's anxiety and the client no longer feels possessed or overwhelmed by unknown, mysterious forces. It should be noted that errors about hypothesized S-R connections at this diagnostic stage usually lead to ineffective treatment, as the treatment will then be focused on treating S-R connections that are *not* involved in perpetuating the maladaptive behavior.

A behavioral analysis begins with the therapist taking a detailed history of the presenting problem, its course, and particularly of its association with current experiences. In making such an analysis it is crucial to obtain specific, concrete details about the circumstances in which the presenting problem arises. If, for example, a client is shy in some situations, it is important to identify the specific interactions in which the client is shy. Furthermore, it is important to determine the reasons the client is shy: Is it because he does not know how to express himself, or is it because he has certain fears? The treatment chosen depends on such information. If the client does not know how to express himself, a *modeling* approach through role-playing might be used. On the other hand, if the client has the response potential but is inhibited by certain fears, a desensitization procedure (described later in this chapter) to reduce these fears might be used.

The objective in doing a behavioral analysis is to identify the antecedent stimuli that are generating the maladaptive responses. Once these connections are identified, these connections are discussed with the client to help the client gain insight and to obtain the client's feedback on possible erroneous connections. The client and the therapist then agree upon the goals for the treatment. The process of how therapy will proceed (along with the techniques to be used) are described to the client. This provides the client with an idea of his role in treatment. Orne and Wender (1968) have found that this knowledge fosters positive outcomes and reduces the dropout rate.

Chambless and Goldstein (1979, pp. 244–45) describe the sources of information for making a behavioral analysis:

The behavior therapist may base the functional analysis on interviews with the client and important people in the client's life or on information gained by having the client keep a journal. Questionnaire data are often useful. Interpersonal problems may be more clearly defined if the therapist and client role play interactions with which the client reports difficulty. When the therapist has a difficult time making the analysis, observing the client in the situation where the problem occurs may lead to a wealth of information. Obviously, there are times when this would be impossible or in poor taste, but direct observation is used much less frequently than it should be.

The remainder of this chapter is focused on presenting some of the most commonly used behavior therapy techniques.

ASSERTIVENESS TRAINING

Assertiveness training has become the most frequently used method in modifying unadaptive interpersonal behavior. It is particularly effective in changing both timid behavior and aggressive behavior. Wolpe (1958) originally developed this approach, and it has been further developed by a variety of authors, including Alberti and Emmons (1970) and Fensterheim and Baer (1975).

In recent years interest has grown enormously, sparked by the recognition that sex-role stereotyping has led to a general lack of assertiveness in women. Assertiveness-training groups are now widely offered. During the past several years an increasing number of men are also getting involved, either individually or through groups, in assertiveness training. Outcome research on assertiveness training has found the approach to be effective in assisting participants to become more assertive (Corimer and Corimer, 1991).

Overview of Assertiveness Training[1]

Do you handle put-down comments well? Are you reluctant to express your feelings and opinions openly and honestly in a group? Are you frequently timid in interacting with people in authority? Do you react well to criticism? Do you sometimes explode in anger when things go wrong, or are you able to keep your cool? Do you find it difficult to maintain eye contact when talking? If you are uncomfortable with someone smoking near you, do you express your feelings? Are you timid in arranging a date or social event? If you have trouble in any of these situations, there is, fortunately, a useful technique—assertiveness training—that enables peo-

ple to become more effective in such interpersonal interactions.

Assertiveness problems range from extreme shyness, introversion, and withdrawal to inappropriately flying into a rage that results in alienating others. A nonassertive person is often acquiescent, fearful, and afraid of expressing his or her real, spontaneous feelings in a variety of situations. Frequently, resentment and anxiety build up, which may result in general discomfort, feelings of low self-esteem, tension headaches, fatigue, and perhaps a destructive explosion of temper, anger, and aggression. Some people are overly shy and timid in nearly all interactions. Most of us, however, encounter occasional problems in isolated areas when it would be to our benefit to be more assertive. For example, a bachelor may be quite effective and assertive in his job as store manager but still be awkward and timid when attempting to arrange a date.

There are three basic styles of interacting with others: *nonassertive, aggressive,* and *assertive*. Characteristics of these styles have been summarized by Alberti and Emmons (1975, p. 24).

In the nonassertive *style, you are likely to hesitate, speak softly, look away, avoid the issue, agree regardless of your own feelings, not express opinions, value yourself "below" others, and hurt yourself to avoid any chance of hurting others.*

In the aggressive *style, you typically answer before the other person is through talking, speak loudly and abusively, glare at the other person, speak "past" the issue (accusing, blaming, demeaning), vehemently expound your feelings and opinions, value yourself "above" others, and hurt others to avoid hurting yourself.*

In the assertive *style, you will answer spontaneously, speak with a conversational tone and volume, and look at the other person, speak to the issue, openly express your personal feelings and opinions (anger, love, disagreement, sorrow), value yourself equal to others, and hurt neither yourself or others.*

Simply stated, *assertive behavior* is being able to express yourself without hurting or stepping on others.

Assertiveness training is designed to lead a person to realize, feel, and act on the assumption that she has the right to be herself and to express feelings freely.

---

[1]This material on assertiveness training is adapted from Charles Zastrow, "How to Become More Assertive" in *The Personal Problem Solver*, edited by Charles Zastrow and Dae H. Chang © 1977, pp. 236–43. Adapted by permission of Prentice-Hall, Inc., Englewood Cliffs, New Jersey.

Assertive responses generally are not aggressive responses. The distinction between these two types of interactions is important. If, for example, a wife has an overly critical mother-in-law, aggressive responses by the wife would include ridiculing the mother-in-law, intentionally doing things that she knows will upset the mother-in-law (not visiting, serving the type of food the mother-in-law dislikes, not cleaning the house), urging the husband to tell his mother to "shut up," and getting into loud verbal arguments with the mother-in-law. On the other hand, an effective assertive response would be to counter criticism by saying, "Jane, your criticism of me deeply hurts me. I know you're trying to help me when you give advice, but I feel when you do that you're criticizing me. I know you don't want me to make mistakes, but to grow, I need to make my own errors and learn from them. If you want to help me the most, let me do it myself and be responsible for the consequences. The type of relationship I'd like to have with you is a close, adult relationship, not a mother-child relationship."

Examples of nonassertive, aggressive, and assertive behavior: You are a social worker driving in a car with an associate to a conference in another city. The associate lights up a pipe; you soon find the smoke irritating and the odor somewhat stifling. What are your choices?

1. Nonassertive response — you attempt to carry on a "cheery" conversation for the three-hour trip without commenting about the smoke.

2. Aggressive response — you increasingly become irritated until exploding, "Either you put out that pipe or I'll put it out for you — the odor is sickening."

3. Assertive response — in a firm, conversational tone, you look directly at the associate and state, "The smoke from your pipe is irritating me. I'd appreciate it if you put it away."

At a party with friends, during small-talk conversation, your husband gives you a subtle "putdown" by stating, "Wives always talk too much." What do you do?

1. Nonassertive response — you don't say anything, but feel hurt and become quiet.

2. Aggressive response — you glare at him and angrily ask, "John, why are you always criticizing me?"

3. Assertive response — you carry on as usual, waiting until driving home, then calmly look at him and say, "When we were at the party tonight, you said that wives always talk too much. I felt you were putting me down when you said that. What did you mean by that comment?"

Steps in Assertiveness Training[2]

1. Examine your interactions. Are there situations that you need to handle more assertively? Do you at times hold opinions and feelings within you for fear of what would happen if you expressed them? Do you occasionally blow your cool and lash out angrily at others? Studying your interactions is facilitated by keeping a diary for a week or longer, recording the situations in which you acted timidly, those in which you were aggressive, and those which you handled assertively.

2. Select those interactions in which it would be to your benefit to be more assertive. They may include situations in which you were overly polite, overly apologetic, timid, and allowed others to take advantage of you while at the same time you were harboring feelings of resentment, anger, embarrassment, fear of others, or self-criticism for not having the courage to express yourself. Overly aggressive interactions in which you exploded in anger or walked over others also need to be dealt with. For *each* set of nonassertive or aggressive interactions, you can become more assertive, as shown in the next steps.

3. Concentrate on a specific incident in the past in which you were either nonassertive or aggressive when you wanted to be assertive. Close your eyes for a few minutes and vividly imagine the details, including what you and the other person said, and how you felt at the time and afterward.

---

[2]These self-training steps are a modification of assertiveness training programs developed by Robert E. Alberti and Michael L. Emmons, *Your Perfect Right* (San Luis Obispo, Calif.: Impact Publishers, 1970), and by Herbert Fensterheim and Jean Baer, *Don't Say Yes When You Want to Say No* (New York: Dell Publishing Co., 1975).

4. Write down and review your responses. Ask yourself the following questions to determine how you presented yourself:

a. Eye contact — did you look directly at the other person in a relaxed, steady gaze? Looking down or away suggests a lack of self-confidence. Glaring is an aggressive response.

b. Gestures — were your gestures appropriate, free flowing, relaxed, and used effectively to emphasize your messages? Awkward stiffness suggests nervousness; other gestures (such as an angry fist) signal an aggressive reaction.

c. Body posture — did you show the importance of your message by directly facing the other person, by leaning toward that person, by holding your head erect, and by sitting or standing appropriately close?

d. Facial expression — did your facial expression show a stern, firm pose consistent with an assertive response?

e. Voice tone and volume — was your response stated in a firm, conversational tone? Shouting may suggest anger. Speaking softly suggests shyness, and a cracking voice suggests nervousness. Tape recording and listening to one's voice is a way to practice increasing or decreasing the volume.

f. Speech fluency — did your speech flow smoothly, clearly, and slowly? Rapid speech or hesitation in speaking suggests nervousness. Tape recording assertive responses that you try out in problem situations is a way to improve fluency.

g. Timing — were your verbal reactions to a problem situation stated at a time closest to the incident that would appropriately permit you and the other person time to review the incident? Generally, spontaneous expressions are the best, but certain situations should be handled at a later time — for example, a challenge to some of your boss's erroneous statements should be made in private rather than in front of a group in which she is making a presentation.

h. Message content — for a problem situation, which of your responses were nonassertive or aggressive and which were assertive? Study the content and consider why you responded in a nonassertive or aggressive style. (At this point it is very helpful to identify the self-talk that led you to act nonassertively or aggressively, and to challenge this self-talk with rational, assertive self-challenges — see Chapter 18.)

5. Observe one or more effective models. Watch the verbal and nonverbal approaches that are assertively used to handle the types of interactions with which you are having problems. Compare the consequences between their approach and yours. If possible, discuss their approach and their feelings about using it.

6. Make a list of various alternative approaches for being more assertive.

7. Close your eyes and visualize yourself using each of the above alternative approaches. For each approach, think through what the full set of interactions would be, along with the consequences. Select an approach, or combination of approaches, that you believe will be most effective for you to use. Through imagery, practice using this approach until you feel comfortable that it will work for you.

8. Role-play the approach with someone else, perhaps a friend or counselor. If certain segments of your approach appear clumsy, awkward, timid, or aggressive, practice modifications until you become comfortable with the approach. Obtain feedback from the other person as to the strengths and shortcomings of your approach. Compare your interactions to the verbal/nonverbal guidelines for assertive behavior in Step 4. It may be useful for the other person to model through role-playing one or more assertive strategies, which you would then, by reversing roles, practice using.

9. Repeat Steps 7 and 8 until you develop an assertive approach that you believe will work best for you and that you are comfortable with.

10. Use your approach in a real-life situation. The previous steps are designed to prepare you for the real event. Expect to be somewhat anxious when first trying to be assertive. If you are still too fearful of attempting to be assertive, repeat Steps 5 through 8. For those few individuals who fail to develop the needed confidence to try being assertive, seeking professional counseling is advised—expressing yourself and effective interactions with others are essential for personal happiness.

11. Reflect on the effectiveness of your effort. Did you "keep your cool?"[3] Considering the nonverbal guidelines for assertive behavior discussed in Step 4, what components of your responses were assertive, aggressive, and nonassertive? What were the consequences of your effort? How did you feel after trying out this new set of interactions? If possible, discuss how you did in regard to these questions with a friend who may have observed the interactions.

12. Expect some success, but not complete personal satisfaction, with your initial efforts. Personal growth and interacting more effectively with others is a continual learning process. Quite appropriately "pat yourself on the back" for the strengths of your approach—you earned it. But also note the areas in which you need to improve, and use the above steps for improving your assertive efforts. These steps systematically make sense but are not to be followed rigidly. Each person has to develop a process that works best for herself.

Helping Others Become More Assertive

Either as a friend or as a counselor, you can be very helpful in assisting another person to become more assertive. The following guidelines are suggested.

1. Together identify the situations/interactions in which the person needs to be more assertive. Get information about such interactions from your observations and knowledge about the person, and from discussing in depth the interactions in which the person feels a need to be more assertive. You may also seek to get information by asking the person to keep a diary of interactions in which he feels resentment over being

nonassertive, and those interactions in which he was overly aggressive.

2. Develop together some strategies for the person to be more assertive. Small assignments with a high probability of successful outcomes should be given first. A great deal of discussion and preparation should take place between the two of you in preparing for the "real event." For a person who is generally shy, introverted, and nonassertive in all interpersonal relationships, it probably will be necessary to explore and explain in great detail the connection between nonassertive behavior and feelings of resentment or low self-esteem. In addition, for very shy people, certain attitudes, such as "don't make waves" or the "meek will inherit the earth," may need to be dealt with prior to developing strategies for the person to be more assertive.

3. Role-playing is a very useful technique in preparing for being assertive. The helper first models an assertive strategy by taking the shy person's role. The shy person concurrently role-plays the role of the person with whom he wants to be more assertive. Then the roles are reversed; the person role-plays himself and the helper plays the other role. An example may make this clearer. Using the illustration cited earlier in which a wife has problems interacting with an overly critical mother-in-law, the helper would play the role of the wife first, modeling an assertive strategy. The wife would concurrently play the role of the mother-in-law. Then the roles would be reversed, the wife practicing various assertive strategies with the helper playing the mother-in-law. The technique is practiced until the wife becomes comfortable with it and develops sufficient self-confidence for the "real event." In addition to the above-mentioned benefits of modeling and practice experience, role-playing has the added advantage of reducing the anxiety that the shy person has about attempting to be assertive. For feedback purposes, if possible, record the role-playing on audio or videotape.

4. Explain the twelve steps described earlier that the person can use on his own to handle future problem situations involving assertiveness. If possible, provide reading material on these steps.

---

[3]Getting angry at times is a normal human emotion, and it needs to be expressed. However, the anger should be expressed in a constructive, assertive fashion. When expressed in a destructive, lashing-out fashion, you are "blowing your cool."

Role-playing assertive behavior in a classroom

Although each person must be able to express himself in his own individual style, there is an additional guideline that is often useful. A good rule is to start sentences with "I feel" rather than making threatening or aggressive statements (I-messages are further described in Chapter 22). Frequently, in our fast-paced society we simply do not take the time to express our real feelings to others; as a result we end up creating serious misunderstandings, hurt feelings, and verbal fights that take ten times as long to work through. Taking the following example of two busy people, a working mother and her fifteen-year-old son.

MOTHER: John, please do the dishes for me tonight.

JOHN: I can't, I'll do them tomorrow.

MOTHER: [*Getting angry.*] You never do anything for me.

JOHN: I said I'll do the dishes tomorrow.

MOTHER: And you always forget. I asked you to clean your room two weeks ago, and you still haven't done that. [*Now angry.*] I just don't know what I'm going to do with you. Just for that you can't go camping this weekend.

And the argument has ignited. Contrast this to the following approach:

MOTHER: John, I feel very tired this evening. I had a bad day at work, and I still have to do all the washing and ironing tonight. Could you please help me out by doing the dishes?

JOHN: I'm sorry you had a bad day. I'm supposed to be at basketball practice in five minutes. I'll be back at 8:30, would it be all right if I did them then?

MOTHER: Yes, if you don't forget.

JOHN: I won't.

The structure of the technique in assertive training is relatively simple to comprehend. Considerable skill (common sense and ingenuity), however, is needed to determine what will be an effective assertive strategy when a real-life situation arises. The joy and pride obtained from being able fully to express oneself assertively is nearly unequaled.

TOKEN ECONOMIES

Tokens are symbolic reinforcers, such as poker chips or points on a tally sheet, which can later be exchanged for items that constitute direct forms of reinforcement, such as candy or increased privileges (for example, an adolescent in a group home being allowed to go to movies). An economy involves an exchange system that specifies exactly what the tokens can be exchanged for and how many tokens it takes to get particular items or privileges. The economy also specifies the target behaviors (such as going to school or making a bed) that can earn tokens and the rate of responding that is required to earn a particular number of tokens. For example, attending school every day for two weeks earns ten tokens at an adolescent group home, and ten tokens can be exchanged for attending a sports event.

Token economies have been successfully used in a wide variety of institutional settings, including mental hospitals, training schools for delinquents, classrooms for students with emotional problems, schools for the retarded, sheltered workshops for the mentally impaired, and group homes for adolescents.

There is considerable evidence to support the effectiveness of token economies (Kazdin, 1977). Token economies have been used to effect positive changes in a wide variety of behaviors, including personal hygiene, social interactions, job attendance and performance, academic performance, domestic tasks such as cleaning, and personal appearance.

At times, token economies are arranged in which clients not only earn tokens for desired behaviors but also lose tokens for undesired behaviors (for example, instigating a fight).

Effective token economies are much more difficult to establish than it appears at first glance. Prochaska (1979, pp. 324–25) summarizes some of the most important factors that need to be given attention in establishing a token economy:

Some of the more important considerations include staff cooperation and coordination, since the staff must be more observant and more systematic in their responses to clients than in a noncontingent system. A variety of attempts at establishing token economies have failed because the staff did not cooperate adequately in monitoring the behavior of residents. Effective token economies must also have adequate control over reinforcements, since an economy becomes ineffective if residents have access to reinforcements by having money from home or being able to bum a cigarette from a less cooperative staff member. Problems must be clearly defined in terms of specific behaviors to be changed in order to avoid conflicts among staff or patients. Improving personal hygiene, for example, is too open to interpretation by individuals, and patients may insist that they are improving their hygiene even though staff members may disagree. There is much less room for misunderstandings if personal hygiene is defined as clean fingernails, no evidence of body odor, clean underwear, and other clear-cut rules. Specifying behavior that are positive alternatives to problem behavior is very critical in teaching residents what positive actions they can take to help themselves rather than relying on just a negative set of eliminating responses. Perhaps most important for more lasting effectiveness of token economies is that they be gradually faded out as problem behaviors are reduced and more adaptive responses become well established. Obviously the outside world does not run according to an institution's internal economy, and it is important that clients be prepared to make the transition to the larger society. Using an abundance of social reinforcers along with token reinforcers helps prepare clients for the fading out of tokens, so that positive behaviors can be maintained by praise or recognition rather than by tokens. Also encouraging patients to reinforce themselves, such as by learning to take pride in their appearance, is an important step in fading out tokens. Some institutions use transitional wards where clients go from token economies and learn to maintain adaptive behaviors through more naturalistic contingencies, such as praise from a fellow patient. In such transitional settings, backup reinforcers are available if needed, but they are used much more sparingly than in the token economies. Without the use of fading, token economies can become nothing more than hospital management procedures that make the care of patients more efficient without preparing patients to live effectively in the larger society.[4]

CONTINGENCY CONTRACTING

Closely related to token economies is contingency contracting. Contingency contracts provide the client with a set of rules that govern the change process. Contracts may be unilateral; that is, a client may make a contract with herself. For example, a person with a weight problem may limit herself to a certain calorie intake, with a system of rewards being established for staying within the calorie limit and negative consequences being set for going over the calorie limit. Contracts may also be bilateral and specify the obligations and the mutual reinforcements for each of the parties.

Kanfer (1975, p. 321) notes that a good contingency contract should contain the following seven elements:

1. A clear and detailed description of the required instrumental behavior should be stated.

2. Some criterion should be set for the time or frequency limitations which constitute the goal of the contract.

3. The contract should specify the positive reinforcements, contingent upon fulfillment of the criterion.

4. Provisions should be made for some aversive consequence, contingent upon nonfulfillment of the contract within the specified time or with the specified frequency.

5. A bonus clause should indicate the additional positive reinforcements obtainable if the person exceeds the minimal demands of the contract.

6. The contract should specify the means by which the contracted response is observed, measured, recorded; and a procedure should be stated for informing the client of his achievements during the duration of the contract.

7. The timing for delivery of reinforcement contingencies should be arranged to follow the response as quickly as possible.

Helping professionals are increasingly finding it very useful to develop contingency contracts (also called *behavioral change contracts*) with clients. Such contracts specify the desired goals, the tasks to be performed to meet these goals, the tasks that will be done by the client and those that will be carried out by the therapist, and the deadline for completing these tasks.

Kanfer (1975) indicates that marriage counseling is one area in which contingency contracts are increasingly being used. In such a contract each spouse agrees to change behaviors that irritate the other, with a system of reinforcements and consequences being specified that will be applied according to the extent to which the contract provisions are met.

Formulating contracts with clients in both one-to-one and in group settings has a number of advantages. The contracts serve as guides to clients as to the specific actions they need to take in order to improve their problematic situations. Contracts tend to have a motivational effect because when people commit to the terms of a contract, they usually feel a moral obligation to follow through on the commitments they have made. In addition, reviewing whether commitments made in contracts are being met provides therapists and clients with one method for measuring progress. If commitments are generally fulfilled, it suggests that

---

[4]James O. Prochaska, *Systems of Psychotherapy*, (Homewood, Ill.: Dorsey Press, 1979), pp. 324–25.

positive changes are occurring; if commitments are generally unfulfilled, it suggests that positive changes are not occurring.

SYSTEMATIC DESENSITIZATION[5]

A useful technique for a person who is unduly anxious about a specific stimulus is systematic desensitization. Most of us have extreme anxiety reactions (phobias) to one or more of the following stimuli: taking exams, snakes, rats, a fear of making love, being alone, fire, heights, walking alone, injections, medications, being in a small place or a crowded place, locked doors, steep stairways, fear of the unknown, fear of death, fear of nightmares, traffic, thunder and lightning, anxiety over talking to authority figures, sexual dysfunctions, speaking in public, fear of criticism, and fear of losing one's mind.

Systematic desensitization was developed by Joseph Wolpe (1969). The basis for this approach is that a person cannot be simultaneously anxious and relaxed. Wolpe uses "relaxation" as a counterconditioner to the feared stimulus. *Systematic desensitization* involves three phases: training in deep muscle relaxation, the construction of anxiety hierarchies, and counterpoising through imagery the anxiety-evoking stimuli and relaxation.

For training in deep muscle relaxation, a modification of Jacobson's (1934) procedures is used. The client, under the instruction of a therapist, is taught how to relax by tensing and then relaxing progressive groups of muscles. This phase is completed when the client is able to relax the muscles through imagery.[6]

The second phase is the construction of anxiety hierarchies. In a series of interviews the therapist seeks

to discover the stimulus situations that elicit fear or anxiety. Suppose that a man has an unreasonable fear of heights. There are apt to be several themes in which the fear arises: being in tall buildings, high-altitude driving, flying in a small plane, amusement park rides. For each theme, a set of stimuli about that theme are ranked according to how fear-producing they are, from the last frightening to the most. For example, rankings of stimuli about flying in a small plane might be the following:

> Thinking about having to fly in a small plane some time in the future.
>
> Knowing that in two weeks you have to fly in a small plane.
>
> Knowing that next week you will have to fly in a small plane.
>
> Thinking about flying in a small plane tomorrow.
>
> Knowing you will have to fly in a small plane today.
>
> Driving to the airport to fly.
>
> Buying a ticket at the airport to fly.
>
> Seeing your luggage put on the plane.
>
> Walking toward the plane.
>
> Getting into the small plane.
>
> Fastening the safety belt.
>
> Hearing the motor start.
>
> Listening to the pilot getting clearance to fly.
>
> Feeling the plane taxi down the runway.
>
> Takeoff.
>
> Feeling the plane gaining altitude.
>
> Looking out the window while gaining altitude.
>
> Reaching the plane's cruise height.
>
> Looking out the window at cruising height.
>
> Encountering a thunderstorm while flying.
>
> Looking out the window during a thunderstorm.

Wolpe indicates that the construction of anxiety hierarchies is the most difficult phase of the desensitization technique.

The third phase is the counterpoising, with imagery, of relaxation and anxiety-evoking stimuli from the

---

[5]This material on systematic desensitization is excerpted from Charles Zastrow, "Systematic Desensitization," in *Talk to Yourself: Using the Power of Self-Talk*, © 1979, pp. 190–93. Reprinted by permission of Prentice-Hall, Inc., Englewood Cliffs, New Jersey.

[6]Muscle relaxation approaches are more fully described in Chapter 22.

hierarchies. The objective of this phase is to replace the fear of each stimulus with relaxation. This is done by having the client imagine each fear-producing stimulus while in the relaxed state. The specific procedures of this phase are these:

1. The client is told that he will be asked to imagine (think about) various scenes from his anxiety hierarchies. The themes are worked on separately, beginning with the least frightening stimulus situation in each theme.

2. The client is told that if he becomes anxious while imagining a stimulus situation to raise the index finger.

3. Taking a theme, the client is then asked to imagine the least frightening stimulus situation in that theme. The client is asked to think about it, then told to relax, then asked to think about it, then told to relax, and so on. The scene and relaxation are counterpoised several times.

3. If the client indicates no anxiety arises, the next scene in the anxiety hierarchy is presented and counterpoised with relaxation. Gradually the client and therapist work their way up the anxiety hierarchy in this manner. If the client indicates anxiety with any stimulus, the therapist instructs the client to relax. After the client is relaxed, a scene lower in the hierarchy is presented and the therapist and the client gradually start working their way up the anxiety hierarchy again.

The advantage of desensitization through imagination is that the appearance of the feared stimulis can be regulated. By encountering the feared stimuli in a step-wise hierarchy in your imagination, you will be less likely to be pushed too far by some event beyond your control. As a clinical technique, systematic desensitization has been found to be highly effective in substantially reducing anxieties, fears, and phobias that are attached to specific conditions (Paul, 1969).

There is also some evidence that systematic desensitization can be used as a self-modification procedure, that is, by a person who is not under the supervision of a therapist (Kahn and Baker, 1968; Migler, 1968; Rardin, 1969). Watson and Tharp (1972) caution that self-desensitization "should be discontinued if the course of anxiety-reduction is not relatively smooth and *it should be immediately discontinued if any increase in anxiety is noted*" (p. 179).

Self-desensitization involves the same stages as systematic desensitization: learning to relax through imagery after learning a muscle relaxation technique, construction of anxiety hierarchies; and counterpoising the anxiety-evoking stimuli with relaxation. (Learning to relax with muscle relaxation techniques is described in Chapter 22.)

In constructing anxiety hierarchies Watson and Tharp (1972) advise that each feared situation be listed on a separate card, and then hierarchies with themes be constructed. For example, phobias of certain animals may include themes of snakes, rats, and dogs. In constructing the themes various types of hierarchies may be used. For example, if a person has a fear of taking exams, hierarchy types might include distance in time before the feared event occurs, importance of the exam, and the exam taker's acquaintance or comfortableness with the anticipated content of the exam.

Desensitization occurs through counterpoising the anxiety-eliciting stimuli with relaxation. A theme is selected and, while deeply relaxed, you present to yourself the lowest fear-producing item in the theme by looking at the card on which it has been written. Keep counterpoising through imagery the item and relaxation. When you feel completely relaxed while imagining the item, you are ready to go on to the next.

IN VIVO DESENSITIZATION[7]

In vivo (from the Latin "in life") desensitization refers to a real-life desensitization process in which a person gradually approaches an actual feared event or stimulus while being in a relaxed state. In order to carry out

---

[7]This material on in vivo desensitization is excerpted from Charles Zastrow, "In Vivo Desensitization," in *Talk to Yourself: Using the Power of Self-Talk*, © 1979, pp. 195–96. Reprinted by permission of Prentice-Hall, Inc., Englewood Cliffs, New Jersey.

in vivo desensitization, the following three steps should be taken:

1. Make a ranked list of fear-producing situations, arranging items from least to most anxiety-producing. (This step is identical to the construction of anxiety hierarchies in systematic desensitization.)

2. Learn to produce or achieve relaxation, perhaps by meditation, muscle relaxation, deep breathing relaxation, or imagery relaxation.[8]

3. Gradually approach an actual feared event while remaining relaxed.

A twenty-two-year-old male college student used this approach in overcoming several situations (themes) connected with a fear of heights. He first became skilled at producing the relaxation response by imagery of his ideal relaxation place. (His ideal relaxation place was lying on the beach in Acapulco. With practice he became skilled relaxing himself by fully focusing his thinking on relaxing in Acapulco.) He then gradually approached feared situations while remaining in a relaxed state with his imagery of Acapulco. He, for example, countered his fear of tall buildings by looking out the window in the lower floors and gradually moving upward while thinking about being relaxed in Acapulco. He also used this approach to overcome his fears of taking amusement park rides and of flying in small planes.

Watson and Tharp (1972) indicate that in vivo desensitization is an effective method in eliminating fear and anxiety reactions associated with specific stimuli (events).

IMPLOSIVE THERAPY

Like systematic desensitization, implosive therapy has the client imagine (think about) anxiety-provoking material. Unlike systematic desensitization, relaxation training is not required or used.

---

[8]All of these techniques to achieve relaxation are described in Chapter 22.

Implosive therapy was developed by Stampfl and Levis (1967). The approach is based on *extinction*. As used by Stampfl and Levis, extinction refers to the gradual reduction in the occurrence of an anxiety response as a result of the continuous presentation of the fear-producing stimulus situation in the absence of the reinforcement that perpetuates the fear.

In using implosive therapy, the therapist first constructs an Avoidance Serial Cue Hierarchy. From interviews with the client, the therapist develops a ranking of important cues involved in the client's fear. For example, if a person has a fear of flying, a cue low on the hierarchy might be driving to the airport, while a cue high on the hierarchy might be taking off in a plane during a thunderstorm. In developing the hierarchy the therapist seeks primarily to include cues thought to be capable of producing a *maximum* level of anxiety in the client. An example of this type of hierarchy is described by Hogan and Kirchner (1967, p. 109).

Fear of rats

Imagine that you are touching a rat in the laboratory. . . . It begins nibbling at your finger . . . and then runs across your arm. The rat suddenly bites you on your arm, and then you feel it run rapidly over your body. . . . It begins biting your neck and swishing its tail in your face . . . then it claws up your face into your hair . . . clawing in your hair . . . you try to get it out with your bloody arm, but you can't. It then goes for your eyes . . . you open your mouth and it jumps in and you swallow it. . . . It then begins to eat away at various internal organs — like your stomach and intestines, causing you great discomfort and pain . . . , etc.

After the hierarchy is developed, the therapist describes implosive therapy to the client. The client is then presented with the scenes, and asked to make every effort to imagine the scenes as vividly as possible, and encouraged to "live" the scenes with emotion.

The objective of implosive therapy is to extinguish fears through having the client produce in his mind frightening experiences of such magnitude that, in the absence of reinforcement, they will *lessen* the fear of the particular situation. Stampfl and Levis (1967, p. 500) state:

An attempt is made by the therapist to attain a max-imal level of anxiety evocation from the patient. When a high level of anxiety is achieved, the patient is held on this level until some sign of spontaneous reduction in the anxiety-inducing value of the cues appears . . . the process is repeated, and again, at the first sign of spontaneous reduction of fear, new vari-ations are introduced to elicit an intense anxiety re-sponse. This response is repeated until a significant diminution in anxiety has resulted.

Sessions end after thirty to sixty minutes, generally after the client experiences a reduction in anxiety to the implosive scenes. Between sessions the client is en-couraged to practice imagining the implosive scenes at home in order to help him realize he can effectively handle the fears.

Morris (1986) indicates that few outcome studies have been conducted on implosive therapy, with the studies showing mixed results. It should be noted that there is a danger that implosive therapy may *increase*, rather than lessen the fear of the particular situation (Morris, 1986). Because of this possibility, the tech-nique should be used only by clinicians who receive extensive training in utilizing this technique.

COVERT SENSITIZATION

Covert Sensitization is an aversive counterconditioning approach that was first developed by J. R. Cautela (1967). Instead of inhibiting anxiety with relaxation as in systematic desensitization, covert sensitization is used to elicit anxiety in certain problematic situations. The technique is claimed to be particularly appropri-ate for treating such behavioral excesses as sexual devi-ations, alcoholism, stealing, overeating, and drug ad-diction (Anant, 1967, 1968; Ashem and Donner, 1968; Sundel and Sundel, 1975).

The first step in covert sensitization is instructing the client in how to relax, for example, by using a mus-cle relaxation technique. (Relaxation techniques are

described in Chapter 22.) The next step is to have the client imagine (visualize) becoming involved in his problematic behavior while at the same time imagin-ing extremely distasteful consequences.

Jehu (1972, pp. 57–58) describes how covert sensi-tization is used with people having a drinking problem:

The patient is relaxed and asked to imagine a se-quence of scenes leading up to the performance of the problem behavior; for example, looking at a glass containing his favorite alcoholic drink, holding the glass in his hand and bringing it to his lips. At this point he signals and the therapist tells the patient to imagine that he begins to feel sick and is vomiting in his drink and all over himself and his companions. He is then asked to visualize the whole sequence and final scene by himself, and to actually feel nauseous as he prepares to drink. Alternate scenes are pre-sented in which the patient imagines himself abstain-ing from drinking and then "rushing out into the fresh clean air," or "home to a clean invigorating shower." The presentation of such relief scenes consti-tutes an escape and avoidance training component in the procedure. After several trials with the therapist, the patient is instructed to repeat the whole procedure on his own and immediately to imagine the vomiting scene whenever he is tempted to drink alcohol.

Prochaska (1979, p. 30) describes using covert sen-sitization with a man who was having homosexual rela-tionships with children:

A thirty-year-old pedophiliac was asked to imagine approaching a ten-year-old boy to whom he was at-tracted. As he approaches the boy to ask him to come up to his apartment, he feels his stomach become nauseous. He feels his lunch coming up into his esophagus, and just as he goes to speak to the boy he vomits all over himself and the boy. People on the street are staring at him and he turns away from the boy and immediately begins to feel better. He begins walking back to his apartment feeling better and bet-ter with each step he takes. He gets back to his apart-ment, washes up, and feels great. After teaching this man the covert scene we had him practice it overtly, including making vomiting noises and gestures. To make the scene even more vivid we had him sit in his apartment window, and when he saw a boy on the street that he would like to approach sexually, we had him go to the bathroom and stick his fingers down his throat and vomit as he imagined propositioning the young boy. Within two months this chronic offender was no longer feeling the urge to approach young boys and he had followed through on our assertiveness techniques for forming adult homosexual relationships.

A word of caution — covert sensitization should be used only by skilled therapists with extensive training in this technique. There is a danger that improper application of this approach may create anxiety reactions in clients (and perhaps lead to other side effects) without accomplishing the goal of eliminating the intended problematic behavior such as overeating or sexual deviation.

AVERSIVE TECHNIQUES

An aversive stimulus is any stimulus that an organism (person) will avoid or terminate if given the opportunity. Examples of such stimuli include electric shock and unpleasant imagery. Covert sensitization is an example of an aversive technique in which the client imagines unpleasant consequences in conjunction with the maladaptive behavior. Covert sensitization results in diminished interest in the formerly desirable stimuli.

In a review of aversive methods Sandler (1986) found aversive therapy has been used in treating self-injurious behavior (such as head banging and self-biting), enuresis, sneezing, stuttering, alcoholism, cigarette smoking, overeating, gambling, sexual deviations (for example, fetishes and transvestism), and aggressive behavior.

The following are some illustrations of aversive techniques:

Vogler, Lunde, Johnson, and Martin (1970) served cocktails to alcoholic clients in a simulated lounge arrangement. Each time a client took a drink, he was given an electric shock and the shock was maintained until the client spat out the drink. The investigators did a follow-up and concluded the treatment led to abstinence.

Corte, Wolf, and Locke (1971) treated four retarded adolescents who exhibited self-injurious behavior (including eye poking, self-slapping, scratching the skin, and hair pulling). Each time one of these adolescents displayed a self-injurious response, he was given an electric shock. The authors report this approach sharply reduced such self-injurious behaviors.

Bancroft, Jones, and Pullan (1966) treated a male pedophile (i.e. child molester) whose sexual deviancy was so serious that he was being considered for brain surgery. The treatment procedure simulated the natural conditions in which the child molesting occurred. In the treatment procedures an instrument called a penile plethysmograph which measures penile volume was used to gauge penile erection. Pictures of young girls were presented to the client and when an erection occurred the client was given a painful shock to the arm. The shock was continued until there was a reduction in the response. Treatment lasted for eight weeks with the treatment procedures being used several times a day. In addition, on every fourth trial the shock apparatus was disconnected and the client was presented with photographs of adult women and the client was encouraged to engage in normal sexual fantasies. Although the results were not a complete success, there was a marked reduction in child molesting activities and an increase in adult-adult heterosexual behavior.

In regard to the use of aversive techniques, Chambless and Goldstein (1979, p. 252) caution:

When reporting on behavior therapy, the popular press emphasizes such techniques and often gives the impression that punishment is the behaviorist's major tool. On the contrary, punishment is used quite infrequently by behavior modifiers even though many clients initially ask for help via punishment in curbing unwanted behavior. To begin with, no behavior should be punished if no alternative behavior is available. For example, if a client complaints of sex-

ually deviant behavior, the first therapeutic intervention is usually directed toward reducing any inhibitions about normal sexual contact. This may be accomplished by a combination of desensitization procedures and training in appropriate expression. Generally the unwanted urges decrease when anxieties about "normal" sex, that is, sex with a consenting partner, diminish.

Such an approach is dictated not only by the moral imperative to employ the least painful method when there is a choice but also by the experimentally demonstrated futility of eliminating behavior through punishment when no alternative modes of satisfaction are available. Opening up alternatives is important in most cases in which punishment might otherwise be used.

Positive reinforcement (reward) approaches are generally more effective than those based on punishment. Punishment is often counterproductive as it can lead to the client's becoming hostile about the treatment procedures. Also, punishment may have only temporary effects. When the client realizes she is no longer under surveillance, she may return to exhibiting the maladaptive behavior.

COGNITIVE BEHAVIOR-MODIFICATION TECHNIQUES

A major trend in behavior therapy in the past three decades has been toward a recognition of the role of cognition (thinking processes) in human behavior. Following the observations of cognitive therapists such as Albert Ellis (1962) and A. T. Beck (1976), cognitive behavior therapists have accepted the notion that changing thoughts will often change feelings and behavior.

The traditional paradigm of behavior therapy has been S (stimulus) $\rightarrow R$ (response). Cognitive behavior therapists insert an additional step in this paradigm:

S (stimulus) $\rightarrow O$ (cognitions of organism $\rightarrow$
R (response)[9]

This section summarizes the following techniques that have been developed to change cognitions: thought stopping and covert assertion, diversion techniques, and reframing.

Thought Stopping and Covert Assertion

Thought Stopping is used for clients whose major problems involve obsessive thinking and ruminations about events which are very unlikely to occur (such as worrying that a plane they will be taking in two weeks will crash, or worrying that they are becoming mentally ill).

In thought stopping the client is first asked to concentrate on and express out loud her obsessive, anxiety-inducing thoughts. As the client begins to express those thoughts the therapist suddenly and emphatically shouts "Stop." This procedure is repeated several times until the client reports that her thoughts are being successfully interrupted. Then the responsibility for the intervention is shifted to the client, so that the client now tells herself "Stop" out loud when she begins to think about the troubling thoughts. Once the overt shouting is effective in stopping the troubling thoughts, the client begins to practice saying "Stop" silently to herself whenever the troubling thoughts begin.

Rimm and Masters (1974) supplemented the thought-stopping techniques with a *covert assertion* procedure. In addition to having the client learn to interrupt the obsessive thoughts with saying "Stop," the client is encouraged to produce a positive, assertive statement that is incompatible with the content of the obsession. For example, a client who worries about becoming mentally ill (when there is no basis for such

---

[9]It is very interesting to note that the paradigm of cognitive behavior therapists [S (stimulus) $\rightarrow O$ (cognitions of organism) $\rightarrow R$ (response)] is very similar to the following paradigm of rational therapists [Events $\rightarrow$ Self-talk $\rightarrow$ Emotions and Actions].

thinking) may be encouraged to add the covert assertion "Screw it! I'm perfectly normal" whenever she interrupts the trouble thinking with "Stop."

Mahoney (1973) successfully used thought stopping and covert assertion as part of a comprehensive
program for overweight clients. Mahoney first instructed the clients to become aware of such self-statements as, "I just don't have the will power" and "I sure
can taste eating a strawberry sundae." The clients were
then trained to use thought stopping and covert assertion to combat these thoughts.

Diversion Techniques

Diversion techniques are used to treat clients who have
strong unwanted emotions such as loneliness, bitterness, depression, frustration, and anger. As indicated in
Chapter 18, unwanted emotions stem primarily from
negative and irrational thinking. When clients with unwanted emotions become involved in physical activity,
work, social interactions, or play, they will usually
switch their negative cognitions to different cognitions
related to their new diversion activities. Once they
focus their thinking on the diversion activities that they
are finding meaningful and enjoyable, they will experience more pleasing emotions.

Diversion techniques are used in both rational
therapy (see Chapter 18) and cognitive behavior therapy. Rational therapy and cognitive behavior therapy
are closely related. In fact, rational therapy is sometimes classified as a cognitive behavioral approach.

Reframing

Reframing involves assisting a client to change those
cognitions that are causing unwanted emotions or dysfunctional behaviors. As the following material describes, there are several categories of cognitions that
may be reframed.

One focus of reframing is on *positive thinking*.
When unpleasant events occur (such as receiving a
lower grade on an exam than we anticipated), we always have the choice of thinking positively or negatively. If we take a positive view and focus on problem

solving, we are apt to identify and initiate actions to
improve the circumstances. On the other hand, if we
think negatively, we are likely to develop unwanted
emotions (such as depression and frustration) and fail
to focus on how to solve the problem. With negative
thinking, we generally do not do anything constructive
and may even engage in destructive behavior.

When a client is thinking negatively, a therapist can
use reframing to assist the client in realizing he is
thinking negatively. At times it is helpful to remind the
client that both negative and positive thinking often become self-fulfilling prophecies (see Chapter 18). Then,
by asking the client to identify some positive aspects of
the situation, the therapist seeks to assist the client in
thinking more positively. (If the client is unable to
identify any positives, the therapist may suggest some.)
The client may then be encouraged to tell himself
"Stop" whenever he begins to think negatively and instead to focus on telling himself positive aspects of the
situation. Some people take a negative view of most
events that happen to them; for such people, reframing
through using positive cognitions is more difficult and
time-consuming. However, if they are successful in
learning to think positively, they often make substantial gains.

A second closely related way in which reframing is
used is *deawfulizing*. When distressing events occur,
most of us tend to awfulize—we exaggerate the negatives. Think about your reactions when someone with
whom you were romantically involved broke up with
you, or when you received a parking or speeding cita-
tion. Did you awfulize and as a result feel angry, hurt,
or depressed? When we awfulize we focus only on the
negatives and do not identify constructive actions to
improve the situation. When a client is awfulizing, a
therapist can usually help the person identify such
thought processes by simply inquiring, "I wonder if
you're awfulizing?" The therapist can then assist the
client, as described in the above material on reframing
with positive thinking, to give himself cognitions that
are more positive and oriented toward problem
solving.

A third reframing focus involves *decatastrophizing*
(Beck and Weishaar, 1989). This technique is used
when clients are catastrophizing over anticipated
feared events. Decatastrophizing involves continually

asking clients "what if" an anticipated, undesired consequence occurs. The following is a dialogue with a twenty-one-year-old college student who fears expressing his thoughts and feelings in class:

THERAPIST: "What do you think will happen if you begin expressing your views in your classes?"

CLIENT: "My voice may crack and the others may laugh at me."

THERAPIST: "It is unlikely that your voice will crack. But even if it does, and the students happen to laugh a little, is that really worse than your anger and frustration over not sharing your thoughts?"

CLIENT: "I don't know."

THERAPIST: "Which is worse when you're asked a question in class? Shrugging your shoulders and appearing tongue-tied, or responding as well as you can even though your voice may crack?"

CLIENT: "I hear what you're saying."

THERAPIST: "What other negative consequences might occur if you begin expressing yourself in class?"

CLIENT: (pause) "None that I can think of."

THERAPIST: "What positives may come from your speaking up in class?"

CLIENT: "I'd probably get more out of the class and feel better about myself. Enough of this. I get the message loud and clear. I will commit myself to speaking up at least once a week in each of my classes."

People who catastrophize usually exaggerate the anticipated feared consequences. Decatastrophizing is designed to demonstrate to clients that even if feared consequences occur (which they seldom do), those consequences are not as severe as feared.

A fourth focus of reframing is to assist clients in *separating positive intents from negative behaviors* so that the positive intents then become linked to new positive behaviors. A parent who is physically abusive to a child has the positive intent of raising his child well, but when he is under stress and the child is misbehaving, that parent may not be aware that he has a number of other options that are much more constructive than physically beating his child. A therapist can

assist such a parent by helping him to reframe his thinking so that when the child misbehaves in the future he focuses his thinking processes on alternative responses, such as asking his wife to handle the child's misbehavior when he is under stress or by punishing the child with a timeout. (This type of reframing is described further in Chapter 21.)

Redefining is a fifth focus of reframing that is used for clients who believe a problem is beyond their personal control (Beck and Weishaar, 1989). A bored person who believes "Life is boring" may be encouraged to think, "The only reasons I'm bored is because I don't have special interests and because I'm not initiating activities. It's not life that is boring; it's my thinking processes that are leading me to feel bored. What I'm going to do is get involved in activities I enjoy and initiate interactions with people I like." Redefining is accomplished as the therapist first demonstrates that emotions, such as being bored, stem primarily from thoughts (see Chapter 18). The therapist next demonstrates that if the client thinks more positively and realistically, he will feel better. Together, the client and the therapist then identify the client's negative thinking patterns that are causing him to believe the problem is beyond his personal control. Finally they identify cognitions that the client makes a commitment to use to counter the cognitions that are (in actuality) causing his unwanted emotions and ineffective behaviors.

Decentering is a sixth focus of reframing that is used with anxious clients who erroneously believe they are the focus of everyone's attention (Beck and Weishaar, 1989). Reframing occurs by having such clients observe the behaviors of others rather than focusing on their own anxiety; thereby they come to realize they are not the center of attention. Beck and Weishaar (1989, p. 310) give an example:

One student who was reluctant to speak in class believed his classmates watched him constantly and noticed his anxiety. By observing them instead of focusing on his own discomfort, he saw some students taking notes, some looking at the professor, and some daydreaming. He concluded his classmates had other concerns.

Additional cognitive change methods are being developed and hold considerable promise for behavior therapists to become increasingly involved in changing unwanted emotions and maladaptive behaviors of clients through changing their troubling thoughts (Hepworth and Larsen, 1986).

It is somewhat difficult to specify what is and what is not a cognitive-behavioral technique. In addition to the techniques described here, Cormier and Cormier (1991) identify the following as cognitive-behavioral techniques: role-playing, problem-solving efforts, meditation, muscle relaxation, imagery relaxation, deep breathing relaxation, and paradoxical suggestions (see Chapter 8 for a description). In Chapter 23 it is asserted that changing irrational and negative cognitions may be the key psychotherapeutic change agent. Since practically all effective psychotherapeutic techniques change cognitions, then in a broad sense practically all psychotherapeutic techniques can be considered cognitive-behavioral techniques.

EVALUATION

It is difficult to make an overall evaluation of behavior therapy. Behavior therapy is composed of a wide range of therapy techniques, some of which are more effective than others. Also, behavior therapy is based on a variety of different learning theories, and there has never been agreement among behavior therapists as to which learning theory should be the main focus of behavior therapy. Particularly controversial among behavior therapists is the learning approach being advocated by cognitive behavior therapists that states that emotions and actions are largely determined by our thoughts. Cognitive techniques are incompatible with the traditional principles of behaviorism, which has ignored cognitive processes because these thought processes cannot be measured and tested. Traditional behaviorism has sought to explain all behavior in terms of stimuli-response connections.

In the past thirty years behavior therapy has had a dramatic growth in the development of new treatment techniques and in the adoption of these techniques by members of the helping professions. Two books that inspired this development were *Science and Human*

Behavior (Skinner, 1953) and *Psychotherapy by Reciprocal Inhibition* (Wolpe, 1958). Numerous books have since been published on behavior therapy. Behavior therapists have developed, and are continuing to develop, more treatment techniques than are emerging in any other psychotherapeutic area. One area that has not yet been mentioned but which has been heavily influenced by using behavior therapy techniques is sex therapy. (The next chapter describes sexual counseling and sex therapy in considerable detail.)

Behavior therapy is to be highly commended for its emphasis on testing the effectiveness of the treatment techniques that are developed. Such an emphasis is consistent with the demand by the public for human services to be accountable. With this emphasis on rigorous testing of therapy techniques, behavior therapy has discarded a number of techniques that have been found to be ineffective. Approaches that have shown effectiveness and are increasingly being used include assertiveness training for people who are shy or aggressive, contingency contracting with clients having a broad range of problems, token economies to change maladaptive behaviors of residents in institutional settings, and systematic desensitization with clients having irrational fears.

The future for behavior therapy is indeed bright. It is anticipated that helping professionals (psychologists, psychiatrists, social workers, guidance counselors, psychiatric nurses) will increasingly be trained in using behavior techniques.

There are also some criticisms that can be made of behavior therapy:

1. The research that has been conducted on many of the techniques has been on applying the techniques to the kind of problems that are readily tested in laboratory situations. Often successful results have been found. However, the kinds of problems that have been treated in laboratory situations are not the kinds of problems that clients commonly face. Prochaska (1979, p. 354) has elegantly phrased this problem:

So what if desensitization can reduce a college coed's fear of white rats? Does that have anything to do with the devastating problems that therapists are confronted with daily in their clinical practices? Whoever sees a snake phobic in a clinic? Most behaviorists would do themselves justice when planning a study if they asked the key clinical question for any outcome research—the so-what question. So what if having college students imagine vomiting in their lunches leads to a loss of a pound a week? So what if some of the loss lasts for four months? There is plenty of evidence that eighty-five percent of the people who lose weight through any means regain it within two years. How come only a tiny fraction of their studies use a two-year follow-up? Are the authors more concerned with completing a thesis quickly or rushing to publish than with establishing a really useful therapy?

2. Many of the problems that clients face in the real world involve arriving at some decision. Should a pregnant seventeen-year-old teenager have an abortion or have the baby? Should a husband and wife who have been married for twenty-one years and have fallen out of love with each other continue living together or seek a new life on their own? How should a recently divorced mother with three children try to support her family? How do you get a person with a drinking problem to admit he has a problem and make a decision to seek help? Should sons and daughters of an aged parent seek to place him in a nursing home? How do you try to help a suicidal person make a decison not to take her life? How do you get a delinquent to make a decision to stop delinquent acts? How do you help a teenager who has run away from home make future plans about where to live? Behavior therapy does not have techniques for helping to arrive at such decisions. The focus of behavior therapy is on changing maladaptive behavior, not at arriving at decisions.

3. The punishment principles of behaviorism have occasionally been used in human services to justify cruel and inhuman treatment. Inmates in some prisons have been placed in isolation for several weeks at a time in environments lacking sensory stimulation. Adolescents in residential treatment centers and patients in mental hospitals have been place in arm and leg restraints for several days at a time. Flogging has been used extensively in some situations. Aggressive residents at institutions for the developmentally disabled have been placed in straitjackets during the waking hours for several months at a time. All of these practices have been justified by the program directors as

being part of a behavior modification program. *It should be noted that well-trained behaviorists are highly critical of such inhumane uses of punishment.*

SUMMARY

The main assumption of behavior therapy is that maladaptive behaviors are acquired primarily through learning and can be modified through additional learning. Behavior therapy is based on learning theory. A number of somewhat different learning theories have been developed, and there has never been a consensus among behaviorists as to which learning theory should be the basis of behavior therapy.

The main trend in behavior therapy in the past two decades has been toward a recognition of the role of cognition in human behavior. Some behavior therapists are now identifying themselves as cognitive behavior therapists and have accepted the notion that changing thoughts will often change feelings and behavior. These theorists are now developing new techniques such as thought stopping, covert assertion, and reframing.

There are some common focuses among behaviorists. One is that maladaptive behavior is the problem and attention needs to be directed at changing the behavior rather than focusing on some unknown underlying causes. Behavior therapists assert that treating the maladaptive behavior will not result in symptom substitution. Another focus is the testing of therapy techniques by rigorous experimental procedures. Baseline levels of maladaptive behaviors are established prior to therapy in order to determine whether the therapy approach is producing the desired change in the rate or intensity of responding.

Behavior therapy is based on the assumption that all behavior occurs in response to stimulation, internal or external. The first task in the therapy process is for the therapist to do a behavioral analysis, which involves identifying the probable stimulus-response connections of the maladaptive behavior that are occurring for the client. Prior to and during the time the therapist is doing the behavioral analysis, the therapist is also attempting to establish a working relationship. Once the behavioral analysis is completed, the findings are discussed with the client and the client and the therapist agree on the goals for the treatment. The treatment procedures and techniques are then described to the client.

This chapter summarizes some of the most commonly used behavior therapy techniques: assertiveness training, token economies, contingency contracting, systematic desensitization, in vivo desensitization, implosive therapy, covert sensitization, aversive techniques, and cognitive behavior-modification techniques. Most of these techniques (particularly systematic desensitization, in vivo desensitization, implosive therapy, covert sensitization, and aversive techniques) should be used only by skilled therapists with extensive training as there is a danger that improper application may intensify the problematic behavior or create undesired side effects.

EXERCISES

1. *Contingency Contracting*

GOAL: This exercise is designed to demonstrate the principles of contingency contracting by having students apply the principles to their own behavior.

Step 1: Describe the goal of this exercise and also explain the principles of contingency contracting.

Step 2: Ask each student to prepare a contract about an area of his behavior he would like to change. The behavior may involve an area such as the following: eating less, drinking less, exercising more, ending procrastination, studying more, or increasing contact with parents and other relatives. In preparing the contract ask the students to write on a sheet of paper answers to the following questions. (Indicate that the students will not be required to reveal what they wrote.)

a.   What behavior do you want to change? (Be as specific as possible.)
b.   What is your behavior goal?
c.   What specifically will you do to achieve this goal?
d.   What are your deadlines for doing these tasks?
e.   How will you reward yourself for doing the tasks necessary to reach this goal?
f.   What adverse consequences will you apply to yourself if you fail to do the tasks?

Step 3: Ask for volunteers to share what they wrote. Have the class discuss the merits and shortcomings of writing such a contingency conrtact.

Step 4: As an added component of the exercise, students may discuss whether they want to attempt to fulfill the conditions they have written into their contracts. If the class decides to do this, a future date (such as four weeks later) may be set for the students to describe their successes and failures in fulfilling the conditions of their contract.

2. *Learning to Be Assertive*

GOAL: This exercise is designed to help students learn how to be assertive in problematic interactions where in the past they were either nonassertive or aggressive.

Step 1: Describe the purpose of this exercise. Explain the differences between nonassertive, aggressive, and assertive behavior. Indicate that everyone is nonassertive or aggressive in some situations in which it would be more constructive to be assertive. Ask each student silently to identify a situation in the past in which he wished he had been assertive, rather than being aggressive or nonassertive. Give some examples such as the following: The situation may involve being told to do something you did not want to do. Or, perhaps someone was smoking a cigarette near you, which bothered you. Or, perhaps someone made a put-down comment about you. Or, perhaps you're unable to express what you feel about certain situations to your parents, or to someone you're dating. Before proceeding further, ask whether the students have identified such a situation in which they wished they had been assertive. Do not proceed to the next step until everyone has identified a situation.

Step 2: State the following: "We will now do a visualization exercise that is designed to help you learn to be more assertive in the situation you identified. There will be no tricks in this exercise. I ask that you close your eyes and keep them closed during this exercise. Get as comfortable as possible in your chair, and slowly take a couple of deep breaths to become relaxed.

"Focus on a specific incident in your past when you wanted to be assertive, but instead were either nonassertive or aggressive. Visualize all the details of what happened. (Pause a few seconds after asking each of the following questions.) What was said to you? What did you fail to say that you wanted to say? What did you say that you didn't want to say? How did you feel about what was said? How do you now feel about this incident? Your nonverbal communication is as important in being assertive as is verbal communication. Think about your nonverbal communiction. What did you communicate with your facial expressions? What did you communicate with your body posture? Did you look down or away from the other person? Did you glare at the other person? What did your gestures communicate? What was your voice tone and volume like? Did your voice crack? Did you yell or speak softly? Did you speak rapidly or with hesitation? During this incident which of your verbal and nonverbal communications were nonassertive? Which were aggressive? Which were assertive?

"Now, let's turn to focus on how to handle this situation more assertively when it arises again. Continue to keep your eyes closed. What might you say that would assertively handle this situation? (Pause.) What changes do you need to make in your nonverbal communication to present yourself more assertively? (Pause.) Is there someone you know who would be good at handling this situation assertively? (Pause.) If there is someone, what would this person say and do? (Pause.) Does this assertive model give you some ideas on how you might assertively handle this situation? (Pause.)

"Continue to visualize various approaches that might work for you. Also, visualize yourself using each of these approaches. For each approach, imagine the full set of interactions that would occur if you were to use the approach. (Pause.)

"Now, seek to select an assertive approach that you believe would best work for you when the nonassertive or aggressive situation arises again in the future. Are you now sufficiently prepared and confident to use this approach in a real-life situation? If not, you may want to visualize further what you might say or do to increase your confidence. Or, you may want to select another approach that you would be more comfortable in using. Or, you may want to role-play your approach with a friend so that you become more comfortable in using the approach. (Pause.)

"The real test will come when you try out your assertive approach in a real-life situation. The next time your problematic situation arises, seek to use your assertive approach. After trying it out, analyze how it turned out. Pat yourself on the back for what you did well. Identify aspects of your nonverbal and verbal communication that you need to improve in order to express yourself more assertively. Visualize ways in which you might more assertively express yourself in the areas you need to work on.

"Above all, congratulate yourself on your efforts to become more assertive. You've earned feeling good about yourself. Learning to express yourself in situations that you're comfortable in is one of the greatest thrills you'll ever experience. OK, gradually open your eyes, and take a little while to relax."

Step 3: Ask whether there are any questions or comments about the exercise. Then ask whether there are any situations they would like to see others in the class role-play. If students suggest some situations, have other students role-play these. If no situations are suggested, ask for volunteers to role-play situations you suggest, such as these:

a. Asking someone to put out a cigarette that is bothering you.
b. Refusing to accept an alcoholic drink that a friend wants to buy for you when you prefer not to drink any more alcoholic beverages that day.
c. Saying no when someone asks to borrow something you don't want to lend, such as a sweater.

3. Expressing Anger Assertively

GOAL: The purpose of this exercise is to help students learn assertive and constructive ways to express their anger.

Step 1: Describe the goal of this exercise. Indicate that many people have not learned to express their anger assertively for a variety of reasons. Some of us have been brought up to believe it is wrong to get angry, so we seek to deny our anger. Some of us, through modeling, have learned to express our anger aggressively, thereby lashing out and hurting others. Indicate that we have a right to all our emotions. It is normal to become angry at times. Others do not have a right to try to convince us that we should not be angry when we are angry.

When anger is not expressed assertively, it is often expressed destructively. We may aggressively hurt others. Or, we may try to deny we are angry, and instead turn the anger inward and become depressed. Or, we may recognize the anger, but fail to express it, which can result in anxiety. Or, anger may lead to guilt if we punish ourselves for getting angry when we erroneously believe we should not get angry. Or, we may seek to relieve our angry feelings through excessive drinking or eating.

Step 2: Explain that there are assertive and constructive ways to express anger. These ways include the following:

a. Expressing our angry feelings assertively so that no one is hurt in the process. When expressing anger assertively it is advisable to use nonblaming "I-messages" rather than "You-messages." (See Chapter 22 for a description of I-messages.)
b. Expressing our angry feelings at the time we become angry so that we do not "stew" about it. If we delay expressing anger, the hostility may build so that we explode and lash out at others.

c. Admitting to ourselves when we are angry, so that we do not try to hide our anger from ourselves. Through acknowledging our anger we are better able to focus on finding constructive ways to express our anger.

d. Blowing off steam nondestructively through such physical activities as jogging, hitting a pillow or punching bag, talking a walk, or lifting weights whenever it is counterproductive to express our anger or when we feel we are apt to explode.

e. Seeking to counter negative and irrational self-talk by writing out a rational self-analysis (see Chapter 18).

Step 3: Ask each student to complete the following three statements on a sheet of paper:

a. Three or four things that make me angry are:

b. I usually express my anger by:

c. Things that I can do to better handle and express my anger are:

Step 4: Have the students form subgroups of three to share what they wrote, and to receive additional suggestions on how to express their anger more effectively. (Indicate that students have a right to privacy and, therefore, they do not have to self-disclose what they want to keep private.)

Step 5: Form a circle and ask the students whether they have any questions or comments about the exercise or about what was discussed in the subgroups.

4. Reframing

GOAL: This exercise is designed to demonstrate to students how to reframe cognitions involving "awfulizing."

Step 1: Describe the concepts of "reframing" and "awfulizing." The instructor should illustrate the process of awfulizing by giving a few examples of occasions when he has awfulized in the past.

Step 2: Instruct each student to record his or her responses to the following questions and instructions on a sheet of paper. Indicate that students will not be required to reveal their responses.

a. Briefly describe a distressing event that occurred to you over which you awfulized.

b. Specify the "awfulizing" cognitions that you gave yourself about this distressing event.

c. For each awfulizing cognition, specify a more positive and realistic cognition that you could give yourself about this event. (Ideally, many of these countering cognitions should also facilitate problem solving).

d. Indicate the approximate length of time that you awfulized over this event.

e. Are you still awfulizing about this event?

f. Do you believe countering the awfulizing cognitions with more positive and realistic cognitions would have shortened the time you spent awfulizing?

Step 3: Ask for volunteers to share their responses to these questions. The exercise may be ended by asking the students to indicate their thoughts on the merits and shortcomings of using reframing in therapy.

20

SEX COUNSELING
AND THERAPY

What is sexuality? To many people, this word connotes a man and a woman, preferably married to each other, having intercourse. To me, sexuality includes many things:

How we feel about ourselves as boys or girls, men or women

Masturbation

Having a baby

Affection

Deciding whether to terminate a pregnancy with abortion

Persons in parental roles using children for their own sexual arousal

Romantic love

A person being biologically of one gender and feeling psychologically of the other gender

"Dirty old men"

Using a condom to reduce the likelihood of contracting AIDS

Babies discovering that touching their genitals gives them pleasure

Rape

Pornography

The wedding night

Erectile dysfunction

Intimacy

A seventeen-year-old male realizing he is sexually attracted to other males and not to females

Jealousy

Getting sexually aroused by erotic thoughts

Predictable physiological responses in our bodies

That warm, goosey feeling we get when we're touched by someone who arouses us

An eighty-five-year-old man making love with an eighty-one-year-old woman

This chapter was especially written for this text by Lloyd G. Sinclair, A.C.S.W. Mr. Sinclair is a Certified Sex Educator, Sex Therapist, and Sex Therapy Supervisor at Midwest Center for Sex Therapy in Madison, Wisconsin.

And many, many more thoughts, feelings, and experiences.

Very few social workers become sex therapists, but most social workers with counseling responsibilities are frequently presented with clients' sexual concerns. Remember a simple adage, "The answers you get depend on the questions you ask." If you're perceived as "askable"[1] by your clients — being comfortable talking about sex, having some knowledge, being sensitive and receptive to clients' sexuality — you will be asked questions about sex. Clients are both perceptive and self-protective — if you're uncomfortable, don't worry. Nobody will bring it up.

This author has been told by many clients who were suffering from sexual problems that in dozens of sessions of previous psychotherapy, the therapist *never asked* them any questions about sex. The client was dying to talk about it, but "it never came up."

The goals of this chapter are (1) to encourage you to see the legitimacy of professional intervention in the sexual area of people's lives, (2) to teach you some basic sex counseling skills, (3) to help you examine and broaden your own comfort and knowledge in this sensitive area, and (4) to teach you some evaluation skills helpful in determining when it might be appropriate to intervene and when referral to a specialist is indicated.

Why is it so important and necessary for social workers to be able to intervene in the area of sexuality? The most compelling reasons are (1) because sexuality is an extremely important aspect of the human personality, indeed a driving biological force; and (2) because many other professionals who *should* be helpful to people with sexual concerns, such as physicians and psychotherapists, often are not. The legitimacy of scientific study of and professional intervention in persons' sexual lives has received widespread recognition only in the very recent past. Consequently, only professionals who have received training in the last ten or fifteen years (either toward a degree or as continuing education) are likely to have acquired skills to assess, treat, or refer persons with sexual problems. The others are "experts" based solely on their personal experiences which, even if the professionals are pretty "experienced," is woefully inadequate. So don't blame the other professionals for not being helpful to persons with sexual concerns — chances are they were never taught these skills. But don't *assume* they are trained either, to use as an excuse for you to ignore the area.

Let's turn our attention now to some important concerns specific to counseling people about sex-related matters.

KNOWLEDGE

The first prerequisite to effective counseling in the area of sexuality, as well in any area, is knowledge. The information necessary to help persons with sexual problems goes well beyond the scope of this chapter. In addition to other resources listed in the footnotes of this chapter, there are two excellent comprehensive surveys of human sexuality: William H. Masters, Virginia E. Johnson, and Robert C. Kolodny, *Masters and Johnson on Sex and Human Loving* (Boston: Little, Brown and Company, 1986), and Ira R. Reiss, *Journey into Sexuality* (Englewood Cliffs, N.J.: Prentice-Hall, 1986).

ASSUMPTIONS

Perhaps more than in any other area, counselors should be extremely careful to avoid making assumptions when clients raise issues about sex. Because people express their sexuality in such a wide variety of ways, because people tend not to talk about their sexual experiences, and because so many people lack good sex education, it is easy to assume that everyone expresses their sexuality like you express yours.

There are basically two dangers in making assumptions. The first is that you can easily draw the wrong conclusions if you don't persevere to determine that

---

[1]The concept of "askable" was developed by Sol Gordon, Ph.D., an Emeritus Professor at Syracuse University, Syracuse, N.Y. Dr. Gordon has written numerous books and articles on various aspects of adolescence and sexuality.

your understanding is correct. For example, if your client talks about masturbation, don't assume every man pleasures himself sexually by rubbing his penis with his hand, and every woman by rubbing her clitoris. Some people masturbate by rubbing against objects, with vibrators, or under streams of water. Some people tie themselves up when they masturbate. Others need to cross-dress (dressing in clothes of the other gender), or exhibit their genitals to strangers to feel aroused. If you assume everyone does it the same way, you may draw too-hasty conclusions based on not enough information.

The second reason to carefully avoid making assumptions is that you risk not being perceived by your client as "safe" to ask questions of. For example, if a man comes to you and says, "Lately I've had trouble getting an erection with my partner," and you ask, "How does *she* feel about it?" you have effectively slammed the door on that client if he happens to be gay. Oh, he'll probably smooth it over nicely and you'll never know you made the mistake, because gay people frequently deal with heterosexual assumptions. But you will not be perceived as a person who is sensitive to the range of human sexual expression. And you will, consequently, counsel only those people who fit *your* stereotypes.

WORDS

Another important consideration is the vocabulary used by the sex counselor. Most counselors develop a vocabulary that they are most comfortable with. It is important to know the scientific language (coitus, fellatio) to understand much of the technical information about sexual response. But the English language contains many more "street" words for sexual expression than any other variety. Many clients are familiar only with those words. You will want to know the meaning of these terms (for example, *makin' it, blow job*) so you will understand them when clients use them and so you won't express shock when you hear them.

You will probably want to find words that describe in a straightforward manner (for example, does sleeping together mean having intercourse, or just sleeping?), in as value free a way as possible, what you are trying to say (for example, intercourse, oral-genital sex).

Many counselors attempt to hide their own discomfort with talking about sex by using medical language. The greatest danger in using words that are unnecessarily scientific is that you are likely not to be understood. Clients are often embarrassed to admit they don't know the meaning of certain words, so they may pretend they do. And if you're not communicating, you're not helping.

Some counselors attempt to hide their discomfort by going to the other extreme—by using street terms to appear "with it." The problem here is that street terms are usually value laden. To some people, the word *fuck* simply means intercourse. But to others, *fuck* is a demeaning, sexist, aggressive, and filthy word.

Another extremely important concept to remember is that persons who are developmentally disabled, in all likelihood, did not develop the same sophisticated use of language about sexuality that we may take for granted. So you may need to be especially graphic in order to be understood. A sensitive counselor may try her vocabulary first, but with the slightest hint of the client's lack of comprehension, she may need to stop talking about "masturbation" and instead talk about "rubbing your penis 'til the white gook comes out," or "rubbing your privates 'til you feel extra good."

One method useful in becoming more comfortable with words that clients might use is to practice saying "street" words out loud, either by yourself or with a friend. If you blush when you say words you were taught to feel uncomfortable about, your client is likely to feel embarrassed too. With practice at desensitizing yourself, you can learn to use the words comfortably.

LEVELS OF INTERVENTION

When a client expresses a sexual concern to a social worker, it is important for the professional to make some preliminary evaluation regarding what the client needs to resolve his problem. Does he need a sentence or two of reassurance, or twelve weeks of intensive sex therapy?

Jack S. Annon has developed an extremely useful conceptual scheme to help professionals make this determination.[2] He believes that very few persons with sexual problems need intensive sex therapy. Rather, they need intervention at the levels he identifies as Permission, Limited Information, and Specific Suggestions.

Permission describes the process of professional reassurance, letting clients know they are normal, OK. The client reports, "My wife and I hear a lot about oral sex. We just aren't interested in doing that. Do you think there's something wrong with us?" The counselor can give permission: "Sex is best when you're doing things you *both* want to do, not because of somebody else's expectations. I would encourage you to do what you both like, and if at some point you want to try oral sex, fine. But if you don't, that's fine too. Enjoy."

While the largest number of people would benefit from intervention at the level of permission, a significant but smaller number need *limited information* to alleviate their sexual concern. A male client reports, "I'm happily married, we have a good sex life, but I still find I masturbate a couple of times a week. Do you think there's something wrong with me?" The counselor might respond with limited information:

You might be interested in knowing a couple of things. First, it's a myth that masturbating indicates there's something wrong with you sexually. In fact, studies show that people who feel good about themselves sexually engage in a larger number of sexual activities of all kinds, including partner sex and masturbation, than people who have a lower sexual self-image. And studies also show that most people masturbate with some frequency throughout their lives. It's simply not true that being in a sexual relationship means all your sexual needs and desires will automatically be met. If you enjoy masturbation, and it's

not used as a weapon in your relationship to try to coerce your partner into being sexual with you, then it can do you no harm. Enjoy![3]

The third level of psychotherapeutic intervention is *specific suggestions*. Annon suggests that in order to make responsible and potentially helpful suggestions, the counselor should take a sexual problem history. This is not a full social-sexual history, but rather data related solely to the specific problem.

First, the counselor must obtain a *description of the current problem*:

"Sally, what brings you to the office today?"
"I'm concerned because when Bill and I have intercourse, it hurts me."
"Can you describe the pain more specifically for me? Is it sharp or dull, shallow or deep?"
"It's more like a chafing pain — not really sharp, but it's sure uncomfortable. And sometimes it's deep, too, almost like he's banging into something deep inside me."

The counselor then asks about the *onset and course of the problem*:

"Has intercourse always been painful to you?"
"No, not always. At first it was a little, but I think that was just because we were new at it. But then for a few years, I wasn't having any pain. But in the past several months, it's hurt."
"Has it been painful every time you've had intercourse in the past few months?"
"No, and that confuses me. Sometimes, particularly when I initiate sex, it doesn't hurt."

Next, the counselor inquires about the *client's concept of the cause and maintenance of the problem*:

"Do you have any ideas about why you're having this problem?"
"Well, not really. I thought for awhile that maybe I was just overtired, or maybe I was making the pain up because sometimes Bill is much more interested in

---

[2]Jack S. Annon, *Behavioral Treatment of Sexual Problems: Brief Therapy* (New York: Harper & Row, 1976) and *Behavioral Treatment of Sexual Problems: Volume 2, Intensive Therapy* (Honolulu, Hawaii: Enabling Systems, Inc., 1975).

---

[3]The counselor might also want to suggest some reading about male sexuality to this client. An excellent book is Bernie Zilbergeld, *Male Sexuality* (Boston: Little, Brown, 1978).

Patty — Counseling for Sexual Abuse

Incest is increasingly being recognized as a major problem in our society. Usually when incest becomes known, the family breaks up. The following case example was selected as it illustrates a recent trend to keep such families intact.

Fourteen-year-old Patty was referred by her teacher to the school social worker because her grades and interest had fallen far below her abilities and previous academic record. The social worker, Ms. White, discussed these concerns one morning with Patty. Patty alluded vaguely to "pressure at home" and, after a good deal of gentle probing, she finally revealed to Ms. White that her father had been having intercourse with her since she was eleven.

Patty was understandably very upset, and yet relieved. She had considered telling someone but had not been able to bring herself to talk about it before. Her father had told her many times not to tell anyone, yet she felt the situation had become intolerable.

Ms. White reassured Patty that she would help her and her family. Since they lived in a state that had a mandatory reporting law for suspected cases of child abuse and neglect, Ms. White telephoned the County Social Service Agency, which in turn notified the police. Social Services sent a social worker, Ms. Fox, their agency specialist in this area, to talk with Patty. Ms. Fox and Ms. White spoke with Patty together.

Both social workers were fully aware that, until a short time ago, incest was considered to be extremely rare in American society. Most people believed that it occurred only in large, rural, economically deprived families. Recent statistics, however, indicate this stereotype of child sexual abuse to be very inaccurate. Sexual abuse is not a rare phenomenon, perhaps because more people are seeking help since more help is available, and perhaps because there has been more publicity about sexual abuse recently, and certainly because there are many more "blended" families (due to the increase in the incidence of divorce, children are more frequently raised by a stepparent who has no biological tie) so that biological aspect of the incest taboo is removed. Indeed, current studies suggest that between one fourth and one half of adult women in the United States were sexually abused as children by someone in an authority position. Whether it is technically incest (a biological tie) or not often makes little difference. The critical issue is that the parent or parent surrogate is using his authority to engage in sexual acts *for the pleasure of the adult*. By definition, no child can give consent for sexual contact with an adult because of the differences in power between them.

Ms. Fox and Ms. White were also aware that sexual abuse in families almost invariably results in severe trauma for the victims, including the inability to trust others or him- or herself. The violation of the important sexual boundary that should exist between generations destroys normal family roles. When father and daughter cease to be father and daughter to become lovers, how can they comfortably switch back and forth? What about mother? What about other children, who feel the favoritism from Dad to daughter, or who may be being sexually abused by him as well?

The typical scenario with a family when sexual abuse becomes known is that the family breaks up. The daughter (and it could have been the son as well) is placed in a foster home "for protection." Dad, whose reputation in the community plummets, generally is jailed briefly and released (pending trial), and is prohibited from seeing his family; this process often takes months. Mother tries to hold the rest of the family together under tremendous economic, social, and emotional strain. And daughter ends up feeling responsible and therefore terribly guilty for destroying the family — "if only I had kept my mouth shut, stayed 'til I was eighteen, and left." With this typical sequence of events, it is easier to comprehend why child sexual abuse can remain "the family secret," often even known or at least suspected by mother, for years.

Patty told Ms. Fox and Ms. White that she was extremely scared, mostly of what her father might do now. She said she had tried to tell her mother, but she just couldn't come right out and say it, so the secret was never broken. Ms. Fox explained that they would do whatever they could to protect her, to help her father, and to keep the family together — as long as the sexual abuse stopped. Ms. Fox arranged to meet with Patty's father shortly after he had been arrested. This mixture of the law — represented by police, the courts, district attorneys, with an emphasis on guilt or innocence — and the helping professions (represented by social workers and other psychotherapists), with an emphasis on mental health — makes for a powerful combination of legal enforcement of mental health improvement. Outcome studies indicate that without the clout of the law, reversal of sexually assaultive behavior is less likely to occur. And most enlightened police officers, judges, and district attorneys are well aware that conviction leading solely to incarceration in prison is often not the most helpful course for any of the parties involved. While it may take the father away from the children so further sexual abuse won't occur, it also takes him and all his *positive* contributions from the family as well. Sexual assault is a criminal violation, so a legal response is appropriate. However, the behavior will generally not change from punishment alone; specific sex offender treatment is required as well.

Mr. Reed, Patty's father, had retained an attorney. While he acknowledged having intercourse with Patty ("for a few months") he denied having forced or even encouraged her. She had been seductive with him, and, he reasoned, "It was better for her to learn about sex at home, the right way, from a man who's had a vasectomy so she won't get pregnant, than from some kid on the street who doesn't care about her. So we went progressively from touching to fondling to intercourse. But don't worry, I've decided to stop and not do it any more."

Once the charges were filed, the district attorney met with Mr. Reed, his attorney, and Ms. Fox. The district attorney agreed to suspend his prosecution of this case if the following conditions were met: (1) Mr. Reed moved out of the family home until his therapist felt he could safely return, and he was not to be alone with Patty (or any other minor children) under any circumstances until treatment had occurred. (The purpose of this is to protect Patty, of course, but also to reinforce Patty's mother's role as parent in the household.) (2) Mr. Reed participated in individual, couple, and family therapy over a period of not less than one year. If either of these conditions were not met, the district attorney would proceed with prosecution and probably gain a conviction.

Continued

CASE EXAMPLE   *Continued*

Mr. Reed was evaluated by a social worker who specializes in the treatment of sex offenders, Mr. James. He knew that some persons who molest children are fixated pedophiles, that is, persons, generally men, whose primary and often exclusive sexual interest is in children, usually boys. In other words, fixated pedophiles aren't sexually interested in adults. They often go to great lengths to place themselves with boys by pursuing occupations or hobbies, such as being newspaper carrier supervisors or baseball team coaches, to gain sexual access to them. But many child molesters are heterosexually oriented men who are married and are sexually aroused to children as well as adults. These men sometimes seek to replace a conflictual adult relationship with involvement with a child. Mr. James believed Mr. Reed was this latter type of offender. He suggested the following goals in the treatment which ensued from the revelation of sexual abuse: (1) Mr. Reed was to take full and complete responsibility for all his deviant sexual behavior; (2) he was to end all sexual abuse; (3) he must understand the emotional and environmental precursors to his sexual assaults and begin to view them as warning signals, thereby changing his thoughts and behaviors early in his abusive cycle; (4) he must strengthen the marital relationship between himself and his wife; (5) he must provide a forum for Patty to express her feelings honestly to her parents; (6) Mr. Reed must make the necessary lifestyle changes to promote his developing relationships with people that are based on mutuality and reciprocity, not manipulation and deception; (7) he must manage the compulsive aspect of his sexual assaults of Patty; and (8) he must assist in rebuilding the family with each family member assuming her or his appropriate role.

The issue of seductiveness often comes up in these cases. In an effort to reduce guilt feelings on the part of the perpetrator of sexual abuse, he can rather easily deceive himself

---

intercourse that I am, but I don't think so. I really don't know."

The counselor explores with the client any *past treatment and outcome*:

"Have you tried anything to alleviate the pain besides coming to see me to talk about it?"

"Yes. I asked my gynecologist about it during my last pelvic exam. He said I was fine. And I've talked with Bill about it a lot, but neither of us knows what to do."

Finally, the counselor is interested in learning the client's *current expectancies and goals of treatment*:

"What would you consider to be a satisfactory resolution of this problem, Sally?"

"I just want intercourse to stop hurting. I used to enjoy it a lot more, and I'm starting to avoid it 'cause it hurts."

The counselor determines from this sexual problem history that intervention at the level of permission alone, or even at the level of limited information, would probably not alleviate the problem. She decides to give some permission, some limited information, and follow up with some specific suggestions:

(Permission) "I'm really glad, Sally, that you had the courage to come in here today to explore this with me. I know that sex is difficult for most people to talk about, and it's especially difficult when you're having a problem with it. And you know, lots of women believe that it's natural for intercourse to hurt, almost

in placing the blame on the victim. The point is that children *are* seductive—for attention, not sexual interaction. Most children learn to attract the attention of significant adults in their lives by whatever means is effective. So an adult who interprets these advances as *sexual* can easily shift the blame to the child. Most counselors believe that it is absolutely necessary for the adult to acknowledge this deception, take full responsibility for his behavior, and say so to the child. This is seen as important primarily to (1) encourage the adult to see himself as in control, not a victim of circumstances, and therefore in control of *stopping* the behavior; and (2) unburdening the child of her guilt for "being seductive" and perhaps becoming aroused by the sexual interactions.

Mr. Reed was seen in group sex offender treatment and in various therapy combinations of father-daughter, husband-wife, and family treatment. Therapy occurred twice weekly for several months, then once weekly, and eventually monthly. Patty saw her own therapist to help her resolve her feelings of guilt, anger, and confusion. Mr. James also organized a self-help group of sexual abusers and their families to encourage mutual sharing and growth. No further incidents of sexual abuse were reported.

Many of the ideas presented in this section are based on the author's clinical experience and are amplified in Anna C. Salter, *Treating Child Sex Offenders and Victims* (Newbury Park, CA: Sage Publications, 1988). Two books on the subject of sexual abuse of children are Sandra L. Ingersoll and Susan O. Patton, *Treating Perpetrators of Sexual Abuse* (Lexington, MA: Lexington Books, 1990), and Ellen Bass and Laura Davis, *The Courage to Heal* (New York: Harper & Row, 1988).

---

as if that's a woman's lot in life. I'm sure glad you're not of that opinion.

"Let me ask you one more question. Do you feel aroused, turned on, ready for intercourse when Bill is ready?"

"No, he seems to be ready for intercourse much more quickly than I am. I could never be as fast as he is."

(Limited information) "That's a pattern I hear from lots of couples. For whatever reason, the man often gets an erection and is ready for intercourse to begin long before the woman is adequately aroused. When you're turned on, your vagina will lubricate and your cervix, at the base of your uterus, will move up and out of the way of the penis. If you're not sufficiently aroused, Bill's penis doesn't slide in easily and

it bumps your cervix, which may be that deeper, sharper pain you talked about."

"So would an artificial lubricant help?"

"Oh, it might help a little, but it wouldn't really solve the problem. What needs to happen is for you to be adequately aroused before you attempt intercourse. It's just as inappropriate for the two of you to be having intercourse if you're not lubricated as it is to attempt to have intercourse when Bill doesn't have an erection."

"What can we do about this?"

(Specific suggestions) "I would suggest that you spend more time concentrating on what you like in the sex play prior to intercourse. Maybe you could tell Bill more about what is particularly arousing to you. Try to stay away from hurrying sex—lots of

*women need a good deal of time before they're ade-
quately aroused and therefore lubricated, and there's
nothing wrong with that. Perhaps if you take more
initiative in directing the sexual encounter, you can
do the things that are most arousing to you. I suspect
one of the reasons you tend not to experience pain
when you initiate sex is because you are likely to be
more aroused then instead of being sexual according
to Bill's rhythms. And most important, don't go ahead
with intercourse until you're really ready."*[4]

The final level of therapeutic intervention described by Annon is *intensive therapy.* Intensive sex
therapy is discussed later in this chapter under "Sexual
Problems."

AIDS

AIDS and the Sexual Revolution

Decades of sexual conservatism emphasizing hetero-
sexuality, marriage, and monogamy gave way to the
sexual revolution of the 1970s. During this period
many persons questioned traditional values and exper-
imented with a variety of sexual behaviors and lifestyles. While some found this sexual revolution to be
liberating, others were distressed at the departure
from the value that sexuality should be expressed only
within marriage.

The 1980s have given way to a sexual revolution of
a far greater scope, growing not from a social move-

ment but from the fear of the sexually transmitted disease Acquired Immunodeficiency Syndrome (AIDS).
AIDS is an infectious disease in which a virus, the human immunodeficiency virus (HIV), attacks the body's
immune system, leaving victims susceptible to a wide
variety of cancers and other diseases. The virus can also
have degenerative effects on the brain, regardless of
whether the immune system has been compromised.
Most disturbing, a diagnosis of AIDS is essentially a
death sentence. While new drugs are being used to alleviate some of the symptoms of AIDS (and thereby
prolonging lives), there is no cure or immediate hope
of discovering a vaccine to inoculate people against the
virus that causes AIDS. To date, 80 percent of victims
have died within two years of a diagnosis of AIDS. The
social, economic, medical, and political consequences
of this disease pose an unprecedented challenge to social workers in the 1990s and beyond.

The 1984 National Association of Social Workers'
Delegate Assembly adopted a policy statement indicating how social workers can pursue action in six areas
related to AIDS (Leukenfield and Fimbres, 1987, p. ix):

Basic epidemiological and clinical research on AIDS.

*The distribution of accurate information on treat-
ment and the medical, financial, and psychosocial
resources that are available.*

*The provision of comprehensive psychological and so-
cial supports to help persons with AIDS, their families,
children, spouses, and loved one.*

*The development of a comprehensive service delivery
system to respond to the AIDS crisis, including suitable housing, home health care, and transportation
services.*

*The protection of the civil rights and right to confi-
dentiality of persons who are diagnosed as having
AIDS or AIDS-related complex (ARC).*

*The protection by the helping professionals and ap-
propriate licensing authorities of the eligibility for
and receipt of benefits by persons with AIDS.*

*There is a great deal of misunderstanding about
AIDS. As misunderstanding, combined with fear, often results in prejudice and even panic, it is incumbent upon social workers to be informed about AIDS.*

---

[4]The counselor might also want to suggest three books by Lonnie Garfield Barbach to this client to help her understand more about
women's sexuality. They are Lonnie Garfield Barbach, *For Yourself: The
Fulfillment of Female Sexuality* (New York: New American Library,
1975); *For Each Other: Sharing Sexual Intimacy* (Garden City, N.Y.:
Anchor Press/Doubleday, 1982); and *Pleasures* (New York: Harper &
Row, 1984).

WHAT WOULD YOU DO IN THE FACE OF AN EPIDEMIC?

☐ IGNORE IT
☐ WAIT FOR IT TO GO AWAY
☑ CALL 777-CARE

AIDS has left few lives in San Francisco untouched. Almost everyone knows of someone, a friend, co-worker or neighbor who has been diagnosed with this life-threatening disease. The Shanti Practical Support Program urgently needs volunteers—men and women from all walks of life—to spend 6 hours a week cooking, cleaning and doing other necessary tasks for people with AIDS. Don't wait any longer, call today.

Tip the scales.

SHANTI PROJECT

Be a Shanti Practical Support Volunteer. Call 777-CARE.

AIDS raises every relevant issue social workers have been taught to face. Left, an ad for the Shanti Project in San Francisco encourages volunteers to enroll in its practical support program; bottom, a counselor meets with a person with AIDS.

Transmission of AIDS

The virus that has been identified as the cause of AIDS is the human immunodeficiency virus (HIV). The first known death from AIDS occurred in England in 1959, and the disease is believed to have entered the United States in 1977. The only way to contract AIDS is for the virus to enter one's bloodstream. The four main ways this occurs are (1) sexual contact; (2) by sharing an infected hypodermic needle; (3) by receiving AIDS-infected blood through transfusion or injection, and (4) by an infected mother transmitting it to her baby during pregnancy. While low levels of the HIV have been found in saliva, "dry" kissing has not been demonstrated to transmit the virus. Less intimate contact will not result in transmission of the virus.

Medical experts have developed guidelines designed to minimize the likelihood of the HIV being transmitted. They include using safer sex practices and refraining from illicit, injected drug use. Safer sex practices involve the following:

- No exchanging of body fluids. Do not allow another person's semen, blood (including menstrual blood), urine, feces, or vaginal secretions to come in contact with your body.

- Use latex condoms for all types of intercourse (oral, anal, vaginal), but be aware that condom failure with HIV may be as high as 17 percent. Therefore, condoms will not eliminate the risk of transmission and must be viewed as a secondary strategy. The most effective condoms are treated with the spermicide Nonoxynol 9.

- Use water-based, never oil-based, lubricants with condoms to reduce the risk of breakage.

- Never mix alcohol or other drugs with sexual activity; drugs may impair your judgment and reduce your ability to make wise decisions.

- Develop a relationship of trust with any person with whom you are going to have sexual contact, and learn as much as you can about his or her sexual history.

- Avoid having sex with multiple partners.

- Choose lower-risk sexual activities.

Symptoms of AIDS

There may be no overt symptoms of AIDS for several years or more after infection. Typical symptoms resemble influenza ("flu") and may include recurrent fever and night sweats; persistent swollen glands in the neck, armpits and groin; unexplained weight loss; recurrent diarrhea; persistent coughing; persistent debilitating fatigue; loss of appetite; unusual oral sores; blotches and bruised areas on the skin that do not go away; a series of infections and illnesses.

Testing for AIDS

There is no actual AIDS test. Rather, a blood test can only register the presence of HIV antibodies, which indicates exposure to the virus that causes AIDS. Therefore, a positive result on the HIV antibody test indicates exposure, not AIDS infection, and that person may or may not develop AIDS. A person with a positive HIV antibody test result can infect others with the virus. The average length of time between HIV infection and onset of AIDS symptoms is approximately ten years. However, this time period is highly variable from person to person. It is also important to note that the HIV antibodies generally take six to twelve weeks to develop, and sometimes longer, following infection. This means that a person who was recently infected with HIV may show an inaccurate "false negative" test result.

There is a great deal of controversy surrounding the testing of persons for the HIV antibodies. Some believe that for certain populations, such as prisoners, persons seeking to immigrate to the United States, or those seeking marriage licenses, the test should be mandatory. Others fear that such widespread compulsory testing will lead to discrimination if results are not kept secret, as well as great emotional upheaval in the lives of individuals who are fearful and confused about the meaning of their test results. Indeed, advertent or accidental public disclosure of positive tests has led to the loss of insurance, marriage and family ties, and housing for certain individuals. Some states require health care providers to report the names of those who test positive for the virus, in order that previous sexual contacts might be notified of their risk. At

Basic Facts about AIDS

Once infected with the AIDS virus (HIV), you are infected *for life*. There is no cure, as yet, for the disease.

Anyone infected with the AIDS virus can transmit the virus to a partner via anal, oral, or vaginal intercourse, or by sharing drug needles.

It takes between three and four months for the HIV to be detectable in one's blood. This means you can carry the virus even though your blood test is negative (that is, okay). On rare occasions it can take up to three years for the HIV to be detectable in blood.

Even though the HIV antibodies are not yet detectable in his or her blood, an infected person can transmit HIV to someone else.

Latex rubber condoms are very effective in preventing the spread of HIV. They should be put on prior to any sexual activity. A space should be left at the tip to accommodate ejaculation, and water-based lubricants and spermicides should be used as well. Condoms, however, are not a fool-proof method.

You cannot get AIDS by donating blood.

It is extremely unlikely that you could become infected with the AIDS virus by receiving a blood transfusion.

You cannot get AIDS by casual contact such as by working or attending school with persons with AIDS, or by sharing eating utensils, toilets, or towels.

Two people who do not have the HIV and who do not use intravenous drugs have *no risk* of contracting AIDS through sexual contact with each other.

the same time, people's fears of testing positive for the HIV antibodies have led some to avoid the health care system, refusing help and trying to live a normal life as a symbol of hope. To circumvent discrimination while increasing people's likelihood of learning their HIV status and accessing health care services as needed, many medical clinics offer anonymous HIV testing. An enormous public policy issue looms: How can the public health and well-being be protected while individual rights are still maintained?

Who Are the Persons with AIDS?

While AIDS is clearly not a gay disease, the majority of persons with AIDS in the United States have been homosexual or bisexual males or intravenous drug users. Some have confused this fact by viewing homosex-

uality as somehow the cause of AIDS, when, in fact, it is homosexuals who have so far suffered the most illness and death. Worldwide, the greatest transmission of the HIV is via heterosexual contact. In the United States, women and adolescents are the groups sharing the largest incidence of new infections. Heterosexual intercourse is especially hazardous for women; one recent study found women who have sexual intercourse with HIV-infected men are fourteen times more likely to contact the virus than are men who have sex with infected women (see Turner, Miller, and Mosed, 1989). AIDS will soon exceed all other causes of deaths, except accidents, for men between the ages of 25 and 44.

Perhaps most tragically, AIDS is increasingly striking groups in the United States who already benefit the least from this society and are the most difficult to help: the poor, minorities, drug abusers, and those with little education.

The health care costs for each individual AIDS patient from the time of diagnosis to death are, on average, about $75,000. Understandably, a diagnosis of AIDS quickly plunges many sufferers into poverty. AIDS thereby presents a challenge of unprecedented magnitude to the health care system in the United States. It has been said that the measure of a society is determined by how well it cares for its least advantaged members. Social workers have been and will continue to be advocates for these very disadvantaged members of our society.

AIDS has changed the social and sexual habits of many people. There has been an increase in sex education programs in institutions as well as in homes. The use of condoms is more widely accepted and they are being advertised in places where previously they were banned. Legislation requiring travelers to certify that they do not carry HIV antibodies is being passed in some countries. There are indications that monogamy and celibacy have increased, particularly in the gay community, and the divorce rate is expected to continue to decline in the heterosexual community.

Social workers have many significant roles to play in the challenges posed by AIDS: developing services; conducting research about social consequences; individual, group, couple, and family counseling; training; educating; planning curricula—the list goes on and on. Indeed, AIDS raises every relevant social issue social workers have been taught to face. The values of the profession—respect for all people, the importance of self-determination, the commitment to community service, ethical responsibility to society, an individual's right to confidentiality, freedom from bigotry and discrimination, and the rights of all persons to adequate physical and mental health care—will serve social workers as they define their individual roles in helping to alleviate the effects of AIDS.[5]

---

[5]For further reading about AIDS, the following books are recommended: Charles Turner, Heather Miller, and Lincoln Mosed, eds., *AIDS: Sexual Behavior and Intravenous Drug Use* (Washington, D.C.: The National Academy Press, 1989); Sasha Alyson, ed., *You Can Do Something About AIDS: New Edition* (Boston, Mass.: The Stop AIDS Project, Inc., 1990); and Gary Anderson, ed., *Courage to Care* (Washington, D.C.: Child Welfare League of America, 1990). A source of excellent, up-to-date pamphlets on AIDS is the Sex Information and Education Council of the United States, 32 Washington Place, New York, N.Y., 10003: phone (212) 673-3850. For information about AIDS, contact the National AIDS Hotline at (800) 342-AIDS.

SEXUAL PROBLEMS

Why do people develop sexual dysfunctions? This author believes that typical patterns of child rearing in America virtually guarantee sexual problems in adulthood. In other words, if you grew up in the United States and learned your lessons well, you'll likely have some sexual problems in adulthood. A little farfetched? Let's look at the evidence.

Young girls in America are encouraged to be sexy (become a cheerleader, attract boys) but certainly not sexual (nice girls don't . . .). They are taught that boys are naturally interested in sex (studs) but girls shouldn't be (because if you are, you're a whore, or at least an easy make). They are taught to attract boys but always to maintain a safe distance, giving sexual favors in a safe progression, always maintaining control.

A woman telephones the sex therapist, stating:

I've been married for five years, I love my husband, we have a delightful child and a happy home. But when we get together sexually I turn on to a point and then, I just go numb. I don't feel anything.

This woman learned to control her sexual feelings so effectively in her earlier experiences that later, when it was no longer functional for her to maintain such control, her body responds, almost reflexively, by shutting down.

Boys, on the other hand, are taught to "sow their wild oats," to have as many sexual experiences as they can. Indeed, it is a status symbol among adolescent boys in American society to "score" whenever, with whomever, however, they can. Most boys have been taught to view virginity as a curse, a condition that must never be admitted. They also learn a contradictory message, however: Don't get caught, by the police, her parents, a pregnancy, or a sexually transmitted disease. And not incidentally, if you don't "perform" at all (when you don't get an erection), you'll be safe.

A man tells the sex therapist:

I love my wife. We've been happily married now for ten years. But my problems don't go away. Oh, at first I thought we just needed to get to know each other better. But even now, after all this time, I sometimes don't get an erection and when I do and enter her vagina, I come to orgasm right away. We're both pretty frustrated by that.

This man learned to associate anxiety with sex and to reach orgasm quickly. He later became a victim of his own, previously functional, pattern.

Under normal circumstances, two people who are sexually attracted to each other will, if they pursue sexual contact, respond well together. This means they will experience erotic feelings that will cause many physiological changes in their bodies and eventually move to high levels of arousal culminating in orgasm for each. But this is the ideal. What happens if

The man is so concerned about his partner's performance that he watches himself and therefore blocks incoming sexual stimulation.

The woman doesn't like her partner, and her sexual value system requires liking someone as a prerequisite to sexual feelings.

The man wants to have intercourse but doesn't know how it is done, nor does his partner.

The woman is with a man, but her sexual orientation is toward women — she is not aroused by men.

The only way the woman can be aroused is when she is physically violent with her partner.

The only people the man is aroused by are children.

The woman is so angry at the man's insensitivity to her needs that she withholds sexual feelings to punish him and maintain her self-esteem.

So you can see that normal, ideal circumstances are often not a couple's norm at all. And just as nothing succeeds like success in sex, nothing fails like failure. In other words, a sexual experience that is seen by the couple as a failure often causes them to watch themselves, fearing the worst. And the worst can rapidly become a self-fulfilling prophecy.

TREATMENT OF SEXUAL DYSFUNCTION

The traditional view of sexuality and sexual problems was largely based on the ideas of the father of psycho-

therapy, Sigmund Freud.[6] He believed that sexuality was an extremely important life force and that sexual problems occurred because one's personality development was incomplete at some life stage. Intervention, therefore, involved the therapist's guiding the client back into that incomplete life stage, gaining *insight* into herself or himself, and therefore completing the development of the personality. And with a fully developed personality, full sexual function would occur.

Perhaps because the theory is faulty, or perhaps because it accounts for only some people's problems, or perhaps because it doesn't adequately account for all problems, including sexual problems, this "traditional" intervention method often failed to help people resolve their sexual problems. So the pendulum swung.

An opposing view of treating sexual problems was first introduced by William Masters, M.D., and Virginia Johnson, in 1970.[7] They suggested that sexual problems can be just sexual problems — that they may have nothing to do with incomplete life stages or any other personality defect. Instead, sexual problems may be solely the result of faulty learning about sex and consequently poor experiences, repeated over and over again. So the intervention dictated by their theory was very much oriented to the present (as opposed to the past). They, therefore, departed from the traditional focus on the *individual* and instead defined and treated the *relationship* as the client, to help persons (1) understand their sexual histories, sexual values, and physical responses more fully; (2) learn what is more interesting and arousing to them sexually and to communicate these things to their partner; (3) reduce goal- and performance-oriented sexual expression, concentrating more fully on the pleasure of the experience rather than the goal of intercourse and orgasm; and (4) reduce their anxiety during sexual experiences.

---

[6]James Strachey, *Sigmund Freud: Three Essays on the Theory of Sexuality* (New York: Basic Books, 1962). Freudian theory is also described in Chapter 13 of this text.

[7]William H. Masters and Virginia E. Johnson, *Human Sexual Inadequacy* (Boston: Little, Brown, 1970). An excellent synopsis of this medical text, written in lay persons' language, is Fred Belliveau and Lin Richter, *Understanding Human Sexual Inadequacy* (New York: Bantam Books, 1970).

Masters and Johnson treated people, often with very long-standing sexual problems, in a two-week intensive therapy program. This was the beginning of *sex therapy*.

By definition, "sex therapy differs from other forms of treatment for sexual dysfunctions in two respects: *first, its goals are essentially limited to the relief of the patient's sexual symptom and second, it departs from traditional techniques by employing a combination of prescribed sexual experiences and psychotherapy.*"[8]

In the 1990s there seems to be a decided trend among sex therapists across the country that might be defined as the pendulum swinging back toward the center. In the past, the pendulum swung from seeking to treat sexual problems by "traditional" methods (that is, by helping the client gain insight into her or his personality and not really talking about sex) to seeking to treat sexual problems in a very programmed, behavioral way. The former approach was generally unsuccessful, while the latter frequently led to improvement—but sometimes only to a point. Some people start to "get better" and then their improvement plateaus, short of their goals. To help clients progress beyond this plateau, sex therapists have increasingly borrowed other methods of intervention frequently used in relationship therapy.[9] A case example of this follows our general discussion of treatment of sexual dysfunction.

SEXUAL DYSFUNCTIONS DEFINED

Sexual dysfunctions can be defined on two levels: specific, behaviorally measurable functional disorders;

and general, often relationship-oriented problems. Problems often occur on both levels.

The specific functional disorders for men are (1) premature ejaculation—the inability of the man "to exert voluntary control over his ejaculation reflex, with the result that once he is sexually aroused, he reaches orgasm very quickly" (Kaplan, 1974, p. 187); (2) erectile dysfunction—the inability to experience erection either at any time or, more commonly, when one is desired for a sexual experience with a partner (usually intercourse); (3) orgasmic dysfunction—the inability to reach orgasm voluntarily at any time, or, more commonly, when one is desired for a sexual experience with a partner (usually intercourse); and (4) dyspareunia—painful intercourse.

The specific functional disorders for women are (1) orgasmic dysfunction—the inability of the woman to experience orgasm voluntarily at any time or when with a partner, (2) dyspareunia—painful intercourse, (3) vaginismus—an anxiety response resulting in the involuntary tightening of the vaginal musculature to prohibit vaginal penetration.

The general dysfunctions include (1) problems of desire and arousal—lack of desire for a certain partner and/or failure to experience arousal with that partner; (2) problems related to aging, physical illness, or disability;[10] (3) fears of intimacy—inability or unwillingness to become close enough to a partner to risk "letting go" sexually; (4) power struggles—aggression with, or withholding of, sex to maintain power in a relationship; (5) communication difficulties—unwillingness or inability to state sexual needs and desire; and (6) lack of an interested and interesting partner.

SEX THERAPY

Steve telephoned the sex therapy clinic and spoke with a male therapist. Steve explained that he had lately be-

---

[8]Helen Sanger Kaplan, *The New Sex Therapy* (New York: Brunner/Mazel, 1974), p. 187.

[9]Sex therapists have also become much more knowledgeable about diagnosing and treating sexual disorders. Books that describe the present state of this knowledge include Helen Sanger Kaplan, *The Evaluation of Sexual Disorders* (New York: Brunner/Mazel, 1983), and John Money, *Venuses Penises* (Buffalo, N.Y.: Prometheus Books, 1986).

[10]Books on sexuality and aging, and physical illness and disability include Edward M. Brecher, *Love, Sex and Aging* (Boston: Little, Brown, 1984); Armando DeMoya, Dorothy DeMoya, Martha E. Lewis, and Howard R. Lewis, *Sex and Health* (New York: Stein and Day, 1983); Alex

come increasingly upset about his marital and sexual problems and, after a particularly heated argument with his wife the previous evening, he realized something must be done. So he talked with his physician, who suggested he call the sex therapy clinic.

The therapist arranged an appointment to see Steve and his wife, Joan, together with his cotherapist. A principle subscribed to at this clinic is that since women and men grow up with such different messages about sex, and since there are obvious physical differences, women can best relate therapeutically to women and men to men. So couples seen at the clinic are seen by a male-female, cotherapy team.

The Intake

At the initial appointment, the therapists asked each person about the nature of the problems occurring in the marriage.

Joan described her general dissatisfaction with the relationship as well as her specific sexual complaints. She felt Steve was preoccupied with his work and generally insensitive to her needs. She felt frustrated at her inability to get him to share his feelings with her. In the past couple of years, she admitted to basically "shutting down" to him and had given up trying to draw him out. She sought and received most of her intimacy needs from their two children. Their sex life had suffered greatly; she professed very little interest in being sexual with Steve or by herself.

Steve, on the other hand, was angry at Joan because he felt he fulfilled his principal role in the relationship—that of breadwinner—and was increasingly being asked to participate in duties around the house and with the children. At the same time, Joan was denying him a sexual relationship. He felt she was unfair in her expectations of him and he had become increasingly more withdrawn.

The therapists learned further that sex, early in the relationship, had been good for Steve and Joan. Lately,

however, their lives had become more complicated: by having children, by additional stresses from Steve's job, and by Joan's increasing lack of satisfaction in her role as housewife. Therefore, the quality and quantity of their sexual intimacy had progressively deteriorated. Intercourse occurred about twice a month now, and there was little physical affection in the relationship outside the sexual encounters.

The therapists felt the couple was motivated to change. Each was frightened by the intensity of their dissatisfactions, but they were committed to each other and seemed eager to learn ways to improve the relationship.

The therapists discussed with Steve and Joan what their entering therapy would mean. They would meet once a week for therapy sessions and would additionally be expected to get together, in the privacy of their own home, three times a week for home experiences prescribed by the therapists. Sex therapy generally lasts for twelve to eighteen sessions. The focus would be on intimacy—how to rebuild, through sexually intimate interactions, the strength of the marriage. There would be no demonstration or observation of sexual behavior in the sex therapy clinic.

Some areas of emphasis for Steve and Joan would be (1) improving verbal communication skills; (2) increasing their knowledge about sex; (3) helping each person individuate—to learn and act on what each wants rather than largely reacting to the other; (4) exploring each person's history to help them understand themselves better, with particular emphasis on parental role models; and (5) exploring the history of the relationship to better understand how the problems developed as they did—to discourage them from developing again.

The therapists encouraged Joan and Steve to discuss, after this initial session, whether they wanted to enter therapy.

The "chicken and egg" question often comes up with sexual problems—that is, has the sexual relationship deteriorated because the marriage is in trouble, or is the marriage in trouble because the sexual relationship has deteriorated? It probably makes little difference. If successful intervention is made in the sexual area—the couple learns to talk honestly about their needs and desires, they learn to cooperate, etc.— improvement in the remainder of the relationship

---

Comfort, *Sexual Consequences of Disability* (Philadelphia: George F. Stickley Co., 1978); and Thomas H. Walz and Nancee S. Blum, *Sexual Health in Later Life* (Lexington, Mass.: Lexington Books, 1987).

Sex therapy

generally occurs. This is because, for most people, sexual intimacy is a microcosm of their entire relationship. They often play out their power struggles, their fears of getting close, their anger, in bed. Intervening in sexuality, furthermore, can be very specific. When a couple is given an assignment to get together for an experience touching each other, the therapists can learn a great deal about motivation, cooperation, communication, ability to give and receive pleasure, and so forth. This promotes the efficiency of therapy by giving a rather concrete focus.

Joan telephoned the therapists two days later to say they had discussed therapy and decided to get started. They scheduled the next appointment.

At the next treatment session, the therapists separated the couple, the male therapist meeting with Steve

and the female therapist meeting with Joan.[11] This was for history taking and would be the only time they would meet separately. Each therapist took an extensive, two-hour social/sexual history.[12]

[11]This case history illustrates the method used most commonly by the author when seeing a couple in intensive sex therapy. Many sex therapists use similar treatment methods, based on principles and techniques originally introduced by Masters and Johnson, *Human Sexual Inadequacy*.

[12]Outlines of sexual histories can be found in Joseph LoPiccolo and Leslie LoPiccolo, eds., *Handbook of Sex Therapy* (New York: Plenum Press, 1978), pp. 103–113, and in Masters and Johnson, *Human Sexual Inadequacy*, pp. 34–51.

The History

The purpose of the history-taking session is to enable each therapist to empathize with and understand as effectively as possible the client she/he will be representing. It also gives the same gender therapists and clients a better opportunity to get to know each other, facilitating openness and trust.

In taking a sexual history the therapists probed each client for her/his goals of therapy, childhood and adolescent experiences (including sexual assault victimization), sexual value systems, the history of the sexual problems, strengths and weaknesses in the marriage, descriptions of typical sexual experiences, and a great deal of other information helpful to the therapists in representing their same-sex client accurately and developing the treatment plan.

During the history-taking session, the therapists were particularly careful to ask specific questions and press for specific, detailed answers. A very important rule for sex counselors and therapists to observe is to avoid *assuming* anything. Because specific, personal sexual experiences are not something people tend to talk about, particularly if there is a sexual problem involved, persons often assume their behaviors are similar to everybody else's. The thorough, careful therapist will avoid serious pitfalls that would have sabotaged the success of therapy had they not been noticed.

The Roundtable

Joan and Steve met the next week for the subsequent therapy session, the roundtable. In this meeting, each therapist reviewed the significant contributions each partner makes to the strengths and weaknesses of their relationship. The areas of misunderstanding resulting from patterns of faulty communication were especially emphasized. The focus was not on whose fault the problems were, or who should feel guilty, but rather what was *dysfunctional* in their unique interactions with each other.

It is important to realize that sexual problems almost never develop in relationships because of some conscious, malicious intent. Instead, these problems are due to patterns of interaction which, as a whole, are dysfunctional. Each piece, taken out of context, might be done with the best of intentions. For example, Steve and Joan had fallen into a pattern of quick sex. This was largely because Steve knew Joan was not particularly enjoying their sexual experiences, so he hurried to get them over with. Unfortunately this served to exacerbate the problem because Joan was less likely to become aroused, and therefore enjoy sex, in a hurried encounter. The therapists pointed this out, along with many other patterns to Joan and Steve.

At the end of the roundtable session, they were asked to abstain from intercourse and were given the following instructions, which were discussed verbally and were also given to the couple in a handout:

Touching Experiences

For many persons, the idea of body touching is thought of only as a preliminary to orgasm. Thinking of touching in this way often causes the touching to become less valued for its own sake. Although the entire body may be pleasant to touch and to have touched, emphasis is usually placed on the breasts and vaginal area or on the penis and testicles. Touching need not be explicitly genital or goal-oriented to be pleasurable. Touching, by yourself or with a partner, can be a joyful expression of discovery and exploration, of giving and getting.

Plan ahead and prepare, together, a quiet and private, warm and comfortable place. Create an atmosphere that is pleasant for you. It may include soft, even colored lights or candles and music or other things that help you relax. Remove your clothing and assume positions that will permit comfort during long periods of touching. Give yourselves a lot of time. Slowly become very familiar with your partner's entire body. Remember, this experience is not one of trying to sexually arouse one's partner. It is designed to give you time to explore your own feelings about touching and being touched. Touch, stroke, squeeze, and caress your partner to explore what you feel. The feeling you receive need not be an arousing one. You will feel something; get in touch with whatever that feeling is.

You may wish to shower together, using pleasant soaps on one another's body, or try to shower in the dark (you must then rely on touch). Try a pleasant tasting, nonalcohol based lotion or oil, or a baby powder. These facilitate the movement of skin on skin and reduce friction. Oils or lotions should first be poured in your hands to be warmed or otherwise warmed beforehand.

Use your fingers, fingertips, your palms, and your full hand to touch and caress in different ways. This is not a massage. Massage is designed primarily to give pleasure to the other person. Remember, the major purpose of this touching experience is to discover feelings for yourself through touching your partner. It may be helpful to close your eyes while touching so you can "get into" your own feelings without observing your partner's response. Try a joyful fantasy, if you like; or pretend you've lost the use of your sight for awhile and must rely on touch alone. The person being touched has only to lie there and concentrate on his or her own feelings of being touched. Sometimes, too, you may want to explore your partner's body visually while you are touching and would feel more comfortable if your partner were to close his or her eyes. If so, ask your partner to do so. If you would like to comb your partner's hair, do so.

Since you are touching your partner for yourself, you need not concern yourself about your partner's reaction, unless it is one of discomfort or pain (if so, your partner must tell you). After each touching experience discuss your feelings with one another; not in a directive or accusatory fashion but with an effort toward understanding each other's feelings about touching and being touched. Do not make assumptions about your partner's feelings. Use "I" language to express your feelings (see next section).

We ask you to have "nongenital touching experiences" a minimum of three times during the first week to reinforce comfortable feelings. We will discuss with you which partner should initiate the first touching experience. After the "initiator" has fully explored his or her feelings from touching the partner's body, change off, the person who was touching will then become the one who is touched. During this first week we do not want the man to touch his partner's breasts, nipples, or vaginal area; nor do we want the

woman to touch her partner's nipples, penis, or testicles. Touching should be done only with the hands during this week period. (Much later you may wish to try touching your partner with other parts of your body: your feet, lips, face, etc.)[13]

Steve and Joan were also given the following instructions to improve their verbal interactions:

Self-Representation: The Use of "I Language"[14]

Most sexually intimate couples think they know considerably more about each other's feelings, attitudes, and behaviors than they, in fact, really do know. They take pride in "outguessing" and in "predicting" their partner's responses without ever really communicating with each other. They believe "since he/she loves me — he/she knows how I feel."

Responsibility for self. We are each responsible for our own sexuality. We should not wait for someone else to discover it for us. We need to explore, discover, and understand our own sexual responses. We are then free to share or not to share our sexuality with another person. If we decide to share our sexuality, we need to be willing to communicate with our partner what we have learned about ourselves . . . to be open . . . to be vulnerable . . . to risk. We also need to be willing to learn about our partner's sexuality from our partner. We cannot make assumptions about his/her needs, feelings, etc., without asking. Too often our guesses are wrong. In order to share a sexual experience on an equal basis we must both have and express knowledge, comfort, and responsibility for our own sexuality. This "responsibility" is necessary to take ownership for our own feelings, attitudes, and ideas as well as our behaviors.

---

[13]Handout, Midwest Center for Sex Therapy, 9 Odana Court, Madison, Wisconsin 53719. This material on touching experiences also appears in "Sexual Counseling and Sex Therapy" by Lloyd Sinclair in Charles Zastrow, *Introduction to Social Welfare Institutions*, 2nd ed. (Homewood, Ill.: Dorsey Press, 1982), pp. 427–29.

[14]"I language" is a verbal communication technique suggested by many therapists. It was developed by Thomas Gordon, *Parent Effectiveness Training* (New York: Peter H. Wyden, 1970). I-language, also called I-messages, is further described in Chapter 22.

Representation of self. *Once we are responsible for our own sexuality and have made a decision to share our sexuality with another person, we need to learn the best ways of representing ourselves clearly to our partner.*

"I language." *It begins with "I," taking responsibility for ourselves, and is followed by a feeling. "I appreciate your tenderness." "I'm upset because you're late, and I've had to delay a fine meal." "I would like to go to that new movie tonight and am curious if you would like to go with me." "I wonder what it would feel like if you touched me like this."*

The purpose of "I" language is not to promote agreement but rather to promote accurate communication and understanding. Only with accurate understanding can you ever know whether you agree or disagree. When you use "I" language you must first be aware of your own feeling, attitude, idea, before you can clearly state it to your partner. Thus, the use of "I" language helps you to get in touch with your own feelings first. All feelings are real for you; they may not always be rational, yet you have them. It is your responsibility to represent your feelings — not your partner's feelings. Do not expect your partner to know your feelings clearly unless you represent them clearly. Through the use of "I" language you minimize putting your partner in a defensive position. You also optimize opening further communication. You speak for you, not for someone else. By openly expressing your feelings you encourage your partner to do the same. Openness often seems risky when used with someone we care about, but the alternative may be years of misinformation. The following are examples of "you" language, succeeded by more effective "I" language:

a. *"You make me so angry when you don't pick up your clothes." (An accusatory statement that is most likely to place your partner on the defensive.)*

b. *"I'm angry because in addition to picking up my own clothes I feel I have to pick your clothes up too." (Permits further communication and represents your feelings.)*

a. *"Let's go out to dinner." (A confused message that takes over your partner's response.)*

b. *"I'd like to go out to dinner and wonder if you would like to also." (Much better.)*

a. *"You're too clumsy when you touch my breasts." (Another accusatory message likely to shut down communication — not open it up.)*

b. *"I get turned off when you touch my breasts that way because it hurts; I'd like to show you what kind of touch feels good."*

a. *"Do you want to go to the movies tonight?" (Answer: "I don't know, do you?" Next response — "I don't know, I asked you first." Result: confusion.)*

b. *"I would like to see _____ tonight, and wonder if you would also like to see that film."*[15]

Finally, Steve and Joan were instructed to take some time, each by himself/herself to explore their bodies through whole-body touching and masturbation. Since masturbation to orgasms was something each of them had done many times before, this was not expected to be difficult. However, talking about masturbation had been awkward before, and each felt some relief to get permission from the therapists and each other to self-pleasure.

The Physiology Session

The next therapy session focused on feedback Steve and Joan shared about their touching experiences.

Both reported feeling awkward at first, but after they got over the feeling that they were touching strictly for the therapists, they enjoyed each session a great deal. Joan felt much more relaxed than she had for some time. Since she wasn't expected to get aroused she felt unburdened by expectations and was able to enjoy the sessions unencumbered by performance demands. Steve was encouraged; Joan initiated two of the three touching experiences they had that week. He had stated, when giving his history, his belief that if *he* never initiated sex, it wouldn't ever happen.

Both had used some "I-language" in discussing issues that came up throughout the week. Steve, particularly, said he needed to remind himself to use it more.

---

[15]This material is in a handout, Midwest Center for Sex Therapy, 9 Odana Court, Madison, Wis. 53719. This material also appears in "Sexual Counseling and Sex Therapy" by Lloyd Sinclair in Charles Zastrow, *Introduction to Social Welfare Institutions*, 2nd ed. (Homewood, Ill.: Dorsey Press, 1982), pp. 427–29.

The therapists explored, very specifically, the touching experiences with Joan and Steve, encouraging them to give each other as much feedback as possible. The emphasis on touching for the pleasure of the active partner, rather than to "turn her/him on," was further emphasized. The assignment for the next week was the same, except touching of breasts and genitals was now permitted. Joan and Steve were encouraged not to place too much emphasis on genital touching, however. They were to integrate genital touching with other touching, to learn and explore, not to arouse. If arousal took place, that was fine; it was *not*, however, the purpose of the experience.

Joan and Steve were further encouraged to continue their private self-stimulation sessions.

In the second half of this therapy session, the therapists reviewed significant information about the physiology of human sexual response, described as follows by this author in a prior article.[16]

The male therapist explained the genital response in the male, using slides and models to illustrate the physical changes. In the first stage of sexual response, excitement, blood flows into the erectile tissue of the penis (vasocongestion), resulting in erection. The scrotum (the sac surrounding the testicles) becomes thicker, more wrinkled, and the testicles move up closer to the body.

The plateau stage of sexual response is characterized by the continuation of erection, although it often waxes and wanes during sex play with a partner. The testicles become fully elevated, rotate toward the front, and become blood-engorged, causing expansion in their size. The Cowper's gland secretes a small amount of clear fluid which comes out of the tip of the penis. The purpose of this fluid is generally thought to be to cleanse the urethra of urine, thereby neutralizing the chemical environment for the passage of sperm.

The orgasm stage in men consists of two phases. The first is ejaculatory inevitability, a short period

during which stimulation sufficient to trigger orgasm has occurred, and the resulting ejaculation becomes inevitable. The second phase, ejaculation, results from rhythmic contractions (myotonia) forcing sperm and semen through the urethra. Simultaneous with this is the very pleasant physical sensation of orgasm.

The final stage, resolution, represents a return to the unstimulated state. In resolution, the penis loses its erection, and the testicles lose their engorgement and elevation.

In women, the excitement stage of sexual response ushers in many changes. The process of vaginal lubrication begins. This response is analogous to the male erection; it is caused by sexual stimulation and is, physiologically, a blood engorgement response. The uterus and cervix begin to move up and away from the vagina. The clitoris and labia minora enlarge and the labia majora spread. Breast size increases slightly and the nipples may become erect.

In the plateau stage, the uterus continues in its movement up and back, the vagina lengthens and balloons at the rear, and the outer third of the vagina contracts, causing a gripping effect. The clitoris retracts under its hood, making it seem to disappear.

At orgasm, the uterus and vagina become involved in wavelike muscular contractions. This response, as well as the subjective pleasure of orgasm, are very similar to the experience of the male.

In resolution, the cervix and uterus drop to their normal positions, the outer third of the vagina returns to normal, followed by the inner two thirds. The clitoris and the breasts also return to normal.

The therapists also discussed the many involuntary extragenital physical responses in men and women. These include muscle tension responses such as facial grimace, spastic contractions of the hands and feet, and pelvic thrusting. Extragenital blood engorgement responses include sex flush, blood pressure and heart rate increases, and perspiration on soles of feet and palms of hands.

Finally, the therapists discussed how aging effects sexual response. They emphasized that persons are capable of experiencing pleasurable sexual response throughout life; while their bodies may slow down, they do not need to stop.

---

[16]Lloyd Sinclair and Charles Zastrow, "Human Sexuality Variations, Sexual Counseling, and Sex Therapy" in Charles Zastrow, *Introduction to Social Welfare Institutions*, 3rd ed. (Homewood, Ill.: Dorsey Press, 1986), pp. 219–20.

Subsequent Treatment Sessions

Joan and Steve saw the therapists weekly for nine more sessions. They were gradually instructed to try new sexual behaviors, with the option to proceed at their own pace. Therapy progressed well until the fifth week.

The fifth, sixth, and seventh therapy session saw Joan reporting sexual interest and sexual arousal, but her progress plateaued. At first, the therapists interpreted the lack of progress as simply rough spots in the process of change. However, after three weeks, deeper exploration was indicated.

During a very intense seventh treatment session, therapists identified a power struggle existing in the relationship that was hampering further progress. Basically, Joan felt *she* was being asked to change for Steve much more than he for her. Since being sexual was what he wanted more than anything from her, and sharing his feeling was what she wanted from him — something she felt he was doing very little of — she was not willing to give further. This was probably an unconscious choice, a way for Joan to protect herself from being fully dominated by Steve. The therapists tested this hypothesis by explaining this power relationship to Steve and working with him to open his feelings more to Joan. Subsequent weeks saw great improvement in this area and the sexual relationship in general.

Therapy was terminated by agreement of clients and therapists, when the couple found that the sexual relationship, as well as the relationship in general, had improved greatly. In addition, they had learned skills to foster further improvement in the months and years to come.

SUMMARY

Any social worker who interacts with clients is presented with opportunities to be helpful in the area of sexuality. Since sex typically elicits concern and anxiety in people in this society, it is incumbent upon social workers to examine their own feelings in this area and become knowledgeable. Further, they need to recognize the legitimacy and importance of their professional intervention in this area.

The first prerequisite to effective counseling in the area of sexuality is knowledge, and therefore social workers need to acquire accurate information in this area. Counselors should be aware that it is a mistake to assume that everyone expresses sexuality in the same way. Social workers also need to learn the technical words involving sexuality and become desensitized to the expression of "street" words in counseling.

Sexual dysfunctions are defined and the various dysfunctions (such as orgasmic dysfunction) are identified. Jack S. Annon has developed a useful conceptual scheme of intervention levels: permission, limited information, specific suggestions, and intensive therapy. The largest number of clients benefit from intervention at the level of permission. Each of these levels is described.

Intensive sex therapy differs from other forms of treatment for sexual dysfunctions in two respects. First, its goals are essentially limited to the relief of the patient's sexual symptom. Second, it departs from traditional techniques by employing a combination of prescribed sexual experiences and psychotherapy. Intensive sex therapy is described in some depth. The stages of intensive sex therapy include problem definition, history gathering, physical examination, information dissemination, prescribed sexual and communication experiences, and ongoing evaluation.

We have explored some basic counseling skills helpful in working with clients about sex. We have examined, through case examples, many areas of knowledge and treatment methodologies that are useful to the social worker. And we hope that we have encouraged you to think about, recognize, and explore your own areas of discomfort. The challenge is yours. Will you further the age-old "conspiracy of silence" in this sensitive area, or will you learn, explore, and help your future clients to enrich this important area of their lives?

EXERCISES

1. Tell Your Neighbor

GOAL: Give students an experiential appreciation for the difficulty people have in talking about their own sexuality, even for those who can easily talk about sex in general.

Step 1: Each student is to pick a partner for the exercise. The person sitting closest is fine; the relationship between the partners is not important. If there is an odd number of students, one group can consist of three members. Be certain all students have partners before proceeding to step two.

Step 2: Instructor gives the following task: "Turn to your partner and tell her/him about a sexual problem *you* have."

Step 3: Instructor interrupts students after a brief period (not to exceed thirty seconds) by saying "Stop" loudly. When the instructor has the attention of the class, she explains that the purpose of the exercise is not to elicit class members' sexual problems, but rather to have them experience their own uneasiness when they are expected to reveal some sexual vulnerability of their own.

Step 4: Instructor leads class in discussion of what occurred when they were faced with the previous task. Typically, students will report they discussed who was going to say their problem first, with each hoping the partner would go first. Other students will likely say they searched their minds for a "safe" problem, one that would not be too threatening to reveal and one that would not be too embarrassing to disclose. The relationship between the partners (whether they are unacquainted or friends, members of the same or the other gender, whether there is a perception on the part of one partner that the other can be trusted with a confidence or will be helpful) has great bearing on how much one is willing to reveal. This exercise should lead students to a heightened awareness of the difficulty faced by a client who must discuss a sexual problem and the qualities they might strive to possess to elicit disclosure from clients.

2. The Word Game

GOALS: (1) Begin desensitizing students to words with which you feel uncomfortable so this discomfort doesn't block their helpfulness with a client. (2) Help students identify a functional language that is comfortable and acceptable to use in a professional setting. (3) Learn new words that may be part of a client's vocabulary and hence should be familiar to the student. (4) Help students realize that the vast majority of words associated with sex are street language and, therefore, many clients are familiar only with those words.

Step 1: The instructor explains the four types of words used when talking about sex: scientific, childhood, common discourse, and street or slang. As described in the text of this chapter, scientific words, such as coitus and fellatio, are very specific. However, they are not commonly used by most people because they have a clinical connotation. Professionals sometimes hide behind these words as a way to diminish their discomfort. (As discussed in the chapter, if you're not communicating, you're not helping.)

Childhood language, such as words like *peepee* and *bottom*, is usually used by anxious parents who are searching for a nonthreatening (to the parents) way to convey their message to their child. When used by adults with each other, they sound ridiculous. Common discourse words and phrases, such as *making love* or *having sex*, are most comfortable for many people. Slang or street words, such as *fuck* or *pussy*, provide graphic descriptions, often laden with hostility. These words are "loaded"; that is, they can mean very different things to different people, depending on the intonation of the voice, the context, the relationship of the people, and other factors. While they are the most commonly used words to express sexual content in this culture, they are also the most powerful and, hence, the most potentially hazardous for a professional to use with a client.

Step 2: The instructor divides the class into two groups, usually by making an aisle down the middle of the room.

Step 3: The instructor puts a word, such as intercourse, breasts, penis, or masturbation on the blackboard. One group is instructed to call out as many words as they can think of that have the same meaning as the word on the blackboard. The instructor writes the words on the blackboard as they are being called out and stops the group after sixty seconds have elapsed.

Step 4: The instructor counts the words and writes the total number on the blackboard.

Step 5: The instructor then challenges the other group to generate a larger number of words than the first group. He writes a new word on the blackboard and repeats this exercise.

Step 6: If appropriate, each group might be given another word and the exercise is repeated.

Step 7: In a debriefing discussion, class members or the instructor can (1) note how many of the words fall into each category described above, (2) discuss the gender bias to particular words, such as those that describe masturbation, and (3) urge the students to practice saying these and other sexually descriptive words to increase their comfort in preparation for their presentation from a client.

3. Answer the Question

GOALS: Help students (1) experience the difficulty in answering a client's questions about sex, even when the answer is known to the students; (2) confront their sexual values as they attempt to respond to the needs of a young person; (3) realize the most commonly asked questions by adolescents about sex are not ones that can be answered factually; rather, they relate to values and are therefore open to many answers.

Step 1: The instructor tells the class that she is going to role-play an inquisitive adolescent, the age and gender of whom will vary with each phase of the exercise. The class is to role-play social workers with whom the adolescent has a trusting relationship.

Step 2: The instructor adopts an insecure and immature affect and asks the first question. Typical questions frequently asked by adolescents include these:

Why do you sometimes get a stiff when you're not thinking about sex?

How tough is that hymen thing?

Will playing with yourself cause problems in intercourse?

How old do you have to be to have intercourse?

How many boys do it? How often? Do girls ever? How would they do it?

Do you automatically know how to have intercourse when you marry?

How do two females have sex together?

Can I use tampons if I'm a virgin?

How do you know if your girlfriend says no when she really means yes?

Why do boys like intercourse more than girls?

If you don't want to have sex before marriage, how far should you go?

Do people have control over their type of sexual behavior, and over how they feel? Is it biological or in your mind?

What does an orgasm feel like?

Class members should be instructed to respond to the questions and to the adolescent's clarifying questions. As the role-play evolves, class members are encouraged to help each other respond to the young person's concerns.

Step 3: When the first question has been exhausted, the instructor leads the class in a discussion of the experience. What was difficult? Where did class members differ with each other on how to handle sensitive matters? How were values dealt with? What reluctances did people have to discuss certain specific areas?

Step 4: The instructor repeats the exercise with a new question, playing a slightly different role. As the role-play progresses, the students should be encouraged to try to determine what the adolescent is really searching for, such as permission to have intercourse or permission *not* to have intercourse.

21

NEURO-LINGUISTIC PROGRAMMING

Neuro-Linguistic Programming (NLP) is a recently developed model of communication that promises to have substantial application in assessing human behavior, in developing rapport, in influencing others (in education, public speaking, and sales), and in changing behavior (psychotherapy). NLP was developed by John Grinder, Richard Bandler, and several other authorities (Lankton, 1980).

Practically all the psychotherapeutic treatment approaches described in this text have been developed by psychiatrists and clinical psychologists. In contrast, NLP has been developed primarily by specialists in communication and linquistics. The roots of NLP can be traced to Gregory Bateson, an anthropologist. Bateson conducted a broad range of research in anthropology, psychiatry, and communication patterns among dolphins. One of Bateson's interests was to synthesize cybernetic ideas with anthropology. *Cybernetics* is the science of communication and control theory; it focuses primarily on the comparative study of automatic control systems — such as comparing the human central nervous system with mechanical-electrical systems.

In 1952 Gregory Bateson received a grant from the Rockefeller Foundation to investigate communication in hypnosis, ventriloquism, animal training, popular moving pictures, the nature of play, humor, schizophrenia, neurotic communication, psychotherapy, family systems, and family therapy. The staff in this project consisted primarily of communication analysts and psychiatric consultants. As this communication research continued, other funding sources provided grants: the Macy Foundation, the Foundations Fund for Research in Psychiatry, and the National Institute of Mental Health (Haley, 1963).

In the 1970s John Grinder and Richard Bandler became involved in these research projects. Grinder and Bandler were specialists in communication and linguistics. Using an approach similar to that of Bateson and his associates, Grinder and Bandler studied the

---

Material in this chapter is adapted from Charles Zastrow, Virginia Dotson, and Michael Koch, "The Neuro-Linguistic Programming Treatment Approach," *Journal of Independent Social Work* 1, (Fall 1986), pp. 29–38. Permission to adapt this material was received from The Haworth Press, Inc.

nonverbal and verbal communication patterns between prominent therapists and their clients. The therapists included Salvador Minuchin (see Chapter 8), Virginia Satir (see Chapter 8), Fritz Perls (see Chapter 15), and Milton Erickson (a leading practitioner of medical hypnosis).

Grinder and Bandler's special genius is the ability to observe the communication patterns of prominent psychotherapists and then to describe in detail what they do, what cues they respond to, and how they go about helping clients make positive changes. Such descriptions, theoretically, make it possible for others to learn how to repeat the same procedures and get similar results.

A number of texts are now appearing that describe the applications of the NLP communication model to business, sales, education, and psychotherapy (Haley, 1973; Bandler and Grinder, 1975, 1976, 1979, 1982; Lankton, 1980; Laborde, 1984). NLP is primarily a model of communication. NLP does not provide a theory of personality development or of psychopathology. The remainder of this chapter will focus primarily on NLP's applications to counseling and psychotherapy.

NLP DEFINED

NLP is the study of the structure of subjective experience (Lankton, 1980, p. 13). It makes explicit patterns of behavior and change that have previously been only intuitively understandable. The components of the term *neuro-linguistic programming* refer to the following:

neuro: nervous system through which experience is received and processed via the five senses.

linguistic: language and nonverbal communication systems through which neural representations are coded, ordered, and given meaning.

programming: ability to organize our communication and neurological systems to achieve specific desired outcomes.

NLP is a model, rather than a theory, of human behavior. A theory is a hypothesis that attempts to explain or interpret the *reasons* things relate as they do. A model, in contrast, is a copy or pattern of already existing phenomena, which, as designed, can be imitated or recreated. A model deals only with what can be observed. For example, a theory of what causes psychotherapeutic changes would seek to specify key variables that lead to positive changes in clients (such as clients being motivated to change). A model, in contrast, would formulate a framework. A framework might be formulated that seeks to represent the verbal and nonverbal communication between people. The framework might then be observed to determine the kinds of verbal and nonverbal messages from a therapist that lead to improved or desired responses from clients.

REPRESENTATIONAL SYSTEMS

Before reading further, take a few minutes to identify what you remember most about the following:

The last grocery store you were in.

What you did on your last birthday.

Your high school days.

Your most enjoyable sexual experience.

Your most enjoyable vacation.

Everyone has, at most, five sensory systems through which they contact physical reality. These senses are the eyes (visual), ears (auditory), skin (kinesthetic), nose (smell), and tongue (taste). For each of the above questions you probably responded with remembrances involving only one or two senses. Taking the grocery store question, you may have had an *image* of fresh fruits and vegetables, or *heard* the hustle and bustle of the activity, or remember *feeling* the Charmin™ bathroom tissue, or remember *smelling* the pleasant aromas of the fresh flowers, or remember *tasting* the free samples of freshly cooked pizza.

Anytime a person interacts with the external world, she does so through sensory representations. Your sensory contact with a grocery store is apt to be quite different from that of your closest friend. The same applies for everyone. Your most enjoyable sexual experi-

CASE EXAMPLE

Sensory Representational Systems

A married couple sought counseling as they felt their sexual relationship was deterio-rating rapidly. After rapport had been established, the counselor asked each, "What tends to turn you on sexually?" The husband mentioned it was hearing romantic things said to him while the wife mentioned it was being softly touched in a variety of areas. Not too surprisingly, the husband was trying to excite his wife by saying romantic things (without touching his wife much), while the wife was seeking to excite her husband by touching him while remaining silent. A simple description of the importance of "joining" with the other's representational system greatly enhanced their love life with the husband spending much more time in tenderly caressing his wife and the wife romantically talking to her husband.

ence may be a visual one, while your partner's may be auditory or kinesthetic.

We operate out of our sensory representations of the world, and not on "reality" itself. Our sensory rep-resentations provide us with a *map* of the territory. But it is important to note that the *map is not the territory*.

NLP asserts that in order to assess another's actions accurately, it is important to identify the sensory repre-sentational system being used by that person. If we are able to identify the other's representational system and "join with" that system in our interactions with that person, communication is apt to flow much more smoothly and rapport is enhanced. On the other hand, if two people are not able to "join" together with the same representational system, communication is apt to be tangential and rapport will be adversely affected. The importance of this point is immense. Successful salespersons, educators and therapists are those who are able to identify and "join" with the representational systems of the persons they are seeking to influence. Once a person (customer, student, or client) has joined with the influencer, the influencer is able to lead the person in the direction he chooses. To a large extent the process of therapy, education, and sales can be de-fined as involving two steps: (1) the influencer's find-ing a way to join with the person to be influenced; and (2) the influencer's leading the person in a new (and, one hopes, positive) direction.

There are several ways for an influencer to join with the person to be influenced. These ways include (a) joining with the person's representational system, (b) talking knowledgeably with the person about sub-jects that interest the person, and (c) mirroring (with-out the person is being consciously aware of the mirror-ing) the person's nonverbal communication — such as the person's posture, gestures, and breathing patterns.

In discussing influencing, it is intriguing to note that there are some remarkable similarities between social workers and sales workers (see Table 21.1 on page 486).

REPRESENTATIONAL SYSTEM PREDICATES

The adverbs, adjectives, and verbs that people select while speaking reveal the sensory system they are most conscious of at that point in time. NLP calls these words *predicates*.

TABLE 21.1

_____

Social Workers and Salesworkers: Similarities and Differences

There are several striking similarities in the essential characteristics of competent social workers and successful salesworkers. I am aware that some social work purists will find it degrading to compare the characteristics of social workers (who seek to enable people to achieve self-fulfillment and social well-being) to the characteristics of salesworkers (who are viewed as being guided primarily to sell more for personal financial gain). In response to such criticism, I urge that such purists reflect on the similarities and differences betweeen these two endeavors. There is considerable evidence that social workers frequently need to "sell" themselves and the services they provide (Lankton, 1980). It appears that competent social workers must possess extensive selling skills.

Contrasting Goals Between Sales and Social Work

There are wide differences between the goals of salesworkers and social workers. The primary goal of salesworkers is to sell products and services. A successful salesworker is viewed as a person who has a high salary and substantial commissions because she or he is very successful in selling products and services. A social worker is a "change agent"—a helper who is employed specifically for the purpose of creating planned change. As a change agent a social worker is expected to be skilled at working with individuals, groups, and families and in bringing about community changes.

In spite of these wide differences in goals between social workers and salesworkers, the following material suggests that several characteristics needed by social workers to accomplish their goals have remarkable similarities to the characteristics needed by salesworkers to accomplish their goal. Theorists who developed neuro-linguistic programming (NLP) have identified the following common characteristics.

Capacity to Influence Is a Key Skill

NLP theorists assert that an essential capacity needed by social workers, salesworkers, psychotherapists, educators, and public speakers is the capacity to influence others.

NLP notes that the process of influencing another involves two steps: (1) the influencer finds a way to "join" with the person to be influenced, and (2) the influencer then leads the person in a new (and preferably positive) direction. Once the influencee (customer, client, or student) has joined with the influencer, the influencer is better able to lead the influencee in the direction desired by the influencer. The concepts advanced by NLP have considerable power in enabling influencers to influence people more effectively.

The Process of "Joining" Involves Forming a Relationship

According to NLP, the first step in influencing someone involves the influencer's forming a relationship with the influencee. This process has also been called establishing rapport.

A number of guidelines have been developed for social workers to use in establishing rapport with clients. Many of these guidelines are summarized here.

1. The social worker should seek to establish a nonthreatening, comfortable atmosphere in which the client feels safe to communicate his or her needs or wants while feeling accepted as a person.

2. The social worker should observe closely nonverbal and verbal communication of the client in order to identify better the needs and wants of the client.

3. In initial contacts with the client, the social worker should "sell" himself or herself—not arrogantly but as a knowledgeable, understanding person who may be able to help and who seeks to find ways to meet the client's needs or wants.

4. The social worker should not laugh or express shock when the client begins to talk about his needs and wants. Emotional outbursts, even if subtle, will lead the client to believe the social worker is not going to understand his or her problems.

5. The social worker should generally be nonjudgmental, not moralistic. The social worker should show respect for the client's values and should not try to sell his or her values to the client.

TABLE 21.1

▬▬▬▬▬▬▬▬▬

(Continued)

6. The beginning of a relationship is often facilitated if the social worker engages in small talk with the client. Such informal conversation sometimes provides information to the social worker about the needs and wants of the client.

7. The social worker should not seek to establish a superior-inferior relationship with the client. Instead, the social worker should convey that the client is a worthy, "equal" person in the relationship. If the client feels he or she is being treated as an inferior, he or she will be less motivated to reveal wants and needs.

8. The social worker should generally not use high-pressure techniques designed to force the client to choose an option he or she may not want. Instead, the social worker should seek to make a variety of options available, help the client assess the merits and shortcomings of each option, and convey that the client has the right and responsibility to make his or her own decision.

9. The social worker should use a "shared vocabulary" with the client. This does not mean that the social worker should use the same slang words and the same accent as the client. If the client perceives the social worker's speech as artificial, the client may be seriously offended. The social worker should use words that the client readily understands and that are not offensive.

10. The tone of the social worker's voice and his or her nonverbal communication should convey that the social worker empathetically understands the client's wants and needs, and cares about the client's feelings.

11. The social worker conveys that the client is an important, worthwhile person.

12. The social worker is a good listener who has skills in identifying the client's needs and wants.

The similarities between essential characteristics needed by social workers and salesworkers can be demonstrated by noting that salesworkers also need to "join with" customers. It is interesting that the guidelines for salesworkers in establishing rapport with customers are remarkably similar to the guidelines for social workers in establishing rapport with clients. This is easily demonstrated by noting that exchanging the words "social worker" for "salesworker" and "client" for "customer" in the guidelines above will provide guidelines salesworkers can use to establish rapport with customers.

As noted earlier, social workers are skilled at working with individuals, groups, and families. They function in roles that include counselor, broker, advocate, and consultant. They also work with administrators, public officials, board members of funding sources, and helping professionals at other agencies. In practically all this work the essence of bringing about positive change involves the social worker's establishing rapport and then seeking to lead the person or persons to be influenced in a new direction.

Differences Between Social Workers and Salesworkers

It would be a serious mistake, however, to conclude that because of the above similarities social workers can also be viewed as salesworkers. There are substantial differences between social workers and salesworkers. These differences include the following:

1. Social workers have the responsibility of helping people find ways to meet their social, financial, recreational, and health needs. Salesworkers, on the other hand, focus on selling products and/or services. Salesworkers are much more guided by the profit motive.

2. Social workers receive substantially more training in the following areas: human behavior, intervention techniques, research, social policy, social problems, and social services. Salesworkers receive more training in becoming knowledgeable about the products they sell and in sales techniques. Some sales techniques are practically never used by social workers, such as lavishly entertaining a customer (client) in the hopes that she or he will be more inclined to make a large purchase.

Continued

TABLE 21.1

(Continued)

3. Social workers focus on improving the lives of people. One of the highest rewards and satisfactions in social work comes from seeing people grow and develop from services that are provided. Salesworkers focus on selling products and services. A major reward for salesworkers is to sell more in order to earn more money.

4. Laborde (1984) in *Influencing With Integrity* makes an important distinction between "influencing with integrity" and "manipulating." In manipulating, the influencer seeks to lead a person in a direction that is in the influencer's self-interest. "Influencing with integrity" involves leading an influencee in a direction that is in the influencee's best interests. Some sales-workers have the image of seeking to influence customers in the salesworker's self-interests (that is, of seeking to sell products or services so that they will benefit financially). On the other hand, social workers have a strong ethical obligation to influence with integrity.

5. Social workers focus on helping clients to assess and identify their personal, social, emotional, health, and financial needs. Once such needs are identified, the role of the social worker is to help clients explore alternatives for meeting these needs. Salesworkers generally do not become involved in assessing and identifying the social-emotional needs of clients. Their focus is on identifying the purchase desires of customers, and then informing customers of products or services they are selling that may meet the purchase desires of customers. Sometimes salesworkers seek to stimulate a purchase desire in customers.

6. The focus of the relationship between a social worker and client is to create a nonthreatening atmosphere in which the client is expected to communicate his or her personal concerns, some of which are highly charged emotionally. In a sales-worker-customer relationship, the customer is expected to share his or her purchase desires. It is generally considered inappropriate for the customer to share highly charged personal concerns.

Usefulness of Comparing Social Workers and Salesworkers

Why is it important to compare the nature of the work performed by social workers to that performed by salesworkers? The primary benefit of this comparison is to emphasize that in establishing relationships with clients a social worker must non-arrogantly "sell" himself or herself as a warm, caring person who has expertise and who may be able to assist clients with difficulties they are experiencing. In this process of establishing a relationship, social workers need to present themselves in a way that has remarkable similarities to the ways in which successful salesworkers present themselves to customers.

This comparison also emphasizes the conceptualization (advanced by NLP) that an essential characteristic needed not only by social workers and salesworkers but also by educators and public speakers, is the capacity to influence others. This influenc-

---

In our culture people use primarily the visual, auditory, and kinesthetic systems. (A few other cultures in other countries place greater emphasis on the senses of smell and taste.) Unless the listener is aware of the sensory representational system the speaker is using, the listener may misinterpret what the speaker is intending. For example, when a client says "I understand you," the intended message depends on the representational system he is in:

Visual: "That looks real good to me"

Auditory: "I hear you clearly"

Kinesthetic: "What you are saying feels right to me"

In the course of growing up, people learn to favor particular representational systems for particular events. People are not totally visual or auditory or kinesthetic. The sense in use depends on the situation, the context. It appears, though, that people tend to

TABLE 21.1

━━━━━━━━━━━━━━━━

(Continued)

ing process involves two steps: "joining with" the influencee, and "leading" the influencee in a new (preferably constructive) direction. In this influencing process the influencer has to give attention not only to verbal communication but also to nonverbal communication so that the optimal conditions will be created for the prospective influencee to want to "join with" the influencer. Aspects of nonverbal communication that the influencer needs to pay attention to include posture, body orientation (the extent to which the influencer faces toward or way from the influencee with head, body, and feet), facial expressions, eye contact, gestures, clothing and personal appearance, and appearance of office (Mehrabian, 1981).

Social workers have an ethical obligation to seek to influence clients with integrity rather than seeking to influence clients for the social worker's personal gain. Some readers may dislike viewing social workers as influencers. They may assert that clients have a right to self-determination and that social workers therefore should not seek to influence them.

In reality, social workers *must* seek to influence clients in constructive directions. If that was not their objective, then their role would be empty and meaningless. Conceptualizing social workers as influencers is *not* inconsistent with clients' rights to self-determination. The right to self-determination holds that clients have a right to express their own opinions and to act upon them, as long as by so doing they do not infringe on the rights of others. In a salesworker-customer relationship it is clearly recognized that the customer retains the right to decide what he or she will purchase, even though the salesworker functions as an influencer. Similarly, in a social worker-client relationship the client retains the right to express his or her opinions, and to make his or her own decisions. A social worker acts as an influencer by using a problem-solving process. The steps in this process include these:

1. Helping clients identify their problems and needs.

2. Helping clients identify alternatives for meeting these difficulties and needs.

3. Helping clients to assess the merits and shortcomings of these altneratives.

4. Urging clients to select and implement one or more of these alternatives.

5. Helping clients to evaluate the outcomes of the strategies implemented, after the strategies have been implemented for a reasonable length of time.

This material is adapted from Charles Zastrow, "Social Workers and Salesworkers: Similarities and Differences," *Journal of Independent Social Work* 4, no. 3, 1990, pp. 7–16.

━━━━━━━━━━━━━━━━

have a primary mode, in that they have a tendency to use more of the one mode than the others (Laborde, 1984, p. 57).

Table 21.2 on page 490 identifies a number of visual, auditory, and kinesthetic "predicates." Mismatched predicates interfere with communication and rapport, as indicated by the following example:

CLIENT: I *feel* so awful! The IRS has just audited me and I just can't *handle* it!

COUNSELOR: I *hear* you. It *sounds bad*, *but tell* me what it is that's so bad.

CLIENT: I just can't *lift* this *feeling*. It's so *heavy*!

COUNSELOR: Yes, but I don't *hear* what the problem is. *Listen* to me and *tell* me what's so bad!

In this illustration, the client is apt to end up viewing the counselor as being insensitive. An example of matched predicates in this situation is the following:

TABLE 21.2

Predicates to Identify Sensory Representational Systems

Visual	Auditory	Kinesthetic
Appear	Audible	Back away
Clear	Buzz	Break down
Colors	Double talk	Bounce
Farsighted	Earshot	Caress
Forsee	Echo	Catch
Glance	Hear	Cold
Hindsight	Hear from	Dig in
Horizon	In tune with	Feel
Illustrate	Listen	Firm
Image	Loud	Grasp
In the dark	Muffled	Handle
Look	Noisy	Hard
Observe	Pronounced	Hold
Overview	Quiet	Iron out
Picture	Resound	Press
Resemble	Rings a bell	Rack your brains
Scan	Roar	Run through
See	Rumbling	Sensitive
Show	Screech	Sensuous
Tint	Sound	Stumble upon
Vague	Sound off	Toss around
Vision	Thundering	Touch
Watch	Whispering	Vibes

CLIENT: I *feel* so awful! The IRS has just audited me and I just can't *handle* it!

COUNSELOR: You *feel* like you're *breaking down* because of the *heaviness* of the audit.

CLIENT: That's exactly it. I'm *stumbling*, but yet *grasping to hold on*.

COUNSELOR: What do you *feel* you need to *hold* on?

CLIENT: *Support* and understanding from my wife, my tax accountant, and you.

In this example the counselor phrases her responses to be consistent with the client's representational system, which leads to better understanding and increased trust and rapport.

EYE-ACCESSING CUES

Listening to the predicates in another's speech is just one reliable way to determine which representational system is dominant at a given time. Eye-accessing cues is another way. Generally the sensory system can be identified by eye accessing cues as displayed in Figure 21.1.

As always with rules there are exceptions: for example, some left handers' kinesthetic representational system is eyes down and to the left, with the eyes down and to the right being their auditory representational system. To test out this information the reader should ask friends or acquaintances questions such as "What do you remember most about your last vacation?" to watch how the eye accessing cues are apt to be consistent with responses that are either visual, kinesthetic, or auditory.

A simple example will illustrate the importance of recognizing eye-accessing cues. When parents are scolding their children, it is common in our society for parents to become additionally angry when the children are looking down. Those parents who become additionally upset are erroneously assuming their children are ignoring what they are saying when they are looking down. They may even yell, "Look at me when I'm talking to you!" In actuality, the eyes being down is a sign that the children are feeling bad about their misbehavior—which is the feeling that parents want their children to have in such situations.

THE FOUR-TUPLE

The four-tuple is a way of representing a person's sensory experience at a moment in time. Its general form is V, K, A, O. These capital letters are abbreviations for the major sensory channels: Visual, Kinesthetic, Auditory, and Olfactory/Gustatory.

FIGURE 21.1

Eye-Accessing Cues

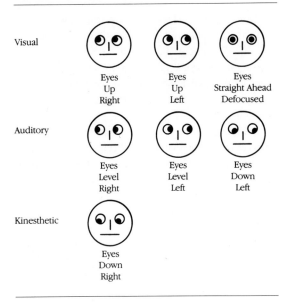

Visual		
Eyes Up Right	Eyes Up Left	Eyes Straight Ahead Defocused

Auditory

Eyes Level Right   Eyes Level Left   Eyes Down Left

Kinesthetic

Eyes Down Right

It is also useful to distinguish between experiences that are internally generated (remembering or imagining a visual image, feeling, sound, or smell), and experiences that are externally generated (sights, sensations, sounds, or smells that we receive from the external world). Therefore the superscript *e* is used to refer to external cues and superscript *i* to internal cues. The experience of someone whose senses are fully turned outward is: V^e, K^e, A^e, O^e. Someone attending fully to an internal event, oblivious of the immediate surroundings is V^i, K^i, A^i, O^i.

Most of us, at any point in time, are generally in a mixed state in which some of our senses are outwardly attending and some of our experiences are remembered or imagined. It is also true that many times one or more of the sensory systems will not be in use. The following example shows how this notational system can be used. Whenever Mrs. Worth *hears* about the Christmas season, she *visualizes* being at her husband's funeral several years ago, two days before

Christmas day. (He was killed in an automobile accident.) She remembers how depressed she *felt* afterwards. These cues in sequence are: A^e, V^i, K^i.

The usefulness of this concept can be readily demonstrated. Think about the last time you said something to someone and received an unusual response. Undoubtedly what happened was that your intended message led the listener to remember auditory, visual, kinesthetic, or olfactory events from the past, which then led the listener to response primarily in terms of the internal cues. NLP makes an important point by asserting: *The meaning of a communication is the response it elicits, regardless of the intent.*

In therapy, an NLP counselor frequently seeks to identify the patterns of the thought processes that are destructive or disturbing to clients and then seeks directly or indirectly to change these patterns. Two of the techniques that are used in this process are metaphors and reframing.

CAUSING CHANGE BY COMMUNICATING IN METAPHOR

NLP uses the term *metaphor* to refer to the use of anecdotes, puns, analogies, and stories in therapy. Metaphors are particularly useful for clients who tend to resist direct suggestions. Metaphors also stimulate the interest of clients. One of the most recognized experts in the use of metaphors was Dr. Milton Erickson, a psychiatrist. (John Grinder and Richard Bandler studied Erickson's techniques extensively while developing the NLP approach.)

Haley (1973, pp. 27–28) provides the following example of Erickson's use of metaphors in working with a married couple who are embarrassed about discussing directly a conflict over their sexual relationship.

He will choose some aspect of their lives that is analogous to sexual relations and change that as a way of changing the sexual behavior. He might, for example, talk to them about having dinner together and draw them out on their preferences. He will discuss with

*them how the wife likes appetizers before dinner,
while the husband prefers to dive right into the meat
and potatoes. Or the wife might prefer a quiet and
leisurely dinner, while the husband, who is quick and
direct, just wants the meal over with. . . . He might
end such a conversation with a directive that the
couple arrange a pleasant dinner on a particular
evening that is satisfactory to both of them. When successful, this approach shifts the couple from a more
pleasant dinner to more pleasant sexual relations
without their being aware that he has deliberately set
this goal.*

I have used storytelling (with some stories being
real and others contrived to fit the clients' circumstances) with a variety of clients. The following are
some examples. A twenty-one-year-old male college
student was thinking of taking his life because his girlfriend had left him to date someone else; he was not
receiving the grades he desired; and he did not know
what he wanted to major in. I asked him to visualize the
following scene.

*Let's assume you slit your wrist this evening and no
one discovers you until you're dead. There will be
blood all over. Tomorrow morning your younger
brother or someone else will discover you in this pool
of blood. For months and years afterward this person
will have nightmares about this scene. Eventually he
may seek to end his nightmares in the same way you
did—that happens! After they find you, a funeral director will be called and he will embalm you, which
involves a variety of unpleasant procedures. Your
parents will be shocked, and will forevermore be
searching for why you did what you did—and
feeling guilty that they had failed you. Your former
girlfriend will be temporarily shocked, but she will experience a sense of relief that you will no longer be
able to seek to manipulate her by threatening suicide.
She'll move on with her life and eventually marry
someone else. People will come to your funeral and
say a variety of things, including the statement that
you didn't have the courage to face life's problems. In
this funeral scene of mental anguish and confusion,
the cover of the coffin will then be closed. You will be
taken to the cemetery. Perhaps it's raining and chilly.*

*You will be lowered into the ground, and slowly your
body will deteriorate. If there is an air leak in the coffin, you will deteriorate much faster—perhaps worms
may enter. Is this what you want?*

Most people who are contemplating suicide think
only about the pain and difficulties they are facing. The
preceding story helps them see that what happens after
suicide may be worse than their present agony. In the
above case the male student stopped thinking about
taking his life and started focusing on resolving the
problems he faced.

For a twenty-one-year-old woman who was dating
a married man (the married man refused to come into
counseling), I vividly told a detailed story about another client who had a miserable life for seven years
while dating a married man; that man refused to leave
his wife for financial reasons and because he did not
want to disappoint his children. This story helped the
woman to give her male friend an ultimatum—either
you leave your wife in thirty days or our relationship is
over. In this case the man refused to leave his wife and
the woman ended the relationship.

For a fifteen-year-old adolescent female who
thought her life would improve if she became pregnant and then had a child who would love her, I arranged for a single working mother (in her twenties)
to talk about the following: young children take love
and affection; they give very little in return; the financial costs of raising a child are enormous; having the
responsibility of being a mother is a full time job that
interferes with dating, partying, forming a relationship
with a male, and developing a career. After this talk, the
fifteen-year-old decided to wait for several years before
wanting to again try to become a parent.

REFRAMING

Reframing involves turning clients' negative behavior,
thoughts, and feelings into resources. The function of
the problem part is simply altered for the client's benefit to get her what she wants more effectively.

CASE EXAMPLE

Reframing

A twenty-eight-year-old wife came into treatment because she wanted her husband to stop drinking so much. She indicated that one or two nights a week her husband would stop off at a bar with other construction workers. The wife indicated that he would usually be two or three hours late for dinner and would be quite intoxicated when he arrived home. She would then chastise him for being late, for spending their scarce money on alcohol, and for ruining her evening by his "foolish talk." The husband generally reacted with name-calling and by verbally abusing his wife in other ways. The wife added that there were generally problems in the marriage only when her husband was drinking. She also stated that her husband denies he has a drinking problem and refuses to join her in counseling. The counselor reframed the positive intent of her behavior in the following manner:

It appears that both you and your husband get along well except when he's been drinking. When he comes home drunk, you definitely want to make the best of the situation. Up until now your wanting to do so has led you to respond by verbally getting on his case for drinking. At that point he probably feels a need to defend himself and a 'blow-up' occurs. Since you want to avoid the heated exchanges with him when he's drunk, I'm wondering if there aren't other actions you can take — such as taking a walk by yourself, going shopping, or going to visit someone when he is intoxicated?

The wife thought about this for a while and concluded the such suggestions might well work. In the next session a month later she reported that the strategy of leaving home when her husband came home intoxicated was working out well. Since she realized she did not have the capacity to stop her husband from drinking, she stated that reducing the difficulties the drinking created was her next best choice.

NLP asserts that it is enduringly useful to presuppose a positive intent behind all behavior. The focus of reframing is to separate the positive intent from the negative behavior so that the positive intent then becomes linked to new positive behavior.

According to NLP "The cure lies within" the client. Clients already have the resources they need to resolve their difficulties. Clients who are in problematic situations are generally making undesirable choices. Reframing is a way to help clients make more constructive choices.

THERAPEUTIC CHANGE OFTEN OCCURS WITHOUT THE CAUSE OF THE PROBLEM BEING KNOWN

Counselors in traditional psychotherapeutic approaches spend considerable time trying to assess the causes of the problematic behavior. NLP asserts that positive changes can occur without intense attention being directed at the causes. Instead, the focus is on first identifying what the client wants and then on helping the client to identify the resources he already has and the ways to achieve his goals.

A college student walked into my office at the start of a spring semester. She stated she was very depressed, and her slumped posture, downcast eyes, and sad facial expressions verified this assessment. She started rambling on about how she had received a speeding ticket over vacation and that she was also sad about seeing a former male friend dating someone else. The following transactions then occurred:

COUNSELOR: "Can you now do anything constructive about these two situations?"

CLIENT: "No."

COUNSELOR: "Do you realize that dwelling on them will only make you more depressed?"

CLIENT: "Yes."

COUNSELOR: "We need instead to focus on what you now want. Do you know what you now want?"

CLIENT: "Yes, to be happy and face this semester with an optimistic outlook."

COUNSELOR: "Good, now we're getting someplace. Tell me about some of the things you could do in the next few hours that are enjoyable for you and that will also get your mind off upsetting things that you can't change."

The client at this point began talking about a variety of things she could do—taking a walk, calling some friends to get together for lunch, and listening to her stereo. The more she talked about these things, the more relaxed she became. After about ten more minutes of talking, she smiled, said good-bye, and proceeded to get involved in her enjoyable activities.

EVALUATION

NLP is indeed rich in new concepts. The concepts described here are some of the more prominent NLP principles, but are only a small subset of the tenets of NLP. The interested reader is encouraged to read fur-

ther in texts (such as those referenced in this chapter) and attend NLP training institutes (a number of such institutes are being offered in various regions of the country).

The concept of studying the verbal and nonverbal communication patterns between prominent therapists and their clients to identify what causes positive changes has considerable merit. NLP includes a number of concepts that are useful in explicating how one person (therapist, teacher, salesperson, public speaker) can influence another. Many of these concepts (e.g., joining with the client's representational system builds rapport) are described in this chapter.

The concepts advanced by NLP have considerable power in enabling influencers to influence people more effectively. There are also some criticisms that can be made about NLP:

1. Little research has been conducted on NLP to test out the principles and concepts it has advanced.

2. NLP is not a theory of human behavior, and therefore it does not have sufficient concepts that can be used independently to assess the causes of emotional and behavioral difficulties. The principles and concepts of NLP are perhaps best viewed as being useful adjuncts to other theories in assessing and changing human behavior.

3. One of the stated goals of NLP is to identify the key psychotherapeutic change agents that result in positive changes for clients undergoing therapy. NLP includes a number of concepts in this area, including the therapist's finding a way to "join" with the client and then "leading" the client in a positive direction. "Joining" and "leading" may well be essential components in the process of influencing. However, I question whether "joining" and "leading" are the key psychotherapeutic change agents for treating emotional and behavioral problems. (I present an alternative explanation in Chapter 23 which asserts that restructuring thinking patterns is the key psychotherapeutic change agent.) With its focus on only what is observable, NLP largely ignores thinking patterns—and thereby NLP may be failing to focus on what may be the key component to changing unwanted emotions and dysfunctional behaviors (see Chapter 23 for an elaboration).

SUMMARY

NLP was developed by John Grinder, Richard Bandler, and several other authorities. NLP is a model of communication that has substantial application in assessing human behavior, in influencing others (in education, sales, and public speaking), and in psychotherapy. Grinder and Bandler studied the communication patterns of prominent psychotherapists with their clients in order to identify the kinds of communication patterns that lead to positive changes in clients. This research led to the development of NLP.

NLP is the study of the structure of subjective experience. It makes explicit patterns of behavior and change that have previously been only intuitively understandable. NLP has advanced a number of concepts and techniques that are useful in assessment, building rapport, and treating clients. These concepts and techniques include sensory representational systems; the map is not the territory; joining with the client's representational system builds rapport; influencing someone involves the influencer joining and then leading the influencee; predicates identify representational systems; eye-accessing cues; four-tuples; use of metaphors in counseling; reframing; and therapeutic change often occurs without knowing the cause of the problem. The principles and concepts of NLP appear to be useful ideas that can be used as adjuncts to other theories in assessing and treating emotional difficulties and dysfunctional behavior.

EXERCISES

1. Eye-Accessing Cues

GOAL: This exercise is designed to demonstrate that visual, auditory, and kinesthetic representational systems can be identified by eye-accesing cues.

Step 1: Prior to this exercise the instructor should study carefully the position of the eyeballs in Figure 21.1 that identify visual, auditory, and kinesthetic representational systems. The instructor begins the exercise by asking for two volunteers. The two volunteers should be seated facing the class. The instructor should sit somewhere with the rest of the class. (None of the students in the class should be informed about eye-accessing cues.) The instructor should then ask the two volunteers to answer silently to themselves the questions that follow. After each question is asked, the instructor should pause for the volunteers to arrive at their answers. The instructor should record after each question the position of the eyeballs — suggesting which representational system is being used. It is likely that some students may use more than one representational system (e.g., both visual and auditory) in answering a question. When this happens, the instructor should record the two or more positions of the eyeballs. The five questions are these":

What do you remember most about _____

1. The last grocery store you were in?
2. What you did on your last birthday?
3. The last time you were really angry?
4. What you did on New Year's Eve?
5. Your most romantic experience?

Step 2: After the questions are asked, the instructor should (for the eye-accessing cues that are fairly identifiable) ask questions of the volunteers according to the following code.

1. Visual—Did you have a visual image or picture of your answer to question _____?
2. Auditory—Did you hear some sounds in your answer to questions _____?
3. Kinesthetic—Did you have a feeling experience in your answer to question _____?

Step 3: The instructor in all probability will be fairly accurate in identifying the representational systems through these eye-accessing cues. The instructor should next ask the class for their ideas on how these representational systems were identified. The instructor should then describe eye-accessing cues.

Step 4: As an optional step, the instructor can assign the students to ask a friend the same, or similar questions, outside of class, requesting the friend to answer silently to himself. The students should then seek to identify (using the same procedures used by the instructors in steps 1, 2 and 3) the sensory representational systems that were used by their friends. The experiences of the students in using eye-accessing cues can then be discussed at the next class period.

2. Joining

GOAL: This exercise is designed to help students learn how to build better rapport with strangers (and future clients).

Step 1: The instructor begins by describing the purpose of the exercise. Explain that NLP asserts that rapport with others is enhanced by (a) using predicates that are consistent with the other person's representational system; (b) mirroring, in a non-noticeable way, the gestures, posture, and breathing patterns of the other person; and (c) talking knowledgeably about topics that are of interest to the other person. Practically everyone is aware of the last-mentioned method.

Step 2: Assign the students the tasks of starting conversations with three different strangers (or three people they do not know very well). During these conversations ask them to try to use predicates that are consistent with the stranger's representational systems and to mirror the gestures, posture, and breathing patterns of the strangers in a non-noticeable manner.

Step 3: At the next class period discuss the following: (a) What were the results of the student's efforts? (b) Did the students have difficulty in using predicates that are consistent with the stranger's representational systems? (c) Did the students have difficulty in mirroring behavior? Do the students think these techniques are useful in building rapport?

22

PROMINENT SPECIFIC TREATMENT TECHNIQUES

P rior chapters in this text have presented treatment techniques that are components of such comprehensive theories of psychotherapy as behavior therapy, transactional analysis, and rational therapy. This chapter summarizes a variety of other treatment techniques that have been used to treat clients who have emotional or behavioral problems. These treatment approaches were developed independently of (were not a part of) a comprehensive theory of psychotherapy; for lack of a better term, the techniques are referred to in this chapter as *specific treatment approaches.*

Therapy techniques covered in this chapter are relaxation approaches, meditation, hypnosis, biofeedback, crisis intervention, task-centered practice, milieu therapy, play therapy, psychodrama, parental education, and mediation. Of these approaches the following have been used by social workers for many years: crisis intervention, milieu therapy, play therapy, parental education, and psychodrama. Mediation is a technique that has existed for some time, but until recently, only a few social workers used the technique. In recent years the approach has increasingly been used by social workers to help resolve conflicts between two or more people. Relaxation approaches, meditation, hypnosis, and biofeedback have been around a long time, but have infrequently been used by social workers; however, with the recognition that stress (and resulting psychosomatic illnesses) is our nation's number one health problem (Pelletier, 1974), there has been a rising interest in training social workers to use these approaches.

MILIEU THERAPY

Milieu therapy involves the creation of a learning/living environment that systematically uses the events that occur in day-to-day living as formats for treating emotional and behavior problems of people. The theory behind the use of a therapeutic milieu is that the person's environment has an immense impact on behavior and can be structured to have a beneficial effect on changing deviant behavior as well as antisocial norms and values.

There are several models of milieu treatment. Milieu programs have been based on a wide variety of intervention approaches including reality therapy, behavior therapy, rational therapy, client-centered therapy, and psychoanalysis. Some milieu programs emphasize using individual therapy as part of the milieu, while others place heavy emphasis on changing behavioral and emotional problems in a group context. A token economy (described in Chapter 19) is one type of a milieu treatment program. Milieu programs typically include a team approach of professional staff members, such as social workers, psychiatrists, psychologists, special education teachers, occupational and physical therapists, and psychiatric nurses.

Although the components of milieu programs vary widely, there are some common focuses. Programs are usually formed on such principles as being democratic, permissive and humanistic, and having reality-oriented living experiences. Milieu programs assume that lasting changes are more likely to take place through group interactional experiences. The community (including the professional staff, nonprofessional staff, and residents) meet and interact regularly, often discussing common problems. An underlying philosophy is that personal problems primarily involve faulty interactions with others, and that an examination of these difficulties through discussion can lead to understanding and resolution. Usually the traditional pyramid of authority is flattened in milieu programs. Generally there is frequent reevaluation of staff roles and ways of functioning (Black, 1977).

Milieu programs have been used with a variety of client populations, including juvenile delinquents, mental patients, mentally retarded children and adults, the elderly, alcoholics and drug abusers, emotionally disturbed children, and correctional clients. Settings in which milieu programs have been used are mental hospitals, day hospitals for the emotionally disturbed, halfway houses, residential treatment centers, day-care programs for disturbed children, nursing homes, group homes, correctional institutions, therapeutic communities for alcohol and drug abusers, and sheltered workshops.

The therapeutic community is one of the treatment programs that is often selected in treating drug addiction in this country. The theory is that drug addiction is a form of behavior that is encouraged by a particular subculture and that therapeutic communities will provide group support to help a person give up his commitment to the drug subculture and also pressure the person to replace previous norms and values with those acceptable to the general society.

PSYCHODRAMA

The primary developer of psychodrama was J. L. Moreno (1946). The objective of psychodrama is to assist a client or client group to overcome personal problems through the use of role-playing, drama, or action therapy. Through these media clients are helped to express feelings of conflict, anger, aggression, guilt, and sadness. Moreno, as did Freud, thought the expression of pent-up emotions had a cathartic effect (eliminated emotional complexes by bringing them to consciousness and allowing the emotional energy to be expressed).

Moreno also thought psychodrama was therapeutic because a person who wants to change maladaptive behavior is presented with feedback about his behavior and allowed to try out and practice new behaviors. Psychodramas can be arranged to have other people model alternative behaviors and then to have the client practice new behaviors that are designed in a particular sequence to ensure success. Thus, the client can practice new behaviors in small bits until he incorporates them into his role repertoire and gains mastery through practice.

Psychodrama is a group therapy approach. Whittaker (1974, p. 230) provides a brief description of psychodrama:

Psychodrama uses four major instruments: the stage, which is both the psychological and physical living space for the subject or client; the director, or worker; the staff of "auxiliary egos," or therapeutic aides; and the audience. Both the auxiliary egos and the audience are made up of other group members. The strat-

Psychodrama, which challenges individuals' self-concepts through role-playing and action therapy, has been used in a variety of settings. At a Lake Tahoe seminar for trial judges attended by police and probation officers, prosecutors, legislators, and convicts, role reversal and other psychodrama techniques were employed in a dialogue on the merits of the American criminal justice system. The workshop, held in the late 1960s, served as a model for similar conferences across the country for the next ten years. Left, criminologist Richard Korn (in white shirt, standing) directs a scene; below, a convict demonstrates how he was frished by police officers after being apprehended.

egy is to enable the subject to project himself into his own world and draw responses from fellow group members. Below are several commonly used techniques:

1. *Self-presentation.* The client presents himself or a figure who is significant in his life.

2. *Direct soliloquy.* The client steps out of the drama and speaks to herself or to the group.

3. *Double technique.* An auxiliary ego acts with the client and does everything the client does and at the same time.

4. *Mirror technique.* An auxiliary ego acts in place of the client as clearly as he can. The client watches from the audience to see himself as others see him.

5. *Role reversal.* The client assumes the role of her antagonist and an auxiliary ego plays the client's part.

The director or worker functions as the producer and as the therapist. As the producer she selects and arranges the scenes and also directs the psychodrama action. The scenes are selected to reflect the client's problem, perhaps an emotionally charged situation for the client or one in which the client is behaving ineffectively or inappropriately. As the therapist, the worker provides the actors with support and clarification; at times she makes interpretations (often with the help of the other group members) of the play action.

Psychodrama presently is used by practitioners who subscribe to a variety of psychotherapeutic theories. Gestalt therapists, in particular, make extensive use of psychodrama. Psychodrama has been used in marital therapy, with children, with drug and alcohol abusers, with people having emotional problems, in prison settings, in training psychiatric residents, in training people with physical and mental impairments; in business and industry, and in education and decision making. (Fine, 1979, p. 487) notes:

We have all had experience with psychodrama. As children, one way we tested and mastered the world was to play roles. Lori put a coronet in her hair and became a queen and her girlfriend became her lady-in-waiting. Gary built satellites and took elaborate interstellar space explorations in his room. Children's play is an enactment of their fantasies in which they practice the social roles of their culture. The action and enacting world of the child is full of energy, excitement, and social learning. . . .

Modern psychodrama is an extension of life in which catharsis and insight are available not only to the audience but to the players as well.

Barocas (1972) provides an illustration of one use of psychodrama. He used this technique to train police officers to handle family crises more effectively. Domestic fights have become a serious hazard to many metropolitan police officers, as the "family disturbance call" has become the single most frequent source of injury and death to these officers. Barocas hired trained actors and actresses to perform skits that were developed from actual family fights reported by police officers. These simulated fights involved arguments around such themes as child abuse, alcoholism, incest, unemployment, and infidelity. After the actors developed the basic fight, the police officer trainees intervened. These psychodrama skits were videotaped and other police officer trainees observed the intervention

approach which was then discussed in a group. The trainees who role-played were also shown the videotape and their performance was then critiqued further. Barocas concluded that this approach was effective in improving the way police officers handled family disputes.

PLAY THERAPY

Play therapy is used with young children. Play is seen as a young child's most natural vehicle for self-expression and is therefore viewed by play therapists as a method for relating to and communicating with young children. Play therapy may serve multiple purposes: diagnosis, relationship formation, ventilation of feelings by the child, working through unwanted emotions, teaching the child desired new behaviors, and providing a format for modeling alternative behavior.

Play therapists vary on a continuum from almost totally nondirective to highly directive. Play therapy can be used by therapists with widely diverging orientations including psychoanalysis, client-centered therapy, reality therapy, rational therapy, transactional analysis, and behavior therapy.

Whittaker (1974, pp. 225–26) gives the following brief description of play therapy:

The therapist may use initial play sessions for diagnostic purposes to observe such things as relationship, attention span, areas of preoccupation, areas of inhibition, direction of aggression, wishes and fantasies, and self-perception. Depending upon orientation, the therapist typically encourages free play with a variety of available materials (paints, dolls, punching bags, puzzles, clay), interprets the child's affect to him ("You seem to be angry at the doll"), and finally offers insights into the child's behavior. The child may experience some regression to earlier levels of functioning while in the play situation and also may practice newly acquired skills and try on new behaviors. A centered notion of play therapy is that the child is expressing symbolically through play the conflicts he is experiencing in the outside world. In the relative

CASE EXAMPLE

Play Therapy

D awn, age seven, was a second grader who was referred by her teacher to a school social worker. Academically and socially she was functioning far behind her peers, even though tests showed she was of normal intelligence. The social worker observed her in her play interactions with peers. She was withdrawn and tried to avoid competitive game situations. Forced to participate she would quit whenever she fell behind. When the social worker discussed Dawn's behavior with her teacher, the teacher indicated that Dawn shied away from doing her assignments and seldom completed any. Dawn was observed for a few sessions in a playroom at school. At one point Dawn held the mother doll and called the baby girl "stupid," and also stated, "You'll never be able to do what your brother does." The social worker felt that Dawn's academic and social problems were resulting from Dawn's having such a low self-concept that she had virtually given up trying. Dawn's interactions with the dolls suggested her mother might be contributing to her low self-concept by disparaging her. Several meetings were then held with Dawn's parents, with Dawn present for two of these. The social worker observed that the mother was highly critical of Dawn without ever praising her. Dawn was placed in a special educational program for the next year and one-half; here she received close attention and considerable praise for her academic and social efforts. The worker also counseled the parents on how they were contributing to her low self-concept and how they needed to praise Dawn for her efforts and to get her more involved in interests she had. On three separate occasions Dawn, her parents, Dawn's brother, and the social worker met in a playroom. The family members were encouraged to play together in various games, and the parents were instructed to praise Dawn whenever she made efforts to participate positively. Also, Dawn's mother was encouraged to refrain from disparaging Dawn. After this intensive program, Dawn was able to rejoin her class at the start of the fourth grade and had become much more outgoing and self-confident.

In *Play Therapy*, now a classic, Axline (1947) provides a number of other case examples in which play therapy has been used for diagnostic purposes, for helping children to understand themselves and their problems better, and to help them grow and resolve their problems.

safety of the play situation, these conflicts can be worked through and — so the theory goes — transferred to the child's real-life situation.

Play therapy generally takes place in a playroom, with usually only the child and the therapist present. At times other children are present, which helps a child learn to interact more effectively with others. Occasionally parents attend the play therapy sessions, which helps them to have a better understanding of their child and to learn more effective interaction approaches with their child. Play materials include such items as a variety of dolls (usually composing a doll family), puppets, clay and finger paints, crayons, sandbox, toy animals, soldiers and weapons, and cutting-out materials. In play therapy children are generally allowed to express themselves as freely as they desire. The principal limits that are set are usually minimal: establishing the duration of the play sessions, forbidding the willful destruction of play materials, and forbidding the child from physically attacking others in the playroom.

In recent years a number of protective services programs have used anatomically correct dolls to gather information from young children who are suspected victims of sexual abuse. A worker first forms a relationship with a child and then asks the child to show, with the dolls, what the alleged perpetrator did. In some jurisdictions this process is videotaped and is available for court use if formal charges are brought against the alleged perpetrator. This use of the doll is primarily for investigative purposes.

PARENTAL EDUCATION: PARENT EFFECTIVENESS TRAINING

The primary goal of parental education programs is to help parents understand child behavior and to develop child-rearing skills. Most programs are based on the assumption that rearing children is a difficult and complex task for which society ill prepares young people. A number of theoreticians have developed somewhat different educational programs: Dreikurs (1964), Ginott (1965), Gordon (1970), Patterson (1971), and Spock (1957). These programs use a variety of educational formats: short courses, small discussion groups, and programmed self-instruction.

Probably the most popular program is Parent Effectiveness Training (PET). The basic concepts of this approach are presented, partly because some of the techniques, such as *Active Listening*, *I-messages*, and *no-loss problem solving*, are techniques that any person can use to interact more effectively with others. PET was developed by Thomas Gordon (1970).

Parent Effectiveness Training (PET) courses are now being offered in hundreds of communities throughout this country and have been endorsed by numerous public and private agencies serving parents and youth. The PET system has been found to work effectively with children of all ages. The program leads to warmer and more harmonious relationships between parents and their children, and children learn to become more responsible. The principles are applicable not only for parents and parent surrogates (such as teachers, principals, counselors, and youth leaders) but can be used also by anyone to improve interactions with others.

Parents Are Persons, Not Gods

Gordon urges parents to be "real" in their relationships with children. "Realness" is much more important than the impossible guidelines of always being consistent in displaying feelings, putting up a "united front," and being unconditionally tolerant and accepting. In a close relationship it is impossible to hide's one's true feelings. It is normal and real for parents to be accepting of some behaviors of their children and nonaccepting of other behaviors. Parents should recognize their true feelings and not attempt to convey false acceptance when they dislike what their children are doing. It is normal and real for one parent to be more accepting than the other, and one parent may feel accepting and the other nonaccepting of the same behavior. Being honest and human in interacting with children will improve a relationship substantially more than trying to convey false acceptance or trying always to be consistent.

Who Owns the Problem?

PET asserts that appropriate parental responses depend on the question: "Who owns the problem?" A person owns a problem only when the situation affects the person's ability to get her needs met in a concrete and tangible way. If the *child* is the owner of a problem, then *active listening* is an appropriate technique for a parent to use. If the *parent* owns the problem, then *I-messages* are appropriate for the parent to use. If the situation involves a conflict between the parent and the child in meeting the needs of both, then *no-lose problem solving* is an appropriate technique. If the situation involves a conflict in values between the parent and the child, Gordon provides guidelines for *resolving collisions of values.*

Active Listening

When a sixteen-year-old son announces "I hate school and I'm going to drop out," parents can respond in a variety of ways: ordering him to stay in school, warning the youth he will be sorry if he goes not, moralizing by saying it would not be proper or right, giving advice by saying the youth should discuss it with the high school counselor, and so forth. Such approaches are generally not effective or productive in helping children to express their feelings, explore their problems, and arrive at a comfortable solution.

Active listening, PET asserts, is a much more effective way of interacting. The following steps are involved in active listening: (*a*) the receiver of a message tries to understand what the sender's message means or what the sender is feeling; and (*b*) the receiver then puts this understanding into her own words and returns this understanding for the sender's verification. In using this approach, the receiver does *not* send a message of her own—such as a question, giving advice, expressing her feelings, or giving an opinion. The aim is to feed back only what she feels the sender's message meant. Active listening is a difficult skill to learn and takes practice to master.

This approach is illustrated below in a set of interactions, with the parent consistently using the active listening technique.

YOUTH: I hate school, and I'm going to drop out.
PARENT: You're fed up with school and thinking about leaving.
YOUTH: Yes I am! My teachers are really bummers this year.
PARENT: You're disappointed with your current teachers.
YOUTH: Especially with my Spanish teacher. He asks us

questions in Spanish and expects us to be able to understand what he's saying. All I hear is words that I can't understand.
PARENT: You're having trouble understanding your Spanish teacher when he speaks in Spanish.
YOUTH: On written exams I've been getting A's and B's, but most of the other students in class appear to understand Spanish better when it is spoken.
PARENT: Your grades show that you are doing well in Spanish, but you have trouble understanding Spanish when it is spoken.
YOUTH: Yes, I wonder what I could do to learn to understand people better when they speak in Spanish.
PARENT: You're wondering how you can better learn to hear and speak in Spanish.
YOUTH: Perhaps I could talk to my teacher about this. He might have some ideas.

Gordon lists a number of advantages for using the active listening technique. It facilitates problem solving by the child, which fosters the development of responsibility. By talking a problem through, a person is more apt to identify the root of the problem and arrive at a solution than by merely thinking about a problem. When a child feels that parents are listening to him, a by-product is that the child will be more apt to listen to the parents' point of view. In addition the relationship between parent and child is apt to be improved because when one feels he is being heard and understood by another person, he is apt to feel warmth toward the listener. Finally, the approach helps a child to explore, recognize, and express personal feelings.

Gordon notes that a parent needs to have certain attitudes in order to use the technique effectively. The parent must view the child as a separate person with his own feelings. The parent must be able to accept the child's feelings, whatever they may be. The parent should genuinely want to be helpful and must want to hear what the child has to say. And the parent must have trust in the child's capacities to handle personal problems and feelings.

In using the technique there are some common mistakes that parents make initially. One mistake is to use the technique with the intention of guiding the child's behavior or thinking toward what the parents think the child should do. If parents have this intention, children are apt to feel they are being manipulated and the approach may be counterproductive. A second mistake is to parrot back the words rather than the intended meaning or feeling. For instance, if a son yells at his father "you stupid jerk," an appropriate response geared to the message would be "you're angry with me," rather than parroting the words "you think I'm a jerk." A third mistake is to use active listening at the wrong time. If a child does not want to talk about his feelings, or is simply too tired, the parent should respect the child's right and need for privacy.

I-Messages

Active listening is used when the child has the problem. However, many occasions arise when the child causes a problem for the parent: for example, a child is talking loudly in church, or getting too close to a precious glass vase, or is about to walk on a new carpet with muddy shoes, or is recklessly driving an auto. In such cases entirely different communication skills are required. Confronted with such situations, many parents send either a *solution message* (they order, direct, command, warn, threaten, preach, moralize, or advise) or a *put-down message* (they blame, judge, criticize, ridicule, or namecall). Solution and put-down messages can have devastating effects on a child's self-concept and are generally counterproductive in helping a child become responsible.

Solution and put-down messages are primarily you-messages: "you do what I say," "don't you do that," "why don't you be good," "you're lazy," "you should know better."

PET advocates that parents should instead send *I-messages* for those occasions when a child is causing a problem for the parent. For example, if a child is walking on a clean carpet with dirty shoes, instead of saying, "John, get off that carpet, you're a pig!" PET urges parents to use an I-message: "I shampooed the living room rug today, and want to keep it clean as long as possible."

I-messages, in essence, are nonblaming messages that communicate only how the sender of the message believes the receiver is adversely affecting the sender. I-messages do not provide a solution nor are they put-down messages. It is possible to send an I-message without using the word "I," as the essence of I-messages involves sending a nonblaming message of how the parent feels the child's behavior is affecting the parent. For example, a parent, riding in a car driven by the seventeen-year-old son who is exceeding the speed limit, may say, "Driving fast really terrifies me."

You-messages are generally put-down messages that convey to a child either that he should do something or that he is bad. In contrast, I-messages communicate to a child much more honestly the effect of the behavior on the parent. I-messages are also more effective because they help children learn to assume responsibility for their own behavior. An I-message tells children that the parent trusts them to respect the parent's needs, that the parent is leaving the responsibility with them, and that the parent is trusting them to handle the situation constructively.

You-messages frequently end up in a struggle between parent and child while I-messages are much less likely to produce an argument. I-messages lead to honesty and openness in a relationship and generally foster intimacy. Children, as well as adults, often do not know how their behavior affects others. I-messages produce startling results as parents frequently report that their children express surprise upon learning how their parents really feel.

For illustrative purposes, some examples of you-messages and I-messages will be given:

You-Messages	I-Messages
1. Don't you ever kick me again; you're a real pain.	Ouch! That kick really hurt me.
2. John, you stop pestering me now!	John, I am very tired today, and I just do not have the energy to play with you this evening.
3. You're a reckless driver and someday you'll kill someone.	I'm afraid to drive with you when you drive so fast.
4. You didn't mow the lawn today as you promised. You're so lazy and never help with the work around here.	I'm upset that the lawn didn't get mowed today. We're having company this evening, and I'm embarrassed about how the lawn looks.

No-Lose Problem Solving

In every parent-child relationship there are inevitable situations in which the child continues to behave in a way that interferes with the needs of the parent. Conflict is part of life and not necessarily bad. Conflict is bound to occur because people are different and have different needs and wants, which at times do not match. What is important is not how frequently conflict arises but how the conflicts get resolved. Generally in a conflict between parent and child, a power struggle is created.

In many families the power struggle is resolved by one of two *win-lose* approaches. Most parents try to resolve the conflict by having the parent win and the child lose. Psychologically, parents almost always are recognized as having greater size, greater authority. When the parent wins it creates resentment in the child toward her parents, leads to low motivation for the child to carry out the solution, and does not provide an opportunity for the child to develop self-discipline and self-responsibility. Such children are likely to react by becoming either rebellious and aggressive or dependent and withdrawing.

In other families (fewer in number) the win-lose conflict is resolved when parents give in to their children out of fear of frustrating their children or fear of conflict. In such families children come to believe their needs are more important than anyone else's, and they generally become self-centered, selfish, demanding, impulsive, and uncontrollable. They are viewed by others as being spoiled, they have difficulty in interacting with peers, and also they do not have respect for property or feelings of others.

Of course, few parents use either approach exclusively. Oscillating between the two approaches is common. There is evidence that both approaches lead to the development of emotional problems in children (Gordon, 1970, p. 161).

The two win-lose approaches are illustrated in the following situation:

Parent wins—child loses:

MOTHER: Since I'm now working we need to divide the work tasks around the house. I'll continue to do most of the work, but from now on I'd like you to wash the dishes in the evening.

JOHN: But I don't like washing dishes.

MOTHER: Well, I don't like cooking, and washing and ironing clothes, but have to do them. We all have to do things we don't like to do.

JOHN: Washing dishes is for girls.

MOTHER: Look, I'm not going to argue with you about this. You're now old enough to help out. In this family we all have to contribute. If you don't do the dishes you won't receive your allowance. In fact, from now on, every evening you do not wash dishes, fifty cents will be deducted from your weekly allowance.

Child wins—parent loses:

MOTHER: Since I'm now working we need to divide the work tasks around the house. I'll continue to do most of the work, but from now on I'd like you to wash the dishes in the evening.

JOHN: But I don't like washing dishes.

MOTHER: Why?

JOHN: Washing dishes is for girls.

MOTHER: But many boys help their mothers with the dishes.

JOHN: Tom and Gary don't help their mothers. What would they say about me washing dishes?

MOTHER: You may be right. Could you instead help me with washing clothes, or dusting, or cleaning your room?

JOHN: Aw—Mom, those things are for girls too.

MOTHER: *(Dejectedly.)* Well, OK, I'll try to do these things while also working.

Gordon seriously questions whether power is necessary or justified in a parent-child relationship. As a child grows older he becomes less dependent and parents gradually lose their power. Rewards and punishments that worked in younger years become less effective as the child grows older. Children resent those who have power over them, and parents frequently feel guilty after using power. Gordon believes that parents continue to use power because they have had little experience in using nonpower methods of influence.

PET suggests a new approach, the *no-lose approach* to solving conficts. The approach is to have each parent and child solve their conflicts by finding their own unique solutions acceptable to both.

The following example illustrates this approach:

MOTHER: Since I'm now working I will have less time to do the work that needs to be done around the house. I would appreciate it if you would help me out with some of the things that need to be done.

JOHN: I think I could help—what needs to be done?

MOTHER: The meals need to be cooked, dishes washed, the house cleaned, grocery shopping done, and the garbage taken out.

JOHN: Let's see. I'd be willing to vacuum the floor and dust. Will my allowance be increased? I'd like to get a new bike.

MOTHER: Yes, since we'll have some more money now that I'm working, we could increase your allowance, with the increase dependent on how much additional work you do.

JOHN: In addition to helping to clean the house, I'd be willing to wash clothes if you show me what to do. I also could carry out the garbage.

The no-lose approach is simple to state: each person in the conflict treats the other with respect, neither person tries to win the conflict by the use of power, and a creative solution acceptable to both parties is sought. There are two basic premises to no-lose problem solving: (*a*) that all people have the right to have their needs met, and (*b*) that what is in conflict between the two parties involved is not their *needs* but their *solutions* to those needs.

Gordon (1970, p. 237) lists the six steps to the no-lose method:

Step 1: *Identifying and defining the needs of each person.*

Step 2: *Generating possible alternative solutions.*

Step 3: *Evaluating the alternative solutions.*

Step 4: *Deciding on the best acceptable solution.*

Step 5: *Working out ways of implementing the solution.*

Step 6: *Following up to evaluate how it worked.*

There are several advantages in this approach. It motivates children to carry out the solution because they participated in the decision. It develops the children's thinking skills and also develops responsibility. It requires less enforcement, eliminates the need for power, and improves relationships between parents.

Resolving Collisions of Values

Collisions of values are common between parents and their children, particularly as the children become adolescents and young adults. Likely areas of conflict include values about sexual behavior, clothing, religion, choice of friends, education, plans for the future, use of drugs, hairstyles, and eating habits. In these areas emotions run strong and parents generally seek to influence their offspring to follow the values the parents hold as important. Teenagers, on the other hand, often think their parents' values are old fashioned and stupid, and declare that they want to make their own decisions about these matters.

Dr. Gordon asserts there are three constructive ways in which parents and teenagers can seek to resolve these conflicts. (For the sake of simplicity, we will use the term *mother* in describing what should be done—a father or a teenager can also use these same techniques.)

The first way a mother can influence her offspring's values is to model the values she holds important. If she values honesty, she should be honest. If she values responsible use of drugs, she should exhibit a responsible model. If she values openness, she should be open. She needs to ask herself if she is living according to the values she professes. If her values and behaviors are incongruent in certain areas, she needs to change either her values or her behavior in the direction of congruency. Congruence between behavior and values is important if she wants to be an effective model.

The second way she can influence her teenagers' values is to act as a consultant to them. There are some do's and don't's of a good consultant. First of all, a good consultant finds out whether the other person would like her consultation. If the answer is "yes," she then makes sure she has all the available pertinent facts. She then shares these facts—once—so that the other person understands them. She then leaves the other person the responsibility for deciding whether to follow the advice. A good consultant is neither uninformed nor a nag; otherwise she is not apt to be used as a consultant again.

The third way for a mother to reduce tensions over values issues is to modify her values. By examining the values held by her teenagers, she may realize their values have merit, and she may move toward their values or at least toward an understanding of why they hold them as values.

In summary, PET concepts are designed to improve relationships between parents and children and to develop the concept of responsibility within children. A large number of parents who have participated in PET courses, or read *Parent Effectiveness Training*, have found them to be effective. In recent years, *these PET concepts have been found useful not only in improving relationships between parents and children but also in improving interactions and communication between people involved in practically any type of transaction.*

CRISIS INTERVENTION

Crisis intervention (CI) postulates that in a crisis situation current levels of functioning may be disrupted and previously manageable internal psychological difficulties stirred up. CI views the emotional disturbances presented by people facing crisis as being the result of (1) the stressful situation which a person faces, and (2) underlying emotional dispositions which come to the surface only in crisis situations. CI postulates that underlying emotional difficulties are ingredients of all personalities. People are viewed as being fairly normal in their general adjustment, with the crisis being a major cause of a person's emotional difficulties.

Figure 22.1 shows graphically the importance to people of successfully resolving crises that arise.

Crisis intervention postulates that a person is most vulnerable to change (either in a constructive or destructive direction) at the point of crisis, and therefore it is at this point that services (such as, counseling) are needed most and have the highest probability of having a positive effect. *Proponents of CI emphasize the*

FIGURE 22.1

The Effects of a Crisis

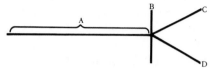

A. Prior to a crisis a person is functioning in a groove; that is, he has a relatively routine, stable kind of living with only minor changes.

B. A crisis arises (for example, being fired from a job) which places a person in an unfreezing position. This unfreezing position is emotionally charged and the person's lifestyle is highly vulnerable to change. In such a crisis, a person may take either the constructive (C) path or the destructive (D) path.

C. This constructive path has the person (perhaps with the assistance of others) gaining an awareness of why the crisis arose. The person develops adaptive ways of handling the crisis and thereby grows through acquiring problem-solving skills that will enable him to solve future crisis situations.

D. If the destructive path is followed, the person does not satisfactorily resolve the crisis. Unsolved aspects of the crisis remain, and the person is apt to develop maladaptive coping patterns. The person remains in an emotionally charged situation and is less able to face future crises that arise. Problems may well begin to snowball (for example, when a single, pregnant woman denies the pregnancy and makes no effort to begin making decisions that she will have to face).

importance of providing services when crises arise and are strongly opposed to agencies' placing people on waiting lists for services.

Golan (1979, p. 500) describes the typical efforts made by a person to resolve a crisis and the emotional reactions to a prolonged crisis:

First, he tries to use his customary repertoire of problem-solving mechanisms to deal with the situation. If this is not successful, his upset increases and he mobilizes heretofore untried emergency methods of coping. However, if the problem continues and can neither be resolved, avoided, nor redefined, tension continues to peak. . . .

As the crisis situation develops, the individual may perceive the initial and subsequent stressful events primarily as a threat, either to his instinctual needs or to his sense of autonomy and well-being; as

CASE EXAMPLE

Crisis Intervention

J ohn Franzene (age twenty-eight) went to work intoxicated one day and was promptly
informed by his supervisor that he was fired. John became incensed and yelled ob-
scenities at his supervisor. He then went to a local tavern and drank until he passed out. A
friend took him home. When his wife found out that John had been fired from his job as a
janitor, she packed her bags that evening and took the two children to live with her mother.
She indicated this was the "last straw."

John is an alcoholic and drinks an average of eight bottles of beer and a pint of whiskey
every day. He has been drinking excessively for the past decade. Three years ago his wife
separated from him because he was abusive to her and the children, both physically and
verbally, when intoxicated. At that time John promised to stop drinking if his wife would
only return; she did, and three weeks later he again began drinking. Five years ago he lost
his position as an elementary school teacher because of his drinking and his frequent absenteeism. Two years ago he lost his driver's license for driving while intoxicated. In the
past five years he has lost three other jobs because of his drinking.

The next day John went to his mother-in-law's home to try to talk his wife into returning home. She refused to speak to him. John, feeling sorry for himself, went to a local tavern and again got drunk. He blamed his supervisor for his current difficulties. While
intoxicated he decided to "straighten this matter out." He went to the office where he was
fired and got into a physical fight with his supervisor. He was arrested. While in jail he got
the "DTs" (delirium tremens), which really scared him. He was transferred to a hospital.
The doctor at the hospital explored his interest in receiving help for his drinking problem.

*a loss of a person, an attribute (status or role), or a
capacity; or as a challenge to survival, growth, or
mastery.*

*Each of these perceptions calls forth a character-
istic emotional reaction that reflects the subjective
meaning of the event to the individual: threat elicits a
heightened level of anxiety; loss brings about feelings
of depression, deprivation, and mourning; challenge
stimulates a moderate increase in anxiety plus a kin-
dling of hope and expectation, releasing new energy
for problem solving.*

Usually within four to six weeks after the onset of
the crisis, a new state of equilibrium is reached. This
state may be better than, the same as, or worse than the
precrisis level of functioning, depending on how well
the person has mastered the cognitive, emotional, and
behavioral tasks inherent in the crisis. During the reorganization phase, new adaptive coping styles may develop to enable the individual to deal more effectively
with future crises. However, maladaptive patterns may
also emerge, which result in decreased ability to cope
in the future.

John indicated he was willing to talk about it to someone, and he was referred to Tom Halaska, the hospital social worker.

For the first time in his life John acknowledged that he had a drinking problem and needed help. Mr. Halaska met with John on several occasions during the next four days. The ways that alcohol was affecting his life (including his job and his family life) were traced and John gained an awareness that he got into trouble only when he was drinking. Mr. Halaska explored the reasons John drank, and it became clear that he drank excessively when he was either with male friends in a tavern or when he sought to relieve unwanted emotions of feeling tense, moody, or depressed. John appeared at this time to be sincerely committed to giving up drinking. Mr. Halaska suggested that one of the things he would have to do to give up drinking was to stop getting together with his friends at a tavern. John indicated that saving his marriage meant more to him than getting together with his male friends. Mr. Halaska arranged a meeting between John and his wife. His wife agreed to return if John would first go one month without drinking, promise never to drink again, and actively participate in AA meetings. John agreed. Mr. Halaska referred him to an AA group and also referred him to the outpatient treatment unit of the mental health center. Among other services, this outpatient treatment service provided marriage counseling services to John and his wife and helped him explore other job opportunities.

John occasionally stops by the hospital to visit Mr. Halaska briefly. It has now been fourteen months since he had a drink. He is a sales clerk at a clothing store and is seeking a teaching position. He reports that he and his wife are getting along better than they ever have.

Additional case examples using crisis intervention are presented in Parad (1965).

Because a person is in an unfreezing position when a crisis arises, crisis intervention services often have a multiple opportunity: to resolve the current crisis and to resolve problems that the person has previously been denying or ignoring. For example, if a person is fired from a job because of drinking problems, services might be focused not only on helping a person obtain another job but also on breaking down the denial that a drinking problem does in fact exist and needs to be dealt with. Golan (1979, p. 500) notes that at the point of crisis

a minimal effort . . . can produce a maximal effect; a small amount of help, appropriately focused, can prove more effective than extensive help at a period of less emotional accessibility.

Crisis intervention services are generally brief and provided primarily during the period when the client is emotionally in desperate need. The specific treatment techniques that are used in crisis intervention are borrowed from other approaches. A few examples are presented here. Role-playing may be used to help a

Suicide prevention is a common form of crisis intervention in many large U.S. cities.

pregnant single woman gain confidence in how to inform her parents and to inform her sexual partner. Confrontation may be used to help a person arrested three times for drunken driving acknowledge that he does have a drinking problem. A person whose three-year engagement has been broken may be instructed on how to counter unwanted emotions by doing a rational self-analysis. A young woman who has been raped may be given immediate medical attention and counseling on legal implications and also on her thoughts and feelings about the assault. A counselor may use the active listening technique in counseling someone who is threatening suicide.

Whittaker (1975, p. 212) provides a summary of crisis counseling services:

Requisite worker skills include the ability to function effectively and efficiently in an emotionally tense atmosphere and to give support and direction while at the same time helping the client to develop autonomous coping skills.

Crisis intervention generally progresses in the following manner: (1) An attempt is made to alleviate the disabling tension through ventilation and the creation of a climate of trust and hope. (2) Next the worker attempts to understand the dynamics of the event that precipitated the crisis. (3) The worker gives his impressions and understanding of the crisis and checks out these perceptions with the client. (4) Client and worker attempt to determine specific remedial measures that can be taken to restore equilibrium. (5) New methods of coping may be introduced. (6) Finally, termination occurs—often after a predetermined number of interviews—when the agreed-upon goals have been realized.

Crisis intervention services are provided by a number of means and in a wide variety of traditional and nontraditional settings, including runaway centers, rape crisis centers, "hot lines," hospital emergency rooms, mental health clinics, suicide prevention services, neighborhood centers, crisis hostels, half-way houses, detention facilities and self-help groups such as Parents Anonymous. CI services are provided not only by professionals but also by paraprofessionals and volunteers.

TASK-CENTERED PRACTICE

The primary developers of task-centered practice are William J. Reid and Laura Epstein, social work faculty members of the School of Social Service Administration at the University of Chicago. Task-centered practice is described in Reid and Epstein (1977).

In the initial interview with a client, the counselor seeks to elicit, explore, and clarify the client's problems. During this interview the counselor may point out problems the client has not recognized, or the consequences of allowing significant problems to go unattended. In the first or second interview the counselor and the client explicitly agree upon the problems to be dealt with. The problems are defined in terms of specific circumstances to be changed. The counselor and the client also agree upon the duration and amount of service to be given. There are usually six to twelve interviews over a two- to four-month time span. The kinds of services agreed upon and the number of interviews to be held form the basis of the service contract, which may be modified by additional agreements as service proceeds.

The counselor and the client then identify tasks the client may undertake to alleviate specific problems. These tasks may be general in nature in that they give the client a direction for action but do not precisely specify the expected behavior — for example, client Jim K will seek to establish a better relationship with his parents. Or, tasks may be very specific — for example, Jim K will inform his parents how much he appreciates their financial support in sending him to college.

During the discussion of the tasks, the counselor may help the client structure the tasks so as to increase their chances of being accomplished. If the client is unable to arrive at alternatives for resolving the problems, the counselor may suggest various possibilities. The counselor's primary roles in this change process are to help the client identify target problems, to help the client identify tasks for resolving these problems, and to then carry out agreed-upon tasks together with the client. The general tasks of clients, in this model, become the client's own goals for change. In this change process the counselor uses relationship skills (which are discussed in Chapter 5) and is apt to utilize a variety of resolution approaches that are suggested by contemporary theories of counseling, such as contingency contracting, assertiveness training, and game analysis.

During the treatment process a substantial amount of the counselor's efforts goes into structuring communication during interviews to keep the client's attention and efforts focused on the tasks. There are a number of efforts to enhance the client's awareness of his problems and to help the client understand obstacles to task performance. The client is given substantial encouragement about constructive actions he is contemplating or is undertaking. The client may also be given suggestions or directions on how to proceed with the task.

Usually in the treatment process there is an emphasis for the counselor to help the client break down general tasks into more specific, operational tasks that clients are then expected to carry out prior to the next treatment session. Incentives for task accomplishment are usually identified. Actions called for by the tasks are rehearsed or practiced (for example, through role-playing). This task-centered approach has been used not only with individual clients but also with families and with groups (Reid and Epstein, 1977).

There are additional distinctive features of this approach. Treatment is short term by plan. It is theorized that when a contract is made with a client for a set number of interviews (usually six to twelve), the client will work hard to resolve his problems during this brief time period.

Another emphasis is to focus treatment sharply on target problems and resolution tasks; that is, there is an emphasis on specifying problems and tasks in operational and measurable terms. With this emphasis, both the counselor and the client are more aware of precisely what needs to be done and what progress is being made during the treatment process in resolving the problems.

A final emphasis is the use of explicit agreements or contracts between the counselor and the clients specifying problems, goals, and tasks to be worked on during the treatment process. The contract is formed in the first or second interview and serves to guide the treatment process. This contract may be oral or written; it may be modified later if both parties agree to changing it.

A number of case examples of task-centered practice are in Reid and Epstein (1977). The task-centered approach has many similarities to the counseling process described in Chapter 5 and to reality therapy described in Chapter 17.

MEDIATION

In the past two decades, mediation has been used increasingly to resolve conflicts between disputing groups. The federal government as far back as 1913 established the use of federal mediators to help resolve issues between employers and employees (Moore, 1986, p. 21). Mediated settlements were expected to prevent costly strikes or lockouts and to protect the welfare and safety of Americans. Federal use of mediation in labor disputes has set a precedent, encouraging many states to pass laws and to train a cadre of mediators to handle intrastate labor conflicts.

Mediation is currently being used in a variety of ways. The Civil Rights Act of 1964 created the Community Relations Service of the U.S. Department of Justice to use mediation to resolve disputes relating to discriminatory practices based on race, color, or national origin (Moore, 1986, pp. 21–22). Diverse private agencies, civil rights commissions, and state agencies now use mediation to handle charges of sex, race, and ethnic discrimination. The federal government funds Neighborhood Justice Centers that provide free or low-cost mediation services to the public to resolve disputes, informally, inexpensively, and efficiently (Moore, 1986, p. 22). Disputes settled through mediation are resolved much more efficiently and creatively than those resolved in court. Mediation is also used in schools and faculty, between faculty members, and between faculty and administration. The criminal justice system uses mediation to resolve disputes in correctional facilities — for example, for prison riots, hostage negotiations, and institutionalized grievance procedures.

Mediation is also used extensively in family disputes involving child custody and divorce proceedings, disputes between parents and children, conflicts involving adoption and the termination of parental rights, and domestic violence situations. Moore (1986, p. 23) states: "In family disputes, mediated and consensual settlements are often more appropriate and satisfying than litigated or imposed court outcomes."

Mediation is used to settle disputes between business partners, private individuals, governmental agencies and individuals, landlords and tenants, businesses and customers, and disputants in personal injury cases.

Many professionals now occasionally act as mediators to help people or groups in conflict to resolve their concerns. Such professionals include attorneys, social workers, psychologists, and guidance counselors. A few social workers, attorneys, and other professionals are working full time as mediators — often in public or private mediation agencies.

Moore (1986, p. 6) defines mediation as follows:

Mediation involves the intervention of an acceptable impartial and neutral third party who has no authoritative decision-making power to assist contending parties in voluntarily reaching their own mutually acceptable settlement of issues in dispute. . . . Mediation leaves the decision-making power in the hands of the people in conflict. Mediation is a voluntary process in that the participants must be willing to accept the assistance of the intervenor if the dispute is to be resolved. Mediation is usually initiated when the partners no longer believe that they can handle the conflict on their own and when the only means of resolution appears to involve impartial third-party assistance.

There are various models of the mediation process (Moore, 1986). An an illustration, the one developed by Joan Blades (1985) is summarized. Blades views the mediation process as involving five stages:

1. *Introduction/Commitment:* This first stage usually is accomplished in a one- to two-hour session. The mediator sets ground rules, describes mediation, answers questions, discusses fees, and seeks to gain a commitment to the process from the two parties. The mediator also seeks to develop an understanding of the more pressing issues, gains a sense of the personal dynamics of the two parties, and tries to ascertain whether they are ready and willing to mediate. If one or both of the parties are not willing to mediate, then the mediation probably should not proceed. If one or both of the parties are hesitant to proceed, the mediator usually describes the alternatives to mediation—such as a lengthy and expensive court battle.

2. *Definition:* The two parties, with the mediator's assistance, define the areas in which they already agree and disagree. Certain disputes, such as divorce mediation, are apt at this stage to require a considerable amount of information.

3. *Negotiation:* Once the two parties agree on the issues in conflict and relevant factual information on these issues is obtained, the two parties are ready to begin negotiating. At this stage the mediator seeks to have the parties focus on one issue at a time. A problem-solving approach is used in which the needs of each party are first identified and alternatives are generated. The mediator recedes into the background when discussions are proceeding well and steps in when emotions intensify or when the two parties are overlooking creative solutions that will meet their needs.

4. *Agreement:* Once alternatives are generated and related facts are evaluated, the two parties are ready to begin making agreements on the issues. The role of the mediator is to maintain a cooperative atmosphere and to keep the two parties focused on a manageable number of issues. The mediator summarizes areas of agreement and pro-

vides legal or other information necessary to a discussion. The mediator helps the two parties examine the merits and shortcomings of the options. During this stage the mediator praises the parties for the progress they are making and gets them to praise themselves for progress made. A mediator seeks to create a positive atmosphere.

5. *Contracting:* In this final stage of mediation the two parties review the agreements and clarify any ambiguities. The agreements are almost always written in the form of a contract, which is available for future reference. Either party, the mediator, or everyone together may do the actual writing of the contract. The contract expresses what each party agrees to do, may set deadlines for the diverse tasks to be completed, and may specify consequences if either party fails to meet the terms of the contract. Mediators seek to have specific agreements stated in concrete form to prevent future controversies. The ultimate goal of mediation is a contract in which no one is a loser and by which both parties willingly abide.

One of the major techniques a mediator uses is a caucus (Moore, 1986). At times a mediator, or either party, may stop the mediation and request a caucus. In a caucus the two parties are physically separated from each other and there is no direct communication between them. In a caucus the mediator meets with one of the parties or with both parties individually. There are many reasons for calling a caucus. A caucus may be used to vent intense emotions privately, to clarify misperceptions, to reduce unproductive or repetitive negative behavior, to seek clarification of a party's interests, to provide a pause for each party to consider an alternative, to convince an uncompromising party that the mediation process is better than going to court, to uncover confidential information, to educate an inexperienced disputant about the processes of mediation, or to design alternatives that will later be brought to a joint session.

Some parties are willing in a caucus to express privately possible concessions. Usually such concessions are conditional upon the other party's making certain concessions. By the use of caucuses, a mediator can go back and forth relaying information from one party to the other and seek to develop a consensus.

MUSCLE RELAXATION APPROACHES[1]

There are now a number of muscle relaxation programs available, described in detail in a review by Bernstein and Borkovec (1973). Muscle relaxation approaches stem from the pioneering work of Jacobson (1934) in teaching people to help themselves deal with stress and anxiety. *Stress* is a state of bodily and mental tension resulting from physical, chemical, or emotional stressors; for example, stress is the state resulting from having a job that is perceived as being filled with "high pressure." (See Chapter 12 for a fuller description of stress and its effects.)

Anxiety has long been recognized as an emotion that accompanies stress. Anxiety is generally described as an emotion consisting of uncomfortable feelings of tension, apprehension, and dread.

Jacobson's investigations led him to the now well-established fact that people are able to regulate certain effects of the automatic nervous system through their own efforts. Specifically, Jacobson discovered that anxiety is associated with the sensation of tension experienced when muscle fibers are shortened or contracted as they are during stress. Jacobson developed an approach to counteract anxiety by muscle relaxation. He demonstrated that anxiety can be sharply reduced by relaxing muscles. The specific approach he developed is an elaborate system for teaching people to progressively tighten and then relax the major muscles of their body. He also demonstrated that anxiety will not exist in the presence of complete muscle relaxation (Jacobson, 1938a).

Jacobson (1934, 1938b, 1959, 1964, 1973) has published many popular books on how to relax, how to handle fatigue, how to sleep well, how to relax while having a baby, and how to help school children relax in the classroom.

Jacobson's approach to relaxation consists of teaching people to relax twenty major muscle groups. Each group is tensed and relaxed in several different ways during a sixty-minute period, practiced every day until the person becomes skilled in the procedure. Jacobson's method is thorough but time-consuming.

Muscle relaxation is a very effective approach in reducing/eliminating both stress and anxiety (Brown, 1977). Practically anyone can learn to reduce both anxiety and stress using muscle relaxation. In recent years shorter programs of muscle relaxation have been developed.

Learning to relax via muscle relaxation is accomplished by having a person first tighten and then relax a set of muscles. When relaxing muscle groups, the person is instructed to think about the relaxed feeling while noting that the muscles are more relaxed than before they were tensed. The following excerpt (Watson and Tharp, 1972, pp. 182–83) provides an illustration of the instructions for muscle relaxation.

Instructions for Muscle Relaxation[2]

Preparation   *Spend a little time getting as comfortable as you can. While you are finding a good position, you will also want to loosen any tight clothing. Loosen your belt or tie if they are not already loose. If your shoes feel tight, you may wish to take them off. Your legs and arms should be slightly apart.*

Slowly open your mouth and move your jaw gently from side to side. . . . Now let your mouth close, keeping

---

[1]This material on muscle relaxation approaches is adapted from Charles Zastrow, "Muscle Relaxation Approaches" in *Talk to Yourself: Using the Power of Self-Talk*, © 1979, pp. 179–83. Adapted by permission of Prentice-Hall, Inc., Englewood Cliffs, New Jersey.

[2]Reprinted with permission of Atheneum Publishers, an imprint of Macmillan Publishing Company, from *Stress Management: A Comprehensive Guide to Wellness* by Edward A. Charlesworth and Ronald G. Nathan, pp. 63–71. Copyright © 1984 by Edward A. Charlesworth and Ronald G. Nathan.

your teeth slightly apart. As you do, take a deep breath . . . and slowly let the air slip out.

While you tighten one part of your body, try to leave every other part limp and loose. Keep the tensed part of your body tight for a few seconds and then relax and let it go. Then take a deep breath, hold it, and as you breathe out, silently say, "Relax and let go." In time, this will be a technique you can use to produce rapid relaxation. Now begin your relaxation practice.

Total Body Tension

First, tense every muscle in your body. Tense the muscles of your jaws, eyes, arms, hands, chest, back, stomach, legs, and feet. Feel the tension all over your body. . . . Hold the tension briefly and then silently say, "Relax and let go" as you breathe out. . . . Let your whole body relax. . . . Feel a wave of calm come over you as you stop tensing. Feel the relief.

Gently close your eyes and take another deep breath. . . . Study the tension as you hold your breath. . . . Slowly breathe out and silently say, "Relax and let go." Feel the deepening relaxation. Allow yourself to drift more and more with this relaxation. . . . As you continue, you will exercise different parts of your body. Become aware of your body and its tension and relaxation. This will help you to become deeply relaxed on command.

Head and Face

Keeping the rest of your body relaxed, wrinkle up your forehead. Do you feel the tension? Your forehead is very tight. Briefly pause and be aware of it. . . . Now, relax and let go. Feel the tension slipping out. Smooth out your forehead and take a deep breath. Hold it. (Briefly pause.) As you breathe out, silently say, "Relax and let go."

Squint your eyes as if you are in a dust storm. Keep the rest of your body relaxed. Briefly pause and feel the tension around your eyes. . . . Now, relax and let go. Take a deep breath and hold it. (Briefly pause.) Silently say, "Relax and let go" as you breathe out.

Open your mouth as wide as you can. Feel the tension in your jaw and chin. Briefly hold the tension. . . . Now, let your mouth gently close. As you do, silently say, "Relax and let go." Take a deep breath. Hold it. (Briefly pause.) As you breathe out say, "Relax and let go."

Close your mouth. Push your tongue against the roof of your mouth. Study the tension in your mouth and chin. Briefly hold the tension. . . . Relax and let go. Take a deep breath. Hold it. (Briefly pause.) Now, silently say, "Relax and let go" as you breathe out. When you breathe out, let your tongue rest comfortably in your mouth, and let your lips be slightly apart.

Keep the rest of your body relaxed, but clench your jaw tightly. Feel the tension in your jaw muscles. Briefly hold the tension. . . . Now relax and let go, and take a deep breath. Hold it. (Briefly pause.) Silently say, "Relax and let go" as you breathe out.

Think about the top of your head, your forehead, eyes, jaws, and cheeks. Make sure these muscles are relaxed. . . . Have you let go of all the tension? Continue to let the tension slip away and feel the relaxation replace the tension. Feel your face becoming very smooth and soft as all the tension slips away. . . . Your eyes are relaxed. . . . Your tongue is relaxed. . . . Your jaws are loose and limp. . . . All of your neck muscles are also very, very relaxed.

All of the muscles of your face and head are relaxing more and more. . . . Your head feels as though it could roll from side to side, and your face feels soft and smooth. Allow your face to continue becoming more and more relaxed as you now move to the other areas of your body.

Shoulders   *Now shrug your shoulders up and try to touch your ears with your shoulders. Feel the tension in the shoulders and neck. Hold the tension. . . . Now, relax and let go. As you do, feel your shoulders joining the relaxed parts of your body. Take a deep breath. Hold it. (Briefly pause.) Silently say, "Relax and let go" as you slowly breathe out.*

Notice the difference, how the tension is giving way to relaxation. Shrug your right shoulder up and try to touch your right ear. Feel the tension in your right shoulder and along the right side of your neck. Hold the tension. . . . Now, relax and let go. Take a deep breath. Hold it. (Briefly pause.) Silently say, "Relax and let go" as you slowly breathe out.

Next, shrug your left shoulder up and try to touch your left ear. Feel the tension in your left shoulder and along the left side of your neck. Hold the tension. . . . Now, relax and let go. Take a deep breath. Hold it. (Briefly pause.) Silently say, "Relax and let go" as you slowly breathe out. Feel the relaxation seeping into the shoulders. As you continue, you will become loose, limp, and relaxed as an old rag doll.

Arms and   *Stretch your arms out and make a fist
Hands   with your hands. Feel the tension in your hands and forearms. Hold the tension. . . . Now, relax and let go. Take a deep breath. Hold it. (Briefly pause.) Silently say, "Relax and let go" as you slowly breathe out.*

Push your right hand down into the surface it is resting on. Feel the tension in your arm and shoulder. Hold the tension. . . . Now, relax and let go. Take a deep breath. Hold it. (Briefly pause.) Silently say, "Relax and let go" as you slowly breathe out.

Next, push your left hand down into whatever it is resting on. Feel the tension in your arm and shoulder. Hold the tension. . . . Now, relax and let go. Take a deep breath. Hold it. (Briefly pause.) Silently say, "Relax and let go" as you slowly breathe out.

Bend your arms toward your shoulders and double them up as you might to show off your muscles. Feel the tension. Hold the tension. . . . Now, relax and let go. Take a deep breath. Hold it. (Briefly pause.) Silently say, "Relax and let go" as you slowly breathe out.

Chest and   *Move on to the relaxation of your
Lungs   chest. Begin by taking a deep breath that totally fills your lungs. As you hold your breath, notice the tension. Be aware of the tension around your ribs. . . . Silently say, "Relax and let go" as you slowly breathe out. Feel the deepening relaxation as you continue breathing easily, freely, and gently. (Briefly pause.)*

Take in another deep breath. Hold it again and again feel the contrast between tension and relaxation. As you do, tighten your chest muscles. Hold the tension. . . . Silently say, "Relax and let go" as you slowly breathe out. Feel the relief as you breathe out and continue to breathe gently, naturally, and rhythmically. Breathe as smoothly as you can. You will become more and more relaxed with every breath.

Back   *Keeping your face, neck, arms, and chest as relaxed as possible, arch your back up (or forward if you are sitting).*

Arch it as if you had a pillow under the middle and low part of your back. Observe the tension along both sides of your back. Briefly hold that position. . . . Now, relax and let go. Take a deep breath. Hold it. (Briefly pause.) Silently say, "Relax and let go" as you breathe out. Let that relaxation spread deep into your shoulders and down into your back muscles.

Feel the slow relaxation developing and spreading all over. Feel it going deeper and deeper. Allow your entire body to relax. Face and head relaxed. . . . Neck relaxed. . . . Shoulders relaxed. . . . Arms relaxed. . . . Chest relaxed. . . . Back relaxed. . . . All these areas are relaxing more and more, becoming more deeply relaxed than you thought possible.

Stomach

Now, begin the relaxation of the stomach area. Tighten up this area. Briefly hold the tension. . . . Relax and let go. Feel the relaxation pour into your stomach area. All the tension is being replaced with relaxation, and you feel the general well-being that comes with relaxation. Take a deep breath. Hold it. (Briefly pause.) Silently say, "Relax and let go" as you slowly breathe out.

Now, experience a different type of tension in the stomach area. Push your stomach out as far as you can. Briefly hold the tension. . . . Now, relax and let go. Take a deep breath. Hold it. (Briefly pause.) Silently say, "Relax and let go" as you slowly breathe out.

Now, pull your stomach in. Try to pull your stomach in and touch your backbone. Hold it. . . . Now, relax and let go. Take a deep breath. Hold it. (Briefly pause.) Silently say, "Relax and let go" as you breathe out.

You are becoming more and more relaxed. Each time you breathe out, feel the gentle relaxation in your lungs and in your body. As you continue to do these exercises, your chest and stomach area will relax more and more. Check the muscles of your face, neck, shoulders, arms, chest, and stomach. Make sure they are still relaxed. If they are not, then tense and release them again. Whatever part is still less than fully relaxed is starting to relax more and more. Soon you will be able to tell when you have tension in any part of your body. You will learn that you can always relax and let go of the tension you may find in any part of your body.

Hips, Legs, and Feet

Now, begin the relaxation of your hips and legs. Tighten your hips and legs by pressing down the heels of your feet into the surface they are resting on. Tighten these muscles. Keep the rest of your body as relaxed as you can and press your heels down. . . . Now, hold the tension. . . . Relax and let go. Feel your legs float up. Take a deep breath. Hold it. (Briefly pause.) Silently say, "Relax and let go" as you breathe out. Feel the relaxation pouring in. Notice the difference between tension and relaxation. Let the relaxation become deeper and deeper. Enjoy the relaxation.

Next, tighten your lower leg muscles. Feel the tension. Briefly hold the tension. . . . Now, relax and let go. Take a deep breath. Hold it. (Briefly pause.) Silently say, "Relax and let go" as you breathe out.

Now, curl your toes downward. Curl them down and try to touch the bottom of your feet with your toes. Hold them and feel the tension. . . . Relax and let go. Wiggle your toes gently as you let go of the tension. Let the tension be replaced with relaxation. Take a deep breath. Hold it. (Briefly pause.)

A yoga class

Silently say, "Relax and let go" as you breathe out.

Now, bend your toes back the other way. Bend your toes right up toward your knees. Feel the tension. Try to touch your knees with your toes. Feel the tension. Hold the tension. . . . Relax and let go. Feel all the tension slip right out. Take a deep breath. Hold it. (Briefly pause.) Silently say, "Relax and let go" as you slowly breathe out. Feel the tension leaving your body and the relaxation seeping in.

Body Review

You have progressed through all the major muscles of your body. Now, let them become more and more relaxed. Continue to feel yourself becoming more and more relaxed each time you breathe out. Each time you breathe out, think about a muscle and silently say, "Relax and let go," . . . Face relax. . . . Shoulders relax. . . . Arms relax. . . . Hands relax. . . . Chest relax. . . .

Back relax. . . . Stomach relax. . . . Hips relax. . . . Legs relax. . . . Feet relax. . . . Your whole body is becoming more and more relaxed with each breath.

Spend a few more minutes relaxing, if you would like. If, during your day, you find yourself getting upset about something, remember the relaxation you have just experienced. Before you get upset, take a deep breath, hold it, and as you breathe out, silently say, "Relax and let go." With practice, you will be able to use this technique to relax whenever you begin to feel the stress of everyday living.

With continued practice of such a muscle relaxation technique, a person is generally able to relax herself whenever anxious simply by *visualizing* (that is, thinking about) her muscles relaxing. The procedure is to think about the tension progressively leaving the various muscle groups. A brief example of this procedure is from Brown (1977):

Think of your lower arm, elbow, and upper arm, all the way up to your shoulders. Picture all the tension just melting away. . . . Think about your stomach and chest, up to your throat and neck. As you continue breathing more deeply, just imagine all the tension flowing out and you are relaxing more and more.

Now think about your throat, neck, and head, feeling limp and relaxed. Relax your facial muscles. Drop the jaw, parting the lips and teeth. Picture yourself completely relaxed (pp. 261–62).

Muscle relaxation approaches in recent years have received increased interest and use in reducing both stress and anxiety by physicians, psychiatrists, psychologists, social workers, and other counselors (Charlesworth and Nathan, 1984). Muscle relaxation is also being used to bring relief to sufferers of both tension headaches and migraine headaches (Goleman, 1976b). Suinn (1976) has demonstrated that relaxation is useful in helping athletes and others reduce stress before participating in important events. It is also useful in reducing hypertension (Shoemaker and Tasto, 1975). Relaxation training is used as a technique in its own right and is also used in conjunction with such other therapy approaches as self-hypnosis, biofeedback, and systematic desensitization.

DEEP BREATHING AND IMAGERY RELAXATION APPROACHES

In addition to muscle relaxation approaches, the relaxation response can be achieved by deep breathing techniques and by imagery of being in a relaxing place. An illustration of the deep breathing technique is described by Brown (1977):

Relaxation Technique: Deep Breathing (Five minutes)

1. *Select a comfortable sitting position.*

2. *Close your eyes and direct your attention to your own breathing process.*

3. *Think about nothing but your breath, as it flows in and out of your body.*

4. *Say to yourself something like this: "I am relaxing, breathing smoothly and rhythmically. Fresh oxygen flows in and out of my body. I feel calm, renewed and refreshed."*

5. *Continue to focus on your breathing as it flows in and out, in and out, thinking of nothing but the smooth, rhythmical process of your own breathing.*

6. *After five minutes, stand up, stretch, smile, and continue with your daily activities (p. 259).*[3]

Brown (1977) presents a relaxation approach using imagery of being in a relaxing place:

Relaxation Technique: Mental Relaxation Place (Five to ten minutes)

1. *Select a comfortable sitting or reclining position.*

2. *Close your eyes, and think about a place that you have been before that represents your ideal place for physical and mental relaxation. (It should be a quiet environment, perhaps the seashore, the mountains, or even your own backyard. If you can't think of an ideal relaxation place, then create one in your mind.)*

3. *Now imagine that you are actually in your ideal relaxation place. Imagine that you are seeing all the colors, hearing the sounds, smelling the aromas. Just lie back, and enjoy your soothing, rejuvenating environment.*

4. *Feel the peacefulness, the calmness, and imagine your whole body and mind being renewed and refreshed.*

5. *After five to ten minutes, slowly open your eyes and stretch. You have the realization that you may instantly return to your relaxation place*

---

[3]From *Stress and the Art of Biofeedback* by Barbara B. Brown. Copyright © 1977 by Barbara B. Brown. By permission of Bantam Books, New York. All rights reserved.

*whenever you desire, and experience a
peacefulness and calmness in body and mind
(pp. 259–60).*[4]

Practice in using any of these relaxation approaches gradually increases the proficiency of achieving the relaxation response. Developing the capacity to achieve the relaxation response is a highly effective approach to alleviating anxiety and stress, and thereby experiencing more pleasing emotions, maintaining health, preventing or coping better with psychosomatic disorders, and probably also extending the number of years you can expect to live. Counselors are increasingly using relaxation approaches to help clients relax in order to reduce anxiety and stress.

MEDITATION[5]

Recorded accounts of meditative practice date back over 2,000 years among Zen monks, Indian yogis, Judaic spiritual leaders, and Christian monks. The earliest known Christian meditators were hermits who lived during the fourth century A.D. in the most isolated areas of the Egyptian desert. Like present-day Indian yogis in the Himalaya Mountains, they sought isolation to communicate with God, free from worldly distractions. The meditative practices of these earliest Christian monks were strikingly similar to practices of Hindu and Buddhist meditators in India at that time (suggesting a cultural exchange). These Christian meditators repeated quietly or silently a selected phrase from the Scriptures. The most popular phrase or *mantra* was "Lord Jesus Christ, Son of God, have mercy on me, a sinner." Many of these monks repeated the short form of this mantra, "Kyrie eleison," silently for hours each day. Today, this form of meditation is no longer practiced among Christians in the West but still sur-

vives in some Eastern orthodox monasteries (Goleman, 1977).

There are numerous meditation approaches being practiced today. The following are described by Goleman (1977) in a review:

Hesychasm: Christianity's Yoga

Kabbalah: Hidden Judaism

Sufism: Muslim Mysticism

Transcendental Meditation: Hinduism for Americans

Patanjali's Yoga Sutras

Bhakti: The Hindu Path of Devotion

Swami Muktananda's Kundalini Yoga

Tantra's Left-Handed Path

The Buddha's Middle Way

Tibetan Buddhism

Zen

Gurdjieff

J. Krisnamurti's Methodless Method

Practically all the approaches seek to achieve a meditative state by having a person concentrate on and/or repeat an object: word, phrase, chant, sound, spiritual value, imagery of an exquisite painting, and so forth. It should be noted that different approaches use different rituals, different objects, have somewhat different goals to be achieved through meditation, and seek to produce somewhat different meditative experiences.

Transcendental Meditation (TM) is used here for illustrative purposes as it is the most popular meditation approach in this country and is one of the most widely practiced forms of meditation in the world. TM first gained popularity in the 1960s when it was practiced by such widely known celebrities as the Beatles and Mia Farrow. TM was developed by Maharishi Mahesh Yogi, a guru (Hindu spiritual leader). TM is a simple Yogic technique.

In TM a meditator lets a mantra repeat itself over and over in her mind. The mantra is a Sanskrit word or sound that is given to meditators by TM instructors. The mantras themselves are not special to TM but come from Sanskrit sources used by many Hindus. Two examples of mantras are "Shyam" (a name of Lord Krishna) and "Aing" (a sound sacred to the divine

---

[4]Ibid.

[5]This material on meditation is adapted from Charles Zastrow, "Meditation," in *Talk to Yourself: Using the Power of Self-Talk,* © 1979, pp. 185–89. Adapted by permission of Prentice-Hall, Inc., Englewood Cliffs, New Jersey.

Meditation

mother). The goal of TM is "passage through a series of advanced spiritual states ending in union with God" (Goleman, 1977, p. 58). Meditators are advised to meditate twenty minutes in the morning, usually before breakfast, and twenty minutes in the evening, usually before dinner.

There is considerable evidence that the reduction of stress and anxiety through meditation derives from a simple set of general procedures that can be learned without elaborate rituals or large expenses (Goleman, 1976a). A strong advocate of this view is Herbert Benson, a Harvard cardiologist who has carefully reviewed the contemporary meditation approaches. Benson (1975) has identified the following four elements as being key to eliciting the relaxation response in any meditation approach:

1. Being in a quiet environment that facilitates tuning out external distractions and internal stimuli.

2. Being in a comfortable position, such as sitting or lying down. The position should be one in which the meditator can feel comfortable for at least twenty minutes.

3. Having an object to dwell on, which also facilitates tuning out thoughts about day-to-day concerns. Examples of suitable objects include one's breathing, a word or phrase chanted to oneself, an audio tape of ocean waves, a symbol to be gazed at steadily, and the sights and sounds of a relaxing place, visualized with one's eyes closed.

4. Having a passive attitude, in which the meditator releases day-to-day concerns. A passive attitude appears to be the key element in eliciting the relaxation response, as people become relaxed when they focus their cognitions on relaxing thoughts and turn loose their day-to-day concerns. If day-to-day concerns drift into the meditator's awareness, he or she should allow them to pass on as effortlessly as possible.

An example of a simplified, noncultic, nonreligious, meditation approach is as follows:

1. Find a quiet environment, such as a quiet room, where you will not be interrupted.

2. Sit quietly in a comfortable posiiton.

3. Close your eyes.

4. Breathe in and out through your nose at a relaxed, natural pace. As you breathe out, silently say the word "Relax" slowly to yourself.

5. Continue this process for ten to twenty minutes: Slowly breathe in, and then as you exhale slowly say "Relax" to yourself.

6. Do not focus your thoughts on day-to-day concerns, and do not worry whether you will achieve a deep level of relaxation. Deep levels of relaxation are gradually achieved with continued practice. The state of being relaxed comes slowly as you let go your worries and concerns. When distracting thoughts enter your mind, allow them to drift away as effortlessly as possible. Focusing your thoughts on your breathing and on silently saying "Relax" as you exhale will facilitate your releasing your worries and concerns.

7. When you finish, sit quietly for several minutes, first with your eyes closed and then with your eyes open. Practice this technique once or twice daily. With practice, you will gradually achieve more rapid and deeper levels of relaxation. A word of caution: walk around for fifteen or more minutes before attempting to drive a car or some other vehicle, as you are apt to be lethargic, with your response reaction time being lengthened considerably.

In reviewing meditation approaches, one notes that meditation and relaxation approaches are closely related. Both techniques are therapeutic because they produce the relaxation response. In addition, certain components of the muscle relaxation and deep breathing relaxation approaches are used by some meditation approaches to aid in producing the relaxation response. Finally, imagery relaxation has characteristics similar to those of meditation and can in fact be considered a meditation approach.

Research has demonstrated that meditation is physiologically and psychologically more refreshing and energy-restoring than deep sleep (Wallace, 1970). Many meditators, in fact, have reported that they needed less sleep after they began meditating, which suggests that a regenerative process occurs during meditation (Bloomfield, Cain, and Jaffe, 1975). Meditation has been used successfully in the treatment of many psychosomatic disorders including hypertension (Benson, Rosner, and Marzetta, 1973) and asthma (Honsberger and Wilson, 1973). It has been effective in decreasing the use of drugs, alcohol, and cigarette smoking (Benson, 1975); alleviating sleep disorders; and accelerating the bodily healing process (Bloomfield et al., 1975).

Meditation has also been found to have a number of other positive effects. It is useful in treating phobias (Boudreau, 1972) and in treating people with emotional problems (Bloomfield et al., 1975). Regular practice of the technique improves learning ability (Abrams, 1974), perceptual motor performance (Blasdell, 1974), ability to recover from stress (Orme-Johnson, 1973), perceptual acuity (Pelletier, 1974), work productivity and job satisfaction (Frew, 1974), and creativity (Bloomfield et al., 1975). Meditation improves psycho-logical health (Shelly, 1973), heightens self-awareness (Bloomfield et al., 1975), increases self-actualization (Ferguson and Gowan, 1974), reduces anxiety, depression, and aggression (Ferguson and Gowan, 1974), reduces reaction time (Shaw and Kolb, 1974), increases recall ability (Abrams, 1974), and improves academic performance (Heaton and Orme-Johnson, 1974).

Meditation's potential medical value in eliciting the relaxation response is dramatically described by Benson (1975):

The prevention of stress-related diseases carries with it enormous significance, certainly for the individual and his family in terms of their own physical and mental well-being, and for society as a whole through huge dollar savings in health expenditures. It is possible that the regular elicitation of the Relaxation Response will prevent the huge personal suffering and social costs now being inflicted on us by high blood pressure and its related ailments (pp. 156–57).

Note: A word of caution. If and when you use meditation (or any relaxation technique) you should walk around for several minutes before driving, as you may be so relaxed that you will have difficulty concentrating on your driving.

HYPNOSIS AND SELF-HYPNOSIS[6]

Many people erroneously believe that the effects produced by hypnotism are the result of some mystical, magical power of the hypnotist. Authorities on hypnotism, however, are in full agreement that the effects result from the thinking processes and imaginative processes of the hypnotized person (Caprio and Berger, 1963; Freese, 1976; Lecron, 1964; White and Watt, 1973).

---

[6]The material on hypnosis is adapted from Charles Zastrow, "Hypnosis and Self-Hypnosis" in *Talk to Yourself: Using the Power of Self-Talk*, © 1979, pp. 197–203. Adapted by permission of Prentice-Hall Inc., Englewood Cliffs, New Jersey.

A clinical hypnosis session

Being hypnotized involves entering a mental state of aroused concentration so intense that everything else is ignored and the hypnotized person goes into a trance. Freese (1976) defines hypnosis as follows:

To understand hypnosis, the trance state, one must always keep in mind this picture of aroused intense concentration. When we concentrate deeply on a book and become completely absorbed in its contents, we're not asleep even though we don't move a muscle, don't hear a think going on about us. . . . In short, hypnosis is a normal state into which we will slip readily during our everyday lives. It's what happens to us every time we become entranced (note

that word) by a movie or a mind-blowing experience, a TV show or a work of art or even a conversation. It's the daydreamer lost in her or his vivid imagery (pp. 37–38).

Caprio and Bergr (1963) note that all hypnosis is self-hypnosis. People who become hypnotized, hypnotize themselves by thinking and concentration. If a person does not wish to be hypnotized, it is almost impossible for a hypnotist to put that person in a hypnotic state. Caprio and Berger note:

Hypnotists do not possess any unusual or mystic powers. A hypnotist is a person who knows that his subject actually hypnotizes himself. The hypnotist is merely a person who has learned or perhaps mastered the science and art of effective suggestion. He teaches the subject how to bring about or self-induce the hypnotic state. Hypnotism has sometimes been called the "manipulation of the imagination."... The hypnotic state is similar to becoming completely absorbed in a movie or a book. In other words, it represents a concentration of attention (pp. 15–16).

Almost anyone can be hypnotized. It takes imagination, a willingness to cooperate with the hypnotist, and a willingness to accept suggestions. Caprio and Berger (1963) add:

To be hypnotized, (1) you must want to be hypnotized; (2) you must have confidence in the hypnotist; (3) you must train your mind to accept suggestion (p. 17).

While under hypnosis a person will not do anything contrary to his or her moral code. The hypnotized person will not commit antisocial acts. Those hypnotized have the power to select the suggestions they are willing to accept, and they will reject improper or unethical suggestions. The hypnotized person also has the power to terminate the hypnotic state at will. There has never been a case in which the hypnotized person did not return to the waking state. Hypnotized people are never in anybody else's power. They won't go into a trance unless they want to. They won't do anything unless they want to. They have the power to come out of a trance whenever they want to (Caprio and Berger, 1963). Caprio and Berger further describe hypnosis and its medical value:

All hypnosis is self-hypnosis. In hypnosis the subject responds to the suggestions of the hypnotist. The subject permits the hypnotist to bring about a state of calmness and relaxation because he, the subject, desires this mental state.

Hypnosis involves (1) motivation, (2) relaxation and (3) suggestion.

In self-hypnosis, the relaxation is self-induced, followed by the hypnotic state. It is the influence of our own minds over our bodies. By including our own hypnotic state, we heighten our suggestibility and are then capable of influencing our body functions....

The phenomena of hypnosis and self-hypnosis explain many of our publicized miracles of faith cures. Self-hypnosis is really a form of psychic healing accomplished through the voluntary acceptance and application of one's own suggestions (p. 19).

There are many techniques that hypnotists use to induce a trance. One technique is relaxation: the hypnotist's voice gradually becomes monotonous (like a lullaby) as the hypnotist keeps suggesting relaxation until the hypnotic state is reached. Another technique is the arm levitation technique in which the hypnotist suggests that the person's arm, fingers, or hand are gradually becoming lighter and lighter, until they "lift by themselves."

In the repetitive movement technique the hypnotist keeps suggesting relaxation and then takes an arm and moves it back and forth while (in a monotonous voice) suggesting that the person perform this movement. A trance state is indicated when the person automatically begins to perform the movement.

The direct state technique is the oldest and perhaps most famous technique but is rarely used today. With this technique the hypnotist stares into the person's eyes and seeks to induce the trance state by using a dominant "Hollywood style" stare.

Freese (1976) documents that over the centuries thousands of different rituals have been used for trance induction. Such rituals include chants or dances of witch doctors, a simple flashing light or a swinging pendulum, or a monotonous beat of a *metronome* (an instrument designed to mark exact time by a regularly repeated tick).

Whatever technique is used to induce a trance, it is important to remember that all hypnosis is self-hypnosis in which a state of aroused intense concentration is achieved because the hypnotized person cooperates with the hypnotist and desires to enter this mental state.

The mechanics of how to induce self-hypnosis and how to help yourself with self-hypnotic suggestions will now be briefly described. The first step is to decide what you would like to use self-hypnosis for: losing weight, reducing drinking, overcoming anger, eliminating jealousy, combating insomnia, relieving a pain, stopping smoking, reducing a phobia, learning to relax in certain anxiety-producing situations—whatever.

The next step is to become very relaxed. Such relaxation can be achieved through using one of the following approaches that have previously been described: muscle relaxation, deep breathing relaxation, imagery relaxation, or meditation. Such relaxation approaches are effective if (and only if) they shift a person's thinking from focusing on day-to-day problems to focusing on calming, monontonous, or relaxing thoughts. This relaxation phase of hypnosis and self-hypnosis is very important because it facilitates the hypnotized person's capacity to accept and follow through on hypnotic suggestions that are given.

The final key component of hypnosis and self-hypnosis is a suggestion (or a set of suggestions) that you give yourself while in a relaxed state. All such suggestions are simply statements in which you tell yourself that you must, can, and will be able to achieve a certain goal: for example, "I can and will stop smoking"; "I will feel no pain"; "I am able to relax myself and fall asleep whenever I need to"; "I am able to relax and reduce my blood pressure"; "I can control my drinking and will never ever take more than two drinks when I go out with friends."

For self-hypnotic suggestions to work, it is essential to give yourself these suggestions daily in order that you keep your attention focused on achieving your goal (for example, telling yourself that you can and will follow a certain diet in order to lose weight).

This phase assumes that what the mind causes, it can cure; or, as Caprio and Berger (1963) note, it is based on the power of telling yourself

I can—I must—I will achieve my goal—that I have the mind-power to accept and carry out certain self-given suggestions which will enable me to overcome almost any handicap, to improve my personality and acquire a healthier philosophy of life (p. 34).

After giving yourself a hypnotic suggestion you can arouse yourself from the self-hypnotic trance by telling yourself that you will "come out" as you slowly count to ten. Hypnotists note it is needless to worry that in the event of an emergency you will not be able to arouse yourself rapidly from the trance. Under hypnosis you

are always able to arouse yourself immediately from the hypnotic state and are rapidly able to respond to the given emergency situation.

Caprio and Berger (1963) provide a number of case examples of hypnosis being successfully used. One involved a noted scientist in his seventies who was hesitant to address audiences because of stage fright. He generally declined invitations to speak. On one speaking engagement he became so frightened that he nearly fainted, and he experienced heart palpitations. This scientist was aware that his fear was largely caused by his thoughts and deduced that if he could learn to control his thoughts, he would in turn control his fear. He practiced a relaxation technique and repeatedly gave himself the following suggestions: "I have nothing to fear—I am going to concentrate on the message I wish to pass on to my audience and not on myself—I have confidence in the power of my mind" (p. 126). He reduced his fear with this approach and subsequently used this self-hypnosis approach before future lectures. He reportedly was able to deliver many talks with this approach and experienced little fear.

Hypnotic and self-hypnotic suggestions have been used for a wide variety of medical and psychological purposes:

To control weight

To alleviate emotional problems

To reduce stress and anxiety

To stop drinking or smoking

To alleviate insomnia

To improve one's sex life

To treat sexual dysfunctions

To alleviate pain

To reduce tension

To relax

To alleviate depression

To improve memory

To increase self-confidence

To improve interpersonal relationships

To improve one's self-image

To reduce fatigue

To treat psychosomatic illnesses

To reduce hostility and anger

To reduce jealousy and guilt

To overcome feelings of inferiority

To conquer fears and phobias

To treat migraine headaches, asthma, arthritis, backaches, bursitis, and allergies

To treat gynecological problems

To anesthetize

To treat stuttering, by reducing anxiety and tension

To alleviate pain during dentistry

To treat hypertension

(A more extensive review of the uses of hypnosis is contained in Caprio and Berger, 1963; Freese, 1976; Lecron, 1964.)

BIOFEEDBACK[7]

Biofeedback is simply a mirror reflecting some aspect of your physiology. Learning takes place only when there is feedback. In the same way your eyes give you feedback when you throw a ball, a biofeedback machine gives you feedback about what you are doing with your body. This feedback is able to gauge levels of arousal or physical change that we usually do not become aware of until a markedly high level of arousal is reached. During an hour interview, for example, your hand temperature is apt to vary by five to seven degrees. A higher hand temperature represents a more relaxed state, while a lower hand temperature indicates a higher level of tension or anxiety. It is unlikely that you will be aware of these gradual changes even though they are graphic indicators of your emotional state.

There are certain things biofeedback can and cannot do. Biofeedback does not alter one's physiological processes, nor does it solve personal or emotional problems, and it definitely does not reveal one's hidden thoughts or fantasies. What it does by meters, lights, or sounds is indicate what is happening in a person's body at that moment.

There is a wide range of biofeedback measures. Some common ones that we generally do not associate with biofeedback are mirrors to reveal how we look, bathroom scales to measure our weight, tape measures to show our height, and fever thermometers to gauge our body temperature. A lie detector test is another common biofeedback machine that measures levels of arousal.

There are many clinical biofeedback measures:

A thermometer to measure hand temperature

Muscle feedback units to measure muscle tension and anxiety

Equipment to measure pulse rate

Galvanic skin response equipment to measure levels of arousal and anxiety

Auditory feedback (using an amplified stethoscope) to measure peristaltic activity in the intestinal tract

Equipment to measure blood pressure levels

Electroencephalogram to measure brain wave activity

Electrocardiograph for recording the changes of electrical potential occuring during the heartbeat

Basically, all of these devices are used to gauge stress (levels of anxiety or arousal) in various parts of the body. The problem that biofeedback training seeks to alleviate is stress and its long-term effects on our feelings, bodies, and thinking processes. Stress is an intense state of physical and emotional arousal that results from a person's perception of being threatened or endangered. It is important to remember that the body prepares itself on the basis of the perception, not on whether the perception is realistic or unrealistic. If the perception is realistic, the physiological and emotional arousal prepares us better to handle the danger. If the perception is unrealistic, we needlessly expend our adaptive energy. Furthermore, prolonged stress is apt

---

[7]This material on biofeedback is adapted from Charles Zastrow, "Biofeedback," in *Talk to Yourself: Using the Power of Self-Talk*, © 1979, pp. 204–10. Adapted by permission of Prentice-Hall, Inc., Englewood Cliffs, New Jersey.

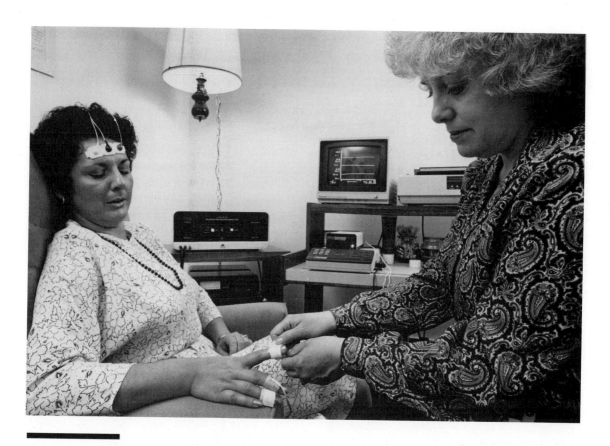

A variety of biofeedback equipment is displayed, with an electromyograph (EMG) being used to monitor muscle tension.

to play a key role in the development and severity of a wide variety of psychosomatic illnesses.

There are three basic ways to cope with high levels of stress and tension:

1. You can seek to change the events that contribute to your high stress level. For example, if you are dating someone and are feeling considerable anxiety over whether your partner is committed to the relationship, you can arrange a time to talk with your partner about committment to the relationship. Often,

however, events that are involved in causing your stress cannot be changed.

2. You can reassess whether you are realistically assessing situations. Doing a rational self-analysis (see Chapter 18) is an example of a structured way of examining the stress-producing self-talk, and of challenging irrational self-talk that generally is involved in prolonging high levels of stress.

3. You can get involved in meaningful activities that will stop you from thinking about the distressing event. Instead, you will think about the enjoyable and meaningful activity that you are involved in, which will reduce your stress level. There are many activities that can help to shift your mental focus: hobbies, exercising, going to a movie, relaxation techniques, meditation, hypnosis, biofeedback, and any other activity that you find enjoyable.

Conceptually, biofeedback is based on two basic priniples: (1) Any biological function that can be monitored and amplified by electronic instrumentation and fed back to a person through any one of his or her five senses can be regulated by that person. (2) "Every change in the physiological state is accompanied by an appropriate change in the mental emotional state, conscious or unconscious; and conversely, every change in the mental emotional state, conscious or unconscious, is accompanied by an appropriate change in the physiological state" (Pelletier, 1977, pp. 264–65).

Biofeedback research has demonstrated that many *autonomic* (that is, involuntary) nervous system processes can be brought under conscious control if a person obtains information about these processes. Such processes include heart rate, muscle tension, brain waves, body temperature, and stomach acidity level.

The following example described by Pelletier (1977) illustrates how it is possible to regulate heart rate via biofeedback.

During the initial stages of electrocardiogram (ECG) or heart-rate feedback, patients are surprised to see how volatile their heart rates really are. At first the pattern seems random. . . . After a relatively short time the patient realizes that minor changes in his physical posture—even flexing an index finger, or changes in his breathing pattern—have a profound effect upon the heart. Breathing in a slow or regular manner or sitting in an upright posture helps to decelerate the heart rate, whereas slouching or breathing shallowly and quickly tends to accelerate it. . . . When thinking of a pleasant or relaxing vacation, he notes that his heart rate begins to decelerate. Conversely, when he thinks about a perplexing or stress-inducing situation, like his income tax or an argument with a close friend, heart rate accelerates. . . . Once this link between internal sensations and their effects upon the cardiovascular system is established,

the individual has a means of regulating this critical autonomic function. (pp. 265–66)

The basic principles of learning how to regulate your heart rate, which are described in the above example, provide a model of how biofeedback can be used to regulate practically all autonomic processes.

Brown (1977) provides another illustration of biofeedback:

The average person can demonstrate to himself the biofeedback phenomenon by using an ordinary thermometer purchased from the drugstore or hardware store. One six to eight inches long and filled with fluid is best. He can tape the thermometer bulb to the fat pad of the middle finger with masking tape, making sure of good contact, but no constriction of circulation. After five or so minutes of quiet sitting, preferably with the eyes closed, note the temperature of the finger. Then, while still sitting quietly, repeat a few autosuggestion phrases to your self, slowly such as, "I feel relaxed and warm," "My hands feel warm and relaxed," "I feel calm and relaxed." Repeat the phrases slowly, allowing the suggestion to take effect, then go on to the next one, and then repeat the series. Every five or ten minutes, take a reading of the finger temperature. Most people will show a rise in finger temperature three to five or even ten degrees, some only a degree. Only a few may not change or may even show a small fall in finger temperature. With repeated practice, everyone can learn to increase finger temperature by using mental activity. (pp. 4–5)

An increase in finger temperature indicates that a person is becoming more relaxed.

Clinical biofeedback can be integrated with other therapy techniques or used as a technique in and of itself. Clinical biofeedback has been successfully used in conjunction with traditional psychotherapy, rational therapy, behavior modification, hypnosis, meditation, and relaxation techniques. (Techniques such as relaxation approaches, meditation, and hypnosis are used at times together with biofeedback to help a person learn how to relax.)

Although biofeedback achieves the same relaxation response as meditation, hypnosis, and relaxation techniques, the essential difference is that biofeedback amplifies biological signals. Pelletier (1977) describes an advantage of being able to amplify biological signals:

An advantage of biofeedback over non-feedback techniques is that the physiological information tells an individual precisely how he is functioning. Interpreting the feedback, a person knows exactly how tense he is in certain muscles, and through trial and error he can discover the means of relaxing those muscles. When he is successful, the feedback lets him know immediately. (p. 260)

Most people are unaware when their body is under moderate stress. Only when they are highly anxious or highly aroused do they consciously become aware of their level of stress. Yet, moderately high levels of stress over extended periods of time can be damaging to physiological functioning and result in breakdown (that is, a psychosomatic illness). Biofeedback shows a person precisely his or her level of stress. It also provides immediate feedback when that level is increased or reduced. Since increases or decreases in stress are caused primarily by our thinking processes, biofeedback immediately provides feedback to a person on the kinds of thoughts that lead to a reduction in stress. Thus, through trial and error, with biofeedback, people can identify what kind of thinking (such as meditating or visualizing being in a relaxing place) will work for them in reducing stress.

Another advantage of biofeedback is that it provides instantaneous feedback on the particular area of affliction. An overall relaxation response usually induces all neurophysiological functions to move toward a state of deep relaxation. Yet the movement toward relaxation may vary considerably in various systems of the body. At times most systems become relaxed, while a few remain tensed. An additional advantage of biofeedback is that a specific physiological process (for example, high blood pressure of a hypertensive person) that needs to be corrected can be monitored, feeding information to the person to help evaluate progress in alleviating this dysfunction.

Brown (1977) describes the therapeutic value of biofeedback:

There are more than fifty major medical and psychological problems in which biofeedback has been used with either greater success than conventional treatments or at least with equal benefits. The mind and body ailments that respond to biofeedback treatment span the entire spectrum of illnesses human beings suffer: emotional, psychosomatic, and physical disabilities. This fact alone speaks to its importance as a fundamental phenomenon of man's nature.

Probably no discovery in medicine or psychology compares in breadth of applications or in scope of implications to the biofeedback phenomenon. More important than its multiple uses, more important than its apparent universality as a cerebral tool of man, is its potential for recasting therapeutics and therapies into new standards of practice in which individual man assumes, or at least shares, responsibility for his own health or illness. (pp. 3–4)

Biofeedback can be used to exert voluntary control over heart rate, skin temperature, blood pressure, muscle tension, brain waves, or any other internal biological function capable of being monitored. Biofeedback is radically altering the doctor-patient relationship in that it requires doctors to instruct patients in being active participants in the healing process.

Brown (1977) provides a summary of disorders that have been reported to respond to biofeedback: problems that are primarily emotional — anxiety, phobias, chronic headaches, tension headaches, hyperactivity, stage fright, insomnia, alcoholism, drug abuse, depression with anxiety; problems that are primarily psychosomatic — asthma, essential hypertension, bruxism (grinding of the teeth), menstrual distress, ulcers, colitis, functional diarrhea; and problems that are primarily physical — muscle spasms with pain, strokes, paralysis, spasticity, cerebral palsy, migraine headaches, and epilepsy.

SUMMARY

This chapter presents a variety of treatment approaches for people with personal problems: milieu therapy, psychodrama, play therapy, parent effectiveness training, task-centered practice, mediation, crisis intervention, muscle relaxation approaches, deep breathing relaxation, imagery relaxation, meditation, hypnosis, and biofeedback. These approaches were developed independent of a comprehensive theory of psychotherapy.

Mediation is being used increasingly by a variety of professions to help resolve conflicts between two or more people. Social workers have used the following treatment approaches for a number of years: crisis intervention, milieu therapy, play therapy, and psychodrama.

Relaxation approaches, meditation, hypnosis, and biofeedback have been around a long time, but only recently have social workers begun to use these approaches. With the recognition that stress (and resulting psychosomatic problems) is our nation's number one health problem, social workers are using these approaches more and more to induce the relaxation response and thereby reduce anxiety and stress (among other objectives).

Parents effectiveness training has four techniques that anyone can use in improving interactions with others: active listening, I-messages, no-lose problem solving, and resolving collisions of values. Task-centered practice is a therapeutic approach that focuses on helping clients to identify and carry out specific tasks that will help them resolve their problems.

EXERCISES

1. Using I-Messages

GOAL: This exercise is designed to demonstrate how to phrase I-messages.

Step 1: Explain the goal of this exercise. Indicate I-messages are a nonblaming description of the effects a person is having on the sender of the message. I-messages do not involve giving a solution message or a put-down messasge.

Step 2: Ask the class how to formulate I-messages in a variety of situations. The following are examples:

a.   Someone is smoking a cigarette near you and the smoke is bothering you.
b.   You're riding in a car that a friend is driving dangerously fast.
c.   Someone is playing a stereo loudly in a building, which is interfering with your studying.
d.   A friend has just made another comment about your being overweight.
e.   A person you're dating continues to write to someone he has dated in the past.

Step 3: Some of the responses given by students may well be "you-messages." If that occurs, ask the class to indicate why the message is a "you-message" and not an "I-message." If the class is having trouble in formulating "I-messages," ask the students to discuss whether we are socialized in our society to use primarily "you-messages."

2. Active Listening

GOAL: To have students practice and further develop their active listening skills.

Step 1: The instructor explains the purpose of the exercise and describes what active listening is and what it is designed to accomplish. The instructor indicates that active listening involves using two types of statements — reflecting feelings and restating content.

Step 2: Students pair off. (If there is someone without a partner, the instructor should participate.) One member of each pair selects a topic to discuss for about ten minutes. The topic may involve (a) a philosophical or moral issue such as abortion, (b) a problem with a friend or a relative, or (c) a problem at school.

Step 3: The member who selects a topic discusses the issue for about ten minutes. The listener should try to respond solely with active listening statements.

Step 4: After the discussion, the presenter should discuss with the listener the quality of the active listening statements. Did the listener make the mistake of making suggestions, asking questions, or beginning to talk about personal experiences? Did active listening motivate the presenter to continue talking? Did the presenter perceive the active listening statements to be primarily "natural" or "artificial"?

The listener should then discuss with the presenter his or her thoughts and feelings about using active listening statements. Did the listener want to make other types of statements? If so, what?

Step 5: The roles should then be reversed and the process repeated.

Step 6: Students form a circle and discuss the merits and shortcomings of active listening. Were there some unique or unusual events that occurred?

3. Meditation and Relaxation

GOAL: This exercise is designed to demonstrate deep breathing relaxation, meditation, imagery relaxation, and muscle relaxation to the class.

Step 1: Describe the goal of this exercise. Indicate that social workers are using meditation and relaxation approaches more and more to help clients handle stress more effectively. Describe the following approaches: deep breathing relaxation, meditation, imagery relaxation, and muscle relaxation.

Step 2: State the following:

I will now lead you in a meditation exercise. The purpose is to show you that through meditating you can reduce stress and anxiety. You can do this exercise by yourself whenever you are anxious or want to relax. You can do it, for example, prior to giving a speech in class, prior to taking a crucial exam, or prior to going to bed at night.

Herbert Benson, who wrote the book, The Relaxation Response, *has identified four key elements common to meditative approaches that help people to relax. These four elements are (1) being in a quiet place; (2) getting in a comfortable position; (3) having an object to dwell on, such as your breathing or thinking about your ideal relaxation place, or a neutral word or phrase that you can continually repeat silently to yourself; and (4) having a passive attitude in which you let go of your day-to-day concerns by no longer thinking about them. Having a passive attitude is the key element in helping you to relax.*

Now, I want you to form a circle. [Wait until a circle is formed.] I will lead you in three types of meditation. First, we will do a deep breathing exercise. Then, we will move into repeating the word "Relax" silently to ourselves. Third, I'll have you focus on visualizing your most relaxing place. We will move directly from the first to the second, and then from the second to the third without stopping. When we do this exercise, don't worry about anything unusual happening. There will be no tricks. Concentrate on what I'm telling you to focus on, while taking a passive attitude where you let go of your everyday thoughts and concerns. Everyday thoughts and concerns may occasionally enter your mind, but seek to let go of them when they do.

Before we start, I want each of you to identify one of your most relaxing scenes. It may be lying in the sun on a beach or by a lake. It may be sitting in warm water in a bathtub reading a book. It may be sitting by a warm fireplace. Is there anyone who hasn't identified a relaxing scene? [Wait until everyone has identified one.]

OK, we're ready to start. [If possible, dim the lights, or turn out some of them.] *First, I want you to close your eyes and keep them closed for the entire exercise. Next, get in a comfortable position. If you want, you can sit or lie on the floor.* [Take five or six minutes for each of the three meditative exercises. Speak softly and slowly. Pause frequently, some-times for twenty seconds or more without saying anything. Feel free to add material to the following instructions.]

First, I want you to focus only on your breathing. Breathe in and out slowly and deeply. . . . Breathe in and out slowly. . . . As you breathe out feel how relaxing it feels. . . . While exhaling, imagine your concerns are leaving you . . . as you're breathing in and out, feel how you're becoming more calm, more relaxed, more refreshed. . . . Just keep focus-ing on breathing slowly in and out. . . . Don't try to be in sync when I'm talking about breathing in and out. . . . Find a breathing rhythm that's comfortable for you. . . . Breathe in slowly and deeply, and then slowly breathe out. . . . You've got the power within you to get more and more relaxed. . . . All you have to do is focus on your breathing. . . . Breathe in slowly and deeply, and then slowly breathe out. . . . If other thoughts happen to enter your mind, just let them drift away as effortlessly as possible. . . . The key to becoming more relaxed is to let go of your day-to-day concerns. . . . To do this, all you need to do is simply focus on your breathing. . . . Breathe in slowly and deeply, and then breathe out.

Now, we will switch to repeating silently to yourself the word "Relax". Keep your eyes closed. . . . just keep repeating to yourself the word "Relax". . . . Keep repeating "Relax" to yourself silently and slowly. . . . If day-to-day thoughts enter your mind, let them. . . . Keep repeating "Relax" to yourself. . . . All of us encounter daily stressors. . . . It is impossible to avoid daily stressors. . . . The important thing to remember about stress management is not to seek to avoid daily stressors but to find ways to relax when we are under high levels of stress. . . . An excellent and very simple way to learn to relax is to sit in a quiet place, in a comfortable position, and silently repeat to yourself the word "Relax" . . . "Relax" . . . "Relax". . . . By simply repeating the word "Relax" to yourself, you have the power within you to become more and more relaxed. . . . Find a nice comfortable pace for repeating the word "Relax" to yourself. . . . The pace should be slow enough that you can relax. . . . But not be so slow that thoughts about your day-to-day concerns enter your mind. . . . Remember, the key to relaxing is letting go of your day-to-day concerns. . . . If such concerns begin to enter your mind, focus more of your attention on repeating "Relax" silently and slowly to yourself. . . . By repeating "Relax" to yourself, you will find it will appear to have magical powers for you, as you will find yourself becoming more and more relaxed and refreshed. . . . [Have the members repeat "Relax" for five or six minutes.]

Now, we will switch to focusing on your most relaxing scene. Don't open your eyes. . . . Focus on being in your most relaxing place. . . . Feel how good and relaxing it feels. . . . Just dwell on how relaxing it feels. . . . Enjoy everything about how calm and relaxing this place is. . . . Feel yourself becoming calmer, more relaxed. . . . Enjoy the peacefulness of this place. . . . Feel yourself becoming more relaxed, more renewed and refreshed. . . . Enjoy all the sights and sounds of this special place for you. . . . Notice and cherish the pleasant smells and aromas. . . . Feel the warmth, peacefulness, and serenity of this very special place for you. . . . Whenever you want to become more relaxed, all you have to do is close your eyes, sit quietly, and visualize yourself in this very relaxing place. . . . The more you practice visualizing being in your relaxing place, the quicker you will find yourself becoming relaxed. . . . It will appear to you that your relaxing place has magical, relaxing powers for you, but in reality you are simply relaxing yourself by letting go of your day-to-day concerns and instead focusing on enjoying the peacefulness of your most relaxing place. . . . If you have to give a speech, or are facing some other stressful situation, you can learn to reduce your level of anxiety by simply closing your eyes for a short period of time and focusing your thoughts on being in your most relaxing place. . . . You always have the power within you to reduce your level of anxiety. . . . All you have to do is close your eyes and visualize being in your very special relaxing place. . . . Feel yourself becoming more relaxed, refreshed, and calm. . . . If you're feeling drowsy, that's fine. . . . Feeling drowsy is an indication that you're becoming more and more relaxed. . . . You're doing fine. . . . Just keep on visualizing being in your very relaxing place. . . . You will become more and more relaxed by simply letting go of your day-to-day concerns and by enjoying this very special relaxing place. . . . [Pause, then continue this exercise for five or six minutes.]

Unfortunately in a minute or so it will be time to return to this class. But there is no hurry. I will slowly count backwards from (5) to (1), and then ask you to open your eyes shortly after we reach (1) . . . (5). Enjoy how relaxed you feel. You may now feel warmer, drowsy, and so relaxed that you feel you don't want to move a muscle. . . . Enjoy this very special feeling. . . . It is healthy to become this relaxed as your immune system functions best when you are relaxed. . . . (4) Slowly begin to return to this class. . . . There is no rush. . . . There is no hurry. . . . Take your time to become more alert. Any time you want to relax, all you need to do is use one of these three meditative approaches. With practice you will gradually get better at relaxing by using these approaches. . . . (3) You should now focus on returning in a short time to this class . . . take your time . . . we still have a half-minute or so. . . . Examine whether you want to make a commitment to using relaxation exercises to reduce the daily stress you encounter. . . . (2) We are nearly at the time to return to this class. . . . You should now work toward becoming more and more alert. . . . (1) Slowly open your eyes. . . . There is no hurry. . . . Take your time to get oriented. A word of caution: If you have to drive some place soon, please walk around for several minutes before trying to drive a car, as you may be so relaxed now that you may not be alert enough to drive safely.

Step 3: Ask questions such as What do you think of these three approaches? How relaxed did you get? Did any of you have trouble getting relaxed? If yes, why? Which of the three approaches did you like better and why? (If the students feel very relaxed and drowsy, they may feel they do not have the energy to respond to these questions. You should respect such a "mood," and not pressure students to respond.) Note: As an additional relaxation technique, you might obtain and play a muscle relaxation tape, with the class going through the instructions to tense and relax different muscle groups. A variety of audiotapes containing muscle relaxation exercises are available from a number of different sources. As an alternative to playing an audiotape, you may choose to lead the class in a muscle relaxation exercise by reading the instructions for such an exercise that are presented earlier in this chapter.

23

ANALYSIS OF THERAPY APPROACHES

The preceding chapters in Part III of this text have focused primarily on describing intervention techniques. This chapter will provide a critique of these approaches, organized under the following headings:

a. Comparison of counseling theories.

b. How effective is counseling?

c. What really causes psychotherapy changes?

d. Does mental illness exist?

e. Effects of mental illness labels.

Some of the material in this chapter is based on research evidence, while other material presents my own theoretical speculations. When the opinions are mine, this will be clearly indicated in the text.

COMPARISON OF COUNSELING THEORIES

This section compares and contrasts the comprehensive psychotherapy approaches presented earlier in the text: psychoanalysis, client-centered therapy, Gestalt therapy, transactional analysis, reality therapy, rational therapy, and behavior therapy.[1]

To begin with a hypothetical case example, let us assume that a forty-six-year-old male seeks treatment for being fairly depressed. We will take a brief look at what would be the diagnostic and treatment focuses of the above-mentioned therapies. (The description given here has been simplified; a therapist with any of the above treatment orientations would look at a broader range of possible causes and perhaps con-

---

[1]There are other comprehensive psychotherapy theories (e.g., see Corsini and Wedding, 1989, or Prochaska, 1979), but the theories reviewed in this text are the primary ones used by social workers. The reader will note that the neuro-linguistic programming approach is not reviewed here. This is because NLP is not designed to be a theoretical framework for assessing unwanted emotions or dysfunctional behavior.

sider using a wider range of treatment approaches than contained in this summary.)

A psychoanalyst would consider the depression a symptom of a more serious underlying problem and would seek to identify unconscious processes (including defense mechanisms) that underlie the depression. Psychoanalysis would explore the possible causative factors such as unresolved, traumatic early childhood experiences that are probably sexual in nature. A psychoanalyst would use hypnosis, dream analysis, free association, and transference to identify the unresolved unconscious processes that are causing the depression. In treatment, a psychoanalyst would seek to bring the memory of the traumatic experiences to the conscious part of the patient's mind in order to release the pent-up emotions and to allow the patient to consciously work through the disturbing thoughts connected with the trauma. Once the pent-up emotions are released and once the patient gains insight into his disturbing thoughts, it is theorized that the patient's personality will be reorganized and the symptom of depression will disappear.

Client-centered therapy would consider the depression to be caused by incongruencies between the client's self-concept and his experiences. The focus of therapy would be to help the client become aware of these incongruencies. Once this insight is achieved, client-centered therapy postulates that the person's self-actualizing motive will foster a reorganization of the self-concept to be more congruent with experiences. Because client-centered therapy asserts that the self-actualizing motive is the best guide for directing the client, client-centered therapists are nondirective. In therapy, the therapist seeks to convey to the client empathy, positive regard, and genuineness or congruence. It is theorized that if a therapist conveys these three attitudes the client will feel free to examine his incongruencies. During therapy the client-centered therapist would seek to help the client gain insight into his thoughts and feelings by using three types of statements: clarification or reflection of feeling, restatement of content, and simple acceptance.

Gestalt therapy theorizes that awareness in the here and now is therapeutic. Gestalt therapy would consider the depression as resulting from inability of

the self-actualization motive to attend to the most important unfinished situations. (Gestalt therapy asserts that the life of everyone is basically an infinite number of unfinished situations; through awareness a person discovers the most urgent unfinished situations to attend to.) Awareness allows the self-actualization motive to give attention to the most important unfinished situations. The goal of Gestalt therapy is to have the depressed client grow and actualize himself. The therapist would seek to frustrate the depressed client, again and again, until the client is face-to-face with his inhibitions. Gestalt therapy postulates that the client's awareness of being stuck, and the awareness of how he is stuck, makes him recover. The focus of therapy is on fostering the client's awareness and on helping the client to sort things out for himself.

Transactional analysis (TA) would consider that the causes of the depression are due, potentially, to a variety of factors. The client may have a self-defeating life script or may be a victim of destructive psychological games that he or others are playing. Or, he may have communication or interaction difficulties. Or, he may be in an inappropriate ego state for what the circumstances warrant. TA would seek first to identify and make the client aware of the intrapsychic and interpersonal problems he has. These problems would be analyzed and interpreted to the client in terms of TA concepts (for example, in terms of psychological game concepts or in terms of life script concepts). Once analyzed, the therapist would make a contract with the client that would specify courses of action to be taken by the client to alleviate the depression. For example, if the client is depressed because his wife has filed for divorce and has made it perfectly clear she wants a divorce, TA would help the client understand how defective communication and interaction patterns contributed to the divorce, and also help the client to examine possible games and life scripts that may have contributed to the divorce. The TA therapist would then make a contract for the client to take specific actions to improve the problematic areas and to help the client make constructive plans for the future.

Reality therapy would consider the depression as being related to the client's view of himself as a failure in some area of his life. A reality therapist would focus on the present and future, as the past cannot be changed. The therapist would seek to have the client understand that what he wants now and in the future, along with his motivation to achieve what he wants, is more important than his past experiences in determining what his future will be. In therapy, the therapist would seek to form a working relationship with the client, explore the nature of the depression in some depth, explore alternative actions that the client could take to alleviate the depression, and finally make a contract with the client for the client to take certain courses of action by specific deadlines. The reality therapist would seek to convey that the client is responsible for his behaviors through asking such questions as "What are you doing that contributes to the depression?" and "What do you intend to do to improve the situation?" For example, if the client is depressed because he is unhappily married, the therapist would ask such questions as "What are you doing to contribute to the marriage?" and "What can you do to reduce your unhappiness?"

Rational therapy theorizes that the depression results primarily from the client's self-talk about events he is facing. The therapist would inform the client that unwanted emotions arise from negative and irrational self-talk rather than from events. The initial focus of therapy would be to help the client identify the irrational self-talk that is the primary source of his depression. The therapist would next inform the client of three different constructive approaches for resolving the depression: (*a*) seeking to change the events associated with his depression, (*b*) getting involved in meaningful activities (such as hobbies or jogging) that would shift his focus from problematic events to more gratifying events, and (*c*) countering the negative and irrational self-talk with rational self-challenges. The client would then be encouraged to make a verbal contract to try out one or more of these alternatives. If the third alternative is selected, the client would be instructed in how to write a rational self-analysis.

Behavior therapy would focus on identifying the stimuli that are eliciting the client's depression. The behavior therapist would seek to identify environmental pressures or stimuli rather than look "inside" the client for internal stimuli. Behavior therapists believe

there are many possible environmental stimuli that may elicit the response of depression—a monotonous job, an unhappy relationship, pressure from relatives or in-laws, being taken advantage of by certain people, and losing money while gambling. The therapist would seek to identify as precisely as possible the stimuli associated with the response of depression. The therapist would then choose those techniques (from a variety of behavioral intervention techniques) that appear to have the best promise of breaking the stimulus-response connection. For example, if the client is being taken advantage of by a colleague at work, the client might be taught through role-playing to be more assertive. If the client is in an unhappy marriage, the wife may be brought in and the client and his wife may be encouraged to develop contingency contracts by which each would seek to do specific things that please the other, and each would seek to stop doing the things that displease the other. If the client is depressed because he is unemployed, he might be given instruction on how to interview and how to look for jobs. Cognitive behavior therapists would seek to identify the cognitions that are leading the client to be depressed, and then use such techniques as "thought stopping" and "reframing" to change these thoughts.

INSIGHT VERSUS RESOLUTION APPROACHES

A useful categorization of therapies is into approaches that emphasize "insight" and those that emphasize "resolution strategies." This categorization is based on a framework originally developed by London (1964). Insight approaches assert that clients will be able to resolve their problems through gaining an understanding or awareness of their problems. Resolution approaches assert that while it is helpful for clients to understand their problems, insight in and of itself will not resolve the problems; clients must also be taught

FIGURE 23.1

Comparison of Insight and Resolution Approaches to Therapy

Characteristics of Insight Category	Characteristics of Resolution Category
1. Behavior is viewed as being largely determined by internal underlying unconscious processes. Therapies adhering to this view seek to identify the cause of a person's actions by looking at internal factors. (Psychoanalysis, client-centered therapy, Gestalt therapy.)	1. Behavior is viewed as being determined primarily by the environment. Therapies adhering to this view seek to identify the causes of a person's actions by looking at environmental or external factors. (Transactional analysis, reality therapy, behavior therapy.)
2. The problematic behavior (e.g., bed-wetting) is viewed as a *symptom* of an internal, unresolved, and unconscious conflict or fixation. (Psychoanalysis, client-centered therapy, Gestalt therapy.)	2. The problematic behavior (e.g., bed-wetting) is viewed as the problem needing to be resolved. (Transactional analysis, reality therapy, rational therapy, behavior therapy.)
3. If only the symptoms are treated it is postulated that the underlying conflicts will cause another symptom. (Psychoanalysis, client-centered therapy, Gestalt therapy.)	3. If the problematic behavior is resolved, it is postulated that symptom substitution will not occur. (Transactional analysis, reality therapy, rational therapy, behavior therapy.)
4. The goal in therapy is to resolve underlying conflicts or disturbing unconscious processes. (Psychoanalysis, client-centered therapy, Gestalt therapy.)	4. The therapy goal is to eliminate the problematic behavior. (Transactional analysis, reality therapy, rational therapy, behavior therapy.)
5. The medical model is used by labeling and interacting with counselees as patients. (Psychoanalysis.)	5. People with emotional and behavioral problems are viewed as being clients or consumers of services. (Practically all therapy approaches except psychoanalysis.)
6. In order to resolve the underlying conflict, it is necessary to probe deeply into patients' past. (Psychoanalysis.)	6. The "here and now" is important; it is not necessary to probe deeply into clients' past. (Practically all therapy approaches except psychoanalysis.)
7. The goal of therapy is to bring the underlying conflict or the disturbing unconscious processes to the patients' awareness so *(a)* the unexpressed energy can be released and *(b)* the person can then consciously deal with the disabling ideas. (Psychoanalysis, client-centered therapy, and Gestalt therapy.)	7. Once the therapist and client understand the problem, specific resolution approaches are explored, with the client selecting and contracting to try an approach. (Transactional analysis, reality therapy, rational therapy, behavior therapy.)
8. Insight into problems is viewed as being curative in and of itself. (Psychoanalysis, client-centered therapy, Gestalt therapy.)	8. Insight is not by itself viewed as being curative; once understanding of the problem is achieved clients need to become aware of available resolution strategies and then select and try one or more. (Transactional analysis, reality therapy, rational therapy, behavior therapy.)
9. Therapy is likely to last for a long time, often a year or more. (Psychoanalysis, client-centered therapy.)	9. Therapy is likely to be considerably shorter in duration. (Gestalt therapy, reality therapy, rational therapy, transactional analysis, behavior therapy.)

Continued

FIGURE 23.1

▬▬▬▬▬▬▬

(Continued)

Characteristics of Insight Category	Characteristics of Resolution Category
10. The medical model is used, which asserts that mental illness exists. (Psychoanalysis, client-centered therapy, Gestalt therapy, and some advocates of transactional analysis, rational therapy, and behavior therapy.)	10. The medical model is rejected and mental illness is viewed as being a myth. This concept will be elaborated on later in this chapter. (Reality therapy and some advocates of transactional analysis, rational therapy, and behavior therapy.)
11. Mental illness is viewed as resulting from internal unconscious processes, such as conflicts, fixations, and use of defense mechanisms. (Psychoanalysis, client-centered therapy, Gestalt therapy.)	11. A learning theory model is used that assumes behavior, including abnormal behavior, is learned. (Reality therapy, rational therapy, transactional analysis, behavior therapy.)
12. The importance of unconscious processes in causing emotional and behavioral problems is emphasized. (Psychoanalysis, client-centered therapy, Gestalt therapy.)	12. Focusing on unconscious processes in understanding human behavior is deemphasized. (Reality therapy, rational therapy, transactional analysis, behavior therapy.)

In a nutshell, psychoanalysis, client-centered therapy, and Gestalt therapy are usually classified as being insight approaches. Reality therapy, rational therapy, transactional analysis, and behavior therapy are usually classified as being resolution approaches.

or learn specific ways of resolving their problems once insight is achieved. Another name that has been used for the resolution category is "learning approaches" (Eysenck, 1961).

It should be noted that the categories "insight" and "resolution" represent *ideal types*. Most therapy approaches do not really fit simply into one or the other of these two categories; they have some characteristics of both of these ideal types.

The characteristics of these two ideal types and the therapy approaches that adhere to these characteristics are listed in Figure 23.1. The purest therapy approach (the one that has nearly all the characteristics) in the insight category is psychoanalysis, while behavior therapy is perhaps the purest illustration in the resolution category. This material is presented to assist the reader in analyzing and comparing the contemporary theories of psychotherapy.

IS COUNSELING EFFECTIVE?

▬▬▬▬▬▬▬

In the future some historian who is studying the twentieth century may amusingly label it "The Age of Psychotherapy." Hundreds of thousands of people in our country are presently engaged in or seeking counseling/psychotherapy. Millions of dollars every year are being spent by our society to train therapists and to pay therapists for their services. The entertainment world—plays, television programs, movies, and novels—dramatically portrays the lives of many people who are receiving psychotherapy. Every year dozens of books are written on the different theories and techniques of psychotherapy. Certainly, many Americans now believe that receiving psychotherapy is a magical and effective way to change one's personality for the better, to relieve one's tensions, to resolve personal problems, and to lead a happier life. But is it really effective? Does it actually cause people to improve?

Most people, including many psychiatrists, social workers, and psychologists, think that this is an absurd question to ask. They point out that many people do improve after receiving psychotherapy. But is psychotherapy the cause of their improving, or is it just coincidentally connected with their improvement? Perhaps the people who improve while undergoing therapy would improve just as much without having therapy. The only way to discover the effects of psychotherapy is to study the process and the outcome of psychotherapy experimentally; ideally this would involve taking two matched groups of people with personal problems, treating one group by giving them therapy, and then testing both groups to see how much they improved. If the therapy group improves more than the control group, then psychotherapy is probably effective; if both groups improve equally, then psychotherapy is probably ineffective.

At first thought, one would expect that therapists would have done many studies on the effectiveness of psychotherapy for several reasons. (*a*) When psychotherapy was first introduced by Sigmund Freud and shortly afterward adopted by others, it received very strong criticism. The best way to have met this criticism would have been to do experimental studies to prove its effectiveness. (*b*) Clinical psychologists, most of whom at least are part-time therapists, have very strongly emphasized the necessity of doing research and have carried out many research studies. One would expect that at least this profession would have done many studies on psychotherapy. (*c*) Since there are so many different theories and techniques on how to perform psychotherapy, the best way for a particular therapist to show that he has the most effective method would be to test the method experimentally. (*d*) Since Americans are so interested in and spend so much money on psychotherapy, one would naturally expect that there would be good proof (by experimental studies) to show that therapy deserves its high position in our society.

However, when we examine the research literature on the effects of psychotherapy, we find that there have been few well-designed studies on this subject. There are numerous reasons for this lack. Many therapists are so convinced of the effectiveness of psychotherapy that they think there is no need to actually demonstrate that it is effective. Another reason is that it is very difficult to design and carry out studies on this subject. Discussing fully all the problems in designing outcome studies on psychotherapeutic approaches is beyond the scope of this chapter. An excellent discussion of these problems is found in Sundberg and Tyler (1962). A few of the problems are mentioned in order to illustrate the difficulties involved in this type of research.

First, the experimenter has to set up some sort of criteria to evaluate the success of treatment. One way to do this is simply to compare the clients' report of their problems when they first come in for help to their report of their problems after therapy has ended. But this is a very subjective method. One of the main difficulties of this method is what Hathaway (1948) has called the "Hello-Goodbye" effect; that is, when clients first ask for help, they try to convince the therapist that they have serious problems and need help; after therapy has ended they give the impression that they have been helped—perhaps because they think it is just common courtesy to say that they have been helped.

Another criterion that can be used is to have therapists rate the progress of each of their clients. Obviously, there is the danger of a strong bias operating here. Or, personality tests can be given before and after therapy to those clients for whom personality change is a goal of treatment. Here, however, one runs into the difficulty that the validity of most personality tests is low (Stuart, 1970). Perhaps the best way to solve the criterion problem is to use several different criteria to rate the improvement.

The second major problem is to set up an adequate control group. It is very difficult to match every person in the experimental group with another in the control group on variables that may influence therapeutic change, such as social status, age, intelligence, sex, motivation for improving, and problems they're having. Then there is the problem of trying to get rid of the *placebo effect*. (The placebo effect refers to the amazing fact that people actually do improve just because they believe they are being treated. For example, an injection of distilled water into some patients will produce the same positive effects that are being claimed for a drug.) Thus, the experimental group may show improvement over the control group, but this improvement may be entirely due to the placebo effect and not to psychotherapy at all.

Then there are many problems caused by the long length of therapy—sometimes two or three years. To do research, including follow-ups, may take five years or longer. Such a long time means that many subjects will probably be lost—perhaps by death or moving away. Losing subjects can easily lead to erroneous results. Also it is hard to motivate researchers to want to do research on something that will take so long to obtain the results.

These problems in research on psychotherapy are indeed serious, but with ingenuity and perseverance they can be overcome. To show the kind of ingenuity that is needed, H. J. Eysenck (1961, p. 701) describes how to get around the ethical problem of withholding treatment from the control group when an experimental study is being designed:

There are several answers to this point. In the first place, the benefits are merely putative, and consequently nothing is being withheld which is known to be of assistance to the patient. The argument assumes that we have already proved what is in fact the point at issue. In the second place it is a universal practice in medicine, whenever a new method of treatment is put forward, that this new method must receive clinical trials, including a control group not treated by means of the new method. If this is ethically admissible in the whole of medicine, even when the most serious disorders are involved and where the a priori probability of effectiveness in favour of the new cure may be rather high, then it is difficult to see why a different set of ethical ideals should apply in psychiatry where disorders are rather less serious. . . . In the third place it is quite untrue that psychotherapy would have to be withdrawn from certain people in order to provide a control group. Of all those who are said to be able to benefit from psychotherapy only a very small number have in fact received it. In the United States, at least, there is a high correlation between

the income of the patient and the choice of therapy; middle-class patients by and large get psychotherapy, working-class patients get physical treatment. It would be very easy indeed to get together large groups of patients who would not in the normal way obtain psychotherapy and to form an experimental and control group from these patients. If this were done the outcome would not be that psychotherapy was withheld, because of the experiment, from people who might otherwise benefit from it; rather, the experiment would be instrumental in bringing psychotherapy to people who would not otherwise have received it.

In fact, some studies, because they were well designed and well executed, have proved that it is possible to do good outcome studies on psychotherapy. The Cambridge-Somerville Youth Study (Teuber and Powers, 1953) is a good example of this. For approximately eight years, from 1937 to 1945, this large-scale treatment effort was directed at the prevention of delinquency—by guidance, counseling, and therapy—in a group of over 600 delinquent boys. The surprising result of this study was that this treatment did not reduce the incidence of delinquency in the treatment group when compared to the control group. But what is important for our present purposes is that this study (*a*) used a control group that was properly chosen and had a large enough number of subjects in each group (control and experimental) to make the results statistically meaningful; (*b*) carried on the treatment and the follow-up over a long period of time in order to obtain meaningful results, (*c*) used objective criteria in order to evaluate the treatment, and (*d*) investigated the process of therapy in a properly controlled and unbiased fashion. Since this study was able to solve the problems of doing good outcome research on psychotherapy, it demonstrated that the effects of psychotherapy can be researched.

When we turn to studies on the effectiveness of psychotherapy, we find some very startling results!

In 1952 H. J. Eysenck first asked the question: "Is psychotherapy effective?" Eysenck wanted to learn whether psychotherapy increased the rate of recovery from neurosis for adults over what might be expected if they received no psychotherapy. To set up his baseline of recovery from neurosis (the rate of recovery of those not receiving therapy) he used two sources of information: (1) Landis, in his study of New York State hospitals from 1917 to 1934, found that the recovery rate of the neurotic patients within these hospitals was 72 percent. It should be noted that this rate of recovery is probably even lower than the recovery rate of all neurotic people because only severe neurotics who have a poor chance of recovering are sent to state hospitals, and because at that time the patients in state hospitals received very little treatment besides custodial care. (2) Denker found that the rate of recovery of 500 disability claimants of the Equitable Life Assurance Society was also 72 percent. These 500 patients were under a physician's care but received no psychotherapy. Thus, Eysenck chose 72 percent at his baseline of recovery from neurosis.

Eysenck then examined the research literature on the effectiveness of psychotherapy and found nineteen studies, covering over 7,000 cases, in which a wide variety of psychotherapeutic techniques had been used. The studies were divided according to whether the treatment was psychoanalytic or less intensive therapy. The percentage of cured or much improved by psychoanalysis was 44 percent if all cases are considered. (If only completed cases are used, the rate was 66 percent.) The percentage of cured or much improved for the other kinds of therapy was 66 percent. These percentages differ significantly from the baseline recovery rate of 72 percent for neurotic people without any therapy — but the differences are not in the predicted direction!

Eysenck (1952, p. 324) sums up this study by stating:

In general, certain conclusions are possible from these data. They fail to prove that psychotherapy, Freudian or otherwise, facilitates the recovery of neurotic patients. They show that roughly two-thirds of a group of neurotic patients will recover or improve to a marked extend within about two years of the onset of their illness, whether they are treated by means of psychotherapy or not. This figure appears to be remarkably stable from one investigation to another, regardless of type of patient treated, standard

of recovery employed, or method of therapy used. From the point of view of the neurotic, these figures are encouraging; from the point of view of the psychotherapist, they can hardly be called very favourable to his claims.

These are, indeed, some very startling results. However, they have been reaffirmed by E. E. Levitt in 1957, who summarized a large number of unpublished and published studies in which children were treated with psychotherapy. Levitt (1957, p. 196) concludes:

The therapeutic eclecticism, the number of subjects, the results, and the conclusions of this paper are markedly similar to that of Eysenck's study. Two-thirds of the patients examined at close, and about three-quarters seen in follow-up have improved. Approximately the same percentages of improvement are found for comparable groups of untreated children. . . . It now appears that Eysenck's conclusion concerning the data for adult psychotherapy is applicable to children as well; the results do not support the hypotheses that recovery from neurotic disorder is facilitated by psychotherapy.

When Eysenck's results were published in 1952, they stimulated more research on this subject. However, it should be pointed out that the increase in research was not as great as might have been expected from such startling results — perhaps therapists thought that Eysenck's results were so erroneous that many just ignored them, or maybe research in this area is so threatening to therapists that they do not want to research something that might show they are providing little or no useful service. Anyway, Eysenck in 1961 examined the studies in this area that had been done since 1952. He found only three studies showing an increase in the rate of recovery from neurosis for those receiving therapy that was higher than 72 percent baseline recovery rate for those not receiving therapy. These three studies were done by J. Wolpe, Lakin Phillips, and Albert Ellis. All three of these therapists base their treatment on learning theory. Eysenck (1961, p. 720) concludes:

With the single exception of the psychotherapeutic methods based on learning theory, results of published research with military and civilian neurotics, and with both adults and children, suggest that the therapeutic effects of psychotherapy are small or nonexistent, and do not in any demonstrable way add to the nonspecific effects of routine medical treatment, or to such events as occur in the patient's everyday experience.

The writer must admit to being somewhat surprised at the uniformly negative results issuing from all this work. In advancing his rather challenging conclusion in the 1952 report the main motive was one of stimulating better and more worthwhile research in this important but somewhat neglected field; there was an underlying belief that while results to date had not disproved the null hypothesis, improved methods of research would undoubtedly do so. Such a belief does not seem to be tenable any longer in this easy optimistic form, and it would rather seem that psychologists and psychiatrists will have to acknowledge the fact that current psychotherapeutic procedures have not lived up to the hopes which greeted their emergence fifty years ago.

A little later in his summary, Eysenck (1961, p. 721) goes so far as to recommend the following:

It would appear advisable, therefore, to discard the psychoanalytic model, which both on the theoretical and practical plane fails to be useful in mediating verifiable predictions, and to adopt, provisionally at least, the learning theory model which, to date, appears to be much more promising theoretically and also with regard to application.

In 1965 Eysenck again reviewed all the studies conducted on psychotherapy and concluded (pp. 135–36):

Neurotic patients treated by means of psychotherapeutic procedures based on learning theory improve significantly more quickly than do patients treated by means of psychoanalytic or eclectic psychotherapy or not treated by psychotherapy at all.

Neurotic patients treated by psychoanalytic psychotherapy do not improve more quickly than patients treated by means of eclectic psychotherapy, and may

improve less quickly when account is taken of the large proportion of patients breaking off treatment.

With the single exception of the psychotherapeutic methods based on learning theory, results of published research with military and civilian neurotics, and with both adults and children, suggest that the therapeutic effects of psychotherapy are small or nonexistent.

A number of other authorities have reviewed the outcome studies conducted on psychotherapy and have arrived at similar conclusions. Stuart (1970), for example, concludes that only therapy approaches based on what we earlier categorized in this chapter as *resolution approaches* appear to be effective; outcome studies generally show that around 90 percent of clients treated by these approaches improve. Also, Stuart concludes that for clients treated by most insight approaches (such as client-centered therapy) the rate of improvement is about the same as for disturbed persons receiving no treatment.

Finally, for clients receiving therapy from the psychoanalytic approach, the rate of improvement is somewhat lower than for people with problems who receive no treatment. Stuart suggests that the reason for this deterioration is the assignment of nondescriptive medical labels (labels such as schizophrenia, unresolved Oedipus complex, psychosis), which are often assigned by psychoanalysts even though the causes of these supposed disorders are not known and even though these labels do not describe specific behavior. Stuart suggests that such labels have a negative effect; they do not suggest a treatment approach and instead lead patients, and often those who interact with the patients, to try to resolve some unknown, nonexistent illness rather than focusing on resolving their personal problems. Also, such labels lead patients to view themselves as different, as having an illness, which leads them to lose their self-esteem and self-confidence and sidetracks them from seeking to be responsible and productive. (More material will be presented on the effects of mental illness labels later in this chapter.)

A recent review of outcome studies on psychotherapeutic approaches is contained in Corsini and Wedding (1989). The results continue to be consistent with those reported in the above material.

Fischer (1973) asked the question, "Is casework effective?" Fischer then reviewed all the outcome studies on casework that used both an experimental group and a control group. Eleven studies were found and reviewed. The findings are similar to the findings of outcome studies on insight approaches to psychotherapy. Fischer (1973, pp. 13–14) reports:

Of all the controlled studies of the effectiveness of casework that could be located, nine out of eleven clearly showed that professional caseworkers were unable to bring about any positive, significant, measurable changes in their clients beyond those that would have occurred without the specific intervention program or that could have been induced by nonprofessionals dealing with similar clients, often in less intensive service programs. In the two additional studies, the results were obfuscated by deficiencies in the design or the statistical analysis. Thus not only has professional casework failed to demonstrate that it is effective, but lack of effectiveness appears to be the rule rather than the exception across several categories of clients, problems, situations, and types of casework.

Fischer (1979) raises the question, "Isn't casework effective yet?" and concludes (p. 245), "There is still no evidence that MSW-level social workers can produce better results with their clients than would occur with no treatment at all."

What do such research findings mean? The author will provide his thoughts on the conclusions to be drawn from these reviews of outcome studies:

1. The effectiveness of casework, psychotherapy, and counseling can no longer be assumed. Additional research is definitely needed to determine which therapeutic approaches are effective, and why they are effective.

2. Available evidence suggests that psychoanalytic approach should either be discarded or at least tested extensively to determine why patients have a lower rate of improvement than the rate for people with problems who receive no treatment.

3. Approaches that only seek to have clients gain insight into their problems appear to have no higher rate of improvement than the rate for people with problems who receive no treatment. (It appears that therapy techniques based on the insight model were largely used by caseworkers in the eleven studies reviewed by Fischer.) These research findings suggest that while insight into a problem may be useful, it is not in and of itself sufficient to bring about positive changes.

4. Therapies that are based on a learning theory approach to helping clients are generally being found to be effective in outcome studies. A crucial component of the learning model appears to be exploring resolution strategies and then having clients select and contract to use a specific resolution approach. Often clients need to be "taught" how to use the strategy (e.g., doing a rational self-analysis) in their daily lives. Approaches that largely use the learning model include behavior therapy, transactional analysis, reality therapy, and rational therapy.

WHAT REALLY CAUSES PSYCHOTHERAPY CHANGE?

Client-centered therapy, psychoanalysis, rational therapy, Gestalt therapy, behavior therapy, transactional analysis, reality therapy, hypnosis, meditation, encounter therapies, and crisis intervention have all been used to treat a wide range of emotional and behavioral problems. Practically all of these approaches have been used to treat people who are depressed, or lonely, or have marital or other interpersonal relationship problems, or who have disabling fears and phobias, or are overly aggressive, or have drinking problems, or who suffer from grief, shame, or guilt. Each of the above therapies differ substantially from every other in treatment techniques and in terms of explaining why therapeutic change occurs. Yet, each of these approaches is used by various practitioners who are able to provide case examples that each of these approaches leads to positive changes.

How can all these distinct and diverse psychotherapeutic approaches produce positive changes in clients?[2] What is it that produces positive changes in therapy? Is there a single explanation that will describe psychotherapy changes that are produced by diverse therapies? (The explanation presented here is one this author and several other writers are advocating but which as yet has not been universally accepted.)

Prior chapters have described the above therapy approaches and presented the explanations advanced by each as to why positive changes occur in counseling. Practically every theory postulates a different view for why positive changes occur. In reviewing this dilemma, Raimy (1977, p. 1) states:

Psychotherapists today are faced with an insistent, nagging problem: since widely diverse methods of treatment for similar problems have their successes as well as their failures, how can one defend a given set of treatment procedures as superior to others? Clearly, since quite different, even contradictory, methods of treatment produce similar results, explanations for the success of treatment must be sought outside the realm of method or technique.

What Causes Disturbing Emotions and Ineffective Actions?

Before attempting to provide an explanation of what produces positive changes in therapy, it would appear important to identify the primary determinants of emotional and behavior problems.

Most people believe erroneously that our emotions and our actions are determined primarily by our experiences (that is, by events that happen to us). A number of authorities (Dyer, 1976; Ellis and Harper, 1977b; Lembo, 1974; Maultsby, 1976), however, have demonstrated that the primary cause of all our emotions and actions is what we tell ourselves about events that happen to us.

All feelings and actions occur according to the following format:

Events: (Or experiences.)
   ↓
Self-Talk: (Self-talk is the set of evaluating thoughts
   | we give ourselves about facts and events
   | that happen to us.)
   ↓
Emotions: (May include remaining calm.)
   ↓
Actions:

This explanation of the primary determinants of our actions is described at length in the material on rational therapy in Chapter 18.

The most important point about the above formula is that our self-talk determines how we feel and act; by changing our self-talk we can change how we feel and act. Generally we cannot control events that happen to us, but we have the power to think rationally and thereby change *all* of our unwanted emotions and dysfunctional behaviors.

The above formula shows that self-talk is the primary determinant of all actions and all emotions, including love, fear, anger, grief, depression, anxiety, shame, happiness, hate, and frustration. Zastrow (1979) has also shown that self-talk is the primary determinant of our self-concept, sense of success, or sense of failure, our personality, and psychosomatic illnesses.

Could Restructuring Thinking Be the Key Psychotherapeutic Agent?

The above conceptualization asserts that discomforting emotions and dysfunctional actions arise primarily from our self-talk, generally self-talk that is negative or irrational. If this conceptualization is accurate, an important corollary is that *any therapy technique that is successful in changing emotions or actions is effective*

---

[2]This section tentatively assumes that all the above-mentioned therapies produce positive changes. The previous section has questioned whether a few of these therapies (particularly psychoanalysis and client-centered therapy) do in fact produce positive changes. The reasons that reported negative changes may be occurring while the client is receiving psychoanalysis are discussed later in this section when psychoanalysis is reviewed.

primarily because it changes a person's thinking from self-talk that is negative or irrational to self-talk that is more rational[3] *and positive.* In other words, self-talk appears to me to be the key therapeutic agent in all approaches that produce positive changes in our emotions and our behaviors. Practically all the contemporary approaches to psychotherapy can be reinterpreted to be consistent with the basic therapeutic principle of producing psychotherapeutic change by restructuring thinking. A few examples are presented below.

PSYCHOANALYSIS   Freud (1924) saw the basic goal of therapy as bringing disturbing, suppressed ideas and emotions to the conscious part of the mind so that the disturbing ideas (now conscious) could be dealt with and the unconscious emotion (energy) could be expressed. Is not Freud, in essence, seeking to help clients become aware of their disturbing ideas (self-talk) so that they can then change this disturbing self-talk? Once such disturbing self-talk is changed, the format presented here suggests that the unwanted emotions generated by the original self-talk (now changed) will be alleviated.[4]

Psychoanalysis asserts that these disturbing ideas are usually unconscious. I agree with this assertion partially, as it appears that clients occasionally may not be fully aware of the "disturbing ideas" that are getting them into trouble, and sometimes considerable probing is needed to identify such "self-talk" (Zastrow, 1979).

BEHAVIOR THERAPY   Originally, behavior modification therapists conceptualized their efforts as being *S* (stim-

ulus) → *R* (response) in nature. Their efforts were focused on identifying and applying stimuli that would change unwanted responses (behaviors). In the past thirty years there has been an increasingly large group of behavior therapists who emphasize the importance of changing cognitions in order to modify human behavior (Beck, 1976; Cautela and Upper, 1975; Craighead, Mahoney, and Kazdin, 1976; Goldfried and Merbaum, 1973; Lazarus, 1971; Mahoney, 1974; Meichenbaum, 1975). These authorities on behavior therapy are now calling themselves *cognitive behaviorists*. Their approach is focused on changing the person's thinking in order to produce changes in behavior. Instead of the old *S* → R conceptualization, they emphasize that behavior changes are best conceptualized as involving a change in a person's thinking, as illustrated in the following format: *S* → O (organism's thinking) → *R*. Thought-stopping and reframing which are described in Chapter 19, are good examples of techniques that are used to change irrational thoughts in order to alleviate unwanted emotions and to change dysfunctional behaviors.

One of the most popular applications of behavior therapy is assertiveness training. All of us are shy or timid in some situations, perhaps in arranging a date, or in talking to an authority figure, or asking someone to put out a cigarette. Authorities on assertiveness training have pointed out that we are shy, or aggressive, because of what we tell ourselves about these situations and that it is necessary to change our cognitions in order to be able to express ourselves assertively (Alberti and Emmons, 1975).

CLIENT-CENTERED THERAPY   The goal of this approach is to help a client gain insight into the inconsistencies between his ideas about self and his experiences, so that the client can then reorganize his self-concept to be more consistent with what he experiences. Is not Carl Rogers saying that clients need to identify the thoughts (self-talk) about themselves that are inconsistent with reality, and then reorganize these thoughts to become more consistent with reality?

OTHER COMPREHENSIVE THERAPY APPROACHES   In *Misunderstandings of the Self*, Raimy (1977) proposes a theory to explain positive changes in counseling that is

---

[3]According to Maultsby (1975), rational thinking and rational behavior (*a*) are based on objective reality, (*b*) help you protect your life, (*c*) help you achieve your short- and long-term goals more quickly, (*d*) help you get out and stay out of significant trouble with other people, and (*e*) help you prevent significant unwanted emotions.

[4]In the previous section research was presented suggesting that psychoanalysis, overall, appears to be less effective than receiving no treatment. How is this explainable? One explanation is that when the therapist uses such terms as *psychosis, Oedipal complex,* and *fixation at the oral stage of development*, the client is sidetracked from focusing his thinking on resolving the real problems he has and instead develops irrational self-talk connected with worrying about having (and trying to resolve) mystical problems that do not exist. Such irrational self-talk, it is hypothesized, may then lead to deterioration.

nearly identical to the self-talk approach presented here. Raimy's main hypothesis is "If those ideas or conceptions of a client or patient which are relevant to his psychological problems can be changed in the direction of greater accuracy where his reality is concerned, his maladjustments are likely to be eliminated." Raimy calls his hypotheiss the *misconception hypothesis* (Raimy, 1977, p. 7). Raimy then proceeds to provide a rationale that positive changes obtained through correcting "misconceptions" account for the changes in the following therapies: Adlerian, rational-emotive, psychoanalysis, transactional analysis, Gestalt therapy, client-centered therapy, and certain behavior modification techniques.

Nontraditional Psychotherapy Techniques

I have presented a rationale that changing self-talk primarily accounts for the positive changes produced with hypnosis, systematic desensitization, biofeedback, meditation, muscle relaxation, deep breathing relaxation, imagery relaxation, in vivo desensitization, acupuncture, electroshock therapy, covert sensitization, sex therapy for sexual dysfunctions, assertiveness training, diet counseling, and therapy for alcoholics (Zastrow, 1979). The rationale for a few of these approaches is summarized below.

MEDITATION   Daniel Goleman (1977) summarizes the contemporary approaches to meditation and describes how each attempts to accomplish its goal. Practically all the approaches seek to achieve a meditative state by having a person concentrate on an object or repeat a sound: a word, phrase, chant, spiritual value, image of an exquisite painting, and so forth. As described in Chapter 22, deep breathing relaxation, imagery relaxation, and repeating the word "one" are all forms of meditation.

Herbert Benson (1975) has noted that the key element in inducing the relaxation response via meditation is having a passive attitude in which the meditator lets go thoughts about his day-to-day concerns. Maultsby (1975) has shown that feelings of stress and anxiety arise primarily from negative and irrational self-talk

about day-to-day problems. Meditation, it is hypothesized here, reduces the feelings of stress and anxiety by having the meditator switch his or her thinking from focusing on day-to-day problems to focusing on the mantra or meditative object. This process can be diagrammed as follows:

A. Event: Concentrating and repeating a mantra while great care is taken to prevent interruptions or distractions.

B. Self-Talk "This is relaxing." (At the same time the person stops thinking about his day-to-day concerns.)

C. Emotion: Feeling of being relaxed.

HYPNOSIS   Hypnosis essentially involves two processes: (a) becoming relaxed so that a person goes into what is called a hypnotic trance; and (b) while in a trance, giving oneself hypnotic suggestions. The hypnotic trance state can be induced by a variety of relaxation techniques, including deep breathing relaxation, imagery relaxation, and other forms of meditation. The hypnotic trance state can be best understood as a state of deep relaxation. As explained in the previous section on meditation, this relaxed state is induced by the meditator's letting go of thinking about his day-to-day concerns.

The second process of hypnosis involves hypnotic suggestions. The therapeutic power of self-talk is dramatically demonstrated by hypnotic suggestions. While in a trance a person can be given a wide variety of instructions or suggestions, many of which are increasingly being used for therapeutic reasons. Nearly all of these hypnotic suggestions are, in actuality, self-talk statements, as the following illustrates:

"I will feel no pain," for those with arthritis or undergoing surgery, for those with terminal cancer, for childbirth, and for practically any type of pain.

"I will relax," for those who are very anxious or tense.

"I will fall asleep after going to bed and counting to ten," for those suffering from insomnia.

"My menstrual period will now be regular," for those with irregular periods.

MUSCLE RELAXATION   Deep muscle relaxation is a technique that people can use when they are tense or anx-

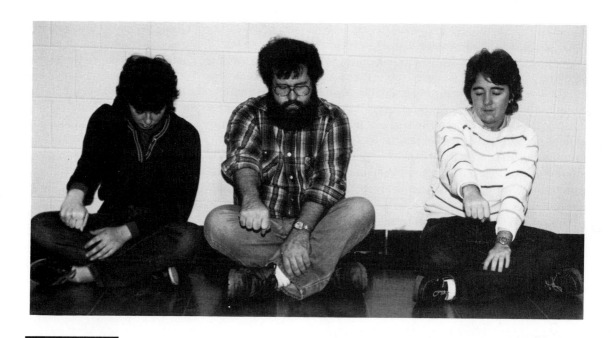

Deep muscle relaxation in a classroom

ious to become more relaxed (Paul, 1966). The technique is learned by having a person first tighten and then relax a set of muscles. When relaxing the muscles the person is instructed to think about the relaxed feeling, while noting that the muscles are more relaxed than before they were tensed. The following excerpt (Watson and Tharp, 1972; pp. 182–83) gives a brief illustration of the procedure.

Make a fist with your dominant hand (usually right). Make a fist and tense the muscles of your (right) hand and forearm; tense it until it trembles. Feel the muscles pull across your fingers and the lower part of your forearm. . . . Hold this position for 5 to 7 seconds, then . . . relax. . . . Just let your hand go. Pay attention to the muscles of your (right) hand and forearm as they relax. Note how those muscles feel as relaxation flows through them (20 to 30 seconds).

After a person learns to relax one set of muscles, he learns to relax other sets (e.g., muslces of the arm,

neck, shoulders, chest, stomach, lower back, hips, thights, and so forth).

Applying the principles of *rational therapy*, it appears that self-talk is a key to achieving a relaxed state:

Event: A person relaxes a set of muscles af-
  ↓   ter having tensed the muscles.
Self-Talk: "This is relaxing." "Feels good."
  ↓   "This is calming."
Emotional
  Consequence: Relaxation.

Advocates of muscle relaxation point out that, with practice, a person can achieve deep relaxation without having to tense muscles — that is, by imagery (Watson and Tharp, 1972). Apparently the following is occurring:

Event: I am imagining my arm (thigh, etc.)
  ↓   muscles first tensing and then be-
                coming very relaxed.
Self-Talk: "This feels good, is relaxing."
  ↓
Emotional
  Consequence: Relaxation.

Muscle relaxation, it is hypothesized here, also reduces the feelings of stress and anxiety by helping a person switch her thinking from focusing on day-to-day problems to focusing on the relaxation exercises.

Consistent with the belief of a number of authorities, it is asserted that discomforting emotions and dysfunctional actions arise primarily from our self-talk, generally self-talk that is negative or irrational. If this conceptualization is accurate, an important corollary is that any therapy technique that is successful in changing emotions or actions is effective primarily because it changes a person's thinking from self-talk that is negative or irrational to self-talk that is more rational and positive.

At this point there is some support (although more research is needed) for the notion that changing negative or irrational self-talk is the key therapeutic agent in psychotherapy approaches. If accurate, the old argument of which therapy approaches are effective and which are not (Eysenck, 1952; Stuart, 1970) may in the near future be refocused to "Which therapy approaches are most effective in changing negative and irrational self-talk?" And "How can present therapy approaches be refined, and new approaches developed, to change negative and irrational self-talk more effectively?"

DOES MENTAL ILLNESS EXIST?[5]

The question of whether mental illness exists was raised earlier in this chapter; it is discussed here at length. Whether mental illness exists has extensive implications for the helping professions.

While working at a mental hospital, I was assigned a case of a twenty-two-year-old male who decapitated his seventeen-year-old girlfriend. Why did he do it? Two psychiatrists diagnosed him as being schizophrenic and a court found him to be "innocent by reason of insanity." He was then committed to a mental hospital. Why did he do it? Labeling him as insane provides an explanation to the general public that he exhibited this strange behavior because he was "crazy." But does such a label explain why he killed this girl, rather than killing someone else, or doing something else that is bizarre? Does the label explain what would have prevented him from committing this slaying? Does the label suggest the kind of treatment that will cure him? The answer to all these questions is, of course, no.

What Is Schizophrenia?

A common definition of *schizophrenia* is a psychotic condition usually occurring during or shortly after adolescence and characterized by disorientation, loss of contact with reality, and disorganized patterns of thinking and feeling. Let us examine this definition. People who are intoxicated, or stoned on drugs, or who are asleep, or who have not slept for over a day experience a loss of contact with reality and their feelings and thinking patterns become disorganized. Are they schizophrenic? No. What about the severely and profoundly mentally retarded who have a mental age of less than two? They have the above symptoms but are not considered to be schizophrenic. What about people who go into a coma following a serious accident? They also fit the definition above but are not considered schizophrenic. The twenty-two-year-old male who committed the bizarre homicide knew the act was wrong, was aware of what he was doing, was in contact with reality, and told me the reasons for doing what he did. Then why was he labeled schizophrenic? Could it be *that there is no definition of symptoms that separates people who have this "disease" from those who do not?*

---

[5]This section is adapted from the following articles: (*a*) Charles Zastrow, "When Labeled Mentally Ill," in *The Personal Problem Solver*, edited by Charles Zastrow and Dae H. Chang, © 1977, pp. 163–69. Adapted by permission of Prentice-Hall, Inc., Englewood Cliffs, New Jersey; (*b*) Charles Zastrow, "Understanding Deviant Behavior," in *Talk to Yourself: Using the Power of Self-Talk*, © 1979, pp. 117–24. Adapted by permission of Prentice-Hall, Inc., Englewood Cliffs, New Jersey.

The Controversy over the Mental Illness Approach

Currently there is a substantial controversy in the mental health field regarding whether mental illness does in fact exist. The use of mental illness labels involves applying medical labels (e.g., schizophrenia, paranoia, psychosis, insanity) to emotional problems. Adherents of the medical approach believe the disturbed person's mind is affected by some generally unknown, internal condition. That unknown, internal condition, they assert, might be caused by genetic endowment, metabolic disorders, infectious diseases, internal conflicts, unconscious use of defense mechanisms, and traumatic early experiences that cause emotional fixations and prevent future psychological growth.

Critics of the medical (mental illness) approach assert that such medical labels have no diagnostic or treatment value and frequently have an adverse labeling effect.

Thomas Szasz (1961) was one of the first authorities to assert that mental illness is a myth—that it does not exist. Beginning with the assumption that the term *mental illness* implies a "disease of the mind," he categorizes all of the so-called mental illnesses into three types of emotional disorders and discusses the inappropriateness of calling such human difficulties "mental illnesses":

1. Personal diabilities, such as excessive anxiety, depression, fears, and feelings of inadequacy. Personal disabilities are unwanted emotions. Szasz says these so-called mental illnesses may appropriately be considered "mental" (in the sense that thinking and feeling are considered "mental" activities), but he asserts they are not diseases.

2. Antisocial acts, such as bizarre homicides and other social deviations. Homosexuality used to be in this category, but was removed from the American Psychiatric Association's list of mental illnesses in 1974. Szasz says such antisocial acts are only social deviations and asserts they are neither "mental" nor "diseases."

3. Deterioration of the brain with associated personality changes. This category includes the "mental illnesses" in which personality changes follow brain

deterioration from such causes as arteriosclerosis, chronic alcoholism, Alzheimer's disease, general paresis, or serious brain damage following an accident. Common symptoms are loss of memory, listlessness, apathy, and deterioration of personal grooming habits. Szasz says these disorders can appropriately be considered "diseases," but are diseases of the brain (brain deterioration), which specifies the nature of the problem, rather than being a disease of the mind.

Szasz (1961, p. 84) states:

The belief in mental illness as something other than man's trouble in getting along with his fellow man, is the proper heir to the belief in demonology and witchcraft. Mental illness exists or is "real" in exactly the same sense in which witches existed or were "real."

In actuality, there are three steps to becoming labeled "mentally ill": (*a*) the person displays some strange deviant behavior; (*b*) the behavior is not tolerated by the family or local community; and (*c*) the professional labeler, usually a psychiatrist, happens to believe in the medical model and assigns a mental illness label. Thomas Scheff (1966) and David Mechanic (1962) provide evidence that whether the family and community will tolerate the deviant behavior and whether the professional labeler believes in the medical model are more crucial in determining whether someone will be assigned a "mentally ill" label than the strange behavior exhibited by the person.

The point that Szasz and a number of other authorities are striving to make is that people do have emotional and behavioral problems, but they do not have a mystical, mental illness. They believe the following terms are useful in describing behavior: *depression, anxiety, an obsession, a compulsion, excessive fear, feelings of being a failure*. Such terms describe personal problems that people have. But they assert that the medical terms (such as *schizophrenia* and *psychosis*) are not useful because there is no distinguishing symptom that would indicate whether a person has, or does not have, the "illness." In addition, Offer and Sabshin (1966) point out there is considerable variation among cultures regarding what is defined as a mental illness. The usefulness of the medical model is also questioned because psychiatrists frequently disagree on the medical diagnosis to be assigned to those who are disturbed (Kolb, Bernard, and Dohrenwend, 1969).

In an intriguing study, David Rosenhan (1973) found that professionals in mental hospitals could not distinguish "sane" patients from "insane" patients. Rosenhan and seven "sane" associates went to twelve mental hospitals in five different states, claiming they were hearing voices. All eight were admitted as patients. After admission these pseudopatients claimed they stopped hearing voices, and they acted normally. The hospitals kept these pseudopatients hospitalized for an average of nineteen days, and all were discharged with a diagnosis of "schizophrenia in remission." The study showed these hospitals were unable to distinguish the "sane" status of the experimenters from the "insane" status of other patients.

The use of such medical labels has several adverse labeling effects. The person labeled mentally ill (and frequently the therapist) believes that the person has a disease for which unfortunately there is no known "cure." The label gives the labeled person an excuse for not taking responsibility for his actions (e.g., innocent by reason by insanity). Since there is no known "cure," the disturbed frequently idle away their time waiting for someone to discover a cure, rather than assuming responsibility for their behavior, examining the reasons that there are problems, and making efforts to improve. Other undesirable consequences of being labeled mentally ill are that those so labeled may lose some of their legal rights (Szasz, 1963); may be stimatized in social interactions as being dangerous, unpredictable, untrustworthy, or of "weak" character (Phillips, 1963); and may find it more difficult to secure employment or receive a promotion (Lemert, 1951).

An even more dangerous effect is that the labeled person may come to view himself as being different, as being "mentally ill," and thereby end up playing the role of a "mentally ill" person for a long, long time. Everyone has a need to evaluate feelings, opinions, and abilities. In the absence of objective, nonsocial means of evaluation, a person will rely on other people to gauge beliefs and feelings. If others define a person as being mentally ill, and react to that person as if he or she were mentally ill, the person may well begin to say, "I must be crazy as other people are relating to me as

being insane." With such self-talk, that person may well define himself as being different or "crazy" and begin playing that role.

A PERSPECTIVE FROM RATIONAL THERAPY

Rational therapy asserts that *any bizarre act can be understood by discovering the self-talk that led a person to do something "strange."* In almost all cases the reasons for the occurrence of any deviant act can be determined by examining what the offender was telling himself prior to and during the time when the deviant act was being committed. The reasons for the deviant act occurring (similar to any action) follow the formula postulated by rational therapy and described in Chapter 18:

Events   (Experiences)
  ↓
Self-talk:
  ↓
Emotions:
  ↓
Actions: (In this case deviant actions)

Furthermore, identifying the "self-talk" that led a person to do something deviant will generally provide information on the kinds of services needed to prevent the deviant behavior from recurring (an example is presented below).

Committing a deviant act (or continuing to display deviant behavior) is not the only reason some people are labeled mentally ill. Mental illness labels are sometimes applied to people who have serious, discomforting emotions such as severe or chronic depression, anxiety, grief, or feelings of inferiority.

Discomforting emotions range on a continuum in severity from mild to extreme. Labelers who adhere to the medical model are forced to draw a line somewhere along this continuum to separate the "insane" from the "sane." All severe discomforting emotions, similar to any emotion, result from self-talk according to the following format:

Events or experiences.

↓

Self-talk.

↓

Emotion.

Rational therapy asserts there is no need to attach a nondescript medical label (such as labeling a severe depression "psychotic") to a severe, discomforting emotion. Such medical labels have no diagnostic or treatment value and may well complicate therapy efforts due to labeling effects.

A Bizarre Murder

Let us return to the twenty-two-year-old male who was labeled "schizophrenic" for murdering his girlfriend. (This murder was briefly described at the beginning of this section on mental illness.) A medical diagnosis should identify the general causes of the medical condition and suggest a treatment approach. In this case the label does not tell us why the murder occurred nor does it suggest what type of rehabilitation is needed. (Incidentally, this male was seen by a psychiatrist a few months prior to this slaying and was viewed as "sane.")

However, after this person described what happened, it was understandable (even though bizarre) why he did what he did and his account also identified the specific problems he needed help with. He described himself as a very isolated person who, except for his girlfriend, had no close relatives or friends. He came from a broken home and was raised by a variety of relatives and foster parents. Because of frequent moves, he attended a number of different schools and made no lasting friends. At age twenty he met the victim and dated her periodically for two years. She provided the only real meaning that he had in life. He held the traditional vision of marrying her and living happily together thereafter.

However, a few months prior to the fatal day, he became very alarmed that he was going to "lose her." She encouraged him to date others, mentioned that she wanted to date others, and suggested that they no longer see as much of each other.

He thought intensely about how he could preserve the relationship. He also realized he had rather intense sexual tensions with no outlet. Putting the two together he naively concluded, "If I'm the first person to have sexual relations with her, she will forever feel tied to me." He therefore tried on several occasions to have coitus, but she always managed to dissuade him. Finally, one afternoon during the summer when he knew they would be alone together, he arrived at the following self-talk decision, "I *will* have sex with her this afternoon, even if I have to knock her unconscious." He stated he knew such action was wrong, but said, "It was my last hope of saving our relationship. Without her, life would not be worth living."

He again tried to have sexual relations with her that afternoon, but she continued to dissuade him. Being emotionally excited, he then took a soda bottle and knocked her unconscious. He again attempted to have coitus, but was still unsuccessful for reasons related to her physical structure. In an intense state of emotional and sexual excitement, he was unable rationally to consider the consequences of his actions. (All of us, at times, have acted dysfunctionally while angry or in a state of intense emotional excitement.) At this point he felt his whole world was caving in. When asked during an interview what he was thinking at this point he stated, "I felt that if I couldn't have her, no one else would either." He sought and found a knife, became further carried away with emotions, and ended up slaying her. He knew it was wrong, and he was aware of what he was doing.

Conversations with this person (and identification of the self-talk prior to and during this bizarre murder) pinpoint certain factors that help explain why the murder took place, including this man's loneliness and isolation, his feeling that continuing a romantic relationship with this young woman was the only source of meaning in his life, his naive thinking that a forced sexual relationship would lead this young woman to feel tied and attracted to him, his lack of any outlet for his sexual drives, and his jealous and possessive desires to go to extreme lengths to prevent this young woman from developing a romantic relationship with another male. Such reasons help to explain why the bizarre behavior took place; the label *schizophrenia* does not.

If the above problems had been known prior to the murder, the slaying might have been prevented. What he needed was to find other sources of interest and other meaningful relationships in his life. Joining certain groups or developing hobbies may well have helped. An appropriate sexual outlet for his passions probably would have also been helpful. Better control of his passions and other sources of finding meaning might have prevented him from losing control of his emotions that afternoon. Reducing the intensity of his jealous and possessive feelings, along with developing more mature attitudes toward romance and sexuality, might also have been preventative. These specific problems are the areas that he needs help with while in a mental hospital, rather than with finding a cure for schizophrenia. In no way does the author feel that this person should be excused for his actions, as implied by the term *innocent by reason of insanity*. But he does need help for the specific problems identified. (In ten or fifteen years he will probably be released and return to society.)

In summary, when a deviant act occurs, asserting that the behavior was due to a "mental illness" does not appear to provide a useful explanation for why the behavior occurred. All such deviant behaviors are understandable, however, when viewed from the actor's perspective.

If the reader wonders how someone could arrive at a point of doing something as bizarre as taking the life of someone he loves, remember it is necessary to attempt to view the situation from the deviant person's perspective. In order to understand such a perspective, it is essential to try to consider all the circumstances, pressures, values, and belief systems of the deviant person. An unusual true example may help the reader to become aware that practically anyone will do something bizarre when circumstances become desperate. Several years ago a passenger plane crashed in the Andes in the wintertime. A number of people were killed, but there were nearly thirty survivors. Rescue efforts initially failed to locate the survivors, who took shelter from the cold in the wreckage of the plane. The survivors were without food for over forty days until they were finally rescued. During this time the survivors were faced with the choice of dying of starvation, or cannibalism of those who died. It was a very desperate, difficult decision. (Psychologically, many people who commit a bizarre act feel they face a comparable decision.) In this situation, all but one of the initial

plane crash survivors chose cannibalism. The one who refused died of starvation.

LABELING AS A CAUSE OF CHRONIC "MENTAL ILLNESS"

Labels have a major impact on our lives. A few examples will be given. If a child is continually called "stupid" by her parents, that child is apt to develop a low self-concept, anticipate failure in many areas (particularly academic), and thereby put forth little effort in school and in competitive interactions with others and end up "failing." If a teenage girl in high school gets a reputation as being promiscuous, adults and peers may label her a "whore," with other girls then shunning her and teenage boys ridiculing her, and perhaps some seeking to date her for a "one-night stand." If a person is labeled an "ex-con" for spending time in prison, that person is likely to be viewed with suspicion, have trouble finding employment, and be stigmatized as being dangerous and untrustworthy, even though the person may be a good family person, be honest, and be conscientious and hardworking.

On another level, labels have an important effect on our day-to-day living. If we fail at a task, we often tend to label ourselves as being a "failure" rather than adopting the more rational perspective of saying that we have only failed at a task. Since we are all fallible, it is irrational either to anticipate perfection or to depreciate ourselves for failing at a task. If we *want* something (e.g., a friend to be attracted to us romantically) we often mistakenly mislabel the want as being a *need*; the problem is that if the erroneously labeled need is not achieved, we then make ourselves deeply depressed by telling ourselves how "awful" our life is because the need is not obtained. A number of people enter a marriage or a romantic relationship assuming that the relationship gives them *ownership rights*; they then interact with their partner in terms of their expectations of what the partner *ought* to do to fulfill their label that the partner is now a *possession* of theirs. One final example will be given. We often assign labels to others that at face value are absurd (names assigned to people include "a jerk," "a bleeding-heart liberal," "a worm," "an animal," "a bully," "a devil," "a son-of-a-bitch," "a queen," "a pig," "a blimp," a "savior," "a doll," "an angel.") But once such labels are assigned, the ridiculous result is that at least some of our interactions are guided by these labels.

It should be noted that labels do have value, as they convey information and are important for categorizing data. When labels accurately categorize data and accurately convey information they are very functional. However, if labels are inaccurate, they have the potential to be immensely harmful and destructive. As indicated in the previous section, mental illness labels may be inaccurate and may interfere with understanding and treating emotional and behavioral problems.

A legitimate question that is sometimes asked is, "If mental illness does not exist, why do some people go through life as if they were mentally ill?" Scheff (1966) has developed a theory that provides an answer. Scheff's main hypothesis is that labeling is the most important determinant of chronic functional "mental illness."

Scheff begins by first arriving at a definition of *mental illness*. He begins by stating (p. 31):

One source of immediate embarrassment to any social theory of "mental illness" is that the terms used in referring to these phenomena in our society prejudge the issue. The medical metaphor "mental illness" suggests a determinant process which occurs within the individual: the unfolding and development of disease. In order to avoid this assumption, we will utilize sociological, rather than medical concepts to formulate the problem.

He states that the symptoms of mental illness can be viewed as violations of social norms, and that for his purposes the term *mental illness* will be used to refer to those assigned such a label by professionals (usually psychiatrists).

Scheff indicates that literally thousands of studies have been conducted in recent years seeking to identify the origins of long-term mental disorders. Practically all of these studies have sought to identify the causes as being somewhere inside a person (e.g., metabolic disorders, unconscious conflicts, heredity factors). These research efforts have been based on medical and psychological models of human behavior. Yet, amazingly, in spite of this extensive research, the determinants of chronic mental disorders (e.g., schizophrenia) are largely unknown.

Scheff suggests that researchers may well be looking in the wrong direction for determinants; instead of seeking causes inside a person, Scheff suggests the major determinants are in social processes (that is, in interactions with others).

Scheff's theory is summarized here. Scheff suggests that everyone, at times, violates social norms and commits acts that could be labeled symptoms of mental illness. For example, a person may on occasion angrily engage in fights with others, or experience intense depression or grief, or be highly anxious, or use drugs or alcohol to excess, or have a fetish, or be an exhibitionist, or commit a highly unusual and bizarre act.

Usually the person who has unwanted emotions or who commits deviant acts is not identified (labeled) as being mentally ill. In such cases, the unwanted emotions and deviant actions are usually not classified as symptoms of a mental illness but instead are ignored, unrecognized, or rationalized in some other manner.

Occasionally, however, such norm violations are perceived by others as being "abnormal." The offenders are then labeled mentally ill, and consequently related to as if they were mentally ill. At the time when people are publicly labeled, they are highly suggestible to cues from others. They realize they have done something unusual and turn to others to obtain an assessment of who they really are. In the absence of objective measures of their sanity, they rely on others for this assessment. If others relate to them as if they are mentally ill, they begin to define and perceive themselves as being mentally ill.

Traditional stereotypes of mental illness define the mentally ill role, both for those who are labeled mentally ill and for people they interact with. Frequently people they interact with reward them for enacting the social role of being mentally ill. They are given such rewards as sympathy and attention, excused from being expected to hold a job, excused from fulfilling requirements of other roles, and excused from being held responsible for their wrongdoings.

In addition, people labeled mentally ill are punished for attempting to return to conventional roles.

They are viewed with suspicion, implicitly considered to still be insane, and have considerable difficulty in obtaining employment or in receiving a job promotion.

Such pressures and interactions with others gradually lead to changes in their self-concept; they begin to view themselves as different, as being insane.

Often a vicious circle is created. The more they enact the role of being mentally ill, the more they are defined and treated as mentally ill; and the more explicitly they are defined as being mentally ill, the more they are related to as if they are mentally ill; and so on. Unless this vicious circle is interrupted, Scheff suggests it will lead to a career of long-term mental illness. Scheff's conclusion is that with this process, labeling is the single most important determinant of chronic mental illness.

If labeling is an important determinant of chronic functional mental illness, significant changes are suggested in certain diagnostic and treatment practices. Mental health personnel are frequently faced with uncertainty in deciding whether a person has a mental disorder. An informal norm has been developed to handle this uncertainty; when in doubt, it is better to judge a well person ill than to judge an ill person well. This norm is based on two assumptions taken from treating physical illness: (*a*) a diagnosis of illness results in only minimal damage to the status and reputation of a person, and (*b*) unless the illness is treated, the illness will become progressively worse. However, both of these assumptions are questionable. Unlike medical treatment, psychiatric treatment can drastically change a person's status in the community; for example, it can remove rights that are difficult to regain. Furthermore, if Scheff is right that labeling is the key determinant in leading to long-term mental illness, the exact opposite norm should be established to handle uncertainty; namely, when in doubt, do not label a person mentally ill. This would be in accord with the legal approach that follows the norm, "When in doubt, acquit," or "a person is innovent until proven guilty."

If labeling is indeed a major determinant of mental illness, certain changes are also suggested in treating violators of social norms. One is to attempt to maintain people with problems in their local community without labeling them mentally ill or sending them to a mental hospital where their playing the role of the mentally ill is apt to be reinforced. The field of mental hygiene has in the past several years been moving in this direction. Another outgrowth of Scheff's theory would be increasing public education efforts to inform the general public of the nature of emotional and behavioral problems, and the adverse effects that result from inappropriate labeling.

The adverse effects of labeling ultimately raise the issue of the value of labeling anyone mentally ill. As indicated earlier, authorities such as Szasz (1961) assert that mental illness does not exist.

SUMMARY

This chapter categorizes comprehensive psychotherapy theories as to whether they have characteristics of the insight approach or the resolution approach to therapy. *Insight approaches* assert that clients will be able to resolve their problems through gaining an understanding or awareness of their problems. *Resolution approaches* assert that clients must be taught or must learn specific ways of resolving their problems once insight is achieved. Psychoanalysis is the purest insight approach; client-centered therapy and Gestalt therapy adhere to most of the principles of the insight approach. Transactional analysis, rational therapy, reality therapy, and behavior therapy adhere to most of the principles of the resolution approach.

There have been few well-designed studies on the effectiveness of psychotherapy. The studies that have been conducted generally show that clients treated by insight approaches have no higher rate of improvement than the rate for people with problems who receive no treatment. Studies have shown that patients treated by psychoanalysis have a lower rate of improvement than people with problems who receive no treatment. Therapies that are based on a resolution or learning approach have generally been found to be effective in outcome studies.

The question "What really causes psychotherapy change?" is raised. The author speculates that any therapy technique that is successful in changing emotions or actions is effective primarily because it changes a person's thinking from self-talk that is negative or irrational to self-talk that is more rational and positive.

The question regarding whether mental illness exists is examined. Szasz (1961) and other authorities assert that mental illness labels have no diagnostic or treatment value and may complicate therapy efforts due to labeling effects. These authorities assert that people certainly do have emotional and behavioral problems, but they do not have a disease of the mind as implied by the term *mental illness.*

Scheff's (1966) theory hypothesizes that labeling is the single most important determinant of long-term mental illness. If the theory is accurate, significant changes are suggested in diagnostic and treatment practices — for example, attempting to maintain people with problems in their local community without labeling them mentally ill or sending them to a mental hospital.

A final word of caution is given in ending this chapter. Many of the therapy techniques described in this text (e.g., psychoanalysis, Gestalt therapy, implosive therapy, intensive sex therapy, aversive techniques, hypnosis, covert sensitization, and systematic desensitization) should be used only by skilled therapists with extensive training because there is a danger that improper utilization may intensify the problematic behavior or create undesired side effects.

EXERCISES

1. Does Mental Illness Exist?

GOAL: The purpose of this exercise is to have students examine whether mental illness exists.

Step 1: Explain the purpose of the exercise. Also explain that the medical approach assumes that mental illness is a disease of the mind. Adherents of the medical approach believe the disturbed person's mind is affected by some generally unknown, internal condition. That unknown internal condition might be due to metabolic disorders, internal conflicts, genetic endowment, unconscious use of defense mechanisms, hormone deficiencies, or traumatic early experiences that cause emotional fixations and prevent future psychological growth.

Step 2: Explain the contrasting approach, first advocated by Thomas Szasz, that mental illness is a myth — that it does not exist. (This approach is described in this chapter.)

Step 3: Ask the students to form subgroups of five and have the subgroups discuss which approach they believe is most accurate. Also ask the subgroups to identify one or more symptoms that will enable professionals to distinguish who is "schizophrenic" or who is "mentally ill" from those who are "sane."

Step 4: Have the subgroups share their conclusions. A debate between subgroups may arise.

2. What Causes Positive Changes in Therapy?

GOAL: This exercise is designed to have students discuss what is the key psychotherapeutic element in counseling.

Step 1: Explain the purpose of the exercise. Indicate that at the present time there is no widely accepted theory as to why such diverse therapies as behavior therapy, rational therapy, meditation, task-centered practice, reality therapy, hypnosis, and transactional analysis are therapeutic.

Step 2: Ask the class if they know of a key psychotherapeutic element that will explain why all these therapies lead to positive changes in clients. Indicate that this question is crucial because if such an element is identified, greater attention can be given in therapy to make certain this element is fully incorporated into the therapeutic process.

Step 3: Indicate that the author of this text asserts that any therapy technique that is successful in changing emotions or actions is effective primarily because it changes a person's thinking from self-talk that is negative or irrational to self-talk that is more rational and positive. Give some examples (as described in this text) that such approaches as behavior therapy, psychoanalysis, client-centered therapy, and meditation can be "reinterpreted" to suggest that restructuring thinking is the key psychotherapeutic element in counseling.

Step 4: Ask the students to discuss whether they believe restructuring thinking is the key psychotherapeutic element. Ask those who disagree what they believe is the key psychotherapeutic element.

3. Assessing and Changing Dysfunctional Behaviors

GOAL: This exercise is designed to have students evaluate the merits and shortcomings of focusing on cognitions in assessing and changing dysfunctional behaviors.

Step 1: Explain the theory, described in this chapter, that thinking processes primarily determine behavior. The theory asserts that the reasons for unusual or dysfunctional behavior can always be identified by determining what the perpetrator was thinking prior to and during the time the act is being committed.

Step 2: Divide the class into several subgroups (ranging in size from three to six). Give each subgroup a different problematic or dysfunctional behavior. Examples include the following: (*a*) alcoholism, (*b*) child abuse, (*c*) bulima, (*d*) date rape, (*e*) suicide attempt, and (*f*) compulsive gambling.

Step 3: Instruct each subgroup to (*a*) identify the *thinking processes* that would lead a person to engage in the dysfunctional behavior that is assigned to its group, and (*b*) identify the interventions that would be most effective in changing the thinking patterns of the perpetrator so as to "curb" the dysfunctional behavior. Instruct each subgroup to identify several intervention strategies or options, as (in one sense) social work practice involves "options planning." Give the subgroups ten or more minutes to arrive at their answers.

Step 4: Ask each subgroup to select a representative to share with the class what the subgroup arrived at for both thinking processes and interventions. Ask a representative to share what his or her subgroup arrived at. Then ask the class to discuss whether the representative identified thinking processes (as the exercise instructed) or focused on describing events and personality characteristics that the subgroup thought were related to the dysfunctional behavior. Also ask the class whether the subgroup may have overlooked some important intervention strategies and options. Continue this process for each subgroup: a representative of the group presents the group's findings, then the class discusses these.

Step 5: After the presentations and discussions end, ask the class for their thoughts on the merits, difficulties, and shortcomings of focusing on cognitions to assess and change dysfunctional behaviors.

4. *Ending the Class*

GOAL: This exercise is designed to bring closure to the class.

Step 1: State the purpose of the exercise. Indicate that there are two things that should be done in ending a class that has been meeting for a number of weeks: (*a*) the students should evaluate the class, and (*b*) goodbye should be said in a way that will be remembered and that will bring closure to the class.

Step 2: Distribute a student course-evaluation form. (There are a number available at all campuses.) Three useful open-ended statements might be added:

a.   The strengths of this class are:

b.   The shortcomings of this class are:

c.   My suggestions for changes in this class are:

(Student-course evaluations should be done anonymously by the students.)

Step 3: The instructor should ask the class to sit in a circle. The instructor may want to express a number of positive thoughts and feelings that she has about the class, and the instructor may mention a few memorable experiences she will fondly remember. Ask the students questions similar to the following:

a.   Is there anything that anyone wants to express before the class ends?

b.   Is there unfinished business we should deal with?

c.   What did you like about this course?

d.   Do you have suggestions for improving the course?

Step 4: Starting from the instructor's left or right, ask each student to express what he will most remember about this course, and/or what he believes he has learned from this course.

Step 5: If the students desire, the class may want to end the class through socializing by going out for dinner, by having a potluck dinner, by having a picnic, or by having a party.

APPENDIX A

THE NASW CODE OF ETHICS*

The National Association of Social Workers, Inc. (NASW), is the professional association that represents the social work profession in this country. Its Code of Ethics summarizes important practice ethics for social workers and is presented as follows:

PREAMBLE

This code is intended to serve as a guide to the everyday conduct of members of the social work profession and as a basis for the adjudication of issues in ethics when the conduct of social workers is alleged to deviate from the standards expressed or implied in this code. It represents standards of ethical behavior for social workers in professional relationships with those served, with colleagues, with employers, with other individuals and professions, and with the community and society as a whole. It also embodies standards of ethical behavior governing individual conduct to the extent that such conduct is associated with an individual's status and identity as a social worker.

This code is based on the fundamental values of the social work profession that include the worth, dignity, and uniqueness of all persons as well as their rights and opportunities. It is also based on the nature of social work, which fosters conditions that promote these values.

In subscribing to and abiding by this code, the social worker is expected to view ethical responsibility in as inclusive a context as each situation demands and within which ethical judgment is required. The social worker is expected to take into consideration all the principles in this code that have a bearing upon any situation in which ethical judgment is to be exercised and professional intervention or conduct is planned. The course of action that the social worker chooses is expected to be consistent with the spirit as well as the letter of this code.

*Reprinted by permission of the National Association of Social Workers, Inc. This code was revised and adopted by the 1979 Delegate Assembly of NASW.

Summary of Major Principles

I. The social worker's conduct and comportment as a social worker
  A. *Propriety.* The social worker should maintain high standards of personal conduct in the capacity or identity as social worker.
  B. *Competence and Professional Development.* The social worker should strive to become and remain proficient in professional practice and the performance of professional functions.
  C. *Service.* The social worker should regard as primary the service obligation of the social work profession.
  D. *Integrity.* The social worker should act in accordance with the highest standards of professional integrity and impartiality.
  E. *Scholarship and Research.* The social worker engaged in study and research should be guided by the conventions for scholarly inquiry.
II. The social worker's ethical responsibility to clients
  F. *Primacy of Clients' Interests.* The social worker's primary responsibility is to clients.
  G. *Rights and Prerogatives of Clients.* The social worker should make every effort to foster maximum self-determination on the part of clients.
  H. *Confidentiality and Privacy.* The social worker should respect the privacy of clients and hold in confidence all information obtained in the course of professional service.
  I. *Fees.* When setting fees, the social worker should ensure that they are fair, reasonable, considerate, and commensurate with the service performed and with due regard for the clients' ability to pay.
III. The social worker's ethical responsibility to colleagues
  J. *Respect, Fairness, and Courtesy.* The social worker should treat colleagues with respect, courtesy, fairness, and good faith.
  K. *Dealing with Colleagues' Clients.* The social worker has the responsibility to relate to the clients of colleagues with full professional consideration.
IV. The social worker's ethical responsibility to employers and employing organizations
  L. *Commitments to Employing Organizations.* The social worker should adhere to commitments made to the employing organizations.
V. The social worker's ethical responsibility to the social work profession
  M. *Maintaining the Integrity of the Profession.* The social worker should uphold and advance the values, ethics, knowledge, and mission of the profession.
  N. *Community Service.* The social worker should assist the profession in making social services available to the general public.
  O. *Development of Knowledge.* The social worker should take responsibility for identifying, developing, and fully utilizing knowledge for professional practice.
VI. The social worker's ethical responsibility to society.
  P. *Promoting the General Welfare.* The social worker should promote the general welfare of society.

In itself, this code does not represent a set of rules that will prescribe all the behaviors of social workers in all the complexities of professional life. Rather it offers general principles to guide conduct, and the judicious appraisal of conduct, in situations that have ethical implications. It provides the basis for making judgments about ethical actions before and after they occur. Frequently, the particular situation determines the ethical principles that apply and the manner of their application. In such cases, not only the particular ethical principles are taken into immediate consideration, but also the entire code and its spirit. Specific applications of ethical principles must be judged within the context in which they are being considered. Ethical behavior in a given situation must satisfy not only the judgment of the individual social worker, but also the judgment of an unbiased jury of professional peers.

This code should not be used as an instrument to deprive any social worker of the opportunity or freedom to practice with complete professional integrity;

nor should any disciplinary action be taken on the basis of this code without maximum provision for safeguarding the rights of the social worker affected.

The ethical behavior of social workers results not from edict, but from a personal commitment of the individual. This code is offered to affirm the will and zeal of all social workers to be ethical and to act ethically in all that they do as social workers.

The following codified ethical principles should guide social workers in the various roles and relationships and at the various levels of responsibility in which they function professionally. These principles also serve as a basis for the adjudication by the National Association of Social Workers of issues in ethics.

In subscribing to this code, social workers are required to cooperate in its implementation and abide by any disciplinary rulings based on it. They should also take adequate measures to discourage, prevent, expose, and correct the unethical conduct of colleagues. Finally, social workers should be equally ready to defend and assist colleagues unjustly charged with unethical conduct.

I. The social worker's conduct and comportment as a social worker.

A. Propriety. The social worker should maintain high standards of personal conduct in the capacity or identity as social worker.

1. The private conduct of the social worker is a personal matter to the same degree as is any other person's, except when such conduct compromises the fulfillment of professional responsibilities.
2. The social worker should not participate in, condone, or be associated with dishonesty, fraud, deceit, or misrepresentation.
3. The social worker should distinguish clearly between statements and actions made as a private individual and as a representative of the social work profession or an organization or group.

B. Competence and professional development. The social worker should strive to become and remain proficient in professional practice and the performance of professional functions.

1. The social worker should accept responsibility or employment only on the basis of existing competence or the intention to acquire the necessary competence.
2. The social worker should not misrepresent professional qualifications, education, experience, or affiliations.

C. Service. The social worker should regard as primary the service obligation of the social work profession.

1. The social worker should retain ultimate responsibility for the quality and extent of the service that individual assumes, assigns, or performs.
2. The social worker should act to prevent practices that are inhumane or discriminatory against any person or group of persons.

D. Integrity. The social worker should act in accordance with the highest standards of professional integrity and impartiality.

1. The social worker should be alert to and resist the influences and pressures that interfere with the exercise of professional discretion and impartial judgment required for the performance of professional functions.
2. The social worker should not exploit professional relationships for personal gain.

E. Scholarship and research. The social worker engaged in study and research should be guided by the conventions of scholarly inquiry.

1. The social worker engaged in research should consider carefully its possible consequences for human beings.
2. The social worker engaged in research should ascertain that the consent of participants in the research is voluntary and informed, without any implied deprivation or penalty for refusal to participate, and with due regard for participants' privacy and dignity.

3. The social worker engaged in research should protect participants from unwarranted physical or mental discomfort, distress, harm, danger, or deprivation.
4. The social worker who engages in the evaluation of services or cases should discuss them only for professional purposes and only with persons directly and professionally concerned with them.
5. Information obtained about participants in research should be treated as confidential.
6. The social worker should take credit only for work actually done in connection with scholarly and research endeavors and credit contributions made by others.

II. The social worker's ethical responsibility to clients.

F. Primacy of clients' interests. The social worker's primary responsibility is to clients.

1. The social worker should serve clients with devotion, loyalty, determination, and the maximum application of professional skill and competence.
2. The social worker should not exploit relationships with clients for personal advantage, or solicit the clients of one's agency for private practice.
3. The social worker should not practice, condone, facilitate, or collaborate with any form of discrimination on the basis of race, color, sex, sexual orientation, age, religion, national origin, marital status, political belief, mental or physical handicap, or any other preference or personal characteristic, condition, or status.
4. The social worker should avoid relationships or commitments that conflict with the interests of clients.
5. The social worker should under no circumstances engage in sexual activities with clients.
6. The social worker should provide clients with accurate and complete information regarding the extent and nature of the services available to them.

7. The social worker should apprise clients of their risks, rights, opportunities, and obligations associated with social service to them.
8. The social worker should seek advice and counsel of colleagues and supervisors whenever such consultation is in the best interest of clients.
9. The social worker should terminate service to clients, and professional relationships with them, when such service and relationships are no longer required or no longer serve the clients' needs or interests.
10. The social worker should withdraw services precipitously only under unusual circumstances, giving careful consideration to all factors in the situation and taking care to minimize possible adverse effects.
11. The social worker who anticipates the termination or interruption of service to clients should notify clients promptly and seek the transfer, referral, or continuation of service in relation to the clients' needs and preferences.

G. Rights and prerogatives of clients. The social worker should make every effort to foster maximum self-determination on the part of clients.

1. When the social worker must act on behalf of a client who has been adjudged legally incompetent, the social worker should safeguard the interests and rights of that client.
2. When another individual has been legally authorized to act in behalf of a client, the social worker should deal with that person always with the client's best interest in mind.
3. The social worker should not engage in any action that violates or diminishes the civil or legal rights of clients.

H. Confidentiality and privacy. The social worker should respect the privacy of clients and hold in confidence all information obtained in the course of professional service.

1. The social worker should share with others confidences revealed by clients, without their consent, only for compelling professional reasons.
2. The social worker should inform clients fully about the limits of confidentiality in a given situation, the purposes for which information is obtained, and how it may be used.
3. The social worker should afford clients reasonable access to any official social work records concerning them.
4. When providing clients with access to records, the social worker should take due care to protect the confidences of others contained in those records.
5. The social worker should obtain informed consent of clients before taping, recording, or permitting third-party observation of their activities.

I. **Fees. When setting fees, the social worker should ensure that they are fair, reasonable, considerate and commensurate with the service performed and with due regard for the clients' ability to pay.**
   1. The social worker should not divide a fee or accept or give anything of value for receiving or making a referral.

III. **The social worker's ethical responsibility to colleagues.**
   J. **Respect, fairness, and courtesy. The social worker should treat colleagues with respect, courtesy, fairness, and good faith.**
      1. The social worker should cooperate with colleagues to promote professional interests and concerns.
      2. The social worker should respect confidences shared by colleagues in the course of their professional relationships and transactions.
      3. The social worker should create and maintain conditions of practice that facilitate ethical and competent professional performance by colleagues.

4. The social worker should treat with respect, and represent accurately and fairly, the qualifications, views, and findings of colleagues and use appropriate channels to express judgments on these matters.
5. The social worker who replaces or is replaced by a colleague in professional practice should act with consideration for the interest, character, and reputation of that colleague.
6. The social worker should not exploit a dispute between a colleague and employers to obtain a position or otherwise advance the social worker's interest.
7. The social worker should seek arbitration or mediation when conflicts with colleagues require resolution for compelling professional reasons.
8. The social worker should extend to colleagues of other professions the same respect and cooperation that is extended to social work colleagues.
9. The social worker who serves as an employer, supervisor, or mentor to colleagues should make orderly and explicit arrangements regarding the conditions of their continuing professional relationship.
10. The social worker who has the responsibility for employing and evaluating the performance of other staff members should fulfill such responsibility in a fair, considerate, and equitable manner, on the basis of clearly enunciated criteria.
11. The social worker who has the responsibility for evaluating the performance of employees, supervisees, or students should share evaluations with them.

K. **Dealing with colleagues' clients. The social worker has the responsibility to relate to the clients of colleagues with full professional consideration.**
   1. The social worker should not solicit the clients of colleagues.
   2. The social worker should not assume professional responsibility for the clients of

another agency or a colleague without appropriate communication with that agency or colleague.

3. The social worker who serves the clients of colleagues, during a temporary absence or emergency, should serve those clients with the same consideration as that afforded any client.

IV. The social worker's ethical responsibility to employers and employing organizations.

L. Commitments to employing organizations. The social worker should adhere to commitments made to the employing organizations.

1. The social worker should work to improve the employing agency's policies and procedures and the efficiency and effectiveness of its services.

2. The social worker should not accept employment or arrange student field placements in an organization which is currently under public sanction by NASW for violating personnel standards or imposing limitations on or penalties for professional actions on behalf of clients.

3. The social worker should act to prevent and eliminate discrimination in the employing organization's work assignments and in its employment policies and practices.

4. The social worker should use with scrupulous regard, and only for the purpose for which they are intended, the resources of the employing organization.

V. The social worker's ethical responsibility to the social work profession.

M. Maintaining the integrity of the profession. The social worker should uphold and advance the values, ethics, knowledge, and mission of the profession.

1. The social worker should protect and enhance the dignity and integrity of the profession and should be responsible and vigorous in discussion and criticism of the profession.

2. The social worker should take action through appropriate channels against unethical conduct by any other member of the profession.

3. The social worker should act to prevent the unauthorized and unqualified practice of social work.

4. The social worker should make no misrepresentation in advertising as to qualifications, competence, service, or results to be achieved.

N. Community service. The social worker should assist the profession in making social services available to the general public.

1. The social worker should contribute time and professional expertise to activities that promote respect for the utility, the integrity, and the competence of the social work profession.

2. The social worker should support the formulation, development, enactment and implementation of social policies of concern to the profession.

O. Development of knowledge. The social worker should take responsibility for identifying, developing, and fully utilizing knowledge for professional practice.

1. The social worker should base practice upon recognized knowledge relevant to social work.

2. The social worker should critically examine, and keep current with, emerging knowledge relevant to social work.

3. The social worker should contribute to the knowledge base of social work and share research knowledge and practice wisdom with colleagues.

VI. The social worker's ethical responsibility to society.

P. Promoting the general welfare. The social worker should promote the general welfare of society.

1. The social worker should act to prevent and eliminate discrimination against any

person or group on the basis of race, color, sex, sexual orientation, age, religion, national origin, marital status, political belief, mental or physical handicap, or any other preference or personal characteristic, condition, or status.

2. The social worker should act to ensure that all persons have access to the resources, services, and opportunities which they require.

3. The social worker should act to expand choice and opportunity for all persons, with special regard for disadvantaged or oppressed groups and persons.

4. The social worker should promote conditions that encourage respect for the diversity of cultures which constitute American society.

5. The social worker should provide appropriate professional services in public emergencies.

6. The social worker should advocate changes in policy and legislation to improve social conditions and to promote social justice.

7. The social worker should encourage informed participation by the public in shaping social policies and institutions.

APPENDIX B

SUGGESTED COUNSELOR'S RESPONSES TO CLIENT'S STATEMENTS

T he following is a suggested response to each of the client's statements in Exercise C in Chapter 5:

1. "I sense that you feel strongly about this, and that you've given this a lot of thought. I'd like to explore this further with you, as I care very much about you as a person. It makes me uncomfortable if you think that the only reason I meet with you is because I'm getting paid. Working with you and with the other clients I have is personally very gratifying to me. Perhaps I have miscommunicated with you, verbally or nonverbally. I'd like to hear more about why you've reached the conclusion that I don't care about you as a person."

2. "You're really feeling like you're caught in a dilemma. Obviously in this situation, as in many situations, you can't please everyone. But, are you aware that the most important person to please is yourself? You're the one who has to live with your decisions. I'm wondering what your feelings are toward Kent, and what your feelings are about getting married at this time in your life. Let's examine each of these one at a time. What are your feelings toward Kent?"

3. "Yes, I did. I took them two summers ago when I was vacationing in the Colorado Rockies. But we're here to talk about you and how your life is going. Let's begin by discussing how you're doing in school. For each subject that you have, could you tell me what grade you received on the midterm report you received this past week?"

4. "I sense this is extremely difficult for you to reveal. You probably are feeling very vulnerable at this point. I'm pleased that you shared this with me, and rest assured that I have an open mind about sexual orientation. It took real courage for you to talk about this, and I now believe we are in a much better position for you to make some decisions about your future. Could you tell me more about this person you are involved with?"

5. "It is true that I am neither black nor have I lived in a ghetto. But I'm interested in you and in working with you. Just because I'm white doesn't mean we can't work together. Everyone, including myself, has personal problems. You, too, have some

personal problems. By taking each one, one at a time and examining them, and then coming up with some realistic ways of resolving them, I firmly believe we can make progress. Just as a teacher does not have to be blind to teach visually impaired students, a counselor does not need to have the same color of skin to work with people who have personal problems. Have I said or done anything to lead you to believe that I am prejudiced against people who have a different color of skin?"

6. "I'm sorry you're still involved with drugs, especially since you were using drugs when you committed the offenses that resulted in you being sent here. I don't like to see you get into trouble, but I have no choice. I have to report this. I made it crystal clear to you at our first meeting that the consequences of drug involvement here would probably be an extension of the time you spend here. As you know we do have a drug treatment program here. I suggest you seriously consider participating in this program. Participation in this program, now, may not only lead to an earlier release, but may also help you to become drug free. Are you interested in participating in this program?"

BIBLIOGRAPHY

Abrams, A. I. 1974. "Paired Associate Learning and Recall." In *Scientific Research on Transcendental Meditation: Collected Papers*, ed. D. W. Orme-Johnson, L. H. Domash, and J. T. Fallow. Los Angeles: MIU Press.

Ackerman, Nathan W. 1966. *Treating the Troubled Family.* New York: Basic Books.

"Acquired Immune Deficiency Syndrome: 100 Questions and Answers." 1985. Albany, N.Y.: AIDS Institute.

"Acquired Immune Deficiency Syndrome: An Annotated Bibliography." 1986. New York: Sex Information and Education Council of the U.S.

Addams, Jane. 1959. *Twenty Years of Hull House.* New York: Macmillan (original publication, 1910).

Administration in Social Work 5, nos. 3 and 4. Fall-Winter 1981. Special issue devoted to computer applications in social work administration.

Aguilar, Ignacio. 1972. "Initial Contacts with Mexican-American Families." *Social Work* 17 (May), pp. 186–89.

Ainsworth, Mary D. et al. 1966. *Deprivation of Maternal Care.* New York: Schocken Books.

Alberti, R. E., and M. L. Emmons. 1970. *Your Perfect Right: A Guide to Assertive Behavior.* San Luis Obispo, Calif.: Impact Publishers.

———. 1975. *Stand Up, Speak Out, Talk Back!* New York: Pocket Books.

Alexander, Chauncey A. 1982. "Professional Social Work and Political Responsibility." In *Practical Politics: Social Work and Political Responsibility*, ed. M. Mahaffey and J. W. Hanks. Silver Spring, Md.: National Association of Social Workers.

Alinsky, Saul D. 1972. *Rules for Radicals.* New York: Random House.

Alyson, Sasha, ed. 1990. *You Can Do Something About AIDS: New Edition.* Boston, Mass.: The Stop AIDS Project, Inc.

American Psychiatric Association. 1987. *Diagnostic and Statistical Manual of Mental Disorders.* 3rd ed., rev. (DSM-III-R). Washington, D.C.: American Psychiatric Association.

Anant, S. S. 1967. "A Note on the Treatment of Alcoholics by a Verbal Aversion Technique." *Canadian Psychologist* 8, pp. 19–22.

———. 1968. "Verbal Aversion Therapy with a Promiscuous Girl: Case Report." *Psychological Reports* 22, pp. 795–96.

Anderson, Gary, ed. 1990. *Courage to Care.* Washington, D.C.: Child Welfare League of America.

Anderson, Joseph. 1981. *Social Work Methods and Processes.* Belmont, Calif.: Wadsworth.

Andreasen, Nancy. 1985. *The Broken Brain.* New York: Harper & Row.

Annon, Jack S. 1975. *Behavioral Treatment of Sexual Problems*. Vol. 2, *Intensive Therapy*. Honolulu: Enabling Systems.

———. 1976. *Behavioral Treatment of Sexual Problems, Brief Therapy*. New York: Harper & Row.

Arlow, Jacob A. 1989. "Psychoanalysis." In *Current Psychotherapies*, 4th ed., ed. Raymond J. Corsini and Danny Wedding. Itasca, Ill.: F. E. Peacock, pp. 18–59.

Asch, S. E. 1955. "Opinions and Social Pressure." *Scientific American* 193, no. 5, pp. 31–35.

Ashem, B., and L. Donner. 1968. "Covert Sensitization with Alcoholics: A Controlled Replication." *Behaviour Research and Therapy* 6, pp. 7–12.

Axline, Virginia. 1947. *Play Therapy*. New York: Ballantine Books.

Baer, Betty L. 1979. "Developing a New Curriculum for Social Work Education." In *The Pursuit of Competence in Social Work*, ed. Frank Clark and Morton Arkava. San Francisco: Jossey-Bass, pp. 96–109.

Baer, Betty L., and Ronald Federico. 1978. *Educating the Baccalaureate Social Worker*. Cambridge, Mass.: Ballinger Publishing.

Baker, Frank. 1977. "The Interface between Professional and Natural Support Systems." *Clinical Social Work Journal* 5 (Summer), pp. 139–48.

Bales, R. F. 1950. *Interaction Process Analysis: A Method for the Study of Small Groups*. Reading, Mass.: Addison-Wesley Publishing.

Bancroft, J. H., Jr.; H. G. Jones; and B. R. Pullan. 1966. "A Simple Transducer for Measuring Penile Erection, with Comments on Its Use in the Treatment of Sexual Disorders." *Behaviour Research and Therapy* 4, pp. 239–41.

Bandler, Richard, and John Grinder. 1975. *The Structure of Magic*, vol. 1. Palo Alto, Calif.: Science and Behavior Books.

———. 1976(a). *The Structure of Magic*, vol. 2. Palo Alto, Calif.: Science and Behavior Books.

———. 1976(b). *Patterns of the Hypnotic Techniques of Milton H. Erickson, M.D.*, vol. 1. Cupertino, Calif.: Meta Publications.

———. 1979. *Frogs into Princes*. Moab, Utah: Real People Press.

———. 1982. *Reframing*. Moab, Utah: Real People Press.

Bandler, Richard; John Grinder; and Virginia Satir. 1976. *Changing with Families*, vol. 1. Palo Alto, Calif.: Science and Behavior Books.

Barbach, Lonnie G. 1975. *For Yourself: The Fulfillment of Female Sexuality*. New York: New American Library.

———. 1982. *For Each Other: Sharing Sexual Intimacy*. Garden City, N.Y.: Doubleday Publishing.

———. 1984. *Pleasures*. New York: Harper & Row.

Barlow, David H., and Michel Hersen. 1984. *Single Case Experimental Designs*. 2nd ed. Elmsford, N.Y.: Pergamon Press.

Barlow, David H.; Steven C. Hayes; and Rosemery O. Nelson. 1984. *The Scientist Practitioner*. Elmsford, N.Y.: Pergamon Press.

Barocas, Harvey A. 1972. "Psychodrama Techniques in Training Police in Family Crisis Intervention." *Group Psychotherapy and Psychodrama* 25, pp. 30–31.

Bartless, H. M. 1970. *The Common Base of Social Work Practice*. New York: National Association of Social Workers.

Bass, Ellen, and Laura Davis. 1988. *The Courage to Heal*. New York: Harper & Row.

Bateson, G.; D. Jackson; J. Haley; and J. Weakland. 1956. "Toward a Communication Theory of Schizophrenia." *Behavior Science*. Reprinted in *Communication, Family and Marriage* I, ed. D. Jackson. Palo Alto, Calif.: Science and Behavior Books, 1968.

Beck, A. T. 1976. *Cognitive Theory and the Emotional Disorders*. New York: International Universities Press.

Beck, A. T., and Marjorie E. Weishaar. 1989. "Cognitive Therapy." In *Current Psychotherapies*. 4th ed., ed. Raymond J. Corsini and Danny Wedding. Itasca, Ill.: F. E. Peacock Publishers, pp. 284–320.

Becker, Dorothy G. 1968. "Social Welfare Leaders as Spokesmen for the Poor." *Social Casework* 49, no. 2 (February), p. 85.

Bellack, Alan S. and Michel Hersen. Eds. 1988. *Behavioral Assessment*. Elmsford, N.Y.: Pergamon Press.

Belliveau, Fred, and Lin Richter. 1970. *Understanding Human Sexual Inadequacy*. New York: Bantam Books.

Bemner, Robert M. 1962. "The Rediscovery of Pauperism," *Current Issues in Social Work Seen in Historical Perspective*. New York: Council on Social Work Education.

Benjamin, Alfred. 1974. *The Helping Interview*. 2d ed. Boston: Houghton Mifflin.

Benson, Herbert. 1975. *The Relaxation Response*. New York: William Morrow.

Benson, H.; B. A. Rosner; and B. R. Marzetta. 1973. "Decreased Systolic Blood Pressure in Hypertensive Subjects Who Practice Meditation." *Journal of Clinical Investigation* 52, p. 80.

Berger, Raymond. 1982. "The Unseen Minority: Older Gays and Lesbians." *Social Work* 27, no. 3 (May), pp. 236–42.

———. 1983. "What Is a Homosexual? A Definitional Model." *Social Work* 28, no. 2 (March–April), pp. 132–35.

———. 1987. "Homosexuality: Gay Men." *The Encyclopedia of Social Work*. Silver Springs, Md.: National Association of Social Workers, pp. 795–805.

Bergman, Ann. 1989. "Informal Support Systems for Pregnant Teenagers." *Social Casework* 70, no. 9, pp. 526–33.

Berlin, Sharon B. 1976. "Better Work with Women Clients." *Social Work* 21 (November), pp. 492–97.

Bernanos, George. 1970. As quoted in J. C. DeBoer, *Let's Plan: A Guide to the Planning Process for Voluntary Organizations.* New York: United Church Press.

Berne, Eric. 1964. *Games People Play.* New York: Grove Press.

———. 1966. *Principles of Group Treatment.* New York: Oxford University Press.

Bernstein, Barton E. 1975. "The Social Worker as a Courtroom Witness." *Social Casework* 56, no. 9 (November), pp. 521–25.

Bernstein, Douglas, and Thomas Borkovec. 1973. *Progressive Relaxation Training: A Manual for the Helping Professions.* Champaign, Ill.: Research Press Co.

Bertcher, J. H., and Frank Maple. 1974. "Elements and Issues in Group Composition." In *Individual Change through Small Groups*, by Paul Glasser, Rosemary Sarri, and Robert Vinter. New York: Free Press, pp. 186–208.

Berwick, D. 1980. "Nonorganic Failure to Thrive." *Pediatrics in Review* 1, pp. 265–70.

Biddle, William W., and Loureide J. Biddle. 1965. *The Community Development Process.* New York: Holt, Rinehart & Winston.

Black, Bertram J. 1977. "Milieu Therapy." In *Encyclopedia of Social Work.* 17th ed. New York: National Association of Social Workers, pp. 919–27.

Blackman, Donald K.; Carolyn Gehle; and Elsie M. Pinkston. 1979. "Modifying Eating Habits of the Institutionalized Elderly." *Social Work Research and Abstracts* 15, no. 3 (Fall), pp. 18–24.

Blades, Joan. 1985. *Mediate Your Divorce.* Englewood Cliffs, N.J.: Prentice-Hall.

Blasdell, K. 1974. "The Effect of Transcendental Meditation upon a Complex Perceptual Motor Test." In *Scientific Research on Transcendental Meditation: Collected Papers*, ed. D. W. Orme-Johnson, L. H. Domash, and J. T. Farrow. Los Angeles: MIU Press.

Bloom, Martin. 1975. *The Paradox of Helping: Introduction to the Philosophy of Scientific Practice.* New York: John Wiley & Sons.

———. 1983. "Empirically Based Clinical Research." In *Handbook of Clinical Social Work*, ed. by Aaron Rosenblatt and Diana Waldfogel. San Francisco: Jossey-Bass, pp. 560–82.

Bloom, Martin, and Joel Fischer. 1982. *Evaluating Practice: Guidelines for the Accountable Professional.* Englewood Cliffs, N.J.: Prentice-Hall.

Bloomfield, H.; M. Cain; and R. Jaffe. 1975. *TM: Discovering Inner Energy and Overcoming Stress.* New York: Delacorte Press.

Blythe, Betty J., and Tony Tripodi. 1989. *Measurement in Direct Practice.* Newbury Park, Calif.: Sage.

Boudreau, L. 1972. "Transcendental Meditation and Yoga as Reciprocal Inhibitors." *Journal of Behavior Therapy and Experimental Psychiatry* 3, pp. 97–98.

Boulette, Teresa Ramirez. 1975. "Group Therapy with Low Income Mexican Americans." *Social Work* 20 (September), pp. 403–5.

Brawley, E. A. 1983. *Mass Media and Human Services: Getting the Message Across.* Beverly Hills, Calif.: Sage Publications.

Brecher, Edward M. 1984. *Love, Sex and Aging.* Boston: Little, Brown.

Breuer, Joseph, and Sigmund Freud. 1895. *Studies in Hysteria.* London: Hogarth Press.

Briar, S. 1973. "Effective Social Work Intervention in Direct Practice: Implications for Education" in *Facing the Challenge.* Plenary session papers from the 19th Annual Program Meeting of the Council on Social Work Education. New York: Council on Social Work Education.

Brieland, Donald; Lela B. Costin; and Charles R. Atherton. 1985. *Contemporary Social Work: An Introduction to Social Work and Social Welfare.* 3rd ed. New York: McGraw-Hill.

Brown, Barbara B. 1977. *Stress and the Art of Biofeedback.* New York: Bantam Books.

Brown, Caree Rozen, and Marilyn Levitt Hellinger. 1975. "Therapists' Attitudes toward Woman." *Social Work* 20 (July), pp. 266–70.

Brown, Edward Garth. 1978. "Minority Content in the First Year Practice Course." In *The Dual Perspective*, Dolores Norton. New York: Council on Social Work Education, pp. 23–30.

Bugliosi, Vincent, and Curt Gentry. 1974. *Helter Skelter.* New York: W. W. Norton.

Burgess, Ann Wolbert; A. Nicholas Groth; Lynda Lytle Holmstrom; and Suzanne M. Sgroi, eds. 1984. *Sexual Assault of Children and Adolescents.* Lexington, Mass.: Lexington Books.

Burgest, David R. 1973. "Racism in Everyday Speech and Social Work Jargon." *Social Work* 18 (July), pp. 20–25.

Burgest, Mwalimu David R. 1983. "Education and Skills for Multi-Racial and Multi-Ethnic Direct Practice." Presented at the Annual Program Meeting, Council on Social Work Education, New York.

Burghardt, Steve, and Michael Fabricant. 1987. *Working under the Safety Net: Policy and Practice with the New American Poor.* Beverly Hills, Calif.: Sage.

Buros, O. K., ed. 1978. *The Eighth Mental Measurements Yearbook* 2 vols. Highland Park, N.J.: Gryphon Press.

Buxton, Edward. 1976. "Delivering Social Services in Rural Areas." In *Social Work in Rural Communities* by Leon Ginsberg. New York: Council on Social Work Education, pp. 28–38.

Campbell, James A. 1988. "Client Acceptance of Single-System Evaluation Procedures." *Social Work Research & Abstracts* 24, pp. 21–22.

———. 1990. "Ability of Practitioners to Estimate Client Acceptance of Single-Subject Evaluation Procedures." *Social Work* 35, pp. 9–14.

Caprio, Frank S., and Joseph R. Berger. 1963. *Helping Yourself with Self-Hypnosis.* Englewood Cliffs, N.J.: Prentice-Hall.

Carrera, Michael. 1981. *Sex: The Facts, the Acts and Your Feelings.* New York: Crown Publishers.

Cartwright, T. J. 1973. "Problems, Solutions, and Strategies: A Contribution to the Theory and Practice of Planning." *AIP Examination Readings.* Washington, D.C.: American Institute of Planners.

Cautela, J. R. 1967. "Covert Sensitization." *Psychological Reports* 20, pp. 459–68.

Cautela, J. R., and D. Upper. 1975. "The Process of Individual Behavior Therapy." In *Progress in Behavior Modification,* ed. M. Hersen, R. M. Eisler, and R. M. Miller. New York: Academic Press, pp. 276–306.

Center for Social Research and Development. 1974. *Analysis and Synthesis of Needs Assessment Research in the Field of Human Services.* Denver: University of Denver.

Chagnon, Napoleon A. 1967. "Yanomamö Social Organization and Warfare." In *War,* ed. M. Fried. M. Harris, and R. Murphy. Garden City, N.Y.: Natural History Press, pp. 109–50.

———. 1968. "Yanomamö, The Fierce People." In *Case Studies in Cultural Anthropology,* ed. G. Spindler and L. Spindler. Chicago: University of Chicago Press.

Chambless, Dianne L., and Alan J. Goldstein. 1979. "Behavioral Psychotherapy." In *Current Psychotherapies,* 2d ed., ed. Raymond Corsini. Itasca, Ill.: F. E. Peacock Publishers.

Charlesworth, Edward A., and Ronald G. Nathan. 1984. *Stress Management.* New York: Ballantine Books.

Christie, R., and F. Geis. 1970. *Studies in Machiavellianism.* New York: Academic Press.

Church, D. 1980. *It's Time to Tell: A Media Handbook for Human Services Personnel.* Washington, D.C.: U.S. Department of Health and Human Services.

Ciminero, Anthony R.; Karen S. Calhoun; and Henry E. Adams, eds. 1977. *Handbook of Behavioral Assessment.* New York: John Wiley & Sons.

———. 1986. *Handbook of Behavioral Assessment.* 2nd ed. New York: John Wiley & Sons.

Clark, Frank W., and Charles R. Horejsi. 1979. "Mastering Specific Skills." In *The Pursuit of Competence in Social Work,* ed. Frank Clark and Morton Arkava. San Francisco: Jossey-Bass, pp. 29–46.

Classification Processes for Social Service Positions: Parts I–IV. 1981. Washington, D.C.: National Association of Social Workers, December.

Cleland, David, and Willian King. 1972. *Management: A Systems Approach.* New York: McGraw-Hill.

Clifton, R. L., and A. M. Dahms. 1980. *Grassroots Administration: A Handbook for Staff and Directors of Small Community-Based Social-Service Agencies.* Belmont, Calif.: Wadsworth.

Cohen, Nathan E. 1958. *Social Work in the American Tradition.* Hinsdale, Ill.: Dryden Press.

Coleman, James W., and Donald R. Cressey. 1990. *Social Problems.* 4th ed. New York: Harper & Row.

Comfort, Alex. 1978. *Sexual Consequences of Disability.* Philadelphia: George F. Stickley Co.

Commission on Accreditation. 1988. "Curriculum Policy for the Master's Degree and Baccalaureate Degree Program in Social Work Education." In *Handbook of Standards and Procedures, 1988.* Washington, D.C.: Council on Social Work Education.

Compton, Beulah R., and Burt Galaway. 1975. *Social Work Processes.* Homewood, Ill.: Dorsey Press.

"Conceptual Frameworks II." 1981. *Social Work* 26 (January), pp. 1–96.

Cook, Thomas D., and Donald T. Campbell. 1979. *Quasi-Experimentation: Design and Analysis Issues for Field Settings.* Chicago: Rand McNally.

Cooley, Charles H. 1902. *Human Nature and the Social Order.* New York: Charles Scribner's Sons.

Cooper, Marlene. 1990. "Treatment of a Client with Obsessive-Compulsive Disorder." *Social Work Research & Abstracts* 26, pp. 26–32.

Coopersmith, Stanley. 1967. *The Antecedents of Self-Esteem.* San Francisco: W. H. Freeman.

Corcoran, Kevin, and Joel Fischer. 1987. *Measures for Clinical Practice: A Sourcebook.* New York: Free Press.

Corey, Gerald, and Marianne Schneider Corey. 1977. *Groups: Process of Practice.* Belmont, Calif.: Wadsworth.

Corimer, William H., and L. Sherilyn Corimer. 1991. *Interviewing Strategies for Helpers.* Pacific Grove, Calif.: Brooks/Cole Publishing Co.

Corsini, Raymond J. ed. 1979. *Current Psychotherapies.* 2d ed. Itasca, Ill.: F. E. Peacock Publishers.

Corsini, Raymond J., and Danny Wedding, eds. 1989. *Current Psychotherapies.* 4th ed. Itasca, Ill.: F. E. Peacock Publishers.

Corte, H. E.; M. M. Wolf; and B. J. Locke. 1971. "A Comparison of Procedures for Eliminating Self-Injurious Behavior of

Retarded Adolescents." *Journal of Applied Behavior Analysis* 4, pp. 201–15.

Coryell, W.; J. Endicott; N. C. Andreasen; et al. 1988. *American Journal of Psychiatry* 145, pp. 293–300.

Council on Social Work Education. 1968. *Working with the Poor: Cultural Differences — Worker and Community.* New York: Council on Social Work Education.

————. 1976. *Teaching for Competence in the Delivery of Direct Services.* New York: Council on Social Work Education.

Craighead, W. E.; M. J. Mahoney; and A. R. Kazdin. 1976. *Behavior Modification: Principles, Issues and Applications.* Boston: Houghton Mifflin.

Criddle, William D. 1974. "Guidelines for Challenging Irrational Beliefs." *Rational Living* (Spring), pp. 8–13.

"Curriculum Policy for the Master's Degree & Baccalaureate Degree Programs in Social Work Education." 1982. New York: Council on Social Work Education, adopted May 24, 1982.

Davenport, Judith, and Joseph Davenport, III. 1982. "Utilizing the Social Network in Rural Communities." *Social Casework* 63 (February), pp. 106–12.

Davenport, Judith, and Nancy Reims. 1978. "Theoretical Orientation and Attitudes toward Women." *Social Work* 23 (July), pp. 306–9.

Davie, J. S., and A. P. Hare. 1956. "Button-Down Collar Culture: A Study of Undergraduate Life at a Men's College." *Human Organization* 14, pp. 13–20.

Davies, Joann F. 1977. "The Country Mouse Comes into Her Own." In *Human Services in the Rural Environment Reader*, by David Bast. (June 1976–May 1977). Madison: University of Wisconsin-Extension, pp. 16–20.

Davis, Larry E. 1979. "Racial Composition of Groups." *Social Work* 24 (May), pp. 208–13.

DeBoer, J. C. 1970. *Let's Plan: A Guide to the Planning Process for Voluntary Organizations.* New York: United Church Press.

Deitel, Harry M., and Barbara Deitel. 1985. *Computers and Data Processing.* Orlando, Fla.: Academic Press.

Delbecq, Andre L., and Andrew Van de Ven. 1971. "A Group Process Model for Problem Identification and Program Planning." *Journal of Applied Behavioral Science* (July-August).

Delgado, Melvin, and Denise Humm-Delgado. 1982. "Natural Support Systems: Source of Strength in Hispanic Communities." *Social Work* 27, no. 1 (January), pp. 83–89.

DeMoya, Armando; Dorothy DeMoya; Martha E. Lewis; and Howard R. Lewis. 1983. *Sex and Health.* New York: Stein and Day.

Deutsch, M. 1949. "A Theory of Cooperation and Competition." *Human Relations* 2, pp. 129–52.

Devore, Wynetta, and Elfriede G. Schlesinger. 1981. *Ethnic-Sensitive Social Work Practice.* St. Louis: C. V. Mosby Co.

DiGiuseppe, R.; N. Miller; and L. Trexler. 1977. "A Review of Rational Emotive Psychotherapy Outcome Studies." *Counseling Psychologist* 7, no. 1

Dilts, Robert; Leslie Cameron-Bandler; Richard Bandler; John Grinder; and Judith DeLozier. 1980. *Neuro-Linguistic Programming.* Vol. 1. Cupertino, Calif.: Meta Publications.

Dolgoff, Ralph, and Donald Feldstein. 1980. *Understanding Social Welfare.* New York: Harper & Row.

Dreikurs, R. 1964. *Children: The Challenge.* New York: Hawthorn Books.

Dumont, Matthew. 1968. *The Absurd Healer.* New York: Viking Press.

Dunn, Judy. 1977. *Distress and Comfort.* Cambridge, Mass.: Harvard University Press.

Dusay, John M., and Katherine M. Dusay. 1979. "Transactional Analysis." In *Current Psychotherapies*, 2d ed., ed. Raymond Corsini. Itasca, Ill.: F. E. Peacock Publishers.

————. 1984. "Transactional Analysis." In *Current Psychotherapies*, 3rd ed., ed. Raymond Corsini. Itasca, Ill.: F. E. Peacock Publishers.

————. 1989. "Transactional Analysis." In *Current Psychotherapies*, 4th ed., ed. Raymond Corsini and Danny Wedding. Itasca, Ill.: F. E. Peacock Publishers.

Dyer, Wayne W. 1976. *Your Erroneous Zones.* New York: Funk & Wagnalls.

Edelwich, Jerry. 1980. *Burn-Out.* New York: Human Sciences Press.

Egan, G. 1982. *The Skilled Helper: Model, Skills, and Methods for Effective Helping.* 2d ed. Monterey, Calif.: Brooks/Cole Publishing.

Ellis, Albert. 1957. "Outcome of Employing Three Techniques of Psychotherapy." *Journal of Clinical Psychology* 13, pp. 344–50.

————. 1958. "Rational Psychotherapy." *The Journal of General Psychology* 58 (January), pp. 35–49.

————. 1962. *Reason and Emotion in Psychotherapy.* New York: Lyle Stuart.

————. 1968. "What *Really* Causes Psychotherapeutic Change?" *Voices: The Art and Science of Psychotherapy* 4, no. 2 (Summer), pp. 90–97.

————. 1973. "Rational-Emotive Therapy." In *Current Psychotherapies*, ed. Raymond Corsini. Itasca, Ill.: F. E. Peacock Publishers, pp. 167–206.

————. 1979. "Rational-Emotive Therapy." In *Current Psychotherapies*, 2d ed., ed. Raymond Corsini. Itasca, Ill.: F. E. Peacock Publishers, pp. 185–229.

————. 1989. "Rational-Emotive Therapy." In *Current Psychotherapies*, 4th ed., ed. Raymond Corsini and Danny Wedding. Itasca, Ill.: F. E. Peacock Publishers, pp. 196–238.

Ellis, Albert, and Robert Harper. 1977a. *A Guide to Successful Marriage*. North Hollywood, Calif.: Wilshire Book Co.

————. 1977b. *A New Guide to Rational Living*. North Hollywood, Calif.: Wilshire Book Co.

Encyclopedia of Social Work. 1971. New York: National Association of Social Work.

Eriksen, Karin. 1979. *Communication Skills for the Human Services*. Reston, Va.: Reston Publishing.

Euster, Gerald L. 1975. "Services to Groups." In *Contemporary Social Work*, ed. Donald Brieland et al. New York: McGraw-Hill, pp. 218–35.

Eysenck, H. J. 1952. "The Effects of Psychotherapy: An Evaluation." *Journal of Consulting Psychology* 11, pp. 319–24.

————. 1961. "The Effects of Psychotherapy." In *Handbook of Abnormal Psychology*. New York: Basic Books, pp. 697–725.

————. 1965. "The Effects of Psychotherapy." *International Journal of Psychiatry* 1, pp. 97–144.

Falck, H. E. 1966. "Integrating the Rural Welfare Department into the Community." In *Can Welfare Keep Pace?*, ed. M. Morton. New York: Columbia University Press.

Federico, R. 1973. *The Social Welfare Institution*. Lexington, Mass.: D. C. Heath.

Fensterheim, Herbert, and Jean Baer. 1975. *Don't Say Yes When You Want to Say No*. New York: Dell Publishing Co.

Ferguson, P. C., and J. Gowan. 1974. "The Influence of Transcendental Meditation on Anxiety, Depression, Aggression, Neuroticism and Self-Actualization." *Journal of Humanistic Psychology*, pp. 51–60.

Ferris, Charles C., and Lorene S. Ferris. 1976. "Indian Children: The Struggle for Survival." *Social Work* 21 (September), pp. 386–89.

Fine, Leon J. 1979. "Psychodrama." In *Current Psychotherapies*, 2d ed., ed. Raymond J. Corsini. Itasca, Ill.: F. E. Peacock Publishers.

Finkelhor, David. 1979. *Sexually Abused Children*. New York: Free Press.

————. 1984. *Child Sexual Abuse*. New York: Free Press.

Fischer, Joel. 1973. "Is Casework Effective? A Review." *Social Work* 18 (January), pp. 5–20.

————. 1978. *Effective Casework Practice*. New York: McGraw-Hill.

————. 1979. "Isn't Casework Effective Yet?" *Social Work* 24 (May), pp. 245–47.

Fischer, John L., and Ann Fischer. 1963. "The New Englanders of Orchard Town, U.S.A." In *Six Cultures, Studies of Child Rearing*, ed. Beatrice B. Whiting. New York: John Wiley & Sons.

Flanagan, J. 1977. *The Grass Roots Fundraising Book: How to Raise Money in Your Community*. Chicago: Swallow Press.

Frank, Jerome D. 1973. *Persuasion and Healing*. 2nd ed. Baltimore: John Hopkins University Press.

Freedman, Norman, and Robert Sherman. 1987. *Handbook of Measurements for Marriage and Family Therapy*. New York: Brunner/Mazel.

Freese, Arthur S. 1976. *How Hypnosis Can Help You*. New York: Popular Library.

French, J. R. P., and B. Raven. 1968. "The Bases of Social Power." In *Group Dynamics: Research and Theory*, ed. Dorwin Cartwright and Alvin Zander. 3rd ed. New York: Harper & Row.

Freud, Sigmund. 1924. *A General Introduction to Psychoanalysis*. New York: Boni & Liveright.

Freudenberger, Herbert J. 1974. "Staff Burn-Out." *Journal of Social Issues* 30, pp. 159–65.

————. 1977. "Burn-Out: Occupational Hazard of the Child Care Worker." *Child Care Quarterly* 6, pp. 90–99.

Frew, D. R. 1974. "Transcendental Meditation and Productivity." *Academy of Management Journal* 17, no. 2 (June), pp. 362–68.

Frey, Gerald A. 1990. "A Framework for Promoting Organizational Change." *Families in Society* 71, no. 3, pp. 142–47.

Friedlander, Walter A. 1968. *Introduction to Social Welfare*. 3d ed. Englewood Cliffs, N.J.: Prentice-Hall.

————. 1974. *Introduction to Social Welfare*. 4th ed. Englewood Cliffs, N.J.: Prentice-Hall.

Galper, J. H. 1975. *The Politics of Social Services*. Englewood Cliffs, N.J.: Prentice-Hall.

————. 1980. *Social Work Practice: A Radical Perspective*. Englewood Cliffs, N.J.: Prentice-Hall.

Garland, James A.; Hubert Jones; and Ralph Kolodny. 1965. "A Model for Stages of Development in Social Work Groups." In *Explorations in Group Work*, ed. Saul Bernstein. Boston: Milford House.

Garland, James A., and Louise A. Frey. 1973. "Application of Stages of Group Development to Groups in Psychiatric Settings." In *Further Explorations in Group Work*, ed. Saul Bernstein. Boston: Milford House, pp. 1–33.

Gartner, Alan, and Frank Riessman. 1980. *Help: A Working Guide to Self-Help Groups*. New York: Franklin-Watts.

Garvin, Charles, and Fred Cox. 1987. "A History of Community Organizing Since the Civil War with Special Reference to Oppressed Communities." In *Strategies of Community Organization*, ed. Fred M. Cox, John L. Erlich, Jack Rothman, and John E. Tropman. Itasca, Ill.: F. E. Peacock Publishers.

Geiss, Gunther R., and Narayan Viswanathan, eds. 1986. *The Human Edge: Information Technology and Helping People.* New York: Haworth Press.

Germain, Carel B., and Alex Gitterman. 1980. *The Life Model of Social Work Practice.* New York: Columbia University Press.

Ghali, Sonia Badillo. 1982. "Understanding Puerto Rican Traditions." *Social Work* 27, no. 1 (January), pp. 98–102.

Gibson, Gwyneth, and Kenneth Ottenbacher. 1988. "Characteristics Influencing the Visual Analysis of Single-Subject Data: An Empirical Investigation." *Journal of Applied Behavioral Science* 24, pp. 298–314.

Gilbert, Gwendolyn C. 1974. "Counseling Black Adolescent Parents." *Social Work* 19 (January), pp. 88–95.

Gilligan, Carol. 1982. *In a Different Voice: Psychological Theory and Women's Development.* Cambridge, Mass.: Harvard University Press.

Gingerich, Wallace J. 1978. "Measuring the Process." *Social Work* 23, pp. 251–52.

———. 1979. "Procedure for Evaluating Clinical Practice." *Health and Social Work* 4, pp. 105–130.

———. 1983a. "Generalizing Single-Case Evaluation from Classroom to Practice." *Journal of Education for Social Work* 20, pp. 78–84.

———. 1983b. "Significance Testing in Single-Case Research." In *Handbook of Clinical Social Work*, ed. Aaron Rosenblatt and Diana Waldfogel. San Francisco: Jossey-Bass, pp. 694–720.

———. 1990a. "Expert Systems and Their Potential Uses in Social Work." *Families in Society* 71, pp. 220–28.

———. 1990b. "Rethinking Single-Case Evaluation." In *Advances in Clinical Social Work Research*, ed. Lynn Videka-Sherman and William J. Reid. Silver Spring, Md.: National Association of Social Workers.

Gingerich, Wallace J., and William H. Feyerherm. 1979. "The Celeration Line Technique for Assessing Client Change." *Journal of Social Service Research* 3, (Fall), pp. 99–113.

Ginott, H. G. 1965. *Between Parent and Child.* New York: Macmillan.

———. 1969. *Between Parent and Child.* New York: Avon Books.

Ginsberg, Leon H. 1976. "An Overview of Social Work Education for Rural Areas." In *Social Work in Rural Communities.* New York: Council on Social Work Education.

Glasser, William. 1965. *Reality Therapy.* New York: Harper & Row.

———. 1969. *Schools without Failure.* New York: Harper & Row.

———. 1972. *The Identity Society.* New York: Harper & Row.

———. 1976. *Positive Addiction.* New York: Harper & Row.

———. 1984. *Control Theory.* New York: Harper & Row.

Glasser, William, and Leonard Zunin. 1979. "Reality Therapy." In *Current Psychotherapies*, 2d ed., ed. Raymond Corsini. Itasca, Ill.: F. E. Peacock Publishers, pp. 302–39.

Golan, Naomi, 1979. "Crisis Theory." In *Social Work Treatment*, 2d ed., ed. Francis J. Turner. London: Free Press, pp. 499–531.

Goldfried, M. R., and A. P. Goldfried. 1975. "Cognitive Change Methods." In *Helping People Change*, ed. Frederick Kanfer and Arnold Goldstein. Elmsford, N.Y.: Pergamon Press, pp. 89–115.

Goldfried, M. R., and M. Merbaum, eds. 1973. *Behavior Change through Self Control.* New York: Holt, Rinehart & Winston.

Goleman, Daniel. 1976a. "Meditation Helps Break the Stress Spiral." *Psychology Today* 9 (February), pp. 82–93.

———. 1976b. "Migraine and Tension Headaches: Why Your Temples Pound." *Psychology Today* 10 (August), pp. 41–42.

———. 1977. "Meditation without Mystery." *Psychology Today* 10 (March), pp. 55–67.

Good Tracks, Jimm G. 1973. "Native American Noninterference." *Social Work* 18 (November), pp. 30–34.

Googins, B.; V. A. Capoccia; and N. Kaufman. 1983. "The Interactional Dimension of Planning: A Framework for Practice." *Social Work* 28 (July-August), pp. 273–78.

Gordon, Thomas. 1970. *Parent Effectiveness Training.* New York: Peter H. Wyden.

Gramick, Jeannine. 1983. "Homophobia: A New Challenge." *Social Work* 28, no. 2 (March-April), pp. 137–41.

Greenberg, Herbert M. 1980. *Coping with Job Stress.* Englewood Cliffs, N.J.: Spectrum.

Grier, William H., and Price M. Cobbs. 1968. *Black Rage.* New York: Basic Books.

Grosser, Charles F. 1973. *New Directions in Community Organization.* New York: Praeger Publishers.

Grotevant, Harold D., and Cindy I. Carlson. 1987. "Family Interaction Coding Systems: A Descriptive Review." *Family Process* 26, p. 49.

Grubb, D. L., and D. R. Zwick. 1976. *Fundraising in the Public Interest.* Washington, D.C.: Public Citizen.

Guthrie, E. R. 1935. *The Psychology of Learning.* New York: Harper & Row.

Haeberle, Erwin J. 1978. *The Sex Atlas.* New York: Seabury Press.

Haley, Jay. 1963. *Strategies of Psychotherapy.* New York: Grune & Stratton.

———. 1973. *Uncommon Therapy.* New York: W. W. Norton.

_____. 1976. *Problem-Solving Therapy: New Strategies for Effective Family Therapy.* San Francisco: Jossey-Bass.

Hall, Calvin S., and Gardner Lindzey. 1957. *Theories of Personality.* New York: John Wiley & Sons.

Hall, Edward T. 1959. *The Silent Language.* Greenwich, Conn.: Fawcett Book Group.

Hansen, James C.; Richard W. Warner; and Elsie M. Smith. 1976. *Group Counseling.* Skokie, Ill.: Rand McNally.

Hare, A. Paul. 1962. *Handbook of Small Group Research.* New York: Free Press.

Harris, Thomas. 1969. *I'm OK—You're OK.* New York: Harper & Row.

Hartford, Margaret. 1971. *Groups in Social Work.* New York: Columbia University Press.

Hartman, Ann. 1989. "Still Between Client and Community." *Social Work* 34, no. 5, pp. 387–88.

Hartman, William E., and Marilyn A. Fithian. 1972. *Treatment of Sexual Dysfunction.* Long Beach, Calif.: Center for Marital and Sexual Studies.

Hathaway, S. R. 1948. "Some Considerations Relative to Nondirective Counseling as Therapy." *Journal of Clinical Psychology* 4, pp. 226–31.

Hauck, Paul A. 1972. *The Rational Management of Children.* New York: Libra Publishers.

Hearn, Gordon. 1979. "General Systems Theory and Social Work." In *Social Work Treatment*, ed. Francis J. Turner, 2d ed. New York: Free Press, pp. 333–60.

Heaton, O. P., and D. W. Orme-Johnson. 1974. "Influence of Transcendental Meditation on Grade Point Average: Initial Findings." In *Scientific Research on Transcendental Meditation: Collected Papers*, ed. D. W. Orme-Johnson, L. H. Domash, and J. T. Farrow. Los Angeles: MIU Press.

Hebb, D. O.; R. Held; A. Riesen; and H. Teuber. 1961. "Sensory Deprivation: Facts in Search of a Theory." *Journal of Nervous and Mental Disorders* 132, pp. 17–43.

Hepworth, Dean H., and JoAnn Larsen. 1986. *Direct Social Work Practice: Theory and Skills.* 2nd ed. Chicago: Dorsey Press.

Hersen, Michel, and Alan S. Bellack. 1981. *Behavioral Assessment: A Practical Handbook.* 2nd ed. Elmsford, N.Y.: Pergamon Press.

_____, eds. 1988. *Dictionary of Behavioral Assessment Techniques.* Elmsford, N.Y.: Pergamon Press.

Hersey, P., and K. Blanchard. 1977. *Management of Organizational Behavior: Utilizing Human Resources.* 3rd ed. Englewood Cliffs, N.J.: Prentice-Hall.

Hite, Shere. 1976. *The Hite Report.* New York: Macmillan.

Hofer, A., and W. Polin. 1970. "Schizophrenia in the NAS-NRC Panel of 15,909 Twin Pairs." *Archives of General Psychiatry* 23, pp. 469–77.

Hogan, R. A., and J. H. Kirchner. 1967. "A Preliminary Report of the Extinction of Learned Fears via Short-Term Implosive Therapy." *Journal of Abnormal Psychology* 72, pp. 106–11.

Hogan, Richard. 1986. "Gaining Community Support for Group Homes." *Community Mental Health Journal* 22, no. 2, pp. 117–26.

Holland. G. 1973. "Transactional Analysis." In *Current Psychotherapies*, ed. Raymond Corsini. Itasca, Ill.: F. E. Peacock Publishers, pp. 353–99.

Hollander, E. P. 1958. "Conformity, Status, and Idiosyncrasy Credit." *Psychological Review*, pp. 117–27.

Hollis, F. 1972. *Casework: A Psychosocial Theory.* New York: Random House.

Honsberger, R., and A. F. Wilson. 1973. "Transcendental Meditation in Treating Asthma." *Respiratory Therapy: The Journal of Inhalation Technology* 3, pp. 79–81.

Hook, Mary Van. 1979. "Female Clients, Female Counselors: Combating Learned Helplessness." *Social Work* 24 (January), pp. 63–65.

Hopkins, Thomas J. 1973. "The Role of the Agency in Supporting Black Manhood." *Social Work* 18 (January), pp.53–58.

Howard, Jane. 1970. *Please Touch: A Guided Tour of the Human Potential Movement.* New York: McGraw-Hill.

Hudson, Walter W. 1978. "First Axioms of Treatment." *Social Work* 23, pp. 65–66.

_____. 1982. *The Clinical Measurement Package: A Field Manual.* Homewood, Ill.: Dorsey Press.

Hull, C. L. 1943. *Principles of Behavior.* New York: Appleton-Century-Crofts.

Hull, G. H. 1978. "The Parents' Anonymous Sponsor: A Professional Helping Role." Paper presented at the Child Welfare League of America Regional Conference, Omaha, Neb.

Humphreys, Griffith E. 1983. "Inclusion of Content on Homosexuality in the Social Work Curriculum." *Journal of Education for Social Work* 19 (Winter), pp. 55–60.

Hyde, Janet Shibley. 1979. *Understanding Human Sexuality.* New York: McGraw-Hill.

Ingersoll, Sandra L., and Susan O. Patton. 1990. *Treating Perpetrators of Sexual Abuse.* Lexington, Mass.: Lexington Books.

Jackson, D. D. 1965. "The Study of the Family." *Family Process* 4, pp. 1–20.

Jacobson, Edmund. 1934. *You Must Relax: A Practical Method of Reducing the Stress of Modern Life.* New York: McGraw-Hill.

———. 1938a. *Progressive Relaxation.* 2d ed. Chicago: University of Chicago Press.

———. 1938b. *You Can Sleep Well: The ABC's of Restful Sleep for the Average Person.* New York: McGraw-Hill.

———. 1959. *How to Relax and Have Your Baby: Scientific Relaxation in Childbirth.* New York: McGraw-Hill.

———. 1964. *Anxiety and Tension Control: A Physiologic Approach.* Philadelphia: J. B. Lippincott.

———. 1973. *Teaching and Learning New Methods for Old Arts.* Chicago: National Foundation for Progressive Relaxation.

James, Muriel, and Dorothy Jongeward. 1971. *Born to Win; Transactional Analysis with Gestalt Experiments.* Reading, Mass.: Addison-Wesley Publishing.

Janis, Irving. 1971. "Group Think." *Psychology Today* 15, no. 6, November, pp. 43–46 and 74–76.

Janis, Irving. 1972. *Victims of Groupthink.* Boston: Houghton Mifflin.

Jayaratne, Srinika, and Rona L. Levy. 1979. *Empirical Clinical Practice.* New York: Columbia University Press.

Jehu, D. 1972. *Behavior Modification in Social Work.* New York: John Wiley & Sons.

Johnson, David W., and Frank P. Johnson. 1975. *Joining Together.* Englewood Cliffs, N.J.: Prentice-Hall.

———. 1987. *Joining Together.* 3rd ed. Englewood Cliffs, N.J.: Prentice-Hall.

Johnson, Louise C. 1986. *Social Work Practice: A Generalist Approach.* 2nd ed. Boston: Allyn and Bacon.

Jones, Richard R.; Russell S. Vaught; and Mark R. A. Weinrott. 1977. "Time-Series Analysis in Operant Research." *Journal of Applied Behavior Analysis* 10, pp. 151–66.

Kadushin. Alfred. 1972. *The Social Work Interview.* New York: Columbia University Press.

———. 1980. *Child Welfare Services.* 3rd ed. New York: Macmillan.

———. 1983. *The Social Work Interview.* 2nd ed. New York: Columbia University Press.

———. 1990. *The Social Work Interview.* 3rd ed. New York: Columbia University Press.

Kahn, M., and B. Baker. 1968. "Desensitization with Minimal Therapist Contact." *Journal of Abnormal Psychology* 73, pp. 198–200.

Kanfer, Frederick. 1975. "Self-Management Methods." In *Helping People Change,* ed. F. H. Kanfer and A. P. Goldstein. Elmsford, N.Y.: Pergamon Press, pp. 309–55.

Kaplan, Helen Sanger. 1974. *The New Sex Therapy.* New York: Brunner/Mazel.

———. 1983. *The Evaluation of Sexual Disorders.* New York: Brunner/Mazel.

Katz, Alfred H., and Eugene I. Bender. 1976. *The Strength in Us: Self-Help Groups in the Modern World.* New York: Franklin-Watts.

Kaufman, Roger, and Susan Thomas. 1980. *Evaluation without Fear.* New York: New Viewpoints.

Kazdin, Alan E. 1977. "Assessing the Clinical or Applied Importance of Behavior Change through Social Validation." *Behavior Modification* 1, pp. 427–52.

———. 1977. *The Token Economy.* New York: Plenum Publishing.

Keith-Lucas, Alan. 1972. *The Giving and Taking of Help.* Chapel Hill: University of North Carolina Press.

Kelly, H. H., and A. J. Stahelski. 1970. "Social Interaction Basis of Cooperators' and Competitors' Beliefs about Others." *Journal of Personality and Social Psychology* 16, pp. 66–91.

Kelman, Herbert C. 1965. "Manipulation of Human Behavior: An Ethical Dilemma for the Social Scientist." *Journal of Social Issues* 21, no 2, pp. 31–46.

Kety, Seymor S. 1976. "The Biological Roots of Schizophrenia." *Harvard Magazine* 78, pp. 20–26.

King, S. W., and R. S. Meyers. 1981. "Developing Self-Help Groups: Integrating Group Work and Community Organization Strategies." *Social Development Issues* 5, pp. 33–46.

Kiresuk, Thomas J., and Sander H. Lund. 1978. "Goal Attainment Scaling." In *Evaluation of Human Service Programs,* ed. C. Clifford Attkisson, William A. Hargreaves, Mardi J. Horowitz, and James E. Sorensen. New York: Academic Press, pp. 341–70.

Knopf, Ron. 1979. *Surviving the BS (Bureaucratic System).* Wilmington, N.C.: Mandala Press.

Knopp, Fay Honey. 1984. *Retraining Adult Sex Offenders: Methods and Models.* Syracuse, N.Y.: Safer Society Press.

Kolb, Lawrence C.; Viola Bernard; and Bruce P. Dohrenwend. 1969. "The Problem of Validity in Field Studies of Psychological Disorder." In *Urban Challenges to Psychiatry,* ed. Bruce P. Dohrenwend and Barbara Snell Dohrenwend. New York: John Wiley & Sons, pp. 429–60.

Konle, Carolyn, and Jane A. Piliavin. 1976. "Vocational Aspirations in Kindergarten Children: Early Sex Differences." *The Wisconsin Sociologist* 13, no. 4 (Fall), pp. 119–24.

Koop, Judy. 1988. "Self-Monitoring: A Literature Review of Research and Practice." *Social Work Research & Abstracts* 24, pp. 8–20.

Kratochwill, Thomas R., ed. 1978. *Single Subject Research: Strategies for Evaluating Change.* New York: Academic Press.

Kravetz, Diane. 1982. "An Overview of Content on Women for the Social Work Curriculum." *Journal of Education for Social Work* 18 (Winter), pp. 42–49.

Krech, David; Richard S. Crutchfield; and E. L. Ballachey. 1962. *Individual in Society*. New York: McGraw-Hill.

Kübler-Ross, Elizabeth. 1969. *On Death and Dying*. New York: Macmillan.

Laborde, Genie. 1984. *Influencing with Integrity*. Palo Alto, Calif.: Syntony Publishing.

Lakein, Alan. 1973. *How to Get Control of Your Time and Your Life*. New York: Signet.

Lankton, Steve. 1980. *Practical Magic*. Cupertino, Calif.: Meta Publications.

Lazarus, A. A. 1971. *Behavior Therapy and Beyond*. New York: McGraw-Hill.

League of Women Voters. 1972. *Know Your Community*. Washington, D.C.: League of Women Voters.

Leavitt, Jerome E. 1974. *The Battered Child*. Morristown, N.J.: General Learning Press.

Lecron, Leslie M. 1964. *Self-Hypnotism*. Englewood Cliffs, N.J.: Prentice-Hall.

Leibert, E. R., and B. E. Sheldon. 1972. *Handbook of Special Events for Nonprofit Organizations: Tested Ideas for Fund Raising and Public Relations*. Washington, D.C.: Taft Corp.

Lembo, John. 1974. *Help Yourself*. Niles, Ill.: Argus Communications.

Lemert, Edwin M. 1951. *Social Pathology*. New York: McGraw-Hill.

Leukenfield, Carl G., and Manual Fimbres, eds. 1987. *Responding to AIDS: Psychosocial Initiatives*. Silver Spring, Md.: National Association of Social Workers.

Levitsky, A., and F. Perls. 1970. "The Rules and Games of Gestalt Therapy." In *Gestalt Therapy Now*, ed. J. Fagan and I. Shepherd. Palo Alto, Calif.: Science and Behavior Books.

Levitsky, A., and J. S. Simkin. 1972. "Gestalt Therapy." In *New Perspectives on Encounter Groups*, ed. L. N. Solomon and B. Berzon. San Francisco: Jossey-Bass, pp. 245–54.

Levitt, E. E. 1957. "The Results of Psychotherapy with Children: An Evaluation." *Journal of Consulting Psychology* 21, pp. 189–96.

Lewin, Kurt. 1952. "Group Decision and Social Change." In *Readings in Social Psychology*, ed. G. E. Swanson, T. M. Newcomb, and E. L. Hartley. New York: Holt, Rinehart & Winston.

Lewin, Kurt; R. Lippitt; and R. K. White. 1939. "Patterns of Aggressive Behavior in Experimentally Created Social Climates." *Journal of Social Psychology* 10, pp. 271–99.

Lewis, Ronald G., and Man Keung Ho. 1975. "Social Work with Native Americans." *Social Work* 20 (September), pp. 378–82.

Lieberman, Morton A.; Ervin D. Yalom; and Matthew B. Miles. 1973. "Encounter: The Leader Makes the Difference." *Psychology Today* 6, pp. 69–76.

Lindblom, Charles. 1959. "The Science of Muddling Through." *Public Administration Review*, Spring, pp. 79–88.

Locklear, Herbert H. 1972. "American Indian Myths." *Social Work* 17 (May), pp. 72–80.

———. 1977. "American Indian Alcoholism: Program for Treatment." *Social Work* 22 (May), pp. 202–7.

Loewenberg, F. M. 1977. *Fundamentals of Social Intervention*. New York: Columbia University Press.

Loewenstein, Sophie. 1980. "Understanding Lesbian Women." *Social Casework* 61 (January), p. 31.

Logan, Sadye. 1990. "Black Families: Race Ethnicity, Culture, Social Class, and Gender Issues." In *Social Work Practice with Black Families*, ed. Sadye Logan, Edith Freeman, and Ruth McRoy. New York: Longman.

London, Perry. 1964. *The Modes and Morals of Psychotherapy*. New York: Holt, Rinehart & Winston.

Looft, William R. 1971. "Sex Differences in the Expression of Vocational Aspirations by Elementary School Children." *Developmental Psychology* 5, p. 366.

LoPiccolo, Joseph, and Leslie LoPiccolo, eds. 1978. *Handbook of Sex Therapy*. New York: Plenum Publishing.

Losoncy, Lewis. 1977. *Turning People On*. Englewood Cliffs, N.J.: Prentice-Hall.

Lowenberg, Frank, and Ralph Dolgoff. 1971. *Teaching of Practice Skills in Undergraduate Programs in Social Welfare and Other Helping Services*. New York: Council on Social Work Education.

Luria, A. 1961. *The Role of Speech in the Regulation of Normal and Abnormal Behavior*. New York: Liveright Publishing.

MacShane, D. 1979. *Using the Media: How to Deal with the Press, Radio, Television*. London: Pluto.

Maddi, Salvatore. 1968. *Personality Theories*. Homewood, Ill.: Dorsey Press.

Mahoney, M. J. 1973. "Clinical Issues in Self-Control Training." Paper presented at the meeting of the American Psychological Association, Montreal.

———. 1974. *Cognition and Behavior Modification*. Cambridge, Mass.: Ballinger Publishing Co.

Maier, N. R. F. 1970. *Problem Solving and Creativity in Individuals and Groups*. Monterey, Calif.: Brooks/Cole Publishing.

Maluccio, A. 1979. "Perspectives of Social Workers and Clients on Treatment Outcome." *Social Casework* 60, pp. 394–401.

Mandino, Og., ed. 1966. *A Treasury of Success Unlimited*. New York: Hawthorn Books.

Manley, Merlin J. 1977. "How to Cope with a Sense of Failure." In *The Personal Problem Solver*, ed. Charles Zastrow and Dae Chang. Englewood Cliffs, N.J.: Prentice-Hall.

March, J. G. 1956. "Influence Measurement in Experimental and Semi-Experimental Groups." *Sociometry* 19, no. 4 (December), pp. 260–71.

Marti-Costa, Sylvia, and Irma Serrano-Garcia. 1987. "Needs Assessment and Community Development: An Ideological Perspective." In *Strategies of Community Organization: Macro Practice*, ed. Fred M. Cox, John L. Erlich, Jack Rothman, and John Trotman. Itasca, Ill.: F. E. Peacock Publishers.

Martinez-Brawley, Emilia, and Joan Blundall. 1989. "Farm Families' Preference toward the Personal Social Services." *Social Work* 34, no. 6, pp. 513–22.

Maslach, Christina. 1976. "Burned-Out." *Human Behavior* 5 (September), pp. 16–22.

_____. 1978. "The Client Role in Staff Burn-Out." *Journal of Social Issues* 34, pp. 11–24.

Maslach, Christina, and Ayala Pines. 1977. "The Burn-Out Syndrome in the Day Care Setting." *Child Care Quarterly* 6, pp. 100–13.

Masters, William H., and Virginia E. Johnson. 1966. *Human Sexual Response.* Boston: Little, Brown.

_____. 1970. *Human Sexual Inadequacy.* Boston: Little, Brown.

Masters, William H.; Virginia E. Johnson; and Robert C. Kolodny. 1986. *Masters and Johnson on Sex and Human Loving.* Boston: Little, Brown.

Mauksch, Hans O. 1975. "The Organizational Context of Dying." In *Death: The Final Stage of Growth*, ed. Elizabeth Kübler-Ross. Englewood Cliffs, N.J.: Prentice-Hall, pp. 7–26.

Maultsby, Maxie C., Jr. 1975. *Help Yourself to Happiness.* Boston, Mass.: Herman Publishing.

_____. 1977. "The ABC's of Better Emotional Self-Control." In *The Personal Problem Solver*, ed. Charles Zastrow and Dae Chang. Englewood Cliffs, N.J.: Prentice-Hall, pp. 3–18.

_____. 1978. *A Million Dollars for Your Hangover.* Lexington, Ky.: Rational Self-Help Books.

McMahon, Frank B. 1971. *The Forty-Eight Item Counseling Evaluation Test: Revised.* Los Angeles: Western Psychological Services.

McQuade, Walter, and Ann Aikman. 1974. *Stress.* New York: Bantam Books.

Mead, Margaret. 1935. *Sex and Temperament in Three Primitive Societies.* New York: Morrow.

Meador, Betty D., and Carl Rogers. 1979. "Person-Centered Therapy." In *Current Psychotherapies*, ed. Raymond J. Corsini. 2d ed. Itasca, Ill.: F. E. Peacock Publishers.

Mechanic, David. 1962. "Some Factors in Identifying and Defining Mental Illness." *Mental Hygiene* 46, pp. 66–74.

Medina, Celia, and Maria R. Reyes. 1976. "Dilemmas of Chicano Counselors." *Social Work* 21 (November), pp. 515–17.

Mehrabian, Albert. 1981. *Silent Messages.* 2nd ed. Belmont, Calif.: Wadsworth.

Meichenbaum, D. 1975. "Self-Instructional Methods." In *Helping People Change*, ed. F. H. Kanfer and A. P. Goldstein. Elmsford, N.Y.: Pergamon Press, pp. 357–92.

Meiselman, Karin C. 1978. *Incest.* San Francisco: Jossey-Bass.

Merkel, W. 1975. "Controlled Research in Transactional Analysis." Unpublished manuscript. Kingston: University of Rhode Island.

Migler, B. 1968. "A Supplementary Note on Automated Self-Desensitization." *Behavior Research and Therapy* 6, p. 243.

Milgram, S. 1963. "Behavioral Study of Obedience." *Journal of Abnormal and Social Psychology*, pp. 371–78.

Mills, Gerald. 1973. "The Wisconsin Mutual Agreement Programming." Paper represented to the 103d Congress of Corrections, Seattle, Wash., August.

Minuchin, Salvador. 1974. *Families and Family Therapy.* Cambridge, Mass.: Harvard University Press.

Minuchin, S., and H. C. Fishman. 1981. *Family Therapy Techniques.* Cambridge, Mass.: Harvard University Press.

Mitchell, James V., ed. 1985. *The Ninth Mental Measurements Yearbook.* Lincoln: University of Nebraska Press.

Mizio, Emelicia. 1972. "White Worker—Minority Client." *Social Work* 17 (May), pp. 82–86.

Money, John. 1986. *Venuses Penises.* Buffalo, N.Y.: Prometheus Books.

Montiel, Miguel. 1973. "The Chicano Family: A Review of Research." *Social Work* 18 (March), pp. 22–31.

Moore, Christopher W. 1986. *The Mediation Process.* San Francisco, Calif.: Jossey-Bass.

Moreno, J. L. 1946. *Psychodrama: Vol. 1.* Boston: Beacon House.

Morris, Richard. 1975. "Fear Reduction Methods." In *Helping People Change*, ed. F. H. Kanfer and A. P. Goldstein. Elmsford, N.Y.: Pergamon Press, pp. 229–71.

_____. 1986. "Fear Reduction Methods." In *Helping People Change*, 3rd ed., ed. F. H. Kanfer and A. P. Goldstein. Elmsford, N.Y.: Pergamon Press, pp. 145–90.

NASW News. 1979. "Bottom Line for Social Work Licensing up in Air." Washington, D.C.: NASW Publications, April.

NASW Practice Digest 6, no. 3 (Winter 1983). Special issue devoted to computers in social work practice.

National Institute of Law Enforcement and Criminal Justice. 1978. *Treatment Programs for Sex Offenders.* Washington, D.C.: U.S. Government Printing Office, January.

Nichols, Ann, and Rebecca Schilit. 1988. "Telephone Support for Latchkey Children." *Child Welfare* 67, no. 1, pp. 49–59.

Norton, Dolores G. 1978. "Incorporating Content on Minority Groups into Social Work Practice Courses." In *The Dual Perspective.* New York: Council on Social Work Education.

O'Connor, Gerald. 1972. "Toward a New Policy in Adult Corrections." *Social Service Review* 46 (December), p. 4.

Offer, Daniel, and Melvin Sabshin. 1966. *Normality: Theoretical and Clinical Concepts in Mental Health.* New York: Basic Books.

Okun, B., and L. Rappaport. 1980. *Working with Families: An Introduction to Family Therapy.* North Scituate, Mass.: Duxbury Press.

Olmstead, Michael S. 1959. *The Small Group.* New York: Random House.

Orme-Johnson, D. W. 1973. "Autonomic Stability and Transcendental Meditation." *Psychosomatic Medicine* 35, no. 4 (July-August), pp. 341–49.

Orne, M. T., and P. H. Wender. 1968. "Anticipatory Socialization for Psychotherapy: Method and Rationale." *American Journal of Psychiatry* 124, pp. 1202–12.

Osborn, A. F. 1963. *Applied Imagination: Principles and Procedures of Creative Problem Solving.* 3d ed. New York: Charles Scribner's Sons.

Palmer, Bonnie, and S. Pablo. 1978. "Community Development Possibilities for Effective Indian Reservation and Child Abuse and Neglect Efforts." In *Child Abuse and Neglect: Issues on Innovation and Implementation,* vol. 1, ed. Michael Lauderdale, Rosalie Anderson, and Stephen Cramer. Washington, D.C.: U.S. Department of Health, Education, and Welfare, pp. 111–15.

Parad, Howard, J,. ed. 1965. *Crisis Intervention: Selected Readings.* New York: Family Service Association of America.

Parsons, Talcott. 1958. "Social Structure and the Development of Personality." *Psychiatry* 21, pp. 321–40.

Parsonson, B. S., and D. M. Baer. 1978. "The Analysis and Presentation of Graphic Data." In *Single Subject Research: Strategies for Evaluating Change,* ed. Thomas R. Kratochwill. New York: Academic Press, pp. 101–65.

Patterson, G. R. 1971. *Families.* Champaign, Ill.: Research Press Co.

Paul, Gordon. 1966. *Insight versus Desensitization in Psychotherapy.* Stanford, Calif.: Stanford University Press.

———. 1969. "Outcome of Systematic Desensitization." In *Behavior Therapy: Appraisal and Status.* New York: McGraw-Hill, pp. 63–159.

Peck, Robert E. 1974. *The Miracle of Shock Treatment.* Jericho, N.Y.: Exposition Press.

Pelletier, K. R. 1974. "Altered Attention Deployment in Meditation." In *The Psychobiology of Transcendental Meditation,* ed. D. Kannellakos and J. Lucas. Hunter, N.Y.: W. R. Benjamin.

———. 1977. *Mind as Healer, Mind as Slayer.* New York: Dell Publishing.

Perls, Frederick. 1969a. *Gestalt Therapy Verbatim.* Moab, Utah: Real People Press.

———. 1969b. *In and Out of the Garbage Pail.* Moah, Utah: Real People Press.

Perls, Frederick; R. Hefferline; and P. Goodman. 1951. *Gestalt Therapy: Excitement and Growth in Personality.* New York: Dell Publishing.

Pfeiffer, J. William, and John E. Jones. 1976. "Role Functions in a Group." In *1976 Annual Handbook for Group Facilitators,* by J. William Pfeiffer and John E. Jones. La Jolla, Calif.: University Associates, pp. 136–38.

Phillips, D. L. 1963. "Rejection: A Possible Consequence of Seeking Help for Mental Disorder." *American Sociological Review* 28, pp. 963–73.

Piers, Ellen V., and Dale B. Harris. 1969. *The Piers-Harris Children's Self-Concept Scale.* Los Angeles: Western Psychological Services.

Pincus, Allen, and Anne Minahan. 1973. *Social Work Practice: Model and Method.* Itasca, Ill.: F. E. Peacock Publishers.

Pinderhughes, Elaine B. 1979. "Teaching Empathy in Cross Cultural Social Work." *Social Work* 24 (July), pp. 312–16.

Pines, Ayala, and Elliot Aronson. 1981. *Burnout: From Tedium to Personal Growth.* New York: Free Press.

Posavac, Emil J., and Raymond G. Carey. 1980. *Program Evaluation: Methods and Case Studies.* Englewood Cliffs, N.J.: Prentice-Hall.

Powdermaker, Hortense. 1933. *Life in Lesu.* New York: W. W. Norton.

Prochaska, James O. 1979. *Systems of Psychotherapy.* Homewood, Ill.: Dorsey Press.

Proctor, Pam. 1978. "The Big Resurgence of Positive Thinking." *Parade.* May 21, pp. 23–24.

Pruger, R. 1978. "Bureaucratic Functioning as a Social Work Skill." In *Educating the Baccalaureate Social Worker: Report of the Undergraduate Social Work Curriculum Development Project* by B. L. Baer and R. Federico, Cambridge, Mass.: Ballinger Publishing Co.

Raimy, Victor. 1977. *Misunderstanding of the Self.* San Francisco: Jossey-Bass.

Ramey, James W. 1979. *SIECUS Report* 7, no. 5 (May).

Rardin, M. 1969. "Treatment of a Phobia by Partial Self-Desensitization." *Journal of Consulting and Clinical Psychology* 33, pp. 125–26.

Rasmussen, S. A., and M. T. Tsuang. 1986. *American Journal of Psychiatry* 143, pp. 317–22.

Rauch, Julia B. 1978. "Gender as a Factor in Practice." *Social Work* 23 (September), pp. 388–96.

Reid, William, and Ann Shyne. 1969. *Brief and Extended Casework.* New York: Columbia University Press.

Reid, William J., and Laura Epstein. 1977. *Task-Centered Practice.* New York: Columbia University Press.

Rein, Martin, and Robert Morris. 1962. "Goals, Structures, and Strategies of Community Change." In *Social Work Practice 1962.* New York: National Conference of Social Welfare.

Reiss, Ira R. 1986. *Journey into Sexuality.* Englewood Cliffs, N.J.: Prentice-Hall.

Richmond, Mary E. 1917. *Social Diagnosis.* New York: Russell Sage Foundation.

————. 1965. *Social Diagnosis.* New York: Free Press.

Riessman, Frank. 1965. "The 'Helper Therapy' Principle." *Journal of Social Work* 10, no. 2 (April), pp. 27–34.

————. 1987. "Foreword." In Thomas J. Powell, *Self-Help Organizations and Professional Practice.* Silver Spring, Md.: National Association of Social Workers.

Rimm, D., and J. Masters. 1974. *Behavior Therapy.* New York: Academic Press.

Ringer, Robert J. 1977. *Looking Out for No. 1.* New York: Fawcett Book Group.

Rogers, Carl R. 1942. *Counseling and Psychotherapy.* Boston: Houghton Mifflin.

————. 1951. *Client-Centered Therapy.* Boston: Houghton Mifflin.

————. 1959. "A Theory of Therapy, Personality, and Interpersonal Relationships, as Developed in the Client-Centered Framework." In *Psychology: A Study of a Science,* ed. S. Koch. Vol. 3. New York: McGraw-Hill, pp. 184–256.

————. 1961. "The Process Equation of Psychotherapy." *American Journal of Psychotherapy* 15 (January), pp. 27–45.

————. 1965. Client-Centered Therapy, film no. 1. In *Three Approaches to Psychotherapy,* ed. Everett Shostrom. (Three 16 mm. color motion pictures) Santa Ana, Calif.: Psychological Films.

————. 1970. *Carl Rogers on Encounter Groups.* New York: Harper & Row.

————. 1984. "A Historic Note–Gloria." In *Client-Centered Therapy and the Person-Centered Approach.* New York: Praeger, pp. 423–25.

Romero, Det P. 1977. "Biases in Gender-Role Research." *Social Work* 22 (May), pp. 214–18.

Rosenhan, David. 1973. "On Being Sane in Insane Places." *Science* 179, pp. 250–57.

Ross, Murray G. 1967. *Community Organization.* 2d ed. New York: Harper & Row.

Rossi, Peter H.; Howard E. Freeman; and Sonia R. Wright. 1979. *Evaluation: A Systematic Approach.* Beverly Hills, Calif.: Sage.

Rothman, J. 1968. "Three Models of Community Organization Practice." In *Social Work Practice.* New York: Columbia University Press, pp. 16–47.

————. 1979. "Three Models of Community Organization Practice, Their Mixing and Phasing." In *Strategies of Community Organization,* ed. F. M. Cox; J. L. Erlich; J. Rothman; and J. E. Tropman. 3d ed. Itasca, Ill.: F. E. Peacock Publishers.

Rounds, Kathleen A. 1988. "Responding to AIDS: Rural Community Strategies." *Social Casework* 69, no. 6, pp. 360–64.

Ruoss, M. 1970. As quoted in J. C. DeBoer. *Let's Plan: A Guide to the Planning Process for Voluntary Organizations.* Princeton, N.J.: Pilgrim Press.

Ryan, W. 1971. *Blaming the Victim.* New York: Pantheon Books.

Sager, Clifford J.; Thomas L. Brayboy; and Barbara R. Waxenberg. 1970. *Black Ghetto Family in Therapy: A Laboratory Experience.* New York: Grove Press.

Salter, Anna C. 1988. *Treating Child Sex Offenders and Victims.* Newbury Park, Calif.: Sage Publications.

Sandler, Jack. 1975. "Aversion Methods." In *Helping People Change,* ed. F. H. Kanfer and A. P. Goldstein. Elmsford, N.Y.: Pergamon Press, pp. 273–307.

Sandler, Jack. 1986. "Aversion Methods." In *Helping People Change,* 3rd ed., ed. F. H. Kanfer and A. P. Goldstein. Elmsford, N.Y.: Pergamon Press, pp. 191–235.

Satir, Virginia. 1967. *Conjoint Family Therapy.* Rev. ed. Palo Alto, Calif.: Science and Behavior Books.

————. 1972. *Peoplemaking.* Palo Alto, Calif.: Science and Behavior Books.

Satir, Virginia; James Stachowiak; and Harvey A. Taschman. 1975. *Helping Families to Change,* ed. Donald Tiffany, Julius Cohen, and Analee Robinson. New York: Jason Aronson.

Schachter, Stanley. 1959. *The Psychology of Affiliation.* Stanford, Calif.: Stanford University Press.

Schafer, Walt. 1978. *Stress, Distress and Growth.* Davis, Calif.: International Dialogue Press.

Scheff, Thomas. 1966. *Being Mentally Ill.* Hawthorne, N.Y.: Aldine Publishing.

Schellenberg, James A. 1970. *An Introduction to Social Psychology.* New York: Random House.

Schinka, John A. 1985. *Personal Problems Checklist for Adolescents*. Odessa, Fla.: Psychological Assessment Resources.

Schoech, Dick J. 1982. *Computer Use in Human Services*. New York: Human Science Press.

Schreiber, Flora R. 1973. *Sybil*. New York: Warner Books.

Schuller, Robert, II. 1973. *Move Ahead with Possibility Thinking*. Moonachie, N.J.: Pyramid Publications.

Schwartz, Gerald. 1989. "Confidentiality Revisited" *Social Work* (May), pp. 223–26.

Schwartz, Marc D., ed. 1984. *Using Computers in Clinical Practice*. New York: Haworth Press.

Schwartz, Ralph, and B. Friedland. 1965. *Linear Systems*. New York: McGraw-Hill.

Sears, R. R.; L. Rau; and R. Alpert. 1965. *Identification and Child Rearing*. Stanford, Calif.: Stanford University Press.

Selye, Hans. 1956. *The Stress of Life*. New York: McGraw-Hill.

Sgroi, Suzanne M., ed. 1982. *Handbook of Clinical Intervention in Child Sexual Abuse*. Lexington, Mass.: Lexington Books.

Shaw, R., and D. Kolb. 1974. "One-Point Reaction Time Involving Meditators and Non-Meditators." In *Scientific Research on Transcendental Meditation: Collected Papers*, ed. D. W. Orme-Johnson, L. G. Domash, and J. T. Farrow, vol. 1, Los Angeles: MIU Press.

Shelly, M. W. 1973. *Sources of Satisfaction*. Lawrence, Kan.: University of Kansas Press.

Sherif, M. 1936. *The Psychology of Social Norms*. New York: Harper & Row.

Sherman, Harold. 1966. "The Surest Way in the World to Attract Success—or Failure." In *A Treasury of Success Unlimited*, ed. Og Mandino. New York: Hawthorn Books, pp. 111–13.

Shimkus, J. R., and J. P. Winship. 1977. *Human Service Development: Working Together in the Community*. Athens: University of Georgia Printing Department.

Shoemaker, James S., and Donald L. Tasto. 1975. "The Effects of Muscle Relaxation on Blood Pressure of Essential Hypertensives." *Behavior Research and Therapy* 13 (February), pp. 29–43.

Shostrom, E. L. 1969. "Group Therapy: Let the Buyer Beware." *Psychology Today* 2, no. 12 (May), pp. 36–40.

Simkin, James S. 1979. "Gestalt Therapy." In *Current Psychotherapies*, ed. Raymond J. Corsini, 2d ed. Itasca, Ill.: F. E. Peacock Publishers.

Simon, B. K. 1970. "Social Casework Theory: An Overview." In *Theories of Social Casework*, ed. R. Roberts and R. Nee. Chicago: University of Chicago Press, pp. 353–96.

Simos, Bertha G. 1977. "Grief Therapy to Facilitate Healthy Restitution." *Social Casework* (June), pp. 337–42.

Sinclair, Lloyd. 1982. "Sexual Counseling and Sex Therapy." In Charles Zastrow, *Introduction to Social Welfare Institutions*. 2nd ed. Homewood, Ill.: Dorsey Press, pp. 412–35.

Sinclair, Lloyd, and Charles Zastrow. 1986. "Human Sexuality Variations, Sexual Counseling, and Sex Therapy." In Charles Zastrow, *Introduction to Social Welfare Institutions*. 3rd ed. Homewood, Ill.: Dorsey Press, pp. 219–20.

Skinner, B. F. 1938. *The Behavior of Organisms*. New York: Appleton-Century-Crofts.

———. 1948. *Walden Two*. New York: Macmillan.

———. 1953. *Science and Human Behavior*. New York: Free Press.

Slaff, James I., and John K. Brubacker. 1985. *The AIDS Epidemic: How You Can Protect Yourself and Your Family—Why You Must*. New York: Warner Books.

Slater, P. E. 1958. "Contrasting Correlates of Group Size." *Sociometry* 21, no. 2 (June), pp. 129–39.

Sloane, R. B.; F. R. Staples; A. H. Cristol; N. J. Yorkston; and K. Whipple. 1975. *Psychotherapy versus Behavior Therapy*. Cambridge, Mass.: Harvard University Press.

Smith, Larry L. 1978. "A Review of Crisis Intervention Theory." *Social Casework* 59, no. 7 (July), pp. 396–405.

Solomon, Barbara. 1987. "Human Development: Sociocultural Perspectives." *The Encyclopedia of Social Work*. Silver Springs, Md.: National Association of Social Workers, pp. 856–66.

Solomon, P.; P. Kubzansky; P. Leiderman; J. Menderson; R. Trumbull; and D. Wexler, eds. 1961. *Sensory Deprivation*. Cambridge, Mass.: Harvard University Press.

Southern Regional Education Board. 1976. "Educational Assumptions for Rural Social Work." In *Social Work in Rural Communities* by Leon Ginsberg. New York: Council on Social Work Education.

Southwestern Cooperative Educational Laboratory. 1968. *Ethno-Pedagogy: A Manual in Cultural Sensitivity with Techniques for Improving Cross-Cultural Teaching by Fitting Ethnic Patterns*. Albuquerque: Southwestern Cooperative Educational Laboratory.

"Special Issue on Conceptual Frameworks." 1977. *Social Work* 22 (September), pp. 338–444.

Spitz, René. 1945. "Hospitalism: Genesis of Psychiatric Conditions in Early Childhood." *Psychoanalytic Study of the Child* 1, p. 53.

Spock, B. 1957. *The Common-Sense Book of Baby and Chhild Care*. New York: Duell, Sloan & Pierce.

Stampfl, T. G., and D. J. Levis. 1967. "Essentials of Implosive Therapy: A Learning-Based Psychodynamic Behavioral Therapy." *Journal of Abnormal Psychology* 72, pp. 496–503.

Standards for Social Service Manpower. 1973. Washington, D.C.: National Association of Social Workers.

Standards for the Classification of Social Work Practice. 1982. Washington, D.C.: National Association of Social Workers.

Standards for the Regulation of Social Work Practice. 1976. Washington, D.C.: National Association of Social Workers.

Starkweather, Cassie L., and S. Michael Turner. 1975. "Parents Anonymous: Reflections on the Development of a Self-Help Group." In *Child Abuse Intervention and Treatment*, ed. Nancy C. Ebeling and Deborah A. Hill. Littleton, Mass.: PSG Pubs.

Steiner, C. 1974. *Scripts People Live.* New York: Grove Press.

Stephenson, M. M. 1983. "The Talking Circle: A Resource for Personal and Community Development." Paper presented at the Eighth Annual Institute on Social Work in Rural Areas, July, Cheney, Washington.

Stone, W. Clement. 1966. "Be Generous." In *A Treasury of Success Unlimited*, ed. Og Mandino. New York: Hawthorn Books, pp. 9–10.

Strachey, James. 1962. *Sigmund Freud: Three Essays on the Theory of Sexuality.* New York: Basic Books.

Stuart, Richard B. 1970. *Trick or Treatment.* Champaign, Ill.: Research Press Co.

Suinn, Richard M. 1976. "Body Thinking: Psychology for Olympic Champs." *Psychology Today* 10 (July), pp. 38–43.

Sundberg, Norman D., and Leona E. Tyler. 1962. *Clinical Psychology.* New York: Appleton-Century-Crofts.

Sundel, Martin, and Sandra S. Sundel. 1975. *Behavior Modification in the Human Services.* New York: John Wiley & Sons.

Szasz, Thomas. 1961. "The Myth of Mental Illness." In *Clinical Psychology in Transition*, comp. John R. Braun. Cleveland: Howard Allen.

———. 1963. *Law, Liberty and Psychiatry.* New York: Macmillan.

Teare, Robert J. 1979. "A Task Analysis for Public Welfare Practice and Educational Implications." In *The Pursuit of Competence in Social Work*, ed. Frank Clark and Morton Arkava. San Francisco: Jossey-Bass, pp. 131–45.

Teuber, H. L., and E. Powers. 1953. "Evaluating Therapy in a Delinquency Prevention Program." *Psychiatric Treatment*, 21, pp. 138–47.

Thomas, Alexander, and Samuel Sillen. 1972. *Racism and Psychiatry.* New York: Brunner/Mazel.

Thomas, E. 1959. *The Harmless People.* New York: Alfred A. Knopf.

Thomas, Edwin J. 1978. "Research and Service in Single-Case Experimentation: Conflicts and Choices." *Social Work Research and Abstracts* 14, pp. 20–31.

———. 1984. *Designing Interventions for the Helping Professions.* New York: Sage.

Thomas, Susan A. 1977. "Theory and Practice in Feminine Therapy." *Social Work* 22 (November), pp. 447–54.

Thompson, George. 1972. "The Identification of Ego States." *Transactional Analysis Journal* 2, pp. 196–211.

Thorndike, E. L. 1913. *The Psychology of Learning.* New York: Teachers College Press.

Thorpe, Louis P., and Barney Katz. 1948. *The Psychology of Abnormal Behavior.* New York: Ronald Press.

Toch, Hans. 1970. "The Care and Feeding of Typologies and Labels." *Federal Probation* 34 (September), pp. 46–57.

Tolman, E. C. 1932. *Purposive Behavior in Animals and Men.* New York: Appleton-Century-Crofts.

Touliatos, John; Barry F. Perlmutter; and Murray A. Straus, eds. 1990. *Handbook of Family Measurement Techniques.* Newbury Park, Calif.: Sage.

Tracy, Elizabeth M. 1990. "Identifying Social Support Resources of At-Risk Families." *Social Work* 35, no. 3, pp. 252–58.

Truax, Charles. 1966. "Reinforcement and Non-reinforcement in Rogerian Psychotherapy." *Journal of Abnormal Psychology* 71, pp. 11–19.

Truax, Charles, and Kevin M. Mitchell. 1971. "Research on Certain Therapists' Interpersonal Skills in Relation to Process and Outcome." In *Handbook of Psychotherapy and Behavior Change*, ed. Allen E. Bergin and Sol L. Garfield. New York: John Wiley & Sons, pp. 299–344.

Tubbs, Stewart I., and John W. Baird. 1976. *The Open Person.* Columbus, Ohio: Charles E. Merrill Publishing.

Turner, Charles; Heather Miller; and Lincoln Mosed, eds. 1989. *AIDS: Sexual Behavior and Intravenous Drug Use.* Washington, D.C.: The National Academy Press.

Turner, John B. 1972. "Education for Practice with Minorities." *Social Work* 17 (May), pp. 112–18.

University of Pittsburg Law Review. 1975. "*Tarsoff v. Regents of University of California: The Psychotherapist's Peril*" 37, pp. 159–64.

Van de Ven, Andrew, and Andre L. Delbecq, 1971. "Nominal versus Interacting Group Processes for Committee Decision-Making Effectiveness." *Academy of Management Journal* 14, no. 2 (June), pp. 203–12.

Van Den Bergh, Nan, and Lynn B. Cooper. 1986. "Feminist Social Work." In *The Encyclopedia of Social Work*. Washington, D.C.: National Association of Social Workers, pp. 610–18.

Vogler, R. E.; S. E. Lunde; G. R. Johnson; and P. L. Martin. 1970. "Electrical Aversion Conditioning with Chronic Alcoholics." *Journal of Consulting and Clinical Psychology* 34, pp. 302–7.

Vygotsky, L. 1962. *Thoughts and Language*. Cambridge, Mass.: MIT Press.

Wachtel, Dawn. 1974. "Structures of Community and Strategies for Organization." In *Strategies of Community Organization—A Book of Readings*, ed. Fred Cox et al. Itasca, Ill.: F. E. Peacock Publishers.

Wallace, R. K. 1970. "Physiological Effects of Transcendental Meditation." *Science* 167, pp. 1751–54.

Walz, Thomas H., and Nancee Blum. 1987. *Sexual Health in Later Life*. Lexington, Mass.: Lexington Books.

Washington, Valora. 1987. "Community Involvement in Recruiting Adoptive Homes for Black Children." *Child Welfare* 66, no. 1; pp. 57–67.

Watkins, Ted R., and Richard Gonzales. 1982. "Outreach to Mexican-Americans." *Social Work* 27, no. 1 (January), pp. 68–73.

Watson, David L., and Roland G. Tharp. 1972. *Self-Directed Behavior: Self-Modification for Personal Adjustment*. Monterey, Calif.: Brooks/Cole Publishing.

Watson, G., and David W. Johnson. 1972. *Social Psychology: Issues and Insight*. 2d ed. Philadelphia: J. B. Lippincott.

Watson, J. B., and R. Rayner. 1920. "Conditioned Emotional Reaction." *Journal of Experimental Psychology* 3, no. 1, pp. 1–14.

Webster's Ninth New Collegiate Dictionary. 1983. Springfield, Mass.: G. & G. Merriam Co.

Weiss, Carol H. 1972. *Evaluation Research*. Englewood Cliffs, N.J.: Prentice-Hall.

Weiss, Joan C. 1990. "Violence Motivated by Bigotry: Ethnoviolence." In *The Encyclopedia of Social Work*. 18th ed., 1990 supplement. Silver Springs, Md.: National Association of Social Workers, pp. 307–19.

Weissman, Harold H.; I. E. Epstein; and Andrea Savage. 1987. "Expanding the Role Repertoire of Clinicians." *Social Casework* 68, no. 3, pp. 150–55.

Wender, Paul, and D. Klein. 1968. *Mind, Mood and Medicine*. New York: Meridian Publishers.

"What Everyone Should Know About AIDS." 1985. South Deerfield, Mass.: Channing L. Bete Co.

White, Robert W., and Norman F. Watt. 1973. *The Abnormal Personality*. 4th ed. New York: Ronald Press.

Whittaker, James K. 1974. *Social Treatment*. Hawthorne, N.Y.: Aldine Publishing.

Wilensky, Harold, and Charles Lebeaux. 1965. *Industrial Society & Social Welfare*. New York: Free Press.

Wiley, Gerry E. 1973. "Win/Lose Situations." In *1973 Annual Handbook of Group Facilitators*, by John E. Jones and J. William Pfeiffer. La Jolla, Calif.: University Associates, pp. 105–7.

Williams, D. A.; T. Jackson; D. Weathers; N. Joseph; and M. Anderson. 1985. "Roots III: Souls on Ice: A Post–Civil Rights Generation Struggle For Identity." *Newsweek*, pp. 82–84.

Wilson, Suanna J. 1978. *Confidentiality in Social Work: Issues and Principles*. New York: Free Press.

Wilson, Terence G. 1989. "Behavior Therapy." In *Current Psychotherapies*, 4th ed., ed. Raymond J. Corsini and Danny Wedding. Itasca, Ill.: F. E. Peacock Publishers, pp. 241–82.

Wiseman, Reva S. 1975. "Crisis Theory and the Process of Divorce." *Social Casework* 56, no. 4 (April), pp. 205–12.

Wofford, J. 1979. "Ebonics: A Legitimate System of Oral Communication." *Journal of Black Studies* 9, pp. 367–82.

Wolpe, Joseph. 1958. *Psychotherapy by Reciprocal Inhibition*. Stanford, Calif.: Stanford University Press.

_____. 1969. *The Practice of Behavior Therapy*. Elmsford, N.Y.: Pergamon Press.

Woodman, Natalie Jane. 1987. "Homosexuality: Lesbian Women." In *The Encyclopedia of Social Work*. Silver Springs, Md.: National Association of Social Workers, pp. 805–12.

Woods, Nancy Fugate. 1979. *Human Sexuality in Health & Illness*. St. Louis: C. V. Mosby.

Wright, B. J., and V. R. Isenstein. 1975. *Psychological Tests and Minorities*. Rockville, Md.: National Institute of Mental Health.

Wright, Chester, and Michael Tate. 1973. *Economic Concepts and Systems Analysis: An Introduction for Public Managers*. Reading, Mass.: Addison-Wesley Publishing.

Yontef, Gary M., and James S. Simkin. 1989. "Gestalt Therapy." In *Current Psychotherapies*, 4th ed., ed. Raymond J. Corsini and Danny Wedding. Itasca, Ill.: F. E. Peacock Publishers.

Zastrow, Charles. 1973. "The Nominal Group: A New Approach to Designing Programs for Curbing Delinquency." *Canadian Journal of Criminology and Corrections* (January), pp. 109–17.

_____. 1977. "How to Counsel." In *The Personal Problem Solver*, ed. Charles Zastrow and Dae H. Chang. Englewood Cliffs, N.J.: Prentice-Hall, pp. 267–74.

_____. 1979. *Talk to Yourself: Using the Power of Self-Talk*. Englewood Cliffs, N.J.: Prentice-Hall.

_____. 1982. *Introduction to Social Welfare Institutions*. 2nd ed. Homewood, Ill.: Dorsey Press.

_____. 1986. *Introduction to Social Welfare Institutions*. 3rd ed. Homewood, Ill.: Dorsey Press.

_____. 1990. "Social Workers and Salesworkers: Similarities and Differences." *Journal of Independent Social Work* 4, no. 3, pp. 7–16.

_____. 1990. "Starting and Leading Therapy Groups: A Beginner's Guide." *Journal of Independent Social Work* 4, no. 4, pp. 7–26.

_____ and Dae Chang, eds. 1977. *The Personal Problem Solver.* Englewood Cliffs, N.J.: Prentice-Hall.

Zastrow, Charles, and Ralph Navarre. 1977. "The Nominal Group: A New Tool for Making Social Work Education Relevant. *Journal of Education for Social Work* 13 (Winter), pp. 112–18.

Zastrow, Charles, and Ralph Navarre. 1979. "Using Videotaped Role Playing to Assess and Develop Competence." In *The Pursuit of Competence in Social Work*, ed. Frank Clark and Morton Arkava. San Francisco: Jossey-Bass, pp. 193–204.

Zastrow, Charles; Virginia Dotson; and Michael Koch. 1986. "The Neuro-Linguistic Programming Treatment Approach." *Journal of Independent Social Work* 1 (Fall), pp. 29–38.

Zauner, Phyllis. 1974. "Mothers Anonymous: The Last Resort." In *The Battered Child*, ed. Jerome E. Leavitt. Morristown, N.J.: General Learning Press.

Zilbergeld, Bernie. 1978. *Male Sexuality.* Boston: Little, Brown.

INDEX

AB design, 267

Abortion, 33–34, 37

Acceptance stage of death and dying, 118, 121–122

Accountability, 49–50

Acrophobia, 17

Action system, 72, 84

Active listening, 502–504, 530–531

Activist role of social worker, 14–15, 20

Addams, Jane, 3–4

Administrative activities, 24–25

Adrenaline, 316–317

Advocacy
 as role of social worker, 14, 20
 as value, 48

African-American clients, 281–283, 290–291

Agenda, for groups, 154

Aggressive behavior, 437, 438

AIDS, 466–470
 sexual revolution and, 466
 symptoms of, 468
 testing for, 468–469
 transmission of, 468

Aim-star technique, 263

Alcoholic game, 384–385

Alcoholism
 in problem assessment, 66
 values and, 34–35

Algophobia, 17

American Psychiatric Association (APA) classifications
 of mental disorders, 15–17

Anal stage of development, 347

Anger
 assertive expression of, 456–457
 as stage of death and dying, 118, 119–120

Antisocial personality disorder, 17

Anxiety, source of, 348

Applied change, 261, 263

Arapesh society, 191

Aristotle, 166

Assertive behavior, 437, 438

Assertiveness training, 130–132, 159, 437–442,
 454–457

Assessment, 12, 56–84
 of change, 261–266
 community, 251
 computers in, 273
 defined, 56
 environmental systems emphasis in, 62–63
 exercise in writing, 82–83
 focusing on strengths in, 58
 knowledge used in making, 61–62
 of needs, 233–235, 251
 of problems, 64–70
 rapid assessment instruments, 258
 sources of information in, 58–61

Assessment *(continued)*
  systems perspective of, 70–78
  in termination phase, 57
Authoritarian leadership style, 167
Autocorrelation, 261
Autokinetic effect, 186–187
Autonomic nervous system, 528
Aversive techniques, 448–449
Avoidance Serial Cue Hierarchy, 446
Awareness, 368, 369, 371, 375, 377–378

Bandler, Richard, 483–484
Bargaining stage of death and dying, 118, 120–121
Baseline designs, multiple, 267–268, 269
Baselining, 259–260, 264
Bateson, Gregory, 483
Behavior
  aggressive, 437, 438
  analyzing, 355
  assertive, 437, 438. *See also* Assertiveness training
  deviant, 418–419, 550–552
  disruptive, 177–178
  ecological model of, 17–19
  measuring, 256
  medical model of, 15–17
  nonverbal, 60, 180
  problematic, 66–68, 348
  sexual, 192. *See also* Sex counseling
Behavioral analysis, 436
Behavioral change (contingency) contracts, 443–444, 454
Behavior modification, 449–452. *See also* Behavior therapy
Behavior therapy, 433–457
  assertiveness training, 130–132, 159, 437–442, 454–457
  aversive techniques, 448–449
  cognitive behavior-modification techniques, 449–452
  comparison with other therapy approaches, 536
  contingency contracting, 443–444, 454
  covert sensitization, 435, 447–448
  evaluation of, 452–453
  founders of, 433–434
  implosive therapy, 435, 446
  in vivo desensitization, 445–446
  reframing, 450–452, 457
  restructured thinking as source of change in, 545
  systematic desensitization, 444–445
  theory of, 435–436
  token economies, 442–443
Beliefs, irrational, 426–428
Benson, Herbert, 521, 546
Berne, Eric, 379. *See also* Transactional analysis
Bilingual clients, 280, 281–283, 291–294, 295

Biofeedback, 526–529
Bipolar disorder, 15
Black clients, 281–283, 290–291
Borderline personality disorder, 17
Brainstorming, 231–233
Broker role of social worker, 14, 19, 247–250
Bulemia, 68
Bureaucracy, 323–327
Burnout, 314–323
  causes of, 317, 318–319
  defined, 315
  prevention of, 319–323, 339
  stress and, 315–323
  symptoms of, 315

Cabot, Richard, 4
Cancer group, case example of, 146–147
Caseloads, 318
Case management, 21
Casework, 20–21
Caseworker, defined, 40
Castration anxiety, 347
Catharsis, 349
Causal analysis, 242
Causality, inferring, 276–277
Change
  applied, 261, 263
  assessment of, 261–266
  causes of, 543–548, 555–556
  experimental, 261–263
  process of, 9–14, 146–147
Change agent, 6, 71, 72, 83–84
Charisma, 166
Charity Organization Society (COS), 3, 4
Chicano clients, 280, 281–283, 288, 291–294, 295
Child abuse, case examples of, 424–425, 462–465
Classification
  of clients, 38–40
  of mental disorders, 15–17
Claustrophobia, 17
Client
  counseling from perspective of, 102–117
  emotional involvement with, 312–314
  explaining confidentiality to, 46–47
  first interview with, 309–310
  identified, 211
  nonverbal behavior of, 60
  reaction to problems, 117–123
  right to self-determination, 40–42
  as source of information, 58–59, 60
  strengths of, 58
  stress caused by, 318
  suggested counselor responses to statements of, 565–566
  values of, vs. social worker values, 37–40

Client-centered therapy, 357–366
  case example of, 362–363
  central concepts of, 358–359
  comparison with other therapy approaches, 535
  congruence in, 358, 359, 360
  empathy in, 358, 360
  evaluation of, 363–365
  limitations of, 364–365
  personality development and, 359–360
  restructured thinking as source of change in, 545
  statements used in, 361–362
  theory of, 360–362
  unconditional positive regard in, 358–359, 360
Client information systems, computerized, 273
Client system, 71–72, 83–84
Clinical change, 261, 263
Clinical evaluation, 254
Code of Ethics, 279, 558–564
Coercive power, 170
Cognitive behavior-modification techniques,
    449–452
Communication
  in community practice, 225–226
  congruent vs. incongruent, 200
  family, 199–201, 215–216
  privileged, 45–46
Communication skills, 235–236
Community, 228
  knowledge of, 226–227, 228–229
  problems of, 225, 226
Community assessment, 251
Community development, 246, 248–249
Community organization, 24
Community practice, 223–252
  fund-raising and, 237–239
  group decision–making skills in, 231–235
  knowledge needed in, 226–231
  of community, 226–227, 228–229
  of funding sources and funding cycles, 230–231
  of organizations, 227, 230
  media and, 236–237
  models of, 246–250
  political activity and lobbying in, 239
  as problem-solving process, 239–244
  public relations skills in, 235–236
  values in, 244–246, 252
Compensation, 345
Competitive groups, 174–175
Compulsions, 264–266, 348
Compulsive personality disorder, 17
Computer applications, 270–274
  client information systems, 273
  clinical assessment, 273
  decision support, 273
  direct intervention, 273

education and training, 274
  electronic networking, 273–274
  information retrieval, 274
  issues in, 274
  office management, 272
  research, 274
Computer Use in Social Services Network, 273–274
Concomitant variation, 266
Conditioned response, 435
Conditioned stimulus, 435
Conditioning
  operant, 434
  respondent, 434–435
  See also Behavior therapy
Confidentiality, 42–47
  absolute vs. relative, 42
  exercise in, 51–52
  explaining to clients, 46–47
  in groups, 180
  law on, 44
  privileged communication and, 45–46
  release of information form, 43
Conflict of interest, 311
Conflict resolution (mediation), 512–514
Conformity, 172–174, 186–187
Congruence, 358, 359, 360
Congruent communication, 200
Consensus, vs. majority voting, 136–137
Consultant, social worker as, 20
Contingency contracting, 443–444, 454
Contracting
  in change process, 12–13
  contingency, 443–444, 454
  in mediation, 513
Control theory, 401–402
Controversy, in groups, 175
Cooley, Charles, 38, 39
Cooperative groups, 174–175, 176–177
Coordinator, social worker as, 20
Council on Social Work Education, 9, 26–27, 279
Counseling, 101–126
  case example of, 112–116
  client reactions to problems in, 117–123
  comparison of theories, 534–538
  effectiveness of, 538–543
  friendship vs., 311–312
  from helpee's perspective, 102–117
  from helper's perspective, 101–102
  principles of, 112–116
  psychotherapy vs., 4
  role-playing and, 123–126
  See also Therapy
Counseling and Psychotherapy (Rogers), 357
Counseling stages
  counselee-counselor relationship, 103–104

Counseling stages *(continued)*
  evaluation, 116–117
  exploring resolution strategies, 110
  implementing resolution strategy, 111, 116
  motivation, 104–106
  problem awareness, 102–103
  problem conceptualizing, 106–110
  selecting resolution strategy, 110–111
Counselor
  counseling from perspective of, 101–102
  emotional involvement of, 104, 312–314
  empathy of, 106–107, 180
  honesty of, 108–109
  relationship to counselee, 103–104
  suggested responses to client's statements,
    565–566
  See also Social worker
Counterconditioning, 435
Covert assertion, 449–450
Covert sensitization, 435, 447–448
Creativity, in groups, 175, 176–177
Credits, idiosyncratic, 173–174
Crisis intervention (CI), 507–511
Criticism, 182
Cross-cultural relationships. *See* Culturally diverse
  groups
Culturally diverse groups, 279–307
  African-Americans, 281–283, 290–291
  gays and lesbians, 283–284, 299–300
  intervention techniques with, 289–302
  knowledge of differences in, 286–289
  Latinos, 280, 281–283, 288, 291–294, 295
  Native Americans, 281, 287–288, 294, 296
  problems and barriers with, 280–281
  rural clients, 284, 300–301
  self-knowledge and, 286, 303–306
  women, 280, 283–285, 286, 296–300

Data
  baseline, 259–260, 264
  sources of, 58–61
Data collection and assessment. *See* Assessment
Death and dying, five stages of, 118–122
Death instinct, 346
Deawfulizing, 450, 457
Decatastrophizing, 450–451
Decentering, 451
Decision making
  computers in, 273
  group vs. individual, 132–134
Decision-making groups, 132–137
Decision-making skills, 231–235
Deep breathing and imagery relaxation approaches,
  519–520, 531–533, 546
Defense mechanisms, 345, 360

Democratic leadership style, 167–168
Denial, 360
  defined, 345
  as stage of death and dying, 112, 118
Depersonalization, and bureaucracy, 324
Depression
  case example of, 79–81
  comparison of treatment by different therapy
    approaches, 534–536
  as stage of death and dying, 118, 121
Desensitization
  in vivo, 435, 445–446
  systematic, 435, 444–445
Designated leader, 169
Development, psychosexual, 346–348. *See also*
  Personality development; Psychopathology
Deviant behavior, 418–419, 550–552
Diagnosis. *See* Assessment
Diagnostic interviews, 86
Direct observation, 255–256
Discriminated operants, 256
Distributed functions approach to leadership,
  168–169
Diverse groups. *See* Culturally diverse groups
Diversion techniques, 450
Double bind, 200, 203, 216
Dreams
  in Gestalt therapy, 373–374
  in psychoanalysis, 350–352
Duration, 256
Dying, Kübler-Ross's five stages of, 118–122
Dyspareunia, 472

Ebonics, 282–283
Ecological model of human behavior, 17–19
Education, computers in, 274
Educational groups, 129–132
Effectiveness
  of counseling, 538–543
  inferring, 265, 266
Ego, 344–346
Electra complex, 347, 348, 349
Electronic networking, 273–274
Ellis, Albert, 413–414. *See also* Rational therapy
E-mail, 273
Emotional involvement, of counselor, 104,
  312–314
Emotional problems, development of, 348
Emotional reactions, 117–123
Empathy
  in client-centered therapy, 358, 360
  sympathy vs., 106–107, 180
Enabler role of social worker, 14, 19
Enchiridion, The (Epictetus), 414
Encounter groups, 143–149

Environmental systems
  emphasis on, 62–63
  model of, 17–19
Erectile dysfunction, 472
Erickson, Milton, 484, 491
Eros, 346
Erythrophobia, 17
Ethics, Code of, 279, 558–564
Evaluation, 253–278
  case example of, 264–266
  clinical, 254
  in counseling, 116–117
  defined, 253–254
  measurement issues in, 258–267
  outcome, 253–254
  planning and, 244
  of programs, 254, 268–270
  single-system approach to, 254, 255–258, 267–268, 269
  subjective, 263
  termination and, 13–14
Evaluative research, 254
Excitement hunger, 383
Excuses, in reality therapy, 406–407
Exercise, and stress, 321
Experimental change, 261–263
Expert power, 170–171
Expert systems, 273
Extended family, 190
Extinction, 435, 446
Eye-accessing cues, 490, 491, 495–496
Eysenck, H. J., 540–542

Failure identity, 38, 332–336, 337, 403–404
Failure to thrive, 58
Family, 189–222
  communication in, 199–201, 215–216
  diverse forms of, 189–192
  extended, 190
  life cycle of, 19
  life script of, 388
  nuclear, 190
  problems in, 192–193
  purpose of, 198
  restructuring, 201–203, 214–218
  sex-role expectations in, 191
  social work with, 193–195
  societal functions of, 192
  values and, 48
Family therapy, 24, 195–218
  approaches to, 199–204
    communication patterns, 199–201, 215–216
    strategic, 203–204, 212
    structural, 201–203
  beginning, 205–210

  case example of, 197
  defined, 195
  problem-solving stages in, 204–218
  in systems perspective, 195–199, 219–222
  terminating, 218
Fantasy formation, 345
Feedback, 146–147, 185
Female clients, 280, 283–285, 286, 296–300
Feminists, 280, 284–285, 296–299
Field placement
  success in, 308–309
  as training, 310
Fixation, 347, 348
Forms
  release of information, 43
  self-report, 59
Four-tuple, 490–491
Free association, 349–350, 355–356
Frequency count, 256
Freud, Sigmund, 15, 343
Freudian theories, 4, 58, 343–354
  concept of mind, 343–346
  defense mechanisms, 345
  dream analysis, 350–352
  evaluation of, 353–354
  free association, 349–350, 355–356
  psychoanalysis, 348–352
  psychosexual stages of development, 346–348
  on sexuality, 346
  transference, 352
Friendship, vs. counseling, 311–312
Funding cycle, 231
Funding sources, 230–231
Fund-raising, 237–239

Games
  analysis of, 393, 394, 398–399
  communication, 215–216
  psychological, 391, 392
  in transactional analysis, 383–386, 391, 392, 393, 394, 398–399
Games People Play (Berne), 379, 385
Gay clients, 283–284, 299–300
Gender. *See* Sex roles; Women
Generalist practice, 8–15
Generalist skills, 225–226
Genital stage of development, 348
Gestalt psychology, 368
Gestalt therapy, 367–378
  awareness in, 368, 369, 371, 375, 377–378
  case example of, 374
  comparison with other therapy approaches, 535
  evaluation of, 375–376
  Gestalt psychology and, 368

Gestalt therapy *(continued)*
  personality and, 369–371
  theory of, 371–375
Gestalt Therapy: Excitement and Growth in
    Personality (Perls, Hefferline, and Goodman), 367
Glasser, William, 400–401. *See also* Reality therapy
"Gloria," 362–363, 364
Goal attainment scaling, 263
Goals
  in evaluation, 255, 264
  group vs. personal, 171–172
  measurable, 70
  operational, 70
  planning and, 242
  setting, 320
  of social work, 19–20
Gordon, Thomas, 502. *See also* Parent Effectiveness
    Training
Great person theory of leadership, 166–167, 168
Grinder, John, 483–484
Griscom, John, 3
Groups, 21–22, 127–188
  agenda for, 154
  case examples of, 130–132, 134–135, 140–141,
    144–145, 146–147
  closeness in, 163, 164
  conformity in, 172–174, 186–187
  controversy in, 175
  creativity in, 175, 176–177
  decision–making skills in, 231–235
  defined, 127
  departure of members, 156–158, 164
  disruptive behavior in, 177–178
  diverse. *See* Culturally diverse groups
  goals in, 171–172
  introductions in, 153–154
  leading, 151–155, 165–169, 179–183
  nominal, 134–135, 159, 233
  preparation for, 149–151, 178
  problem-solving approach in, 176–177
  reality therapy in, 408–409
  roles in, 154, 165, 187
  seating arrangements in, 153
  sessions of
    ending, 182–183
    planning, 151–152
  size of, 178
  social power bases in, 169–171, 187
  stages in development of, 163–165
  starting, 149–151, 179–180
  terminating, 155–158, 164, 183–185
  types of, 128–149
    competitive, 174–175
    cooperative, 174–175, 176–177
    decision-making, 132–137

    educational, 129–132
    encounter, 143–149
    involuntary, 177, 179
    membership, 161–163
    problem-solving, 132–137
    recreation, 128–129
    recreation-skill, 129
    reference, 162, 163
    self-help, 138–142
    socialization, 142, 144–145
    therapeutic, 142–143, 146–147, 148
    voluntary, 179
  win-lose approach in, 175–176
Group therapy, 24, 142–143, 146–147, 148, 408–409.
    See also names of specific therapies
Groupthink, 134–136
Guthrie, E. R., 433

Haley, Jay, 203–204
Hardware, computer, 271
Helper therapy, 24, 138, 142
Hidden agenda, 171
Hispanic clients, 280, 281–283, 288, 291–294, 295
History
  sexual, 475
  social, 85–86, 87–88, 89, 99–100
  of social work, 3–6
  validity and, 266
HIV test, 468–469
Homeostasis, 71, 317, 369
Home visits
  assessment and, 60
  interviewing and, 90–91
Homophobia, 283
Homosexual clients, 283–284, 299–300
Honesty, 108–109, 181, 236
Hot seat therapy technique, 373
Hull, C. L., 433
Humanism, 357
Humor
  in dealing with bureaucracy, 326
  stress and, 323
Hypnosis, 349, 351, 522–526, 546
Hypochondriasis, 15

Id, 344, 346
Ideal self, 358
Ideal types, 538
Identification, 345, 347
Identified client, 211
Identity
  development of, 329–337, 339–340
  need for, 402–404
Identity theory, 402–404
Idiosyncratic credits, 173–174

Imagery, 519–520, 531–533, 546
I-messages, 200, 504, 530
Implementation
  planning and, 243–244
  of resolution strategy, 111, 116
Implosive therapy, 435, 446
Impotence, case example of, 374
Incest, 35, 462–465
Incongruence, 358, 359–360
Incongruent communication, 200
Index of Self-Esteem, 271, 272
Individualization, principle of, 38–40
Informational interviews, 85–86
Information retrieval, 274
Information sources, 58–61
  collateral, 59
  forms completed by client, 59
  home visits, 60
  nonverbal behavior of client, 60
  psychological tests, 59–60
  social worker's intuition, 60–61, 107, 180
  verbal report from client, 58–59
Innate response, 435
Insight vs. resolution approaches to therapy,
    536–538
Institutional orientation, 47–48
Intake, 9, 12, 473–474
Intervention, 13, 260–261, 264
  computers in, 273
  multiple, 267
  See also Counseling; Therapy
Intervention strategies, 30–31
Intervention techniques, 289–302
Interviews, 85–100
  closing, 93–94
  diagnostic, 86
  with first client, 309–310
  informational, 85–86
  location of, 90–91
  note taking in, 96
  opening, 92–93
  questioning in, 94–96
  social history, 85–86, 87–88, 89, 99–100
  students' concerns about, 309–311
  tape recording, 97
  therapeutic, 86, 89–90
  videotaping, 97–99
Intimacy, in transactional analysis, 383
Introjection, 359, 370
Intuition, 60–61, 107, 180
In vivo desensitization, 435, 445–446
Irrational thinking, 312–313
Isolation, 345

Johnson, Virginia, 471–472

Knowledge
  in assessment, 61–62
  of community, 226–227, 228–229
  of differences of culturally diverse groups,
    286–289
  of funding sources and funding cycles, 230–231
  of organizations, 227, 230
  of self, 286, 303–306
  of social worker, 25–27
  values vs., 36–37
Knowledge statements, 37
Kübler-Ross's five stages of death and dying, 118–122

Labeling, 39, 415–416, 427, 550, 552–554
Laissez-faire leadership style, 168
Latency, 256
  as stage of development, 347–348
Latino clients, 280, 281–283, 288, 291–294, 295
Leader, group, 149–158
  departure of, 157–158
  designated, 169
  guidelines for, 154–155
  introducing, 153
  preparation of, 149–151, 178
  relaxing before meetings, 152
  role clarification by, 154
  session planning by, 151–152
  traits of, 166–167
Leadership approaches, 165–169
  distributed functions, 168–169
  style, 167–168
  trait, 166–167
Leadership styles
  authoritarian, 167
  democratic, 167–168
  laissez-faire, 168
Learning processes, types of, 434–435
Legitimate power, 170
Lesbian clients, 283–284, 299–300
Libido, 346
Life scripts, 386–389, 394–395, 397–398
Listening, 109–110, 502–504, 530–531
Lobbying, 239
Locality development approach to community
    practice, 246, 248–249
Looking glass self-concept, 38, 39, 330, 415
Love, in reality therapy, 403

Machiavellianism, 166–167
Macro practice, 20
  generalist skills and, 225–226
  group decision-making skills and, 231–235
  values and, 244–246, 252
  See also Community practice
Maintenance roles, 165, 187

Maladjustment, psychological, 358
Management by objectives (MBO), 50
Manson, Charles, 418–419
Marriage
    communication in, 199–201
    trial, 191
    See also Family
Masters, William, 471–472
Masturbation, 35–36, 37
Maturation, 266–267
Mead, Margaret, 191
Measurable goal, 70
Measurement, 258–267
    methods of, 255–258
        direct observation, 255–256
        self-anchored rating scales, 256–257
        standardized measures, 257–258
    reactivity of, 258–259
    reliability of, 258
    repeated use of, 258
    validity of, 258, 266–267
Measures
    selecting, 255, 264, 275–276
    standardized, 257–258
Media
    barriers to effective use of, 236
    relationships with, 236–237
    skills for utilization of, 237
Mediation, 512–514
Medical model of human behavior, 15–17
Meditation, 520–522, 531–533, 546
Meetings, group, 152–155
Membership groups, 161–163
Mental health days, 321
Mental illness
    APA classifications of, 15–17
    existence of, 548–552, 555
    labeling and, 550, 552–554
    in medical model of human behavior, 15
    in reality therapy, 403–405
Metaphor, communicating in, 491–492
Mezzo practice, 20
Micro practice, 20
Milieu therapy, 497–498
Minahan, Anne, 71
Mind, Freudian conception of, 343–346
Minority groups. *See* Culturally diverse groups
Minuchin, Salvador, 201–203, 484
Misconception hypothesis, 546
Misunderstandings of the Self (Raimy), 545–546
Modeling, 435
Models
    of community practice, 246–250
    ecological, 17–19
    of family therapy, 203–204, 212

    medical, 15–17
    Pincus-Minahan, 71–78
Monitoring, 13, 243–244, 260–261, 264
Moreno, J. L., 367, 498
Motivation, in counseling, 104–106
Multiple baseline designs, 267–268, 269
Multiple intervention interference, 267
Multiple personality disorder, 350–351, 353–354
Mundugamor society, 191
Murder, 548, 551–552
Muscle relaxation approaches, 514–519, 531–533,
    546–548

Narcissistic personality disorder, 17
National Association for the Advancement of Colored
    People (NAACP), 279
National Association of Social Workers
    Code of Ethics of, 279, 558–564
    on definition of social work, 6, 8
    formation of, 4
    on knowledge of social worker, 25–26
    on skills of social worker, 28–29
    on values of social worker, 28–29
National Urban League, 279
Native American clients, 281, 287–288, 294, 296
Needs assessment (NA), 233–235, 251
Negative reinforcer, 434
Negotiation, 513
Nervous system, 528
Networking, electronic, 273–274
Neural probes, 108, 181
Neuro-Linguistic Programming (NLP), 483–496
    defined, 484
    development of, 483–484
    evaluation of, 494
    eye-accessing cues in, 490, 491, 495–496
    four-tuple in, 490–491
    metaphors in, 491–492
    predicates in, 485–490
    reframing in, 492–493
    representational systems in, 484–485
Neutral stimulus, 435
New Horizons, 144–145
New York Charity Organization Society, 4
New York School of Philanthropy, 4
NIMBY (Not In My Back Yard) syndrome, 223
Ninth Mental Measurements Yearbook, 258
NLP. *See* Neuro-Linguistic Programming
No-lose problem solving, 505–506
Nominal groups, 134–135, 159, 233
Nonassertive behavior, 437, 438
Nonconformity, 173–174, 186–187
Nondirective therapy. *See* Client-centered therapy
Nonverbal behavior, 60, 180

Nonverbal cues, 108, 181
Note taking, in interviews, 96

Objectives, 242–243
Observation, direct, 255–256
Obsessions, 348
Obsessive-compulsive disorder, case example of, 264–266
Oedipus complex, 347, 348
Office management, computers in, 272
On Death and Dying (Kübler-Ross), 118
Operant conditioning, 434
Operational goal, 70
Oral stage of development, 346–347
Organizational change, 230
Organizations, knowledge of, 227, 230
Orgasmic dysfunction, 472
Osborn, Alex, 232
Outcome evaluation, 253–254

Paperwork, 318, 319, 327
Paradox, systemic, 201–202
Paranoia, 15, 16
Parent Effectiveness Training (PET), 39, 502–507
Parents Anonymous, 140–141
Passive-aggressive personality disorder, 17
Pauses, 108, 180–181
Pavlov, I., 433
Perls, Frederick (Fritz), 367–368, 484. *See also* Gestalt therapy
Personality development
   in client-centered therapy, 359–360
   in Gestalt psychology, 369–371
   in psychoanalytic theory, 346–348
   in rational therapy, 414–419
   in reality therapy, 401–404
   self-concept formations and, 415–417
   in transactional analysis, 380–382
Personality disorders, 16, 17, 350–351, 353–354
Personal Problems Checklist for Adolescents, 59
Person-in-environment model, 17–19
Person-in-family model, 19
Phallic stage of development, 347
Phobias, 17, 197
Physiology
   self-talk and, 428–429
   sex therapy session on, 477–478
Piers-Harris Children Self-Concept Scale, 59
Pincus, Allen, 71
Pincus-Minahan model, 71–78
Placebo effect, 539–540
Planning, 240–244
   in community practice, 226
   contracting and, 12–13

group sessions, 151–152
implementation and, 243–244
preplanning, 240–241
in reality therapy, 406
Play therapy, 500–502
Political activity, 239
Positive affirmations, 431–432
Positive reinforcer, 434, 449
Positive thinking, 320, 328–329, 340, 450
Power, 169–171, 187
   coercive, 170
   expert, 170–171
   legitimate, 170
   referent, 170
   reward, 169–170
Precipitating events, 67–68
Preconscious, 343–344
Predicates, 485–490
Prejudice, 287. *See also* Culturally diverse groups
Premature ejaculation, 472
Preplanning, 240–241
Privacy Act of 1974, 44
Privileged communication, 45–46
Probationers
   counseling vs. friendship with, 311
   explaining confidentiality to, 46–47
   self-determination of, 41
Problems
   alternative solutions to, 181–182, 243
   awareness of, 102–103
   client reactions to, 117–123
   conceptualizing, 106–110
   exploring in depth, 180–181
   personal vs. community, 225
Problem solving
   in community practice, 239–244
   in groups, 132–137, 176–177
   no-lose, 505–506
   skills in, 19, 226
   in social work, 20
   stages of, 204–218
Problem-solving groups, 132–137
Problem systems, assessment of, 64–70
Program developer, social worker as, 20
Program evaluation, 254, 268–270
Projection, 345, 371
Psychoanalysis, 348–356
   case example of, 350–351
   comparison with other therapy approaches, 535
   dream analysis in, 350–352
   evaluation of, 353–354
   free association in, 349–350, 355–356
   hypnosis in, 349, 351
   reality therapy vs., 410

Psychoanalysis *(continued)*
   restructured thinking as source of change in, 545
   transference in, 352
Psychoanalytic theory, 342–348
   defense mechanisms in, 345
   ego in, 344–346
   evaluation of, 353–354
   id in, 344, 346
   stages of development in, 346–348
   superego in, 344, 346
   unconscious in, 343–344
Psychodrama, 367, 395, 498–500
Psychological games, 391, 392. *See also* Games
Psychological maladjustment, 358
Psychological tests, 59–60
Psychopathology
   in client-centered therapy, 359–360
   in Gestalt therapy, 369–371
   in psychoanalytic theory, 348
   in rational therapy, 414–419
   in reality therapy, 401–404
   in transactional analysis, 389–391
Psychosexual development, 346–348
   anal stage of, 347
   genital stage of, 348
   latency stage of, 347–348
   oral stage of, 346–347
   phallic stage of, 347
Psychosocial drives, in transactional analysis, 382–383
Psychotherapy. *See* Therapy
Psychotherapy by Reciprocal Inhibition (Wolpe), 452
Public relations, 235–236
Punishment
   in behavior therapy, 448–449, 453
   in reality therapy, 407

Questioning, 94–96

Rape, case example of, 10–12
Rap group, 144–145
Rapid assessment instruments, 258
Rating scales, self-anchored, 256–257
Rationalization, 345, 360
Rational Self-Analysis (RSA), 420–421, 422–423
Rational therapy, 320, 413–432
   case examples of, 422–425
   comparison with other therapy approaches, 536
   evaluation of, 428–430
   irrational beliefs and, 426–428
   personality development and, 414–419
   perspective on deviant behavior, 550–552
   self-talk in, 414–415, 416, 417–418, 420, 421,
      422–423, 428–430
   theory of, 419–428

Reaction formation, 345, 347
Reactivity, 258–259
Reality therapy, 400–412
   case example of, 408–409
   comparison with other therapy approaches,
      535–536
   control theory and, 401–402
   evaluation of, 410–411
   identity theory and, 402–404
   personality development and, 401–404
   psychoanalysis vs., 410
   theory of, 404–410
Recognition hunger, 382
Recreation groups, 128–129
Recreation-skill groups, 129
Redefining, 451
Reference groups, 162, 163
Referent power, 170
Referrals, 185
Reform approach to social work, 17
Reframing
   in behavior therapy, 450–452, 457
   in family therapy, 204
   in Neuro-Linguistic Programming, 492–493
Refreezing, 148
Regression
   as defense mechanism, 345
   statistical, 267
Reinforcement, 434, 449
Relationships
   concept of, 71
   in reality therapy, 405
Relaxation techniques
   deep breathing and imagery, 519–520, 531–533,
      546
   for group leader, 152
   muscle relaxation, 514–519, 531–533, 546–548
   in stress management, 321, 322
Reliability, 258
Representational system, 484–485
Representational system predicates, 485–490
Repression, 344, 345, 347
Rescue fantasy, in psychotherapy, 40–41
Research
   computers in, 274
   evaluative, 254
Residential view of social welfare, 47–48
Resolution strategies
   exploring, 110
   implementing, 111, 116
   selecting, 110–111
Resolution vs. insight approaches to therapy,
     536–538
Respondent conditioning, 434–435

Response, in respondent conditioning, 435
Responsibility
  in Gestalt therapy, 371
  in reality therapy, 404, 407
Reward power, 169–170
Richmond, Mary, 4
Ritual, 383
Rogers, Carl, 357. *See also* Client-centered therapy
Role playing
  in assertiveness training, 440
  exercise in, 123–126
  in Gestalt psychology, 370
  for interview with first client, 310
Roles
  in groups, 154, 165, 187
  maintenance, 165, 187
  sex, 191, 387–388
  of social worker, 14–15, 20
  task, 165, 187
Roundtable, 475–477
Runaway center, 144–145
Rural clients, 284, 300–301

Salesworkers, vs. social workers, 486–489
Satir, Virginia, 196, 199–201, 215–216, 484
Scapegoat, 211
Schizoid personality disorder, 17
Schizophrenia, 15, 16, 17, 548, 551–552
School behavior problems, case examples of, 13,
    74–78, 501
School phobia, case example of, 197
Schools without Failure (Glasser), 400
Science and Human Behavior (Skinner), 452
Script analysis, 394–395, 397–398
Seasonal affective disorder (SAD), 67
Seating arrangements, in groups, 153
Self, and incongruence between experience, 358,
    359–360
Self-actualization motive, 358
Self-anchored rating scales, 256–257
Self-concept
  defined, 358
  formation of, 415–417
  looking glass, 38, 39, 330, 415
  positive, development of, 332–336, 339–340
Self-determination, client's right to, 40–42
Self-esteem
  of children, 58
  index of, 271, 272
Self-fulfilling prophecies, 340
Self-help groups, 138–142
Self-hypnosis, 523–526
Self-knowledge, 286, 303–306
Self-report forms, 59

Self-talk
  boundaries of, 429–430
  developing positive self-concept and, 334–337
  emotions and actions and, 544
  physiological effects of, 428–429
  in rational therapy, 414–415, 416, 417–418, 420, 421,
      422–423, 428–430
  as source of change, 544–548
Sensitivity training groups, 143–149
Sex and Temperament in Three Primitive Societies
    (Mead), 191
Sex counseling, 458–482
  AIDS and, 466–470
  assumptions in, 459–460
  case example of, 462–465
  levels of intervention in, 460–466
  vocabulary in, 460
Sexism, 280, 284–285, 296–299
Sex roles, 191, 387–388
Sex therapy, 472–479
  intake interview in, 473–474
  physiology session in, 477–478
  roundtable in, 475–477
  sexual history in, 475
  termination of, 479
Sexual abuse, case example of, 462–465
Sexual behavior, 192
Sexual dysfunction, 470–479
  defined, 472
  treatment of, 471, 472–479
Sexual history, 475
Sexual instincts, 346
Sexuality, Freud on, 346
Sherman, Harold, 328–329
Single-system approach to evaluation, 254, 255–258
Single-system designs, 254, 267–268, 269
Skills, 27–29
  communication, 235–236
  generalist, 225–226
  group decision-making, 231–235
  media utilization, 237
  public relations, 235–236
Skinner, B. F., 433
Social action
  as approach to community practice, 247, 248–249
  as value, 48
Social comparison, 263
Social Diagnosis (Richmond), 4
Social history
  interviews, 85–86, 87–88, 89
  writing, 99–100
Socialization groups, 142, 144–145
Social planning approach to community practice,
    246–247, 248–249

Social policy, 20
Social Security Act of 1935, 4
Social service broker, 247–250
Social services, knowledge of, 229
Social support systems, 322–323
Social welfare, vs. social work, 6–7
Social work
  career in, 8, 314
  defined, 6
  enjoying, 327–337
  generalist practice of, 8–15
  goals of, 19–20
  history of, 3–6
  as profession, 8
  social welfare vs., 6–7
  variety in, 323
Social worker
  activities of, 20–25
  burnout of, 314–323
  education of, 9
  intuition of, 60–61, 107, 180
  knowledge of, 25–27
  responses of, 13, 565–566
  roles of, 14–15, 20
  salesworker vs., 486–489
  skills of, 27–29
  values of, 29, 37–40
Social Work Practice: Model and Method (Pincus and
  Minahan), 71
Social Work Research and Abstracts, 274
Society for the Prevention of Pauperism, 3
Software, computer, 271
Standardized measures, 257–258
Statistical change, 261–263
Statistical regression, 267
Stimulus
  aversive, 448–449
  in respondent conditioning, 435
Stimulus hunger, 382
Stone, W. Clement, 328
Strategic model of family therapy, 203–204, 212
Strengths, focus on, 58
Stress
  adrenaline and, 316–317
  burnout and, 315–323
  causes of, 318–319
  defined, 316
Stress management, 319–323, 339
  changing stressful thoughts, 320–321
  exercise, 321
  goal setting, 320
  humor, 323
  outside activities, 321
  pleasurable goodies, 321
  positive thinking, 320

relaxation techniques, 321, 322. *See also* Relaxation
  techniques
  social support systems, 322–323
  time management, 320
  variety at work, 323
Stressors, 316, 317
Structural analysis, 392
Structural hunger, 382
Structural school of family therapists, 201–203
Students
  attitude problems of, case example, 74–78
  behavior problems of, 13, 74–78, 501
  common concerns of, 308–314, 338
  school phobia of, 197
Style approach to leadership, 167–168
Subjective evaluation, 263
Sublimation, 345, 346
Success identity, 331, 336, 403, 404
Superego, 344, 346
Supervisor, social worker as, 20
"Surest Way in the World to Attract Success — or
  Failure" (Sherman), 328–329
"Sybil," 350–351, 353–354
Sympathy, vs. empathy, 106–107, 180
Systematic desensitization, 435, 444–445
Systemic paradox, 201–202
Systems analysis, 73–81
  in clinical setting, 79–81
  in school setting, 74–78
Systems theory, 70–78
  family therapy and, 195–199, 219–222
  overview of, 70–71
  Pincus-Minahan model, 71–78
Szasz, Thomas, 549

Tact, 181
Tape recording, of interviews, 97
Tarasoff v. Regents of the University of California, 44
Target system, 72, 84
Task-centered practice, 511–512
Task roles, 165, 187
Tchambuli society, 191
Terminal illness, Kübler–Ross's five stages of,
  118–122
Termination phase, 13–14
  assessment in, 57
  of family therapy, 218
  of group, 155–158, 164, 183–185
Tests, psychological, 59–60
Thanatos, 346
Therapeutic groups, 142–143, 146–147, 148
Therapeutic interviews, 86, 89–90
Therapy
  behavior, 433–457, 536, 545
  causes of change in, 543–548, 555–556

client-centered, 357–366, 535, 545
comparison of approaches to, 534–538
counseling vs., 4
effectiveness of, 538–543
family, 24, 195–218
gestalt, 367–378, 535
group, 24, 142–143, 146–147, 148, 408–409
implosive, 435, 446
insight vs. resolution approaches to, 536–538
milieu, 497–498
play, 500–502
psychoanalysis, 342–356, 410, 535, 545
rational, 413–432, 536
reality, 400–412, 535–536
rescue fantasy in, 40–41
sex, 472–479
transactional analysis, 379–399, 535
Thinking
positive, 320, 328–329, 340, 450
as source of change, 544–548
See also Self-talk
Thorndike, Edward, 433
Thought stopping, 449
Three Approaches to Psychotherapy, 362–363
Time management, 320
Time-outs, 318
Time-sampling methods, 256
Token economies, 442–443
Tolman, E. C., 433
Topdog vs. Underdog, 370, 388
Training
computers in, 274
field placement as, 310
Trait approach to leadership, 166–167
Transactional analysis (TA), 379–399
comparison with other therapy approaches, 535
evaluation of, 395–397
games in, 383–386, 391, 392, 393, 394, 398–399
life scripts in, 386–389, 394–395, 397–398
personality development in, 380–382
psychopathology and, 389–391
psychosocial drives in, 382–383
theory of, 392–395
types of transactions in, 383–385, 390, 391
Transactions, 383–385
complementary, 390
crossed, 390–391
Transcendental Meditation (TM), 520–521
Transference, 352
Treasury of Success Unlimited, A (Stone), 328
Trend, 261
Trial and error approach to career, 314

Trial marriage, 191
Trust walks, 145, 159–160
Twin studies, 17

Unconditional positive regard, 358–359, 360
Unconditioned stimulus, 435
Unconscious, 343–344
Undoing, 345
Unfreezing, 144–146
Unlearned response, 435
U.S. Supreme Court, on confidentiality, 44

Vaginismus, 472
Validity, 258, 266–267
Value dilemmas
abortion, 33–34, 37
of clients vs. social workers, 37–40
of helping professionals vs. bureaucracies, 325
Value judgments, 406
Values, 33–54
accountability, 49–50
advocacy and social action, 48
client, 37–40
in community practice, 244–246, 252
confidentiality, 42–47
exercises for clarifying, 52–54
family, 48
institutional orientation, 47–48
knowledge vs., 36–37
resolving collisions of, 506–507
of social worker, 29, 37–40
Variability, 261
Variation, concomitant, 266
Variety, importance of, 323
Videotaping, of interviews, 97–99
Visual analysis, 261–263
Vocabulary, shared, 104, 180
Voting, consensus vs. majority in, 136–137

Welfare, knowledge of services in community, 229
Wholeness, 71
Wilbur, Cornelia, 351
Win-lose approaches, 175–176, 505
Withdrawal designs, 267–268
Women, life scripts of, 387–388
Women clients, 280, 283–285, 286, 296–300
Word association, 355–356
Worth
conditions of, 358, 359
in reality therapy, 403

You-messages, 504

PHOTO CREDITS

p. 5: Prints Old & Rare, San Francisco

p. 8: Courtesy Senior Services of Seattle/King County; photo © Richard Heyza/Seattle Times

p. 21: © Michael Weisbrot and Family; Stock Boston

p. 22: *top left* — © Michael Weisbrot and Family; Stock Boston

p. 22: *bottom left* — Author

p. 22: *top left* — Courtesy National Association of Social Workers

p. 22: *top right* — David Valdez/HUD

p. 22: *bottom left* — Courtesy San Francisco Child Abuse Council, Inc.

p. 22: *bottom right* — Courtesy National Association of Social Workers

p. 34: © Alan Carey/The Image Works

p. 35: © Patsy Davidson/The Image Works

p. 49: © Paul Conklin/Monkmeyer Press Photo Service

p. 64: Courtesy HUD

p. 89: © Ken Light

p. 90: Kit Hedman/Jeroboam

p. 91: © Ken Light

p. 103: © Ken Light

p. 105: Tom Ballard/EKM-Nepenthe

p. 109: Madison General Hospital

p. 128: Courtesy YMCA Archives

p. 129: Courtesy YMCA Archives

p. 133: © Ken Light

p. 143: Bill Powers/Frost Publishing Group

p. 162: Jean-Claude Lejeune/Stock Boston

p. 168: Author

p. 196: © Comstock

p. 224: © Ken Light

pp. 271, 272: Courtesy of Psychological Assessment Resources, Inc.

p. 282: Bohdan Hrynewych/Stock Boston

p. 293: Author

p. 319: Family Service of the East Bay, Oakland, California

p. 322: © Bohdan Hrynewych/Stock Boston

p. 343: The Bettmann Archive

p. 352: The Metropolitan Museum of Art, Gift of M. Knoedler & Co., 1918. Photographic Services, The Metropolitan Museum of Art, New York, N.Y. 10028

p. 372: Courtesy Cyndy Sheldon, Gestalt Institute of San Francisco; photo © Shelly Dunnegan

p. 380: Author

p. 381: Author

p. 419: AP/Wide World Photos

p. 441: Author

p. 467: *top* — Courtesy Shanti Project, San Francisco

p. 467: *bottom* — © Eugene Richards/Magnum Photos

p. 474: Social Services Council

p. 499: © Eva Korn